The
Malcolm X
Encyclopedia

Painted portrait of Malcolm X. Courtesy of Albert Smith and the Pyramid Gallery, Little Rock, Arkansas.

THE
MALCOLM X
ENCYCLOPEDIA

EDITED BY
Robert L. Jenkins
CO-EDITED BY
Mfanya Donald Tryman

GREENWOOD PRESS
Westport, Connecticut • London

Library of Congress Cataloging-in-Publication Data

The Malcolm X encyclopedia / edited by Robert L. Jenkins, co-edited by Mfanya Donald Tryman.
    p. cm.
   Includes bibliographical references and index.
   ISBN 0–313–29264–7 (alk. paper)
   1. X, Malcolm, 1925–1965—Encyclopedias. 2. Black Muslims—Encyclopedias. I.
Jenkins, Robert L., 1945– II. Tryman, Mfanya Donald.
BP223.Z8.L57+
320.54'092—dc21   2001023318
[B]

British Library Cataloguing in Publication Data is available.

Library of Congress Catalog Card Number: 2001023318
ISBN: 0–313–29264–7

First published in 2002

Greenwood Press, 88 Post Road West, Westport, CT 06881
An imprint of Greenwood Publishing Group, Inc.
www.greenwood.com

Printed in the United States of America

The paper used in this book complies with the
Permanent Paper Standard issued by the National
Information Standards Organization (Z39.48–1984).

10 9 8 7 6 5 4 3 2 1

CONTENTS

PREFACE

Numerous works have fueled the scholarly rebirth of Malcolm X since his murder on February 21, 1965. Although he fell that day, his reputation and status have risen higher than ever. Clearly an icon among black Americans, his reputation and image have enjoyed mass appeal even among whites, ironically a class that in general was hardly friendly toward the controversial leader during his short life.

While many studies of Malcolm have been biographical in nature, assessing his life as a political and religious force or evaluating his untimely death during a period of political upheaval, other important works have revealed Malcolm through his own writings and speeches. The approach to this volume is different than previous publications on Malcolm in that it represents an encyclopedic coverage of the world that he helped shape and that helped shape him. It literally addresses Malcolm's life from his childhood in the Midwest to his adulthood and maturation as one of America's most renowned leaders, through his "afterlife" as a bona fide American icon. Although his stature as a national and international leader was brief, he undoubtedly met and influenced a wide range of people, visited many places, and commented on a diverse number of issues and events that impacted on the lives of people of color the world over. Hence, included in this study are accounts of the major public figures, personalities, institutions, issues, places, and events that were a part of Malcolm's world and life. Included as well are entries about a number of less known people, issues, events, and places that also affected and were affected by him. Many of the nuances of his life are also here. While at first glance one might question why some of these obscure subject pieces are part of our coverage, it is important to understand that collectively they helped to define who Malcolm was and what he became in life and death to others. Consequently, even minor entities in Malcolm's inner and outer circle cannot and should not be readily disregarded because they give to a study of this kind the breadth and depth that it deserves.

The encyclopedia represents an interdisciplinary approach. Consequently, it involves the work of scholars who are primarily in the fields of history, political science, sociology, education, literature, and black studies. Represented also are several lay contributors from varied backgrounds who maintain a serious interest in Malcolm's life. When working with a comprehensive edited volume of this size and nature over several years, as we have, some of the entries may give the appearance of being dated material, especially with respect to obscure personalities who may now be deceased or who have changed their names and/or their allegiances. Our intent, however, has been to ensure that the volume is as comprehensive as possible without being able to control some of these factors. Hence, we have also striven to ensure factual accuracy but have deliberately avoided straitjacketing authors into a singular interpretative approach to the various threads sewn into Malcolm's life. Further, while we endeavored to remove duplication, by the very nature of this work, it has not been entirely possible to do so. In cases where some overlap does occur in several entries, we have chosen not to edit out the duplication completely because Malcolm's world cut across so many paths, and the duplication gives substance, insight, and greater understanding for the specific entry.

A comment on organization: Readers will note that—following a brief chronology—the volume begins with an introduction. Written by Hanes Walton, one of the nation's most reputable political science scholars, it explains the societal racism that gave rise to someone so articulate and charismatic as Malcolm X. This introduction provides the foundation upon which the entries are built. Several thematic essays in the beginning of the work assist in building from this foundation and attempt to capture the most important aspects of Malcolm's thinking and political philosophy. Their subject matter, we think, readily conforms to what helps to broadly define Malcolm X. Slight deviation from this thinking might be noted in the essay examining Malcolm on the Internet. We include it as thematic not only because of its novel approach but also because it tells us how enduring interest in Malcolm is and how knowledge about Malcolm and its distribution is evolving and will continue to evolve in the twenty-first century. Asterisks adjacent to names and terms in the text indicate cross-referenced entries.

For the coeditors this volume has been a labor of love. Long before we began our work on this project, we held Malcolm in great regard. We were youths in the period that Malcolm was alive and had the greatest impact on America, and though we were not mature enough to understand all that he meant to a segment of people, or foresightful enough to realize what he would eventually become, we came away from the period no less enamored of the man and his message, respectful of the passion for his work and the compassion for his people. It is easy to understand that he did not have all the answers to the social ills of black America caused by white racism. No one did. But he sounded an alarm about the inhumanity of inertia and of the pitfalls of enduring practices against the oppressed. And that alarm remains as timely (and perhaps ominous) in the early twenty-first century as it was in the last half of the twentieth century. As it was some forty years ago for those of us who read his works and heard his voice, it remains incumbent on all to remain attentive and not to disregard his warnings about the potential consequences today and tomorrow of racism and oppression.

ACKNOWLEDGMENTS

It goes without saying that a work the size of this one required the help of many people. Some might not be aware of how much their input meant to the final production of the encyclopedia, but whatever of quality readers find in the pages of this volume is owed largely to the collective efforts of those who contributed in a substantial way and those whose contributions were minor. Perhaps no one has been more efficiently associated with this project in the past two years than part-time Department of History secretary Patsy Humphrey at Mississippi State University. It was Patsy who did yeoman administrative and often tedious work regarding the encyclopedia. She typed, she retyped, she assembled, she advised, and most important, she strove to ensure that we as editors stayed focused and organized in the effort to see this project through. Energized by her midmorning bag of microwave popcorn and overseeing a dish filled with assorted flavors of Life Savers, she waded through stacks of often illegible editorial comments without allowing telephone interruptions to break her concentration regarding the task at hand. And through it all she never stopped smiling; she never stopped encouraging. Thanks, Patsy. You made it all so much more bearable. For Peggy Bonner, the Department of History's main secretary, seeing to fruition the manuscripts of faculty members became almost an official responsibility. Seldom did we have to ask for her assistance; it became expected. Less demanding departmental chores simply waited, because as Peggy said, "We're going to get this done, Dr. Jenkins." Through it all, her wise counsel and vast experience helped us to avoid the minor as well as the most glaring mistakes. Without Peggy, completing this project would have been vastly more difficult. We also appreciate part-time Department of History secretary Lonna E. Reinecke. In her quiet, unassuming demeanor, Lonna just went to work and spent many afternoon hours reading, suggesting editorial ideas, and typing as we moved closer to our deadline submission.

Over the years that we worked on the encyclopedia, several undergraduate work-study students helped immeasurably. Natisha D. Moore, now a professional educator and part-time graduate student, worked with this project almost from the outset. It was largely Natisha upon whom we relied so heavily in the beginning for typing and general computer-related work. Precocious for her age, we came to respect Natisha not only for her technical computer skills but also for many of her suggestions that made this volume better. Thanks is also due to former undergraduate student Andrea Miller, whose typing contributions at various stages along the way greatly facilitated the completion of this book. The editor's former work-study students Leah Parham and Atoya Collins were always willing to go the extra mile for the project, never complaining when we needed their assistance at the computer or in the library well after they had worked their allotted weekly hours. Current assistant Kim Riley stepped in to continue the fine effort and contributions of these former workers. To Deborah Hill, who also typed draft copies of the manuscript and who says that she learned much about Malcolm, thank you. We also appreciate the assistance of former graduate student, currently professional historian, Curtis Austin, himself a contributing author to the volume, and graduate students Dwyane Jones and Randy Burnside for library work and other chores. Mississippi State University library outreach coordinator Gail Peyton helped immeasurably in securing valuable library and Internet resources, as did interlibrary loan librarian Brenda Valentine. We would also like to thank Réne Goodvin, assistant librarian at Mississippi State University, for her meticulous work related to helping us complete the bibliography.

We are also greatly indebted to the Department of History for its considerable financial assistance to this project. Largely due to the commitment of Charles Lowery, now retired as department head, this project was finalized. From financing postage and costly phone bills to funding travel to libraries and defraying interlibrary loan and copying costs, the assistance that Lowery and the Department of History provided was critical at every stage. Thanks, Charles, for believing in the importance of this work. Similarly, we also acknowledge the financial assistance of the Mississippi State University Political Science Department and head Doug Feig. Important funding assistance from the Political Science Department during the last year of this project clearly helped to ease the prospect of considerable personal financial burdens for the editors. We would also be remiss not to acknowledge the support, both morally and financially, of Godfrey Uzoigwe, current head of the Department of History. Uzoigwe is new to Mississippi State University, but he is himself a first-rate scholar and has shown great regard for the professional development of others by his commitment to the completion of this work. Thank you, Godfrey. We are clearly indebted to you. We also thank the director of the Mississippi State University Graduate Program, William "Bill" Person, whose funding support of graduate work-study students allowed us access to valuable assistance at often critical stages of the work.

We must also thank Greenwood editor Cynthia Harris for her assistance. She believed strongly in the merits of the encyclopedia. There were times, we are sure, that Cynthia must have believed that she would never see *The Malcolm X Encyclopedia* manuscript, but she never communicated any negative energy about our missing deadlines, and her commitment to see the project completed never wavered. For this, we are most appreciative.

Finally, the many hours completing a task of this sort require that other people, especially family members, also make sacrifices. What they give up is often taken for granted in the process. Hence, this book certainly could not have been completed without the support and sacrifices of the editor's wife Barbara Jenkins and their children Gwendolyn, Robert Jr., Taryll, and Brittany. Barbara occasionally questioned the long and seemingly continuous hours that her spouse put into this project, but she never questioned the significance he placed on Malcolm's life and work as an advocate of human rights and his commitment to see the book finished. Only Brittany is a minor in the Jenkins household, but young adulthood did not free Gwendolyn, Robert, and Taryll from the needs and benefits of father-child interaction and especially the kinds of counsel that only a "pops" can provide. They, too, expected and made demands for the editor's time. Unfortunately it was not always there to give, though promises for amends still abound. Similarly, Myesha and Subira Tryman, the daughters of coeditor Mfanya Donald Tryman, came to understand why Malcolm X was consuming the attention of their father. This was particularly difficult for him as a single parent and father balancing a number of roles and duties. Because of his age and maturity, his older son Nyerere was much more understanding as a freshman in college. All of them occasionally had to listen to discussions of various aspects of Malcolm X's world during rides to and from the Mississippi State University campus, at each other's homes, or to and from distant shopping centers. We only regret that we could not have played a better balancing act when it came to giving time to all of them. However, their willingness to accept what we do as important helped to make the effort easier and, ultimately, to make the understanding of Malcolm and his role in American society more important than ever before.

CHRONOLOGY

May 10, 1919	Earl Little, originally from Georgia, marries Louise Norton, originally from Jamaica.
December 1924	The Ku Klux Klan visits the Littles' house at night and tells Louise Little, in her husband's absence, that her family had better move because of the black nationalist activities of her husband, who was affiliated with the United Negro Improvement Association.
May 19, 1925	Malcolm Little is born to Louise and Earl Little in Omaha, Nebraska.
January 1928	The Littles buy a house in Lansing, Michigan.
November 1929	Amid threats from the Black Legion, a white Ku Klux Klan–like hate group, the Littles' house is burned to the ground by two white arsonists as Earl Little shoots at the departing perpetrators.
December 1929	Earl Little builds a four-room house by himself on the outskirts of East Lansing, Michigan.
August 1930	W. D. Fard, the founder of the Nation of Islam (NOI), establishes Temple Number One in Detroit, Michigan.
September 31, 1931	It is rumored that the Black Legion killed Earl Little after his body is found on the tracks, run over by a streetcar.
1939	Unable to cope with the murder of her husband, white racism, attempting to work several jobs, and raise her children during the Great Depression, Louise Little is committed to a mental institution in Kalamazoo, Michigan. Malcolm completes the eighth grade, his last year of formal school, and becomes alienated after Mr. Ostrowski tells him that a "nigger" could not really expect to be a lawyer, which Malcolm aspired to become.

1940–41   Visits his half sister Ella Collins in Boston during the summer
                   of 1940, which leaves a lasting impression on him. Lives in
                   several foster homes, including that of Mr. and Mrs. Swerlin,
                   after returning to Michigan, only to leave Michigan to live with
                   sister Ella, where he holds several jobs and becomes involved
                   in crime.

Spring 1943   Moves to New York after briefly living in Flint, Michigan, and
                   gets a job with the New Haven Railroad, where he is fired after
                   a brief stint. Hired by Small's Paradise Club in Harlem as a
                   waiter.

Fall 1943   Rejected by the U.S. Army for military service because of his
                   mental condition after registering several months earlier. Be-
                   comes involved in hustling, numbers running, and other petty
                   crimes as Detroit Red.

Fall 1944   Works briefly on a job after returning to Boston but quits after
                   several weeks, only to get involved in larceny, where he is
                   caught, given a suspended sentence, and placed on probation for
                   a year.

Winter 1945–46   Malcolm becomes involved with his good friend Malcolm
                   "Shorty" Jarvis in a burglary ring in which white women are
                   used to "case" houses in white neighborhoods. After getting
                   caught attempting to pawn a stolen watch, he is indicted, tried,
                   and found guilty. Begins serving his sentence at Charlestown
                   Prison.

1947–52   Reads extensively in prison and joins the Nation of Islam,
                   headed by Elijah Muhammad. Malcolm joins a prison debate
                   team that takes on student competition from nearby universities,
                   including Harvard and Yale University. He is transferred to three
                   different prisons during his incarceration.

Summer 1952   Paroled from Charlestown Prison. Hears Elijah Muhammad
                   speak in person in Chicago, Illinois. Shortly thereafter, he re-
                   ceives his "X" and formally becomes known as Malcolm X of
                   the NOI.

June 1953   Appointed by Elijah Muhammad as Assistant Minister of Detroit
                   Temple Number One and in the fall of the same year becomes
                   Minister of Temple Number Eleven in Boston.

1954   Becomes very involved in Temple activities and organizing in
                   Boston, New York, and Philadelphia. Appointed as the Minister
                   of Philadelphia's Temple Number Twelve and New York's
                   Temple Number Seven.

1955   Interviewed by the Federal Bureau of Investigation (FBI). Be-
                   comes heavily involved in recruiting new members for the NOI
                   amid rumors that Elijah Muhammad is involved sexually with
                   women outside of his marriage.

1956	Betty Sanders becomes a member of the NOI at Temple Number Seven and gets her "X" shortly thereafter.
Spring 1957	Brother Hinton X Johnson is brutally beaten by the police in New York and taken to the police station after trying to break up a fight. Malcolm has the Fruit of Islam (FOI) stand in rank formation at the 123rd Street Police Station until given assurances that Johnson will receive proper medical attention. The FOI and NOI in New York get widespread attention.
January 1958	Betty X marries Malcolm X in Lansing, Michigan. They live in a home in East Elmhurst, Queens. Their first child, Attallah, is born in November.
Summer 1959	Malcolm heads an NOI delegation to the Middle East and Africa, visiting five countries and learning more about orthodox Islam. A New York television station airs "The Hate That Hate Produced," a documentary by Mike Wallace and Louis Lomax, which gives the NOI national attention and new recruits.
December 1960	On Christmas Day, Malcolm and Betty's second daughter, Qubilah, is born.
1962	On April 27, Ronald Stokes, a member of the NOI in Los Angeles, is killed by the police after an altercation. Six other NOI members are wounded, and Malcolm, seeking revenge, is sent instead with orders from Elijah Muhammad to reduce tensions. Rumors again surface of adultery by Elijah Muhammad. Malcolm dialogues with three former secretaries of Muhammad that had his children through adultery. A third daughter, Ilyasah, is born to Malcolm and Betty in July.
May–August 1963	Several famous interviews, with *Playboy*, James Baldwin, and Kenneth B. Clark, take place with Malcolm. Malcolm attends the March on Washington in August.
Fall 1963	On November 10 Malcolm X addresses an alternative to the civil rights conference in Detroit and delivers to the Northern Negro Grass Roots Leadership Conference one of two of his most important speeches, entitled "Message to the Grass Roots." On November 22 President John F. Kennedy is assassinated, and Malcolm states that it is a question of the "chickens coming home to roost." On December 4 Malcolm is suspended from the NOI by Elijah Muhammad for the statement.
Winter 1963–64	At the invitation of Cassius Clay, who will soon become Muhammad Ali, on January 15, 1964, Malcolm and his family visit his Florida training camp for a week as Clay prepares to fight Sonny Liston for the heavyweight title. On March 8, 1964, Malcolm holds a press conference to announce his formal departure from the NOI and the creation of his new organization, the Muslim Mosque, Inc. (MMI).

Spring 1964   Malcolm meets with Martin Luther King, Jr., in Washington,
                           D.C. for their first and only meeting during congressional debate
                           of the 1964 Civil Rights Act. Lawyers for the NOI start eviction
                           proceedings to have him removed from the East Elmhurst home.
                           On April 13 Malcolm again travels to the Middle East and Af-
                           rica, makes the Hajj to Mecca, Saudi Arabia, and visits a number
                           of other Middle East and African countries where he tours and
                           lectures regarding human rights and race relations in the United
                           States. As an international figure, he is given the treatment of a
                           chief of state in Saudi Arabia, the Republic of Ghana, and other
                           countries. Returns to New York in the middle of increasing ten-
                           sions with the NOI on May 21, 1964.

Summer 1964   Malcolm announces the creation of the Organization of Afro-
                           American Unity (OAAU) as a formal entity. In July he again
                           travels abroad to Africa and the Middle East, attempting to mo-
                           bilize support for his campaign of human rights violations
                           against the United States. He addresses the Organization of Af-
                           rican Unity (OAU), making his case to the thirty-four delegates
                           from various countries to support the cause of African Ameri-
                           cans in the United Nations. He also addresses a number of par-
                           liaments in several countries on this same issue. On September
                           1 a New York judge hands down a decision that Malcolm must
                           move from the East Elmhurst home.

December 1964   His fourth daughter, Gamilah, named after Gamel Abdel Nasser,
                           is born.

Winter 1964–65   Malcolm flies to Paris, France, on February 9, 1965, for a speak-
                           ing engagement but is denied entry by the French government,
                           and rumors abound that the U.S. Central Intelligence Agency
                           (CIA) may have planned an assassination on French soil. On
                           February 14 Malcolm's house is firebombed in the middle of
                           the night. The police blame him for the firebombing. On Feb-
                           ruary 18, 1965, Malcolm's family is evicted from the East Elm-
                           hurst house.

February 21, 1965   Malcolm is assassinated at the Audubon Ballroom in Harlem.

February 22, 1965   Elijah Muhammad denies any involvement of the NOI in the
                           assassination of Malcolm X, although the three arrested for the
                           shooting are alleged members of the NOI.

February 27, 1965   Malcolm is funeralized at the Faith Temple Church of God in
                           Christ, given formal Islamic last rites, and buried at Ferncliff
                           Cemetary in Hartsdale, New York.

March 11, 1965   A grand jury indicts Talmadge Hayer, Thomas 15X Johnson,
                           and Norman 3X Butler for the death of Malcolm X.

November 5, 1965   Betty Shabazz gives birth to twin girls, Malaak and Malikah.

Winter 1966

The murder trial in the assassination of Malcolm X starts January 12. On March 11 all three of the defendants are found guilty in the murder of Malcolm X, and on April 14, Judge Charles Marks sentences all three convicted assassins to life imprisonment.

INTRODUCTION

Hanes Walton

COMPROMISING MORALITY: THE CREATION OF THE POLITICAL LEADERSHIP OF MALCOLM X

Man's inhumanity to man in the American experience created Malcolm X and his enduring legacy. He is not, as E. Victor Wolfenstein claims, the result of Marxist dialectic materialism. He was not the sole result of Sigmund Freud's intrapsychic tensions and childhood maturation. Or the results of Harold Lasswell's thesis about the power seeker syndrome. The journalistic theory of CBS reporter Mike Wallace* of "The Hate That Hate Produced"* is far from the mark. In fact, Harold Cruse's theory of culturalism does not quite explain the rise and perpetuation of Malcolm X; neither will the theories of racial oppression and subordination of Frantz Fanon.* And perhaps most important, nor will the religious cosmology of Elijah Muhammad do the job, or the autobiographical insights of Alex Haley* about a streetwise hustler armed with a righteous cause and calling. They all leave him pretty much where they found him, in "the here and now," a man responding to his present crisis in a different and unique fashion. This leaves him as a one-dimensional figure in an era dominated by Martin Luther King, Jr.'s* leadership. Clearly, it does not come close to explaining his continuing relevance, popularity, and legacy well beyond his time and place on the historical stage. And without his continuing presence, the intellectual and popular community would not need this important and timely new book.

COMPROMISING MORALITY: THE ROLE OF THE FOUNDING FATHERS

At the May 1787 Constitutional Convention in Philadelphia the Founding Fathers* treated the slavery issue as a "political instead of a moral question"

and therefore delayed its destruction and elimination as a task for future generations when they would supposedly be more enlightened. Hence, the Founding
Fathers created a republican form of democracy that compromised in its formative years with morality and thereby set into motion a major precedent, one
that each succeeding enlightened generation would embrace in their solution to
a racial crisis. Their voice was and is clear: Compromise the nation's morality
and solve the matter in piecemeal fashion. Thus, each solution to a racial crisis
in the Republic has been a compromised "morality solution." Slavery gave way
to racial segregation,* while segregation gave way to desegregation, and desegregation has for the moment tumbled into affirmative action. And this status for
African Americans is being undercut and mended because it supposedly dis-
advantaged whites. Currently, the onslaught to this status is being led by African
Americans who claim that they know in their heart of hearts that the affirmative
action status and state for African Americans is wrong because it makes them
dependents and wards of the state. Sadly they have no plan for dealing with the
past, current, and future problems that are derived from the compromised morality given to the nation–state by its Founding Fathers and their political and
social heirs. Yet it is this endless reality of compromised morality that created
the political leadership and enduring legacy of Malcolm X. Therefore, the question can be raised: What is this matter of compromised morality? Essentially,
as John P. Roche put it when he made his extensive analysis of the 1787 Convention, it is not one of asking if the treatment of African Americans under
these various social systems is right or wrong but one of asking what is politically feasible at the moment in dealing with this less-than-humane treatment.
In approaching this problem, the Founding Fathers created at the 1787 Constitutional Convention two distinct tendencies and realities: (1) a movement toward
democracy and (2) a movement toward tyranny. Although the nation's psyche
has failed to recognize these two tendencies that emanated from the 1787 Convention, Malcolm X saw not just the American Dream but also the American
Nightmare, which was made possible by the Founding Fathers' compromise with
morality.

COMPROMISING MORALITY AS THE CONTEXTUAL
ROOTS OF MALCOLM X'S LEADERSHIP MANTLE

Regarding the results of the 1787 Convention and the Constitution, historian
John Hope Franklin notes that an examination of the period from the advent of
the Constitution to the Civil War, perusing the Founding Fathers, the embryonic
Republic, and its great leaders in the first half of the nineteenth century, finds
that they never pursued a policy that would lead to citizenship or equality for
free blacks and slaves. Moving beyond the period discussed and analyzed by
Franklin, historian, attorney, and former chair of the U.S. Civil Rights Commission Mary Francis Berry, adds:

The Founding Fathers created a framework of government that has served many purposes. In protecting slavery and assuming racial inequality, they made African Americans outsiders from the beginning. They also provided a rationale that could be used by non-African Americans to assume the basic worthlessness, powerlessness, and inhumanity of African Americans as a part of the nation's legacy. Even though by the time of the centennial there had been a great deal of violence and their work had been modified and improved upon, the pall of slavery's influence remained. The pall was still present at the Constitution's bicentennial, although it had diminished somewhat.

She continues: "The African American vision of the Constitution as it was written in 1787 can be characterized as an affirmation of exploitation and exclusion. By 1887 the Constitution had come to represent inclusion in language but exclusion in reality. Today African Americans see in it a continuing struggle for inclusion. Our lives begin and end taking into account that vision of us crafted by the Founding Fathers in the Constitution."

Collectively, both Franklin and Berry see that compromised failure as continuing and as the source for the African American freedom struggle. And it is this contextual reality that gave birth first to an oppositional culture and to one of its greatest articulators and leaders, Malcolm X. But first a word about the nature, scope, and significance of this contextual environment.

Of all the descriptions of the context in which African Americans lived and died and hoped and prayed, one of the most poignant is that one described by political scientist Richard Bardolph:

Whites, including not a few liberals, were hurt and angered when blacks continued to raise their demands after a decade and a half of civil rights victories in courts and legislatures had made concession after concession. They failed to understand that the concessions should not have been necessary in the first place, and that they had not, after all was said, made very much difference. The ultimate reason for seeking admission to unsegregated schools and buses and theaters had been the imputation of racial inferiority which segregation so clearly proclaimed. But after the courts decreed an end to segregation the implication was still there . . . in private and personal ostracism; in shabby employment opportunities; in inferior schools; in ghetto stores where shoddy merchandise was sold at inflated prices to a trapped clientele.

It was this context, the near uniform and universal nature of it, that existed throughout the nation–state for almost all African American communities. Over time it created a culture of opposition, and that culture generated its own spokespersons and mobilizers. It had to, and it still does.

The social, economic, legal, and political system known as segregation was more than a constitutionally condoned system of "separate but equal" reality. First, it was never an equal system. It was in every way and from top to bottom a system of inferiority and oppression. It had no intentions of being—nor could it be—a system of equality. The very section of the nation–state that was its originator, perpetuator, and constant guardian could not economically afford to make it "a separate but equal" system. But more important, the social and political philosophy of the region, white supremacy, could and would not ever let it be "separate but equal." This philosophy insisted on a system of hierarchy and value priorities. Hence, the African American material, economic, social, and political position had to be less than, subordinate, lower, under, secondary, poorer, second-rate to, mediocre, substandard, and of a poorer quality than whites'. The very inherent nature of this philosophy could not accept anything more. Therefore, the very essence of white leadership in the region committed itself to ensuring this constant reality. Beginning with the politics of redemption when southern whites recaptured the southern governments from African Americans and the Republicans until the present time, regional leadership sought not only to protect their social system from outside interference and intervention by the national government but to persuade the rest of the nation to accept and implement in their own area the social system of segregation. Their instrument of persuasion, transformation, and protection was the Democratic Party.* It was their outreach tool and device.

In the 1880 presidential election, the South went solidly Democratic and maintained this status until 1928 and 1948, when there were momentary cracks, and each time thereafter the region returned to its solid status until 1964. Then the cracks began to take on a permanent status, as the 1960s, 1970s, 1980s, and 1990s would prove. The South became solidly Republican, save when the Democratic Party nominated a southern native son candidate, in the likes of Lyndon B. Johnson,* William Carter, and William Clinton, and Al Gore. Yet even with these native sons the cracks remained. And in the 1994 election when the region transformed itself from just presidential Republicans to congressional and gubernatorial Republicans, the thrust of the changes was to maintain the new social system of desegregation if not roll back to the old days via the destruction of affirmative action.

But the second major instrument of persuasion, transformation, and protection besides the Democratic Party was African American leadership itself. This tool and technique also began in the Era of Redemption and finally consolidated itself with the emergence of Booker T. Washington and those of similar views. These selected and anointed leaders taught the already heavily impacted African American communities to accept and accommodate themselves to their inferior status until southern whites were ready to change their system of white supremacy. In different ways and via different philosophical arguments, these accommodation leaders urged their communities to go along in order to get along and survive. But despite the nature and brand of these philosophies, they all had the same thesis—accept a system with an inferior, second-class, subordinate context and leave the initiative of change to southern whites. This was then, as now, a bitter pill to swallow.

The third but little acknowledged instrument of persuasion, transformation, and protection came from the white population itself, along with all of its institutions and organizations. At the center of all of this, however, was the white individual. The preeminent historian of this social system of segregation and its philosophy of white supremacy is C. Vann Woodward. He says unequivocally that Jane and Jim Crow put the power of the state into the hands of every ordinary white person. They, at both the informal and formal bases of society, had a stake in the maintenance and perpetuation of segregation. White journalists John Griffin and Grace Haskell changed the color of their skin and went south to discern what this social system was really like on a day-to-day basis. In their two classical works on the world behind the veil—W.E.B. Du Bois* had in his classic *The Souls of Black Folks*, with as much elegance of language as he could muster, told White America what life behind the veil was like—Griffin in *Black Like Me** and Haskell in *Soul Sister* describe a context that was at the very least the heart of darkness.

Of the unique role that the individual white masses played, Griffin and Haskell discovered the strange and rarely discussed device of the "hate stare," that is, the look that whites gave African Americans in public and in private on a daily basis simply because they were African American. For African Americans this stare was given even if they had not breached any of the social boundaries of the social system of segregation. This hate stare was indiscriminate. It was given to those who violated the system of segregation as well as to those who religiously tried to obey and accommodate it. And to those who obeyed, it was more than unsettling. But, then, it was intended to be. It was a psychological weapon meant to terrorize, since the recipients did not know what they had done to deserve such a terrible response; and it was designed to convey without even speaking that this black person was less than human. It was the white man's inhumanity to the black man. It was merciless. It was frightening. It was anger, bitterness, and viciousness. It was vilification and meanness. It created a context that, in the words of Malcolm X, blamed the victim for his or her own victimization. The hate stare was the ultimate put-down of another human being. Segregation—and its ensuing counterpart, desegregation—was not simply "separate and unequal"; it was unrelenting psychological terror and oppression. Thus, it is into this context that Malcolm X was born and evolved.

The fourth and deadly technique of persuasion, transformation, and protection was that of violence. It could be both legal, as implemented by the white justice system and its legitimate police force, and extralegal, as implemented by the Ku Klux Klan,* a white mob, or a single white individual on a racial vendetta. However it was implemented, it was a form of social control that was bloodthirsty, murderous, and the very epitome of racial brutality. This technique worked to ensure few breaches of the social system of segregation and desegregation. This, too, shaped the context in which Malcolm X evolved.

COMPROMISING MORALITY GENERATES AN AFRICAN AMERICAN OPPOSITIONAL CULTURE AND LEADERSHIP

Collectively, these four dominant instruments, along with several minor ones, kept the southern culture and way of life known as white supremacy intact for another hundred years after the collapse of slavery. And even when desegregation appeared, these instruments helped to continue a modified version of the system in place until the turn of the twenty-first century. These instruments and devices were able to beat back and beat down any attacks, modifications, and breaches in the social system of segregation that African Americans were able to mount. And if parts of this system were destroyed and overrun, these instruments would immediately repair it, prop it up, and recast the system so as to minimize the damage and disintegration. These instruments kept the system from sustaining any permanent damage and rearrangement. These instruments proved, in a word, to be resilient. But neither did they nor their proponents go without a challenge. The African American community responded to its systematic and comprehensive oppression.

Caught up in such a vortex of both psychological and physical terror and violence, the African American community created a culture of opposition. With meager resources and precious few allies, and with all of the techniques and devices that it could muster, the African American community generated a long and protracted struggle to shake off and eliminate its oppressors. At the cultural level, African Americans went after their own leadership that had been turned against them. Since this leadership had not been selected or elected or anointed by the community, they had to find a way to neutralize and isolate this white clientage leadership in the African American community.

A popular procedure in this culture of opposition was the use of African American newspapers to decry, denounce, deride, diminish, dethrone, decloak, deny, and defame this clientage leadership. These newspapers stereotyped, ridiculed, and satirized these clientage leaders into either reconversion—shaming them into quitting or neutralizing themselves and embarrassing their followers into moving on—and/or abandonment by whites formerly supporting them. Although this was an imperfect control tactic, it was not without its effects. It was a central feature of this culture of opposition.

Coupled with this diverse tactic of the dismissal of clientage leaders, the culture of opposition generated its own inbred and in-house leaders that defied and confronted the system of segregation and its philosophy of white supremacy. Such leaders, dubbed "Bad Niggers" by the African American community and "Militant Negroes" by the white community, flaunted the customs and conventions of the system of segregation and desegregation and spoke the truth to power. They called it as they saw it and demanded not slow progress but immediate changes. Most important, they were uncompromising. The white community quickly isolated and refused to deal with these leaders or simply had them eliminated. But as quickly as they were expunged, new ones emerged to take their place. And the process was not helter-skelter. Such leaders had to earn their stripes and their recognition. They had to acquire followers and respect and then achieve recognition to rise to the top. They had to find a way to get noticed and accepted. They had to earn community adulation and admiration. The road to this pinnacle could be diverse and unconventional, but a road had to be taken. There was one and only one requirement: They had to engage in plain speaking about the horrors and terrible conditions and disquietude, the endless frustrations, indignities, and the inhumanity inside the context of the African American community. The solutions to these problems did not matter as much as the lack of straight talk about the conditions. These would-be leaders had to speak of the nightmare nature of the American Dream in the African American community. They had to speak of the "hate stare" in their daily lives. They had to be indelicate about these matters in their discussions with and engagement of the white community. These would-be leaders, these "Bad Niggers," these "Militant Negroes," had to persuade their potential followers in the African American community that when they came into contact with the white community, they would not embrace comity in their exchanges about the nature and scope of the problem. When these leaders persuaded their potential followers, they were on their way. Again, the culture of opposition could not and did not elevate its confrontational leaders in a straightforward and linear fashion. Nor could it always generate them quickly and immediately. But it would eventually push them to the forefront.

David Walker and Henry Highland Garnet came out of the antislavery movement. Martin Delany came out of the colonization movement. W.E.B. Du Bois came out of education and the Booker T. Washington movement. Chief Albert Sam and Marcus Garvey* came out of the Back to Africa movement. Jack Johnson came out of boxing and athletics. A. Philip Randolph* came out of the railroad labor movement. Elijah Muhammad* came out of the Moorish Temple movement, and Malcolm X came out of the streets, prison,* and the Black Muslim* movement. Different confrontational leaders arrive from different points from within the African American community with different outlooks, philosophies, and tactics but with a common core reality, which was speaking the truth to power about the conditions under which African Americans lived and suffered and persevered. Each in his own way spoke of the nightmare nature of the American Dream. Each earned his reputation as a leader according to the dictates of the culture of opposition.

COMPROMISING MORALITY: THE MOMENT OF MALCOLM X LEADERSHIP AND LEGACY

The African American culture of opposition had to rely on the African American press and its church to reinvigorate and rejuvenate its confrontational leadership. Technological changes in communication like the radio in the 1920s were seized upon by white supremacy leadership because of its control of advertising revenue and used to further stereotype African Americans via shows like *Amos and Andy* and via white products with such names as Aunt Jemima, Uncle Ben, and Niggerhead Shrimps. Only sport shows where African American athletes like Jesse Owens in the 1936 Olympiad, Joe Louis* in his defeat of German boxer Max Schmeling, and Jackie Robinson's* outstanding performances in baseball games fed into and reinforced the oppositional culture. Radio, in a

word, did not advance the culture of opposition as did African American institutions. But soon a new communication technology would arrive, television.
And television, like radio, came with stereotypical sit-coms and product advertising. However, this new electronic medium had one feature that was different:
It had news programming that was global in scope and focus. In and of itself,
this would not have been useful. What made it useful was that after the Albany
Movement of 1961 and its less-than-successful achievement of national public
policies to eliminate the social system of segregation, African American civil
rights* leaders designed their future protest so that it could effectively exploit
the new technological medium of television. This had not happened with radio.
However, the use of television as a tool of African American social protest was,
without a shadow of a doubt, dramatic. The images and pictures of the 1963
March on Washington,* the pictures and images of the peaceful nonviolent 1963
Birmingham protest and the brutal violence, and the white inhumanity needed
to maintain and perpetuate the system of segregation were there for everyone
to see. As Martin Luther King, Jr., remarked, television brought out in the open
and to the light what African Americans constantly experience behind the veil.
Television captured the straight talk and plain speaking that scores of African
American leaders had not been able to convey to the rest of the world. Television
revealed that "separate but equal" was not about that but truly about white
supremacy at all cost. Television brought the true nature of the segregation
holocaust to full and complete and comprehensive view. It could no longer be
swept under the rug and kept in the shadows with generous and kind and dis-
arming phrases like "You know we are making progress" and "We have to be
patient a little bit longer" and "Full citizenship, full freedom is just around the
corner." The 1965 Selma March demonstrated that no such intention, at least in
the South,* was under way. In television the culture of opposition got a major
ally. And unlike liberals, who were unreliable, the eye of television was un-
blinking.

Yet again it was not television itself. This new technology came of age at the
very moment of the civil rights movement.* In the 1960s, this brooding and
simmering and sometimes halting movement had finally started to coalesce and
unify and organize to effectively tackle all four instruments employed by white
southerners and their allies, so as to shatter their grip on the institutions of power
and force. This culture of opposition had come into its own. Instead of its rather
meager thrust of the past, it had finally fostered a challenge of major proportions
and magnitude. This was unexpected.

But more important, the soldiers of segregation, as in the past, sought a new
crop of clientage leaders. Television joined in the search and found an unexpected phenomenon, the charismatic and confrontational leadership of Malcolm
X. Television introduced him not only to the soldiers of segregation and the
white community but to the African American community as well. If Malcolm
was a surprise to the soldiers of segregation and the white community, he came
as no surprise to the African American community. But to this community, here

was the "Bad Nigger" in the flesh. Here was the "Militant Negro Leader" in the flesh. Here was the pop-culture hero—Shaft—in the flesh. All during their lifetimes, they had heard of such a figure, had hoped for such a figure. They had been willing to accept fictional and mythic characters in this role. Finally, they had accepted the written word about him in the shape of an autobiography. But television went one better. Now television provided a real image of a real person. And Malcolm X did not disappoint them. He was all that people had hoped for and more. Malcolm X fitted the myth perfectly. Malcolm X was the myth. This was like the coming of the messiah, the promised one.

Malcolm arose during the dynamic leadership of Martin Luther King, Jr. Hence, the African American community could compare this myth, the hoped-for plain-speaking leader, the uncompromising leader, with the mighty King. He was just as awesome. He was just as needed and just as important. The culture of opposition had long taught and socialized the African American community into understanding that the sole successful African American leader could become corrupted or coopted or, worse, eliminated. One needed a check and countercheck. One was needed in the wings and/or on stage to be the opposite. For the soldiers of segregation this was not only unsettling; it meant that their search for, in the words of Federal Bureau of Investigation* director J. Edgar Hoover,* a reliable Negro leader responsible to whites only would have to be more overt and obvious than in the past. This also meant that such a clientage leader would have no place to run and hide or be effective in a context where Malcolm and King dominated.

Yet despite the elegance and dynamism of King and his lieutenants, the community also needed a Malcolm X, and no one knew this more than Malcolm himself. The times and the community needed someone to speak of the nightmarish frustrations and anguish and gothic horrors gripping the segregated communities of African Americans. Malcolm X "made it plain." He told it like it was. He proved to be the match for television. He was, literally, the right man at the right time. The existence of King gave Malcolm his moment, and Malcolm helped to give King his moment. Theirs was a moment of reciprocity. Even so, Malcolm seized the moment and made it his. And for that capture of the arresting moment, the African American community extended their mantle of leadership to Malcolm X.

It was not just King and the technology that made Malcolm X alone. Nor was it just the capture of the moment by Malcolm X. The culture of opposition had first enlisted the enlightened, the elites, the well-placed, and the talented. Then it penetrated to enlist the masses in its struggle. By the 1960s it had recruited and enlisted the rising intelligentsia, the college students. The culture of opposition had attracted those least attached to and connected with this system of segregation. And in a moment, these students became the shock troops of the freedom movement and became consciously aware of this crucial position as well as the need to be the shock troops. Thus, they acquired their own heroes and heroines who, like them, had shock value. The confrontational leader had shock value. Malcolm X had shock value. Without him knowing it, they took Malcolm out of his religious environment, out of the Nation of Islam* and away from Elijah Muhammad, and put him in the midst of the mainstream civil rights movement and struggle. Television aided in this transformation process, as did the conversion of popular boxer Muhammad Ali.* Soon Malcolm X was speaking not just for Muhammad, the Temple, and Allah*; he was speaking for the entire African American community. The culture of opposition had always used even reluctant leaders to assist in its own cause and salvation. Malcolm X simply became the new spokesperson. And this reposition and transformation of Malcolm soon led to his break with Muhammad. And his reconversion as an Islamic spokesperson became embedded in the culture of opposition. This departure soon led to his assassination and murder. The confrontational leader died at the hands of African Americans. His counterpart, King, died the same way but at the hands of whites. With their deaths, the die was cast. A legacy was born. Malcolm X became bigger than life itself.

Numerous forces merged to give Malcolm X his moment. Or, in the words of the old Baptist preachers, a variety of things called Malcolm X to a leadership role. Put in the vernacular of behavioral, social, and political science, a rare combination of independent variables caused him to play a major leadership role in the 1960s. And then his questionable destruction and demise ensured his legacy for all future generations. The reason for this perpetual legacy lies in the very nature of the culture of opposition in the African American community.

During Malcolm's unique and exceptional moment of leadership, he became the myth. He became one with the uncompromising leaders. He became that mythic figure, and he did not live long enough after that to contradict or deny his presence as the personification of that myth. Malcolm, at the moment of his death, became encased and entombed in a long and enduring myth in the African American community. Malcolm the fearless one. Malcolm was the man. And despite his death and the way of his death, Malcolm had already become a legend in his own time. He was the ultimate living legend. Therefore, his death merely enhanced and enriched that legend.

Of Malcolm X's role and function in and for this culture of opposition, cultural theorist and leader Maulana Karenga* declares:

Of all of Malcolm's contributions to African American political and intellectual history, none is more central than his critique of domination and the oppositional logic which informs and impels it. . . . Malcolm's critique includes a moral judgement against the social constraints on human freedom, i.e., on the human person's capacity for rational self-determination in community.

Karenga adds to this instructive insight by noting that

Malcolm sees behind the image and illusion of the American dream, an American nightmare for the oppressed, below the illusion of integration, a tokenism of symbolic placement of selected and cooperative members of the oppressed and beyond the claims of democracy, a race- and class-determined social order.

In Karenga's opinion, Malcolm both represents and advances the culture of opposition. He both symbolizes and energizes it. The rise of Malcolm X legitimatizes the culture of opposition. He moved it from the abstract and the potential to the real and the practical. Malcolm X gave the culture of opposition a meaning, a new purpose, a raison d'être.

But in the end, would it have all happened if the Founding Fathers had not compromised their morality at the 1787 Constitutional Convention? Would there even be a Malcolm X leadership and legacy, had equality been extended to all Americans? Yes, it is conceivable that there might have been a Malcolm X in an Islamic movement, but surely he would have been different than the one that arose in the Black Muslim movement. And that defining moment in the 1960s— would it have appeared along with King if the Founding Fathers had not failed at Philadelphia in 1787? Would there have been a culture of opposition created by the African American community and its allies, had moral concerns over African Americans as humans not been compromised?

Compromised morality led to the creation of, as well as the perpetuation of, man's inhumanity to man, the white man's oppression of the black man with the social systems of slavery, segregation, and desegregation. Compromise led to the creation of secular religions of the above social forms. And this secular religion justified the inhumanity of man to his fellow man and allowed the duality of morality, one for blacks and one for whites. In his 1997 essay "Moral Man and a Moral Journey," Political Scientist Hanes Walton in a reference to this secular religion practiced by famed educator and Morehouse College president Benjamin Elijah Mays and his students Martin Luther King, Jr., and classmate Samuel Du Bois Cook noted that:

This secular religion gave whites a dominant place, position, and function while simultaneously placing African Americans in a lower, negative, demeaning, and inadequate spot. This secular religion gave whites dominion over African Americans. God on earth had a white skin and face. And this secular religion was ever insistent that this article of faith be accepted and believed. The unaccepting and the unwashed and the nonbelievers would suffer a life of great pain and suffering behind the veil.

Ultimately, however, this secular religion led to the development of a culture of opposition and to an unaccepting and unwashed and nonbelieving leader known as Malcolm X. This leader confronted this secular religion in its segregation manifestation and denounced the prophets, soldiers, and fellow travelers of this religion of segregation. And in his moment of opposition, he reached back through time and exposed how the Founding Fathers of the nation–state had flawed their democracy by compromising moral issues related to slavery.

THE VALUE OF THIS ENCYCLOPEDIA ON MALCOLM X

If Malcolm X is important to the past, to the present, and to the future, as the introduction has shown and called one's attention to, then this volume that covers Malcolm X literally from A to Z will provide current and future generations with an invaluable tool to understand not just the man and his times and his organizations and the movements but the very essence of democracy and how flawed institutions can lead to unexpected consequences.

The coeditors and authors of this volume are to be congratulated for correctly using their time and scholarly talents to revisit this democracy and its institutions. Likewise, they are to be congratulated for not looking in the usual places and at the conventional leadership for insights into this democracy and its attendant problems. For by looking into some of the unusual places and at nonconventional leaders, they are able to offer up unused and bold new solutions to continuing and long-term unsolved problems.

In the end, this group of scholars have, because of their focus and approach, given more to the promise and spirit of democracy than those who continue to round up the usual suspects and institutions. With this work, future generations will be able to better understand and put into perspective the Malcolm X legacy and what the promise of democracy means. Flawed democracies carry with them not just dreams but simultaneously nightmares. And these burdens have long-term consequences and meanings not just for the slighted and demeaned groups but for the nature and promise of that democracy itself. These must be overcome, or clearly the democracy will fail.

This volume is a scholarly attempt to see that the worst of this democracy does not continue to prevail in time and space and institutions of the future. As Americans reach out into space and time to conquer and order new worlds and planets, new political arrangements should not continue to render man's inhumanity to other humanity. This volume is a bold effort to render that possible scenario harmless. Such is scholarship at its very best. No one could ask for or hope for more. This volume on Malcolm X is the right place to start.

SELECTED BIBLIOGRAPHY

Bardolph, ed., 1970; Berry (Franklin and McNeil, eds.), 1995; Carter, 1996; Franklin (Franklin and McNeil, eds.), 1995; Karenga, 1993; Malcolm X (Breitman, ed.), 1965; Malcolm X with Haley, 1965; Malcolm X (Perry, ed.), 1989; Roche, 1965; Walters and Smith, 1999; Walton, 1971, 1985, 2000; Walton (Trotter, ed.), 1997; Wolfenstein, 1993; Woodward, 1974.

THEME ESSAYS

ELIJAH MUHAMMAD, SR.

Irvin D. Solomon

It is virtually impossible to consider the evolution of Malcolm X and his role in the 1960s as a black leader without recognizing the importance of Elijah Muhammad* in his life. No one seemed to have had a greater influence in shaping what Malcolm became than Muhammad, a reality that Malcolm often repeated. Malcolm "loved" Muhammad, his world revolving around him for much of his adult life, and he was unashamed to admit it. But in many ways, Malcolm did as much to forge Elijah Muhammad as a major force in twentieth-century Black America as Elijah did for himself.

While serving time for burglary at a Massachusetts prison in the late 1940s, Malcolm X learned from his brother Reginald (Little)* and his sister Hilda (Little)* about an exciting religion based on black nationalism* and headed by its frail and dynamic leader Elijah Muhammad. Malcolm soon converted to this religious sect, the Nation of Islam (NOI),* more commonly known as the Black Muslims.* Elijah Muhammad lived in Chicago, Illinois,* at the time, but his converts resided primarily in the ghettos of large northern cities and in prisons. The NOI dramatically affected Malcolm in various ways until his death in February 1965.

Malcolm converted to the Black Muslim religion after extensively reading Muhammad's literature and after receiving a personal letter from Elijah Muhammad encouraging him to become a member of "the true knowledge religion." Like many of his fellow prisoners, Malcolm quickly evolved into a devoted follower of Elijah Muhammad and his religious sect, strictly following the Muslim* creed of racial separation* and prohibitions against the use of tobacco, alcohol, drugs, and the consumption of pork.* This regimen of personal absti-

Elijah Muhammad, Sr., shown speaking to his membership, was a beloved figure by most of his followers, none perhaps more devoted to him than Malcolm X before the break in their relationship in 1963. Library of Congress.

nence, coupled with Malcolm's unquenchable thirst for reading and studying Muslim literature, dramatically shaped Malcolm's psyche and persona for the rest of his life. From the time of Malcolm's release from prison* in 1952, he became a devoted follower and close personal associate of Muhammad until their well-publicized rift in 1963. Malcolm not only preached the tenets of Islam* throughout most of his adult life, but he exemplified the basic doctrines of the religion through his strict personal habits and lifestyle grounded in the Muslim faith. In this sense, Malcolm had become Elijah Muhammad's most popular lieutenant and effective proselytizing force.

Muhammad, whom Malcolm studiously referred to as "The Honorable Elijah Muhammad" during his Black Muslim years, had become both a powerful and controversial symbol of black nationalism by the midtwentieth century. Born Elijah Poole, the son of tenant farmers in rural Georgia, the uneducated Poole moved to Detroit, Michigan,* in 1923, where he met W. D. Fard* (Wali Farad, Master Farad Muhammad), a self-proclaimed "Allah"* or God and founder of the "Lost-Found Nation of Islam in the Wilderness of North America." In 1934,

Poole replaced Fard (who had mysteriously disappeared) as leader of the small black sect. Shortly thereafter, Poole adopted the name Elijah Muhammad and other honorific titles, including the "Prophet," the "Messenger of Allah," and the "Supreme Minister of the Nation of Islam." By sheer force of his personality, Muhammad molded the fledgling group into one of the most controversial American religious sects of the twentieth century. Imprisoned in 1942 for failing to register for the Selective Service, Muhammad's incarceration rallied members of the NOI further and helped to publicize the organization's views.

Elijah Muhammad's magnetic attraction to followers like the young Malcolm X came through his espousal of the doctrines of racial solidarity, self-help, self-defense,* and racial dignity. Under Muhammad, the Muslims also adopted an anti-assimilationist doctrine that alarmed moderate civil rights* leaders and organizations. The idea, as prescribed by Muhammad, that black Americans were the descendants of a superior African race that was destined to rule the white race and the world through violent upheaval proved equally disturbing to civil rights moderates.

Although significantly different from the teachings of orthodox Islam, the doctrine of the NOI advocated by Elijah Muhammad proved a powerful attraction to disaffected blacks like Malcolm, who had experienced firsthand the trials and tribulations of being black in a "White man's America." Based on Elijah Muhammad's forceful delivery of the Muslim message, and the energetic recruiting of new members by "the Prophet's" devoted lieutenant Malcolm X, the Chicago-based group grew to an estimated 250,000 followers nationwide by the early 1960s.

Many Muslims and non-Muslims alike were mesmerized by the dynamic leadership of Elijah Muhammad. Although he was hardly Malcolm's equal as a speaker, Muhammad was effective and frequently delivered his powerful speeches and messages in person and in the weekly tabloid *Muhammad Speaks*,* which Malcolm founded. Yet in the civil rights movement* of the 1960s, the angry prophet Elijah Muhammad was a divisive pariah in the eyes of black moderates but an apostle of cultural nationalism to black militants, many of whom had come to mold his teaching with the basic tenets of Black Power.* Even though Elijah Muhammad had tempered his rhetoric and placed the NOI on a more moderate ideological footing by the mid-1960s, most observers continued to see the Black Muslims as outside of the mainstream of the civil rights movement until the death of Muhammad in the mid-1970s.

Elijah Muhammad's popularity among blacks, and his influence over his most talented advocate Malcolm X, declined dramatically in the summer of 1963, when the press reported that two former secretaries had accused the sixty-seven-year-old "Messenger of Allah" of fathering their children. As disturbing as the disclosures were to rank-and-file Muslims, they proved fatal to the once bedrock loyalty of Malcolm. A growing crisis of confidence appeared between leader and disciple. It culminated in a much publicized eruption between the two after Muhammad had stripped Malcolm of his Muslim credentials for purportedly making an impolitic statement about the death of President John F. Kennedy* in November 1963. Shortly thereafter, Malcolm renounced his affiliation with the Muslim leader and created his own rival religious movement based on black nationalism and brotherhood.

The growing tensions between Malcolm and Elijah Muhammad culminated in the assassination of Malcolm X in February 1965, purportedly by dissenting Black Muslims. Elijah Muhammad vehemently denied rumors of involvement in Malcolm's assassination until his own death ten years later to the month. Even though speculation about Elijah Muhammad's possible complicity in Malcolm's death persists, the record is clear that the Black Muslim leader had a profound effect on the evolving philosophy and impact of Malcolm X until his violent death in 1965.

SELECTED BIBLIOGRAPHY

Clegg, 1997; Lincoln, 1973; Malcolm X (Westin, ed.), 1964; Malcolm X with Haley, 1965; McCartney, 1992; McCloud, 1995; *New York Times*, February 26, 1975.

NATION OF ISLAM

Nancy-Elizabeth Fitch

The Nation of Islam (NOI), popularly known as the Black Muslims,* a name given to it by the renown historian of the movement, C. Eric Lincoln,* reportedly to the dismay of NOI officials, was founded during the Great Depression* years in the midwestern part of the United States. In 1930, a man known at the time as Wallace D. Fard* came to an economically depressed section of Detroit, Michigan,* called "Paradise Valley."* He began preaching to the community's black working class, many of whom had recently migrated from the South,* seeking a better life. He spoke of the unfair and oppressive conditions that had been the lot of black people since they were forcibly brought to North America as slaves.

In order to counter the ill effects of the legacy of slavery, "Master" Fard preached that black pride* needed to be restored in black people and that blacks were a nation. The message, though presented in religious terms, had a distinct racial ideology. It also had social and economic importance. Around 1931, the NOI—or what members sometimes called the "Lost-Found Nation of Islam in the Wilderness of North America"—was born. The Black Muslim movement would be one that historian Lincoln, in his seminal work *The Black Muslims in America*,* called a dynamic social and religious protest movement.

Fard, known as the Prophet, spread his message generally among African Americans who were or had been Christians. He proclaimed, however, that there were religions more appropriate to the black experience that did not come from Europe* but from Asia and Africa. With teachings from the Bible* and the Holy Qu'ran,* and a new theology based on the concept of the divinity of black

Members of the Chicago Nation of Islam, including leader Elijah Muhammad (dark glasses), in a photo session outside the national headquarters. Courtesy of Kamal Karriem Jr.

people, he proselytized and converted many to an unorthodox form of Islam.* The message was especially directed at men in the inner city. Consequently, men constituted (and continue to do so) the greatest number in the NOI. The NOI, then, was structured as a black nationalist religious organization advocating black separatism, not only in the spiritual but also in the social and political spheres of African American life. Fard instructed his followers that just as the United States was not really their country, and therefore not owed any black allegiance, Christianity* was not the religion of blacks but of people whom he said were white "devils."* Fard identified a nexus between the peoples of Africa and Asia and used *black* as an all-inclusive term, excluding only the Caucasian. Islam, he taught, was the black man's natural religion.

According to NOI doctrine, the Caucasian race was created by a "mad" black scientist named Yacub.* Yacub had disobeyed Allah* or God by creating a nonblack race that replaced the hegemony of the black man with that of the white man. What is significant about this is that the NOI also preached that the present political and economic dominance of the Caucasian was "temporary," and a revived black nation would, in the future, reclaim its past and dominant position in the world. To accomplish this, the NOI saw that its mission was also to instruct the black masses in the history of the race. It proclaimed that white society had practiced "tricknology" in order to brainwash black men and deprive them of their self-knowledge as the original source of human civilization. These circumstances led, according to NOI ideology, to the existence and plight of the so-called Negro.* This so-called *Negro* is the derogatory term the NOI and Malcolm used to describe African Americans unsympathetic to its black nationalist teachings and who maintained a fundamental belief that America would eventually provide them the same opportunities and human rights* that it provided white citizens.

Initially, the NOI met in the homes of its members. Master Fard subsequently rented a hall, in Detroit, which he called the Temple of Islam. The Prophet's form of Islam, not recognized by mainstream practitioners of the religion, had its own theology and political creed complete with rituals and dogma specific to the racial uplift of black people. The NOI focused on the urban poor African Americans who were a scorned underclass in the United States. The philosophical teachings of the NOI are contained in two manuals written by Master Fard. *The Secret Ritual of the Nation of Islam* is presented in mathematically coded language and requires what Lincoln has called "special interpretation" to be understood. The second work, *Teaching for the Lost-Found Nation of Islam*, is presented through oral instruction that is memorized. Elements of secrecy and mystery are integral parts of NOI operations. As an example, even the number of its members can only be estimated. At the death of Fard's successor, Elijah Muhammad* in 1975, the figure ranged from 25,000 to 250,000.

In addition to the Temple of Islam, Fard created several other institutions. One of the first was the University of Islam,* in Detroit, a primary-secondary educational institution that promulgated his teachings. Another one was the Muslim Girls' Training Classes* that instructs young women in home economics and the appropriate demeanor for NOI women and their proper place within the family. And last but not least was the Fruit of Islam (FOI),* a paramilitary organization of able-bodied men whose original role was to defend the organization's members and property from non-Muslims. The FOI would later increase its authority within the NOI itself by policing and disciplining the membership.

One of Fard's first devotees, and the man he would appoint his Chief Minister of Islam, was Elijah Poole, a migrant from rural Georgia. Poole eventually became the spiritual leader of the NOI and would elevate Master Fard, after his mysterious disappearance in 1934, from Prophet to God or Allah, giving flesh to the idea of the divinity of the black man. Poole, whose name was changed by his mentor to Elijah Muhammad, would become the Messenger of Allah until his own death in 1975. No one knows what happened to Master Fard. Some have even speculated that his disciple, Elijah Muhammad, might have been involved in a power play to replace him. Regardless, with Fard's absence, dissension arose within the NOI—and not for the last time. Accompanied by his followers, Elijah Muhammad, who had been threatened by some of the

Detroit membership, left that city and retreated to Chicago, Illinois,* and Temple Number Two, which would become the national headquarters of the NOI.

Under Muhammad, the NOI identified itself as more than a separatist organization by addressing issues such as black economic self-sufficiency, black self-knowledge and racial self-identification,* and black nationhood. As a mass movement, the NOI had similarities to such early black nationalist groups as the Moorish Science Temple, Marcus Garvey's* Universal Negro Improvement Association (UNIA),* and Father Divine's Peace Mission Movement. In fact, Lincoln wrote that many of Fard's early converts came from the membership of these organizations. Further, none of these groups, including the NOI, were led by a black middle-class elite or by a desire to be integrated into America's dominant white society. Though it surely did not support legalized racial segregation* within the United States, the NOI did see blacks as a "separate" nation that should forge its own destiny. Unlike Marcus Garvey, who wanted to found a nation for African Americans on the African continent, Elijah Muhammad wanted a nation carved from the South where black people had worked free for centuries.

The NOI addressed the daily concerns of its membership who had a limited education. It instructed them in individual and group discipline, which included strict moral behavior in relations between Muslim* men and women and with non-Muslims, encouraged conservative dress, and stressed the importance of the family and the primacy of the man within it. The NOI also extolled the virtues of body cleanliness and the work ethic and established dietary restrictions that took pork,* considered unhealthy, out of diets as a former "slave" food. In addition, it proscribed the use of tobacco, drugs, and alcohol.* Schools of the NOI were among the first to teach courses in black history,* albeit some of it mythical, and provide instruction in Arabic. This puritanical and moralistic regimen, which constituted in many ways a constructive, though rigid, lifestyle for people afflicted by poverty and the accompanying despair and temptations of city life, was combined with a fundamental distrust of white society. The potential was there for violent, or at least confrontational, situations both inside and outside the NOI as a result of this duality.

In terms of self-identity and providing the foundations of black nationhood and racial separateness, entering Muslims were given the surname "X," which stood for their unknown African family name. Part of the mythology of the NOI was that African Americans in the United States were descendants of the Shabazz Tribe.* This surname was Malcolm X's, whose Muslim and Arabic name, after making his Hajj,* or pilgrimage to the Holy City of Mecca,* was El-Hajj Malik El-Shabazz.* In relinquishing their European last names, which was part of the legacy of American black slavery,* members of the NOI were told they were "exs": ex-slaves, ex-Negroes, and ex-Christians. By abandoning what was considered white Christianity, and embracing the NOI, they would also have a religion where God was a black man who resembled them.

In addition to establishing temples, or mosques, and parochial schools in major cities in the United States, the NOI was also involved in economic and business affairs in their communities. It established small businesses that included bakeries, restaurants, grocery, clothing, and drug stores, publishing companies, and dry-cleaning plants. When Malcolm X became the National Minister, he established the NOI's official newspaper, *Muhammad Speaks.** It necessitated FOI hawkers to sell the paper on street corners or buy them if they could not meet their sales quota. These efforts supported the rhetoric of black economic self-sufficiency.

Under Elijah Muhammad's forty-one-year leadership, the NOI grew. The Messenger proselytized among the working poor, among dissatisfied Christians, and among those who supported no organized religion. His ministers "fished" among prostitutes and pimps, in nightclubs and pool halls, among those with drug addictions, and among the criminal class. The NOI found many of its recruits in the prison* systems where Muslim ministers would go to preach and convert. Malcolm Little, who later became Malcolm X, was himself a prison convert and would later lead a successful prison ministry. It was Malcolm who, as the National Minister, was responsible for mobilizing and organizing the large membership on the national level.

Malcolm X first became acquainted with the NOI between 1947 and 1948, while serving a prison sentence for burglary. His brothers, Philbert (Little)* and Reginald (Little),* were already Muslims. They wrote him about the strict laws of the NOI, convincing him that he could benefit from self-discipline and could start by giving up smoking and eating pork. His brother Reginald told him that in this religion God, or Allah, was a black man and that he had talked to his Messenger, Elijah Muhammad. Malcolm's brothers also encouraged Malcolm to learn about the history of black people, indicating a link between a lack of self-knowledge and the oppression of the black man in the United States.

While still in prison, Malcolm took on a course of self-instruction and self-discovery, begun by reading and defining every word in the dictionary. He increased his vocabulary and improved his writing skills. Though he had been a good student in school, he had not gone beyond the eighth grade. By the time he was released from prison, in 1952, and working on behalf of the NOI, he was a self-taught, well-read, articulate, and charismatic speaker. The future spokesman of the NOI was careful to read everything he could get his hands on, including books by writers who might not give objective accounts about people of color. He needed to know how they thought too, he reasoned, in order to refute their ideas.

As Malcolm was preparing himself for life as a free man, Elijah Muhammad was often in Detroit* reestablishing Temple Number One. In Detroit, Muhammad often stayed with Wilfred Little,* another of Malcolm's brothers. Through these family connections with the NOI, Muhammad and Malcolm became frequent correspondents while Malcolm served his term. This was nothing new for Muhammad, because he often wrote to prison inmates, sometimes even sending money to them. He encouraged and fueled Malcolm's rehabilitation and became a second father figure to him. The two men met for the first time soon after Malcolm's release. Within a year, Malcolm had become Assistant Minister at Temple Number One and was fishing* for new recruits on Detroit streets. By 1954, when he became Minister of Temple Number Seven* in Harlem,* he had gained considerable experience, having served as Minister in the Boston and Philadelphia temples. Elijah Muhammad recognized Malcolm's organizing potential and charismatic personality. In addition to being Muhammad's spokesman and the first National Minister of the NOI, Malcolm X, in effect became second in command in the NOI and, even more important, the symbol of the NOI itself. During his twelve years as an active NOI member, in addition to founding *Muhammad Speaks*, Malcolm dramatically increased its membership and, through his very public adversarial and confrontational critique of American society, made the NOI an ideological and philosophical force to be reckoned with in the non-Muslim community in the United States as well as abroad.

The 1950s were an important period in the country's racial history. The *Brown v. Board of Education, Topeka, Kansas** Supreme Court decision outlawed segregated public schools and served as a catalyst to the twentieth-century mass protest movement for civil rights.* With the ascendancy of Dr. Martin Luther King, Jr.,* as the premier civil rights leader in America also came a rise in black militancy and debate within the black community itself over the respective virtues of racial integration* versus racial separation.*

The NOI, with Malcolm X as its foremost public symbol, presented the country with a clear choice: the nonviolent civil rights movement,* whose goal was integration and complete American citizenship, or increasing Black consciousness and calls for Black Power* and racial separation. Malcolm X crystallized the differences in the philosophies and tactics of the two movements and for a time took the NOI and a segment of the black community on the latter path.

This dialectical relationship, however, was really between the civil rights establishment and Malcolm X. Though it might have been beneficial to the country, in the long term it did not bode well for the NOI's National Minister. Elijah Muhammad had proscribed participation in, and confrontations with, American political and civil rights matters. By speaking out, as spokesman for the NOI, Malcolm drew the organization into the fray, provoking unwelcome criticism and scrutiny. At the same time, as Malcolm became more of a celebrity, he seemed more important than the Black Muslim movement and certainly more prominent than its leader. The final straw for Muhammad was Malcolm's unflattering remarks about the assassination of a beloved American president, John F. Kennedy.*

In 1963, Elijah Muhammad suspended his protégé, ostensibly for disobedience in speaking about the Kennedy assassination. Among certain elements in the NOI, Malcolm was also shunned. He left the NOI in 1964, became a Sunni Muslim, and established the Muslim Mosque, Inc. (MMI)* and later the Organization of Afro-American Unity (OAAU).* He also disavowed the NOI's tenet that whites were devils and said that he would work with militant Caucasians and non-Muslims toward goals they had in common. These events were perceived as challenges to the NOI and to the message of Elijah Muhammad and created dissension again within its ranks. Further, by discussing the alleged marital infidelities of Muhammad, Malcolm questioned his moral authority. When this is combined with the jealousy that existed among his former colleagues, there are reasonable grounds for some, including his deceased widow Betty Sanders Shabazz,* to believe that the NOI was involved in the 1965 assassination of Malcolm X.*

In the ten years between Malcolm X's death and that of Elijah Muhammad, in 1975, Malcolm's protégé and successor at Temple Number Seven in Harlem, Louis X, who later became Minister Louis Farrakhan,* assumed leadership as the National Minister. After Elijah Muhammad's death, Wallace Muhammad* became the new spiritual leader and changed the nature of the organization tremendously. He opened the former NOI to Caucasians, abandoned the demonization mythology about them, allowed that his father was not a holy Messenger but a mere mortal man, adopted orthodox Islam, divested the NOI of many of the financial assets acquired in the forty years of his father's leadership, and abolished the FOI, which he reportedly called the "punch your teeth out" branch of the NOI. Instead of a social protest movement, Wallace Muhammad remade the former NOI into a Sunni Islamic religious organization, no longer racially separatist and now involved in American political life and civil rights efforts.

These changes did not please everyone. Farrakhan was removed from his position as Minister of Temple Number Seven and posted to Chicago. Because of these changes, dissension in the ranks soon emerged again, and Farrakhan appeared to be in the forefront of it. In 1978, Minister Farrakhan led a group of followers out of what is now known as the American Muslim Mission* and resurrected the Nation of Islam in its original form, including the Fruit of Islam. He also became and remained in the 1990s its spiritual leader, a position he maintained in the year 2001.

Thus, much of this prior to Farrakhan was the Nation of Islam that came to be identified with Malcolm X. Clearly Malcolm left the greatest influence on the national character of the NOI movement, and the story of the organization cannot be legitimately told without acknowledging the impact that this charismatic figure had on the sect and the international world that he influenced.

SELECTED BIBLIOGRAPHY

Carson (Gallen, ed.), 1991; Clegg, 1997; Evanzz, 1999; Friedly, 1992; Gardell, 1996; Lincoln, 1968, 1973; Mamiya and Lincoln (Lippy and Williams, eds.), 1988; R. Turner, 1997.

MALCOLM X AND THE ROLE OF WOMEN

Mamie Locke

According to C. Eric Lincoln,* the Nation of Islam (NOI)* defined sex, morality, and the role of women in puritanical terms. No Muslim* woman could be left alone in a room with any man except her husband. She was forbidden to wear provocative or revealing dress or makeup. Muslim males were to be on constant guard for any interest shown in Muslim women by white men. It was believed that for white men sex was a degraded obsession. Muslim women were also taught the sect's version of the proper role of women, that is, how to sew, cook, rear children, care for their husbands, keep house, and behave under Muslim moral codes.

Initially, Malcolm X upheld the Muslim tradition of excluding women from full participation in leadership, keeping them mainly in the home and sharing only those responsibilities. He was a sexist who accepted the patriarchal views of traditional Western culture. Malcolm once stated that man by nature was strong and women were weak. Although men were required to respect women, they also had to control them.

Malcolm's attitude was derived not only from his Muslim teachings but also from the misogynist street culture that influenced his attitude. He often blamed women for the conditions of black men. He referred to black women as tricksters, evil, and tools of the devil; women, he once said, were satanic in nature. Throughout his sermons, when he preached in Temple Number Seven* in Harlem,* he criticized women for their gossip and excessive talking, for their sometimes "half-naked" attire, and for their use of body language to attract the attention of men. With such views, he understandably held women who conceived children out of wedlock in contempt. He was often criticized by women in the NOI for the harshness of his attitude and statements regarding them. According to Malcolm, however, his views were not meant to simply criticize but to emphasize the importance of women deferring to men. Any woman who dominated a man, he said, would also destroy him.

While in the NOI, Malcolm indicated that he so strongly supported the moral issues indoctrinated in him by Elijah Muhammad* that he was often accused of being "antiwoman." He stated that his teaching came directly from his belief that Muhammad was the very embodiment of moral, mental, and spiritual reform among black people. When he was faced with Elijah Muhammad's adultery, he indicated that his mind refused to even contemplate something so grotesque coming from an individual whom he so admired and respected. However, once he discovered the truth, he had to accept the fact that Muhammad had not only betrayed him but all Muslims. Included in this betrayal, in his mind, was the degradation of women—women who had struggled hard to rid themselves of drug habits and prostitution (working with Muslim sisters) to qualify morally to become registered Muslims.

Malcolm changed his views over time, ultimately supporting the full democratic transformation of all organizations dedicated to progressive social change. That meant the inclusion of women into all facets of society. In the last year of his life he rejected sexism and moved toward a more revolutionary position that insisted on the principle of absolute equality between men and women. He often repeated the revolutionary idea that progress in a society could best be measured by the condition of the women in that society. A truly revolutionary society could exist only when women had been freed from the bonds of male supremacy and patriarchy.

In an interview in Paris, France, in 1964, Malcolm stated his view about the role of women in advancing a society. If a country was progressive, he said, so were its women. If the country supported the advancement of education, it was because women insisted upon a consciousness of the need for education. Malcolm asserted that he was convinced of the importance of giving freedom to women through education and any other means that would advance them in society. This was because women would be the ones to instill the spirit, culture, and values in future generations. He was proud of the contributions that women had made in the struggle for freedom and felt that they should be given all of the opportunities necessary to advance in society. Malcolm claimed that women had, in many instances, made greater contributions to social movements than men.

Ironically, many of the changes in Malcolm X's attitude came as a result of his travels to Africa and the Middle East,* parts of the world where the submissive status of women in patriarchal societies had occurred for centuries. Malcolm X saw in many of these countries the roles women played in promoting and sustaining revolutionary movements. He was, for example, very complimentary of W.E.B. Du Bois's* wife, Shirley Graham Du Bois,* for the work she was doing in the Republic of Ghana.*

Malcolm also witnessed the roles of women in the civil rights movement* and within the NOI itself. In December 1964, Malcolm heard Fannie Lou Hamer* speak at an ad hoc committee meeting supporting the Mississippi Freedom Democratic Party (MFDP),* an organization that she cofounded. He condemned black men for allowing the brutality that Hamer and other women and children had experienced in Mississippi.* He spoke of her strength as a black woman for taking a leading role in the movement. At a meeting of the Organization of Afro-American Unity (OAAU)* held later that same evening, he called Hamer a brave freedom fighter, an individual at the forefront of the struggle in Mississippi. At this same meeting he spoke of the Mau Mau* uprising in Kenya and how blacks in the United States needed to be proud of them, not only the brothers (men) but the many brave sisters (women) who were also a part of the struggle to liberate Kenya. As an indication of his changing views of women, Malcolm stated that one need not be a man to fight for freedom; one need only be an intelligent human being. Fannie Lou Hamer and women of the Mau Mau were those kind of human beings.

In the aftermath of his split with the NOI, Malcolm X completely changed his views on the issue of women's rights. He went beyond the religious and moral context of their roles but emphasized the pressing need to mobilize all forces in order to bring about revolutionary change in society. He insisted that women be given clearly defined and prominent roles in the OAAU. He came to fully understand the African proverb "Educate a woman and you educate an entire family."

SELECTED BIBLIOGRAPHY

Alkalimat, 1990; Cone, 1991; Malcolm X (Breitman, ed.), 1970a; Malcolm X with Haley, 1965; Marable, 1985; B. Perry, 1991.

"MESSAGE TO THE GRASS ROOTS"

Najee E. Muhammad

Malcolm X (El-Hajj Malik El-Shabazz) delivered over twenty-six public orations that included his position as the national spokesman for the Nation of Islam (NOI)* founder of the Organization of Afro-American Unity (OAAU)* and the Muslim Mosque, Inc. (MMI).* Of those orations, four, delivered during the period between 1963 and 1965, stand out as perhaps the most significant: "Message to the Grass Roots" on November 10, 1963, in Detroit, Michigan*; "The Ballot or the Bullet,"* April 3, 1964, in Cleveland, Ohio; "The Oxford Debate," December 3, 1964, in Oxford, England; and what is commercially advertised as "The Last Message," February 14, 1965, in Detroit, Michigan. Of these four, three revealed a profoundly analytical, quick, observant, incisive, evolving intellect of one whose social critique of the political infrastructure of the United States and the international political infrastructure remains unrivaled in the latter half of the twentieth century and the beginning of the twenty-first century. "Message to the Grass Roots" provided the infrastructure for the other three major oratorical discourses. In doing so, it opened the window to Malcolm's critical intellectual capacity.

In 1963, two months after the March on Washington,* the Detroit Council for Human Rights organized a Northern Leadership Conference that was held in Detroit, Michigan, on November 9–10, 1963. When the council's chairperson the Reverend C. L. Franklin attempted to exclude the advocates of black nationalism,* Reverend Albert B. Cleage, Jr.,* pastor of the Shrine of the Black Madonna and a council member, resigned. In collaboration with the Group on Advanced Leadership (GOAL) and the Freedom Now Party,* an all-black political party, Reverend Cleage called for another conference—the Northern Negro Grass Roots Leadership Conference*—to be held in Detroit at the same time as the Northern Leadership Conference. The Northern Leadership Conference, integrationist in nature, attracted approximately 3,000 persons to its meeting site at Cobo Hall and featured as its main speaker Congressman Adam Clayton Powell, Jr.* The nationalist two-day conference, which attracted approximately 2,000 people, mostly of African descent from the United States and non-Muslims, was held at the King Solomon Baptist Church featuring Malcolm X as its main speaker. Appearing on the program with him were James Boggs* and his wife Grace Lee from Detroit; William Worthy,* journalist and head of the New York Freedom Now Party; civil rights* activist Gloria Richardson Dandridge*; and Reverend Cleage.

Malcolm X's "Message to the Grassroots" spoke plainly but clearly to the root of the problem confronted by African people in the United States. While this discourse spoke specifically to the problems of African people, so-called Negroes in the United States, it would be the first time that Malcolm would include the issue of ethnic diversity and ethnic unity in one of his addresses, and it indicated a major shift in his political orientation. Malcolm noted in "down to earth" language that people of color in the United States were a problem because they were not wanted in the country. He spoke to the root of issues faced by the critical masses of people of color internationally and called for common folk, "the grass roots," to put aside their differences and embrace their commonality by forming a united front in the face of common oppression. He stated the blacks caught hell because they were black, nothing more or less, and as ex-slaves had a common enemy and common oppression.

Unlike the previously delivered public discourses, this speech was different in context and content. Malcolm spoke as a leader of the African masses by explaining what was needed for liberation. For the first time since his affiliation with the NOI he did not speak primarily as their spokesman. While he used the stock phrase "the Honorable Elijah Muhammad teaches us," it was used sparingly, leaving the content of the speech politically beyond the teachings of Muhammad; indeed, he emerged as a significant "master teacher," social critic, and international theorist. Two weeks later, on November 22, 1963, President John F. Kennedy* was assassinated in Dallas, Texas, and Elijah Muhammad* issued a "gag rule" directive to all ministers of the NOI not to comment on the president's death. Despite the directive, when Malcolm, at a rally conducted by the NOI, was asked by a reporter about the assassination he gave his famous "chickens coming home to roost"* comment and was "silenced" for ninety days for the indiscretion that initially led to his break from the NOI. Therefore, his grassroots speech is one of the last public orations that Malcolm gave before leaving the NOI. According to Malcolm X scholar and theologian James H. Cone, after the break, Malcolm requested Milton Henry (Gaidi Obadele)* to eliminate all references to Muhammad from the tape recording of the speech. Apparently Henry complied with Malcolm's request.

The speech indicated Malcolm's shift from being a domestic theorist to an international theorist, establishing himself as a Pan-Africanist. Actually, this shift was a return to his familial Garveyite upbringing and existence. It was the first speech where he addressed the issue of international ethnic diversity and suggested the coming together of black people as a united front to combat white supremacy using the Bandung Conference* as the methodological template for his often-made call to unity. This 1959 conference held in Indonesia brought nations of color together under the banner of unity and excluded the white man. Malcolm's attendance at the Grassroots Leadership Conference and the speech itself suggested his willingness to broaden his scope beyond the NOI to address the liberation struggle of African people in the diaspora. It also suggested his willingness to ally himself with others outside of the NOI by putting differences aside for the purpose of unifying against a common oppressor.

He would repeat his willingness to work with anyone toward this goal. Malcolm defined revolution and dispelled the contextual romanticism associated with the term by giving a political and historical overview of the revolutions that took place in the United States, France, Russia, China, and Africa. He pointed out that the term *revolution** was used too loosely without understanding what it really means and that once one understood its meaning and how to successfully achieve revolution, they would accordingly change the context of how they used the term.

Malcolm noted that the foundation for revolutions was land, which is the basis for independence, freedom, justice, and equality. In his discourse on revolution, Malcolm as an educator taught about revolution and described, rather than supported, such action. In closing, Malcolm noted the significance of history as an educational and emancipatory tool for political liberation, pointing out that once blacks understood how others got their freedom, they would understand how to straighten out their own problems. Not only was "Message to the Grass Roots" one of Malcolm's best speeches, it was well received by the audience at the Northern Grass Roots Leadership Conference.

SELECTED BIBLIOGRAPHY

A. P. Bailey, 1990; Branham, 1995; Carson (Gallen, ed.), 1991; Cone, 1991; DeCaro, 1996; Goldman, 1979; Malcolm X (Breitman, ed.), 1965; R. Wright, 1994.

COALITION BUILDING

Lauren Larsen

The Voter Education Project (VEP) was established in 1961 as an early cooperative effort between the major civil rights organizations* and the U.S. Department of Justice (DOJ). Aides within the Kennedy administration, through contacts with liberal philanthropic foundations, arranged to help provide financing for nonpartisan voter registration campaigns throughout the South.* This was headed by the Southern Regional Council, a private interracial agency based in Atlanta, Georgia. A black civil rights* lawyer from Arkansas, Wiley Branton, was named to direct these efforts and to get the support of all the major civil rights organizations. These combined efforts led to the registration of 287,000 potential black voters. However, most of the new black registrants came mainly from southern urban areas and not the targeted rural black belt where repression of the race was most severe. The act of trying to bring about political reform often led to violent confrontations between the civil rights workers and southern law enforcement officials. The failure of the federal government to protect the civil rights workers dampened their efforts and generated their resentment toward the DOJ.

Other attempts at bringing about cooperative efforts led to frustration and disillusionment by civil rights activists. From 1961 to 1962 the Student Non-Violent Coordinating Committee (SNCC)* joined with the National Association for the Advancement of Colored People (NAACP),* the Southern Christian Leadership Conference (SCLC),* and other black organizations of Albany, Georgia,* to establish the Albany movement for desegregation. Bob Moses was instrumental in organizing the Council of Federated Organizations (COFO) in the state of Mississippi.* COFO was essentially a coalition of the Congress of Racial Equality (CORE),* NAACP, and SNCC organizers. Moses consistently instituted many registration drives in spite of strong white opposition. Throughout the South, CORE local groups cooperated with SNCC in organizing voter education and registration campaigns. These attempts at cooperation were short-lived as Malcolm X's ideas and organization began to attract a following that cut into the initiatives of established civil rights organizations. By late 1963 Malcolm's militancy was having an impact on many CORE and SNCC chapters, as some were seriously considering his suggestions for self-defense* within the black communities. At least one year before his break with the Nation of Islam (NOI)* Malcolm had established ties with the more radical elements of SNCC. In 1962 Stokely Carmichael,* an active member of SNCC and head of the Non-violent Action Group (NAG), invited Malcolm to debate longtime civil rights activist Bayard Rustin* and to speak before the student body of Howard University.* This subsequently led to other meetings between Malcolm and members of SNCC in Washington, D.C. as the group prepared to participate in the 1963 March on Washington.*

As civil rights activism progressed, Malcolm came to realize that the NOI's goals of racial and religious separation were ineffective in advancing the African American community in the United States. He recognized that his early criticism of the civil rights leaders and their techniques of protest and activism had underestimated the potential of grassroots activities to emerge as a force for social and political change. Malcolm eventually abandoned his post as a vehement critic of civil rights activities to establish a closer working relationship with others who had successfully mobilized mass protest movements. Although he had severely criticized many civil rights leaders, he often made overtures for dialogue with them. In 1960, he had invited Martin Luther King, Jr.,* and Roy Wilkins* of the NAACP to attend and speak at a Muslim-sponsored education rally in New York. Occasionally, Malcolm approved of non-Muslim protest activities: He supported the efforts of A. Philip Randolph* in the struggles of black and Spanish-speaking workers; he took part in a Harlem* rally against police brutality*; and he attended a rally in Birmingham, Alabama,* in 1963 to protest the bombing of a black church that killed four black girls.

By August of 1963 Malcolm had clearly developed a more conciliatory tone toward the nation's civil rights leaders. He called again for dialogue and for putting their minor differences aside to seek a solution to common problems. The conflict and eventual break with the NOI led to Malcolm's greater promotion of his black nationalist ideology. On March 8, 1964, when Malcolm announced his split from the NOI, he also indicated his support for, and his willingness to be actively involved in, the civil rights struggle. Although some civil rights leaders were receptive, others reacted with ambivalence.

To maintain his credibility and viability as a religious leader, Malcolm established the Muslim Mosque, Inc. (MMI).* Initially, the MMI was fashioned to attract membership from all classes and groups in the African American community. This was Malcolm's first attempt in building a black coalition. To achieve this, he had to become associated with the civil rights movement* and subsequently had to find an honorable way of working with black middle-class* leaders. In several public statements, Malcolm said that his goal was to work with other African American leaders to find a solution to the problems faced by blacks in the United States. However, he soon realized that an institution based on religion would not attract the broad base of support necessary to realize his objectives.

Malcolm believed that the most efficient way to achieve unanimity was not to challenge the established civil rights leadership but to form a united front with them in the context of an umbrella organization. Malcolm did not dismiss the reformist strategies of the civil rights movement. He felt that the limits of reform strategies had to be tested and challenged so that African Americans might be encouraged to transcend them. On June 28, 1964, shortly after returning to the United States from a pilgrimage to Mecca,* he established the Organization of African American Unity (OAAU)* to unite African Americans in a nonreligious, nonsectarian program for human rights.*

The new organization was patterned after the Organization of African Unity (OAU),* the first major attempt in the 1960s by revolutionary Pan-African nationalists to form a black united front. Malcolm's group was designed, in part, to be a revolutionary nationalist alternative within the established civil rights movement. Its purpose was to engage in activities that would bring international recognition to the African American freedom struggle. It sought to achieve a comprehensive agenda of goals by attacking the internalization of black oppression through improved education for the African American community (developing alternative schools, cultural centers, and other educational institutions); enhancing black political power through voter registration campaigns and the election of independent black candidates for public office; promoting better housing conditions for blacks; eliminating organized crime; and establishing community programs to help drug addicts and unwed mothers.

Another objective included developing a working relationship between the civil rights movement and the OAAU. In this respect, Malcolm invited Roy Wilkins and other civil rights leaders to an OAAU meeting in June 1964. He assured them in his overture that the intent of the OAAU was not to compete with other existing civil rights groups. Shortly thereafter, in one of its first official acts, the OAAU sent messages to both Dr. Martin Luther King, Jr., and SNCC executive director James Forman,* pledging its willingness to help with their civil rights agenda. At the time, King was engaged in SCLC's nonviolent St. Augustine, Florida, campaign, while Forman and SNCC were involved in the Mississippi Freedom Summer* project. Little in a positive way came from Malcolm's and his OAAU overtures to these established national leaders, although many of Harlem's political, educational, and cultural leaders responded affirmatively.

The OAAU resulted from the evolution of Malcolm's political ideology from black nationalism* to Pan-African internationalism. By 1963, after almost ten years of activism, the civil rights movement was faced with the dilemma of determining which direction it should take. The problem was whether or not to continue with the efforts toward reform through nonviolent means or move in a direction toward a program of extreme radicalism. Nationalist ideology became a significant issue at this crucial stage of development. This stage required three things: that the civil rights movement be expeditiously transformed into a formal organization as part of a national movement; that the southern regional character of the movement assume one that had a national appeal; and that the movement successfully attract a broader base of groups and classes that were inactive in the earlier stages of the struggle. The OAAU was the first attempt in the 1960s to build an African American coalition based on nationalist ideology. Although it was based in a northern urban environment, its leadership and membership represented new social groups that were drawn into the struggle for freedom.

By creating the OAAU Malcolm hoped to cultivate three groups: progressive elements of black middle- and working-class activists that came together to oppose exploitation of the African American urban community; allies in Africa and other parts of the world who could get worldwide acknowledgment for his organization; and friends in the civil rights movement who favored Malcolm's wishes for reconciliation. In formulating the OAAU, Malcolm put together a brain trust composed of students, writers, politicians, academics, celebrities, professors, professionals, former Black Muslims, and developing revolutionaries, whose mission it was to devise an organization and a political program around the concept of black nationalism. The OAAU was especially attractive among the youth groups associated with the civil rights movement. These groups also provided access to radical white students who would ultimately serve as allies.

Malcolm also organized several chapters of the OAAU among expatriate communities in the Republic of Ghana,* Kenya, Egypt,* and Paris, France. These chapters provided African Americans living abroad with the opportunity to relate to the mission of the OAAU and to take part in events occurring in the United States. Malcolm developed a tremendous following among African American students abroad and Middle Eastern and African students. The support from foreign students came directly as a result of his two trips to Africa and the Middle East* in 1964. Malcolm enlightened the students about the struggles of African Americans for freedom, which he often equated with the attempts at ending colonialism in Africa and the Caribbean.

Malcolm was able to establish a connection to the more militant civil rights leaders who were uncomfortable with the pace of reform and the programs of their parent organizations. In March 1964, prior to the formal establishment of the OAAU, a coalition of militant leaders from the traditional civil rights organization invited Malcolm to attend a rally being held in Chester, Pennsylvania. Present at this rally were Stanley Branch, leader of a militant local NAACP chapter in Chester; Gloria Richardson Dandridge,* head of the civil rights protest that had occurred in Cambridge, Maryland; and Julius Hobson of the Washington, D.C. CORE chapter. Milton Galamison* and Lawrence Landry, who had led school boycotts in Brooklyn and Chicago, respectively, also attended this gathering. Malcolm guaranteed his support for their cause and committed himself to any future demonstrations that they might plan.

In early 1965, Malcolm met with a group of civil rights leaders in a meeting organized by Juanita Poitier, wife of actor Sidney Poitier. Present at this meeting was labor leader A. Philip Randolph, Whitney Young* of the National Urban League (NUL),* and Dorothy Height of the National Council of Negro Women. The discussion centered on Malcolm's philosophy and how to attract more people to the ongoing struggle. Other influential blacks in attendance who attempted to bridge the gap between Malcolm and the established civil rights leadership included Ossie Davis* and Ruby Dee,* official representatives of the Association of Artists for Freedom.

Malcolm's second visit to Africa in October 1964 led to a coincidental meeting with two SNCC officials in Nairobi, Kenya. John Lewis* and Donald Harris* were members of SNCC, who were sent by their parent organization to tour several African countries. Malcolm spoke to them about the significance of viewing the civil rights struggle from a human rights perspective and emphasized the role that Africa could play in supporting the efforts of African Americans for human rights. These discussions led to a renewed determination by Malcolm to establish an ongoing dialogue with SNCC and other groups involved in the struggle. In December 1964, Malcolm spoke in Harlem,* along with Fannie Lou Hamer,* a SNCC official and symbol of the Mississippi freedom struggle. Malcolm extended an invitation to Hamer to address an OAAU rally scheduled for that same evening. He offered the assistance of the OAAU to the efforts of SNCC and the Mississippi Freedom Democratic Party (MFDP)* in their efforts at registering African American voters in the Magnolia state. Malcolm also had an opportunity to address a group of young SNCC Mississippi activists who were visiting New York. In early February 1964, at the request of SNCC, Malcolm addressed a group of civil rights activists at a church in Selma, Alabama. Clearly, SNCC and the more militant direction in which the organization moved offered Malcolm an enhanced opportunity to mend bridges with the older civil rights groups and extend his efforts at coalition building.

Among the student groups, Malcolm's influence grew precipitously. Perhaps nowhere was this becoming more evident in 1964 than at Fisk University in Nashville, Tennessee, a longtime hotbed of student activism. In the spring of 1964 militant students at Fisk University formed the Afro-American Student Movement (ASM). Fisk's ASM grew out of an earlier Afro-American Student Conference on Black Nationalism held on the campus. The students at this gathering wanted to integrate a self-defense* component into the southern civil rights struggle, a view that certainly paralleled Malcolm's views about blacks protecting themselves. In April 1964, Malcolm had urged civil rights activists to form rifle clubs to defend the black community against the violent actions of whites. An integral part of the students' self-defense approach included the politics of black empowerment based on nationalist values. The conference supported Malcolm's position of presenting the cause of African Americans directly to the United Nations* and called for a black cultural revolution. The conference also outlined Thirteen Points for Implementation, several of which reflected the Basic Aims and Objectives of the OAAU.

In response to the self-defense initiative proposed by the students, SNCC chairperson John Lewis approved an experimental self-defense project in Greenwood, Mississippi. In late 1964 SNCC invited Malcolm to speak and visit their operations in Greenwood, Mississippi, and Selma, Alabama. Malcolm was being increasingly recognized as the spokesperson for the self-defense units being organized. On February 3, 1965, he addressed several thousand Tuskegee students and on the following day addressed another group of student activists in Selma, Alabama, at an event sponsored by SCLC. After a speech that charged the emotions of the Selma students, he reassured Coretta Scott King,* wife of Martin Luther King, Jr., that his purpose was to complement Dr. King's work. White America, he said, must be reminded to accept King's nonviolent ideology or risk the alternative that he, Malcolm, had always advocated. During the week in which he was assassinated, Malcolm was scheduled to go to Mississippi to explore ways in which the OAAU might more effectively cooperate with SNCC in that state.

Shortly before his death, Malcolm had begun to develop a message to white students in the United States whom he felt could relate to the human rights struggle. He was impressed with their openness and honesty, and he believed that they could demonstrate collective guilt and open rebelliousness against their parents, who were the ones that were really responsible for the sad state of race relations in America.

During his lifetime, Malcolm made significant strides in bridging the gap between his black nationalist views and organization and more traditional civil rights organizations. This was by his participation in a number of activities sponsored by these civil rights groups. In addition, Malcolm made a clear attempt to reach out to young black activists. It was obvious near the end of his life that he had a great vision of coalition building that possibly included young white activists, as well. His death ended the best opportunity to forge the disparate elements of black leadership in the 1960s.

SELECTED BIBLIOGRAPHY

Carson (Gallen, ed.), 1991; Goldman, 1979; Lawson, 1991; Malcolm X (Breitman, ed.), 1965; Malcolm X (Clarke, ed.), 1990; Marable, 1984; McAdam, 1985; Sales, 1994.

"THE BALLOT OR THE BULLET"

Robert L. Jenkins and Mfanya Donald Tryman

For more than a century after their emancipation from slavery, black Americans strove for full admission into the American mainstream. To be sure, in the period during the Reconstruction of the former Confederate states, where the bulk of African Americans continued to live, there was promise that America might indeed live up to the ideals embodied in the Constitution. The experiment, however, was brief, and in the end, the optimism and expectations proved to be more apparent than real. In the decades that followed, improvement in their status certainly occurred, but for most blacks, confronting white racism and its emasculating effects was almost a daily occurrence. Consigned to a castelike system with its poor economic conditions, segregated in virtually every facet of social life, and politically powerless, black southerners grew increasingly defiant during the twentieth century and moved aggressively to change their condition.

Outside of the South,* the northern ghettos sweltered under similar frustrations. Poor employment opportunities, deplorable housing conditions, substandard and essentially segregated schools, and frequently deadly encounters with the police made life for most blacks appealing only on the surface. Largely left out of the surging tide of social activism that gripped such places as Jackson and McComb, Mississippi,* Birmingham and Selma, Alabama, and Albany and Augusta, Georgia, northern urban leaders nevertheless understood that there was little difference in the practices and effects of white southern and white northern racism. Accordingly, they too worked to remove its existence from their midst.

Perhaps no black American in the twentieth century more effectively articulated the depths of this racism and its effect on the black masses than Malcolm X. To Malcolm, the nexus of southern and northern white racism had always been clear: It was simply American, historically embedded in the fiber of the nation. During the early 1960s at the height of the modern civil rights movement,* Malcolm and the Nation of Islam (NOI),* with whom he was most identified and for whom he officially spoke, stood on the fringes and condemned the nation's racial order in the most strident terms. With their views about self-defense,* they also advocated an alternative voice to the nonviolent method to social change championed by the movement's most respected leadership. Uncompromising in their views, understandably it was easy to label them, especially Malcolm, as racists themselves.

Officially forbidden to vote or participate in direct action tactics, Malcolm nevertheless flirted with these practices and moved ever closer to endorsing them as he acquired independence from the NOI and called for black liberation "by any means necessary." It was during his independent status as the head of his own black nationalist political group, the Organization of Afro-American Unity (OAAU),* that he articulated a sense of urgency about the importance of America improving how it treated its largest racial minority group. His expression of this sense of urgency consistently conformed to Malcolm the man and his philosophy, especially after 1963. If not through one of his best orations, it nevertheless manifested itself clearly through the ideas articulated in his memorable 1964 "The Ballot or the Bullet" speech.

It was the noted black novelist James Baldwin* who once said that color was more of a political than racial issue. Malcolm would not likely have agreed entirely with his friend's analysis, preferring to call the condition that color consigned to black Americans a human rights* issue. That he was beginning to accept more traditional political approaches to black American powerlessness, however, clearly manifested itself. During the last year of his life he toyed with the idea of running for political office himself, specifically under the banner of the black Freedom Now Party.* More precisely, however, he talked increasingly about black voting rights. In Selma, Alabama, where he had gone to speak to young Student Non-Violent Coordinating Committee (SNCC)* workers, Malcolm spoke convincingly about his "100 percent" endorsement of their voter registration efforts. He told audiences of his support for the Mississippi Freedom Democratic Party (MFDP)* and its goals to enfranchise black Mississippians and replace the whites-only regular Democratic Party* in the state. He volunteered to go personally to the South and help lead black voter registration efforts and promised to use his young OAAU as a conduit to further black voting aims wherever there was a need. Understandably, this effort would also include his own backyard of Harlem,* where he endorsed a registration drive that would sign residents up as independents. For those who failed to take seriously their registration responsibility, Malcolm promised to run them out of the community. Freed of the constraints of the NOI, Malcolm was clearly in transition and seeking a greater definition of his future activist role as a black leader.

There is nothing to indicate that Malcolm did not choose the title "The Ballot or the Bullet" for his speech without some thought. To him, America clearly had a choice. In a less formal way, he had, of course, addressed the choices before. America, he had frequently said, could choose to embrace black Americans and honor what was already constitutionally theirs or run the risk of eruption and bloodshed. In many ways the civil rights movement and the gains it generated, however slowly and begrudgingly made, were a reflection of the choice. But Malcolm regarded the results halfhearted at best and the price paid too much to have surrendered for the outcome. Black victimization was pervasive and painful, from the numerous deaths of civil rights* workers to the bombing murder of young and innocent girls worshiping in a church service; from the callous use of police dogs and fire hoses on peaceful women and children demonstrators to random acts of northern police brutality* under the guise of law enforcement. Still, from the occasional tone of his remarks, hope was not entirely lost that law-abiding whites, a powerful federal government, and a politically savvy African American electorate could not collectively allow the ballot to be used effectively to empower blacks and do for them what it was intended to do for all Americans.

In his speech, delivered in Cleveland, Ohio, on April 3, 1964, at the Cory Methodist Church, Malcolm talked about the importance of black unity. It made little sense for black people, regardless of their background and their religious and political orientation, or where they resided regionally, not to face the reality that racism victimized them all equally. Speaking the harsh truth about the nature and extent of black suffering in America because of white racism should not be interpreted as reverse racism, he said; rather, it should be interpreted as opposition to black exploitation, black degradation, and black oppression. He pointed out the hypocrisy in practicing the American creed that accepted white Europeans (whom he called "hunkies" in one of the earliest usages of a term that black militants later popularized and derisively used to refer to whites) entering the nation immediately as citizens, while denying the same benefits to millions of blacks whose presence went far into the national past.

Malcolm's speech was certainly a timely one because 1964 was a presidential election year, and as usual the candidates were vying for the black vote. Moreover, the Congress was debating the historic 1964 Civil Rights bill, and southern leaders were making a last-ditch stand to thwart its passage. Hence, it was a good opportunity to score white politicians and the two-party system for their failures to deliver their promises to black people. He did so aptly, especially against the Democrats, whom he routinely degraded as Dixiecrats.* But he also roundly criticized blacks who had been duped by the appeals of both parties. They had, he said, literally thrown away their votes, on southerners like Lyndon B. Johnson,* whose home state of Texas had no better record in its violent treatment of blacks than Mississippi,* a state that Malcolm criticized more than he did any other. He reminded them that it was the African American who had made the difference in the 1960 victory of John F. Kennedy* over Richard M. Nixon* and that they had the balance of power in the upcoming election as well.

Malcolm certainly made no effort to endorse either party or candidate, and that essentially meant that he had no practical suggestion out of the same dilemma that typically constricted black voting choices when it came to the two-party system. On the one hand, he made clear his lack of confidence in black people ever being treated as true Americans. On the other hand, however, he emphasized the importance of black voters regarding the ballot as synonymous with freedom and demanding vigorously all that the term meant in defining American citizenship. They must not be reluctant, he said, about reminding white America of the consequences of continuing to deny them the ballot.

Malcolm used the Cleveland forum as an opportunity to further emphasize some of his often-stated ideas. Themes of anticolonialism, American military aggression, black self-defense, and a duplicitous criminal conspiracy between the federal government and racist southern white politicians to deny blacks their rights, for example, permeated his remarks. Moreover, the speech was also the occasion to largely begin his initiative to regard black mistreatment as human rights rather than civil rights violations. In the waning weeks of his life, he would pursue this line and the effort to gain a hearing before the United Nations* more vigorously. But clearly, it was the sound of urgency that clamored ominously from his presentation. The year 1964, he warned, would be a difficult one for America, difficult because blacks had grown tired of their lowly status and the criminal way that they were being treated.

Violence was not something that Malcolm openly advocated. But he warned that he would not be nonviolent with those who were violent with him. He posited that not only would blacks arm themselves, but they would also engage in guerrilla warfare* in the future if their rights were not granted. Malcolm had often expressed the idea of blacks forming rifle clubs as protective measures. This position was quickly attacked by civil rights leaders and the white media* and conveniently distorted for their own purposes. In his "The Ballot or the Bullet" speech, Malcolm countered by noting that the government could limit the prospect of blacks arming themselves by simply doing its job of protecting African Americans. Like himself, he warned, many blacks were willing to die defending themselves and for the cause of black political liberation. To Malcolm, it was the young black nationalists, who numbered more abundantly than most Americans realized, that white America had to be most concerned about. Angry and frustrated, they were demanding substantive change and hence constituted the real fuse to the nation's "racial powder keg." The streets of Jacksonville, Florida, witnessing black civil disturbances about the same time of his speech, were not only indicative of black impatience but a harbinger of things to come. For blacks and America, it must be, he said more emphatically, either "the ballot or the bullet."

Malcolm's views turned out to be prophetic in a number of ways. While he stated that it would be the ballot or the bullet in 1964, it turned out to be the ballot and the bullet in that year and in the years after 1964. In the summer of 1964, SNCC led a voter registration drive in Mississippi called Freedom Summer.* Their efforts were met with white violence and terror. Three civil rights workers, two of them northern whites, were murdered near Philadelphia, Mississippi. Mississippi civil rights and grassroots leaders formed the MFDP, held mock statewide elections since blacks were not able to vote, and unsuccessfully

challenged the segregated all-white state Democratic Party at the 1964 Democratic National Convention in Atlantic City, New Jersey. The 1965 Voting
Rights Act* passed Congress, surely the most powerful voting rights legislation
in American history. At the time of its passage, there were only approximately
200 black elected officials; thereafter, their numbers rose steadily, comprising
more than 8,000 in the year 2000. The vast majority of the total are southern
blacks, with Mississippi, ironically, leading the way. Blacks have voted as a
bloc, as Malcolm argued that they should, and this has influenced the outcome
of local, state, and national elections, including presidential elections.

The metaphorical bullet that Malcolm predicted was indeed witnessed in 1964
and thereafter as well. It, too, manifested itself in many ways. Beyond Jacksonville, Florida, American cities went up in flames as the angry black revolt that
Malcolm spoke of spread widely during several long hot summers during the
mid- and late 1960s. Sniper fire (guerrilla warfare) occurred frequently when
police and fire departments answered calls in numerous black ghetto outbursts.
Militant black organizations advocating armed self-defense and revolution,* including the Revolutionary Action Movement (RAM),* the Black Panther Party
for Self-Defense,* the Black Liberation Army,* the Republic of New Africa,*
and US,* gained notoriety in the late 1960s and attention from the Federal
Bureau of Investigation (FBI)* and their Counter-Intelligence Program (COIN-
TELPRO).* In 1967 black leaders held the first Black Power Conference in
Newark, New Jersey, composed of black nationalists, Pan-Africanists, conventional political and religious leaders, and other groups from across the nation.
A second conference, the National Black Political Convention, assembled in
Gary, Indiana, in 1972. To be sure, these gatherings were an outgrowth of
Malcolm's call for a black nationalist conference in Cleveland and were instru-
mental in developing agendas and other organized efforts to further the cause
and address some of the issues he articulated in his ballots or bullets speech.

Like "Message to the Grass Roots," Malcolm's other major speech during the
last year of his life, "The Ballot or the Bullet" speech proved to be among his
most respected and enduring orations. Spoken in his typical passionate style,
much of what he said was, of course, characteristically "Malcolmnesque." But
in many ways the logic behind his words, the force of his warning, and the
immediacy of his concerns resonated in ways different than previously. Malcolm
was certainly not the only black leader in 1964 who understood the powder keg
that continued civil rights wrongs and black powerlessness threatened to detonate. Because of who he was and what he had long advocated and represented,
however, his voice was certainly more foreboding. Admittedly, it was he who
was "spreading the gospel of Black nationalism" with all of its threatening implications to the white status quo. Moreover, the philosophy, he said, was poised
to spill over and influence people of color the world over who suffered similarly
under the yoke of white racism. Only the most astute and observant on the
American social scene who heard his speech, or subsequently read its content,
were receptive to many of the ideas that he suggested or understood the sense

of urgency that he articulated. America in the months and years after his April speech, however, had little choice but to take note of the nation's racial course. These were, in fact, alarming times for the United States, and to many, the angry displays threatened the very fabric of the American democratic experiment. All that Malcolm and other leaders had preached for and about, including the goals and the consequences, did not ultimately come to pass, but some positive change for black America had to occur, and it did, inspired by both the ballot and the bullet. In the new century, seventy-five years after his birth, Malcolm would surely have acknowledged this.

SELECTED BIBLIOGRAPHY

Berry and Blassingame, 1982; Bracey, Meier, and Rudwick, eds., 1970; Branch, 1988, 1998; Carson, 1981; K. Clark, ed., 1985; Goldfield, 1997; Haines, 1988; Hampton and Fayer, with Flynn, eds., 1991; Leeming, 1994; Malcolm X (Breitman, ed.), 1965, 1967; Malcolm X (Clark, ed.), 1992; Malcolm X with Haley, 1965; Marable, 1991; T. Perry, ed., 1996; Van Deburg, 1992; Woodard, 1999.

MALCOLM X AND THE "LONG HOT SUMMERS"

Robert L. Jenkins

One of the most important views expressed by Malcolm X was his preachments to America that the racial ills from which it suffered could not be adequately resolved from legislation alone. To Malcolm, white racism was so deeply ingrained in the national fabric that it was impossible to eliminate its existence altogether. Hence, he believed for most of his public career that resolving the problems caused by white American racism could occur only when the races physically separated from each other. At one time he held closely to the Nation of Islam (NOI)* line about blacks establishing their own state within the United States, but eventually he abandoned the idea in support of his black nationalist position of African Americans remaining in their separate local communities and controlling from within them every aspect of their political, social, and economic affairs. But Malcolm was a keen observer of the American social order, and he understood the masses perhaps unlike any other black leader of his era. Sweltering under the effects of oppressive urban environments, blacks had neither the patience nor the inclination to wait for the slow pace of civil rights* legislation, or even black nationalism,* to quicken. Injustice and unequal treatment of black people demanded immediate attention, and if it was not forthcoming, then America, Malcolm would say, must expect consequences. Malcolm was hardly a soothsayer, but he read well the temper of the 1960s and he was able to predict with considerable accuracy the turbulence that so frequently characterized the era. It remains among the main currents that emanate from his legacy.

Perhaps no period in American history has been fraught with more interracial tensions than the 1960s. During the decade, more than 300 American cities were affected by violent uprisings. To be sure, the 1960s were hardly isolated years. Following World War I, black and white racial violence flared nationally, initiated by the bloody 1919 Red Summer. During that period, 25 American cities convulsed from the rioting spurred by economic competition and social strains in the aftermath of the war. It was, up to then, the greatest rash of rioting in the nation's history. Property damage and loss of life were certainly pronounced during the tumultuous postwar era, but the destruction and human casualties did not compare to the outbreaks of the 1960s. A half-million blacks were involved in the 1960s eruptions, and these affairs consumed tens of millions of dollars in property damage and prompted some 50,000 arrests, 5,000 injuries, and 250 deaths.

During the 1960s as activists confronted the denial of black civil rights in the South,* African Americans in the northern urban ghettos smarted over a variety of problems of their own. The generic culprit that lit these urban torches was systematic racial discrimination. High unemployment, poor housing, economic and political exploitation, and police brutality* punctuated a general sense of hopelessness for many of them. Malcolm X spoke to their despair and helped to shed light on their suffering. Although his was hardly a singular voice in addressing their issues, none seemed as prophetic as his in predicting the consequences for White America if relief for these black ghetto dwellers was not forthcoming. In a 1963 conversation with National Urban League* leader Whitney M. Young,* Malcolm criticized the nation's unstable racial climate and warned of a probable eruption. Ever present beneath the surface of the black ghetto, Malcolm would say, was the existence of an anger that would not and could not be long contained. White racism made the American economic and political system impossible to include black people; hence, the African American condition, which so closely resembled conditions in Third World countries like Algeria,* would respond similarly: in explosion and terrorism.

On July 18, 1964, Malcolm's own backyard of Harlem* erupted in the decade's first important rebellion. As so frequently would occur, the provocation for Harlem's riot was an incident involving the police; an off-duty officer shot and killed a fifteen-year-old black boy. Angry rioters targeted small white-owned neighborhood businesses—especially furniture and clothing stores, pawn shops, and groceries—with looting and fire bombings. These were typically the businesses that Harlemites accused of selling them poor-quality goods at gouging prices.

Malcolm had always been quick to advise his listeners not to equate his predictions about impending long hot summers with instigation. He would have no such luck. He was, in fact, blamed by many for elevating the city's violently charged atmosphere, although he was in Africa on his second trip to the continent at the time of the Harlem riot. Likewise, his absence during the height of the troubled summer made him a target of critics, some of whom were his close associates in the Organization of Afro-American Unity.* According to Ethel N.

Minor, a former secretary in the office, many of these critics thought that Malcolm had picked a time to be out of the country when he was most needed at home; Harlem was burning and Malcolm was simply becoming "another bourgeois nigger" hobnobbing with African heads of state. Nothing from the trip, they complained, would bring benefits to black Americans.

To be sure, Malcolm's African visit had come at a critical juncture in the 1960s social milieu of black Harlem, but of course he had no way of knowing that the cauldron would boil exactly when it did. Yet when informed of the uprising, he understandably expressed neither surprise nor culpability. What had taken place, in Malcolm's opinion, was simply the loosening of pent-up anger and frustrations that were bound to erupt violently. Blacks were promised jobs but instead got welfare checks. In the process, they had lost their dignity. Malcolm scored the New York press for depicting the rioters as hoodlums and criminals. He acknowledged their looting and destruction of private property but maintained that these were hardly common thieves, bent on violating community-minded business owners. In Malcolm's opinion, the rioters had been justified in targeting these businesses because their owners were neither residents of Harlem nor concerned about its welfare; they were exploiters, "organized thieves" who took money from the community and gave nothing in return. The press had it wrong, Malcolm proclaimed; it was not the looters who were the criminals, or the landlords and store owners who were victims. Rather, it was the other way around, and the white press needed to consider the riot's root causes. It was a "miracle," he said, that with all of the resources at their disposal, blacks restrained themselves and did not do more damage than they did.

Harlem's riot was the beginning of a series of "Long Hot Summers," a popular term that Malcolm and other black leaders used euphemistically to describe the violent ordeal, largely through race rioting, to which blacks would subject their squalid urban settings. Malcolm's declaration from afar, and with greater frequency upon his return to the United States four months after the riot, that 1964 would be the bloodiest year in the nation's history certainly seemed on target. In the same summer, rioting erupted in Brooklyn's Bedford-Stuyvesant section and Rochester in New York, several New Jersey cities, including Jersey City, Union City, and Paterson, Philadelphia, Pennsylvania, and Dixmoor, Illinois. With even greater certainty, he forecast the same thing for 1965 because nowhere in urban America had the problems been resolved. Unable to control their own communities, blacks were having to deal with a series of broken promises about jobs and upgrading inferior schools and housing in the only way that they knew how, he told listeners and readers. Since old methods were not working, they would have to continue trying the "new" more violent methods. Hence, the explosions would be greater, the bloodshed more widespread. And, he said, the disruptions would be exported to affect directly the white business community in white neighborhoods.

Malcolm would not live to see his predictions about the long hot summer of 1965 unfold. His death in February 1965 occurred nearly six months before tumult in the Watts community of Los Angeles awakened white America to the pervasive disaffection existing in the nation's black ghettos. Idyllic Los Angeles with its movies stars, sunshine, and relaxed lifestyle was far from the northern urban centers where historical patterns of racism had, during the twentieth century, occasionally precipitated racial upheavals. (The Harlem riot of 1964, for example, was the third such eruption to grip that community in the twentieth century.) But black Los Angeles was hardly immune from the repression encountered in other urban centers. Ignited by a police brutality incident, the Watts riot, in many ways a misnomer because it extended well beyond this highly populated working-class area, resulted in 4,000 arrests, hundreds of injuries, thirty-four deaths, and approximately $35 million in property damage. After the very first day of rioting, the sparks were fanned by the popular disc jockey Nathaniel Montague, affectionately known by his listeners as the "Magnificent Montague." The recent arrival from New York, who had known Malcolm X in Harlem, had always used the term "burn baby, burn!" as part of his commentary in reference to the music he played and the artists that he featured. Unknowingly, repeated usage of the phrase in the initial stages of the rioting unfortunately inspired the arsonists as they too often repeated the popular words during the looting and burning. Strongly influenced by Malcolm's militant philosophy and his admirable courage, these revolters were, as a federal riot commission report later stated, characteristically young and combative, unafraid to confront official authority. It was, as Malcolm predicted, a display of truly explosive energy and, up to then, the "hottest" summer in consequences in American history.

Subsequent disorders in the summer months in the remainder of the decade gripped virtually every major urban center, including some in the South. The worst occurred in Newark, New Jersey, in 1967 where twenty-five persons, mostly blacks, died and property damages approximated $15 million. More tragic and costly was Detroit, Michigan,* a city closely associated with Malcolm during his early work in the Nation of Islam. There, beginning in mid-July of 1967, rioters and looters in five days of wrath over yet another police harassment spark, razed the city and caused more than $54 million in damages. In its wake there were 7,000 arrests and forty-three persons killed. Collectively, with Newark and Detroit leading the way, the Long Hot Summer of 1967 with its uprisings in sixty-five cities in thirty-two states and eighty-two deaths made the Red Summer of 1919 with its scores of dead and millions of dollars in property damage pale.

In the aftermath of the long hot summers the federal government studied the riots—their causes, immediate and long-range effects, and potential solutions. In a comprehensive report, the National Advisory Commission on Civil Disorders*—the so-called Kerner Report—described in one of several findings the profile of these rioters. They were, the report said, mostly young, disillusioned urban ghetto youth angry at white America for causing their oppressive conditions and at the black middle class for their accommodation to the plight of the black masses. They mistrusted white political leaders and the local police. Proud of being black, these rebellious youth were no less "acutely conscious of the discrimination they suffered." This was, in fact, a vivid description of what also had made Malcolm one of "Black America's angriest men" and a portrait of the very people for whom he personified and spoke.

Martin Luther King, Jr.,* referred to these annual summer outbreaks as simply language articulated by "the unheard." Malcolm would likely have agreed. Because so much of it was black blood, Malcolm would hardly have relished the "blood in the streets" of the decade's persistent rioting, had he lived to see it. But revolutions were in and of themselves bloody, Malcolm frequently said, and it would have been difficult for him not to see what was happening in the streets as a phase of the black liberation struggle in America. Moreover, at the very least, he would have likely acknowledged that the logic of what he was trying to teach America about the oppression, despair, and anger of Black America was being vindicated.

SELECTED BIBLIOGRAPHY

Carmichael (Minor, ed.), 1971; Cashman, 1991; Conot, 1967; Dickerson, 1998; Horne, 1995; *The Kerner Report*, 1968; Lawson, 1991; Malcolm X (Breitman, ed.), 1970a; Malcolm X (Perry, ed.), 1989; Malcolm X with Haley, 1965; *Militant*, January 18, 1965, August 23, 1965; Powledge, 1991; Warren, 1965.

CONSPIRACY THEORIES OF THE ASSASSINATION OF MALCOLM X

Mfanya Donald Tryman and Lawrence H. Williams

Malcolm X's death on February 21, 1965, was not completely unexpected. Three Black Muslims,* Talmadge Hayer,* Thomas 15X Johnson,* and Norman 3X Butler,* were indicted and found guilty of murdering Malcolm X "in cold blood" before his wife and children and hundreds of supporters who were part of the audience on that day. Evidence shows that the assassins were affiliated with New Jersey mosques, particularly the Newark mosque,* and that some of those who plotted the assassination were recruited from the streets of Paterson, New Jersey. Even before Malcolm's assassination, a number of attempts had been made on his life by Black Muslims (and perhaps coordinated with others) associated with the Nation of Islam (NOI).* This occurred in Los Angeles as Muslims* awaited his plane arrival from New York, his departure from Los Angeles on his return flight, and at his home in East Elmhurst,* Queens, New York City. In the latter case, he rushed his family out into the cold winter night in February 1965, only a week before his actual assassination, as firemen put out the fire that had been started by an arsonist. He escaped an assassination attempt in Boston as a car he was in sped through a tunnel trailed by a car of Black Muslims; another foiled effort occurred when Anas "Brother" Luqman,* an ex-military explosives expert, was instructed by Elijah Muhammad* faithful

Captain Joseph to put a bomb under the car of Malcolm X that would explode when he turned the ignition. All of these incidents occurred after his break with the NOI and after a number of death threats had been made on his life by members of the NOI, primarily through *Muhammad Speaks*,* the official newspaper of the NOI. Minister Louis X Farrakhan,* along with other Black Muslim ministers, wrote a series of articles in the paper, and Farrakhan stated that Malcolm was "worthy of death." While Farrakhan has continuously denied any involvement in the actual death of Malcolm X, he has admitted on the CBS news program *60 Minutes* broadcast in the spring of 2000 that he contributed to the violent climate that precipitated Malcolm's death.

During the last year of his life Malcolm stated on a number of occasions and confided with a number of friends that he did not have long to live because assassins were trying to kill him. Yet he refused police protection. He refused offers from heads of state in other countries that invited him and his family to come and live there, avoiding the sure fate that awaited him back in the United States. In fact, Malcolm toured Africa and the Middle East* in 1964 partly to get away from the violent atmosphere in New York and the intensifying attempts to kill him. Yet he refused to allow his security detail to frisk audience participants shortly before he was gunned down by assassins.

The Federal Bureau of Investigation (FBI),* utilizing its COINTELPRO* program, had advance information on attempts on the life of Malcolm X. However, these agencies refused to intervene and arrest Elijah Muhammad, who stated with regard to Malcolm that it is time to "shut his eyes," and deliberately exacerbated the hatred and jealousy that Muhammad developed for Malcolm through FBI agents and NOI confidantes close to Muhammad. In this respect the FBI contributed to the violent atmosphere between the NOI and supporters of Malcolm. Further, the FBI continuously monitored and tapped the phones of Elijah Muhammad as well as Malcolm. During the last months of his life, Malcolm stated that he no longer felt that it was just the Black Muslims who were trying to kill him, that some of the things that were happening to him were beyond the capabilities of the NOI. The insinuation was that the U.S. government, which Malcolm criticized incessantly, was implicated in his impending demise.

In his autobiography, Malcolm X told Alex Haley* that the Muslims were not responsible for either his house catching fire or Malcolm's being denied entrance to France in February 1965. However, the author of one of the most thorough examinations of the assassination, journalist Peter Goldman,* concluded that the justice system was correct in its prosecution of the three Black Muslims. But Eric Norden, a Malcolm X biographer, has argued that the FBI, the Central Intelligence Agency (CIA),* and the New York Police Department (NYPD) were guilty of Malcolm's death because he was in the process of taking the case of black Americans to the United Nations,* arguing that their human rights* were being violated. Both Norden and George Breitman,* who has written and edited extensively the works on Malcolm, argue the "second man theory," suggesting that there was another assassin at the scene who was let go by police and who has never been accounted for. The implication is that this second man was an agent of the government.

While there is no doubt that the NOI wanted Malcolm dead, and had made a number of attempts on his life, just because members of the NOI pulled the triggers that killed him does not necessarily mean that there were not other conspirators inside and outside of the NOI intricately involved. These elements might have helped to plan Malcolm's death or gave the orders for the assassination that Sunday afternoon. Jealousy ran rampant inside the NOI toward Malcolm, even before he left the organization. The public associated the NOI with Malcolm, not Muhammad. Newsmen and reporters interviewed Malcolm frequently and rarely wanted to interview the sect's official leader. Malcolm's establishment of the Muslim Mosque, Inc.* after his break with the NOI only increased tensions, as a number of Malcolm loyalists exited the NOI to join him in the new organization. The founding of the Organization of Afro-American Unity (OAAU)* was the proverbial straw that broke the camel's back. But Malcolm was also stirring up dust in other quarters. With the formation of the OAAU, one of his primary goals was to bring the case of human rights violations against African Americans before the United Nations. These plans were being formulated at the height of the struggle for full civil rights* for African Americans in the United States, and the international spotlight continued to focus on the mistreatment of African Americans. The United States boasted and labeled itself as the greatest democracy on earth as racial atrocities continued to occur, but nothing would have been more embarrassing than for the American government to be brought before an international body and condemned, if not sanctioned, for its treatment of black Americans.

Consequently, it is not hard to imagine that the FBI or the CIA may have played a role in the death of Malcolm. The timing just seems too coincidental. The exposure of COINTELPRO and its subversive activities and the fanatical and racist hatred that FBI director J. Edgar Hoover* expressed for black leaders surely add credence to this government assassination scenario. Norden and George Breitman argue that the FBI, CIA, and NYPD acted in concert in killing Malcolm. The dubious actions and exposure of the CIA abroad in allegedly causing, contributing to, or playing a direct hand in the assassination of foreign heads of state and revolutionaries who were considered too radical, or did not want to be manipulated by the U.S. government, cannot be discounted in the death of Malcolm, given his political behavior and planned actions in the international arena. During his travels in Africa in 1964, it is known that Malcolm was "shadowed" by the State Department*; it monitored every move that he made and everywhere that he went. This occurred at a time when Malcolm was lining up support among African countries for his human rights campaign. While Malcolm was visiting Cairo, Egypt,* as part of an African tour, he became violently ill and had to be rushed to the hospital and have his stomach pumped.

Undoubtedly, he was a victim of food poisoning, but the question remains, How was he poisoned and was it done intentionally?

In addition to the NOI and the U.S. government, a third political actor may also have conspired to have Malcolm assassinated. When Malcolm joined the NOI, he developed puritanical habits. Not only did he give up alcohol, drugs, tobacco, pimping, and other criminal acts, but he became a role model* for every black man and woman to aspire to become. He never "backslid" into recidivistic ways. In fact, he exhorted all African Americans to forego drugs, alcohol, promiscuity, and other vices and constantly preached this message to the large black ghettos in America. This brought him into direct conflict with the international drug cartel and the Mafia,* which had a vested interest in a number of vices in the lower-class black community, including drugs, prostitution, gambling, and the numbers racket. Malcolm, more than any other individual in America, represented a direct threat to profits by the Mafia. Malcolm held a number of Harlem street corner rallies* exhorting public crowds of thousands of people to get rid of the drug pushers by chasing them out of the black community. No one in Harlem,* except perhaps Adam Clayton Powell, Jr.,* had more influence among blacks than Malcolm in the 1960s. According to James Farmer,* who headed the Congress of Racial Equality (CORE)* and was one of the civil rights leaders of the 1960s whom Malcolm grew to respect, Malcolm's influence was drying up a multimillion-dollar racket. He argued that the international drug cartel was responsible for Malcolm's death. Supposedly, the cartel was opposed to Malcolm X's war on drugs. Farmer also implicated the Chinese Communists who were concerned, he said, because the American demand for Asian drugs would decrease from Malcolm's crusade. Farmer's theory could not be proven, and he later changed his thinking, saying Harlem drug dealers were responsible. A former Freedom Rider* who was a Fisk University senior met Farmer during his 1965 visit to the Republic of Ghana* and informed him of an assassination plot against Malcolm X, which she said would be blamed on the NOI. Likewise, a Quaker friend told Farmer the NYPD had arrested the wrong people at the Audubon Ballroom.* This man said that he saw two other men commit the crime, not Johnson and Butler. He informed the police, but they would not listen to him.

It may never be known for sure who murdered Malcolm. Journalist and biographer Karl Evanzz has made convincing arguments that several entities wanted him dead. It is possible that the government and Mafia conspired in getting NOI members as the "fall guys" in the murder of Malcolm. Thomas Hayer, one of the convicted assassins, claims that three other black men were the assassin plotters* in the murder of Malcolm, not the two other convicted assassins, 15X Johnson and 3X Butler, who were in the Audubon Ballroom on the day of the murder. While this may sound far-fetched to some, it is well known that the CIA conspired with the Mafia to assassinate Fidel Castro,* and conspiracy theorists argue that the Mafia was responsible for the death of President John F. Kennedy.* Given the nature of conspiracies and their clandestine origins, claims of conspiracies will continue to abound regarding Malcolm's assassination.

SELECTED BIBLIOGRAPHY

Blackside/PBS, 1994; Breitman, Porter, and Smith (Miah, ed.), 1976; Carson (Gallen, ed.), 1991; CBS News, 1992; Evanzz, 1992, 1999; Friedly, 1992; Gallen, ed., 1992; Goldman, 1979; Karim with Skutches and Gallen, 1992; Lomax, 1968; B. Perry, 1991; Sales, 1994; Waldron, 2000; Xenon Studio, 1991.

MALCOLM X IN CYBERSPACE

Abdul Alkalimat

As more and more information about and by Malcolm X is digitized and published on the Web, he is being reborn. This is part of the new information revolution. Malcolm X created *Muhammad Speaks,** a newspaper that became a major communication tool for the black liberation movement of its time. One may assume that Malcolm would have been a cyberorganizer for the information revolution.

The memory of humanity is being relocated in a new brain, a silicon-based electronic environment, a global asynchronous cluster of images, sounds, and text that represents all that is documented about his life and work. This is the main way that humanity will experience Malcolm in the future. This "CyberMalcolm" represents a new reality.

Cyberspace is new and different from the spaces humans have occupied, so one must distinguish how people have been living—the actual—from the new opportunities of cyberspace—the virtual. The actual has been shaped in terms of capitalist practices, the private ownership of property, the sale of goods and services for profit, and the hegemony of the power and knowledge of the capitalist class. New principles are emerging in cyberspace.

Cyberspace is the battleground of the information revolution. In cyberspace three principles define the greatest potential: cyberdemocracy—everyone has access to cyberspace; collective intelligence—everyone's voice can be heard; and information freedom—information is available to all for free.

The digitization of the black experience includes black intellectual history. Since the 1960s, the study of black intellectual history has included biographies, anthologies, reprints, and archives. The most important projects have been to publish the collected works of key historical figures. So far this includes Frederick Douglass, W.E.B. Du Bois,* Booker T. Washington, Marcus Garvey,* and Martin Luther King, Jr.* Each of these collected works began as book projects, and now all include major Web sites. It is imperative that Malcolm X join the list because his importance cannot be overlooked.

As of March 2000, the Web included at least 150 sites and several thousand

Web pages devoted to Malcolm X. Search engines returned 24,522 pages (altavista.com) and 29,800 pages (google.com). Malcolm pages are posted in the following countries: Australia, Burkina Faso, Canada, Denmark, England, Germany, Italy, Netherlands, Sweden, Switzerland, and the United States. The two most comprehensive and inclusive digital collections of materials concerning Malcolm X are a listserv for online discussions maintained by F. Leon Wilson and a research Web site maintained by the author, "Malcolm X: A Research Site" (http://www.brothermalcolm.net), launched May 19, 1999, and maintained by the Africana Studies Program of the University of Toledo. The introduction to this site states:

This web page is designed to be a resource for scholarship in Black Studies and the political development of activists in the Black Liberation Movement. *Malcolm X: A Research Site* has been developed in the spirit of *Academic Excellence and Social Responsibility*, intending to make a contribution toward preserving the radical Black tradition. We are interested in growing this site based on mass participation.

The site averaged 1,000 hits per day during February 2000 and averaged 600 hits per day through spring 2000. The site includes a family section with data on six generations. The source for the early family history is a book by Rodnell Collins,* *Seventh Child: A Family Memoir of Malcolm X* (1998). Collins is the son of Ella Collins,* half sister of Malcolm X. The six generations begin with the African progenitor from Mali, a Bambara man named Ajar. Ajar's son Tony had twenty-two children. Tony's son John had six children. John's son Earl had eleven children. And Earl's son Malcolm himself had six children. As of April 2000, there were four Web pages on Malcolm's parents and nine Web pages on his brothers and sisters.

There are links to twenty-four Web pages about Betty Shabazz,* the wife of Malcolm X. These are organized into the following categories and respective pages: chronology (1), memories of Malcolm X (4), speeches-interviews (3), tributes-honors (6), and death (10). Malcolm and Betty had six daughters. Twelve pages on the site discuss three of the daughters.

The research site includes a rich chronology, a day-by-day accounting of the life of Malcolm X. As with all parts of the site, the number-one source for this chronology was *The Autobiography of Malcolm X.** A second most useful source was contemporary newspapers, especially the *New York Times.** This leads to the crisis of authenticity that arises from using official government surveillance reports acquired under the Freedom of Information Act. The material has to be considered, but it is dangerous to use it as the sole source. Overall, of the nearly forty years that Malcolm lived information is posted on thirty-two of those years.

The research site also lists books, CDs, and videos about Malcolm X. There are a total of 129 links to these materials including bibliographies, biographies, words by Malcolm X, youth-oriented books, struggle, doctoral dissertations, CDs, and videos. Each link allows for online purchasing. This is vital for global distribution of these materials. While it does require a buyer to have a credit card in a hard international currency, this e-commerce system is the best commercial approach seen thus far in distributing material about Malcolm X worldwide.

Malcolm X: A Research Site links to pages that digitize the words of Malcolm X. A total of 132 texts are cited: speeches, articles, letters, interviews, and an autobiography. Fifteen links are to full-text pages. Twenty-two links are to audio clips. The citations are from 1941 to 1965.

Date	Text Cited	Text Online	Audio Clips
1941–59	19	2	0
1960–63	28	6	6
1964	47	7	13
1965	38	0	3
Total	132	15	22

The pioneering cyberorganizer F. Leon Wilson established the Malcolm X Listserv in 1997. This is the definitive discussion list on Malcolm X in cyberspace. In the first post to the list on May 3, 1997, Wilson stated its purpose:

The purpose of this list is to identify, examine and separate the myths about Malcolm X from his actual philosophical beliefs and values and to develop a clearer understanding of his works. Malcolm X has come to symbolize power, solidarity and self-empowerment within the Black community. As this millennium draws to a close, it becomes more compelling to understand the agents of change which have shaped African Americans' thought, rhetorical bases and collective actions within the confines of Western culture. The icon "X" has come to signify one man's words and ideals. It is important that Malcolm X's concepts and ideas of group empowerment, rebellion against injustice and the ultimate refusal to assimilate, not be overshadowed by commercial exploitation and other romantic notions of Malcolm X.

The Malcolm X Listserv is a free discussion list maintained at St. Johns University. It started out as a monitored list and is now open and unmonitored. Full logs are published on the Web, searchable by month. As this list is open to the general public, it combines scholarship about Malcolm X with personal opinion. What can be considered information is mixed with ideological discussion and debate.

As of April 10, 2000, 171 people subscribed to the list. Posts to the list include at least four basic types of discussion: those newly exposed to Malcolm X, ideologies who contend other points of view, nonblacks who resurrect the role of whites in the black movement, and questions from the international community that put Malcolm in a global context. This listserv demonstrates that the power of the Internet as global interaction is cheap, fast, and possible—certainly for those who want to discuss the life and meaning of Malcolm X.

Malcolm X in cyberspace is essential for the current organization of knowledge. This is a real way for knowledge to be democratic, as there is little like-lihood that physical books can be acquired by all libraries to make up for the inequalities. The Internet is a different story. Most institutions are coming online and will have equal access to whatever is on the Web. CyberMalcolm is avail-able to whoever can participate in those institutions—especially schools, uni-versities, and libraries—on an equal basis.

Yet there are several critical problems that define the limits of Malcolm in cyberspace. The first limitation is that the core texts are under copyright, in the hands of private owners. This became a major issue in the precyberspace era, up to and including legal action against efforts to share the words of Malcolm. (See, for example, the supplement to the study guide on Malcolm X: A Research Site.)

The second limitation is that most of the archived materials—letters and other unpublished matter—are also in private collections. This has been essential, for without private collectors much of this material would have been lost. The best example is Preston Wilcox of Harlem,* New York, who has maintained the newsletter-based Malcolm X Lovers Network for decades. Since information technology provides us the opportunity to practice collective intelligence and information freedom, we must begin to consider ways to consolidate the archives in cyberspace by putting them online and building links between Web sites. Malcolm X spoke whenever he could to every possible type of audience. We have the responsibility to make his words and deeds available to all.

The third issue is the need to establish an international commission, served by a staff of serious academics, to oversee the development of an official Web site for the collected words and actions of Malcolm X. CyberMalcolm means more than just the person of Malcolm X. An official Web site would be an anchor for the radical black tradition as a whole. All scholars recognize that Malcolm X is a critical nodal point linking historical traditions with the contem-porary diversity of ideological positions. His life, his ideas, and his philosophical context are together the beginning in defining the traditions of black liberation theology, Pan-Africanism,* black nationalism,* black Marxism, and black fem-inism. Material online about and by Malcolm is essential if the great debates of black intellectual history are to be presented in cyberspace: the emancipation debate (as expressed in the National Negro Convention Movement), the self-determination debate (Du Bois, Booker T. Washington, and Marcus Garvey), and the black liberation debate (Malcolm X and Martin Luther King, Jr.).

The purpose of an archive is to preserve material for future generations and enable people from all points of view to examine materials and make an as-sessment. We all learn from preserving our history. Up to the twenty-first cen-tury, this has been done in limited-access institutions usually reserved primarily for formal academic scholars. Now cyberspace gives us the opportunity to save everything on a given subject and make it available to everyone at all times. The only requirement is being hooked up to the Internet, and in the United States this is available in almost every public library. For everyone concerned about Malcolm X, the primary focus must turn to cyberspace and the birth of CyberMalcolm.

SELECTED BIBLIOGRAPHY

Alkalimat, ed., 1990; Alkalimat, 1992; Archives of Malcolm-X Listserv Discussion, http://maelstrom.stjohns.edu/archives/malcolm-X.html; Collins with Bailey, 1998; Cone, 1991; Malcolm X: A Research Site, http://www.brothermalcolm.net; Sales, 1994.

MALCOLM X—LESSONS FROM THE LEGACY

Mfanya Donald Tryman and Robert L. Jenkins

More than thirty-five years have passed since the assassination of Malcolm X on a wintry afternoon at the Audubon Ballroom* in Harlem,* New York, in February 1965. Yet his legacy and influence appear to be greater than ever on America and particularly the African American. When alive, although some of his ideas were moderate, Malcolm had pronounced views regarding white America, racial separation,* black supremacy, black pride,* and black nationalism,* and for this he was considered by some blacks and most whites as a hate monger. He was often depicted as an advocate of violence, largely because he was uncompromising in his view about the right of all people to defend themselves against wanton violent attacks by anyone who sought to do them and their families bodily harm. Understandably, when America was seeking to adjust to the demands that black America was making about acceptance into the mainstream, these were not easy views for most people to embrace. Could it be that most of America misunderstood Malcolm? But who really was Malcolm X? And why, if he held such unpalatable views about race and the place of blacks in America, could he be the icon that he is today? What was the legacy that Malcolm left and how important is it in the lives of black and white America in the new millennium?

At first glance, Malcolm X appears to be a complex figure, difficult for those who failed to study him to understand. To be sure, there were many sides to Malcolm X; he was hardly a shallow man with few interests and fewer ideas. But in reality, he was a very simple man with simple but logical solutions to the oppressed conditions that confronted black people wherever they lived. He articulated them simply and logically, albeit often in the most acrid way. His anger often clouded our understanding of him, and while it is easy to grasp even the logic behind his anger, given Malcolm's and our own understanding of the historical place of blacks in their relationship to Europeans and the Euro-Americans, we must look beyond his indignation to fully comprehend his legacy.

It was Malcolm's close associate Peter Bailey* who perhaps more graphically than anyone gives insight into who Malcolm was in life and in essence what he has become in death. Bailey, a journalist, worked with Malcolm in his fledgling

Organization of Afro-American Unity (OAAU)* and tells us that Malcolm must be remembered for what he was: a master teacher. It is apt as a description, for Malcolm taught us much.

Malcolm gave us a consciousness about the universality of oppression. His task was first to deal with the problems that black Americans encountered, but he soon came to understand how pervasive this oppression was. Malcolm eventually saw black American oppression as not merely a racial phenomenon but as a human rights* issue. It was not just civil rights* that white America denied its black citizens, but these were human rights denials. Hence, he sought to make America accountable for how it treated black people by taking them before the United Nations.* His initiative was thwarted by his death, but the attention that he called to human rights violations gave greater currency to the importance of addressing human rights violations the world over. Even Martin Luther King, Jr.,* would increasingly call attention to the plight of the black poor and the nation's prosecution of the Vietnam* War in essence as human rights violations. More significantly, although the American government would never acknowledge the validity of Malcolm's claims, or equate the racial dilemma along the same lines that he did, it nevertheless became more concerned about how other nations handled domestic dissidence, frequently condemning their practices as human rights violations. At home, it officially moved to endorse black civil rights claims as legitimate goals for the nation to achieve.

Malcolm taught us how important it was to be aware of who we are and from whence we as black people came. A student of history, Malcolm was diverse enough in his interest to study the glorious past of many civilizations, for he understood that black history* did not exist in a vacuum; it was part and parcel of human history. He was keenly interested in the African American past, and though he knew that it had its own dynamic, he also knew that it was influenced not only by the history of Euro-Americans; blacks also shaped the historical development of the United States. When no other black leader told their followers how important it was to "know thyself," Malcolm taught them to understand their history as a key to understanding not only why they were oppressed but what they had been able to accomplish in a nation that had a long history of racial oppression.

And the accomplishments, he emphasized, were hardly negligible. Black people, he said, should be proud of what they had done and of who they were. It was a cord that Marcus Garvey,* one of Malcolm's predecessors and someone very much associated with his family's history, had used to exalt and encourage his people in the 1920s.

While it cannot be attributed entirely to Malcolm, the importance that he placed on blacks studying themselves certainly influenced the Black Studies Movement* of the 1960s and 1970s and the explosion of scholarly knowledge about black people in the years since then. Unlike in Malcolm's youth, when the only history of black people that seemed acceptable to whites or accessible to blacks were their roles as slaves, thirty years after his death no one can deny that we know infinitely more than ever about the true role of blacks in human history.

As black men, Malcolm taught us how to be men. When actor Ossie Davis* eulogized Malcolm by proclaiming that he was "our Black manhood," it was a recognition in part that as black men Malcolm also taught us how to be men. During an era when blacks looked to passivity as the key to achieving their "freedom," Malcolm refused to abandon one of the historical themes in the quest for black freedom—respect for his manhood. When he dared to look white men in their eyes and condemn even those that considered themselves well meaning—"white liberals"*—for their historical oppression of his people, respect for his courage welled up in the hearts and minds of many African Americans. And he condemned them with a logic that was difficult to dispute and that magnified the deference that many felt about him. To Malcolm, it mattered little whether one was a religious or a social hero or a president; when he felt compelled to criticize them, he often did so scathingly in the most public venue.

To Malcolm, being a man also meant defending himself whenever he or his family was threatened. He never apologized for the right to arm himself to accomplish this. It was not just a legal or constitutional right to do so; as a man, it was simply common sense to do so. Even Islam,* he once said, taught its adherents not to turn the other cheek.

But Malcolm was hardly a violent man, despite the media image that depicted him as such. Certainly during the years of his life as a black leader, Malcolm never instigated an incidence of violence. In fact, Malcolm diffused violent situations and confrontations between the black community and the police on more than one occasion. But he tenaciously clung to the idea that black people, and particularly black men, had the right to defend themselves, their families, their communities, and their race "by any means necessary."

Malcolm was in many ways the example of black manliness, and because of it, it is easy for one to overlook another side of him. Malcolm understood that manliness was not always about courage and dominion. It is also about being confident enough in one's masculinity to also be loving and caring. Because of his assertive public persona and his long working hours, it is often overlooked that Malcolm was still a devoted and loving husband and father. When he was with his family, he spent uncounted hours playing with his little girls and providing the social and emotional support for his wife. Although he certainly believed that there were clear roles for men and women to play as husbands and wives, and as fathers and mothers, Malcolm was not the sexist that many feminists have attempted to portray him as. This was evident in his OAAU, in which women played important roles as decision makers. Malcolm, in death, made it clear to African Americans, and especially African American males, that the strong image of black manhood that he projected did not contradict his role as a passionate and understanding family man.

In fact, these roles are not and cannot be contradictory. Rather, they are complementary. No one knew this side of Malcolm better than his wife, Betty Sanders Shabazz,* who often spoke and wrote about the loving and caring husband and father that Malcolm was in his private life. As many black families have disintegrated or separated, Malcolm remains the prototype for black males as fathers and husbands.

In a period of our nation's history when many prominent black men and women willingly accept the accolades of an endearing public, yet bemoan and reject the reality of their influence on the lives of others, especially young people, Malcolm, without being aware of it, himself was the moral example of what he wanted for black people. Clearly, he served as one of the most positive role models for African Americans in the twentieth century. He showed us how one can literally rise from the gutter of the streets as a petty criminal, as a drug addict, hustler, and dope pusher, and become one of the most dynamic, influential, and articulate leaders of the twentieth century. In this respect, he gave us hope, and when his life's example is used adequately and effectively, it can guide many of our young, regardless of their race, from paths in life that lead ultimately to dead end or destruction.

Not only did Malcolm leave a legacy as a scholar, educator, leader, convert, organizer, minister, and nationalist, but he was uncompromising in his religious and political convictions. Once he became a Muslim,* no one could ever legitimately accuse him of "backsliding" or vacillating with regard to his principles. He never went back to his street ways as Detroit Red, never again used drugs, smoked, or used alcohol. He was never accused of womanizing or abusing women. Most commendable, Malcolm could not be bought—for any price—although he often accused black leaders of selling out the cause of black freedom, justice, and equality. There simply is no evidence that Malcolm ever took a bribe or payoff to silence his continuous attacks on racism, imperialism, colonialism, and political oppression. It is a self-evident truth that Malcolm continued to speak out aggressively against injustice and racial oppression until assassins on that fateful winter day in 1965 silenced him.

To be sure, Malcolm taught us much. But perhaps the greatest legacy he left to those who are willing to learn from it was that he taught us how to die. During the last months of his life, Malcolm knew that his death was imminent. But as he had said to Shirley Graham Du Bois,* while visiting West Africa, he was willing to die if by his death he would advance the cause of black people. He never ran from the inevitable, although many people, including the actress Ruby Dee,* Ghana's president Kwame Nkrumah,* and perhaps Gamal Nasser* and Fidel Castro,* offered to give him refuge from the stalkers who eventually destroyed him. In the face of his crisis, he remained filled with life and enthusiasm for the causes that he had championed for the previous ten years of his life. To the end, Malcolm unfortunately refused to think of himself and his family and about how much his living meant and would continue to mean to black people. He simply failed to realize how much more he could have contributed in life than in death. It was a fatal flaw in his thinking. But how he confronted the dangers that swirled around him and came to accept his death is as much a part of his legacy as the force of his life and work.

As did so many of Malcolm's supporters and followers, Lewis Michaux,* one of his closest friends and the owner of a bookstore in the heart of Harlem, honored Malcolm shortly after his death. In one of the last stanzas in a poem that Michaux penned about Malcolm, he wrote "that every goodbye ain't gone." For more than thirty-five years, lessons of the legacy that Malcolm left to all of us who have been willing to accept them prove Michaux's words to be prophetic.

SELECTED BIBLIOGRAPHY

Barboza, 1994; Clarke, ed., 1990; Collins with Bailey, 1998; Goldman, 1977; Malcolm X with Haley, 1965; T. Perry, ed., 1996; Strickland (Greene, ed.), 1994; Stull, 1999; Warren, 1965; Wood, ed., 1992.

THE ENCYCLOPEDIA

A

ABERNATHY, RALPH DAVID, SR. Ralph David Abernathy was a veteran of World War II,* a Baptist minister, and a committed participant in the modern civil rights movement.* He was close and second in command to Dr. Martin Luther King, Jr,* and the Southern Christian Leadership Conference.* Malcolm X was critical of the nonviolent direct action tactics endorsed by leaders like Abernathy and King. While he was especially critical of King, nothing appears in his writings or speeches specifically criticizing King's lieutenant. Malcolm spoke against racial integration* and initially was opposed to the civil rights movement, yet Abernathy respected Malcolm's overall contributions to the movement and the quest for equal rights in America. Following King's assassination in 1968, Abernathy preached a sermon entitled "My Last Letter to Martin" in which he asked Dr. King to look for Malcolm X in heaven. Abernathy preached that Malcolm supported equal rights and the uplift of his people, though he may have had different methods and a different philosophy.

SELECTED BIBLIOGRAPHY

Abernathy, 1989; Fairclough, 1987; Kharif (Lowery and Marszalek, eds.), 1992; *New York Times*, April 18, 1990.

Gerald L. Smith

AFRICAN LIBERATION MOVEMENTS. Malcolm X's active involvement in Africa lasted for only six years (July 1959–February 1965) before he was tragically killed by assassins. Before 1964 it would appear that his perspectives on Africa and the black revolution derived from the Garveyite brand of black nationalism,* which he inherited from his family and from his voracious reading of the literature on Africa at the time. His extensive visit to the African continent in 1964, during which he had discussions with two of independent Africa's revolutionary leaders, Gamel Abdel Nasser* and Kwame Nkrumah* respec-

Ralph Abernathy, Martin Luther King, Jr.'s chief lieutenant in the Southern Christian Leadership Conference. Library of Congress.

tively, apparently reinforced his hatred of white racism and capitalist exploitation.

That Malcolm was destined to play a leading role in the rise and shaping of black nationalism in the United States in the 1960s should surprise no one. Soon he became known as the "Prince of the Black Revolution," and the Nation of Islam (NOI)* to which he belonged can be described as "the oldest and most powerful" of all the organizations espousing the new black nationalist movement of the 1960s. It is important, however, to appreciate the movement and the place of the NOI and Malcolm X in its proper historical context.

This new black nationalism was like an old wine in a new bottle. It still exhibited essentially two faces, one American and the other African, or what W.E.B. Du Bois* described as double-consciousness. What occurred in the 1960s, and in the 1970s especially, differed from its earlier manifestations. This difference did not necessarily occur in terms of its fundamental animation and message, or in the level of sophistication, eloquence, depth of consciousness, and fulminations of both its radical and moderate articulators. What happened in its peculiar manifestations should be comprehended in the context of the changing political climate in the United States, the winds of political change in Africa brought about by forced European political retreat from Africa, the greater number of the various people involved in it, and the extensive coverage the movement received in an age when increasing worldwide literacy in the English language as well as the advances in information science and technology were approaching dimensions hither to nonexistent. Like the historical individual that he was, Malcolm X saw the possibilities of the movement, put himself at the head of it, and, following his return from a long tour of Africa in 1964, tried to change its direction.

Between May and June 1964 Malcolm X toured Africa. He had private audiences with several African leaders including Nasser of Egypt, Nkrumah of the Republic of Ghana, Nnamdi Azikiwe of Nigeria,* Julius Nyerere of Tanzania, Charles Kenyatta* of Kenya, Milton Obote of Uganda, and Ahmed Ben Bella* of Algeria.* The details of these discussions are not known. He also gave several public speeches and granted several interviews to the print media as well as to radio and television establishments. On May 14, 1964, he was given the special honor of addressing Ghana's Parliament. He also visited Liberia, Senegal, and Morocco. The experiences influenced him tremendously and helped to transform him from a "home-made" black nationalist in the mold of Elijah Muhammad* to a Pan-Africanist in the mold of George Padmore and W.E.B. Du Bois: an internationalist who perceived the African American struggle for equality as part of the global struggle against racism, colonialism, and capitalism.* The oscillation in Malcolm X's sociopolitical thought between racial Pan-Africanism* and the common origins of all black peoples in Africa, and the new, wider identification of all oppressed peoples everywhere was to be a hard sale among his African American audiences, however.

Nevertheless, in spite of this dualism he proceeded to articulate what is said to be his African strategy. To help actualize this strategy, Malcolm X established on June 28, 1964, the Organization of Afro-American Unity (OAAU),* modeled on the Organization of African Unity (OAU).* On July 17, 1964, he attended an African Summit Conference as a representative of the OAAU at which he appealed to the African delegates to bring the plight of African Americans before the United Nations (UN).* Between September and November he toured eleven African countries and addressed most of their parliaments. His main purpose was to better familiarize himself with problems on the continent. On February 8, 1965, he addressed the First Congress of the Council of African Organizations in London and articulated his new message. Less than two weeks later he was dead.

Throughout his speeches, interviews, and writings Malcolm X emphasized more than any of his contemporaries the oneness of black peoples wherever they lived and a sense of African identity and pride in things African. He linked the African American struggle for civil rights* and human rights* with the liberation struggle in Africa. He made African Americans aware of the winds of change in Africa and assured them that ultimately their power lay in political unity with Africans. African Americans, he said, could not know themselves until they knew Africa, and hatred of Africans meant hatred of themselves. Therefore, he preached mutual respect and love among all blacks. And since their struggle could not be separated from that of continental Africans, he urged them to continue to support African liberation movements. He stressed that although to be successful the black struggle must be internationalized in the United States, the struggle's primary "supportive base" must be Africa, just as black America must be the primary support base of African liberation movements. Hence, he set up a Pan-African Secretariat of North America and planned to organize international Pan-African propaganda on the African continent. This was to be based in Tanzania. Its purpose was to spread information about the struggles of Africans in the West to Africans at home and politicize diasporan Africans about the struggle in Africa. This was one way of carrying out Garvey's work.

Malcolm tried, unsuccessfully, to persuade African leaders to bring the African American struggle before the UN, a factor that was a matter of concern to the American government. These leaders were reluctant to support Malcolm because of their dependence on economic aid from the United States and the West. He also hoped to destroy America's "divide and conquer" strategy: namely, that neither Africans nor African Americans cared for each other. Finally, he was determined to explode the myth that the conditions of blacks in America were better than those of their kin folk in Africa.

It is difficult to say how well these exhortations resonated among African Americans. It is even more difficult to measure the real impact of Malcolm X on colonialism in Africa. On the one hand, his rise to prominence as a black nationalist leader came too late in the day to impact decisively on the anticolonialist movement. On the other hand, his strident and eloquent denunciation of racism and white oppression of blacks gave a fillip to the revolutionary struggles in those parts of Africa—South Africa,* Southern Rhodesia (Zimbabwe), Northern Rhodesia (Zambia), Angola, Mozambique, and Algeria—still controlled by racist, hard-core European settlers who had formed themselves into formidable prefabricated collaborating groups with continental European colonialists and their sympathizers in white America. Nevertheless, perhaps more than any other African American personality, Malcolm's leadership helped to bridge the social, cultural, psychological, and political gaps between Africans and African Americans.

SELECTED BIBLIOGRAPHY

Clarke, ed., 1990; Essien-Udom, 1971; Gallen, ed., 1992; T'Shaka, 1983.

G.N. Uzoigwe

AFRICAN NATIONALISM. Malcolm was deeply influenced in his views on African nationalism by his sojourns to the Middle East* during the Hajj* and later on a tour of African countries. Both of these trips occurred during the last year of his life. After the Hajj, Malcolm visited Lebanon, Egypt,* Algeria,* Morocco, Nigeria,* and Ghana.* His travels across much of Black Africa had a profound impact on his nationalist philosophy. Writing from Lagos, Nigeria, in May 1964, he argued that black Americans must return to Africa philosophically, psychologically, and spiritually. Hence, Malcolm began to advocate a link between African American nationalism and African nationalism.

During the 1960s two major events confronted African people: one, the struggle to regain independence from European colonialism; and two, the struggle for civil rights* in the United States. Independence for African nations meant the presence of numerous African representatives at the United Nations,* several visiting African dignitaries, African liberation movement* activists, and students. These contacts afforded Malcolm the opportunity to exchange political, social, economic, and cultural ideas with them. It was in these exchanges that Malcolm began to link systemically African nationalism with African American nationalism and saw the struggle for independence going on in African countries as one and the same as the struggle going on in the United States. Africans were Africans, whether in Africa or in the United States. Malcolm was especially fond of Patrice Lumumba,* an African nationalist freedom fighter for independence in the Congo* (now Zaire). Citing fighters like Lumumba allowed Malcolm to realize the strengths and weaknesses in liberation strategies, and he also pointed out that some Africans were like Moise Tshombe,* who had betrayed Lumumba, which resulted in the latter's death.

Malcolm established the Organization of Afro-American Unity (OAAU)* in the United States on June 28, 1964. It was patterned after the Organization of African Unity (OAU)* that had been established in May 1963 in Addis Ababa, Ethiopia. When he visited Egypt in July 1964 he sought unsuccessfully to formally address the OAU at its first annual summit in Cairo. This summit brought together such notable leaders as Emperor Haile Selasie and Presidents Gamal Abdel Nasser,* Kwame Nkrumah,* Modibo Keita, Sekou Touré,* Julius Nyerere, and Ahmed Ben Bella.* Two points were made clear by Malcolm in his dialogue with and memorandum to summit leaders, however: one, that African problems were American problems and must be solved by both peoples and, two, that African leaders should help secure an investigation by the United Nations* into human rights* abuses against black people. The African tour allowed Malcolm to highlight the African American struggle while at the same time sharpen his experience with the tenets of African nationalism. Clearly, Malcolm's contact with African leaders and experience with them in the United States and Africa allowed him to link and merge African nationalism as an intercontinental concept related to Pan-Africanism.*

SELECTED BIBLIOGRAPHY

Malcolm X (Breitman, ed.), 1992, 1993; Clarke, ed., 1990.

Zuberi Mwamba

AFRO-ASIAN-ARAB BLOC. One of the messages that Malcolm constantly preached was black unity. During many of his lectures, he frequently told his audiences that blacks in general and black Americans more specifically would be able to achieve little as long as they remained divided. It was this division, apparent in individuals and in black organizations, that limited black progress. One of the reasons, Malcolm would say, that whites were not welcome to join his Organization of Afro-American Unity* was his view that blacks must first come together as a people and do things for themselves before seeking help for their elevation outside of the race. To Malcolm, the crux of this division was a lack of black pride* and the influence of whites who profited by keeping black people the world over divided. In the United States, this white influence to divide and conquer first manifested itself in the slave era, and it involved emasculating black peoples' sense of self and cultural roots. But Malcolm would also include in his messages words of hope. That hope was emanating from the vast pride that black Americans were beginning to experience from the African independence movements of the 1960s. Blacks throughout the diaspora were starting to understand their common connections to the African homeland. Black Americans, he said, could also take inspiration from the Bandung Conference* of 1955 where Asiatic, Arabic, and African leaders from emerging Third World countries came together in a dramatic and unprecedented show of unity to push for an end to European colonialism. These leaders put aside their religious, cultural, and political differences to fight the damaging effects of their common imperialist enemies. From this meeting there emerged a permanent association of nonaligned nations, which Malcolm termed the Afro-Asian-Arab bloc, that maintained the Bandung theme of unity and continued to fight for nationalist causes and other common interests. It was in the United Nations,* Malcolm claimed, that the coalition made its presence felt most in the 1960s. In the United Nations the bloc maintained a place among other groups based on race and common issues. There was much from this association of Third World countries, devoid of many of the attributes of powerful nations, Malcolm believed, that blacks could learn from in overcoming their own American oppression.

SELECTED BIBLIOGRAPHY

Breitman,1968; Malcolm X (Breitman, ed.), 1970a; Malcolm X (Karim, ed.), 1971; Malcolm X (Perry, ed.), 1989.

Robert L. Jenkins

AHMED, AKBAR MUHAMMAD (Maxwell Stanford; Max Stanford). Akbar Muhammad Ahmed, formerly Maxwell Stanford before his conversion to Islam, a founding member of the Revolutionary Action Movement (RAM)* and a contemporary of Malcolm, was a known radical leader in his own right. Stanford, Grace Lee Boggs, her husband James Boggs,* veteran journalist William Worthy,* and black feminist Patricia Robinson met with Malcolm X in a small Harlem* café in the spring of 1964 and received a stern lesson about his strict moral, social, and cultural standards. Malcolm had recently broken with the Nation of Islam (NOI),* and the group met with Malcolm to ask him to help form a political organization to fight for black liberation. Malcolm started the conversation by emphasizing the importance of being on time and not breaking the law, then using racism as an excuse for irresponsible behavior. Malcolm stressed that those who were serious about political struggle must conquer their own internal weaknesses first.

In a classic Federal Bureau of Investigation (FBI)* Counterintelligence Program (COINTELPRO)* memo on black nationalists and hate groups dated March 4, 1968, Stanford was targeted as someone who aspired to the position of messiah of a black revolution. In the FBI's estimation, Malcolm had almost assumed this status before his untimely assassination. The Counterintelligence Program outlined in this famous memo sought to direct the state's effort against the coalition of militant black nationalist groups that had revolutionary potential. The memo specifically profiled Stanford as one who could unify the militant black nationalist movement, along with Martin Luther King, Jr.,* Stokely Carmichael,* H. Rap Brown,* and Elijah Muhammad.* To prevent the long-range growth of militant black organizations, especially among youth, the memo called for the execution of specific tactics to prevent those elements from converting young people.

Stanford and the RAM he founded in 1962 appeared as a primary target of COINTELPRO because it represented one of the most violent and radical groups of the 1960s. RAM had as one of its goals the overthrow of the U.S. government. The FBI characterized his influence and RAM as nationwide in scope. Malcolm X himself probably knew very little about Stanford and his ideas about leading revolutionary warfare inside the United States. He probably would have associated him with the vibrant, left-wing, labor-oriented culture of Detroit, Michigan,* but little else. Their names became linked following Malcolm's assassination as bizarre stories of Stanford having something to do with a plot to kill Malcolm X circulated.

Stanford would use Malcolm's martyrdom when he felt it helped him, but immediately after Malcolm's death, he did not seek to be the reincarnation of Malcolm X nor to represent RAM as carrying out the black nationalist or internationalist revolution that Malcolm had so brilliantly and passionately died articulating and organizing. Stanford continued to build RAM after Malcolm's death until 1968, when, according to most accounts, he faded from the national scene and RAM started on the road to nonexistence. FBI COINTELPRO activities played a large part in Stanford's eventual incarceration and RAM's disintegration. His failure to change and grow, which was a hallmark of Malcolm X's persona, at a time of extreme state repression of blacks suspected of subversive activity, undoubtedly hastened his political demise.

SELECTED BIBLIOGRAPHY

Bracey, Meier, and Rudwick, eds., 1970; Cohen, 1972; Glick, 1989; Kelley, 1999; O'Reilly (Gallen, ed.), 1994.

Amilcar Shabazz

AHMED, OSMAN. Osman Ahmed met Malcolm X when Ahmed was a student at Dartmouth University. After talking to each other on several occasions, they became good friends. Malcolm and Ahmed, nevertheless, had major differences in the way that they viewed Islam.* As a member of the Nation of Islam (NOI),* Malcolm's beliefs as taught by Elijah Muhammad,* the leader of the NOI, were quite different than those of Ahmed's, an orthodox Muslim* from the Middle East.* After prayers at the Islamic Center on Riverside Drive in New York City, Malcolm would often sit and talk with Ahmed as well as the Center's director, Dr. Mahmoud Shawarbi,* about these differences. These talks, and Malcolm's association with orthodox Muslims, occurred several years before Malcolm made the Hajj* (or pilgrimage) to Mecca,* required of every Muslim who can afford to go, and the last of the Five Pillars of Islam upon which the religion is based.

While Ahmed and Malcolm had major religious differences between them before Malcolm converted to an orthodox Muslim, Ahmed had nothing but praise for Malcolm as a person and political leader. Ahmed recalled that given Malcolm's reputation nationally and internationally, he could have had virtually anything that he wanted. However, Malcolm was neither materialistic nor status conscious. Hence, Ahmed viewed Malcolm more in a spiritual sense and as one of a number of prophets, rather than as an ordinary human being. Ahmed noted that because of Malcolm's reputation he was one of the most sought-after speakers on college campuses in the United States and abroad. He recalls that when Malcolm made a presentation at the American University in Beirut, Lebanon, he spoke to an overflow crowd of students and Lebanese people. Ahmed observed that Malcolm was considered a major Muslim leader from the United States when he visited the Middle East and was given the recognition normally accorded to a state leader. As such, he felt that Malcolm represented the ambitions of people in most of the Third World. They remained friends until Malcolm's death in February 1965.

SELECTED BIBLIOGRAPHY

Hitti, 1970; Strickland (Greene, ed.), 1994; R. Turner, 1997.

Mfanya Donald Tryman

ALBANY, GEORGIA. In November 1961, the Albany campaign to end racial segregation* was started by local leaders, including Dr. William G. Anderson, who was assisted by Student Non-Violent Coordinating Committee (SNCC)* field workers Charles Sherrod and Cordell Reagon and students from Albany State College. On December 10, 1961, ten freedom riders* on an integrated train attempted to desegregate the local terminal and were arrested. A ruling desegregating the bus terminal was tested, causing this southwest Georgia city of 56,000 people, with a 40 percent African American population, to become nationally prominent. Martin Luther King, Jr.,* led a demonstration in Albany and was arrested, focusing more attention on the city's strained race relations. Yet

Albany proved to be a failure for the civil rights movement,* in part, when an open feud developed among SNCC, the National Association for the Advancement of Colored People,* and the Southern Christian Leadership Conference (SCLC).* After the Albany movement discontinued, bus service was discontinued, and parks and theaters remained segregated. Malcolm X responded to the failure in Albany in his "Message to the Grass Roots"* speech delivered in Detroit, Michigan,* in late 1963. No friend of the conventional civil rights movement or its goals, especially racial integration,* Malcolm X said that the failure to desegregate Albany was important because it signaled an all-time low in the civil rights movement. SCLC was in financial trouble, and nationally known black civil rights leaders "became fallen idols." In turn, local black leaders began to take charge of agitating the masses. Malcolm relished this new local militancy and self-determination displaying itself after Albany in such cities as Cambridge, Maryland, and Danville, Virginia, because it showed that the national civil rights leadership was running its course.

SELECTED BIBLIOGRAPHY

Carson (Gallen, ed.), 1991; Malcolm X (Breitman, ed.), 1965; Oates, 1982; Solomon (Lowery and Marszalek, eds.), 1992.

Lawrence H. Williams

ALGERIA. On May 19, 1964, Malcolm X visited Algeria, the last stop on an African tour before returning to the United States. The visit highlighted his thirty-ninth birthday and came after Malcolm had left the Black Muslim* movement. Algeria had recently achieved independence from France, and Malcolm was impressed with Algeria's success. He saw in the former colony a model for the black African's quest for power. He advocated, as an example, the Algerian model as the only solution to the black South African problem of white domination and apartheid. This was a direct reference to the eight-year liberation war led by Algeria's National Liberation Front. Some white American leaders were fearful that Malcolm's fondness for Algeria would garner him support from that country, which, in turn, could be utilized in the United States for revolutionary purposes. This, however, never occurred.

While in Algeria, Malcolm had the opportunity to talk with the Algerian ambassador to the Republic of Ghana,* the revolutionary Taher Kaid.* After visiting with Kaid he would change his emphasis from "black nationalism"* to "Afro-Americanism," a more neutral term that Kaid, as a white, could support. During this visit he was also given the opportunity to walk through the casbah of Algeria, which Malcolm equated with New York's Harlem* community.

Malcolm claimed that Algeria was the base for a new type of political power that was socially inclusive rather than exclusive. It was this type of power balance that Afro-Americans needed, he argued. During the time that he spent in Algeria, Malcolm was also impressed with the spirit of brotherhood and understanding that he witnessed. He remarked that in Algeria he had encountered neither closed minds, closed hearts, nor closed doors.

SELECTED BIBLIOGRAPHY

Goldman, 1979; Malcolm X (Breitman, ed.), 1970b, 1992; Malcolm X (Clark, ed.), 1992.

Ronnie Tucker

ALI, JOHN (John 4X). On December 1, 1963, at a rally in New York, Malcolm replied to a question from the floor that the slain U.S. president John F. Kennedy* was a victim of "chickens coming home to roost."* Malcolm made the statement in defiance of Elijah Muhammad's* edict that no Muslim* minister should comment on Kennedy's assassination. Muhammad reasoned that blacks loved and respected the president so much that any negative Muslim comment might turn them against Muslims. John Ali (also known as John 4X), then the National Secretary of the Nation of Islam (NOI),* who attended the rally, reported to Elijah Muhammad in Chicago, Illinois,* that Malcolm had spoken out against the dead president. On December 6, 1963, Muhammad suspended Malcolm for ninety days for his comment. John Ali's information also caused Malcolm's isolation within the organization, an act that forbade other Muslims to speak to him.

Ali was once one of Malcolm's closest friends in the NOI. It had been Malcolm who recommended Ali to the National Secretary post with its commanding responsibility of managing NOI finances. Ali was aware of how important Malcolm was to the financial security of the organization, so he and Malcolm were in constant contact with each other. After Malcolm's break from the organization, however, he soon came to regard Ali as one of his greatest enemies. Ali publicly denounced Malcolm, and prior to Malcolm's death, he responded to a telephone caller on a radio show in Boston, stating that Malcolm deserved to die for the troubles he had caused Elijah Muhammad and the NOI.

SELECTED BIBLIOGRAPHY

Breitman, Porter, and Smith (Miah, ed.), 1976; Carson (Gallen, ed.), 1991; Goldman, 1973.

Kenneth A. Jordan

ALI, MUHAMMAD (Cassius Clay). Muhammad Ali is arguably the best heavyweight boxing champion of all time. He was born Cassius Marcellus Clay, Jr., to Cassius and Odessa Clay, who worked as a sign painter and domestic, respectively. Ali developed an interest in the sport of boxing at an early age. He proved to be a dedicated and successful amateur boxer. In 1960 he won the gold medal for the 178-pound division during the Rome Olympics. Later that year, Clay won his first professional fight, defeating Tunney Hunsaker in a six-round decision. Following this victory, Clay's professional career soared rapidly.

Other major developments were taking shape in Ali's personal life as well.

World heavyweight boxing champion Muhammad Ali speaking to a group of his admirers during the mid-1970s. Courtesy of Iman Johnny Hasan.

In 1959, he had heard about Elijah Muhammad* during a Golden Gloves Tournament in Chicago, Illinois.* Then in 1961, while training in Miami, a Black Muslim, Captain (Sam) Saxon (now Abdul Rahaman), invited him to a local meeting. Clay was impressed and inspired by the teachings of the Nation of Islam (NOI).* The following year, he met Malcolm X in Detroit, Michigan.* Malcolm considered Clay a likeable and clean-cut grassroots youngster. But he also had great respect for Ali's mind. Malcolm considered Ali a shrewd man who could easily fool people with his imitations of a clown. To Malcolm, Ali had a considerable amount of "untapped mental energy" to go along with his great physical talents.

Over the next several months Clay would sneak into NOI meetings. Eventually the press got word of Ali's interest in the NOI. Then, on February 7, 1964, the *Miami Herald* quoted Clay's father, saying his son had joined the NOI. (Actually, however, Clay had secretly joined the NOI three years earlier and was educated in the Muslim* creed by Miami's Minister Ishmael Sabakhan and the NOI's Deep South coordinator Jeremiah X.*) This news came within three weeks of Clay's scheduled championship bout with Sonny Liston. Clay invited Malcolm X and his family to Miami to celebrate the couple's sixth wedding anniversary. Malcolm's presence at Clay's camp became a huge distraction. Fight promoter Bill McDonald blamed slow ticket sales on Clay's connection with the Muslims. McDonald, along with one of Clay's friends, asked Malcolm to leave the city. Muslims in Chicago also wanted Malcolm to leave Miami, but for different reasons. They, along with Elijah Muhammad, believed Clay would lose the fight and consequently embarrass the NOI. However, Malcolm returned to Miami in time for the February 25, 1964, fight. Malcolm gave Clay spiritual encouragement by explaining the significance of his fight with Liston. Malcolm compared the fight to a modern Crusades, in which the whole world would be watching.

Ali defeated Sonny Liston for the heavyweight championship. In press conferences following the fight, Ali announced that he was a Muslim. On March 6, 1964, during a radio broadcast, Elijah Muhammad gave Cassius Clay the name Muhammad Ali. Initially, there was a reluctance to recognize the champion by his new name. On March 20, Ali was a spectator during a fight at Madison Square Garden where the announcer refused to introduce him to fans by his new name. Ali left the arena in protest. And though he drew criticisms from the crowd in choosing to leave the arena that night, his popularity and success as heavyweight champion continued. He defeated Sonny Liston easily for a second time on May 25, 1965, in Lewistown, Maine.

As the 1960s progressed, Ali's commitment to the NOI increased. He attended meetings, he studied, and he helped spread the teachings of the NOI. When Malcolm X and Elijah Muhammad split because of ideological differences, Ali chose to remain loyal to Elijah Muhammad. Yet Malcolm did not easily surrender his friendship with Ali. Although Ali rebuffed Malcolm when the two encountered each other in Accra, Ghana, following his trip to Mecca,* Malcolm sent Ali a telegram advising him not to allow people to exploit him. But Ali continued to distance himself from Malcolm; the rejection deeply sorrowed Malcolm. Ali, who had been one of Malcolm's most treasured relationships, even refrained from offering comments in the days after Malcolm's murder. Many speculated, including former boxing champion and Ali title fight loser Floyd Patterson,* that Malcolm's death trapped Ali in the NOI. It was fear, Patterson said, that kept Ali quiet about Malcolm and tied to Elijah Muhammad.

The most significant test of Ali's devotion to the NOI came during America's war with Vietnam* in 1966 and 1967. Because of his religion, Ali claimed he was a conscientious objector and could not serve in the army, a political position that Malcolm had once advocated. Ali refused to be inducted into the United States Armed Forces and was banned from boxing for three and a half years before he won his case on appeal in a decision by the U.S. Supreme Court. Thereafter, he returned to the ring and once again became heavyweight champion. By the time that he ended his career in 1981, he was clearly one of the greatest boxers of all times.

SELECTED BIBLIOGRAPHY

Branch, 1998; Hauser, 1991; Patterson with Talese (Early, ed.), 1998; Plimpton (Early, ed.), 1998; Wiggins (Gorn, ed.), 1995.

Gerald L. Smith

ALI, NOBLE DREW, AND THE MOORISH SCIENCE TEMPLE (Timothy Drew). Noble Drew Ali was born in 1886 in North Carolina. Before he adopted his Muslim* name he was originally known as Timothy Drew. After working as a laborer on a New Jersey railroad, Ali formed the Moorish Science Temple in Newark in 1913. The Moorish Science Temple combined the philosophies of various Eastern religions and black nationalism.* Members, who came largely from the working class, were taught that African Americans were not "Negroes" but "Moors," descendants of the Moroccans before their New World enslavement. Ali also referred to his teachings as Islam,* but it was not based strictly along the Islamic orthodoxy. Although Ali was semi-illiterate, he nevertheless held great influence among most of his followers, and the organization gained considerable popularity among blacks in the midwestern states during the 1920s. Ali and his "Moor" supporters were credited with helping to elect Chicago's black congressman Oscar DePreist in 1928. However, bitter rivalries fractured this organization, and Ali was jailed for an alleged role in the murder of one such rival in 1929. Ali died shortly after his release from prison on bond later that year.

Most students of W. D. Fard* and Elijah Muhammad* claim that they were members of the Moorish Science Temple before Fard founded the Nation of Islam (NOI),* of which Malcolm X was the national spokesman in the early 1960s. Similarities between the NOI and the Moorish Science Temple have been well documented, including their endorsement of black nationalism, the organizational structure of their temples, the symbolism associated with their dress and rituals, and their dietary habits. Both groups placed significance in the symbolism of members' names; the NOI replaced surnames with the alphabetical letter "X," while members of the Moorish Science Temple added to their surname the word "bey." Both groups were highly critical of Christianity,* and both claimed a racial heritage that derived originally from ancient Asia. Like all members of the NOI, Malcolm X was a beneficiary of the historical and practical legacy of Noble Drew and his Moorish Temple. But if he had much to say in acknowledging the historical linkage between the two groups, it was not done outside of his own temple teachings. In the year 2000, there were several thousand members of the Moorish Science Temple, mostly in the Mid-Atlantic states.

SELECTED BIBLIOGRAPHY

Bontemps and Conroy, 1945; Essien-Udom, 1962; Evanzz, 1999; Marsh, 1996; Pinkney, 1976.

Damon Fordham

ALLAH. Before Malcolm X publicly converted to orthodox Islam* in 1964, he believed as a member of the Nation of Islam (NOI),* as taught by Elijah Muhammad,* that all whites would suffer the wrath of Allah (Arabic for God) as a result of their treatment of people of color. Malcolm initially believed that black people in America, like Judaism's* belief about Jews,* were Allah's "chosen people." Muhammad taught Malcolm that he had an intimate relationship with Allah in the form of W. D. Fard,* who was selling silks in Detroit, Michigan,* in the 1930s. Black people were considered divine by nature and the primogenitor of everything that is in existence. Allah is a black man, and all black people are physical embodiments of Allah as taught by the NOI. Allah, Malcolm was taught, exposed white people as the devil incarnate. Hence, like Allah, the devil is not just a spirit but has a physical form as well. It was this divine teaching, according to members of the NOI and Malcolm as the national spokesman, that explained the Muslim's reference to all people of the Caucasian race as "white devils."* References to Allah were often interlaced with economic development, and fund-raising events were considered the will of Allah.

The meaning of Allah took on quite a different connotation for Malcolm after he converted to orthodox Islam and became a Sunni Muslim* near the end of his life. He no longer believed that Allah recognized blacks as a chosen people over all of humanity, nor that whites were by nature demonic and would be destroyed by Allah. Malcolm now believed that Islam is a color-blind religion.

According to orthodox Islam, Allah gave the divine and biblical teachings to the Prophet Muhammad,* who was illiterate and resided in Mecca* in the seventh century, and Muhammad's recitation of Allah's revelations are found in the Holy Qu'ran,* the sacred book that Malcolm and all Sunni Muslims believe in.

SELECTED BIBLIOGRAPHY

Hitti, 1970; M. Lee, 1988; Muhammad, 1965; R. Turner, 1997.

Mfanya Donald Tryman and Abdul Al-Barrak

ALLEN, MAYNARD. In 1937, Maynard Allen, a white state official in Michigan, took Malcolm X to the detention home that was run by Mr. and Mrs. Swerlin* following his expulsion from Lansing's West Junior High School. In his autobiography, Malcolm maintained that Allen was nice to him as they drove to the detention home in Mason, Michigan.* Allen consoled Malcolm by pointing out to him that the detention home was not the bad place that some portrayed it. Rather, it was a place where an individual like Malcolm could overcome his behavioral problems.

Although he had great admiration for Allen, Malcolm X declared that Allen still held the belief that blacks were responsible for all of their own problems. Malcolm felt that Allen's attitude toward him was paternalistic. Against this background, Malcolm X would declare, prior to his death, that while he welcomed the support of progressive whites in the struggle to improve the plight of blacks, blacks must be in absolute control of the effort.

SELECTED BIBLIOGRAPHY

Karim with Skutches and Gallen, 1992; Malcolm X (Breitman, ed.), 1965; Malcolm X with Haley, 1965; Warren, 1965.

Amos J. Beyan

AMEER, LEON 4X. Leon 4X Ameer was born in New York City in 1933 and served as a captain of the New Haven, Connecticut, Fruit of Islam (FOI)* of the Nation of Islam (NOI).* He also served as a former press secretary to Muhammad Ali.* He defected to Malcolm X's entourage from Muhammad Ali's entourage. Before his defection, he used his expert skills to train Black Muslims* in the art of self-defense.* With his defection, he brought news to Malcolm of an assassination plot Black Muslims were planning against Malcolm. Malcolm looked upon this act by Ameer as a sign of loyalty, and Ameer became one of Malcolm's most trusted followers after Malcolm's split from the NOI. Ameer served as one of Malcolm's lieutenants. During Malcolm's time as a minister of the NOI, Ameer became a target of the Black Muslims and received several vicious beatings at the hands of them. Malcolm considered attacks on Ameer as a harbinger of things to come and literally as a message to him that he would suffer a similar fate or worse.

In the final months before Malcolm's death, Ameer served as a representative of the Organization of Afro-American Unity* in Boston, an organization founded by Malcolm after his split with Elijah Muhammad.* Speculation has it that the beatings Ameer suffered were in retaliation for his defection. After Malcolm's death, Ameer stated that it confirmed his belief that the Muslims were capable of murder and that his life was worth nothing. Ameer predicted openly that Elijah Muhammad's days were numbered. The New York Police Department picked up on this implicit threat and informed the Chicago Police Department, who in turn informed Muhammad, and a heavy presence of security materialized outside and around his mansion.

Near the end of his own life, Ameer lived under a cloud of intimidation and threats created by the NOI. He changed his opinion, however, regarding who was responsible for the death of his friend and mentor Malcolm X. Ameer now felt that the government conspired to kill Malcolm, as opposed to the NOI. Some conspiracy theorists have speculated that Ameer, who was found dead in a Boston hotel room in March 1965, was killed by the government because he got too close to the real reason why Malcolm X was assassinated.

SELECTED BIBLIOGRAPHY

Friedly, 1992; Gallen, ed., 1992; Goldman, 1979.

Byron E. Price

AMERICAN DREAM OR AMERICAN NIGHTMARE. On April 3, 1964, Malcolm X, while delivering his "The Ballot or the Bullet" speech at Cory Methodist Church in Cleveland, Ohio, stated that he was not an American but one of 22 million black victims of Americanism, and as a victim, he did not experience the American Dream but the American Nightmare. Unlike Martin Luther King, Jr.,* who gave the "I Have a Dream" speech at the March on Washington* in 1963, Malcolm felt that he and black Americans were living a nightmare. The sharp contrast between a dream and a nightmare is generally recognized as a comparison of two opposing "visions" of the United States and contrasted most sharply by King and Malcolm, respectively. One vision was of good things to come; the other, of ugly things as they were and would be. King's vision was a world of tomorrow, a world constructed out of a Christian faith that grew ever more palpable as its God appeared to become further removed from the lives of its true believers. King, perhaps because he was living in a world that consistently rejected his conception of justice, raised his eyes above the white supremacist quagmire in which his people were submerged and fixed his imagination upon a utopia, an ideal world, where words prevailed over actions, and faith in justice triumphed over the reality of injustice.

Malcolm also had a vision of the future, a dream of sorts, but a dream that was formed out of the quicksand in which he found himself and his people. For Malcolm, escape from oppression was not the product of faith in a God who was either unwilling or incapable of parting the waters for blacks, as he once parted the Red Sea for Moses* and the Hebrews. Rather, escape from oppression and the nightmare would be the product of a cooperative effort by blacks to gain control over their socioeconomic environment.

Malcolm explained in his "Message to the Grass Roots" speech how blacks could escape from the American Nightmare through revolution,* which is based upon land acquisition, and he reminded his audience that the so-called Negro Revolution* of the 1950s and 1960s was a historical and unrealistic path to freedom. He also reminded his audience that revolutions, like the American Revolution, are violent and bloody and that land and liberation are historically inseparable as a basis for independence. The American Nightmare was not just how blacks were treated in this country and remained passive but how violent blacks could become when "Uncle Sam"* sent them abroad to Korea, the South Pacific, and Germany to fight against people they did not even know. Yet they remained nonviolent when their own churches were being bombed and little black girls were murdered in Alabama.

The vision of America as a dream or nightmare arose out of a common reality—living while black in America—but a disparate vision arises from the two metaphors. While King concentrated his vision on his hopes for what America could become—the dream—Malcolm concentrated his vision on what America had already become—the nightmare—but he showed his people how they could awaken from it.

SELECTED BIBLIOGRAPHY

Clarke, ed., 1990; Collins (Wood, ed.), 1992; Cone, 1991; Malcolm X (Breitman, ed.), 1965, 1967; T'Shaka, 1983.

Peter Jackson and Mfanya Donald Tryman

AMERICAN NAZI PARTY. The formal name of this group is the National Socialist White Peoples Party. It is popularly referred to as the American Nazi Party, so named because of its admiration for the former German fascist leader Adolf Hitler* and the party's adherence to the Nazi German's racial ideology. The party was not only anti-Semitic and anticommunist; it was also antiblack. The party was founded in 1958 by George Lincoln Rockwell,* who served as its commander until his assassination by a disgruntled follower in 1967.

During the 1960s the party railed against the civil rights movement* and its leaders. In many ways it was similar to its older associate in the white supremacist movement, the Ku Klux Klan.* This was also true in the amount of interest that the party garnered from the Federal Bureau of Investigation (FBI)*; the party was one of a number of white hate groups targeted by the FBI for surveillance and disruption. However, the party found much in common with the Nation of Islam (NOI).* NOI leader Elijah Muhammad* and Rockwell flirted with each other because of their similar views regarding interracial marriage* and the philosophy of racial separation.* The two exchanged letters and on one occasion even met secretly to work out an agreement regarding mutual cooperation, though apparently nothing of substance resulted. Malcolm, apparently unaware of the meeting, was supposedly informed about it by Congress of Racial Equality (CORE)* chief James Farmer,* and he was noticeably angered over the prospects of it having occurred.

Still, the Nazis were fascinated with Malcolm. Malcolm was not only a dynamic speaker; he spoke the language that the Nazis wanted to hear philosophically. On the occasion of a speech entitled "Separation or Death" that Malcolm delivered in Washington, D.C.'s Urline Arena, Rockwell and twenty of his fully uniformed "storm troopers" joined some 8,000 blacks to hear Malcolm's talk. Rockwell and a number of his followers would also hear a speech given by the Messenger during the NOI's annual convention in 1962 and made a generous contribution to the offering.

Neither Malcolm nor Muhammad were Nazi Party supporters. Indeed, from information that he acquired, Malcolm once warned CORE of an impending Nazi protest outside of CORE's national headquarters. After Malcolm broke with the NOI, he sent a telegram to the Nazi Party chief indicating that he no longer believed in the kind of separation espoused by Elijah Muhammad. Increasingly moving toward recognition as an internationalist, he could not jeopardize the coalition he was forging by strongly associating with hate groups like the American Nazi Party. Perhaps more important to Malcolm, he simply considered the Nazis indistinguishable from the Klan who lynched and perpetrated other heinous crimes against southern blacks. The American Nazis were a grim reminder of the kind of racists who had victimized the Little family in the Midwest during the 1920s and who likely killed Malcolm's father.

SELECTED BIBLIOGRAPHY

Bridges, 1994; Clegg, 1997; Farmer, 1985; Haley (Fisher, ed.), 1993; Malcolm X (Brietman, ed.), 1992, 1993; Schmaltz, 1999; Simonelli, 1999.

Zuberi Mwamba and Robert L. Jenkins

ANGELOU, MAYA. Maya Angelou was born in St. Louis, Missouri, on April 4, 1928. Angelou is a poet, literature professor, author, actress, and civil rights* activist. She is among the first African American women to publish best-selling books and earn Pulitzer Prize and National Book Award nominations.

Angelou first heard Malcolm speak in his familiar spot before a large crowd during one of his street corner rallies. She was immediately impressed with him and the extent to which he appealed to his audience. She then sought him out for a personal meeting at his temple restaurant in Harlem.* At the time, Angelou was working for Martin Luther King, Jr.'s* Southern Christian Leadership Conference* as its northern representative. The meeting with Malcolm was an effort to understand the Black Muslim* position on the assassination of the Congo's* Patrice Lumumba.* Malcolm had been outspoken regarding Lumumba's murder, blaming not only his African rival Moise Tshombe* but also the U.S. State Department* and the Central Intelligence Agency* in a conspiracy. Malcolm rebuffed Angelou's overtures to join her and other outraged marchers in a demonstration at the United Nations* in protest over the Congo issue (a demonstration the day before led by black nationalist Carlos Moore* ended in a near riot with New York police). Muslim* policy did not permit members to participate in demonstrations and marches.

In 1964, Malcolm made two tours of Africa that ended in the Republic of Ghana,* where African American expatriates like Angelou now lived and worked. Angelou referred to this expatriate community as "Revolutionist Returnees." She and Julian Mayfield,* a notable black author, nationalist admirer of Malcolm, and target of Federal Bureau of Investigation* surveillance, organized Malcolm's visit and appointments with various African diplomats, Ghanian ministers, and key journalists. It was a whirlwind tour that left Malcolm impressed with Ghana and Ghana impressed with him. On his second African tour, Malcolm established chapters of his Organization of African-American Unity (OAAU)* on the continent. He also recruited members and began appointing women to leadership positions. Malcolm valued Angelou's administrative talents and African connections as assets to the OAAU. Impressed with Malcolm's intelligence, dignity, independence, compassion, devotion to family, and commitment to the struggle, she accepted his offer in a leadership position in the OAAU.

Angelou's Pan-African spirit complemented Malcolm's Pan-African vision, and she looked forward to working with him. She returned to the United States only two days before his fateful speech at the Audubon Ballroom* and spoke with him by phone from the airport. Malcolm informed her about the life-threatening problems he was encountering with the Nation of Islam,* and Angelou tried to ease his mind about the troubles. She suggested to him a brief respite at her mother's home in California, which he apparently refused. His death not only prevented her from working with him but anguished her as well. It was not until the early 1990s, she once said, that she was able to get beyond her anger with Malcolm for dying.

SELECTED BIBLIOGRAPHY

Angelou, 1981; CBS News, 1992; Gallen, ed., 1992; Malcolm X (Karim, ed.), 1971; J. Smith, 1992.

Lehlohonolo Tlou and Robert L. Jenkins

APOLLO THEATRE. Formerly an old vaudeville house located in Harlem,* New York, the Apollo Theatre showcased black and white entertainment throughout the early 1900s. During the mid-1930s, however, Frank Schiffman, a white Harlem entrepreneur, acquired the popular night spot and began featuring jazz and rhythm and blues groups. For most of its history, the Apollo was the premier theater for both established and up-and-coming black performers.

During the early 1940s, Malcolm X moved to Harlem. There he made his living committing petty robberies and selling marijuana. In the evenings, he often visited the Apollo, where he saw such performers as Billie Holiday* and Lionel Hampton.* Malcolm X made fast friends with the Apollo's musicians and singers, many of whom became his regular customers.

SELECTED BIBLIOGRAPHY

D. Lewis, 1981; Malcolm X with Haley, 1965; B. Perry, 1991.

Phillip A. Gibbs

ARMAGEDDON. Popularly noted to mean the destruction of the world during the 1960s Cold War era, the term Armageddon was frequently used to describe what many believed would be the results of an eventual nuclear clash between the superpowers, the United States and the Soviet Union. The Nation of Islam (NOI),* however, variously referred to Armageddon as the Judgement, the Fall of White America, and the Second Hell. Central to NOI ideology, the term's meaning, regardless of its synonyms, consisted of a rather complex and peculiar explanation of the destruction of White America and the emergence of blacks to a state of supremacy. Rooted in tenuous connections with Old Testament theology, and outlined by NOI founder W. D. Fard,* Armageddon was God's final battle with the devil—his final destructive punishment of white America because of its historical treatment of black people, God's chosen people. The Muslims* taught that this destruction would have occurred in 1914, but a merciful Allah* gave a reprieve of seventy years for white wrongs to be righted. According to NOI teaching, prior to the apocalypse, Allah would warn blacks who had not accepted Islam* of the impending calamity by generating a series of deadly natural disasters. Invariably, both blacks and whites would suffer in the unleashing of this First Hell, though the brunt of the suffering would be inflicted on whites. Black people could escape God's wrath only by accepting Islam and completely separating themselves from whites. Subsequently, the Second Hell, which would be carried out by a spacelike aircraft, "The Mother Plane," filled with smaller versions of the aircraft, all armed with incendiary bombs, would make much of the earth a veritable lake of fire. The final act of destruction would come directly from Allah, who, the Muslims claimed, would cause a gigantic atmospheric explosion, setting off additional fires that would burn for nearly 400 years. The cooling process would require another 610 years, keeping the earth, except for 144,000 righteous black people, unfit for human habitation until then. Thereafter, however, a new nation of black people would emerge from the ashes of the destroyed white-dominated one to reclaim their rightful place as the world's dominant people.

As an NOI minister, Malcolm X certainly taught the sect's account of Armageddon. And he respected the symbols important in the story. In Malcolm's administered Temple Number Seven,* as with other NOI mosques, two flags, one Islamic and the other one the U.S. flag, were always in place. On a nearby blackboard, also on constant display, was the question, "Which flag will survive the Armageddon?" Consistent with the NOI's tenets, he held the line in the prophesied battle of right conquering wrong, of good over evil, which translated to mean blacks mastering whites and the restoration of the proper order of the races.

There is much to indicate, however, that Malcolm did not buy into much of the sensationalism associated with the Armageddon story. At least publically, however, his version of Armageddon differed somewhat from the story as formulated. It was not the natural disasters that gave indication of the coming War of Armageddon but the rising of black people. The signs were pervasive worldwide, Malcolm taught in the early 1960s, and reiterated in a *Playboy Magazine* interview, of this inevitable destruction of the white world because courageous blacks in their liberation struggles were defying white customs and power. Regardless of what one called it, "colonialism," "westernism," "Europeanism," or simply "white-ism," white supremacy, as were those who benefited from it, was disappearing, and what people were seeing was the end of white world supremacy and hence the fulfillment of prophecy. It was this line of approach to Armageddon that Malcolm continued to support after his departure from the NOI and the formulation of his own group.

SELECTED BIBLIOGRAPHY

Carson (Gallen, ed.), 1991; Clegg, 1997; DeCaro, 1998; Goldman, 1979; Haley (Fisher, ed.), 1993; Lomax, 1963; Malcolm X (Karim, ed.), 1971; Muhammad, 1963.

Robert L. Jenkins

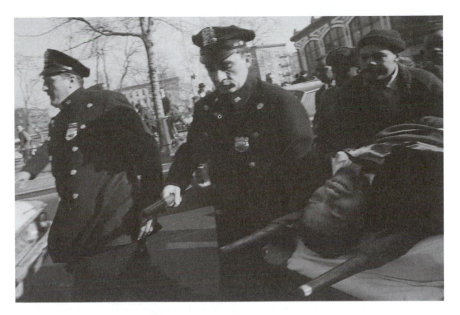

Malcolm's body being transported to a nearby hospital in Harlem following his assassination. © Bettmann/CORBIS.

ASSASSINATION OF MALCOLM X. Since the death of Malcolm X, a number of conspiracy theories have advanced to explain who or what organization or government entity was behind his death. Ever since the ouster of Malcolm from the Black Muslims* in November 1963 after making his chickens coming home to roost* statement about the assassination of President John F. Kennedy,* animosity toward him increased. This was evident inside the Nation of Islam (NOI)* and the hostility of officials toward Malcolm. Elijah Muhammad* and Louis Farrakhan* both showed open contempt toward the former Muslim.*

But it was not until Malcolm decided to expose Elijah Muhammad having fathered six children by his personal secretaries that it became clear from a number of statements made by Black Muslims that the NOI preferred Malcolm dead. Many of these statements appeared in *Muhammad Speaks,** the national newspaper for the organization. Malcolm reiterated on a number of occasions during the last year of his life that he was a marked man. Several ominous signs suggested that the loss of his life had become imminent. One had to do with members of the Fruit of Islam,* who Malcolm had trained and recognized, waiting for his flight to come in at the Los Angeles International Airport, apparently waiting for the opportunity to kill him. Malcolm was able to avoid and lose them, however. A second incident had to do with the firebombing of Malcolm's home in Queens, New York. He had to wake up his children and rush them out into the cold winter night to avoid this disaster. The New York police later accused Malcolm of attempting to make it appear that someone else had torched his house when he actually had done it. In a third incident, a car approached the one that Malcolm was in with companions on a Los Angeles freeway and only backed off when Malcolm stuck the end of a black walking stick out of his window, pretending to have a gun.

Hence, many believe that the Black Muslims had him killed. There is no doubt that the three men who pulled the gun triggers in the crowded Audubon Ballroom* on that fateful Sunday in 1965 were Black Muslims. Talmadge Hayer,* also known as Thomas Hagan, Norman 3X Butler,* and Thomas 15X Johnson,* all of whom were arrested, were later tried and found guilty of killing Malcolm X.

Prior to Malcolm's speaking engagement that day, several Black Muslims had been in the auditorium that Malcolm was to appear in. It is thought that their purpose in coming there before Malcolm's speaking engagement was to walk through and act out the assassination that would take place. They took their seats on the front row, in similar places that they would sit on the day of the shooting. At the time, Black Muslim followers and bodyguards of Malcolm X did not give much attention to their presence.

On the day of the assassination, Malcolm had instructed personnel not to frisk and check people for weapons, which was a policy to which his followers normally strictly adhered. As it turned out, the would-be assassins again had front row seats. A weary Malcolm, after a brief introduction by one of his followers, appeared on stage and opened with his traditional Arabic greeting of "A Salaam Alaikum." Many in the audience responded in kind. As Malcolm began his opening statements, he was distracted by a commotion at the far end of the first row. One man said to another, "Get your hand out of my pocket." Malcolm looked over and informed the brothers that they should "cool it." No sooner than he had been distracted, three other men in the front row stood up with guns in front of Malcolm and, at point blank range, began shooting numerous rounds of bullets into his face and chest. Oddly enough, one of Malcolm's last words was "brother," directed unknowingly at the men who were a part of the death squad.

SELECTED BIBLIOGRAPHY

Evanzz, 1992; Friedly, 1992; Lomax, 1968; *New York Times*, February 22, 1965; *Militant*, March 4, 1965.

Mfanya Donald Tryman

ASSASSINATION TRIAL. The rift with his former mentor and friend Elijah Muhammad,* Allah's* Messenger in the Nation of Islam (NOI),* became so deep that Malcolm X readily acknowledged the danger to his life. Months before his murder, Malcolm predicted to those in and outside of his circle that his death was imminent. Even the New York Police knew, Malcolm claimed, that the highly charged atmosphere surrounding him meant that his life was in serious danger. Threatening telephone calls and letters, suspicious followers and stalkers, and the firebombing of his home were all part of a series of ominous incidents that gave foreboding credibility to Malcolm's premonition. What Malcolm predicted about his death became a reality on February 21, 1965. At the beginning of his weekly Organization of Afro-American Unity* address in Harlem's* Audubon Auditorium,* he was brutally murdered before an audience of some 400 people, including his wife and young children. By the time of his murder, however, he was no longer convinced that his death would occur at the hands of disgruntled members of the NOI. Indeed, there was much in his mind to convince him that what he and his family were experiencing in the final weeks of his life came from quarters more powerful than the NOI, perhaps from the federal government itself. Nevertheless, those believed to be involved in his assassination had no discoverable connection with the federal government. Immediately arrested for the murder was a young black man, known variously as Talmadge Hayer* or Thomas Hagan. Hayer, who was shot at the scene by one of Malcolm's bodyguards while trying to flee, was saved by the arrival of policemen from a sure lynching by an angry crowd who had witnessed Malcolm's demise. In the course of the next ten days, police arrested two other men, Norman 3X Butler* and Thomas 15X Johnson,* and also charged them in Malcolm's murder.

Originally on the docket for December 1965, the preliminary trial began on January 12, 1966, nearly a full year after the assassination. The New York prosecutor's office tabbed Vincent Dermody,* a veteran assistant prosecutor with an impressive murder conviction record, to argue the state's case. Black court-appointed attorneys William Chance and Joseph B. Williams* represented Butler; Joseph Pinckney and Charles B. Beavers comprised Johnson's legal team. Hayer's family provided the funds to hire white attorneys for his defense, seventy-two-year-old trial attorney Peter L. F. Sabbatino,* reputable for his murder defense skills, and a lesser known, Peter Yellin. Veteran judge Charles Marks* presided over the case. The jury, consisting of nine whites and three blacks (nine men and three women) and equally represented by working-class and white-collar "peers" of the defendants, would sit for nearly two months and hear more than two dozen witnesses, including Malcolm's widow Betty Shabazz* and the three accused.

Clearly, the state intended to rely heavily on the testimony of one of Malcolm's bodyguards, Cary 2X Thomas.* Thomas, who had provided the police with information that led to the arrest of both Butler and Johnson, had himself been arrested shortly after Malcolm's murder and held in jail for nearly a year as a material witness. In three days on the stand, he provided testimony filled with inconsistencies and contradictions from his grand jury statements. This was especially true about the roles of the men in starting the diversionary tactics prior to the shooting and who actually held and fired the shotgun that killed Malcolm. Although he claimed to have known Hayer as a member of the NOI, he gave conflicting testimony about Hayer's membership in the New York mosque and the more anti-Malcolm mosque in Newark, New Jersey. Indeed, it was never substantiated in the trial that Hayer was actually a member of the NOI, an affiliation that Hayer would consistently deny. Nevertheless, Thomas was the only witness whose testimony seemed decisive and credible in indicting the three men. And the story that he told corresponded with that spun by the prosecutor Dermody.

The prosecutor was aggressive in pushing his case. Unconcerned about conjectured conspiracies or motive, he sought merely to prove that the three defendants did in fact commit the murders. His presentations about the evolution of events in Malcolm's life leading up to his murder were spirited, his questioning simple and direct, and his expectations of "yes" or "no" answers from witnesses reflecting the skill of a seasoned prosecutor who fully expected the accused to be convicted. Although she provided little that was factually significant to the trial, Dermody allowed Malcolm's widow on the stand for her to give emotional testimony. No doubt, it gave a more compelling human dimension to the prosecutor's case.

Although the attorneys for the accused fought for their clients, they were hardly matches for Dermody. Their case was clearly hampered by the inability to acquire access to considerable specific information about the prosecution's witnesses, an acceptable and expected practice in court cases. But besides a friendly judge who frequently sided with the prosecution on many of the motions, the defense was unimaginative and understandably found it difficult to refute some of the evidence. This was especially true of Hayer's role; most damaging was his capture at the scene after attempting to flee, confiscation of a pistol clip from his coat pocket, a witness's discovery of Hayer's .45 automatic pistol used in the shooting replete with his fingerprints, and the diversionary smoke bomb, also laden with his fingerprints. On the stand, the twenty-eight-year-old accused perjured himself by denying membership in the NOI and claimed nothing to do with the murder. There was similar testimony by both Butler and Johnson about their involvement. The two men had been arrested away from the murder scene, and there was hardly definitive testimony about their being in the auditorium. Indeed, one of Malcolm's lieutenants, Benjamin Karim,* whose speech opened the Audubon rally prior to Malcolm's appearance, maintained that because both Butler and Johnson were so well known as Fruit of Islam (FOI)* enforcers and hence potentially threatening to Malcolm, they could not have entered the arena undetected and undetained. Unfortunately for the two, Karim was not called to testify. Moreover, Butler, whose alibi placed him at home doing the Audubon rally, was also under a doctor's care from a recent shooting. He was badly hobbled at the time of his arrest and consequently appeared an unlikely perpetrator capable of escaping quickly from a murder scene. Four witnesses, including his wife and medical doctor, testified to such in his behalf. Nevertheless, a large number of witnesses besides Thomas placed both men at the Audubon and fingered each of them as one of the shooters with Hayer.

Unexpectedly after his initial testimony, Hayer took the stand a second time and confessed to the murder. In the process, he sought to absolve Butler and Johnson of any involvement in the murder. Only the confession came as a surprise to observers, for the physical evidence certainly made it difficult to deny Hayer's role. Yet the confession also surprised his attorney, who professed genuine belief in his client's innocence and quickly urged the jury to disregard the confession as an untruthful but noble effort on Hayer's part to exonerate the other two defendants. Dermody, understandably, had little trouble with the merits of the confession but refused to accept Hayer's version that the other two men were not guilty. The prosecutor's position prevailed. On March 11, 1966, the jury, after twenty hours of deliberation, found all three men guilty of Malcolm's murder. Since New York had no death penalty, each of them received an automatic life sentence, though parole was possible after they had served twenty-seven years of their term. Butler, a model prisoner in the places where he was incarcerated, was paroled in June 1985; Johnson and Hayer won release shortly thereafter.

As Malcolm had been in life and death, his assassination trial attracted the attention of the media, both black and white, from across the nation. For two months, Malcolm's friends, followers, and interested observers awaited the trial's conclusion to divulge the details of his murder. To be sure, there was much to substantiate the crime's commission by Hayer even before his admission, but in many ways the trial left as many questions unanswered as it answered. Most significantly, the question of who was actually behind the murder was left for considerable speculation. Many came to believe that the three men convicted in the murder could not have been more than pawns in a larger conspiracy. Hence, over the years since Malcolm's murder and trial, numerous theories evolved, including allegations against the NOI, the New York Police, Mafia* drug lords, the Central Intelligence Agency (CIA),* and even agents of foreign governments. Hayer himself helped to fan the flame of conspiracy, when on the stand for the second time he claimed that he and four others had been hired to kill Malcolm, but he refused to identify them. No conclusive evidence ever emerged to validate the various conspiracy theories. While in prison, however, Hayer in a 1977 interview with notable civil rights* attorney William Kunstler* gave considerable detail about the four accomplices mentioned in his trial confession. All of them were FOI members from the Newark Mosque,* but none were identified as Butler and Johnson. The information, however, added more grist to the mill about complicity in the murder. Still, it was deemed insufficient to warrant reopening the case.

What most Malcolm X students have essentially concluded is that both Butler and Johnson were merely victims, largely railroaded into prison by a justice system bent on convicting more than Hayer for Malcolm's murder. In the end,

Malcolm himself, like these two men, became a casualty of the justice system that he so often railed against and for which he demanded reform. He would not likely have been surprised at the outcome.

SELECTED BIBLIOGRAPHY

Breitman, Porter, and Smith (Miah, ed.), 1976; Farmer, 1985; Friedly, 1992; Goldman, 1979; Kondo, 1993; Laurino (Gallen, ed.), 1992; Lomax, 1968; Malcolm X with Haley, 1965; *Militant*, January 24, 1966; *New York Amsterdam News*, March 13, December 14, 1965, February 12, March 12, 1966, April 29, 1978.

Robert L. Jenkins

ASSASSIN PLOTTERS. Talmadge Hayer,* Thomas 15X Johnson,* and Norman 3X Butler* were convicted of the assassination of Malcolm X. But Willie (or William) X, Talmadge Hayer, Robert X, Benjamin Thomas (Ben X), Leon X Davis, and Wilbur X McKinley allegedly were the men who had plotted and participated in the assassination of Malcolm X. One of the actual assassins alleged that these men were the real assassins and were recruited off the streets of Paterson, New Jersey, and the Newark mosque* in New Jersey to kill Malcolm during the late spring of 1964. Hayer admitted in 1977 in a sworn affidavit while still in prison for the murder of Malcolm that these other men were involved, but questions remained regarding the veracity of Hayer's affidavit because of his statement under oath during the assassination trial.* Hayer admitted in the affidavit that he told a number of lies during the trial to make the Nation of Islam (NOI)* as well as himself appear innocent in Malcolm's murder. In his new version, Hayer asserted that Willie X used the shotgun in the killing, and Leon and himself used large-caliber weapons. Ben and Wilbur created a disturbance in the back of the room to distract attention and ignited a smoke bomb to create confusion once the plot actually unfolded.

In 1978, Hayer signed a second sworn affidavit related to the killing that further correlated with the actual physical evidence collected for the assassination trail. Hayer claimed that the other two convicted assassins, Thomas 15X Johnson and Norman 3X Butler, were not even at the Audubon Ballroom.* This latter assertion was corroborated by Benjamin Goodman (who later changed his last name to Karim), a close friend of Malcolm who scanned the audience on the day of the assassination, in an affidavit he signed swearing that Johnson and Butler were nowhere in the audience. Nevertheless, all efforts, legal as well as political, to have the case reopened with the names of the new alleged assassins failed.

SELECTED BIBLIOGRAPHY

Evanzz, 1999; Friedly, 1992; Laurino (Gallen, ed.), 1992; Morrison, 1965.

Mfanya Donald Tryman

ATKINS, CLARENCE. Clarence Atkins was a personal friend of Malcolm X's during the years that Malcolm lived in Harlem* as a pimp and hustler in the

1940s. He recalls that a number of black women liked light-skinned black men with a reddish complexion. Malcolm, with such a complexion and a reddish "conk"* or processed hair, met that prototype for black women. This was in spite of the fact that such men often had more than one female that they called their "woman." The fact that Malcolm was tall and handsome added to his allure. Atkins described Malcolm as a person who was very wild at this point in his life and who did not care about anything or anyone.

On a number of occasions, Malcolm spoke to Atkins regarding his upbringing in a family in which his father was a follower of Marcus Garvey* and the United Negro Improvement Association* in the 1920s. While Malcolm was not involved in political organizations or politics in Harlem, Atkins recalls, he was still very political and shrewd as a person. Malcolm often spoke of the incident with his eighth-grade teacher, who told Malcolm that a "nigger" could not be a lawyer, as Malcolm aspired to be at the time, and that he should be more realistic in looking for a career, such as carpentry.

But Atkins also remembers lighter moments with Malcolm in which they went to Sammy "Pretty Boy" McKnight's apartment, where Sammy cooked and they smoked marijuana and listened to the jazz greats of the time, including Charlie Parker and Dizzy Gillespie. This was one of the few places in which Malcolm had a respite from the dangerous nightlife of Harlem, where he hustled and pimped women for a living before his Islamic conversion.

SELECTED BIBLIOGRAPHY

DeCaro, 1996; Malcolm X with Haley, 1992.

Mfanya Donald Tryman

AUDUBON BALLROOM. The Audubon Ballroom, located in uptown Manhattan or what is commonly known as Harlem,* is famous in its own right. It was here that so many big band celebrities of the 1930s and 1940s played to large crowds seeking entertainment in the black nightlife. It was also here that many other entertainers, including comedians, charmed audiences with some of their best performances. Nipsey Russell, Redd Foxx,* Moms Mabley, and Slappy White were among the comedic regulars at the famous ballroom. Clearly, the Audubon was not only a stepping-stone for aspiring artists but also indicative of one's status as an accomplished star.

It was at this ballroom that Malcolm X, street-smart and still living with values associated with the same, shined shoes and had the opportunity to associate with the big names of the day. It was also at the Audubon that Malcolm used drugs and saw well-known celebrities using drugs.

The Audubon Ballroom was not just a place for social events. Malcolm held a number of press conferences there later in his career. He also used it as a forum for a number of his speaking engagements. It was at this ballroom that Malcolm was slated to speak on that fateful day in the winter of 1965 when he

Contemporary outside view of the Audubon Ballroom where Malcolm was assassinated. The building is under renovation to house the Malcolm X Museum. Author's collection.

was assassinated. The names Audubon and Malcolm have become inextricably linked since that day.

SELECTED BIBLIOGRAPHY

Breitman, Porter, and Smith (Miah, ed.), 1976; Malcolm X with Haley, 1965; Spitz, 1965.

Mfanya Donald Tryman

THE AUTOBIOGRAPHY OF MALCOLM X. Since the publication of Booker T. Washington's *Up from Slavery* in 1901, no other autobiography of an African American has been as widely acclaimed or read as Malcolm X's. Based on a series of interviews over two years with Alex Haley,* who, at the time, was a freelance reporter for the *Pittsburgh Courier,* * *The Autobiography of Malcolm X* has generally been interpreted as a commentary on militant black manhood.* Through the autobiographical genre, Malcolm provided compelling testimony as to the meaning, scope, exigencies, and horrors of being black and male in America and the accompanying anger and rage that it engenders.

Further scrutiny and analysis of the autobiography indicates that it is enormously complex and revealing on a number of different levels. The work's two dominant themes are the concept of "self" and the issue of change. As suggested by Malcolm in the autobiography, the idea of self is rational; it perceives the rest of the world as objects to be understood and then manipulated or managed. In other words, the self engages in conquest of the external or material world, learning its principles and using them to practical ends, namely, solving problems and creating things. The ultimate definition of self is not so much qualitative as it is the record of its measurable accomplishments.

Consider, for instance, Malcolm's account of his conversion to the Nation of Islam (NOI).* The whole account dwells hardly at all on the subjective nature of the experience. Instead, it focuses on measurable daily, monthly, and annual achievements related to learning. This is at the expense of sleep and the neglect of meals. Quite literally, his account of the conversion is told in terms of words learned, letters penned, penmanship improved, grammar mastered, correspondence courses completed, books read, and debates engaged in and won. In short, the self served to empower.

An empowered self also contributed to change. In the autobiography, readers are made to understand how Malcolm evolved from a troubled but promising youth in crime and drugs to a dynamic and forceful agent of social redemption. The developing pattern of change in Malcolm's life tended to be almost messianic in dimension. Indeed, there are patterns in his autobiography that support at least an interpretation of Malcolm as a magnificent antihero, an existentialist saint, and a mythic witness to America's oppressive racism. Much of what Malcolm had to say in his autobiography deliberately veiled the truth. In many cases, Malcolm simply sought to protect the personal lives of many who played a role in shaping his life. This, however, has never distracted from its importance of being the beginning of any effort to understand Malcolm and what he became in America. While the book has earned tens of thousands of dollars, Malcolm and his family derived only minimal financial gain from its publication, previously in the form of the advance the publisher gave to him during the writing phase. Profits from most of his ventures were almost automatically assigned to the NOI. *The Autobiography of Malcolm X* reminds all who read it that Malcolm's life was a drama—a saga of conflict conditioned and informed by racism, domination, and injustice. Even so, Malcolm's life was one of achievement through willed action and reflection in the face of hostile forces. Surely, though, Malcolm was not a creature of circumstances. Rather, he was a man in search of humanism, credibility, enlightenment, wisdom, and vision while endeavoring to lead and motivate others.

SELECTED BIBLIOGRAPHY

Benson, 1974; Cone, 1991; Flick and Powell, 1988; Glanville, 1964; Goldman, 1973; Knebel, 1969; R. Miller, 1972; Ohmann, 1970; B. Perry, 1991; Rummel, 1989; B. Shabazz, 1969; T'Shaka, 1983.

Demoral Davis

AZZAM, OMAR. During the spring of 1964, Malcolm X made his famous religious life-changing Hajj* to Mecca.* He had succeeded in making the pilgrimage only after securing the support of important orthodox Islamic leaders in both the United States and Saudi Arabia.* One of the most important of these was Mahmoud Shawarbi,* a member of the faculty of the University of Cairo and director of the Federation of Islamic Associations in the United States and Canada. It was Shawarbi who gave Malcolm a book to read in preparation for his trip written by one of Saudi Arabia's most outstanding scholars on Islam,* Dr. Abd ar-Rahman Azzam, an Egyptian national and close adviser to Saudi Crown Prince Mohmaed Al-Faysal.* Azzam's son Omar Azzam, a resident of the city of Jedda, hosted Malcolm in his home before Malcolm actually entered Islam's holiest city. Malcolm had been confined to the city's airport, unable to enter Mecca immediately until he was cleared by a religious court.

Malcolm's visit to Azzam's home and his subsequent experience in Jedda and Mecca were transforming experiences for him. From the outset, he recognized the physical differences between himself and Omar, but he gave little significant thought to the fact that Omar was white and he was black. Omar, who was an engineer by profession, was the brother-in-law of the Arabian ruler, so he was an obvious member of the nation's upper class and well versed in social etiquette. Malcolm basked in Azzam's hospitality, capped by a dinner in his honor and an overnight stay in the elder Azzam's luxurious Jedda hotel suite, but he seemed more moved by the genuine display of Muslim* warmth toward him, a perfect stranger in the midst of distinguished persons. Malcolm recorded his relationship with the Azzams in his diary and wrote affectionately about it in his autobiography.

SELECTED BIBLIOGRAPHY

Clarke, ed., 1990; DeCaro, 1996; Malcolm X with Haley, 1965.

Robert L. Jenkins

B

BABU, ABDUL RAHMAN MOHAMMAD. Abdul Babu was an East African revolutionary leader from the island of Zanzibar. In 1963, the Cuban-influenced political movement that he helped lead successfully seized power in Zanzibar to achieve the country's independence. The independent nation then united the next year with nearby Tanganyika to form the Republic of Tanzania. Babu served Tanzania's president Julius Nyerere as Minister of Commerce and Co-operatives. Malcolm, as with other Third World revolutionaries, knew of Babu's background but did not meet him until his second visit to Africa in the latter half of 1964. Their relationship budded, largely as a result of their mutual friendship with the Cuban revolutionary Che Guevara.* Babu respected Malcolm as someone willing to tell the truth about the real condition of black Americans and as the first black leader to take the emerging African nations seriously enough to make a sustained visit to the continent. While in Tanzania, Malcolm recruited Babu to help him in his effort to bring the plight of African Americans before the United Nations* and invited him to speak during a rally of the Organization of Afro-American Unity (OAAU).*

Babu made an appearance before Malcolm's organization on December 13, 1964. Malcolm's introduction of the African revolutionary indicated that he valued their association, and he contended that the audience had much to learn from someone like Babu, who understood the tactics and methods necessary in pursuing a real revolution.* The enthusiastic crowd received with approval Babu's presentation about the historical connection between Africa and the United States and the importance of strengthening the Pan-African relationship between blacks of Africa and North America.

SELECTED BIBLIOGRAPHY

J. Anderson, 1997; T. Davis (Chapnick, ed.), 1993; Evanzz, 1992; Goldman, 1979; Sagay and Dawson, 1978; Sales, 1994.

Robert L. Jenkins

BAILEY, PETER. One of Malcolm X's closest aides in the Organization of Afro-American Unity (OAAU),* Peter Bailey was by training and profession a journalist. For much of his career, he served as associate editor of *Ebony* magazine, for many years Black America's premier monthly, but he wrote for other journals as well. During the 1990s Bailey traveled extensively, lecturing on the life and legacy of the man with whom he worked so closely.

Once a member of several of the traditional black civil rights* groups, including the National Association for the Advancement of Colored People* and the Congress of Racial Equality,* Bailey became a devoted Malcolm follower almost from the time that he first encountered him. This occurred shortly after his move to Harlem* from Chicago, Illinois,* in 1962. On the first night of his arrival, Bailey went walking and by chance happened upon one of Malcolm's street rallies, gatherings that Malcolm had made common occurrences during the summer months. Bailey, of course, knew of Malcolm, but he had never heard him speak; he was struck by Malcolm's eloquence—the forcefulness and logic of his words. It was as though, he said, that he "was hearing the truth" for the first time, and he left the gathering "stimulated." Thereafter, Bailey returned each Saturday to hear Malcolm lecture, often following up his attendance at the rally by visiting the public library to acquire reading material that was mentioned during the speech. Exactly how the friendship between the two men bloomed is not clear, but doubtless it developed into something special for Bailey. He extolled the virtues of Malcolm as "a master teacher," who held classes that benefitted the masses right out of the "university of the streets." In many ways, he came to see Malcolm as part of a historical continuum that began with the black nationalist Civil War and Reconstruction leader Martin Delaney, who sought to forge a greater linkage between African Americans and Africa.

Activism in other black uplift groups had left Bailey unfulfilled, and he eventually withdrew from them. Although he never joined the Nation of Islam,* he was elated over the opportunity for a non-Muslim to work closely with Malcolm in his new black nationalist–oriented OAAU. Bailey maintains that Malcolm first began to conceptualize of such a group as early as December 1963, long before the commonly held view of the March 1964 permanent break with Elijah Muhammad* as the germinating factor. Bailey was a part of the earliest secret meetings, held initially in a New York motel, that evolved into the OAAU. Thereafter, he played a major role in helping to shape the organizational structure of the new group, and he edited its official newsletter, the *Blacklash.**

Bailey was often in Malcolm's company in the weeks before his death and sat in the Audubon Ballroom* audience the afternoon of his friend's assassination. To him, Malcolm's murderers had a larger message to send in their act: They perpetrated their dastardly deed in public, he claimed, as a means to intimidate Malcolm's followers in the OAAU. If indeed that were the case, their intent largely succeeded. Bailey and the others closely associated with Malcolm and his embryonic organization quickly faded from the scene. Students of Malcolm, however, owe much to Bailey for his accounts of what Malcolm experienced in the last days of his life.

SELECTED BIBLIOGRAPHY
Blackside/PBS, 1994; Clarke, ed., 1990; T. Davis (Chapnick, ed.), 1993; Friedly, 1992; Hampton and Fayer with Flynn, eds., 1991; Sales, 1994; Strickland (Greene, ed.), 1994.
                                                        Robert L. Jenkins

BALDWIN, JAMES. James Baldwin is considered by many scholars as one of the leading literary figures of the twentieth century. He attended Frederick Douglass Junior High School and DeWitt Clinton High School in New York City. As a teenager, Baldwin became a Pentecostal preacher. As a professional writer, he produced a number of books and critical essays. His most seminal novels are *Go Tell It on the Mountain, Notes of a Native Son,* and *Giovanni's Room.* In *Fire the Next Time,* a plea to America to address the nation's racial nightmare, Baldwin reveals much about his views and relationship with the Nation of Islam (NOI)* and, to some extent, Malcolm personally.

James Baldwin's career was partially generated by the thrust of the civil rights movement.* Indirectly, this is the context concerning his relationship to Malcolm X. To the American public, Baldwin appeared to be the alternative from the radical nationalist faction of the NOI and its prolific national spokesman Minister Malcolm X. As such, Baldwin shared conflicting and common views with Malcolm X. Simply put, the common ground between the two men ideologically was an applied aesthetic for social change.

Malcolm and Baldwin had first met in 1961 when they were guests on a New York radio program hosted by Isivic Goldman. Because the two often articulated parallel views, Baldwin soon came to regard himself and Malcolm as "soul mates." Malcolm respected Baldwin, especially the black writer's independence, and like Malcolm, Baldwin found it difficult to trust the motives of liberal whites in their support of black causes.

Baldwin's analysis of race relations had a point of resemblance to that of Malcolm X. Baldwin often expressed that Malcolm's critical analysis in examining racial, gender, and class issues was effective. In an interview with psychologist Kenneth Clark,* on May 24, 1963, Baldwin was queried on non-violent strategies and the tactics of civil rights organizations.* Referring to Malcolm X and the NOI, Baldwin cited how Malcolm's approach reached student protest groups and developed their critical thinking skills in examining the constituents of power and the distribution of the economic pie. He made reference to the point that Malcolm X instilled a reaffirming spirit in African Americans by telling them they should be proud of their blackness and heritage.

Hence, when further queried in making a comparative analysis between Martin L. King, Jr.,* and Malcolm X's civil rights tactics, Baldwin favored the approach of Malcolm X, by saying that Malcolm's appeared more dangerous because it was more effective.

In general, Baldwin expressed the idea that Malcolm's articulation of civil rights* presented a context for black Americans to describe and evaluate social, political, and economic issues from their own historical experiences. Baldwin stated that Malcolm reinforces their real world and who they are. Therefore,

Malcolm X's message of liberation and equality for blacks connected a sacred and secular expression of a precursory black liberation theology. Although there exists conflict in the theological repertoire between Malcolm X and James Baldwin, there appears to be commonality in their analysis and perspectives on civil rights and black liberation. Upon Baldwin's death in 1987, he left an unpublished biography and screen play on Malcolm X that film director Spike Lee* produced in 1993, entitled *X*.

SELECTED BIBLIOGRAPHY

Baker, 1988; Baldwin, 1962; Brigsby, 1980; K. Clark, 1963; Leeming, 1994; O'Reilly (Gallen, ed.), 1994.

James L. Conyers, Jr.

"THE BALLOT OR THE BULLET." *See* Theme Essay "The Ballot or the Bullet."

BANDUNG CONFERENCE. On April 15, 1955, twenty-nine countries of Asia and Africa, most of them having recently become independent, sent representatives to the former Dutch colony of Indonesia for the first Asian-African conference. The conference, as much a celebration to recognize the waning of colonialism in the Third World as it was a response to strategize solutions to common economic, social, and political problems, was heralded as a dawning of unity for peoples of color on the two continents. In no uncertain terms, delegates condemned the exploitive nature and white supremacy character of colonialism. They were less successful in finding permanent solutions to many of their problems, however.

Although the conference was held prior to Malcolm's emergence as an international figure, he was aware of the gathering's symbolic meaning. Colored peoples had come together, totally without the participation or influence of their former white colonial rulers, an indication, in Malcolm's opinion, that Elijah Muhammad's* prediction about the black man's inevitable emergence from white enslavement and domination was creditable. Malcolm especially relished the progress toward nationalism emanating from the Asian and African continents, and he extolled the virtues of the conference for prompting it in Black Africa. Indeed, the conference had left such an impression on Malcolm that a couple years afterward he initiated on behalf of the Nation of Islam* a large gathering that addressed colonial and neocolonial issues. Also in attendance were official delegates from five African and Arabic governments; the conclave made one of its last activities the dispatch of an official greeting from NOI leader Elijah Muhammad to a Cairo, Egypt,* international assemblage of Afro-Asian emissaries just beginning their conference.

More important, Bandung's unity theme was never lost on Malcolm. He occasionally hoisted it as an example of what blacks in the diaspora, but especially in the United States, could do to achieve greater rights. In numerous speeches he recalled the "spirit" of Bandung as a challenge for blacks to emulate in throwing off their Euro-American oppressors. Clearly, there was a lesson to be learned from Bandung. Despite their differences, he said, Africans and Asians of all kinds—Buddhist and Hindus, Christians and Muslims,* socialists and capitalists—all saw in the European a commonality of oppression and evil, and they were willing to put their differences aside to fight for racial progress and nationalism.

As early as 1959, in front of CBS television news cameras, Malcolm called unsuccessfully for a Bandung Conference of Negro Leaders to be held in Harlem.* Nothing could be achieved for black Americans, he said, if these leaders were not willing to agree first that their common enemy in America was the white man. In later years, Malcolm would abandon much of his rhetoric about the evil nature of all whites in America, but he would continue to emphasize his aversion for the evil that whites often did against black Americans. Equally, he remained committed to establishing a united black front to address this evil, and the Bandung Conference was the model that he advanced.

SELECTED BIBLIOGRAPHY

Carson (Gallen, ed.), 1991; Cone, 1992; Evanzz, 1992; Fanon, 1968; Malcolm X (Breitman, ed.), 1965; Malcolm X (Clark, ed.), 1992; Malcolm X (Perry, ed.), 1989; Marsh, 1984; Plummer, 1996; Wright, 1956.

Robert L. Jenkins

BARAKA, IMAMU AMIRI (LeRoi Jones). No one's legacy influenced the Black Power* movement and the Black Arts Renaissance more than Malcolm X. Standing at the junction between those two movements, Imamu Amiri Baraka (LeRoi Jones) was greatly affected by Malcolm X in many ways and on several levels: personal, cultural, and political. At the personal level, Baraka had meetings with Malcolm X, including the pivotal one with both Malcolm X and the Tanzanian hero of the Zanzibar revolution Abdul Rahman Mohammad Babu* in New York City in January 1965, where they held an all-night discussion of an international united front strategy for black liberation.

At both the personal and cultural level, Malcolm X's assassination in February 1965 was a turning point in Baraka's life. After leaving his first wife, Hettie Jones (formerly Hettie Cohen), and daughters in Greenwich Village, Baraka wrote the evocative paean to Malcolm X, "Poem for Black Hearts," which addressed the fearless leader's outspoken truths and the tragedy of his death. Since then Baraka has written probing poems, plays, and essays exploring the meaning of Malcolm X: for instance, the poem "X," the drama "The Death of Malcolm X," and the essay "The Legacy of Malcolm X, and the Coming of the Black Nation."

Malcolm X was one of the most important paradigmatic figures for Baraka's cultural and political self-transformation. Moving to Harlem,* Baraka carried Malcolm's lessons with him as he pioneered the Black Arts Movement by

founding the experimental Black Arts Repertory Theatre/School (BARTS). The
Black Cultural Revolution that Baraka insisted upon in the Black Arts Movement took aim at the "Novocain" of nonviolence that Malcolm X attacked in
his "Message to the Grass Roots,"* arguing for self-defense.* Furthermore, due
to the influence of Malcolm X and hundreds of urban uprisings, the major
protagonists in much of the work of the Black Arts Movement are from the
"grassroots." Baraka also insisted that the Black Arts Movement take aim at the
enticing reformism that was intended to calm the radical fervor of the black
revolt, just as Malcolm explained that too much cream would undermine the
jolt of a hot black cup of coffee—too black, too strong. Baraka often made
reference to Malcolm X's "The Ballot or the Bullet"* during his work in the
Newark political arena. For instance, during a heated 1970 political contest for
municipal power, with rumors spreading that powerful forces might steal a black
grassroots electoral victory, Baraka insisted that if African Americans could not
take power in Newark legally with the ballot, then they would seize it with the
bullet.

Above all, Baraka believed that in the Black Power movement the revolutionary culture that took its cue from "the music" was essential in forging the
politics of liberation. In his last days, Malcolm X insisted that in developing a
new politics the best model was black music, given the creativity of African
Americans in the past. Malcolm felt that such creativity could be used in constructive ways in the political, social, and economic arenas for black progress.
Baraka's cultural contributions to the Black Power movement were improvisations and experiments in the politics of liberation—attempts to create the conditions for the emergence of new strategies for self-emancipation. Thus, the
black conventions were all political improvisations to fashion united fronts and
to create the flowering of a new politics of liberation: the 1968 Newark Black
Political Convention and the 1969 Black and Puerto Rican Convention in Newark, the 1970 Congress of African People* in Atlanta, and the 1972 National
Black Political Convention in Gary, Indiana. One suggestion of the content of
such a new politics is the "Gary Agenda," the manifesto and program developed
out of the National Black Political Convention in Indiana.

Later, when Baraka rose to national leadership at the head of the Modern
Black Convention movement, his international diplomatic strategy was influenced by the guidance of Malcolm X and Babu. Particularly important were
Malcolm X's teachings about an international united front of anticolonial forces,
along the lines of the historic Bandung Conference.* Furthermore, Malcolm X's
strong teachings about the virtues of black nationalism* and Pan-Africanism*
were major factors in Baraka's stance on the right of self-determination. Moreover, whereas Malcolm X's Organization of Afro-American Unity* sought
United Nations* status, later Baraka's Congress of African People became a
nongovernmental organization (NGO) at the United Nations. And, in line with
Malcolm X's message, Baraka, Huey P. Newton,* H. Rap Brown,* and others
signed a United Nations petition in 1967 charging the United States with human

rights* violations against the African American people. Finally, it was no accident that Malcolm X's birthday on May 19, 1972, was chosen for the unveiling of the Gary Agenda and the launching of the African Liberation Support Committee devoted to the emancipation of colonial Africa. Thus, for a generation of Black Power and Black Arts leaders such as Amiri Baraka, Malcolm X was the definitive symbol of black liberation, and they tried to live up to his standards in their own work.

SELECTED BIBLIOGRAPHY

Baraka, 1966, 1984, 1995, 1996; W. Harris, ed., 1991; Van Deburg, 1992; Woodard, 1999.

Komozi Woodard

BARNETTE, AUBREY. Aubrey Barnette, a graduate of Boston University with a degree in business administration, was attracted to the Nation of Islam (NOI)* because it offered him the prospect of not only spiritual growth but also economic empowerment. After hearing Malcolm X speak, Barnette became a member of the NOI in 1962 and was appointed Secretary of the Boston Mosque. Within a few years, the demands on his time and the financial pressures from the NOI tithing requirements led him to quit. When Malcolm left the NOI and his life was threatened, Barnette also defected and remained a loyal supporter of Malcolm.

Barnette later wrote an article in the *Saturday Evening Post* in which he accused the Black Muslims of strong-arm tactics and of deceiving African Americans. The exposé resulted in a severe beating, presumably by NOI loyalists from the Boston temple, angered over his departure from the organization and the embarrassing article. On February 18, 1965, shortly before the article appeared, Malcolm and Barnette were invited as guests of the WINS Radio show in New York. On the show, Malcolm X corroborated Barnette's claim against the NOI and further contended that Islam* as a religion did not discriminate but that Elijah Muhammad* had used race as the measuring stick in the NOI. Three days later Malcolm was murdered.

Barnette's initial problems with the NOI occurred during the tense atmosphere of the Malcolm X–Elijah Muhammad conflicts. Like numerous other dissidents who suffered from violence during the period, Barnette's attack made more credible charges from the general public that Malcolm's death was the result of loyal supporters to Elijah Muhammad.

SELECTED BIBLIOGRAPHY

Evanzz, 1992; Friedly, 1992; B. Perry, 1991.

Lehlohonolo Tlou

BASIE, WILLIAM "COUNT." "Count" Basie was an accomplished keyboardist and a leader of the "Swing" era (1935–45), when mergers between jazz and popular music led to the emergence of "big bands." Basie's Swing bands and ensembles first appeared in the national consciousness at Boston's Roseland Ballroom* in 1936. Basie's 1940s band was known for its rhythm section, "riff-phrasing," and arrangements, coming from the Kansas City Swing tradition featuring improvisation in trumpet, trombone, and saxophone sections. There were many star soloists on its roster, including Lester Young, Buddy Tate, and Buck Clayton.

Malcolm X, known in his youthful hipster days as "Detroit Red," enjoyed jazz and dancing. Working in Boston at the Roseland Ballroom in the early 1940s, he met such jazz greats as Duke Ellington* and Lionel Hampton.* Jimmy Rushing, Basie's renowned blues vocalist, introduced Malcolm to many of Basie's sidemen. Known for his acumen on the dance floor, Malcolm, during a Roseland dance, won a Lindy Hop* contest with the Basie band performing the "Showtime" segment, when the best dancing couples competed against one another.

SELECTED BIBLIOGRAPHY

Deffaa, 1989; Malcolm X with Haley, 1965; Tirro, 1977.

Nancy-Elizabeth Fitch

BAZARIAN, BEATRICE CARAGULIAN. Prior to his imprisonment, religious conversion, and "rebirth," Malcolm lived a fast life, replete with crime, liquor, and women. One of the many women with whom he kept company while living in Boston was Beatrice Caragulian. She was white and an aspiring nightclub dancer. Malcolm met her at a local tavern called the Tic Toc Club, where he initiated the encounter. She was not particularly beautiful—her face reflecting the residual effects of a broken and unhappy home as a child. Perhaps what attracted Malcolm to her was that she dressed elegantly, suggesting that she had money or access to it.

Malcolm paraded her around as a "showpiece" to stir the envy of other men and to make him feel superior. Beatrice's involvement with Malcolm was, likewise, self-serving. She thought of him as a black "stud," a role he seemingly relished. The relationship was on occasion an abusive one with Malcolm beating Beatrice. Still, she maintained the relationship with him, albeit intermittently, for nearly five years. Interestingly enough, though, in 1944, she married Mehran Bazarian, her former dancing partner, while he was home on leave from the military.

Beatrice and Malcolm continued their involvement, nonetheless. She still bought him clothes and gave him money in exchange for sexual favors. The beginning of the end of their relationship started several weeks before Christmas of 1945 when Malcolm and a group of male cohorts, along with Beatrice and her sister, set out on an ambitious house burglary scheme in Arlington, a white Boston suburb. The entire ring was caught within a month, and everyone involved, except Malcolm and his friend Malcolm "Shorty" Jarvis,* either got probation or spent little time in jail. Beatrice, for example, spent only seven months of a five-year sentence in jail after her trial because she turned state's evidence and testified against Malcolm. Malcolm saw and met Beatrice for the last time at his second trial on the burglary charges in April 1946.

SELECTED BIBLIOGRAPHY

Clarke, ed., 1969; Malcolm X with Haley, 1965; B. Perry, 1991; B. Shabazz, 1969.

Dernoral Davis

BEAN PIE. As was the case with orthodox Muslims,* members of the Nation of Islam (NOI)* maintained strict dietary habits. For both health and religious reasons, sect leader Elijah Muhammad* set the NOI's standards of diet and eating habits, which he formally proclaimed in many of his presentations and which were taught in the organization's schools and training classes. Muslims, for example, were discouraged from eating more than one meal per day and from consuming too much meat. More restrictive, they were required to refrain entirely from eating pork* (considered to be "the filthiest" domesticated animal) and certain bottom-feeding or trash-eating fish such as catfish and carp. Even some vegetables, such as black-eyed peas and collard greens, both centuries-old favorites among black Americans and generally considered assets to health by nutrition and food experts, were disdained by the Muslim leader.

Perhaps no vegetable was more favorably regarded by Muslims, however, than the navy bean, and Muslim housewives and cooks found creative ways to make bean dishes. One of the most popular of these bean dishes was the bean pie. Similar in taste to the sweet potato pie, the dish was considered a delicacy even among nonblack Muslims, and many from the community would drive miles to purchase one from Malcolm's combination restaurant-office in Harlem.* While Malcolm never hawked bean pies in the neighborhoods and on street corners for profit, as so many Muslims would do in the large urban cities, he was certainly a fan of the lowly bean, during both his tenure in the NOI and after he left the organization. The multicourse Sunday dinner meals in his East Elmhurst,* New York, home, to which he frequently invited friends and associates following one of his evening lectures, were considered real "occasions" where bean dishes, including the bean pie topped with ice cream, Malcolm's favorite food, were standard fare. Although many of Malcolm's food choices and his once-a-day eating habit resulted largely from his association with the NOI, he continued to adhere to the practice until his death because he found it personally redeeming.

SELECTED BIBLIOGRAPHY

Gallen, ed., 1992; Karim with Skutches and Gallen, 1992; Lomax, 1963; Muhammad, 1967; B. Shabazz, 1969; Tate, 1997.

Robert L. Jenkins

BEMBRY (BIMBI), JOHN ELTON. John Elton Bembry was convicted for burglary and was serving time in 1947 in the Massachusetts Charlestown State Prison when Malcolm Little (later Malcom X) met him while also serving time for burglary. Both men worked in the prison* license plate shop. Bembry operated the machine that stamped the numbers on the license plates, while Malcolm worked the conveyor belt where the numbers were painted on the finished plates. Bembry became the prison guru, who often held a captive audience of both inmates and prison guards intrigued and spellbound by his oratorical abilities and vast knowledge of history, literature, and theology.

Malcolm was impressed with Bembry's speaking ability and his command of the attention of audiences. Bembry fascinated Malcolm with his knowledge of religion and word derivatives. Bembry's knowledge renewed Malcolm's interest in education and stimulated in him an insatiable thirst for knowledge. Under Bembry's tutelage, Malcolm came to realize the importance of reading, writing, and being articulate. Bembry convinced Malcolm that language and literacy were essential skills in becoming an intellect. He encouraged Malcolm to take advantage of the prison library and to sign up for the correspondence courses that were available to the inmates.

Bembry's discourses on word derivatives influenced Malcolm to take courses in Latin and English. While in prison, Malcolm began a lifelong habit of voracious reading and extensive note-taking. Even after his emergence as spokesman for the Nation of Islam,* Malcolm often visited and consulted with his friend John Bembry, who had moved to Queens, New York, after his release from prison.

SELECTED BIBLIOGRAPHY

Malcolm X with Haley, 1965; B. Perry, 1991.

Lauren Larsen

BEN BELLA, AHMED. Malcolm X was a close friend to Ahmed Ben Bella, the African leader of Algeria,* and Ben Bella's propagandist Mahmoud Boutiba* was a personal adviser to Malcolm. It was Ben Bella who opened Malcolm's eyes to the international context of racism and its devastating effects on the Third World by Western powers. Ben Bella broadened Malcolm's scope and view of racism, which had been myopic in nature based upon Malcolm's experience in a black and white context in American society.

Ben Bella invited Malcolm to an international conference of the world's revolutionaries of color in February 1965, in which Malcolm and Che Guevara,* a Cuban revolutionary, would be the keynote speakers. Malcolm had planned to introduce his petition regarding U.S. human rights* violations to the United Nations* at the conference in order to get approval by the attendees. In addition to Malcolm and Guevara, revolutionary organizations including the South West African Peoples Organization (SWAPO), the Palestinian Liberation Organization, and leaders of sixty-five other revolutionary movements were invited.

Malcolm was considered the American link with black Americans that would be willing to fight wars of liberation on the continent of Africa. Guevara was to coordinate this linkage with Malcolm. However, the untimely death of Malcolm and the removal from power of Ben Bella in a military coup constituted a serious blow to Guevara's plans.

SELECTED BIBLIOGRAPHY

Evanzz, 1992; Malcolm X (Clark, ed.), 1992; Segal, 1995.

Mfanya Donald Tryman

BIBLE. From the time of his imprisonment until his death, Malcolm was a lifelong learner. His interests were varied, and according to his wife, he read incessantly and widely from the classics to anthropology, from the history of ancient Africa to issues of contemporary Africa. Malcolm was also an ardent student of religious history, particularly Christianity.* Accordingly, he became well versed in the Bible, and he studied it often. Although one might suspect that he derived an early interest in the Bible because his father had been a Baptist preacher, Malcolm actually began a determined effort to read and understand the Bible while serving his prison term. After he became a Muslim* minister, he continued to study, something that he seemed proud to tell audiences in the black Christian churches, where he occasionally spoke. While much of his interest in the Bible might have resulted from a naturally inquisitive nature, Malcolm had practical reasons for becoming familiar with the Bible. As a leader in a small sect existing in the midst of the black Christian urban community, he often had to defend himself and his own religion from Christian believers. Numerous questions invariably came from these Christians, among whom he was forced to "fish" for new recruits. Hence, knowledge of the Bible was imperative when it was necessary to answer those questions or to make comparisons between Christianity and Islam* and between the Holy Qu'ran* and the Holy Bible itself.

Typically, Malcolm and other Muslim ministers gave the Bible a central place in their teaching. As a Black Muslim,* however, Malcolm could never admit to an affinity for Christianity. Although he would occasionally declare that Jesus was a black man, normally he condemned Christianity as a white man's religion based on white supremacy. Yet Malcolm readily acknowledged his respect for numerous Christian biblical figures, especially the prophets, and he often mentioned them in his presentations before Muslim and non-Muslim audiences alike. These men included Abraham, considered by Muslims as the "father of all prophets" and the religious link between "Christians, Jews and Moslems," and Jesus himself, whom Islam regards only as a prophet but not as divine.

From Malcolm's perspective, there was much for black people to learn from the Bible, "a good book," about their station in life. It was not to the Jews* that the Bible referred when it dealt with issues of "strangers in the land," he said, for example, but to black people. African Americans especially needed to know where they fit into biblical history, and Malcolm readily found scripture to both reveal this and to amplify his ideas about liberation and oppression. Occasionally, he chided blacks for not reading it enough. Their failure to study the Bible in more depth, he would say, kept them unenlightened, but it was also the reason for so many of their lost blessings.

SELECTED BIBLIOGRAPHY
Branch, 1988; DeCaro, 1998; B. Shabazz, 1969.

Robert L. Jenkins

BILL, CREOLE. Creole Bill, sometimes referred to as Creole Pete's, was an after-hours "speakeasy" located in Harlem.* Once many of the clubs that operated legally closed down for the night, including one of Malcolm's favorites, Small's Paradise,* there was still Creole Bill's to go to for additional entertainment. Creole Bill obtained the name because, in fact, he was a Creole with New Orleans roots. His after-hours club was actually his apartment, which he had partially converted to give more of the appearance of a small club. Malcolm recalls that both food and drinks were plentiful, and one could get practically any alcoholic concoction desired. Creole Bill specialized in Louisiana and Creole spicy dishes, which his customers loved to eat. After Creole Bill and Malcolm became close friends, Malcolm had some of his earliest practice at "steering" (men seeking sexual encounters) to Creole Bill's apartment. Fast-spending affluent whites who enjoyed the black nightlife of Harlem were eager for more of the same, and Creole Bill's place offered that to them. Malcolm would guide them to Creole Bill's.

SELECTED BIBLIOGRAPHY
Malcolm X with Haley, 1965; B. Perry, 1991.

Mfanya Donald Tryman

BIRMINGHAM, ALABAMA. Incorporated in 1871, Birmingham, Alabama, was nicknamed "The Magic City" because of its rapid growth. With its railroads and rich deposits of coal and iron ore, Birmingham symbolized the industrial progress of the Deep South. Yet the city gained a reputation for being "the most segregated city in America" and was referred to as "Bombingham" as the result of racial violence directed toward civil rights* workers and blacks. A group of businessmen and professionals, the Young Men's Business Club, sought to advance conditions in Birmingham. They convinced voters to abolish the commission form of government and vote on a mayor and city council. Elections for the new government were set for the spring of 1963. About the same time in April and May 1963, the Southern Christian Leadership Conference (SCLC)* led a dramatic and carefully planned civil rights protest movement in Birmingham, known as Project "C," which stood for confrontation. The Birmingham demonstrations were nationally televised as Eugene "Bull" Connor* ordered his

A black demonstrator during the Birmingham, Alabama campaign being attacked by a police dog, the kind of police violence that Malcolm often brought to light. Copyright, Photo by *The Birmingham News*, 2001. All rights reserved. Reprinted with permission.

officers to use police dogs and fire hoses to end the protest. Malcolm X was in New York and watched the Birmingham demonstrations on television with the rest of America.

Jeremiah X,* the leader of the Birmingham temple, claimed that Malcolm was coming to the city to lead rallies, but this visit never materialized. However, Malcolm criticized Dr. Martin Luther King, Jr.'s* decision to allow women and children to participate in the Birmingham protests. He referred to King as a "chump, not a champ." Malcolm was also angry that it took the Birmingham demonstrations to force the federal government to take a stronger stand on civil rights. The Kennedy administration, according to Malcolm, was actually concerned with protecting white property and lives, as evidenced in the unfolding of events in Birmingham. In Malcolm's opinion the real heroes in Birmingham were the local activists who put their lives on the line for the sake of freedom and equality. Yet Malcolm realized that the violence in the streets of Birmingham was just the beginning of larger racial disturbances.

SELECTED BIBLIOGRAPHY

Branch, 1988; Garrow, 1986; Malcolm X with Haley, 1965; Nunnelley, 1991; Porterfield (Bullard, ed.), 1989.

Gerald L. Smith

BIRMINGHAM'S SIXTEENTH STREET BAPTIST CHURCH BOMBING. Few southern cities during the 1960s civil rights movement* claimed as much attention from activists as Birmingham, Alabama.* Located near Alabama's geographical center, the city during the period boasted a significant black population and, with its major coal ore and steel industries, was the state's largest industrial-urban complex. Civil rights* leader Martin Luther King, Jr.,* whose Southern Christian Leadership Conference* mounted the major campaigns to desegregate the city, realized the difficulty involved. King called the steel city the South's* most segregated city; clearly, it was also one of the most dangerous to civil rights interests. Long a bastion of violent Ku Klux Klan* resistance to civil rights demands, the city was often referred to as "Bombingham," a reference to the frequent use of dynamite to deter black demands for substantive change in the racial status quo.

Perhaps no event in the 1960s outraged Malcolm X more than a bombing incident in Birmingham. Still convulsing over King's violently resisted 1963 summer desegregation campaign, the city again stepped into the national limelight on September 15, 1963, when four young girls died in the basement of the Sixteenth Street Baptist Church from a massive dynamite blast during Sunday school class. Twenty others were injured in the church bombing, targeted because it was an important staging center for many of the downtown demonstrations. Occurring less than three weeks after King's "I Have a Dream" speech during the historical March on Washington,* the four deaths initiated one of the most emotional national responses to the city's persistent pattern of violence.

King feared a major outbreak of black-white confrontations in the bombing's aftermath. Black Harlem* was enraged over the incident and, according to one observer, could have easily resorted to street violence, had Malcolm not interceded to maintain cooler heads. Although he claimed that he never spoke out against the church bombing as forcefully as he should have, presumably because Nation of Islam* leader Elijah Muhammad* did not approve, Malcolm was, nevertheless, in the forefront of criticizing the murders. In his temple lectures, and in numerous speeches and writings in the months that followed, especially after his separation from the NOI, Malcolm denounced the Klan and the climate of racial hate that sanctioned the girls' deaths. These people, he quipped, were a part of a "society of criminals," and their misdeed represented the greatest violation of decency and human rights.* Protesting the deaths of these "four babies" as civil rights crimes made little sense, he would admonish the Student

Birmingham's Sixteenth Street Baptist Church after the Ku Klux Klan's bombing that killed four young black girls attending Sunday School services. Birmingham Public Library, Department of Archives and Manuscripts (Catalog Number 85.1.9).

Non-Violent Coordinating Committee.* Addressing these murders properly belonged in the realm of the United Nations.*

As he so frequently did with other fallen blacks, Malcolm raised the issue of the youths' deaths in Birmingham to call greater attention to his condemnation of white racism and the failure of white justice to adequately address the violent repression of black people. (Although several klansmen were indicted, it would take more than two decades after the murders before Alabama successfully prosecuted a perpetrator of the bombing.) To tell his listeners that these innocent girls were killed by white Christians literally while praying to Jesus was a potentially powerful reminder to the frustrated and disillusioned blacks that his message in addressing the African American plight in unconventional, even nonviolent, ways was both meaningful and logical.

SELECTED BIBLIOGRAPHY

K. Clark, ed., 1985; Malcolm X (Breitman, ed.), 1970a; Malcolm X (Clark, ed.), 1992; Malcolm X with Haley, 1965; Manis, 1999; Sikora, 1991; Strickland (Greene, ed.), 1994.

Robert L. Jenkins

BLACK CELEBRITIES. Throughout Malcolm X's life black celebrities seemed to gravitate to him. This was evident even in his hustling* days in New York, where he came to know on a first-name basis black entertainers of renown, including musicians Duke Ellington,* Lionel Hampton,* Count Basie,* Dinah Washington,* Billie Holiday,* Billy Eckstine, Ella Fitzgerald, and the comedian John Elroy Sanford (Redd Foxx),* although the latter had not yet attained the television star status that he would achieve in the 1970s. Such personalities came to know Malcolm largely because he was a fixture on the dance floor and in the party atmosphere of popular ghetto night spots in the 1940s like the Roseland Ballroom* in Boston, or Harlem's* Savoy Ballroom,* Small's Paradise Club,* or the Onyx Club. Malcolm loved music and this heyday of the big bands provided considerable opportunity to patronize those places where it was abundantly played. It is not unreasonable to assume that some of these celebrity relationships were also based on the opportunity to secure from Malcolm some of the illicit drugs that he regularly sold as part of his successful hustle. Those were heady days in Malcolm's life when he basked in the energetic frivolity of his youth, but he clearly relished the association with these celebrities. After he attained considerable prominence as a black leader during the 1960s, he continued to both attract and court them as friends. Some were no more than casual acquaintances, though he might refer to them as friends, as he frequently did with many prominent people that he barely knew; others had a greater presence in his inner circle. During the 1960s these included such celebrities as athletes Jim Brown and Muhammad Ali,* singer Sam Cooke, the actors Sidney Poitier, Ruby Dee,* and Ossie Davis,* the comedian Dick Gregory,* and literary and intellectual figures like Maya Angelou,* John Oliver Killens,* Chester Himes,* and Kenneth Clark.*

Malcolm realized that many of these personalities had much to lose in terms of fan loyalty and financial support for too strong an alliance with him, and though he did little to flaunt publically his ties with many of them, he clearly valued the existence of several close relationships. As he did with prominent black political and civil rights* leaders who failed to address issues he thought of critical concern to the black masses, however, he frequently labeled some of the entertainment community little more than Uncle Toms* and Aunt Thomasines, middle-class blacks* who sought more to cater to whites. This was especially true of personages such as Harry Belafonte, Sammy Davis, Jr., Eartha Kitt, and Lena Horne, who he condemned largely for their interracial marriages.

As close as he and Dick Gregory became, Gregory was not initially beyond Malcolm's scorn and criticism. Admittedly Malcolm liked Gregory's comedic talent but once expressed disdain and concern over white America's tendency to regard people like Gregory as a "Negro leader" simply because of their celebrity status. Before they established a close relationship, Malcolm regarded Gregory as nothing more than "a clown" and like many other well-known black stars of the 1960s a "puppet" of whites.

SELECTED BIBLIOGRAPHY

Angelou, 1981; CBS News, 1992; Davis and Dee, 1998; Early, ed., 1998; Goldman, 1979; Himes, 1976; Malcolm X (Perry, ed.), 1989; Malcolm X with Haley, 1965; Xenon Studio, 1991.

Robert L. Jenkins

BLACK HISTORY. To Malcolm X, knowledge was regarded as a redeeming force. He understood the value of acquiring knowledge not only as a means of self-improvement* but, just as important, as a way to fight oppression. Perhaps because he had done little in his youth to complete a formal education, during the remaining years of his life he took learning seriously and became an avid reader. No topic seemed to interest him more than black history. It was during his incarceration that his interest in black history first manifested itself. As an inmate he read incessantly, relying on the various works of amateur historian Joel A. Rogers,* a favorite among members of the Nation of Islam.* At a time when the systematic study of African Americans had not reached the popularity that it would later enjoy, Malcolm found the time to enmesh himself in the study of black people, even with a hectic travel and speaking schedule. This interest included educating himself about the African linkage to the earliest of man, to the contributions and contemporary status of people of African descent throughout the diaspora. While he was hardly an expert on the varied aspects of black history, he knew enough to teach about the important role and contributions of blacks to the development of the world in his temple classes, public lectures, and small gatherings. He chided blacks for not knowing enough about their past and told them that their ignorance about their own history not only helped whites relegate them to a subordinate status, but it also factored in their acceptance of this subordinate place. Whites, he claimed, had deliberately stolen, distorted, or lied about the black past as part of their program to oppress and control blacks, but black people had much to be proud of, and learning the truth about their history meant that whites could not easily dupe them about what the race was capable of accomplishing in the contemporary world. Hence, he often reminded blacks of their contributions to biblical history, of their role in the establishment of the magnificent Egyptian civilization, and about the many contributions that inventive black minds made to world advancements in government, science, and technology. He often recalled historical facts about black and white race relations whenever he sought to make a decisive point in answering questions or asserting a position. And despite his general distaste for black intellectuals, he frequently referenced their work and was close to several, including the notable black historian John Henrik Clarke,* an expert on African history.

SELECTED BIBLIOGRAPHY

Lomax, 1963; Malcolm X (Breitman, ed.), 1970b; Malcolm X with Haley, 1965; Xenon Studio, 1991.

Robert L. Jenkins

BLACKLASH. As a national black leader, Malcolm X was almost always associated with newspapers. It was Malcolm who was responsible for starting the official paper of the Nation of Islam (NOI),* *Muhammad Speaks.** He not only wrote journal pieces for this paper, but he also penned numerous articles articulating NOI views for papers such as the *Chicago Defender*,* the *New York Amsterdam News*,* and the *Los Angeles Herald-Dispatch*.* He understood the power of words, whether spoken or printed. Hence, it was almost natural that once Malcolm began his own organization, he would establish an official publication.

Initially he sought an organ that would be tied to his religiously oriented Muslim Mosque, Inc.,* and planned *The Flaming Crescent*, a name chosen, he said, because he wanted it "to set the world on fire." The paper, however, never materialized. Instead, following the formation of the Organization of Afro-American Unity (OAAU),* Malcolm established the biweekly *Blacklash* as the group's official organ. As was intended with *The Flaming Crescent*, Malcolm likely associated social meaning to the title *Blacklash*. The "paper" made its initial appearance shortly after the 1964 outbreak of racial violence in Harlem,* making plausible a view that the title reflected Malcolm's frequently stated predictions about violent black upheaval in response to white racism. Thereafter published infrequently, the paper was little more than a newsletter of four to five pages per edition on a ditto machine. Seldom did its printing exceed 200 to 300 copies, most of them available to OAAU members and visitors to his rallies; it sold at a modest $.05 per copy. Experienced journalist Peter Bailey* served the paper as editor.

The paper's format was hardly appealing, something that Malcolm recognized as a limiting factor in its value as a propaganda organ, but it was, nevertheless, in great demand. Typically, it carried stories about Malcolm's trips abroad, his speeches, and affairs in the developing OAAU. In the end, it had a shorter life than did Malcolm's organization. Almost immediately after his death the paper ceased operation.

SELECTED BIBLIOGRAPHY

DeCaro, 1996; Malcolm X (Breitman, ed.), 1970a; *Militant*, October 5, 1964; Sales, 1994.

Robert L. Jenkins

BLACK LEGION. During the 1920s, the Ku Klux Klan* enjoyed a resurgent popularity that flourished not only in the South,* where it had first appeared during Reconstruction, but also in numerous northern and midwestern states. One of the notable aspects of Klan history is the existence of numerous parallel organizations that functioned simultaneously. Although their names might have differed, such groups were so similar in their philosophies, goals, and tactics that only the most casual observer might find it difficult to distinguish between them. In Michigan, one of the spiritual sons of the Klan was the Black Legion. Like the Klan, the Black Legion was anti-Catholic, antiblack, and anti-Semitic.

Strongest in cities like Pontiac, according to Malcolm X, the group also maintained a presence in the Lansing–East Lansing area where his family first encountered them. Malcolm's father, Earl Little,* was an organizer for Marcus Garvey's* black separatist Universal Negro Improvement Association* and attracted the Legion's attention for supposedly spreading discontent among the area's blacks. Little had previously been forced to flee from Nebraska because his activism raised the wrath of Omaha's Klansmen. Like the Klan, the Legion was prone to violence against those perceived as their enemies. According to Malcolm, they were responsible for the death of his father, who was found badly beaten, his body literally severed on the trolley tracks near his home. Malcolm and his mother accused the Black Legion of throwing his father's dying body on the tracks, where it was then mutilated.

Though police evidence never substantiated Black Legion responsibility, the mysterious death of Little left a lasting effect on Malcolm. He was only six years of age when his father died, but he never swayed from his belief that the Legion was the perpetrator. It might have been this early family experience with the Legion that helped to stamp an indelible hatred for such Klan-like organizations as the White Citizen's Council* and the American Nazi Party,* both of which he denounced in the 1960s for their crimes against southern blacks.

SELECTED BIBLIOGRAPHY

Chalmers, 1965; Malcolm X with Haley, 1965.

Robert L. Jenkins

BLACK LIBERATION ARMY (BLA). After his death in 1965 a number of militant black organizations emerged that gave credit to Malcolm X for their ideology. One such organization that believed that they were the true inheritor of Malcolm's legacy was the Black Liberation Army (BLA). A revolutionary nationalist group during the Black Power* movement, the BLA was founded by a group of Eldridge Cleaver's* followers after Cleaver began to experience problems in the Black Panther Party for Self-Defense.* Shortly after its founding, the organization suffered major problems with its leadership. A number of them were indicted and convicted of various crimes.

As a result of its reputation as a revolutionary organization, the government classified the BLA as the most violent of the militant African American organizations of the Black Power movement in the late 1960s and early 1970s. According to government reports, members of the BLA committed eight murders from 1971 to 1973. The government also conducted congressional hearings on the organization, classified it as a terrorist group, and labeled it as a threat to national security.

Reports on the organization claimed that it was carrying out acts against the law enforcement community. As a result, the federal government authorized the Federal Bureau of Investigation* to penetrate the organization. This led to the arrests of the group's leading members and the eventual demise of the organization.

The members of the organization adopted Malcolm X's earlier rhetoric regarding a violent black revolution.* However, Malcolm changed his revolutionary tone in later years and did not automatically support a violent revolution.

SELECTED BIBLIOGRAPHY

Malcolm X with Haley, 1965; Pearson, 1994; Shafritz, Gibbons, and Scott, 1991.

LaVonne Jackson

BLACK LIBERATION FRONT (BLF). The impact of the thinking of Malcolm X on the Black Power* movement is undeniable. Malcolm's insistence on the use of violence in self-defense* captured the hearts and minds of young protesters throughout the United States, who were disillusioned over the nonviolent civil rights movement* in the 1960s. His attempts to internationalize the black freedom struggle also brought more support to the Black Power movement. The Black Liberation Front (BLF) represented one of the groups whose ideology reflected the influence of Malcolm X.

Organized in 1964 by eighty-four students returning from a visit to Cuba,* the group advocated the use of violence to achieve freedom for blacks. Some scholars argue that the BLF favorably responded to Malcolm's ominous conclusion that "revolutions by nature are bloody." Led by Robert Steele Collier, a Boston native living in New York, the group claimed that blacks had been raped, discriminated against, brutalized, and murdered because of their skin color and because they were weak and disorganized.

Like Malcolm, the members of this group believed that their survival depended on the use of violence. They argued that violence and the threat of violence kept blacks in their "place." Although Malcolm never publicly advocated the use of violence as an offensive weapon, he believed that blacks would never achieve their goals using nonviolent tactics. Taking this belief to its extreme, a group of BLF members, including Robert Collier, Walter Bowe, and Khaleel Sayyed, set out to obtain recruits and to draw attention to the poor condition of black communities by bombing the Statue of Liberty, the Liberty Bell, and the Washington Monument. However, the New York City Police Department, using the Bureau of Special Services (BOSS),* apprehended this small group of insurgents before it could execute its plans.

BOSS, a secret body charged with monitoring subversive or potentially violent groups, infiltrated the BLF as much as it had already infiltrated the Nation of Islam* and Malcolm X's Organization of Afro-American Unity (OAAU).* Just as Ralph White, a police informant, had entered the inner circles of the OAAU, Raymond Wood, a black rookie patrolman, infiltrated the BLF. After several months of spying, Wood had the group set up to be arrested and, through his work, effectively caused the demise of the organization.

Malcolm's influence can be seen in the BLF's internationalist orientation and in its insistence that blacks acquire freedom "by any means necessary." The group's members, like Malcolm, neither wanted to reform nor to integrate with the capitalist system. Finally, the idea that either Malcolm or the BLF might succeed prompted law enforcement officials to infiltrate and destroy both entities. It is significant, however, that both Malcolm and the BLF thought that the political and economic system in the United States had to be destroyed before true liberation could be realized. Despite their revolutionary ideology, both entities lacked the resources to convince large numbers of people that their brand of violence differed considerably from the violence of those they labeled oppressive.

SELECTED BIBLIOGRAPHY

New York Times, February 17, 1965, May 20, May 25, 1965; Van Deburg, 1992.

Curtis Austin

BLACK LIKE ME. In late 1959, southern-born journalist John Howard Griffin embarked on one of the most fascinating personal adventures for a white man in the twentieth century. Griffin successfully interested the publishers of *Sepia* magazine, at the time one of the nation's most prominent black monthlies, in his plan to chemically alter his skin color and travel the South* to experience life as an African American. In return for the magazine's financial support of his project, Griffin proposed to publish in *Sepia*, and in book form, the truth about white racism and its effects on him as a disguised "Negro." Traveling throughout the Deep South states of Louisiana, Mississippi,* Alabama, and Georgia, Griffin's experience occurred at a time when America was on the verge of a veritable revolution* in modifying the racial order. But change did not occur without immense danger to the southern black population, and Griffin in his travels was certainly exposed to the potential danger that was the daily ordeal of millions of other blacks. For more than two months, he experienced the taut color line that subjected African Americans to segregated and inferior public facilities and the scorn emanating from a general atmosphere of white hostility to black aspirations. Many southern whites subjected him to considerable abuse and serious threats on his life after his searing published account, *Black Like Me*, appeared in book form in 1960. A best-seller, Griffin's book has subsequently gone through five printings, sold more than 10 million copies, and been made into a Hollywood docudrama.

Malcolm, like thousands of others, read Griffin's book in the early 1960s. The journalist's book appeared during a period in Malcolm's life when he was evolving from his blind allegiance to Elijah Muhammad* and the Nation of Islam* to a more creditable status as a black leader in his own right. Malcolm was struck by Griffin's bravery and revealing but "frightening" account. In his autobiography, he commented about the popularity of Griffin's book among Middle East* Arabs interested in the black American plight but indicated his response to their queries that Griffin's experience had occurred only as a "make-believe" black man. The African American horror in the South, he said, was real, and its reality had confronted them for more than three centuries.

Malcolm was a prolific reader with diverse interests. His exposure to books such as Griffin's *Black Like Me* not only indicates his marked determination to keep abreast of contemporary issues and literature but, with all of the demands on his time, reveals him as a man of extraordinary energy as well.

SELECTED BIBLIOGRAPHY

Griffin, 1960; Malcolm X with Haley, 1965.

Robert L. Jenkins

BLACK MANHOOD. Published writings furnish a wealth of information that dramatize the fierce teachings about manly race pride exemplified by Malcolm X. His teachings inspired his followers to feel that, no matter how far they had fallen, black manhood meant that they could still raise themselves up to bear any burden, to surmount any obstacle, and to become one people politically and psychologically.

Malcolm's iconoclastic style and tenacious resolve against the white power structure literally transformed blackness from what had commonly been re-garded as a badge of shame into a symbol of pride. Malcolm, in his prime, became synonymous with pride in black manhood, defined by many observers in terms of physical strength, physical ability, raw courage, and uncompromising racial pride. It was this kind of race pride that compelled Malcolm to organize an ecumenical organization called the Organization of Afro-American Unity,* based on the belief that black Americans could and should use their political and economic strength to change their status in the United States. Malcolm recognized the role of black manhood in the liberation of black people in the United States and in the development and implementation of an action program sensitive to the good of the entire black community and for the betterment of the community "by any means necessary."

In order to fully grasp Malcolm's perception of black manhood, one must not lose sight of the fact that his behavior often failed to conform to his image. For example, even when Malcolm sensed that his life was being threatened, he refused police protection and would not request protection from his own men. While pride deterred him from requesting protection because of his fearless image, he was also sometimes a tender and solicitous husband who taught his wife Betty Shabazz* how to live and to love as a woman, how to be true to herself and her responsibilities as a mother, and how to use her spiritual, ma-terial, and intellectual capabilities to help build a better human society.

Malcolm did not oratorically invoke black rage to forge a romantic, masculine image of the black man but rather to emphasize the black community's deter-mined quest for political power as a responsibility of black manhood. Malcolm's overall approach was to allow black manhood to serve as proxy for the nation and for African Americans of both genders. The resulting conflation of blackness, masculinity, and political astuteness set the stage for some of the main ideas of black nationalism* that Malcolm advocated.

Further, Malcolm defined black manhood in terms of the capacity and will to employ violence as a legitimate means of self-defense* in resisting illegitimate and state violence perpetrated against black men. He blamed this violence on the white males who dominated positions of political power in the United States.

Malcolm's politics concerning black manhood was couched in the perception that revolutionaries are tough and manly. And since revolutions are usually violent, being a true revolutionary meant being willing to succeed "by any means necessary," even if that meant ending up dead or martyred to advance the cause of liberation and freedom from immoral but legally sanctioned racial oppression. He felt that the essence of being a black man translated into the willingness to be a freedom fighter and undaunting courage even in the wake of dominant forces arrayed against one. To Malcolm, black manhood was viewed as a struggle to liberate one's self inwardly by liberating one's people politically. His belief that it takes a man to stand and not be afraid to bleed transformed the debate about political violence and a question of strategy into an issue of masculinity. He maintained that the crucible of manhood is the willingness to employ violence as a strategy for achieving progress, but he cautioned that one must sit down and carefully analyze the likelihood of success or failure before embarking on a path of violence. His equating willingness to commit violence with virility must be understood within the context of the view that blacks should never initiate violence but should do so only when hostile whites forced them to employ it as an act of self-defense. The models of black manhood and masculinity that black people have inherited from Malcolm have nurtured the understanding that the threat of violence was often more effective than the use of it, particularly when the threatening party had to lead from a position of weakness.

The concept of black manhood and masculinity implicitly demands that black men define it for themselves rather than internalizing a white definition, which Malcolm emphatically warned against. Malcolm's view of black manhood conjures up an image of a black man as well dressed, confident, assured, articulate, independent, and capable of doing something for the black community as well as himself. Malcolm envisioned black men as business owners, electricians, manufacturers, traders, producers of their own newspapers, heterosexuals, militants, sexually supreme, proud, and self-determined. In Malcolm's thinking, the goal of black men is to have the power and privilege of white men but with a black face and identity. Black manhood meant developing the intellectual skills and acquiring the cultural capital necessary to nurture, protect, and defend black survival. To Malcolm, asserting one's manhood meant being willing and able to defend one's turf at the expense of sacrificing one's own life. To his detractors, his conception of black manhood connotes the preservation of an antiquated, patriarchal, heterosexist belief system, while his idolaters observed an icon with a brand of manly racial pride that defined manhood in a way that compelled him to defend his beleaguered people far better than he defended himself.

The impact of his expressions of manhood, primarily through the practice of political fearlessness, has been such that it allowed him almost single-handedly to change the terms of the debate about the means that could be used by black Americans to achieve the goal of equal opportunity. In the process, he helped transform America.

SELECTED BIBLIOGRAPHY

Gallen, ed., 1992; Malcolm X with Haley, 1965; B. Perry, 1991; Rummel, 1989; Wood, ed., 1992.

Kenneth A. Jordan

BLACK MEDIA. The black media emerged in 1827 with the first black newspaper, *Freedom's Journal*. Since that time, there have been 2,700 black newspapers alone, reaching their peak in the 1950s. Simply by virtue of numbers, most of the public attention that Malcolm received was from the white media,* but the black media, particularly newsprint, covered the activities of Malcolm on a regular basis. The white media tended to be more hostile and to distort statements Malcolm made. While the black media were not overtly hostile, they were not beyond taking out of context statements that Malcolm made or criticizing his actions or statements.

When he advocated that blacks form rifle clubs for self-defense* against groups like the Ku Klux Klan,* the *Chicago Defender** ran the article "Negroes Need Guns, Declares Malcolm X," and the *New York Amsterdam News** in an editorial excoriated Malcolm for advocating violence rather than peaceful protest. There were no black-owned television stations while Malcolm was alive, and black appearances on white-owned television were limited mostly to comedy, entertainment, sports, and similar programs.

Elijah Muhammad* had most of the black radio stations covering his own speeches nationwide on a regular basis in the 1960s. This was mostly in the evening and in many cases on the weekend, when majority-black audiences could tune in to hear Muhammad. While Malcolm did not have the same captive audience, he made a number of appearances on black radio, but interviews and articles on him consistently appeared in black-owned newspapers and magazines more than any other black medium. This included four black newspapers that Malcolm specifically endorsed for their fearlessness, outspoken style, and uncompromising nature. These were the *New York Amsterdam News*, the *Los Angeles Herald-Dispatch*,* the *Pittsburgh Courier*,* and the *New Jersey Herald News*. *Ebony* and *Sepia* magazines were two black monthly publications that carried major articles on Malcolm during his life as well as after his death.

When Malcolm was a member of the Nation of Islam,* he not only started their black weekly newspaper *Muhammad Speaks*,* but he initially appeared in it on a regular basis and wrote a number of articles for publication. During the

Malcolm awaits a press conference in Washington, D.C., in 1964. Library of Congress.

early 1960s, Malcolm's weekly opinion columns in the *New York Amsterdam News* and the *Los Angeles Herald-Dispatch* gave him an opportunity to present his own views without distortion by the white press. Although the terms *Afro-American* and *African American* had been used as early as 1892 by the black media, as a nationalist, Malcolm helped to reintroduce the former term in the black media in the 1960s. In death, Malcolm's influence in the black media has increased in stature, and he has been elevated to the status of a martyr.

SELECTED BIBLIOGRAPHY

Goldman (Gallen, ed.), 1994; Lincoln, 1994; Massaquoi, 1964; Pohlmann, 1999; P. Turner, 1999.

Mfanya Donald Tryman

BLACK MUSLIMS. The term Black Muslim is a reference to the Nation of Islam (NOI)* that was led by Elijah Muhammad* until his death in 1975. Controversy has swirled historically around the Black Muslims because religious scholars as well as orthodox Muslims* believe that the group does not practice the real religion of Islam.* Under the leadership of Elijah Muhammad, the NOI believed that all Caucasians were white devils,* a people who were inherently evil. This was based upon a mythology that argued that whites were created by a vindictive scientist named Dr. Yacub,* who created them as an evil race 600,000 years ago. According to the myth, whites would rule the world until the early twentieth century. Malcolm often taught this mythology in temple classes and to new recruits that he brought into the NOI.

During the period when Malcolm was at the height of his power in the NOI in the early 1960s, the Black Muslims were growing nationally with temples in almost every major city in the country. Nevertheless, while Mike Wallace* and Louis Lomax* were producing the documentary "The Hate That Hate Produced"* that aired on national television in 1959, the Black Muslims were denounced by the Federation of Islamic Associations in Chicago,* in part because of their emphasis on white devils and Elijah Muhammad as "The Messenger of Allah." Malcolm vehemently denounced the federation as an organization of blue-eyed devils who were mostly of European origin. Similarly, Talib Ahmed Dawud,* a rival of the NOI and leader of the Muslim Brotherhood USA, accused Elijah Muhammad of being a fake. Shortly after the documentary, members of the NOI were referred to as Black Muslims, and this term became commonly accepted. This was particularly true after religion scholar C. Eric Lincoln* published his classic study on the group in 1961, *The Black Muslims in America.** Malcolm, however, greatly disdained the name, initially criticizing its usage as derisive.

True Islam is color blind. After Malcolm made the Hajj* in 1964, his pilgrimage to Mecca,* he no longer believed in the religious tenets that distinguished the Black Muslims from orthodox Muslims. Even while he was a member of the NOI, he referred to himself not as a Black Muslim, but as a

Muslim. Though he never acknowledged the title Black Muslim as a proper way to identify the NOI, he increasingly used it himself when commenting about the group, especially after his break with Elijah Muhammad.

SELECTED BIBLIOGRAPHY

DeCaro, 1998; Lincoln, 1961; Lomax, 1963; Malcolm X with Haley, 1965.

Mfanya Donald Tryman

BLACK MUSLIMS AND POLITICS. Although attempts were being made by such organizations as the Southern Christian Leadership Conference* and the Student Non-violent Coordinating Committee* to gain the franchise for blacks in the South* at the height of the civil rights* era of the 1950s and 1960s, the Black Muslims* refused to exercise the right to vote. Believing the United States was "corrupt and doomed," they did not participate in the political process. Instead, they adhered to a millennial view of history, which taught that the day of judgment was near when "the white devils"* would be punished. Malcolm was quick to point out, however, that the lack of Nation of Islam (NOI)* political activity did not mean the same thing as "political ignorance" or political "lethargy." In the meantime, God had sent Elijah Muhammad* to prepare blacks for their day of destiny. For this reason, the Muslims,* primarily a northern organization, had assumed an apolitical position and adopted a philosophy of black nationalism* similar to Booker T. Washington and Marcus Garvey,* prominent leaders early in the twentieth century. They were awaiting the "Battle of Armageddon," in which blacks would be victorious.

The Black Muslims developed an economic plan based on land. Elijah Muhammad believed the federal government should provide a separate territory for a black nation, either in the United States or Africa. In the meantime, Muslims were to tithe, establish businesses, and invest only in all-black banks. By 1960 the (NOI) was estimated as being worth $70 million based on small businesses and newspaper sales. There were sixty-nine temples in twenty-seven states. Nonparticipation in the voting process was also one way of keeping their actual membership secret.

Despite not exercising the vote, the Black Muslims became a powerful domestic force. In August 1960, Malcolm X invited Martin Luther King, Jr.,* Jackie Robinson,* Adam Clayton Powell Jr.,* Thurgood Marshall,* Hulan Jack,* and Roy Wilkins* to a Harlem* debate. But only Jack, a Harlem politician, came. However, earlier Powell, a congressman from Harlem, who considered himself to be a friend of Malcolm, had attended a Muslim leadership conference. Powell also stated that although the Black Muslims did not actively participate in politics, their drawing power could not be disregarded when political decisions were made in Harlem. It was believed that Malcolm X and Temple Number Seven* in Harlem potentially had enough power to decide Powell's successor.

Malcolm X became dissatisfied with the nonpolitical philosophy of the Black

Muslims and grew to believe noninvolvement was not the proper course. He believed that the NOI was ideologically separating itself from 22 million blacks in the United States at the time. This difference in political philosophy partially led to Malcolm X's departure from the NOI in March 1964.

SELECTED BIBLIOGRAPHY

Goldman (Franklin and Meier, eds.), 1982; Hall, 1978; Lincoln, 1961, 1968; Lomax, 1971; *New York Amsterdam News*, April 18, 1963.

Lawrence H. Williams

THE BLACK MUSLIMS IN AMERICA. *The Black Muslims in America* represents a seminal sociological study of the Nation of Islam (NOI),* formally known as the Lost-Found Nation in the Wilderness of North America but most often referred to as the Black Muslims.* The original study was published in 1961, with two subsequent editions appearing in 1973 and 1994. Written by C. Eric Lincoln,* a notable scholar of theology, *The Black Muslims in America* is a comprehensive look at this twentieth-century religious sect. The work is divided into ten chapters, including a postscript. The book opens with a play entitled *The Trial*, written by Louis X, who is now known as Louis Farrakhan.* Subsequent chapters discuss such issues as the beginning of the religious movement in Detroit, Michigan,* with the appearance of W. D. Fard,* organization doctrine, internal factionalism, the rise of Elijah Muhammad* to power, and the role and influence of Muhammad and Malcolm X in building the NOI into a national spiritual and sociological force.

The third edition of Lincoln's study addresses issues not covered in the previous editions. Not only does it analyze events that led to the death of Malcolm X, the activities of civil rights organizations* during the 1960s, which Malcolm roundly criticized, and the rise of the Black Panther Party for Self-Defense* in Oakland, California, but this edition also addresses events and issues since the death of Elijah Muhammad in 1975. This includes the various splits and splinter groups in the NOI, its takeover by Wallace D. Muhammad* following his father's death, the transition of the NOI to orthodox Islam,* and the resurgence of Louis Farrakhan as the new leader of the NOI. Farrakhan, as NOI leader, instituted a number of changes that included naming the first female minister, running Muslim* candidates for political office, registering blacks to vote, expanding Muslim mosques to African countries, and involving the NOI in addressing contemporary social issues such as the mediation of gang wars. A number of Farrakhan's reforms were activities that Malcolm wanted the Muslims to implement during the 1960s, but he was restrained from doing so by Elijah Muhammad. Malcolm involved himself in some of these activities only after separating from the NOI and creating the Muslim Mosque, Inc.* and the Organization of Afro-American Unity.* Clearly, despite the animus that existed between Malcolm and Farrakhan during Malcolm's final years, it is obvious that Malcolm left an indelible imprint on Farrakhan's programs and the NOI.

SELECTED BIBLIOGRAPHY
Lincoln, 1961, 1994; Magida, 1996.
                          Wanda T. Williams and Mfanya Donald Tryman

BLACK MYSTICS. A number of black mystics have appealed to a segment of the black community over time. These mystics claimed to be God, who had simply taken human form. Father Divine of New York, Nobel Drew Ali* of Chicago,* and Bishop Sweet Daddy Grace of Washington, D.C. all fall under this category. With their preaching of deliverance and salvation, these mystics had a special appeal to African Americans, who historically have been, with the Native American, one of the most oppressed racial groups in America. This was particularly true during the Great Depression,* which had a disproportionate economic impact on black Americans.

W. D. Fard* was one of these mystics who had the greatest impact on African Americans with the establishment of the Nation of Islam (NOI).* Indeed, the NOI has always been cloaked in mysticism with regard to its origin and its leaders, especially Fard and Elijah Muhammad,* successor to Fard. Muhammad, who was known to his followers as the Messenger, claimed that a man from the Middle East* had come to him selling silk materials and exposed him to Islam.* Among other things, this man, W. D. Fard, according to Muhammad, preached the message that Islam was the true religion of the black man. While his message was revealing in many respects, Fard disappeared as strangely and suddenly as he had appeared. Malcolm was exposed to the same story about this enigmatic figure by the Messenger while still in prison. Consequently, Malcolm was greatly moved and influenced by the story about W. D. Fard as part of his conversion to Islam.

In fact, Malcolm claimed to have had a similar experience while in prison. A mystical figure appeared, sitting in a chair by his bed while he lay in it. The figure had a light brown complexion, with slick black hair, and appeared to be of Asiatic or Middle Eastern descent. He said nothing. He did nothing. Malcolm was almost in a hypnotic state. And suddenly, just as he appeared, he disappeared. This experience occurred while Malcolm felt that he was caught between the loyalties of Muhammad and his own brother Reginald (Little),* who had been disciplined by Muhammad. Later, Malcolm believed that the man sitting in the chair was W. D. Fard, the same man who had mysteriously visited Muhammad.

SELECTED BIBLIOGRAPHY
Fauset, 1971; Malcolm X with Haley, 1965; R. Turner, 1997.
                                          Mfanya Donald Tryman

BLACK NATIONALISM. Black nationalism is an ideology that emphasizes black people's racial and cultural pride, their demand for social, economic, and political justice, their right to self-determination, and their common experiences with enslavement and racism. Black nationalism originated on the coast of West Africa beginning with the Trans-Atlantic slave trade in the 1500s. It was first manifested by those West Africans who died in defense of their freedom in the capturing process in West Africa and during the Atlantic voyage from West Africa to the Americas.

Slave uprisings in New York and South Carolina in the early 1700s and the ones headed by Virginians Gabriel Prosser in 1800 and Nat Turner in 1831 were continuations of this form of black nationalism. This could also be said about those blacks who, between 1773 and 1795, were developing an inclination to leave America for Africa. Their nationalism was empirically expressed when Paul Cuffee, a successful black New England merchant, sailed with some thirty-eight blacks in 1815 to Sierra Leone, a colony for freed slaves that had been established by the British on the west coast of Africa in the 1780s. Publications such as *Freedom's Journal*, the first black journal that was edited by John Russwurm and Samuel Cornish in 1827, David Walker's *Appeal*, a militant antislavery pamphlet released in 1829, and the bold attack of Henry McNeal Turner* on American racism show that black nationalism was expressed in various forms in America in the nineteenth century.

This view could be applied to the nationalist sentiments of black intellectuals and creative artists such as John E. Bruce, Carter G. Woodson, W.E.B. Du Bois,* William L. Hansberry, Monroe Work, Langston Hughes, Claude McKay, Countee Cullen, and many others. They not only condemned the various injustices blacks experienced; they also emphasized black cultural nationalism and Pan-Africanism* in their respective publications from the 1890s through the 1950s.

Malcolm X continued the articulation of black nationalism in the 1960s. Like those of Turner and Marcus Garvey* before him, Malcolm's brand of black nationalism emphasized racial and cultural pride, self-protection, self-determination, advancement, and identification with Africa. One of Malcolm's first concrete expressions of black nationalism occurred when he replaced his last name, Little, with the letter "X"* that symbolized his African family name that had been taken away by the Atlantic slave trade and American black slavery.* For Malcolm X, black nationalism meant black people having their own nation. Against this background, he was not opposed to African Americans emigrating to Africa, the land of their ancestors, though he was more supportive of the Nation of Islam's (NOI)* position of black Americans receiving a separate state in the United States. As a cultural and social black nationalist, Malcolm X was to tell his people to be proud of every aspect of their African features. Another example of Malcolm's manifestation of black nationalism was his establishment of the Organization of Afro-American Unity (OAAU).* The objectives of the OAAU included the right of black people to self-defense;* complete independence for blacks everywhere; and the promotion of black voting rights and African American studies in America. The OAAU called for the sending of a petition to the United Nations* Human Rights Commission requesting the prosecution of the United States for the oppression of African Americans.

Fundamental to Malcolm's black nationalism was the economic, political, and cultural liberation of blacks. Therefore, he declared that black people had the right to be recognized, respected, and treated like human beings, and blacks were to seek this aggressively by any method needed. Even his Pan-Africanism was informed by his nationalism, for he believed that by identifying with Africa, African Americans would not only be enhancing their struggle for cultural identity, but they would also be broadcasting the base of their civil rights movement,* since Africa, which was becoming a new force in the international political system in the 1960s, was their ancestral home.

Malcolm's brand of black nationalism was a synthesis of the different forms of black nationalism that had been manifested from the beginning of the slave trade on the West African coast in the 1500s through the 1950s. Such a synthesis was being informed by Malcolm's militancy that was a by-product of both his personal experiences and what he described as gross exploitation of blacks by whites in America and elsewhere. For Malcolm X, the exploitation, subjugation, powerlessness, alienation, and impoverishment of blacks were perpetuated through violent means. Malcolm X, therefore, declared that blacks would have to employ "any means necessary" to overcome the oppression that they' had historically experienced.

SELECTED BIBLIOGRAPHY

Berry and Blassingame, 1982; Essien-Udom, 1962; F. Miller, 1975; Moses, 1978; Pinkney, 1976; Stuckey, 1987, 1994.

Amos J. Beyan

BLACK PANTHER PARTY FOR SELF-DEFENSE. Founded in 1966, by Huey P. Newton* and Bobby Seale,* the Black Panther Party for Self-Defense set out to implement the strategies and ideas Malcolm X formulated in the last years of his life. Over time, Malcolm's thinking evolved from an emphasis on the hatred of whites to a genuine understanding of the problems affecting the oppressed. He believed that unrestrained capitalism* lay at the roots of the world's social problems. As a result, Malcolm began to work with a number of individuals and groups, regardless of color, to achieve "freedom by any means necessary."* These ideas later became the basic foundation of the Black Panther Party (BPP).

Seeing themselves as the "heirs of Malcolm X," Panther leaders believed that Malcolm had come up with a solution to the problems of the oppressed. They subsequently adopted his ideas on liberation and self-determination and tried to put them into practice. Having organized ghetto residents to vote, implemented community service programs, and armed themselves, the Panthers sought to eliminate the historically state-sanctioned violence directed against blacks. The

Panthers believed that police and other official violence prohibited significant social, political, and economic advancement among the vast majority of blacks. Because Malcolm insisted that failing to defend oneself from unprovoked attack was criminal, the Panthers sought to help the oppressed by violently responding to police violence. Panther tactics, however, exacerbated violent police responses protesters sometimes encountered.

For example, the Panthers shadowed the police and patrolled the ghettos with shotguns, cameras, and law books in an effort to prevent acts of police brutality* and harassment. These actions inevitably drew the Panthers into a series of violent confrontations with law enforcement. Indeed, in 1968, the Panthers' limited success in these shootouts compelled state governments to establish Special Weapons and Tactics (SWAT) teams specially designed by armed forces personnel to combat the well-trained and heavily armed revolutionaries. While dozens of Panthers died as a result of shootouts with the police, the Panthers wanted to demonstrate that black Americans would no longer resist violent oppression with love and nonviolence. Their philosophy and actions coincided with Malcolm's suggestion that blacks need to respond to state-sanctioned violence with a force even greater than that used against them. It is clear, however, that the group's efforts helped to encourage the growth of police review boards and other bodies that allowed citizens to participate in the political lives of their communities.

In the area of education, the Panthers had followed Malcolm's lead by stressing the importance of African and African American history and culture in their liberation schools. Because Malcolm X considered black history* and culture indispensable weapons in the fight for freedom, the Panthers urged members of the black community to learn everything they could about these subjects. They frequently quoted Malcolm when he stated that a people who are not conscious of their history and culture are essentially a dead people.

Having realized that most American blacks knew little or nothing about African or African American history, the Panthers sought to remedy the problem. Their first attempts at teaching these subjects to residents in the black community occurred when they instituted the Free Breakfast for Children Programs. As the children ate hot breakfasts before school, party leaders delivered minihistory lessons. Using the party as their focal point, these speakers explained to black children, and often their parents or guardians who welcomed the free breakfasts, the reasons black Americans remained subordinate to Euro-Americans. The Panthers, like Malcolm before them, told the children that their success in life depended on them having an accurate and balanced view of the past. Their rationale was that if black Americans continued to look at themselves as only the descendants of slaves, then they would never reach their full potential and therefore would never free themselves from the shackles of ignorance and poverty. Over time, these early morning history lessons mushroomed into Panther liberation schools for children and political education classes for adults. The Panthers use of this type of educational tactic clearly demonstrates that they believed that Malcolm's admonishment to blacks to learn about the past could have tangible benefits for the present. The Panthers hoped that disseminating this information via the classes and its newspaper *The Black Panther* would create a revolutionary consciousness among impoverished individuals.

The decision to use violence, however, ensured the group's demise. Using a vast array of agents provocateur and electronic surveillance, U.S. law enforcement agencies, including the Federal Bureau of Investigation,* Central Intelligence Agency,* Alcohol, Tobacco and Firearm, and the Internal Revenue Service, succeeded in discrediting, neutralizing, and eventually destroying the BPP. Under the guise of maintaining law and order, state, local, and federal officials outgunned the Panthers in city streets throughout the nation. Shootouts with police in California, Illinois, Michigan, New York, North Carolina, Tennessee, and Louisiana, among others, left the party with demoralized, jailed, and dead members. What Panther leaders and perhaps Malcolm X failed to realize is that unless they converted a sizable majority of middle- and upper-class whites to their cause, they would never realize their goals. Simply relying on the largesse of well-to-do college students and a few rich actors and directors failed to bring about the material improvement of the people they sought to liberate.

The BPP's existence can clearly be attributed to the example set by Malcolm X. The group occupies a central position in the Black Power* movement that Malcolm helped to spawn. While the party experienced success and failure, no one can deny that it sought to bring Malcolm's dream of a color-blind liberation movement to fruition. Like Malcolm, though, the group's limited success invited the armed reaction of the authorities. In the end, assassins' bullets killed both Malcolm and the Panthers. Those Panthers lucky enough to escape this violent demise ended up incarcerated and/or mentally and spiritually exhausted and therefore unable to continue the struggle on such a grand scale. In recent years, however, the legacies of both Malcolm X and the Black Panthers have enjoyed considerable attention in the media and among scholars. Perhaps this rediscovery of their hopes, aspirations, and activities will be translated into a better tomorrow.

SELECTED BIBLIOGRAPHY

Jones, ed.,1998; Pearson, 1994; Van Deburg, 1992.

Curtis Austin

BLACK POETS. The life and times of Malcolm X attracted black poets to examine his sociopolitical philosophy within a structural analysis. Much of the poetic literature produced on Malcolm X attempted to locate his ideas in a certain space, place, and time. Hence, the personal attributes of Malcolm X have been described and evaluated in a number of genres to assess his personal discipline, critical intellect, spiritual sobriety, moral conduct, black nationalist ideology, and unyielding emphasis on self-determination, self-respect, and self-defense.* From an analytical point of view, Malcolm X refused to accept a truncated vision of American history. He understood clearly that to accept a singular view of black subordination contributed to the creation of black oppression. Malcolm X illustrated a critical interpretative analysis in describing the historical experiences and mental conditioning of African Americans. For black poets, this social and political rhetoric evolved into a radical poetic that initiated black pride,* self-esteem, and a lens to examine reality from a black prism. To some, Malcolm X is referred to as a cultural hero. To others, his ideas challenged young poets to rethink their position and to create a body of knowledge that reaffirmed African Americans historically and culturally.

The Black Arts movement of the 1960s was a significant movement for black poets to express their ideas concerning the relativity of African culture to African American heritage. From a historical point, there were two schools of thought that existed among black writers, artists, and poets: the committed art school and the detached art school. Writers of the Black Arts movement were located in the committed school; traditional and older writers were in the detached school of art. Ironically, on the one hand, there were (are) black poets from the traditional school of art who wrote of and about Malcolm X with severe reservations. Nevertheless, these poets were in a minority, and much of their analysis was predicated on an assimilationist module. On the other hand, the committed school of artistic poets wrote about Malcolm X in the form of an epic. His ideas and philosophy of Black Power* and African American advancement were reaffirmed in a genre that articulated a political and cultural satire. Accordingly, these schools of thought provide a context to locate the repertoire of black poets writing and discussing the ideologies of Malcolm X.

The Black Arts movement provided a forum and literary repertoire for black poets to read, write, and debate on social issues affecting African Americans throughout the diaspora. Unequivocally, Malcolm X became the symbolic motif and scientific paradigm of intellectualism for a radical black consciousness espoused by black poets. As black poets searched to query the concept of "human reason," they simultaneously initiated a quest to define, defend, and reaffirm the idea of a black aesthetic. Malcolm X became the criterion, on which young black poets assessed the critical meanings of their works. In fact, the Black Arts movement was generated out of a thrust by young black poets to connect scholarship with activism, simultaneously creating a dialectic for black liberation.

Indeed, Malcolm X can be considered the centerpiece of the Black Arts movement and black poets' repertoire to query the legitimacy of white male supremacy. Three general areas in which black poets located Malcolm X's embodiment were change, responsibility, and action. Some poets have focused on attributes of Malcolm X's aura, his appearance, and his originality in espousing a rhetoric that challenged the enforcement of civil rights* and Black Power. Thus, his place in American history provided an ambidextrous method of theory and praxis to advance social and political change in America.

In general, black poets have been successful in capturing the essence of the Malcolm X persona and his political perspectives in a twofold manner involving

African American political thought and black political behavior. This analysis illustrated a practical approach to examine the variables of the sacred and secular components of African diasporic history and culture. Louis Young, Jr., refers to Malcolm X as an ancestor who provides a context to develop an understanding of the black ethos as a prerequisite to critically examine black consciousness thought for black poets. Sonia Sanchez* refers to Malcolm X's critical, analytical, and philosophical skills. These attributes presented a plethora of discourse concerning white nationalism. In summary, her quest captures the idea that we do not know of what could have been because he was struck down in the prime of his intellectual advancement.

The central thesis of Malcolm X's sociopolitical philosophy rested in a critique for the destruction of white male supremacy. Malcolm X exposed the systematic creation and consequences of a subordinate group status for African Americans, and he articulated these reservations through a rhetoric of liberation, challenging scholars, students, and community activists.

SELECTED BIBLIOGRAPHY

Christian, 1995; Neal, 1989; Semmes, 1992.

James L. Conyers, Jr.

BLACK POWER. During the 1960s, perhaps no term did more to alarm white America and the conservative black leadership than did the term "Black Power." First uttered in 1966 by Student Non-Violent Coordinating Committee (SNCC)* activist Stokely Carmichael* during a demonstration along a Mississippi* delta highway—the James Meredith March against Fear*—the term *Black Power* was an ambiguous one that had as many different meanings as it eventually had users of the phrase. Initially Carmichael explained the term to mean the need for blacks to unify and develop their own communities and to celebrate their heritage. Subsequently, however, he defined Black Power to mean for African Americans self-determination and community control when it came to their own goals, value systems, organizations, and institutions. Regardless of who uttered the term or sought to define its meaning, Black Power was conceived by most whites as an aggressive move, even a violent one, toward black separatism and disassociation from even their most liberal white allies in the civil rights* struggle.

To be sure, the slogan was initially uttered by blacks like Carmichael and others as an articulation of their anger and frustration about the goals and moderate gains of the nonviolent civil rights struggle. Much of this anger and frustration came in the wake of the southern white backlash, both legal and extralegal and frequently violent, against black demands for change through peaceful demonstrations and voting rights activism and the failure of the federal government to protect activists. While there were clearly gains being made, even Martin Luther King, Jr.,* was disturbed over the white response, the federal government's inertia in safeguarding movement workers, and the general slow pace of the accomplishments. Hence, increasingly, many of the young civil rights activists, especially those affiliated with SNCC and the Congress of Racial Equality,* veered from King's nonviolent philosophy and articulated through the slogan of Black Power a decidedly more militant stance in the pursuit of black liberation.

However one came to define Black Power, at the very least advocates wanted for black people an opportunity to define and seek their destiny in America on their own terms and to have a greater degree of control in managing the affairs of their community. They insisted that this power be achieved without the abandonment of their value as men and women. In this respect, the essence of Black Power goes deep into the African American experience. That a black consciousness during the last third of the twentieth century chose to articulate Black Power in the militant and often threatening way that it did, however, must be ascribed to the influence of Malcolm X. Indeed, Malcolm's exposition on black nationalism* encompassed much of the same meaning as it pertained to his belief about African Americans recognizing their heritage and shaping with dignity the world in which they daily functioned. Frequently in his speeches he reminded his audiences about the racial origin and basis of their powerlessness and emphasized the importance of their demanding positive change. Fearless himself, in no uncertain terms, he told black people, they should not compromise their manhood but acquire their rightful place in America regardless of the method and personal sacrifice it required. That many of the most ardent proponents of Black Power considered Malcolm X as the quintessential defender, supporter, and interpreter of the concept, and themselves successors to his beliefs and strident leadership, reflected his place as the vanguard of the philosophy, symbolic of its resurgence before and after his death.

SELECTED BIBLIOGRAPHY

Blackside/PBS, 1987; Carmichael and Hamilton, 1967; Carson et al., eds, 1991; Haines, 1988; Hampton and Fayer with Flynn, 1991; Lincoln, 1994; McCartney, 1992; Sales, 1994; Van Deburg, 1992; Wagstaff, 1969.

Robert L. Jenkins

BLACK PRIDE. One of the cruelest acts in the oppression of blacks in the United States was the purposeful denial of information that told black people who they were, where they came from, and the contributions of their ancestors to the development of the modern world, including the United States. According to Malcolm X, this act contributed to a lack of racial identity and racial pride that served to divide not only Africans in the United States but African people worldwide. Malcolm taught that having pride in oneself and one's heritage was essential to knowing one's self and what the person was capable of doing. Consequently, Malcolm was a lifelong student of black history* himself, determined to know more about his past and the history of his people. It was clearly a lack of pride and a denial of his blackness that Malcolm said resulted in his denigration during his hustling* years in Boston and New York when he "conked" his hair, wore the Zoot Suit,* and peddled and used drugs.

Malcolm regarded black pride as an important part of the black liberation struggle. He once noted that African Americans who had black pride were less likely to accept characterizations of themselves that inhibited their ability to work together. Morever, having pride in themselves would help African Americans understand their relationship with the U.S. political system and what they should do as a people to achieve their liberation.

Malcolm X also referred to black pride when discussing the need for world-wide revolution.* The liberation struggles in Africa, the Caribbean, and Latin America were frequently used as examples of positive images for African Americans. According to Malcolm X, these positive images would serve as incentives for African Americans to intensify their struggles for freedom. For Malcolm, his connection to Africa and its struggle and the pride in his ancestral homeland were highlighted on a trip to the continent in 1964. He was honored with a new name in Nigeria,* Omewale, a Yoruba word that means "the child who has come home." The honor, he later said, was the highest treasury bestowed upon him.

SELECTED BIBLIOGRAPHY

Cwiklik, 1991; Malcolm X (Breitman, ed.), 1965; Malcolm X with Haley, 1965; Malcolm X (Perry, ed.), 1989.

Franklin Jones

BLACK SELF-HATRED. Malcolm X and the Nation of Islam (NOI)* frequently claimed that the most destructive result of white oppression of black people was self-hatred. The long-standing white racial system caused numerous problems for black America, Malcolm claimed, but white barbarity and cruelty perpetrated no greater crime against blacks than teaching them to hate themselves. Historically, blacks learned from whites to idealize everything white and to despise as inferior everything black. Malcolm believed that this self-hatred manifested itself in many ways among the race, the most obvious being in criminal behavior and vice. Black people often struck out against the system that continued to oppress them, but they frequently could find release only by lashing out against their own kind. Having learned to despise themselves through a pattern of oppression and discrimination, Malcolm maintained, they inflicted greater victimization on themselves as a result of drug addiction, alcoholism, smoking, and gambling. These were widespread problems in the black community, but no less destructible and visible was the frequency of black men and women in abandoning their families and denigrating themselves physically by chemically altering their hair and skin. The ultimate malaise pervasively affecting the black community, Malcolm said, was ignorance, poverty, and apathy for race solidarity. Malcolm X frequently called attention to these black self-destructive problems as both a way to indict white racism for its historical

Malcolm often reminded his black audiences that they were modern-day slaves, "bought" and "sold" as graphically depicted in this illustration. Library of Congress.

pattern of oppressive power against blacks and as a way to explain a dysfunctional behavior and mentality, thereby identifying the cure. As he had himself done, Malcolm said that blacks must first recognize these problems and seek correction initially through their own efforts.

SELECTED BIBLIOGRAPHY

Blackside/PBS, 1987; Essien-Udom, 1962; Library Distributors of America, 1993; Malcolm X (Clark, ed.), 1992; Silberman, 1964.

Robert L. Jenkins

BLACK SLAVERY. Perhaps no aspect of the African American experience left a more negative effect on black Americans than the institution of slavery. Long after the demise of slavery in 1865, the haunting legacy of the system not only influenced the thought of black Americans about their contemporary American circumstance but in many ways vitally factored in their subsequent oppression by white Americans. As a student of American history, especially black history,* Malcolm readily recognized the impact that slavery had on the black condition. As a youth, his study of slavery in grade school was filled with the standard fare of "lazy" and "shiftless" blacks before and after their emancipation. Much of his later thinking about the system, however, was informed by his study of the works of professional historians such as Dwight Dumond, whose scholarship on antislavery was highly regarded among slavery specialists, John Hope Franklin, author of the textbook *From Slavery to Freedom*, which was considered by many people as the most authoritative and balanced work on the history of black Americans, amateur historian J. A. Rogers,* and black sociologist E. Franklin Frazier. Malcolm called American black slavery the "world's most monstrous crime" and felt compelled to teach his followers about the "total horror" that was the essence of the system. In his frequent discourse describing and analyzing the black American plight and his ideas about improving their status, Malcolm often talked about slavery, both physical bondage and how blacks functioned under it, and its lingering effects on the black mind. In one of his longest lectures prior to his death, Malcolm talked in-depth about the origin and nature of black slavery and its impact on black Americans. He condemned the white slave traders and those who purchased slaves as "criminals." Slaveholders, including the Founding Fathers* George Washington and Thomas Jefferson, he said, were "artful liars," who tried to justify their involvement with slavery as "humanitarian" gestures to liberate Africans from an imagined savagery. He talked about the role that race played in the enslavement of blacks and emphasized how important the established churches were in securing the system. He scored docile blacks of contemporary America who sought to please whites with their "respectful" ways and efforts "to act responsibly" when whites did not respond to them similarly. Such actions, he maintained, paralleled the slave mentality of living to benefit the slave master; consequently, most black Americans were still in bondage.

Malcolm occasionally praised the boldness of black slave rebels such as Nat Turner, who resorted to violence in their quest for freedom and respect. The virtues of his comparison of slavery's "Field Negro"* and "House Negro"* were so frequently repeated during the 1960s and 1970s that the terms became a virtual lexicon in the rhetoric of young militant blacks disillusioned with the nonviolent civil rights movement.* That Malcolm often declared himself a Field Negro, prepared to do whatever it took to maintain his human dignity, was consistent with the strident and brave positions that he took asserting his own manhood, and it did not go unnoticed by those who admired and sought to emulate him. To Malcolm, slavery was a brutal and evil system, and he left no doubt about his views on it and about those who enslaved blacks. He did so as a tool to condemn whites for their historical and contemporary treatment of Blacks, to attack compliant members of his own race who refused to fight more assertively for their human rights,* and as a way to educate and encourage blacks about what they had accomplished and were capable of accomplishing despite their historical ordeal.

SELECTED BIBLIOGRAPHY
Lomax, 1963; Malcolm X (Breitman, ed.), 1970b; Malcolm X (Epps, ed.), 1991; Malcolm X with Haley, 1965; Strickland (Greene, ed.), 1994; Xenon Studio, 1991.
                                                            Robert L. Jenkins

BLACK STUDIES MOVEMENT. Perhaps no person inspired the Black Studies movement more than Malcolm X. Malcolm was a prodigious reader and intensively studied world history as well as African history, black history,* culture, politics, and related subjects while in prison.* His desire for knowledge continued after his release in 1952 when he joined the Nation of Islam (NOI).* In many of Malcolm's speeches, sermons, debates, and public arguments, he often made reference to the scholarly study of blacks and Africans and in NOI mosque lectures often made reference to Egyptology and related subject matter. As a black nationalist, Malcolm was ensconced in developing a strategy of black political power and liberation.

In the late 1960s, shortly after Malcolm's death, a movement developed on college campuses calling for programs and departments that would have what pejoratively came to be known as Black Studies, although such programs and departments differed from campus to campus and came under different rubrics, such as African Studies, Afro-American Studies, and Pan-African Studies. Malcolm X's name was often intertwined with the movement, and his legacy was reflected in the orientation of the programs themselves, which often called for racial separatism, demands for black faculty, separate buildings just for black students and professors, and black student empowerment. Students as well as faculty involved in the Black Studies movement often cited and quoted Malcolm to justify some action that they were undertaking or to raise black student consciousness. The Black Studies movement utilized a number of tactics in order to have "nonnegotiable demands" met, which included sit-ins, building takeovers, campus demonstrations, and political rallies, tactics some of which, given his own public statements, Malcolm surely would have approved.

SELECTED BIBLIOGRAPHY
Allen, 1969; Baraka (Wood, ed.), 1992; McEvoy and Miller, 1969.
                                                      Mfanya Donald Tryman

BLOOD BROTHERS. Malcolm X frequently criticized the philosophy of nonviolent resistance. Convinced that such a philosophy was both unmanly and ineffectual, he called for blacks to defend themselves. In the eyes of some he seemed to encourage blacks to go beyond self-defense.* As a result, Malcolm X's critics often held him responsible for specific incidents of black violence against whites.

In May 1964, for example, six black teenagers attacked a middle-aged white couple in New York City. Although the man escaped serious injury, the woman died from multiple stab wounds. The *New York Post* reported that the black youths were part of an antiwhite Muslim* gang who described themselves as "blood brothers." When the press asked him about the youths and the killing, Malcolm X maintained that all blacks were his blood brothers and that there was no reason for him to be remorseful over white deaths. Although he discouraged members of his own organization from taking up arms against whites unless it was self-defense, his comments suggested that he favored open warfare against whites. Malcolm actually knew little about the supposed Harlem* hate group, having heard their name only while in Nigeria* on his African tour. But he would not disavow them publicly.

SELECTED BIBLIOGRAPHY

Goldman, 1979; *New York Post*, May 8, May 10, 1964; B. Perry, 1991.

Phillip A. Gibbs

BOGGS, JAMES. James Boggs was a theoretician who published numerous articles related to Black Power* and black politics and was the author of *The American Revolution*, which has been translated into several languages. He was considered a black socialist, and his writings were influenced by Malcolm X. Boggs realized that any revolutionary effort must involve youth at the core of the movement. Boggs built on the efforts of the Revolutionary Action Movement (RAM)* in the mid-1960s that had attempted to combine some elements of Marxism with black nationalism.* He argued that a Leninist black vanguard party must develop and have a core cadre that focused particular potential on the political cognizance and revolutionary commitment of such youth. Malcolm did not live long enough to develop this line of thinking in detail. Before his death, Malcolm had realized the potential of "street youth" in revolutionizing American society. The question was one of how to harness such energy into a functional organizational form. In this regard, some of Boggs's ideas paralleled those of Malcolm concerning youth.

Boggs had political thoughts similar to the ideas Malcolm possessed, especially regarding race. In one of his most definitive works, *Racism and the Class Struggle*, he argued that young whites could not be part of an alliance with young blacks in a black revolution* to obtain Black Power. America represented a fascist state with a "master majority race." Black Power, his reasoning went, was the scientific recognition that there is no historical basis for thinking that white workers would join the black proletariat against the white capitalist bourgeois or elite ruling class. If this were done it would be, to paraphrase one of Malcolm's pet phrases, to invite the fox into the henhouse. Boggs argued that blacks in the rural black belt in the South* and urban ghettos of the North would have to struggle not only against capitalists but the white workers and middle class as well. As social critic Harold Cruse argued, Boggs's thinking was limited because it was too dogmatic in its Marxist notions. At the time of Malcolm's death, he was rethinking what role whites may be able to play in changing American society. But he held steadfast to the view that blacks must be in a leadership role. Boggs, like Malcolm, questioned how far social reform could go in a stagnant and decadent political system.

SELECTED BIBLIOGRAPHY
Boggs, 1970; Cruse, 1967; Sales, 1994.

Mfanya Donald Tryman

BOSTON TO NEW YORK. In 1941, Malcolm Little began working for the New Haven Line Railroad Company located in Boston, Massachusetts. Although only sixteen years old at the time, Malcolm convinced the personnel officer that he was twenty-one years old. Malcolm was hired while living with his sister, Ella Collins,* who encouraged an elderly Pullman porter* named Roundtree to recommend him for the railroad job. The job with the railroad not only provided Malcolm with an income, but it was also a means to avoid being drafted by the U.S. Army.

Malcolm was hopeful that the employment with the railroad would yield an opportunity for him to visit Harlem.* All of his life, he had heard about the "Big Apple," New York City. He had especially heard about Harlem, the mecca of black life in New York. His father had often described Harlem with considerable pride and had shown him pictures of the famous Harlem parades, led by Marcus Garvey.*

However, Malcolm's first assignment as a fourth cook (dishwasher) was on the "Colonial" that ran from Boston to Washington, D.C. Nevertheless, Malcolm had an opportunity to see New York. Shortly after he began work, he replaced a sandwich man on the "Yankee Clipper" that ran from Boston to New York. He would work every other day for four hours selling sandwiches.

It was during his first stay over in New York that Malcolm was finally able to visit Harlem. Malcolm was so impressed during this visit that he wanted to live there permanently. For the moment, however, the excitement of the gala affairs in Harlem gave him new aspirations as the sandwich man on the Boston to New York train.

Thus, he sold sandwiches, coffee, candy, cake, and ice cream as fast as the commissary department could supply them. As a result, he became the regular sandwich man on the "Yankee Clipper." The cooks and waiters gave him the name of "Sandwich Red," one of several nicknames* associated with Malcolm.

Unfortunately, Malcolm began to exhibit unusual behavior while working on the Boston to New York train. As a result his coworkers made bets as to how long it would be before he would be fired. He had been labeled as an uncouth, wild, young Negro. He used profanity widely, and he was abusive toward the customers. He especially disliked servicemen. During one adventure with a drunk serviceman, Malcolm talked his way out of a fight by convincing the fellow that he, Malcolm, had on too many clothes to fight.

The complaints against Malcolm increased. Although he was granted several opportunities to improve his conduct on the job, he continued to come to work talking loud, acting wild, half-high on liquor or reefers.* The complaints mounted as passengers and conductors expressed their disapproval of his behavior, and consequently, Malcolm Little was fired from the New Haven Line. He never worked the railroads again.

SELECTED BIBLIOGRAPHY

Clarke, ed., 1990; Goldman, 1979; Malcolm X with Haley, 1965.

Ronnie Tucker

BOUTIBA, MAHMOUD. Mahmoud Boutiba was a personal adviser and close ally of Ahmed Ben Bella,* who was the leader of Algeria* after the Algerian Revolution in 1959. Boutiba was a part of the Ben Bella government and a propagandist for Algeria. The Federal Bureau of Investigation (FBI)* postulated that Boutiba was a longtime personal adviser to Malcolm on international affairs. When Boutiba visited the United States, every move he made was watched closely by the FBI because of his expertise in spouting propaganda. Boutiba shared and spoke on platforms with Malcolm on a number of occasions, which only confirmed the thinking of the FBI that Boutiba had persuasive powers over Malcolm. The radical and revolutionary ideas of Boutiba and other Third World revolutionaries and leaders, who Malcolm rubbed shoulders with in various instances, influenced Malcolm's thinking on black nationalism,* internationalism, and liberation in the United States. These leaders were patrons of the Nation of Islam (NOI)* while Malcolm was a member of the sect and continued to be associated with Malcolm when he formed his own political and religious organizations.

SELECTED BIBLIOGRAPHY

Sales, 1994; R. Turner, 1997.

Mfanya Donald Tryman

BRAATH, ELOMBE. Elombe Braath was a cartoonist in the early 1960s for a radical black newspaper known as the *Citizen-Call* in New York City. Braath noted that, in the case of Malcolm X, most people either loved or hated him, and depending on one's perspective, he was considered almost mythically as either a Godsend or Satan incarnate. One of Braath's most notable cartoons in 1963 was that of Malcolm who had written on the blackboard 100 times that President John F. Kennedy* was not a devil, holding his wrist and wringing it while Raymond Sharrieff,* not far away, is leaning over and whispering into the ear of Elijah Muhammad.* The cartoon suggests a conspiracy between Sharrieff and Muhammad based upon the controversial statement that Malcolm had made about the "chickens coming home to roost"* after the death of Kennedy. Shortly after Malcolm made the statement, he was suspended, first for ninety days, and eventually permanently, from the Nation of Islam.*

Although Braath was a cartoonist, he was immensely moved by the thinking, charisma, and oratory of Malcolm and pointed out that Malcolm's militancy, his Pan-Africanism,* his philosophy of black nationalism,* and his revolutionary thinking all combined to have an immense impact upon African Americans, particularly those in large northern cities and ghettos. And Braath pointed out, Malcolm's legacy and influence are greater than ever, as witnessed by larger and larger street rallies commemorating him and what he stood for. Braath notes that he has become a fan of Malcolm and is one of a number of people who attends these street rallies.

SELECTED BIBLIOGRAPHY

Fredrickson, 1995; Karim with Skutches and Gallen, 1992.

Mfanya Donald Tryman

BRADLEY, EDWARD. A close friend of Malcolm X who had known him for more than ten years, Bradley never hesitated when asked to provide transportation for Malcolm when he visited Los Angeles in January 1965. Malcolm flew in to meet with two of the former secretaries of Elijah Muhammad.* These women had filed paternity suits against Muhammad, and Malcolm wanted to check on their welfare. After a bizarre incident at the airport terminal, in which Bradley and Hakim Jamal,* Malcolm's cousin, reported to airport security that members of the Nation of Islam (NOI)* were stalking Malcolm for an assassination attempt, Malcolm was whisked away in Bradley's car after a diversionary tactic at the airport. As Bradley drove Malcolm to his hotel, Malcolm responded to a number of questions about scandals and corruption in the NOI and funding by right-wing millionaire H. L. Hunt for extremist causes, including the NOI. Bradley listened in disbelief.

When Bradley got Malcolm to his hotel, they were followed by Black Muslims* that had gotten out of another car. Bradley was questioned alone by the pursuing Muslims about his association with Malcolm when Malcolm went to the registration desk. Bradley would have several close encounters with Black Muslims over the next twenty-four hours, who had completely surrounded Malcolm's hotel on foot and parked on every side street nearby. The next morning Bradley found himself barricaded in Malcolm's hotel room with him because NOI members had again surrounded the hotel inside and out. Later, they were able to escape, but as Bradley took Malcolm back to the airport for a flight to Chicago,* a high-speed chase ensued in which two cars full of Black Muslims pursued them on the freeway. As one of the cars closed in on Bradley's, Malcolm stuck his black walking cane out of the window, giving the impression that it was a rifle barrel. The pursuing car slowed down and began to drop back. As they entered the airport by foot, Bradley and Malcolm were approached by two Black Muslims, but policemen interceded. Malcolm's farewell words to his friend conveyed thanks and were given in rather solemn tones. Bradley's own sources inside the NOI made him realize how serious these encounters were. Both Bradley and Jamal would publish their own accounts of these incidents.

SELECTED BIBLIOGRAPHY
Evanzz, 1992; Jamal, 1971; Lomax, 1968; *Washington Evening Star*, February 24, 1965.
                                                   Mfanya Donald Tryman

BREITMAN, GEORGE. A self-educated journalist and political activist, member of the Socialist Workers Party,* and editor of its official organ the *Militant* from 1941 to 1943, George Breitman committed the latter part of his life to ensuring that Malcolm X's words were preserved and read, if not heard. Ironically, he never met Malcolm X and, in fact, never heard him speak in person. Beginning with the premise that Malcolm X was primarily a speaker, not a writer, Breitman prioritizes listening to him speak "in his own words." As a result, he compiled and edited, initially by default, two seminal collections of Malcolm's speeches and statements: *Malcolm X Speaks* (1965), reprinted as *Malcolm X Speaks: Selected Speeches and Statements* (1965) and the more analytical but brief *The Last Year of Malcolm X: The Evolution of a Revolutionary* (1967). Breitman readily concedes that the printed speeches do not adequately convey Malcolm's greatness "as a speaker," how they affected listeners, "and the resulting interplay" evident between Malcolm and his audience.

Both collections of Malcolm X's speeches are valuable and include such classics as "Message to the Grass Roots"* (1963), "The Ballot or the Bullet"* (1964), and "A Declaration of Independence" (1964). In these speeches Malcolm announces his formal break with Elijah Muhammad* and the Nation of Islam (NOI),* describes himself as a black nationalist, and declares his intention to organize the Muslim Mosque, Inc.* Speeches before the leftist Militant Labor Forum* and those delivered at the Organization of Afro-American Unity (OAAU)* and political rallies appear in *By Any Means Necessary* (1970), a phrase used in one of his speeches that served as a rallying cry for Black Power* advocates after Malcolm's death. Breitman's collections also include excerpts of letters written by Malcolm during his pilgrimage to Mecca* and the history-making memorandum Malcolm submitted to the African heads of state involved in the Organization of African Unity,* whose assistance he solicited in bringing the plight of African Americans before the United Nations.* Breitman's prefatory notes that introduce each entry provide useful insights, historical details, and background information.

Breitman's *The Last Year of Malcolm X*, on the other hand, is written as a complementary text to the popular *Autobiography of Malcolm X*,* written by its amanuensis Alex Haley.* In many ways, Breitman's text is also corrective, for he maintains that constraints were placed on Haley by his personal and orthodox views. Although he does not question the veracity of Haley's representation (although Malcolm worked directly with Haley, the autobiography was published posthumously without Malcolm approving the last draft), Breitman finds it incomplete, if not muted or terribly flawed. For example, it fails to take into account and represent accurately the myriad of philosophical and ideological changes Malcolm underwent in the final months of his life, specifically after May 1964. Breitman maintains that many of Malcolm's new ideas diverged from the *Autobiography*, which he began more than a year before his death. In order for these ideas not to be mistaken as Malcolm's final word, Breitman attempts to eliminate the ambiguities and provide a more objective account of Malcolm's legacy.

Breitman's essay "Malcolm X, the Man and His Ideas," which appears in *The Assassination of Malcolm X* (1976, Malik Miah, editor), amplifies the ideas found in *The Last Year* but in a more biographical form. He provides general information about Malcolm's early life without being repetitious. He remains most interested in setting the record straight about the total Malcolm, especially about the split from Elijah Muhammad and the Nation of Islam. Breitman describes Malcolm X as a man close to blacks because he was one of them and spoke for them. In many ways, students, followers, and critics of Malcolm continue and will continue to understand exactly what the former black leader said on behalf of those for whom he spoke because of Breitman's published works.

SELECTED BIBLIOGRAPHY

Breitman, Porter, and Smith (Miah, ed.), 1976; M. Dyson, 1995; Malcolm X (Breitman, ed.), 1965, 1967, 1970a, 1976.

Wilfred D. Samuels

BROTHERS AND SISTERS. As an adolescent, Malcolm, like many young blacks, was faced with learning society's dividing line when it came to his proper place as a black man. The message became clear as he witnessed the treatment of blacks based on class, gender, and even skin complexion, from ebony to "high" yellow.

A culmination of his experiences manifested itself later in his life when he embraced the religion of Islam* in his assessment of the condition of the black man. He would often address his audiences using the phrase "brothers and sisters." It was his intent to use nationalism as a means to achieve racial unity. Malcolm's use of the phrase "brothers and sisters" had symbolic implications and reached beyond the United States and into the African diaspora. His intent was to bridge the cultural gap that he claimed was made by whites as a result of colonization and other forms of dominance over blacks. All blacks, he said, should be considered as his brothers and sisters.

Through his nationalist ideology and religion, he stressed the importance of men and women of African descent in understanding that they shared a common bond of oppression. He concluded that the oppression of black men and women anywhere in the world sent a message that it was acceptable to oppress black men and women in other parts of the world.

SELECTED BIBLIOGRAPHY

Lincoln, 1967; Malcolm X with Haley, 1965.

Wanda T. Williams

BROWN, BENJAMIN (Benjamin X). Benjamin Brown, also known as Benjamin X, was the head of an embryonic Muslim* mosque located in the Bronx during the early 1960s that was affiliated with neither Malcolm X nor Elijah Muhammad.* Brown's organizational activities occurred at a time when Malcolm had already broken with the Black Muslims* and a number of former followers of Muhammad had defected from the Nation of Islam (NOI)* to Malcolm's rival organization, the Muslim Mosque, Inc.* Brown had also earlier defected from the NOI. He was targeted for physical retribution by the NOI, although there was no evidence that he was attempting to undermine Muhammad. In fact, in his sermons, he still used Muhammad's name in a positive context.

After NOI members made at least one attempt to intimidate Brown verbally, he was shot in the back while walking down the street with several followers after leaving his mosque. Although Brown required hospitalization, his wounds were not fatal. This incident occurred a month before the assassination of Malcolm X. At the time he was shot, Brown had still expressed loyalty to the NOI, though he was not directly connected to the organization. Two of the three triggermen found guilty in the assassination of Malcolm X, Norman 3X Butler* and Thomas 15X Johnson,* were arrested in the Brown incident. All three were affiliated with Temple Number Seven* in New York, where Malcolm had once served as minister. The case against the trio lingered in criminal court in New York but never went to trial, and the suspects were eventually released. Both Brown and Malcolm were perceived as threats to the organizational control of the Black Muslims and Elijah Muhammad.

SELECTED BIBLIOGRAPHY
Friedly, 1992; Goldman, 1979.

Mfanya Donald Tryman

BROWN, HUBERT GEROLD (H. "Rap"; Jamil Abdullah Al-Amin). By the late 1960s, H. Rap Brown espoused the two revolutionary ideologies of black separatism and the transformation of racist white society "by any means necessary," which Malcolm X had once so forcefully trumpeted. Brown's own angry rhetoric and militant leadership of the Student Non-Violent Coordinating Committee* attracted national attention, especially when he stated that black violence was necessary. Violence, according to Brown, was as American as cherry pie. Like so many black militants who emerged in the mid-1960s, Malcolm's rhetoric and the legacy of his manhood played a vital role in shaping Brown's militancy. For Brown, Malcolm was certainly a "spiritual heir."

Throughout the 1960s, Brown had been in trouble with the law in several states. In 1971, he received wounds during a gun battle with police in New York City after an attempted armed robbery. Following a controversial, high-profile trial, Brown began serving a prison sentence in 1973. Paralleling Malcolm's religious development as a convict, Brown converted to Islam* in prison and

Student Non-Violent Coordinating Commettee's H. Rap Brown, one of a number of young civil rights leaders who became an admirer of Malcolm and moved closer to his militant views. Library of Congress.

adopted the Arabic name of Jamil Abdullah Al-Amin. Upon his release from prison, Brown sought to maintain a low public profile, but he continued to be criticized as one of the civil rights movement's* "self-defeating extremists" of the 1960s.

SELECTED BIBLIOGRAPHY

H. Brown, 1969; Haines, 1989; Van Deburg, 1992.

Irvin D. Solomon

BROWN v. BOARD OF EDUCATION, TOPEKA, KANSAS. In 1954 the U.S. Supreme Court rendered one of the nation's most momentous and historic legal decisions known as *Brown v. Board of Education, Topeka, Kansas.* The decision, which grew out of several public school desegregation lawsuits, declared the half-century practice of segregating black and white children in the public schools as a violation of the U.S. Constitution. The Court's pronouncement not only eventually affected the racial configuration of the nation's public schools but spearheaded a massive challenge to racial segregation* and race-based inequities in other aspects of American life.

Malcolm X saw little that was impressive about the Court's decision. A recent parolee from prison,* he had already become a committed convert to Elijah Muhammad's* separatist Muslim* sect and hence philosophically could not support the principle of racial integration.* This essential position remained unchanged throughout most of his career as a spokesman for black rights, though he moderated his views some once he separated from the sect and made the Islamic pilgrimage to Mecca.* As the pace of southern school desegregation moved slowly in the face of overt and masterful white resistance, the decision was easy prey for Malcolm's criticism. To him, the Court's decision not only was a mistake against the natural order of racial orthodoxy; he regarded the justices' decision as insincere and hypocritical. These men, he railed, handed down a "pitiful" ruling because they deliberately left loopholes for southern states to escape implementation. Malcolm claimed that the Court could have stated with clarity and decisiveness that school integration would occur immediately and hence there would be no need for civil rights* activism more than ten years later to desegregate the schools in the South.* The justices were white liberals,* he said, and like all liberals simply pretended to support black people. What they had proved, he frequently stated, was that they were little more than masterful practitioners of "legal phraseology" and "deceit." Although he would remain substantially correct for nearly a decade, his prediction that the public schools in places like Mississippi* would never be desegregated has proved off the mark.

SELECTED BIBLIOGRAPHY

Carson (Gallen, ed.), 1991; Kluger, 1975; Library Distributors of America, 1993; Malcolm X (Breitman, ed.), 1970a; Malcolm X (Clark, ed.), 1992; Malcolm X (Perry, ed.), 1989.

Robert L. Jenkins

BUNCHE, RALPH. To Malcolm X, those who spoke disparagingly about the Nation of Islam (NOI)* and Elijah Muhammad* were fair game for his blistering denunciations. However, prior to 1961 Elijah Muhammad thought it best that neither he nor his ministers attack the civil rights* leadership because it would further divide African Americans.

In 1959, several African American leaders were asked to comment on the significance of the Black Muslim* movement. Nearly to a person, the established black leadership denounced the NOI. Ralph Bunche was the most noted black leader on the national and international stage. He had received the Nobel Peace Prize in 1950 for his role in negotiating the armistice agreement between the Arabs and Israelis, ending the first war between the two nations. In the Muslim* world, Bunche was portrayed as a sellout to the white world because the settlement divested land from the Palestinian people and set up the state of Israel. In Africa, Ralph Bunche was accused of white complicity in the Congo,* the Republic of Ghana,* and other countries attempting to overthrow colonialism. Malcolm referred to Bunche simply as an international Uncle Tom.*

Bunche abhorred what he called the hate teaching of the NOI. He had little respect for Malcolm's views on racial segregation,* publicly rebuking him as someone in the "form of a racist virus" during a 1963 speech at Mississippi's* Tougaloo College. To Bunche, Malcolm was no less "poisonous" and "vicious" in his racism than Mississippi's segregationist governor Ross Barnett and members of the White Citizen's Council.* Bunche and Malcolm clearly disliked each other, as Malcolm countered with the snake analogy. He fervently suggested that if someone and their relatives were repeatedly bitten by a snake, and others were warned about the snake, then it would be ridiculous to accuse someone of teaching hate regarding snakes. Malcolm claimed that Bunche could have put his time to better use than going to Mississippi and attacking blacks rather than whites. To Malcolm, Ralph Bunche represented on the international level what Roy Wilkins* represented in America, a sellout of black America.

SELECTED BIBLIOGRAPHY

Evanzz, 1992; *New York Amsterdam News*, November 2, 1963; Urquhart, 1993.

Horace Huntley

BUREAU OF SPECIAL SERVICES (BOSS). The Bureau of Special Services (BOSS) was an intelligence agency within the New York Police Department (NYPD). Although its lineage in various forms and under different names predates the 1960s, it was during this decade that the organization was reconstituted and rejuvenated to address the numerous militant student and political groups and personalities that appeared in the city. With its elite corp of agents and sophisticated equipment and operations, in many ways BOSS resembled a scaled-down version of the Federal Bureau of Investigation (FBI).* It maintained such a high level of secrecy regarding its agents and their work that most of their colleagues on the police force had no idea about their identity. The agency considered Malcolm X a subversive and, like the FBI with which it worked closely in its surveillance operations, maintained an extensive dossier on the black leader that captured much about the man, his life, and his activities even before his arrival in Harlem* as minister of Temple Number Seven.*

The agency had a cadre of paid informants that it utilized to gather information about their targets, but it tended to use more effectively their own undercover officers. In 1963 or 1964, just prior to Malcolm's establishing his Muslim Mosque, Inc. (MMI)* and the Organization of Afro-American Unity (OAAU),* BOSS assigned Gene Roberts* to join and work in Malcolm's group as an undercover operative. He would later infiltrate the Black Panther Party for Self-Defense.* Supposedly, Malcolm knew that his telephone was tapped and suspected that he was being watched closely by different agencies, especially federal agencies, though he could hardly prove it. Roberts, who disguised himself as a clothing salesman, gained considerable credibility among the other "brothers" in Malcolm's inner circle and, as one of his bodyguards, came to know Malcolm well himself. Hence, it was through his clandestine operations close to the center of power in the MMI and OAAU that BOSS acquired much of the specific information regarding Malcolm's work. Similarly, informants and agents planted in the Harlem* Nation of Islam (NOI)* mosque revealed much to BOSS headquarters about the strained relationship that existed between the NOI and Malcolm and the imminent danger that surrounded Malcolm in late 1964 and 1965. Upon the agency's recommendation, the NYPD, according to one Malcolm X biographer, sought on several occasions in the last weeks of Malcolm's life to provide him twenty-four-hour protection. Although Malcolm had on occasions worked with the police in a cooperative spirit, he was also a well-known and frequent critic of the tactics that policemen employed against blacks. Consequently, from a political standpoint, Malcolm would have found it difficult to accept their offer of protection, and accordingly, either he or his closest associates refused to do so. Beyond outside monitoring during Malcolm's speeches at OAAU meetings, New York's police force took no significant steps on its own to protect Malcolm adequately.

Roberts and several other BOSS undercover agents were in the Aubudon Ballroom* the evening that Malcolm was shot; Roberts immediately sought to revive him. Although Roberts had seen much of the affair, he was not called to testify in the trial of the men who were indicted for the murder. Given the hostile milieu in which Malcolm faced the final days of his life, Malcolm's own security team and New York's elite BOSS component had done precious little to save him.

SELECTED BIBLIOGRAPHY

CBS News, 1992; Evanzz, 1992, 1999; Gallen, ed., 1992; Goldman, 1979.

Robert L. Jenkins

BUTLER, NORMAN 3X (Muhammed Abdul Aziz). Norman Butler, who later changed his name to Muhammad Abdul Aziz, was indicted by a grand jury on March 11, 1965, for the murder of Malcolm X. He was indicted along with two other accomplices identified as Thomas 15X Johnson* and Talmadge Hayer,* now known as Mujahid Abdul Halim. Norman 3X Butler was a karate-trained "enforcer," who had performed yeoman service as Malcolm's "security guard" when Malcolm was minister of Harlem's* Temple Number Seven.*

On the afternoon of Sunday, February 21, 1965, Malcolm held a meeting of his struggling Organization of Afro-American Unity* in the Audubon Ballroom* on West 166th Street in Harlem, New York. Malcolm X rose to speak and shortly after the ritual greeting, "Asalaam Alaikum, brothers and sisters," was cut down by shotgun and revolver fire by assassins sitting in a front row of the audience.

The three men cited earlier were arrested in the case and tried for first-degree murder. Hayer, also known as Thomas Hagan, denied Black Muslim* connections, but both Johnson and Butler were identified as members, Butler as a lieutenant in the "Fruit of Islam"*—the bodyguards and paramilitary unit of the Nation of Islam.*

At the time of Malcolm's assassination, Norman 3X Butler was already under indictment for shooting Benjamin Brown,* a defector who had been trying to establish his own mosque in the Bronx. Butler's criminal record also included three arrests and one felony conviction. Although Benjamin Brown was not affiliated with Malcolm, he supplied information to the police that enabled them to arrest three suspects in the shooting of Brown, including Butler and Johnson. At the time, Johnson had a twelve-year-long criminal record, including eight arrests and six convictions. Thomas Johnson did not disguise his enmity for Malcolm and asserted, after Malcolm's death, that he deserved to die. On March 11, 1966, Hayer, Butler, and Johnson were convicted after twenty hours of jury deliberation of first-degree murder in Malcolm's death; they were all sentenced to life imprisonment.

More than thirty years after Malcolm's death, the identity of the triggermen who killed Malcolm is still hotly debated. Famed criminal defense attorney William Kunstler,* who represented the two codefendants Butler and Johnson in 1966 in an attempt to secure them a new trial, argued that the two men were not even in the hall on the afternoon of the shooting. It was Kunstler's opinion that the crime against Malcolm was committed by members of the Newark mosque,* which included Thomas Hayer. At the trial, Hayer testified that he and four accomplices had been hired to assassinate Malcolm. Although he refused to name the four accomplices during the trial, he insisted that both Butler and Johnson were innocent. After the trial, Hayer named all of his accomplices and told where they lived. The information was deemed insufficient to warrant a new trial, however, because no one wanted a new trial except Butler and Johnson. The district attorney was satisfied, the judge was satisfied, and Betty Shabazz* was satisfied. The court would not endorse any evidentiary hearings to have Hayer come back to court and talk about this new evidence on the witness stand because all other parties wanted the case closed. All attempts by

Butler to obtain a new trial failed, and he remained behind bars serving a twenty-five year to life sentence for his role in assassinating the man whose fearlessness helped transform America and made him an icon in the process.

SELECTED BIBLIOGRAPHY

Breitman, Porter, and Smith (Miah, ed.), 1976; Carson (Gallen, ed.), 1991; Goldman, 1973.

Kenneth A. Jordan

C

CAMPBELL, JAMES. Prior to meeting Malcolm in 1964, James Campbell, a South Carolina native, was a civil rights* activist who worked with such organizations as the Student Non-Violent Coordinating Committee * in their sit-ins and voter registration campaigns. Once he began his association with Malcolm, however, he became a Pan-Africanist and leftist internationalist. As a Malcolm X ally he is remembered for creating the Organization of Afro-American Unity's (OAAU) Liberation School* in June 1964. The Liberation School's ultimate goal, however, was to make the African American community aware that other minorities in the world suffered from white capitalist oppression as well. Students who graduated from the school received certificates bearing Malcolm's signature.

After Malcolm's assassination, the OAAU soon fell apart. Quietly and quickly many of Malcolm's former lieutenants, including James Campbell, disappeared into obscurity.

SELECTED BIBLIOGRAPHY
Malcolm X with Haley 1965; Sales, 1994.

Craig S. Piper

CAPITALISM. Capitalism is an economic system marked by unrestricted competition in a free market, in which the means of production and distribution are privately owned. Since the beginning of its development in the 1500s, capitalism has been praised by some and indicted by others. Included among its chief critics from 1870 to 1905 were black intellectuals such as Peter H. Clark, T. Thomas Fortune, Stewart D. Stroker, and Beverly C. Ranson. They argued that capitalism was responsible for the exploitation and subjugation of blacks. Ranson called upon blacks in 1905 to endorse socialism,* since, according to him, its structural arrangements allowed justice for all. He reasoned that blacks would eventually turn against capitalism once they had a thorough understanding of the crimes committed against them by the system.

Other blacks like A. Philip Randolph* and Chandler Owen continued the foregoing debate. Even black creative artists like Claude McKay and Richard Wright,* who initially had reservations about the arguments against capitalism, moved to the prosocialist camp. This could also be said about W.E.B. Du Bois,* who wrote periodically on blacks' experiences in America. Du Bois concluded that the terrible conditions of blacks were mostly a product of capitalism and that while capitalism and racism were simultaneously reinforcing each other; the former was the lifeblood of the latter. Du Bois, and later Eric Williams, a famous West Indian scholar, had argued that the transatlantic slave trade that brought some 12 million Africans to the Americas was a manifestation of capitalism.

Malcolm X reemphasized this indictment of capitalism when he declared in 1964 that capitalism not only produced racism; it was also responsible for the degradation, powerlessness, and impoverishment of blacks. Before a cheering crowd in the Audubon Ballroom* in June 1964, he made his views clear when he declared that capitalism could not secure freedom for African Americans. The system had been the product of black slavery,* and capitalism could in turn "only produce slavery." Malcolm's trip to Guinea and the Republic of Ghana,* where the leaders of the two West African nations were moving to the socialist camp, was to reinforce his anticapitalist convictions. Following his return from Africa to the United States in 1964, Malcolm X told blacks that the U.S. government did not want them to be internationally informed, since such exposure would make them receptive to socialism. Indeed, before his death in 1965, Malcolm X was in the process of redefining black nationalism,* which some interpreted as having socialist leanings in light of the fact that capitalism had painfully failed blacks. In this sense, it could be reasonably argued that Malcolm's indictment of capitalism was a manifestation of his ongoing criticisms of the political and economic system of the United States.

SELECTED BIBLIOGRAPHY

Allen, 1969; Boggs, 1970; Breitman, 1968; W.E.B. Du Bois, 1903; Foner, 1977; *Militant*, June 15, 1964; Ofari, 1970.

Amos J. Beyan

CARLOS, JOHN. Malcolm X's influence on the Black Power* movement, which developed out of the black nationalist movement of the 1960s, was monumental. His rhetoric, strength of character, courage, and ideas about black people taking charge of their own destiny were distinctive attributes subsequently adapted by proponents of black nationalism.* The fist and raised arm soon became one of the most recognized symbols of Black Power advocates.

Malcolm's influence on Black Power exponents was clearly evident at the 1968 Olympics in Mexico City, when several African American athletes used the fist and raised arm in protest of how African Americans were treated in the United States. One of those athletes was John Carlos. Carlos was a sprinter from San Jose State University and a member of the U.S. Olympic Team. He and teammate Tommie Smith* were at the award platform to receive their bronze and gold medals, respectively, after having competed in the 100 meters dash. John Carlos's fist and raised arm also stood for solidarity and respect for all peoples of African descent across the world. The black-gloved fist and lowered head represented the increase of power in the black community and America's denial of African American socioeconomic parity in the United States.

John Carlos's political protest was a stand for justice, truth, and the rightful uplift of African Americans. Malcolm's stance as a black man in America influenced the actions and thoughts of John Carlos. Malcolm's legacy of political and socioeconomic protest became the model for the Black Power movement.

SELECTED BIBLIOGRAPHY

Gallen, ed., 1992; Page, 1991.

Saul Dorsey and Robert L. Jenkins

CARMICHAEL, STOKELY (Kwane Ture [or Toure]). Stokely Carmichael, former Prime Minister of the Black Panther Party for Self-Defense* and later known as Kwame Toure, was born in the Port of Spain, Trinidad, in 1941. As leader of the Student Non-Violent Coordinating Committee (SNCC),* Carmichael contributed the term Black Power* to the vocabulary of the country during the height of the civil rights movement.* Carmichael, a student activist, also coauthored a book with political science scholar Charles V. Hamilton entitled *Black Power.* In his youth, Carmichael was not impressed with Malcolm X's philosophy and informed Malcolm personally of his distaste for his political views. Later, Carmichael and members of SNCC invited Malcolm to Howard University* in Washington, D.C. to address college students and to debate veteran civil rights* strategist Bayard Rustin.*

Observers assert that Carmichael was Malcolm's spiritual descendant after his death and that Carmichael attempted to pick up where Malcolm left off. By then Stokely's ideology and political views were certainly very similar to Malcolm's. A review of Stokely's concept of Black Power reveals that it evolved from the black nationalist perspective that Malcolm articulated on many occasions. Both Malcolm and Carmichael advocated self-defense,* a rejection of white support in black movements, black self-determination, and an uncompromising opposition to, and challenge of, racism in the United States. Moreover, each alienated civil rights leader Martin Luther King, Jr.,* with their fiery rhetoric. Like Malcolm, Stokely criticized King and the other civil rights leaders for advocating nonviolence, seeking racial integration,* and their pacifist methods.

The phrase Black Power made famous by Carmichael reminded civil rights leaders and whites of Malcolm X, and many civil rights leaders refused to share the dais with Carmichael, just as they had refused to share a political platform with Malcolm. Carmichael did, however, distinguish himself in one area from Malcolm X: Carmichael's Pan-African emphasis went further than Malcolm in linking African emancipation to African American freedom. But this may be due to the fact that Malcolm met an early death, though he had argued a number of years before Carmichael even came on the scene that African and African American freedom were interconnected.

SELECTED BIBLIOGRAPHY

Hamilton and Carmichael, 1967; Johnson and Gallin, eds., 1990; Sales, 1994; Wolfenstein, 1989.

Byron E. Price

CARTER, RUBIN "HURRICANE." Rubin Carter was a middleweight professional boxer who reached his pinnacle of success in the mid-1960s. He adopted the name "Hurricane" because of the speed and ferocity of his punches, as well as his ability to knock out opponents. Born in Delawanna, New Jersey, in May 1937, Carter had a number of run-ins with the law as a youth and served time in prison* after coming out of the military for a crime spree he admits to openly. Carter, like Malcolm X, was a strong advocate of self-defense,* and did not go along with Martin Luther King's* nonviolence philosophy,* refusing an invitation to join King for the March on Washington* in 1963. Carter's ring persona, a muscular, very dark male, sporting a shiny and pointed bald head, a mustache that attached to his full beard, and a scowling look on his face as he stepped through the boxing ring ropes in a black, full-length hooded robe, was intimidating enough. But this image was matched by his public statements and militant image in which he, like Malcolm, often railed against white racism, police brutality,* and racial injustice and exhorted blacks to fight to the death if they were attacked. Like Malcolm and King, Carter believed that he became a target of the Counter-Intelligence Program (COINTELPRO)* run by the Federal Bureau of Investigation* because of his views.

Like Malcolm, Carter's family had a confrontation with the Ku Klux Klan* in Georgia. While in prison a second time for killing (ultimately he was exonerated) three white bar patrons in Paterson, New Jersey, in 1966, Carter, like Malcolm, spent most of his time in the library and studying (mostly law books to obtain his freedom), even at night, utilizing a dim light from the corridor that came into his cell. Carter read *The Autobiography of Malcolm X** while incarcerated and was so impressed by Malcolm's perspicacity and breadth of knowledge that he ordered his friends to bring him every book to read that was available that Malcolm had also read while imprisoned. Because Malcolm was so rebellious and spent time in solitary confinement, he was referred to as Satan. Carter received the same experience for his rebelliousness and refused to wear the uniformed prison garb the entire time he was in prison, almost twenty years (prison officials allowed him to wear an all-white uniform during his first incarceration). Like Malcolm, Carter took the idea of revolution* seriously and felt that the prison riots and rebellions of blacks he was incarcerated with were just a facade; inmates really did not understand what a revolution is all about. After a second trial, in which he was convicted of murder again, his case was appealed on a number of grounds in federal and state courts and eventually overturned. Malcolm was the second most sought after college speaker in 1964. Carter was one of the most popular campus speakers in the 1990s. Malcolm and Carter shared many similarities, though Malcolm was slain at the young age of thirty-nine when he was assassinated at the Audubon Ballroom* on February 21, 1965. At thirty-nine, Carter had served just over half of his prison time.

SELECTED BIBLIOGRAPHY

Carter, 1976; Chaiton and Swinton, 2000; Hirsch, 2000; Malcolm X with Haley, 1965.

Mfanya Donald Tryman

CASTRO, FIDEL. On January 1, 1959, a revolutionary leader in Cuba* named Fidel Castro overthrew the procapitalist government of Fulgencio Batista and immediately nationalized the country's industries and casinos. Castro instituted a socialist government in Cuba, embraced Marxist-Leninism, and alienated a number of economic elites in the process.

During his visit to New York in 1960 to attend Cuba's induction into the United Nations,* Castro was denied accommodations in many of the leading hotels and singled out to pay for his lodging expenses in advance. He protested, threatening to sleep on the streets. He eventually resided at the Hotel Theresa* in Harlem.* Malcolm X, who had expressed a great deal of respect for the revolutionary leader, was a member of a committee that invited Castro to stay at the famous black-owned hotel. The hotel was then the finest in downtown New York that accepted black patrons. Castro was confined to Manhattan by the U.S. government, never dreaming that he would stay in Harlem.

Castro achieved a psychological coup over the U.S. government and gained the admiration of the black community, who identified with his treatment as a person of color. Malcolm X, in his capacity as a member of the welcoming committee of the Twenty-eighth Precinct Community Council of Harlem, helped to organize a reception for Castro. Castro later met with Malcolm X and several members of the black community in his room at the Hotel Theresa. Few of the details of Malcolm's meeting with Castro are known, but a former close associate of Malcolm claimed that the Black Muslim leader "fished" Castro, appealing to the Cuban leader to join the Muslim* organization. According to Benjamin Karim,* Castro did not accept Malcolm's invitation, but he did not say no, either. Malcolm's face-to-face meeting with Castro was the only time the two leaders had personal contact with each other.

SELECTED BIBLIOGRAPHY

Clarke, ed., 1969; Evanzz, 1992; Goldman, 1973; Karim with Skutches and Gallen, 1992; Malcolm X with Haley, 1965.

Morgan Ero

CENTRAL INTELLIGENCE AGENCY (CIA). The role of the Central Intelligence Agency (CIA) in the assassination of Malcolm X remains a matter of much speculation but few verifiable facts. To many, that the CIA plotted and executed Malcolm's murder is almost an article of faith. Radical writers George Breitman* and Herman Porter,* who covered the trial of Malcolm's alleged assassins for the Trotskyite *Militant*,* first postulated a "state conspiracy" theory involving the CIA, the Federal Bureau of Investigation (FBI),* and the New York City Police Department. Following his break with the Nation of Islam (NOI),* they claimed, Malcolm's increasing outspokenness against America's interventionist foreign policy in the Third World made him a danger to national security and a prime target for assassination. Another radical writer, Eric Norden, added weight to their theory by quoting an anonymous North African diplomat who claimed that the French government had barred Malcolm's admission to that country earlier in 1965 because it had discovered that the CIA was planning a "hit" on French soil. In a 1968 book, journalist Louis E. Lomax* also indicted the CIA for his friend's assassination.

More recently, Karl Evanzz utilized declassified FBI and CIA documents to bolster the state conspiracy theory. Evanzz showed that Malcolm had, indeed, become an object of CIA surveillance by 1964, because of his connections with such anti-American Third World nationalist leaders as Fidel Castro* of Cuba* and Patrice Lumumba* of the Congo,* both of whom were themselves targeted for assassination by the U.S. government. Mercenaries murdered Lumumba in January 1961. According to Evanzz, Malcolm's effort to mobilize African protests in the United Nations* against U.S. violations of African American human rights* was the last straw for the intelligence establishment. The CIA deliberately exaggerated Malcolm's financial backing from Third World nationalists in order to justify his elimination. Evanzz did not explicitly identify the link between the CIA and Malcolm's assassins, but he noted that the murder occurred shortly before Malcolm was scheduled to speak before a gathering of revolutionary leaders in Algeria.*

Other studies of Malcolm X's death have been highly skeptical of CIA complicity and have endorsed the official verdict of the alleged assassins' trial: that Malcolm X was murdered by order of the NOI. Both Peter Goldman* and Michael Friedly conceded that Malcolm's efforts to internationalize the African American struggle were certainly an annoyance and embarrassment to the U.S. government and that his foreign connections undoubtedly attracted CIA attention. Malcolm, however, never posed such a threat to national security as to warrant assassination by the CIA. Both authors emphasized the later sworn affidavits by convicted killer Talmadge Hayer* as evidence that the assassination was plotted and executed by Black Muslims* rather than government agents. The definitive explanation of CIA involvement in Malcolm X's murder, however, must await the opening of all relevant government files.

Elijah Muhammad of the Chicago Nation of Islam and several of his bodyguards. © Bettmann/CORBIS.

SELECTED BIBLIOGRAPHY

Breitman, Porter, and Smith (Miah, ed.), 1976; Evanzz, 1992; Friedly, 1992; Goldman, 1977; Jeffreys-Jones, 1989; Lomax, 1968.

Richard V. Damms

CHICAGO, ILLINOIS. Chicago is one of the United States' largest black-populated cities. It was also the site of the headquarters for the Nation of Islam (NOI),* in many ways a logical choice to locate the headquarters for the militant organization. In 1959 the annual income for the NOI was estimated at $3 million. Beyond Temple Number One in Detroit, Michigan,* the birthplace of the NOI, there were few other mosques in the country. By 1961, through the efforts of Malcolm X, eight temples had been founded in the eastern states. These temples, along with Malcolm's Temple Number 7* in Harlem,* contributed tens of thousands of dollars to the new headquarters in Chicago in the following years.

As a high-ranking official in the NOI and the chief lieutenant to the group's leader, Malcolm visited Chicago to confer with Muhammed at least once monthly. But Chicago would come to have additional significance for Malcolm X. It was in Chicago that Malcolm's relationship with Elijah Muhammad* ended, disillusioned over rumors about Muhammad's private life—specifically, that he had fathered several children with former secretaries. Moreover, it was in Chicago that Elijah Muhammad silenced Malcolm for commenting on the death of President John F. Kennedy.* Malcolm felt that the punishment was part of a conspiracy initiated by the "Chicago officials" to have him removed from the NOI. Wallace Muhammad,* one of Elijah's sons, stated that the Chicago officials were jealous of Malcolm's national popularity and power and his closeness to Muhammad.

Malcolm's views were in conflict with the Chicago officials because he saw the NOI as an organization that needed to be involved in resolving the social and political issues affecting black people in the United States. Elijah Muhammad and other officials did not see the NOI as a political organization. Through the influence of the Chicago officials, who told Muhammad that Malcolm was challenging him for power and control, and that the NOI was becoming "Malcolmnized," Elijah Muhammad felt he could no longer trust Malcolm X. Thus, from his Chicago headquarters, he used Malcolm's comment about Kennedy's assassination to begin the break with his alleged rival.

SELECTED BIBLIOGRAPHY
Cone, 1991; Malcolm X with Haley, 1965; J. White, 1985.

Mamie Locke

CHICAGO DEFENDER. Begun in 1905 by Robert S. Abbott—"Black Abbott," as his friends knew him—the *Chicago Defender* has been one of the twentieth century's premier newspapers. Although at its founding the weekly paper was intended to serve primarily Chicago's* growing black population, which the paper was noted for helping to increase, it soon expanded its readership and distribution area, becoming essentially by the 1920s national in circulation. By then, the thirty-two-page paper had a circulation that topped more than 180,000 copies weekly. Its phenomenal growth helped to make Abbott one of black America's first millionaires. In 1940 Abbott's nephew John H. Sengstacke assumed control over the paper, developed it into one of the country's few black dailies in the 1950s, and continued its position as one of the most well-read and trusted organs in the national black community. With its diverse coverage of news affecting black America, the paper took a natural interest in the Nation of Islam,* no less influenced by the fact that it was published in the city of the organization's national headquarters. But despite the existence of their proximity to each other, and the extremely large black population in the nation's second largest populated city, the paper was hardly flooded with news about the Nation or its most charismatic leader, Malcolm X. This was despite the fact that Malcolm was frequently in the city, even during the last week of his life. Neither Malcolm nor his mentor Elijah Muhammad* published a regular column in the paper, and no journalist made a reputation for himself, as it was with several other large city black newspapers, shadowing Malcolm for regular copy in his frequent trips to Chicago. To be sure, as it was with a number of other journals, however, the *Defender* printed stories about the various scandals that affected Muhammad's personal and spiritual family and the internal problems associated with the sect, including the rift between Malcolm and Muhammad that prompted the permanent rupture and eventually Malcolm's murder.

SELECTED BIBLIOGRAPHY

Carson (Gallen, ed.), 1991; Evanzz, 1999; Lomax, 1987; Senna, 1994.

Robert L. Jenkins and Keith O. Hilton

"THE CHICKENS COMING HOME TO ROOST." Perhaps the most famous and quoted phrase by Malcolm X, except for "by any means necessary," was the statement that Malcolm gave in response to a question regarding the assassination of President John F. Kennedy* in November 1963 at a Muslim* rally in New York City only a week after the death of Kennedy. His answer was that Kennedy's death was a question of "the chickens coming home to roost." After the death of Kennedy, when questioned, Elijah Muhammad* had initially stated that his death was of no concern to the Nation of Islam (NOI),* and he made reference, as was standard Black Muslim terminology, to Kennedy as a "white devil."* However, it quickly became apparent that the white as well as black public were in deep mourning regarding his death. In response, Muhammad soon instructed all of his Muslim ministers nationwide that there were to be no derogatory public comments about the assassination.

According to Malcolm, his "chickens" statement had more than one interpretation. He felt that Kennedy's assassination was the result, in part, of the political climate that existed in national and international affairs. A number of assassinations of heads of state had occurred in the world arena. On the national scene, civil rights* activists were brutalized and killed, yet the Kennedy administration had not brought any of the murderers to trial or initiated such proceedings in southern states. As a results of Malcolm's statement, he was initially "silenced" and forbidden from making any public statement or granting interviews for ninety days, although he would retain his ministry over his Harlem* mosque. Malcolm soon learned that his suspension would be much longer. It is clear, however, that ministers of the NOI had often made outrageous statements about whites as devils and about Allah's* (God's) retribution upon the white race for the way that they had treated African Americans.

Malcolm's silencing and suspension from the NOI, nevertheless, had more than one interpretation. Rival groups within the NOI had become increasingly jealous of Malcolm, including some of Muhammad's siblings, and felt that he was not only too close to Muhammad, but he was also trying to take over the NOI. This jealousy was often fed to Muhammad, who had himself become

Malcolm with one of his daughters shortly before
his assassination. © Bettmann/CORBIS.

resentful of Malcolm's increasing public stature while his own appeared to be
in decline.

SELECTED BIBLIOGRAPHY

Boggs, 1970; Gallen, ed., 1994; Lomax, 1968; Wolfenstein, 1993.

Mfanya Donald Tryman

CHILDREN OF MALCOLM X. Malcolm X and his wife Betty Shabazz* had
six daughters: Attallah (1958); Qubilah Bahiyah (1960); Gamilah Lamumbah
(1964), named for her father's heroes, Egypt's* Gamal Nasser* and African
nationalist Patrice Lumumba*; Ilyasah (1962); and twins Malaak Saban and
Milikah Saban (1965), born after their father's death. The four elder children,
the oldest at the time only six, witnessed the assassination of their father at the
Audubon Ballroom* in Harlem* on February 21, 1965. They were also with
their parents in their house in East Elmhurst,* New York, a week earlier when
their home was firebombed.

Attallah has said she is the only child with a clear memory of their father.
Because of his busy schedule as National Minister and spokesman for the Nation

of Islam (NOI),* and later as he was establishing the Organization of Afro-American Unity,* Malcolm was unable to spend as much time with his family as he would have liked. But Malcolm loved his children dearly and was quick to show pictures of them that he carried in his wallet to almost anyone that he thought might be interested, nearly to the point of exasperation for the onlooker, as Maya Angelou* recalled. Alex Haley,* his collaborator on *The Autobiography of Malcolm X,* recalled how working with Malcolm on the book one evening Malcolm remembered Attallah's birthday was the next day. Knowing her father would not have time to shop, Haley gave Malcolm a doll to give to the child as a present.

Malcolm's wife Betty had the main responsibility for raising the children. Whenever Malcolm was away from home, especially abroad, Betty gave the girls a map that she kept on a wall showing exactly where Malcolm was at the time. It was a way for her and the children to remain connected to Malcolm. After his assassination, Betty worked very hard to provide the children with a normal life and to protect them from harm. Attallah has recounted, for example, how her mother hid copies of the *Autobiography* because she thought it would be too painful for her children to read. Attallah said she read it for the first time when she was sixteen, although she was never able to read it to the end at the time.

Attallah and Dr. Martin Luther King Jr.'s* daughter Yolanda, both in the arts community as performers and producers, in part because of their shared experiences as children whose fathers were assassinated, became friends and professional colleagues in the 1980s. Together, they formed a performing arts troupe known as Nucleus Inc. and have collaborated on several plays that showcase their social as well as artistic interests.

In January 1995, Malcolm's daughter Qubilah Bahiyah was arraigned in Minneapolis for allegedly participating in a conspiracy to assassinate Minister Louis Farrakhan,* spiritual leader and head of the NOI and her father's former protégé. Minister Farrakhan is thought to have had some involvement in Malcolm X's assassination; in fact, Mrs. Shabazz publicly accused Farrakhan of involvement in Malcolm X's death. At a press conference, Farrakhan himself suggested Qubilah's arrest was part of a government plot to divide the black community. He said that he believed Miss Shabazz, whom he had known since she was a child, was innocent. Indeed, many civil rights* activists including Martin Luther King's widow, Coretta Scott King,* believed Quibilah was framed by the Federal Bureau of Investigation (FBI)* as a part of a continuous government plot to discredit prominent black leaders, including her husband in death. Charges were eventually dropped against Qubilah, and she resumed her life in relative obscurity. Apparently, there remains little contact between the NOI and Malcolm's children.

SELECTED BIBLIOGRAPHY

Angelou, 1986; *Clarion-Ledger* (Jackson, MS), February 1, 1995; Hopkins, 1989; R. Nagel (Smith, ed.), 1993; B. Shabazz (Clarke, ed.), 1990.

Nancy-Elizabeth Fitch

CHINESE REVOLUTION. Malcolm X was a philosopher, creative thinker, and a revolutionary. He often referred to the need for a worldwide black revolution that was based on the quest for independence through the acquisition of land. He chided those that were afraid of revolution* and invited African Americans to look beyond their borders for redemption. Internationalization of the political struggle for racial justice was Malcolm's wish. Malcolm made references to the Mau Mau* of Kenya, the Algerian Revolution as described by Frantz Fanon,* the Cuban Revolution, and the Chinese Revolution as models for the black struggle in the United States. He praised Chinese leaders for being the most familiar with the African American struggle. The "Negro Revolution,"* according to Malcolm, was unlike the "Black Revolution," in that the former sought inclusion in a "burning house" rather than building its own house.

Malcolm often cited not only the Chinese Revolution but the Chinese's international involvement in the political struggle with people of color. He was influenced in his views by a film of the Chinese Revolution while in Africa. This is also evident in Malcolm's writings and speeches. Malcolm considered "House Negroes"* symptomatic of division and confusion. His suggestion was that this had been a similar problem in China, but the Chinese dealt harshly with "Uncle Tom* Chinese," thereby purging the country of that type of character. Consequently, he held the Chinese Revolution up to descendants of Africa as one concrete example of an effort to gain independence and self-sufficiency, even with falsely created divisions among the people. Malcolm saw black nationalism* as the solution to the African problem worldwide.

SELECTED BIBLIOGRAPHY

Malcolm X (Clark, ed.), 1990; Malcolm X with Haley, 1965; *Militant*, December 21, 1964.

Horace Huntley

CHRISTIANITY. The son of a Baptist minister and an avid reader, Malcolm X knew the Bible* as well as, and probably better than, some Christian ministers. Indeed, Charles Kenyatta,* a longtime Malcolm associate, claimed that Malcolm could quote the entire scriptures "from heart." If true, this was likely the result of the extensive study that he committed himself to while imprisoned during the 1940s. Malcolm was highly critical of Christian leaders who failed to practice what they preached and ministers who allowed themselves to be manipulated by whites to misuse the Bible in order to brainwash African Americans.

Since most blacks in America were nominal Christians, whether they supported the church or not, Malcolm's audience, outside of those in his mosque lectures, were Christians. He saw his ministry as a calling to enlighten and correct the distorted teachings blacks had received from Christian ministers and teachers. Malcolm repudiated Christianity as the prime adversary that impeded racial justice and equality. He accused black preachers of being criminals in sheep clothing, pretending to champion the interest of blacks while in reality ingratiating themselves with whites for personal gain. He argued that Christianity had a long legacy of believers who used religion to enslave blacks and that the scripture served to inoculate them into docility.

Malcolm denounced the cross, which is the central symbol of Christianity. To him, this symbol dramatized the disgraceful religion the white man was feeding African Americans. He contended that as long as blacks adhered to Christianity, they would continue to be subordinate to the white race.

It was difficult for Malcolm to comprehend how well-meaning black Christians could embrace such a hypocritical religion. He exhorted blacks to disavow a religion that offers Jesus while the white man controls the world. He viewed black Christians as the contemporary Lazarus under the table of the rich man begging for crumbs in the midst of plenty.

Like his black nationalist predecessor Marcus Garvey,* Malcolm taught that Jesus had been a black man. Whites had murdered him, he said, but unlike Christian doctrine taught, Jesus had not risen from the dead; neither would he return to save mankind. Only the Nation of Islam (NOI)* leader Elijah Muhammad* could save the black man.

Malcolm expressed the same contempt for the civil rights movement* as he had for the black church. He lamented the fact that blacks were still begging for civil rights* in a so-called Christian nation. He regarded it as inconceivable that a few white southerners could prevent the rest of the nation from giving African Americans the rights that were already granted in the Constitution. He was critical of civil rights leaders who taught their people to "love thy neighbors" when there was not a single white man in America who practiced the Golden Rule mandated by Christianity. He accused Christianity of teaching blacks to love others while hating themselves; being patient with others while being impatient with themselves; and finding unity with others while finding disunity with themselves.

It was Malcolm's long-range goal to win all blacks to the Islamic faith. However, he failed to realize that the majority of African Americans have known no religion other than Christianity. Historically, Christianity has been a survival mechanism and citadel of hope for the masses of blacks on the brink of despair. Consequently, any other religion not strongly interlaced with at least lip-service sympathy to the Christian tradition of meekness and love will find the black masses generally unreceptive.

In spite of Malcolm's failure to win massive numbers of converts from Christianity, however, he was appreciated and greatly admired by many black Christians. He counted numerous black preachers as his friends, including Adam

Clayton Powell, Jr.,* and many of his public speeches were held in the sanctuary of black Christian churches. The actor Ossie Davis,* who eulogized Malcolm, reported after the funeral that his Baptist pastor thought highly of Malcolm, a man who was "a giant in a sick world." He was admired by blacks in general for his courage to articulate what many of them felt about race matters. Despite his anti-Christian rhetoric, his personal rapport with Christianity was usually respectable, if not warm. Once he remarked that he loved no subject more than Christianity, and in the last years of his life he was an avid reader of the scriptures, especially the Book of Revelation. One young Christian who became acquainted with Malcolm over lunch at Harlem's* Hotel Theresa* even described him as bearing a likeness to Christ.

The death of Malcolm caught the eye of *Christianity Today*, the leading white conservative evangelical magazine of the period. The magazine that had never mentioned him before pointed out that Malcolm, although an orthodox Muslim,* had his funeral held in a Christian church in Harlem.

SELECTED BIBLIOGRAPHY

O. Davis (Clarke, ed.), 1990; DeCaro, 1996; Goldman, 1979; Karenga, 1969; Krieg, 1979–80; Lincoln, 1994; B. Perry, 1991; Plimpton, 1964; Protz, 1964.

L. Henry Whelchel

CIVIL RIGHTS. Civil rights initially was of little concern to Malcolm X. For blacks, he felt that the U.S. government was the problem, not the solution. Hence, the problem of inadequate civil rights for black Americans was created by the very government that civil rights advocates were appealing to for freedom. Malcolm felt that the government that created the problem could not solve it because it was morally bankrupt. After all, it was the American government, a world power, that could not or would not protect innocent black men, women, and children from murderous assaults by law enforcement officials, many of whom were Ku Klux Klan* members, during protest marches and demonstrations within its own sovereign borders.

Racial integration* was equated with civil rights by most black leaders in the 1950s and 1960s. However, Malcolm did not necessarily relate racial integration with freedom. He felt that the right to sit down by a white person in a restaurant did not necessarily make one free. Freedom was much more complex than that. Hence, he argued that integration as a tool to achieve civil rights was misleading. Political and racial separation,* rather than racial integration, were the keys to real black freedom. Strength would be achieved through racial unity in a separate political entity, or nation–state. Malcolm often used the analogy of a cup of coffee to make his case. He stated that he liked his coffee black. When one adds cream to coffee, it becomes diluted and thus weak. Malcolm felt that racial integration to achieve civil rights on terms set by the government would also lead to a denigration of black culture and black pride.*

Nevertheless, Malcolm did see the issue of civil rights as an opportunity to get black Americans involved in the struggle for freedom. He wanted the Black Muslims* to participate in limited and focused activities. This included voting and certain forms of public protest. However, Elijah Muhammad* would not allow Black Muslims to participate in any political activities whatsoever, and he made this clear to Malcolm on a number of occasions. Consequently, even though Malcolm saw the issue of civil rights as an opportunity to advance the cause of Black Americans in certain arenas, he was not allowed to do so by the leader of the Nation of Islam.*

SELECTED BIBLIOGRAPHY

Brisbane, 1970; Condit and Lucaites, 1993; Malcolm X with Haley, 1965.

Mamie Locke

CIVIL RIGHTS ACT OF 1964. For the greater part of his public life, Malcolm X was hardly a friend of civil rights.* Frequently, he bitterly and roundly denounced the concept of civil rights and its advocates. The concept of nonviolence, the core of civil rights activists' strategy, was similarly without merit in Malcolm's view. Its application simply made blacks more vulnerable to white violence, placing them in harm's way unnecessarily, as in Birmingham, Alabama,* in 1963. It was certainly no strategy for revolution.* Revolution, Malcolm often remarked, is "bloody," "hostile," and "without compromise."

If there was any doubt as to Malcolm's feelings regarding civil rights, his reaction to the March on Washington* in 1963 certainly cleared the air. He variously depicted it as a "Chump March," a "farce on Washington," a "circus," and a "picnic." Even so, by 1964 Malcolm was evidently somewhat ambivalent, as opposed to being outright hostile toward the historic Civil Rights Act of 1964. Originally conceived by President John F. Kennedy,* the legislation would gain impetus and momentum only after his death. His successor, Lyndon B. Johnson,* was left to push for its passage. By votes of 328 to 74 in the House of Representatives and 79 to 18 in the Senate, bill H.R. 6400 became law on August 6, 1964. The new legislation outlawed racial discrimination in all forms of public accommodations and conveniences.

Malcolm seemed unusually interested, if not intrigued, by this legislation. He was concerned that the "Big Six" civil rights leadership (heads of the major civil rights organizations*) had been relatively quiet about the Senate filibuster on the measure. He wanted to hear for himself the argument of "Dixiecrats"* in their opposition to the bill, so in March 1964, he flew to Washington to observe the Senate debate. Afterward, he commented that the proceedings were a "con game." He likened the bill to "a counterfeit check" that would likely bounce on Congress. If the measure did not pass, Malcolm predicted "hell," and if it did pass, there would also be "hell" because the bill had nothing in it for northern blacks. Characteristically, he labeled the senators "hypocrites" debating whether black people "should be free." However, another reporter quoted him as saying he wanted the bill to pass "exactly as is." The seemingly contradictory

Malcolm deep in thought in a Washington, D.C., hotel during congressional considera- tion of the Civil Rights Act of 1964. Library of Congress.

comments were the early signals of a philosophical or possible tactical meta- morphosis. Either appears likely, especially given Malcolm's brief meeting with Martin Luther King, Jr.,* while in Washington during debate of the bill. To be sure, over the next year, from March 1964 to February 1965, Malcolm would give glaring indications that his thinking on a whole range of issues was under review with an eye toward possible revision. This even included civil rights, an issue on which he moved increasingly to support in his public statements and in his overtures to some of the recognized black leaders that he once criticized.

SELECTED BIBLIOGRAPHY

Boulware, 1967; Cone, 1991; Khan and Rustin, 1966; Kly, 1986; Malcolm X (Perry, ed.), 1989; *Militant*, March 23, 1964, April 6, 1964, May 6, 1964; *New York Amsterdam News*, March 28, 1964.

Dernoral Davis

THE CIVIL RIGHTS MOVEMENT. Among the general populace of almost any given society, social reform movements are as apt to be as unpopular as

Blacks of Birmingham line up to register to vote. In his last year, Malcolm often pledged to work for voter registration in the South. Birmingham Public Library, Department of Archives and Manuscripts (Catalog Number 827.1.1.12.59).

popular. Americans of the civil rights era, for instance, were sharply divided over the relative merits of that movement. Many, perhaps even most, whites equated agitation for civil rights* with domestic unrest, anarchy, communism, and ultimately, irreparable damage to the nation's social and institutional fabric. At the very least, many whites were unalterably convinced that the struggle over civil rights meant a blurring of America's racial divide and potentially a modicum of, if not widespread, social engineering. Moreover, such a misreading of the movement cast it in a particularly disparaging light among whites, resulting in a popular perception of civil rights as un-American and subversive.

By contrast, most African Americans were sufficiently persuaded that the civil rights movement was thoroughly in the American tradition, in both its thrust and objectives, especially because it challenged the nation to live out the full measure of its founding creed. Indeed, for blacks the struggle was fundamentally about birthright and the failure of America to make room for them at the nation's table of opportunity. Not all African Americans, however, shared such convictions. Arguable, their ranks had no more articulate and eloquent a spokesperson than Malcolm X.

Malcolm launched a repeated and sustained denunciation of the orthodox civil rights movement, emerging in time as the most cynical counterpoint to the movement in its heyday of the 1950s and 1960s. The impetus for his blistering assault on the civil rights movement and leadership sprang from the teachings of Elijah Muhammad.* Muhammad taught first and foremost that whites were devils. That being the case, blacks should not and must not anticipate harmonious relations with whites. Furthermore, Muhammad taught that faith in a culturally integrated society was sheer folly, a pipe dream at best. The goals of social integration and cultural assimilation were likewise bankrupt to the core, leading only to disappointment, rejection, and the alienation of blacks.

Black civil rights leaders, Muhammad often insisted, and Malcolm reiterated in his fiery and forceful oratory, were but "White minded, brainwashed Uncle Toms."* Perhaps not surprisingly, Martin Luther King, Jr.,* was singled out for special criticism. Malcolm dubbed him a "religious Uncle Tom," as well as other derogatory terms. The message of King and other civil rights leaders was particularly disquieting for Malcolm because of the impact he felt it had on the black psyche. It was utterly ludicrous, Malcolm concluded, to counsel blacks to turn the other cheek and to love one's enemy, because their enemies were incapable of loving them in return. Indeed, Malcolm further observed, it was abnormal to love one's enemy.

The alternative vision and hope Malcolm advanced as a counterdistinction to that of King and other civil rights leaders was predicated on racial separation.* According to Malcolm, separation was neither a temporary nor tactical position but an ideological commitment. He often told black audiences that there is an important distinction between racial segregation* and separation. Segregation, he maintained, is when one's life and liberty are controlled by someone else. Separation is that which is done voluntarily. Separation was preferred because it allowed blacks to develop independently, using their own talents and strengths. But given the prevailing ethos of integration, Malcolm's effort to clarify the distinction between the two terms generally failed.

Malcolm did not, however, fail to make clear his views regarding the March on Washington.* He was bitterly critical of the 1963 March on Washington and was less than congratulatory of King's receipt of the Nobel Prize for Peace. Malcolm, nevertheless, became decidedly less harsh in his castigation of civil rights and its leadership after 1963. He even met and briefly conversed with King in Washington after attending a session of the Senate's debate on the 1964 Civil Rights Bill. This apparent overture was part of a larger pattern of less stridency that his subsequent Hajj* to Mecca* helped to nurture. Indeed, references to whites as devils became less frequent and the castigation of civil rights advocates less pronounced. Malcolm was apparently experiencing a philosophical metamorphosis in which he sought both ideological clarity and the possible building of new relational bridges. Admittedly, he never became a public advocate of civil rights, only more open, perhaps, to the promise(s) it offered. In death, his bequest, and part of his legacy, was a style of leadership, complete with a polemical vernacular that resonated with young blacks then and in the decades since.

SELECTED BIBLIOGRAPHY

Clark, ed., 1969; Cone, 1991; Goldman, 1979; Lincoln, 1973; Malcolm X (Breitman, ed.), 1967; Malcolm X with Haley, 1965; B. Perry, 1991.

Dernoral Davis

CIVIL RIGHTS ORGANIZATIONS. The major civil rights organizations originated in the early twentieth century, beginning with the National Association for the Advancement of Colored People (NAACP),* which protested the treatment of black Americans, especially in the South,* where they were frequently victimized by lynchings. Other civil rights organizations that formed from this time period up to the 1960s included the National Urban League,* the Congress of Racial Equality (CORE),* the Southern Christian Leadership Conference (SCLC),* and the Student Non-Violent Coordinating Committee (SNCC).* These organizations were, for the most part, racially integrated and fought for constitutional rights, jobs, racial integration,* and better living conditions.

During the 1950s and 1960s, as the struggle for civil rights* intensified, these organizations engaged in a number of nonviolent tactics designed to advance goals related to racial integration and racial equality. This included sit-ins, boycotts, marches, public demonstrations, public and church rallies, and other activities. While the tactics appeared assertive, the underlying philosophy was one of passive resistance. Hence, members of these organizations would not physically attempt to defend themselves if attacked by antagonistic whites.

It was this method and philosophy of nonviolence that disturbed Malcolm X. He did not understand how civil rights organizations could counsel their members to remain passive and not defend themselves when attacked and brutalized. Malcolm felt that force had to be met with force. He was especially critical of Dr. Martin Luther King, Jr.,* leader of the SCLC, who led numerous marches and encountered violent resistance from racists and segregationists. Malcolm stated that the only thing a nonviolence philosophy* proved was how violent the white man was. He questioned the wisdom of civil rights organizations leading marches that resulted in beatings with billy clubs, attacks by police dogs, the use of pressurized water hoses, tear gas, and cattle prods on peaceful marchers.

In addition, Malcolm felt that civil rights organizations were going to the very people to ask for justice that had committed the crimes. He argued that the federal government perpetuated racial injustice and inequality directly and indirectly by failing to pass adequate legislation to ensure black rights and to protect them when they marched for their rights.

Malcolm could not understand how real men in civil rights organizations could lead women and children in demonstrations where white violence against them was a certainty. The fact that numerous blacks were harmed, some fatally, as a result of this philosophy proved to Malcolm that the tactics and overall strategy of nonviolence simply did not work. He argued that these types of protests by civil rights organizations were really cowardly and revealed the absence of black manhood.*

The zenith of Malcolm's criticism of civil rights organizations occurred in 1963 as the result of the "March on Washington."* He argued that the march had been coopted by President John F. Kennedy,* who had called civil rights leaders to the White House to get assurances that the march would be peaceful and orderly. Malcolm felt that once Kennedy became involved, the march and protest lost their effectiveness.

Although Malcolm was extremely critical of civil rights organizations and their leaders, in 1964 he began to rethink his position with regard to the public criticisms that he launched on them. He began to realize that it may have been counterproductive, suggesting that the media and whites wanted to see blacks publicly fighting and criticizing each other. He suggested that in the future he and spokespersons from the civil rights groups should not air their differences in public but in a private forum and, when they emerged in public, present a united front.

SELECTED BIBLIOGRAPHY

Brisbane, 1970; Lawson, 1991.

Lauren Larsen and Mfanya Donald Tryman

CLARK, KENNETH B. A social psychologist, educated at Howard University* and Columbia University where he earned his Ph.D. in experimental psychology, Clark began what would be a lifelong passion to fight racism even before he left college. In 1931 he was among a number of Howard students arrested for protesting racial segregation* in restaurants located in the U.S. capitol building. During the 1940s, along with a core of black scholars, he contributed to the research of Swedish sociologist Gunnar Myrdal's path-breaking race relations study *The American Dilemma*. It was, however, his authoritative research and testimony before the U.S. Supreme Court on the detrimental consequences of segregation on the development of black children, so effectively used by the National Association for the Advancement of Colored People* in its successful legal bid to desegregate the nation's public schools, that brought him greater notoriety as a scholar. By then, he had already begun what would be a long teaching tenure at City College in New York, one of the few black professors at a predominantly white college. He was a prolific author whose publications included the accomplished study of Harlem* segregation and ghetto life, *Dark Ghetto*. Popularly known as the "scholar of the civil rights movement,"* during the 1960s, he became a close ally of Martin Luther King, Jr.,* the black struggle's most recognizable symbol.

In a relationship that went back to the early 1960s, however, Clark came to know King's nemesis, Malcolm X, relatively well. Although he often railed against "the danger of the Black Muslim* movement," especially its anti-Semitism demagoguery, he nonetheless admitted that much of what the Nation of Islam (NOI)* said about white racism and the victimization of blacks was true. It was precisely because of their basic premises regarding the maintenance of white America's racial system of barbarity and cruelty and the effectiveness of the NOI's condemnation of it, he said, that made the group so dangerous.

None did a better job of conveying the Black Muslim line than Malcolm X, and Clark developed a real affection for him. By the end of Malcolm's life Clark had publically met and debated, interviewed, or privately visited with Malcolm as much as, if not more than, any personality who was not in Malcolm's orbit. A television interview that Clark had with Malcolm in June 1963 was published in a book by Clark, along with interviews he conducted with King and acclaimed black novelist, poet,* and activist James Baldwin,* himself a notable Malcolm X fan. While Malcolm tended to refer to black Ph.D.s as "puppets," "yard Negroes," or "twentieth century Uncle Thomases," he apparently did not use these terms as criticisms of Clark. As a King associate, Clark clearly did not adhere to Malcolm's philosophy about how best to liberate black people, but there is much to indicate that the two men genuinely admired and respected each other. Indeed, Clark's son, a college student at Columbia University, became so enamored with Malcolm that he began to spend a considerable amount of time around Malcolm's office and neglected his studies. This prompted the Muslim* leader to reassure Clark that he would make no effort to influence the budding youth toward Islam,* something that Clark claims did as much as anything to strengthen their existing friendship.

That each was comfortable with the other attests to the complexities inherent in personal relationships, even those where the philosophical and political chasms separating the individuals are notably deep. Understandably, Clark was saddened over Malcolm's death, and he lamented the loss as a major blow to the cause of black justice. In the years following Malcolm's murder, as the black icon became an increasingly popular figure, Clark, through his speeches and writings, helped to give insight and perspective about Malcolm's life and contributions to the crucial 1960s period.

SELECTED BIBLIOGRAPHY

Clark, ed., 1985; Gallen, ed., 1992; Goldman, 1979; Kluger, 1975; Malcolm X with Haley, 1965; Samuels, 1963; Silberman, 1964; Southern, 1987.

Robert L. Jenkins

CLARKE, JOHN HENRIK. Clarke was a noted Harlem* African American historian and Pan-African activist. Although Clarke taught history at New York's Hunter College, most of his "teaching" role was outside of the academy walls. An occasional poet with strong ties to the literary movement embodied in the Harlem Writer's Guild, he was also a scholar who authored numerous studies dealing with African and African American history, the latter from the often controversial Afrocentric perspective. Clarke was one of several Harlem-based intellectuals in Malcolm's inner circle. The "shadow cabinet," as Clarke referred to these people, consisted of a diverse group of scholars, including specialists in history, politics, and sociology. The cabinet, Clarke maintained, paralleled that of a good university faculty. For both Clarke and Malcolm, their association grew in mutual admiration and respect.

Although neither a Muslim* nor a separatist, Clarke nevertheless bought into Malcolm and his ideas. He considered Malcolm a true but rare revolutionary, evidenced by his 1964 Detroit, Michigan,* speech "Message to the Grass Roots," which linked black progress to landholding and the concept of nation-hood. Clarke was especially supportive of Malcolm's idea of the Organization of Afro-American Unity (OAAU).* In fact, it is claimed that it was Clarke who suggested using the Organization of African Unity* as the model for Malcolm's group and who was responsible for the similar name. Moreover, it was in Clarke's Harlem* apartment where Malcolm met with Clarke and another associate, Lynn Shifflet,* to draft the final version of the OAAU's Aims and Objectives. Thus, in many ways, Clarke, who regarded the OAAU as one of twentieth-century America's most important achievements because it brought real linkage of black America to the emerging nations of black Africa, played a critical role in the development and evolution of Malcolm's short-lived signature organization.

In the immediate years after Malcolm's death, Clarke became a pioneer advocate of the Black Studies* and African Studies movements. An intellectual initiative largely demanded by young black college students inspired by the civil rights movement* and the cultural renaissance of the 1960s, and Malcolm's views about black history,* black pride,* and black nationalism,* Black Studies made a major and pervasive appearance on college campuses nationwide, especially after 1970. Clarke also continued to ensure that Americans not forget about Malcolm and his work to uplift blacks and to eradicate white racism. He spoke frequently on programs that sought to honor Malcolm and assess his political and economic impact on the consciousness of both the national and international community. Perhaps the most significant contribution of Clarke to Malcolm's legacy was his editorship of a 1969 book entitled *Malcolm X: The Man and His Times*. A collection of essays by scholars, associates, and admirers of Malcolm, its appearance occurred during a time when many who knew little about the Muslim* firebrand were struggling to understand how and why Malcolm came to influence an age. The book helped to give insight into that influence.

SELECTED BIBLIOGRAPHY

Clarke, ed., 1969; Cruse, 1967; Evanzz, 1992; Gallen, ed., 1992; Sales, 1994; Strickland (Greene, ed.), 1994; Thorpe, 1971.

Robert L. Jenkins

CLEAGE, ALBERT B., JR. (Reverend Jaramogi Abebe Agyeman). Now known as the Reverend Jaramogi Abebe Agyeman, Cleage is a minister and pastor of Detroit's* Shrine of The Black Madonna, the founding church of the Pan-African Orthodox Christian Church. Agyeman founded this African American denomination in 1972 and leads it as the Holy Patriarch. A black nationalist churchman, Agyeman believes that the liberation of black people is at the core of the Gospels and that Jesus, whom he identifies as non-Caucasian, was a black revolutionary sent to liberate the black "nation." In the 1960s, Reverend Cleage also founded the all-black Freedom Now Party (FNP)* and ran for governor of Michigan on its ticket.

In 1968, Cleage published a collection of sermons, *The Black Messiah*, in which he identified God and Jesus as "Black" and, in 1972, outlined a black liberation theology in *Black Christian Nationalism: New Directions for the Black Church*. A prominent Christian Black Power* advocate and spokesman at the time, he urged more traditional churches to place African Americans in leadership positions and provide financial support for the improvement of inner-city communities.

Cleage was one of the first black churchmen to embrace Malcolm X when he was spokesman for the Nation of Islam (NOI).* However, after Malcolm made his Hajj* in 1964 and opened the door to cooperative efforts with non-Muslims and nonblack militants, Cleage came to believe that Malcolm, who had changed his name to El-Hajj Malik El-Shabazz, had lost his way. In 1963, after the March on Washington,* Cleage, on behalf of the FNP and another organization, the Group on Advanced Leadership (GOAL), invited Malcolm X to give what would become a seminal address where he talked about a "Black" versus "Negro" revolution* in America and scored the nonviolent practices of the civil rights movement.* In giving his "Message to the Grass Roots"* speech, Malcolm was becoming a more independent thinker, gradually moving away from the NOI's proscriptions against public discussions about political and civil rights* issues.

Malcolm's invitation was a result of Cleage leading a group out of the Detroit Council for Human Rights (DCHR), because the organization was excluding black nationalists from the upcoming Northern Negro Grass Roots Leadership Conference.* This would be one of Malcolm's last public speeches as a member in the NOI before his suspension by Elijah Muhammad,* ostensibly for intemperate remarks about the assassination of President John F. Kennedy.*

Cleage supported Malcolm's proposal to bring the African American case before the United Nations,* but he would later claim that Malcolm underestimated the extent of white American institutional racism. It was this very power, Cleage said, that controlled the United Nations and hence would have made Malcolm's effort to internationalize the African American struggle difficult.

Eldridge Cleaver, one the most well-known leaders in the Black Panther Party whose membership considered themselves as "heirs" of Malcolm X. Library of Congress.

SELECTED BIBLIOGRAPHY

Clarke, ed., 1990; Cleage, 1972; Cone, 1991; Murphy, Melton, and Ward, eds., 1993; *New York Times*, November 10, 1968; Ward, 1969.

Nancy-Elizabeth Fitch

CLEAVER, ELDRIDGE. Eldridge Cleaver was born in Wabbaseka, Arkansas. During the height of the Great Depression* his family, looking for a better life, eventually moved to East Los Angeles, where Eldridge grew up. Finding his new environment challenging, he soon gravitated to a life of crime. He was first arrested in 1947 and sent to reform school in 1949 and again in 1952. By the time that Eldridge was eighteen, he was serving his first jail term. Released in 1956, he began to assault white women. Remanded to California Folsom State Penitentiary for these crimes in 1957, Cleaver, influenced by the teachings of the Nation of Islam (NOI)* and its spokesperson, Malcolm X, joined the NOI and became a disciple of Malcolm X. When the schism between Malcolm and

Elijah Muhammad* occurred, Eldridge sided with Malcolm and became interested in the Organization of Afro-American Unity (OAAU),* Malcolm's new political and human rights* organization.

Cleaver was paroled in 1966 and became a staff writer for the San Francisco–based radical magazine *Ramparts*. After Malcolm's death in 1965, he wanted to revive the OAAU on the West Coast but did little in this regard. He eventually joined Huey Newton* and Bobby Seale* in Oakland, California, where they established the Black Panther Party for Self-Defense;* Cleaver became the party's chief publicist and one of its main theoreticians.

Cleaver's participation in the Black Panther party was stormy. He fled to Algeria* in 1968, eventually returning in the mid-1970s, when he began to involve himself in right-wing conservative causes. It was, however, Cleaver's association with the Black Panthers and his searing account of his life and ideas entitled *Soul on Ice*, written while he was in prison, for which he is most remembered.

SELECTED BIBLIOGRAPHY

Cleaver, 1968; *Ebony*, March 1988; Pearson, 1994.

Charles Pete Banner-Haley

COALITION BUILDING. *See* Theme Essay "Coalition Building."

COINTELPRO (Counter-Intelligence Program). COINTELPRO (Counter-Intelligence Program), though not formally organized until after Malcolm's death, was an operation the Federal Bureau of Investigation (FBI)* initiated in 1956 to discredit and disrupt political groups that Director J. Edgar Hoover* and his top associates considered subversive. At this time and into the early 1960s, the FBI was more concerned with leftist internal subversives and generally did not view the Nation of Islam (NOI)* as a major threat to national security. If anything, the FBI's concerns lay with communist infiltration into the civil rights movement.* Still, the FBI's counterintelligence program launched in 1962 what became a long-term surveillance and investigation of the NOI. Wiretaps, informants, scripted public attacks, and well-placed anonymous "leaks" about the NOI, and especially about Elijah Muhammad's* out-of-wedlock children, all sought to exploit the Muslim* group and neutralize their popularity and effectiveness.

Although not initially a target of COINTELPRO actions, Malcolm X's association with Elijah Muhammad, the leader of the NOI, had earlier attracted the Bureau's attention. The NOI had interested the FBI largely because of its opposition to military service. Ultimately, the agency added Malcolm's name to its important security index and accumulated some 3,600 pages of documents on Malcolm X. Once the breach between Malcolm and Elijah Muhammad occurred, COINTELPRO operatives sought to exploit it with rumor and intrigue to make the rift permanent. It was the Organization of Afro-American Unity

(OAAU),* however, that the program was most concerned about because of its potential to unify blacks on a global basis. Malcolm's association with socialists made the counterintelligence program of disruption and harassment against him more credible.

In the years following Malcolm's death, the rise of urban racial violence and the increasing involvement of black nationalists in mass activism concerned the agency. Dissatisfaction with the progress of civil rights* led many in that movement to adopt a more militant stance, many of them identifying with the ideas of Malcolm X. In particular, his call for armed self-defense* in the face of racist aggression and police brutality* appealed to many discontented urban blacks.

On August 25, 1967, FBI Director Hoover extended COINTELPRO activities to so-called black nationalist hate groups. Among those listed as targets of the operation were the Deacons for Defense and Justice,* the Nation of Islam, the Congress of Racial Equality,* the Southern Christian Leadership Conference,* the Student Non-Violent Coordinating Committee,* and the Revolutionary Action Movement.* One of the program's goals was to prevent the rise of a "messiah" who would unify the more militant Black Power* movement. Hoover speculated that had Malcolm X lived, he might have played such a role, and the director further suggested that Martin Luther King, Jr.,* Stokely Carmichael,* and Elijah Muhammad aspired to that position. In this new phase of the program, FBI leaders attempted to disrupt and discredit organizations and leaders associated with the new forms of racial militancy that characterized black activism in the late 1960s.

COINTELPRO especially sought to exacerbate conflicts among the various factions that identified themselves with the views of Malcolm X. One such group, the Black Panther Party for Self-Defense,* a paramilitary organization founded in 1966 that capitalized on the growing militancy in urban black areas, was the major target of the agency's efforts against black groups. Hoover perceived the Panthers as the greatest threat to national security, and consequently the FBI mounted a national campaign to disrupt the group's activities. By the late 1960s most of the black militant groups had been weakened by police raids as well as internal dissent. Contributing to this decline were the activities of COINTELPRO operatives, their actions provoking conflict and violence that otherwise may not have occurred.

SELECTED BIBLIOGRAPHY

Branch, 1998; Carson, 1981; Carson (Gallen, ed.), 1991; Lowery and Marszalek, eds., 1992; O'Reilly, 1989; B. Perry, 1991; Sales, 1994; J. Williams, 1987.

Horace D. Nash

COLLINS, ELLA LITTLE. Besides his mentor Elijah Muhammad* and his wife, Betty Shabazz,* perhaps no person had a greater influence on the life of Malcolm X than his half sister Ella Little Collins. The first daughter of Mal-

Malcolm's half sister Ella Collins (left) along with his widow Betty Shabazz, attorney Percy Sutton (with hat), and an unidentified man shortly after Malcolm's murder. © Bettmann/CORBIS.

colm's father Earl Little, Sr.,* with his first wife Daisy Little, Ella was one of four half siblings of Malcolm. Ella lived on Sugar Hill* in the black middle-class* section of Roxbury,* Boston's black ghetto. Relatively well known in the community, she was a dark-skinned, strong-willed woman who, according to Malcolm, exuded black pride.* She was among a small number of "affluent" blacks, primarily employed in service-related jobs, who owned their own homes. In fact, Ella owned several significant blocs of property in Boston and, with her considerable business acumen, did well for a while as part owner of a neighborhood store. It was Ella with whom Malcolm spent the summer in 1939 following a difficult period of his life. With his father dead and his mother Louisa Little* committed to a mental hospital, the family was disrupted; Malcolm was forced into a foster home run by whites in Mason, Michigan,* and never made the adjustment well. His visit with Ella had impressed him so favorably that he soon requested and received her permission to live with her and two elderly aunts permanently. Strongly family oriented and noted for helping numerous family members in both the North and in her native state of Georgia, she simply could not resist the opportunity to help remove Malcolm from his white environment.

Ella sought to shape Malcolm's life into that of a respectable black professional, but Malcolm had other ideas. He found little interest in the black bourgeois lifestyle, preferring the offerings of street life and the association of the masses in the lower Roxbury ghetto. Despite her efforts to thwart it, Malcolm soon gravitated to criminal activity and was eventually imprisoned for his misdeeds. Ella, however, refused to abandon him. She visited him frequently in prison* and successfully worked to get him transferred to a more rehabilitative environment, one with better educational facilities where he could improve a notably bright mind. She was gratified over his conversion to Islam,* not because she believed in Elijah Muhammad's* philosophy but because of the positive change that the Nation of Islam (NOI)* was forging in Malcolm's life.

Following Malcolm's release from prison, he relocated first to Michigan and subsequently to New York, but in the interval he made frequent visits to Ella's home in Boston in his capacity as the organizer of the Boston temple and as an NOI minister and national spokesman. In turn, she visited Malcolm frequently in Harlem,* often getting together with him in Lewis Michaux's* Harlem bookstore where Malcolm read voraciously, or riding along with Malcolm in his drives throughout New York City, or simply talking late into the night with him in his home. According to her son, Rodnell Collins,* Ella was immensely proud of Malcolm's accomplishments in the NOI, but she was not, by Malcolm's own admission, easy to convert. When she did become a Muslim,* she did so, Collins said, more out of respect for the work that Malcolm and his brothers were doing in the NOI for black people rather than a belief in the divinity of Muhammad.

Once she committed to the NOI, Ella worked in the Boston mosques with women and children programs. She was responsible for establishing numerous activities in the temple and in the process was recognized as an important leader in her own right. Many of the temple's members sought her out for advice and leadership, which angered Louis Farrakhan,* the minister of the Boston temple, and this eventually breached their relationship. Under orders from Elijah Muhammad, Malcolm worked to resolve the dissension, but both Farrakhan and Ella were strong-willed, and the problems never truly ended between them.

Throughout Malcolm's work in the NOI and as a black leader, Ella was steadfast in her support of him. Never devoutly tied to Elijah Muhammad and the NOI, she was pleased with Malcolm's defection from the sect, though angry over his agony for doing so, especially his occasional equivocations about the separation from Muhammad. According to one Muahmmad biographer, Ella smarted over Muhammad's refusal to comply with a promise to name her minister or a female captain in the Boston temple. Hence, her lack of respect for Muhammad and her squabbles with Farrakhan made her own departure from the group easier. Committed to Malcolm's growth in Islam and as a black leader, she delayed her own plans to make the legendary Hajj* to finance Malcolm's pilgrimage to Mecca,* and helped support his two sojourns to Africa in 1964.

Like thousands of other Malcolm followers, Ella grieved over her brother's assassination, but she remained determined to carry on his work. From the outset, she strove to advance his efforts in launching the Muslim Mosque, Inc.* and the Organization of Afro-American Unity (OAAU),* and shortly after his death, she announced in a news conference that, as Malcolm had wished, she was assuming leadership of the OAAU and would work closely with Malcolm's chief assistant, James Shabazz (James 67X),* who was elected president of the Muslim Mosque, Inc. Collins's son maintains that she continued to lead Malcolm's OAAU until the early 1970s. But the organization was in its embryonic stage, and without the charismatic and capable leadership of Malcolm available, there were actually few followers left to lead. After a long debilitating illness, Ella Collins died in August 1996 at age eighty-two.

SELECTED BIBLIOGRAPHY

Blackside/PBS, 1994; Collins with Bailey, 1998; DeCaro, 1996; Evanzz, 1999; Malcolm X with Haley, 1965; *Militant*, March 22, 1965; Sales, 1994; Strickland (Greene, ed.), 1994.

Robert L. Jenkins

COLLINS, RODNELL. Several letters written by Malcolm X to Ella Collins,* his half sister, when he was in prison* during the 1940s and when he traveled after becoming a Muslim* minister suggested that a very close relationship existed between the two of them. Perhaps the closeness could be traced back to the family tragedies that occurred during the early years of Malcolm's life. At age six Malcolm's father Earl Little, Sr.,* was mysteriously killed in Lansing, Michigan,* in 1931, only three years after the family had moved there from Milwaukee, Wisconsin. Eight years later his mother, Louise Little,* was declared insane and committed to a mental institution for twenty-six years. After being placed in several foster homes, Malcolm eventually moved to Boston to live with his sister Ella for almost two years.

Much of the close relationship that Malcolm and Ella enjoyed and a number of other important family issues are revealed in an important book on Malcolm, written by Rodnell Collins, the son of Kenneth Collins and Ella. In his book *Seventh Child: A Family Memoir of Malcolm X*, Rodnell revealed that his first memory of Malcolm was sitting on his uncle's knees when his mother visited with him in prison in the mid-1940s. During Malcolm's association with the Nation of Islam (NOI)* he was in Boston a great deal and was frequently in the Collins's home, where his private side as an affable and humorous person was expected and accepted. Malcolm was easy to relate to, and he enjoyed being around his relatives, which included two other half siblings and aunts, in a family setting. This personal portrait of Malcolm provided by his nephew shows a side of Malcolm that is usually hidden by the public persona normally presented of him.

Rodnell viewed his uncle Malcolm both as a big brother and as a source of knowledge. He reported that he was taught much about African American history, Africa, Asia, self-determination, self-defense,* and white supremacy by his uncle Malcolm in Nation of Islam (NOI) workshops. He was, he said, influenced to a great extent by Malcolm's teachings. Rodnell's account of Malcolm's final hours prior to his assassination on February 21, 1965, is equally interesting. He described how despondent and dejected Malcolm appeared to be at his friend Tom Wallace's* home in New York on the evening before his death. An extended conversation with Rodnell's mother in Malcolm's car late that evening in front of the Wallace home revealed that Malcolm believed that the Central Intelligence Agency (CIA)* was the primary threat to his life. Rodnell, as so many other students of Malcolm's life have done, stokes the fire of conspiracy in Malcolm's murder, resolving little about the controversy but leaving much to continued speculation.

Rodnell's account of his relationship with Malcolm X is historically significant. Indeed, his perspective will help historians and other scholars further define and clarify the complexity and impact of the life of Malcolm X.

SELECTED BIBLIOGRAPHY

CBS News, 1992; Collins with Bailey, 1998; Malcolm X with Haley, 1965; http://www.brothermalcolm.net.

William A. Person

COMMEMORATIVE POSTAGE STAMP. In the more than thirty-five years since his death, Malcolm X's stature has grown not only in the black community but in the larger American community as well. Considered a pariah by conservatives of both black and white America during much of his adult life, since 1965 Malcolm has increasingly attained a level of respectability that influenced how even the federal government, once the target of some of his most scathing criticisms, came to regard him. Perhaps nothing has more graphically illustrated the moderation in attitude of white America in general, and the federal government specifically, about Malcolm than the decision of the United States Postal Service to honor him with the issuance of the Malcolm X Commemorative Stamp. As a matter of policy, the images on postal stamps are reserved for only those individuals of marked historical and cultural achievement. Appearing in early 1999, Malcolm's likeness on the nearly 100 million printed stamps is the twenty-second stamp issued by the service in its Black Heritage series; he joins such honorees as his contemporary Martin Luther King, Jr.,* and other black greats like Harriet Tubman, Frederick Douglass, Booker T. Washington, George Washington Carver, Mary McCleod Bethune, Ida Wells Barnett, Ernest E. Just, and W.E.B. Du Bois.* Identified on the stamp by his orthodox Muslim* name of El-Hajj Malik El-Shabazz, the Malcolm X postage stamp was unveiled in a ceremony at New York's Apollo Theatre,* a place Malcolm frequented for entertainment during his youthful hipster days. Unveiling ceremonies occurred in other cities as well, including Detroit, Michigan.*

During the Apollo Theatre ceremony, a celebrated crowd of family, friends, and followers heard Attallah Shabazz, Malcolm's eldest daughter, talk about

Malcolm's legacy and proclaim that most of America, unlike the time that her father was alive, was ready to hear about Malcolm's work. Others also spoke glowingly of Malcolm, including the Postal Service Governor S. David Fineman, who praised him as a committed "modern day revolutionary" opposed to oppression, and media notable Mike Wallace,* a former critic and friend of Malcolm who honored Malcolm with a special tribute as a man and leader. Part of the celebration and its significance was recorded by Attallah in the introduction of the 1999 edition of *The Autobiography of Malcolm X.**

SELECTED BIBLIOGRAPHY

Black Media News, Summer 1999; Malcolm X with Haley, 2000; http://www.brothermalcolm.net

Robert L. Jenkins

COMMUNIST PARTY. Malcolm X never developed close relations with the Communist Party of the United States of America (CPUSA), although at least one Federal Bureau of Investigation (FBI)* informant claimed that Malcolm had been a communist. Perhaps this view grew out of statements that Malcolm had made in an ambiguous and critical letter to President Harry S. Truman in June 1950 while in Charlestown (Massachusetts) Penitentiary. In the letter he claimed to have been a longtime communist who also tried to enlist in the Japanese army during World War II.* Of course, none of this was true. In more than one instance, Malcolm, who was well read, claimed to know very little about Marxism.

Throughout the 1950s, the CPUSA leadership remained wary of black nationalism* and black separatism. Taking its cue from Moscow, the CPUSA officially viewed most African Americans as "peasants," necessarily condemning them to a "bourgeois nationalist" outlook contrary to the Marxist class struggle. The communists, therefore, encouraged integrating blacks into White working-class organizations and threw their support behind the liberal integrationist approach of Dr. Martin Luther King, Jr.,* as a tactic for promoting worker solidarity.

Malcolm initially viewed communists as atheistic white radicals who had no interest in genuine black liberation. He believed that racism, not the class struggle, was the primary evil in America. Only after his break with the Nation of Islam* and his overseas trips to Africa and the Middle East* did Malcolm incorporate into his thinking political ideas that paralleled more of the Marxist critique of American and European capitalism and imperialism. He noted the interdependence of capitalism* and racism and hinted at his preference for a socialist politicoeconomic system. Nevertheless, Malcolm insisted that black people had to find answers to their own problems and not simply adopt ideological constructs borrowed from their white oppressors. There could be no worker solidarity until black solidarity had been achieved. Blacks and whites could best help each other, he believed, by working separately within their own communities.

SELECTED BIBLIOGRAPHY

Carson (Gallen, ed.), 1991; Cone, 1991; Evanzz, 1992; Horne, 1994; Malcolm X (Breitman, ed.), 1970a; Malcolm X with Haley, 1965; *Militant*, April 20, 1964; Strickland (Greene, ed.), 1994; Weinstein, 1975.

Richard V. Damms

THE CONGO. Achieving its independence from Belgium in 1960, the Congo suffered from a violent and unstable political structure during its first decade of autonomy. Malcolm X became extremely critical of the actions of the United Nations* in this central African nation and the Central Intelligence Agency's* interference in Congolese affairs. He denounced the American-Belgium involvement in Congolese affairs as criminal. In 1964 the Congolese People's Republic (CPR), under the leadership of Christophe Gbenye, began a leftist revolution against the seated government and Premier Moise Tshombe.* After the CPR captured several hundred foreign nationals and began to use them as political hostages, the United States and Belgium dropped paratroopers into Stanleyville, the national capital, in the successful effort to free approximately 500 prisoners (Operation Red Dragon). Malcolm claimed President Lyndon B. Johnson's support of "Tshombe's hired killers" created the military situation in the Congo. The deaths of thirty hostages at the hands of the CPR were, therefore, Johnson's responsibility. Malcolm also stated that while the deaths of the white hostages were unfortunate, it should be remembered that as a result of white massacres black Congolese were frequently murdered victims. Tears should be shed for the Congolese, too. To many, Malcolm sounded callous in a statement reminiscent of his comment about the death of President John F. Kennedy.* Malcolm often cited the Congo and other problems that resulted from the decline of European colonialism* in Africa as evidence supporting the need for Pan-Africanism.* The Congo became the Republic of Zaire in 1971.

SELECTED BIBLIOGRAPHY

Epstein, ed., 1965; Meditz and Merrill, eds., 1994; *Militant*, December 7, 1964; *New York Times*, November 25, 1964; Wagoner, 1980; Weissman, 1974; Wolfenstein, 1993.

James W. Stennett

CONGRESS OF AFRIKAN PEOPLE (CAP). After his assassination in 1965, Malcolm X's views regarding Pan-Africanism* and self-determination were a springboard for the Pan-Africanist and black nationalist movements that developed in the late 1960s. Africana Studies Professor Maulana Karenga,* who was a part of those movements, argues that Malcolm X served as a model for countless nationalist groups and leaders. One such group that was an outgrowth of the national Black Power* conferences (held between 1967 and 1969) was the Congress of Afrikan People (CAP), created in September 1970 in Atlanta, Georgia. The driving force behind the organization was poet/playwright Imamu Amiri Baraka* (formerly LeRoi Jones), who knew Malcolm personally and was heavily influenced by him. Baraka argues in an essay entitled "Malcolm as Ideology" that Malcolm X, even years after his murder, continues to be at the center of the ideological development of the Black Liberation movement.

CAP organized workshops on economics, law, and especially politics. The organization sought to develop resolutions for conflicts facing African Americans. CAP spearheaded a National Black Political Convention, convened in March of 1972 in Gary, Indiana, to set a black agenda and become an aggressive force in the 1972 presidential election. It was clear that some of the sentiments voiced at the convention were borrowed from Malcolm. As a result of the black nationalist and Pan-Africanist movements, Malcolm's ideologies continue to echo in the twenty-first century.

SELECTED BIBLIOGRAPHY

Baraka, 1972; Baraka (Wood, ed.), 1992; Gilliam, 1975; Hampton and Fayer with Flynn, eds., 1991; Sales, 1994.

Nancy J. Dawson

CONGRESS OF RACIAL EQUALITY (CORE). The Congress of Racial Equality (CORE) is a civil rights organization* founded in 1942. The founding organizer and leader was James Farmer.* CORE invoked a new climate among blacks of open, nonviolent defiance against social injustice. The organization rallied students and activists alike to its cause. It is believed that CORE originated the civil rights* tactic of the "sit-in" in a Chicago* restaurant in 1943. The entity took part in sponsoring numerous other activities, including the freedom riders,* the March on Washington,* and protest at the 1964 World Fair in New York City. In 1967, CORE came up with a fifteen-point program that involved political, economic, cultural, educational, and international objectives. During the civil rights period from the early 1940s when it was founded until the late 1960s, CORE was perhaps the most militant and strident of the traditional civil rights organizations, though nonviolence was its official policy.

Malcolm detested this philosophy of nonviolence by CORE and other civil rights groups and often lashed out against these organizations and their leadership. However, Malcolm respected James Farmer as a leader because Farmer was the only one willing to debate Malcolm on civil rights. Malcolm contended, nevertheless, that organizations like CORE were being hoodwinked by whites. He felt that neither the federal government nor white supporters of these organizations were genuinely interested in obtaining human rights* for blacks. According to Malcolm, CORE and other organizations were only fighting for racial integration* and civil rights, not human rights. Malcolm thought that CORE and other protest and civil rights organizations genuinely concerned with freedom, justice, and equality for African Americans should bring charges against the

United States in the United Nations* for violating the human rights of blacks. However, he was unsuccessful in persuading civil rights organizations to do so.

SELECTED BIBLIOGRAPHY

Gallen, ed., 1992; Karim with Skutches and Gallen, 1992; Malcolm X (Clark, ed.), 1992; Ploski and Kaiser, eds., 1971.

Patricia Jernigan and Mfanya Donald Tryman

CONK. Prior to the 1970s, one of the most popular black male hair fads was what is often called the "conk," also known as the "process," the "do," and the "Marseille." Based on a blend of lye, eggs, and white potatoes, the conk is an often painful hair-straightening process that found its niche beginning in the 1930s, most prominently in the black entertainment community but also among black youths. Because of the latter, many came to associate the conk with black criminal behavior. In the early 1940s, during his hipster experience, Malcolm X conked his hair. Malcolm's closest Roxbury* friend, Shorty,* who sported a conk himself, prepared the chemical mixture and placed the first conk on Malcolm's hair. It was, as expected for any first-time user, an excruciatingly painful experience for Malcolm, which he readily described in his autobiography. With a runny nose and watery eyes and his head virtually on "fire," Malcolm withstood the pain and was pleased with what the mirror revealed: shiny red hair, limp like the hair of whites. The process would be repeated numerous times during the years of his street life, occasionally with subdued humor. Once in the midst of a Michigan winter, frozen pipes prevented him from getting water from the bathroom wash basin to rinse the mixture from his scalp and necessity prompted improvisation: He turned to the toilet bowl, flushing it several times to remove the mixture.

Conking his hair was one of the few examples of Malcolm's life, even in his hipster days, that he did something to deny his blackness. As he did with so many other aspects of his street life, however, Malcolm would later speak disparagingly about the conk. As he came to understand more about himself and his heritage, he regarded the conk as one of the most shameful displays of black denial of self. Whenever he saw black men wearing conks, it reminded him of his own personal experience of buying into white opinions about their racial superiority and the African American's acceptance of white standards of beauty. Consequently, he was not hesitant to speak disdainfully about what he saw. Nothing, in Malcolm's view, was more emblematic of the black man's shame of himself and his race than chemically disposing of his kinky hair and defacing himself by wearing this hairstyle. Considerable evidence supports the fact, however, that the style was a "Negro-idiom" influenced by the desire not to be more like the Anglo-Saxon but to emulate the wavy-haired darker-skinned "Latin Don Juan type."

Malcolm died on the eve of an emerging national black pride* movement of the mid-1960s. African Americans no longer consciously sought to deny their roots and heritage, and they extolled the virtues of their black physical characteristics. A significant component of this social and cultural renaissance was the abandonment of the conk and the substitution of the "natural" or Afro hairstyle. Its popularity crossed class and economic lines, including even the upper- and middle-class Blacks,* groups that Malcolm frequently condemned incorrectly for their supposed tendency to emulate whites. Malcolm's articulation of issues related to this mass movement, including his criticism of the conk, arguably helped to set the stage for its emergence.

SELECTED BIBLIOGRAPHY

DeCaro, 1996; Kelley (Wood, ed.), 1992; Levine, 1978; Malcolm X with Haley, 1965; Morrow, 1973; Murray, 1970; Smitherman, 1994; White and White, 1998.

Robert L. Jenkins

CONNOR, THEOPHILUS EUGENE (BULL). The son of a railroad dispatcher, the man who would become a Birmingham, Alabama,* police commissioner and politician first became a celebrity in 1922 when he began recreating the Birmingham Baron's baseball games in front of the telegraph office. He gained the nickname "Bull" because of his booming voice. He won election to the Alabama legislature in 1934, and in 1937 he began his long career as Commissioner of Public Safety, where he established his anti-integration reputation. For many, Connor symbolized the determination of white supremacists to make no concessions in what was often described as the South's* most segregated city.

In the early 1960s when Martin Luther King, Jr.,* began leading civil rights* demonstrations in Birmingham, and Connor retaliated with fire hoses and police dogs, Malcolm X repeatedly spoke out in protest. Malcolm frequently drew criticism from the civil rights leadership for his scathing indictment of southern racism and the strategy employed to combat it but never participating in the battles. There was speculation, however, that he would be in Birmingham during the demonstrations, invited by the local Muslim* temple minister, who owed his appointment to Malcolm. Elijah Muhammad,* however, would not permit it, and Malcolm could do little more than comment. Malcolm condemned Connor "as an international thug" for the brutal tactics used against women and children in King's 1963 Birmingham campaign. Malcolm seldom referred to Connor by name, but the frequent comments in his speeches about the violence in Birmingham against defenseless demonstrators left his audiences with little doubt about his views of Connor, whose job it was to maintain the city's racial status quo.

SELECTED BIBLIOGRAPHY

Malcolm X (Clark, ed.), 1992; *Montgomery Advertiser*, March 11, 1973; *New York Times*, March 11, 1973; Nunnelley, 1991; B. Perry, 1991; *Washington Post*, March 12, 1973.

John F. Marszalek

Birmingham's public safety commissioner Bull Connor (right foreground), a noted symbol of official white resistance to civil rights advances, confronts black demonstrators at the Trailways bus terminal. Birmingham Public Library, Department of Archives and Manuscripts (Catalog Number BPH1).

CONSPIRACY THEORIES OF ASSASSINATION. *See* Theme Essay "Conspiracy Theories of the Assassination of Malcolm X."

COOKS, CARLOS A. Carlos A. Cooks was born in the Dominican Republic. Early in his life, Cooks came under the influence of the philosophy of Marcus Garvey.* His father, a successful businessman, and one of his uncles were among the early members of the United Negro Improvement Association* on the island nation of the Dominican Republic. Cooks's early life was comfortable, though interrupted by the recurring political upheavals in his native land. He attended school in the Dominican Republic and completed his education in New York City when he arrived there in 1929.

Cooks joined the Garvey movement in the United States, becoming a frequent speaker in Harlem* for the cause of African nationalism.* In 1941, he organized the African Nationalist Pioneer Movement (ANPM), a Pan-Africanist organization. He remained a popular street lecturer, frequently climbing atop a stepladder, as was the custom in Harlem in those days, to address the people congregating nearby. Military service took him overseas, and the ANPM became dormant until he reactivated it in 1949. Between 1939 and 1957 he irregularly published *The Street Speaker* as the official magazine of his movement and the Garveyite philosophy.

Followers of Cooks later insisted that he was the major influence on Malcolm X's thinking, even more significant than Elijah Muhammad.* This claim is doubtful. Malcolm and Cooks appeared together on several occasions, and their black nationalist ideology was similar, but there is no hard evidence of a close association. Cooks, for example, receives no mention in Malcolm's autobiography. Second, Malcolm's Black Muslim* ties were totally different from Cooks's antireligious approach. Finally, Cooks was hardly viewed as Malcolm's heir after the latter's assassination. When Cooks died the next year, his death received little notice outside his small group of followers, though Betty Shabazz,* Malcolm's widow, did come to the funeral home and signed the book of condolences.

SELECTED BIBLIOGRAPHY

Harris, Harris, and Harris, eds., 1992; Malcolm with Haley, 1965; *New York Times*, May 7, 1966.

John F. Marszalek

CUBA. In 1959 insurrectionary forces led by Fidel Castro* overthrew Cuban leader Fulgencio Batista and installed a communist regime in Cuba. Thereafter, Castro quickly moved the small Caribbean island into the Soviet Union's orbit, which exacerbated its relationship with the United States. The ideological differences and political estrangement between revolutionary Cuba and the United States made Castro a natural ally of black American militants during the 1960s. Consequently, the island became a popular asylum for some of them seeking refuge from prosecution by the federal government for alleged crimes. Malcolm X was never in serious enough trouble with the law to ever contemplate moving to Cuba, though supposedly the Cuban authorities once invited him to live there permanently.

There was much about Cuba, however, that Malcolm found praiseworthy. To Malcolm X, Cuba was regarded as a veritable "giant killer" for its determination to challenge America. The Cubans had not only confiscated American investments and nationalized American businesses, but they had also succeeded in gaining support for their anti-American policy from other Latin American nations, and this clearly impressed Malcolm. Moreover, though Malcolm seldom had much to say about the major Cold War antagonists, he regarded Cuba's right as a sovereign nation to accept the Soviet Union's influence no less legitimate than the right of the United States to extend its influence to African and Asian nations.

As he did in regard to the Chinese Revolution,* Malcolm praised the accomplishments of Cuba's revolution and hoisted it as an example for black Americans to emulate in their struggle against white racism. Malcolm had considerable respect for the two personalities that represented the essence of the Cuba revolution, Castro and Ernesto "Che" Guevara.* In June 1960, the Muslim* minister made national headlines when he conferred with Castro for two hours in Harlem's* Hotel Theresa.* Castro, who was on a visit to the United Nations,* was denied lodging in New York's upscale hotels, and as an alternative, he chose to stay in Harlem. No detailed account of what the two men talked about exists, but the meeting was an act that further endeared the Cuban leader to black American urbanites. It was Che, a high-ranking Cuban official and a close confidante of Castro, however, that Malcolm seemed more enamored with. Although not a Cuban national, Guevara had made a considerable international reputation for himself through his support of exporting a Cuban-styled revolution* to Latin American, African, and Middle East* countries. Both he and Malcolm railed against imperialism, and he made no qualms of his support for armed struggle against the worldwide influence of the United States. Guevara knew Malcolm and his work and, after accepting an invitation from Malcolm, planned a speaking engagement before one of Malcolm's Organization of Afro-American Unity (OAAU)* meetings. The appearance of such an international force as Guevara would have done much to give Malcolm's fledgling organization greater visibility, but Malcolm had to settle for reading a message that Guevara wrote to the body because last-minute security concerns prevented him from attending.

Malcolm could certainly relish the fact that Cuba effectively snubbed its nose at the powerful United States, but he hardly lauded the less-than-ideal race relations that he knew existed on the island. One Black Panther Party leader claims that on the eve of Malcolm's murder Malcolm was making plans to visit the island nation to personally learn more about conditions there. His death precluded the opportunity. If, however, Malcolm had little chance to learn much about Cuba and its people before his death, they, like so many others from both inside and outside of the United States, learned much about him after his death. Cubans have found Malcolm and his philosophy fascinating qualities, and more than thirty-five years after his assassination, Malcolm is one of Cuba's most popular and widely read black American leaders of the twentieth century.

SELECTED BIBLIOGRAPHY

Evanzz, 1992; Lomax, 1963; Malcolm X (Breitman, ed.), 1965; Mealy, 1993; Moore, 1988; Reitan, 1999; Tyson, 1999.

Robert L. Jenkins

D

DANDRIDGE (RICHARDSON), GLORIA. Gloria Dandridge was a native of Baltimore, Maryland. She gained national notoriety during the 1960s as a civil rights* activist in Cambridge, Maryland. Although born into a privileged family, Dandridge early in life felt the effects of racism in Cambridge, a small town of some 11,000 located on the Chesapeake side of Maryland's Eastern Shore, where she was reared. In her youth, her father died because he could not receive proper medical attention in the town's segregated medical facilities. Racial segregation* kept her and the town's other blacks from the best public accommodations and schools. And though college educated at Washington, D.C.'s Howard University,* Dandridge's disinterest in becoming a schoolteacher meant other forms of professional employment were effectively closed to her in a segregated society. It was largely because of these patterns of racism that Dandridge was prompted to activism. In 1962 she became the major catalyst in launching the Cambridge Movement, a grassroots effort to improve the status of the city's black poor, increase meaningful employment opportunities, and eliminate the city's discriminatory practices of segregated schools and housing. Outspoken and uncompromising, Dandridge, whom many compared to the historic figure Joan of Arc, and her community-based Cambridge Non-violent Action Committee (CNAC) encountered stiff white resistance to the massive demonstrations and other forms of direct action protest; concessions were made grudgingly. The result was a serious outbreak of violent black-white confrontations in 1963 that required the long-standing presence of a National Guard peacekeeping force in the city.

Dandridge first encountered Malcolm X in Detroit, Michigan,* in November 1963. The occasion was a black leadership conference that attracted many of the major establishment civil rights leaders. Malcolm was part of a rump session that split from the official body and met at the church of one of his close associates, the Reverend Albert Cleage,* who was a black nationalist. It was during this meeting that Malcolm made perhaps his most influential speech, "Message to the Grass Roots,"* and it left an indelible impression on Dandridge, who had also defected from the mainstream group. To be sure, she was already aware of his views and how much they affected militant movement activists in Cambridge. Student Non-Violent Coordinating Committee (SNCC)* colleagues working with her local group had encouraged her to steer clear of Malcolm during Cambridge's struggle, but she publicly supported his views about blacks arming themselves in self-defense.* Doing so, she said, was a "practical" policy, a good "deterrent" to white violence. Dandridge's views made her one of the first of her gender to reject nonviolence as a tactical method for civil right gains; by then, she was referring to herself as "a radical revolutionary."

Impressed with Malcolm's ideas and he with her militant reputation, their mutual admiration for each other soon led to a closer association. By 1964 the two had certainly established a working relationship. Dandridge recruited Malcolm in the spring of 1964 to work as a consultant with a new militant northern civil rights organization called *ACT* (not an acronym), and he would mention her fondly in some of the speeches he made during the year. Obviously, she did not accept SNCC's heeding in Cambridge, and it would be totally rejected when she got married and left the town for New York in July 1964 at the height of her fame. There she took an activist role in turning the attention from the sole concentration on black problems in the South.* She also began an affiliation with Malcolm's fledgling Organization of Afro-American Unity (OAAU).* Presumably, she was one of several intellectuals and militant outcasts of the established movement to help prepare the charter for Malcolm's organization. That Malcolm held Dandridge in high regard was further demonstrated by the fact that during his travels in the last year of his life he occasionally sent her postcards containing brief words of wisdom about the course of the black struggle. Typically, only those that he regarded as his friends or admired as activists in the liberation movement were singled out as addressees from abroad. Clearly, the admiration between the two was mutual.

SELECTED BIBLIOGRAPHY

Blackside/PBS, 1987, 1994; Brock (Crawford, Rouse, and Woods, eds.), 1990; Cone, 1991; *Ebony*, July 1964; Giddings, 1984; Goldman, 1979; Malcolm X (Breitman, ed.), 1970; Strickland (Greene, ed.), 1994.

Robert L. Jenkins

DAVIS, ANGELA. Angela Davis was born in Birmingham, Alabama.* Davis is a social activist and educator. Her teaching, research, speaking, and political activism demonstrate her commitment to the liberation struggle of all oppressed peoples, especially people in the African diaspora. It was in Davis's senior year, at Brandeis University, that she heard Malcolm X speak. Davis became aware at an early age of the problems created by poverty and racism. However, it was Malcolm's articulation of the black liberation struggle that roused her pride and stirred her mind. Malcolm X had a profound impact on her political development and awakened in her a black feminist consciousness. While Malcolm was not necessarily a feminist (when he was a member of the Nation of Islam*), Davis recognized that he loved women and had the highest respect for them. The world's rediscovery of Malcolm X has compelled Davis to formulate analyses on popular culture, the iconization of Malcolm X, and gender. She argues that popular culture is historically incorrect in iconizing Malcolm amid profane and vulgar references to women.

SELECTED BIBLIOGRAPHY

A. Davis (Wood, ed.), 1992; J. Smith, ed., 1992; M. Williams, ed., 1993.

Lehlohonolo Tlou

DAVIS, OSSIE. Ossie Davis was born in Cogdell, Georgia. Davis's father worked as a construction laborer and minister. Both of his parents influenced him with their storytelling skills and church activities, which provided the groundwork for his acting career.

After Davis graduated from high school he attended Howard University* in Washington, D.C., where he met the so-called mid-wife of the Harlem* Renaissance, Alain Locke, a drama critic and philosophy professor. As Davis's mentor, Locke persuaded him to pursue an acting career with the Rose McClendon Players. Shortly thereafter, Davis made his acting debut in the McClendon Players's presentation of *Joy Exceeding Glory*. After the success of this play, he unexpectedly joined the army when World War II* began. His stint in the army delayed his acting career. However, as soon as the war ended, he resumed acting and won his first lead role in 1946 in the play *Jeb*. He also met his future wife during the performance, Ruby Ann Wallace, whose stage name was Ruby Dee.* They became active in the civil rights movement* long before it was fashionable.

Davis produced plays throughout the 1950s and 1960s, including *Alice in Wonder, The Big Deal*, and *Purlie Victorious*, his most notable production. Although Davis was opposed to the teachings of the Black Muslims,* Malcolm attended *Purlie Victorious* on one occasion and complimented Davis's performance. This was the beginning of a long association between the two men.

Along with his impressive acting career, Davis found time to maintain contact with black activists like Malcolm X. In 1962, Malcolm visited Davis and his wife, Ruby, at their home in Mount Vernon, New York. Davis perceived this as an opportunity to learn more about Malcolm's program for the black struggle. Although Malcolm did not answer all of the questions Davis posed, Malcolm left a lasting impression on Davis as a man with high morals and integrity. The respect and admiration he had for Malcolm developed thereafter and continued to grow.

Davis delivered Malcolm's eulogy on February 27, 1965. He emphasized that Malcolm represented the manhood of black America. He further elaborated on

Malcolm's leadership and the honor he brought the black community. Davis understood that Malcolm was a rare black man who deserved the honor and salute he gave to him in his eulogy.

In justifying why he eulogized Malcolm, Davis emphasized that he knew him personally and held him in high esteem. He regarded Malcolm as one of the most fascinating and charming men he had ever met. Most important, Davis elected to deliver Malcolm's eulogy because he loved, respected, and admired Malcolm for what he represented in the black struggle for freedom, justice, and equality. He especially cherished his affiliation with Malcolm in the movement.

Davis's eulogy of Malcolm enhanced his acting career. He has appeared on television starring in a number of television series including *The Defenders, The Nurses, The Doctors, The Fugitive, Bonanza*, and *Evening Shade*. His film career was also boosted, appearing in such films as *Let's Do It Again* in 1976 and *Jungle Fever*, produced by black film director Spike Lee.* Davis and his wife have both received numerous awards.

SELECTED BIBLIOGRAPHY

Clarke, ed., 1990; Davis and Dee, 1998; Hampton and Fayer with Flynn, 1991; Myers, 1993; C. Nagel, ed., 1994; Ploski and Williams, 1989.

LaVonne Jackson

DAWSON, WILLIAM L. William L. Dawson was born in 1886 in Albany, Georgia. A graduate of Fisk University and Northwestern University Law School, Dawson began his interest in politics during the early 1920s in Chicago, Illinois.* A decorated veteran of World War I, he had recently returned from the European conflict where he had suffered injury from a mustard gas attack. Success in the political arena, however, did not occur until much later in his life. During the 1950s and 1960s, he became the recognized leader of the Chicago black political community. A member of the U.S. House of Representatives, Dawson's election in 1942 made him only the third black American elected to that body in the twentieth century. A Democrat, he introduced few pieces of legislation and did little materially to advance the status of black Americans, though he did occasionally speak admirably on their behalf. He was, however, an extremely powerful political figure in Chicago, where he spent a considerable amount of his time dispensing patronage and overseeing his strong political machine. Malcolm X tended to be highly critical of Democratic politicians, and he did not exclude black political figures, most of whom he regarded as little more than pawns for white leaders. Malcolm, who visited frequently the home of Nation of Islam* leader Elijah Muhammad* and the sect's headquarters in the "Windy City," was aware that Dawson's real source of power derived from his alliance with the powerful white political machine in Chicago, and that made him an easy target for Malcolm's criticisms. Though Malcolm eventually came to soften his views about black America's most notable national leader, Harlem* Congressman Adam Clayton Powell, Jr.,* Malcolm had little trouble characterizing Dawson as an "Uncle Tom"* and among those blacks who helped to keep his own people in bondage.

SELECTED BIBLIOGRAPHY

Clay, 1992; V. Franklin, 1996, Malcolm X (Breitman, ed.), 1970a; Malcolm X (Epps, ed.), 1991.

Robert L. Jenkins

DAWUD, HAJJ TALIB AHMED. During the height of their popularity in the 1960s, Elijah Muhammad,* Malcolm X, and the Nation of Islam (NOI)* were frequently the source of biting criticism. Much of the venom came from the civil rights* community because of the NOI's harsh separatist views and their blunt and caustic indictment against whites as the historical oppressors of black people. Occasionally, however, Black Muslims* were the source of criticism because their version of Islam* was at great variance with more orthodox beliefs. In the United States, orthodox Islamic groups did not recognize Muhammad's sect as legitimately Islamic in their practices and philosophy. Even Malcolm admitted his embarrassment over the fact that he understood little of the doctrines and prayer rituals consistent with the religion when he made the Hajj* in the spring of 1964.

Malcolm's specific problems with traditional Islamic practices while in Mecca* were unknown to his American critics until he later revealed them in his autobiography. In general, however, perhaps there was no one more aware of Malcolm and the NOI's shortcomings as Muslims* than Talib Ahmed Dawud. His determination to air these faults made him one of the sect's greatest nemeses. Dawud, who came to the United States from Antigua in the West Indies when he was a young boy, was a self-styled Imam who became a Muslim in 1940. Before his conversion, he made his living as a jazz musician. He soon abandoned the career, however, and dedicated himself to spreading Islam in the United States. By 1950, he had established his first mosque in Philadelphia, Pennsylvania, and helped to form the Muslim Brotherhood in America, Inc., a loose alliance of numerous Islamic groups. Although grossly exaggerated, reportedly Dawud would eventually have more than 100,000 followers. Ever faithful to Islamic tenets, Dawud was quick to point to the NOI's lack of orthodoxy, and for several years during the late 1950s and early 1960s, he was involved in a rancorous exchange with Muhammad and the NOI over their religious practices and racial doctrines. He denounced both Elijah and the founder of the NOI, W. D. Fard,* as charlatans and former convicts, and Dawud even tried to have the presidential administration of Lyndon B. Johnson* arrest Muhammad as a serial murderer, claiming that the NOI leader caused the death of Noble Drew Ali,* founder of the Moorish Science Temple, a distant forerunner of Fard's movement. Muhammad countered Dawud, emphasizing Dawud's jealousy of the success of the NOI movement and making aspersions against Dawud's wife, Dakota Staton, a notable blues singer of the era.

Dawud, who had himself made the Hajj, claimed that the reason Malcolm had not visited Mecca during his first visit to the Middle East* in 1959 was because both pilgrimage and Saudi Arabian authorities realized that he was not a true Muslim and denied his entry into the Holy city. To be sure, much of the hostility that Dawud and Muhammad expressed toward each other resulted from their competition for followers. As Muhammad's closest lieutenant during the controversy, Malcolm was unable to absolve himself from the fray, and in characteristic style, he leveled a blistering response to Dawud. The dispute, however, also prompted Malcolm to make overtures to Dawud to resolve his differences with his mentor. Black people were already experiencing enough trouble with whites because of their racism, he wrote in the *Los Angeles Herald-Dispatch*;* it made little sense for African Americans to fight among themselves. In an effort to help legitimate Muhammad, Malcolm led a fund-raising drive to help finance his mentor's Hajj and to prepare him for the pilgrimage. Unfortunately, the NOI's problems with Dawud, as they did with other critics, lingered well into the 1960s, long after Malcolm's death.

SELECTED BIBLIOGRAPHY

Clegg, 1997; Essien-Udom, 1971; Lincoln, 1994; Malcolm X with Haley, 1965.

Robert L. Jenkins

DEACONS FOR DEFENSE AND JUSTICE. A black self-defense* group formed in Bogalusa, Louisiana, in early 1965. The Deacons reflected Malcolm X's belief that African Americans had the right to defend themselves against white violence and terrorism. Black citizens, Malcolm maintained, had the right to protect themselves by whatever means necessary whenever the government was either unable or unwilling to protect them. Despite the concerns of moderate civil rights* leaders like Martin Luther King, Jr.,* the Deacons participated in the James Meredith* march in Mississippi. The Student Non-Violent Coordinating Committee (SNCC)* and the Congress of Racial Equality (CORE)* invited armed Deacons to provide protection for the marchers. The Federal Bureau of Investigation* kept a file on the Deacons for Defense and sent reports to Louisiana authorities about the group's activities. Malcolm X and the Deacons for Defense influenced the later-formed organization, the Black Panther Party for Self-Defense,* who adopted their notions of the right to self-defense.

SELECTED BIBLIOGRAPHY

Breitman, 1967; Carson, 1981; Malcolm X (Breitman, ed.), 1965, 1970a; O'Reilly, 1989; J. Williams, 1987.

Horace D. Nash

DeBERRY, CLIFTON. Clifton DeBerry, a blond, extremely fair-skinned African American, was a Socialist Workers Party* candidate for the U.S. presidency in 1964 and a black nationalist. Though Malcolm did not endorse

DeBerry's presidency the veteran socialist remained close to Malcolm during the last month's of Malcolm's life. He lauded Malcolm X's stand on the need for blacks to develop their nationalistic political potentials. DeBerry supported Malcolm's formation of the Muslim Mosque, Inc.,* in Harlem* and the Organization of American Unity.* The latter organization had chapters in the United States, Europe, and Africa. After Malcolm formed his new groups, DeBerry, as leader of the party, frequently extended Malcolm invitations to speak at the party's political forums, which Malcolm accepted as good public platforms to further his movement.

DeBerry accused New York City Police Commissioner Michael J. Murphy and the media of deliberately distorting the speeches of Malcolm by claiming that he was calling for "bloodshed and armed revolt." He argued that the distortion of Malcolm's words was an attempt to justify the New York police's inflicting violence on civil rights* activists.

DeBerry and Malcolm embraced black nationalism,* which they described as African Americans building their own organization and selecting their own programs and leadership. Both advocated blacks defining their identity. They credited black nationalism for promoting black pride* and unity in the 1960s, not the white liberals* and black integrationists. DeBerry believed Malcolm could have played a more pivotal role in unifying the black community, had he lived.

Malcolm was always courteous to DeBerry and the socialists. Critical of capitalism,* he understood the role of socialism and how it was helping to resolve problems in many Third-World countries. But despite his occasional leftist rhetoric, Malcolm held no inclinations for Marxism in his own political ideology. As much as DeBerry and the socialists could have benefitted from Malcolm becoming a card carrying member of the Party, DeBerry made no effort to recruit him and Malcolm made no effort to join.

SELECTED BIBLIOGRAPHY

Friedly, 1992; Goldman, 1979; Militant, March 16, 1964, March 23, 1964, March 1, 1995; New York Amsterdam News, July 1964.

L. Henry Whelchel

DEE, RUBY (Ruby Ann Wallace). For more than fifty years Ruby Dee has been one of America's most recognizable Hollywood screen stars. Although popular in her own right, she has enjoyed even greater notoriety because of her long time marriage to Ossie Davis,* himself a widely known actor-writer-producer, with whom she has teamed on numerous occasions in movies, in theater, on television, and as a producer. Dee's most acclaimed screen and theater credits include *Purlie Victorious*, *The Jackie Robinson Story*, and the Broadway hit, *A Raisin in the Sun*. Socially conscious about the victimization and oppression of the African American, she played an important, persistent, and often highly visible role as a non-violent civil rights* activist. It was also as an artist that she voiced her disillusionment with the American racial order. Yet,

Dee and Ossie Davis were among a small group of black celebrities* that maintained a long-standing relationship with Malcolm X. Like so many other blacks, her first awareness of Malcolm occurred through the 1959 television documentary "The Hate That Hate Produced."* Though both she and her husband hardly expected Malcolm to be any more than a fast-rising but equally fast-falling star, their immediate impressions of his extraordinary intelligence, breadth of knowledge about the black American historical condition, and ability to articulate the race's frustrations more effectively than Martin Luther King, Jr.,* grew increasingly. Dee met Malcolm sometime shortly afterward through her brother Edward Wallace,* who had become a member of the Nation of Islam (NOI)* and invited her to hear Malcolm speak at his New York Temple Number Seven.* Thereafter, their relationship budded; as Dee and Ossie wrote in their autobiography, "It was difficult not to like Malcolm X."

For many years she and her husband kept a residence in Harlem,* New York, where Malcolm visited often during both his tenure in the NOI and after the break with the group. Malcolm also benefitted from the relationship, for it was through the acting couple, who knew personally many of the prominent civil rights leaders like Roy Wilkins* and Whitney Young,* that Malcolm was invited to participate in an informal meeting Ossie and Ruby hosted to formulate civil rights strategy. Although it was officially frowned upon by Elijah Muhammad* and the Muslim* sect, Malcolm attended Ruby and Ossie's stage performances and praised their work as artists and social commentators through their acting roles.

It was especially during his last days that Ruby and Ossie became important sounding posts for Malcolm as he confided in both of them and seemingly prepared himself for his death. Devoted to Malcolm as a wise and courageous friend, understandably Dee lamented the ordeal that Malcolm experienced in the last months of his life. She claims to have suggested secure hiding places for Malcolm to escape the personal danger he was expecting and was prepared to fund the effort. Apparently, however, Malcolm did not seriously consider the suggestions, or they could not be finalized. Like her husband, who delivered a stirring eulogy of Malcolm, Dee played a prominent role in the funeral service. During the simple service, in a few words she spoke affectionately about her departed friend and read selectively from some of the hundreds of messages of condolences that his family received. In the weeks that followed, she worked with other celebrity friends to raise funds to help secure his family financially.

SELECTED BIBLIOGRAPHY

A. Alexander, 1999; Davis and Dee, 1998; DeCaro, 1996; *Los Angeles "Not Born Yesterday" Citizen*, June 1999; Myers, 1993.

Robert L. Jenkins

DEFECTORS. When Malcolm publicly split from the Nation of Islam (NOI),* a cleavage developed between his followers and Elijah Muhammad.* The NOI had a policy of violently attacking former members who they felt had betrayed them. Beatings and even assassinations were used as a means of intimidation for others who may have contemplated a similar exit. This was just as true of defectors that sided with Malcolm when he decided to form his own organization. Consequently, a number of former Black Muslims* were brutally beaten and in some cases even killed by members of the Fruit of Islam (FOI),* the NOI's paramilitary arm.

Those viciously beaten included Thomas 13X Wallace,* who had quit the Harlem* mosque in 1964 to join Malcolm's new organization. Wallace was the brother of actress Ruby Dee,* who was a good friend of Malcolm's. Leon 4X Ameer,* a former member of the FOI, was brutally beaten by Black Muslims in front of hotel guests in Boston for siding with Malcolm. A policeman who was passing by broke up the one-sided attack. Later that same evening, a second group of Black Muslims attacked Ameer in his hotel room and beat him unconscious, leaving him bloodied in a bathtub. In a separate incident in 1964 in Boston's Roxbury* district, a ghetto area, Aubrey Barnette,* a college graduate and Black Muslim who dared to defect, had his car cut off in heavy traffic. Surrounded by thirteen powerful and well-built Black Muslims, they took turns punching and kicking Barnette, who only stood five feet six inches tall and was slightly built. Bystanders and drivers from other cars came to his aid but not before he suffered a number of internal injuries and bone fractures for which he had to be hospitalized.

After the death of Malcolm, Barnette coauthored a major publication in the *Saturday Evening Post* entitled "The Black Muslims Are a Fraud," which detailed the incident surrounding his beating by the FOI. Benjamin X Brown* left the sect and established a storefront mosque and put Muhammad's picture in the storefront window. When he refused to remove the picture after being ordered to do so by NOI members, he was shot in the chest just above the heart with a shotgun, but, like Ameer, he survived. Hamaas Abdul Khaalis,* a former member of the NOI and close friend of Malcolm's, publicly spoke out against the organization, referring to it as a "fake." Members of his family in Washington, D.C. were killed as a result at his home by NOI followers. A number of other beatings and shootings occurred against former NOI followers by the FOI. In one sense, the FOI had become enforcers of the sect's doctrine rather than protectors of their followers. It is rather ironic that Muhammad's organization taught that whites were the devil, yet almost all of their victims, including Malcolm X, were black.

SELECTED BIBLIOGRAPHY
Evanzz, 1992, 1999; Friedly, 1992; A. Wilson, 1990.

                                                          Mfanya Donald Tryman

DEMOCRATIC PARTY. After more than seventy years of solid support of the party of Lincoln and emancipation, black Americans during the 1930s began an allegiance to the Democratic Party that has lasted past the end of the twentieth century. Their turn to the Democrats occurred as a direct result of the favorable promise of race advancement that began with the administration of Franklin D. Roosevelt. In virtually every election where their votes counted since the Great Depression* era, especially at the national level, the black vote was firmly in the Democratic column. Although black Democrats in New York were not opposed to inviting Malcolm to speak before their party gatherings, they would find no black leader in the early 1960s more stridently opposed to the Democratic Party than Malcolm X. This was particularly true after his break with the Nation of Islam (NOI)* when he became increasingly more politically oriented. It was largely because black voters were so predictable that Malcolm X criticized both the party and blacks who elected their candidates. African Americans, he said, were simply being taken for granted because the Democrats realized how strongly they supported the party. The Democrats made promises to them at election time but never fulfilled them. He held special contempt for prominent Democrats, especially Presidents John F. Kennedy* and Lyndon B. Johnson.* These men wore the Democratic Party label, but they were really Klansmen or Dixiecrats,* Malcolm reasoned, leaders who held the same attitude about black advancement as most white southerners. The party, he would often say, was under the complete control of powerful southern congressmen, who not only shaped party and national policy, particularly civil rights* policy, but who also greatly influenced the presidents. Malcolm's suggestion to African Americans not to sell themselves short by blind allegiance to the Democratic Party was a simple message, one that numerous other black leaders would deliver during both his lifetime and the years that followed his death.

SELECTED BIBLIOGRAPHY

Carson (Gallen, ed.), 1991; Malcolm X (Breitman, ed.), 1965, 1970a; *Militant*, July 13, 1964; *New York Amsterdam News*, June 22, 1963.

Robert L. Jenkins

DERMODY, VINCENT. Vincent Dermody, New York City's assistant district attorney, served as the chief prosecutor in the Malcolm X assassination trial.* Dermody, the son of a New York policeman, was a veteran prosecutor whose legal career spanned more than three decades. In New York's criminal trial circles, no one in the prosecutor's office was regarded as his superior in trying murder cases. Dermody's task involved prosecuting three men, Talmadage Hayer* (also know as Thomas Hagan), Norman 3X Butler,* and Thomas 15X Johnson,* who were indicted for Malcolm's murder. All three of them were Muslims,* though only Butler and Johnson were proved to be members of the Nation of Islam (NOI).* Neither of the three men were personally close to Malcolm, although both Butler and Johnson were well known to Malcolm's security force. A thorough, crafty and tenacious cross-examiner, Dermody found proving a motive against the trio dubious at best. Yet, his case against the men seemed solid and their conviction appeared a foregone conclusion. This was particularly true when it came to Hayer. Numerous witnesses identified him as being in the Audubon Ballroom* audience the evening of Malcolm's murder; he was clearly seen pumping bullets into Malcolm's felled body and after attempting to flee the scene, he was apprehended outside the building after having been shot, ostensibly by one of Malcolm's bodyguards. Hayer subsequently confessed but to no avail tried to exonerate the other two men. Although many questions existed about Dermody's evidence against both Butler and Johnson, a sympathetic trial judge, Charles Marks,* a generally hostile view of Black Muslims* by the jury, and what turned out to be creative presentations against the defendants helped to make the prosecutor's case against the twosome as well. Convinced of their guilt, Dermody felt the life sentences that all three of the defendants received were justified.

SELECTED BIBLIOGRAPHY

Breitman, Porter, and Smith (Miah, ed.), 1976; Friedly, 1992; Goldman, 1979.

Robert L. Jenkins

DETROIT, MICHIGAN. Detroit was one of urban America's most attractive cities for blacks during the first half of the twentieth century. With its numerous automobile factories, it was a veritable magnet for southern black migrants seeking to escape the poverty associated with tenant farming and the often violent racial atmosphere of a white supremacy–dominated region. The city, however, was hardly a mecca of ideal race relations, because occasionally during the twentieth century it, too, convulsed over race conflict growing out of black-white adjustments to changing demographic factors. It was in the black neighborhoods of Detroit that W. D. Fard* began the organization that would be so closely associated with Malcolm; the city would play a crucial role in Malcolm's evolution and growth as a minister in the Nation of Islam (NOI)* and as a national leader.

As a youth during his hipster life, Malcolm had spent some time in the Motor City, and it was this relationship with Detroit generally that earned him the nickname of Detroit Red among some of his street friends and acquaintances. After his release from prison* in the summer of 1952 he relocated to Detroit, where his brother Wilfred Little* lived. Wilfred had helped to convert Malcolm to the NOI while he was incarcerated, and he helped his younger brother find employment at a furniture store that he, Wilfred, supervised. Malcolm also worked temporarily in a wood industry plant and briefly on the assembly line of the Ford Motor Company. But it was on behalf of the NOI and Elijah Muhammad* that Malcolm would throw most of his energy into Detroit. Muhammad, who had communicated frequently with Malcolm while he was in prison, was impressed with Malcolm and encouraged Detroit's temple leader Lemuel Hassan* to give Malcolm an appointment as a student minister. Malcolm worked diligently, carrying Muhammad's message to the streets where his aggressive "fishing"* techniques brought in numerous new members to the NOI. Thereafter, his rise was rapid. Within ten months he had become assistant minister of the temple and shortly thereafter left the city to begin organizing new mosques in other cities. By the summer of 1954, he had risen to the coveted position of minister of the Harlem,* New York, Temple Number Seven* and would soon gain international stature as the national spokesman for the NOI. Periodically, Malcolm would return on official business and speaking engagements to the city that launched him as an international figure. It was in Detroit, for example, where on November 10, 1963, he would give perhaps his most influential speech to date, "Message to the Grass Roots,"* at the Northern Negro Grass Roots Leadership Conference.*

SELECTED BIBLIOGRAPHY

Bontemps and Conroy, 1966; Evanzz, 1992; Marsh, 1984.

Robert L. Jenkins

DIXIECRATS. "Dixiecrats" is a term derived from the 1948 southern Democratic Party* split from the national party over the issue of civil rights.* The party would run unsuccessfully South Carolina governor Strom Thurmond as a presidential candidate against the incumbent, Harry S. Truman. While the party no longer existed on the national level in the 1960s, the resistance to racial and social change that had largely prompted the defection remained unchanged among southern Democrats. Most of the region's congressmen consistently opposed legislation that sought to advance the civil rights of blacks. Malcolm often railed against these southern leaders. He typically referred to members of the Democratic Party as Dixiecrats, including Presidents John F. Kennedy* and Lyndon B. Johnson.* He held in great contempt Senators James Eastland of Mississippi* and especially Georgia's Richard Russell for their strident opposition to civil rights for blacks, but President Johnson was frequently singled out because he was a southerner and, according to Malcolm, under the thumb of Russell. These southern white supremacists, he told his audiences, were dominant in both congressional houses, commanding chairmanships over key committees and the Democratic Party. Consequently, according to Malcolm, black people could never acquire real solutions to their political and economic status in America through the traditional civil rights course.

SELECTED BIBLIOGRAPHY

Goldman, 1979; Malcolm X (Breitman, ed.), 1970a.

Robert L. Jenkins

DRESS CODE. From the time that Malcolm X left prison* in 1955 and became a Muslim* leader, he carried himself in the most dignified manner. Tall, handsome, and almost regale in appearance, his persona was enhanced by an adherence to a dress code that left little doubt that he considered being well groomed central to self-improvement* and self-esteem. In virtually every situation, whether in the temples teaching, making presentations at public rallies, or hosting guests at home or in the popular eateries that he frequented, Malcolm was always impeccably attired. Like most Muslims influenced by Elijah Muhammad's* Nation of Islam (NOI)* doctrines, Malcolm's clothing of choice was normally a dark suit, usually black, blue or gray, worn with a white shirt, though he often deviated from the typical red necktie that Muslims wore. Except for formal occasions or official NOI celebrations, these ties were seldom ever the bow tie so identifiable with his mentor Elijah Muhammad, and other Black Muslim* members. Occasionally a multi-colored sports coat broke his solid jacket-wearing routine, especially after he left the NOI. Captain Joseph X Gravitts,* who headed the security force in Temple Number Seven* and eventually became a bitter Malcolm foe, remembered that Malcolm loved to wear expensive shoes, his style of choice during his youth manufactured by Florsheim, the so-called "ghetto Cadillac" of shoes, and during his later years from the well-known Stacy Adams line. Malcolm wore his clothing well, and even in places such as West Africa, where he usually dressed less formally in apparel like the dashiki, it is easy to see his concern about outward appearance. His well-shined shoes, close-cropped hair style, and brilliant smile complimented his dress.

Understandably, Malcolm's dress as a Muslim was a great departure from the more flashy zoot suit* attire that he wore during his hipster lifestyle on the streets of Roxbury* and Harlem.* But even then his identity with this form of black urban popular culture clothing enhanced his reputation as a "good dresser," an attribute particularly appealing to some women. In Malcom's case, as an adult and a Muslim, clothes hardly made the man, but he obviulsy took great pride in being well dressed and he preached the virtues of this in lectures to his followers as a part of both NOI doctrine and personal commitment.

SELECTED BIBLOGRAPHY

A&E Entertainment, 1995; Angelou, 1986; CBS News, 1992; Davis (Chapnick, ed.); Lincoln, 1994; Lomax, 1963; Malcom X with Haley, 1965; Strickland (Greene, ed.), 1994.

Robert L. Jenkins

DRUGS AND ALCOHOL. During his days as hustler on the streets of Roxbury* and Harlem,* Malcolm X was not only a drug pusher; he was also an abuser of drugs and alcohol. Such behavior was not unusual for persons like Malcolm who spent considerable time in the nightlife establishments of these communities and who consorted with numerous reputable and disreputable personalities who were users and small-time criminals themselves. Malcolm would later say that this was the most degrading and unfulfilled part of his life. As a member of the Nation of Islam (NOI),* Malcolm reformed himself and abstained from any use of alcohol and drugs. It was not just the sect's ban against its members' usage of these substances that inspired his abstinence, however; his own personal experience with the self-deprecating effects of drugs and alchohol played a role in his teaching about the importance of shunning their use. Malcolm "fished" for membership heavily from this downtrodden part of the black ghetto population; and he was good at reaching them because of his own background. Malcolm combined his message of these substances' negative effects on the users with what he considered a commonsense approach. The profits from the purchase of these products, he said, enriched only the white suppliers who were responsible for bringing them into the black community and who sought to keep black people subjugated by their heavy consumption and addiction. After blacks consumed these products, he said, white authorities then invaded their community and arrested them for using them. These people, Malcom would tell his listeners, were the true enemy of African Americans.

Many people overlooked Malcom's proselytzing rhetoric on behalf of the NOI and marveled instead over of the success rate that he achieved in rehabilitating the lives of scores of fallen men and women consumed by these products. Only fear about a posible backlash over the controversy that surrounded Malcolm and the NOI's antiwhite doctrine prevented white officials in New York's social service community from allowing Malcolm to expand his substance in New York's social service community from allowing Malcolm to expand his substance abuse work among those whom their program served.

SELCECTED BIBLIOGRAPHY

Collins with Bailey, 1998; Davies, 1990; Goldman, 1979; Karim with Skutches and Gallen, 1992; Library Distributors of America, 1993; Malcolm X with Haley, 1965.

William A. Person

DU BOIS, DAVID GRAHAM. David Graham Du Bois, the son of Shirley Graham Du Bois* and the stepson of W.E.B. Du Bois,* was a novelist, lecturer, and journalist. For a period during the 1960s, Du Bois lived in Accra, Ghana, with his parents, where his mother was employed as an official in the Ghanaian government and W.E.B. Du Bois was living out his remaining years as a celebrated international scholar and preparing his long-planned, though never finished, *Encyclopedia Africana*. It was while Malcolm was visiting Africa following his Hajj* to Mecca* during the spring of 1964 that he and Du Bois first encountered each other. At the time Du Bois was living in Cairo working as a journalist for the Egyptian News Service and several other international news bureaus. Malcolm had stopped in the Egyptian capital to meet with government officials, and he also spent time with Du Bois. What the two talked about is largely unknown, but Malcolm, as he did with so many others that met him for the first time, apparently left a great impression on Du Bois, who supposedly warned him of the real potential for physical harm once he returned to the United States. In Malcolm's subsequent summer visit to Africa he and Du Bois were together for more extensive discussions. During their meetings, Malcolm often related to him some of his innermost feelings about Islam* and his former mentor Elijah Muhammad.*

After Du Bois himself returned to the United States he took residence in the San Francisco Bay area, long a hotbed of radical protest, and moved increasingly toward a more militant activist stance. He identified with the escalating Black Power* movement during the late 1960s and early 1970s and joined the Black Panther Party for Self-Defense,* serving as one of its spokesmen; in 1972 he became editor in chief of the party's intercommunal news service. As such he expanded and diversified news coverage of the official newspaper *The Black Panther*.

Both the Black Power movement and the Black Panther Party owed much of their existence to Malcolm, whose views about black nationalism* and self-defense,* established the ideological foundations upon which they functioned. It was also during this period that Du Bois wrote his first novel, *And Bid Him Sing*. The book was a historical novel depicting the lives of a Cairo black American expatriate community, unique for the existence of a character in that it closely resembled Malcolm and his life's work. In 2000, Du Bois served on the Black Studies faculty at the University of Massachusetts.

SELECTED BIBLIOGRAPHY

Angelou, 1986; Davenport (Jones, ed.), 1998; DeCaro, 1996, 1998; D. Du Bois, 1975; C. Jones, ed., 1998; Page, comp., 1977.

Robert L. Jenkins

DU BOIS, SHIRLEY GRAHAM. As an accomplished playwright and dramatist, Shirley Graham Du Bois wrote and directed several plays focusing on the black experience and culture such as *Tom Toms, It's Mornin'*, and *Dust to Earth*. Later, she wrote several biographies including one of international actor and civil rights* activist Paul Robeson* and another of her husband, the black intellectual giant W.E.B. Du Bois.* A former American Communist Party* activist, she also was founding editor of *Freedomways*, a major national journal of black literature and culture.

Prior to, during her marriage, and after the death of her husband, she worked with the Pan-African movement, Africa's fight for liberation, and the fight for justice and world peace. Like her husband, she was committed to uplifting people of African ancestry and preserving black history* and culture. In 1963 she participated in the chartering of the Organization of African Unity.*

Apparently Du Bois was much impressed with Malcolm. Well respected by the Ghanaian government, she was part of a small group of black American expatriates who worked with Ghanaian officials in 1963 to give Malcolm a celebrated welcome in the West African country. On the occasion of their first meeting Du Bois and Malcolm stole away in an adjacent room from the main party, where they talked for nearly an hour. When she returned, she indicated that she had become a real Malcolm fan, seeing him as a brilliant man worthy of being her son. She saw many parallels between Malcolm and President Kwame Nkrumah.* Obviously, Malcolm was similarly impressed with her. At the time of Malcolm's visit to Ghana, Du Bois was working as Ghana's Director of Television, and being "family-close" to President Nkrumah, she had a personal pipeline to African authority. Hence, it was Du Bois who arranged Malcolm's personal meeting with the African president, something no other American had been able to accomplish.

Because of her political astuteness and work and commitment for liberation and justice, Malcolm noted Du Bois's unique professional status and observed that she was one of the most intelligent women he had ever met, a woman people of African ancestry should be proud of.

SELECTED BIBLIOGRAPHY

Angelou, 1986; DeCaro, 1996; S. Du Bois, 1971; Malcolm X (Perry, ed.), 1989; Perkins, 1985; B. Perry, 1991.

LaVerne Gyant

DU BOIS, W.E.B. Arguably, W.E.B. Du Bois was twentieth-century America's greatest black intellectual. Born in Great Barrington, Massachusetts, shortly after the end of slavery, Du Bois lived a rather privileged life. He was educated at Fisk University, studied in Germany, and earned a doctorate degree at prestigious Harvard University.* By education and training, he was a historian, but he made his greatest scholarly contributions in sociology. He taught for thirteen years at Atlanta University, where he influenced its status as one of the nation's foremost black colleges. His philosophical differences with black educator Booker T. Washington in the early twentieth century over the proper course for black progress helped endear him to many African Americans. It was his lifetime of activism in the cause of black uplift, however, that solidified his stature in American history. Despite his own background, Du Bois understood the plight of America's black oppressed and worked to change their conditions. He began a formal and systematic effort in this respect in 1905 with the establishment of the Niagara Movement. This civil rights* initiative, however, soon gave way to the more successful and enduring National Association for the Advancement of Colored People (NAACP),* which Du Bois also helped to found. From 1910 to 1934 he served as the editor of the organization's official organ, the *Crisis*.

Although Du Bois supported the racial integration goals of the NAACP, he was also a promoter of black nationalist ideals advocating black unity and advising blacks to play a more decisive role in leading and shaping their own communities. An advocate of Pan-Africanism,* he helped to organize five Pan-African gatherings between 1919 and 1945. His dissatisfaction with America and the negative effects of its political and capitalistic system on blacks influenced him to join both the Socialist and Communist Parties. The greatest display of his disillusionment, however, would occur in 1960 when at age ninety-two

W.E.B. Du Bois was arguably the twentieth
century's greatest black intellectual. Library
of Congress.

he emigrated to the Republic of Ghana,* where he hoped to write his long-anticipated *Encyclopedia Africana*.

Du Bois died in 1963, the year before Malcolm X made his life-changing visit to Ghana and several other African countries. Like most knowledgeable leaders, however, he was certainly aware of Du Bois and his position on some of the same ideas that he also championed. Malcolm was an avid reader, and in his effort to educate himself by studying the works of the great scholars of history, philosophy and culture, he did not avoid reading Du Bois, who was a prolific author. Indeed, Malcolm may have been influenced by Du Bois's thought more than many have acknowledged, for it was Du Bois who, in 1947, first announced a plan to take the plight of black Americans to the United Nations* as an example of human rights* violations. In most of Malcolm's life as a black leader, he certainly sought to emphasize to the world the reality of Du Bois's prophetic 1903 comment that the greatest issue the twentieth century would confront would be "the problem of color line." During Malcolm's stay in Accra, he met extensively with Du Bois's widow, novelist Shirley Graham

Du Bois,* serving at the time as a civil servant in the Ghanaian government, and told her how much he had admired her husband and his work. Du Bois's wife was impressed with Malcolm and he with her, but given Malcolm's life of opposition to racial integration* and activist politics before the full impact of his Hajj,* and the later modification of his views about participatory democracy, it is not unlikely that his favorable comment about Du Bois was primarily an act of courtesy.

Supposedly, Ghanaian President Kwame Nkrumah* wanted to help Malcolm through his life-threatening ordeal by inviting him to live permanently in Ghana as a government employee and complete Du Bois's work on the encyclopedia. Malcolm was flattered by the invitation but declined it, determined to continue the fight on behalf of black human rights* in the United States.

SELECTED BIBLIOGRAPHY

Angelou, 1986; Blackside/PBS, 1994; Broderick, 1959; Cruse, 1967; W.E.B. Du Bois, 1903; Evanzz, 1992; Lewis, 1993, 2000; Marable, 1986.

Robert L. Jenkins

E

EAST ELMHURST. East Elmhurst is an area of Queens, a borough of New York City. After January 1958, Malcolm had moved to this area with his family to a small home owned by the Nation of Islam (NOI).* Controversy arose over the ownership of the home after the split between Malcolm and the NOI in late 1963. Not long before his assassination in New York, the NOI had tried to have him evicted from this residence.

One week before his actual assassination, on February 14, 1965, Malcolm's home in East Elmhurst was firebombed during the night, before Malcolm rushed his three small children and pregnant wife out into a cold, wintry night. However, after police and fire department officials rushed to the scene and put the fire out, the police accused Malcolm of starting the fire himself. One official had noticed a whiskey bottle of gasoline that was still sitting on the dresser in the children's bedroom in the house and inferred that Malcolm must have intended to use this gasoline as well in starting the fire, since he was inside at the time that the fire had started. While the police, fire officials, and the NOI pointed the finger at Malcolm, there were other rumors that the police, the Federal Bureau of Investigation,* or the NOI was responsible for the firebombing. However, none of this was ever proven.

SELECTED BIBLIOGRAPHY

Gallen, ed., 1992; Haley (Fisher, ed.), 1993; Strickland (Greene, ed.), 1994.

Mfanya Donald Tryman

EBONY MAGAZINE. *Ebony* magazine is America's oldest African American–oriented news and variety entertainment monthly. Established in 1945 by John H. Johnson in Chicago, Illinois,* the monthly magazine became an immediate hit and helped to spin off other successful publishing ventures by Johnson's publishing company, including the weekly variety magazine *Jet*, which first

Malcolm's modest home in East Elmhurst, New York. Library of Congress.

appeared in 1951. Johnson had already established himself as a rising publishing entrepreneur when he launched his first print news venture, the *Negro Digest* in 1942, later renamed the *Black World.*

By the 1960s, with their wide range of coverage of black personalities in virtually every walk of life, at home and abroad, and articles dealing with black history* and current affairs, both *Ebony* and *Jet* were read in nearly a million black American homes. One of America's most provocative and controversial personalities, Malcolm X, already a source of considerable interest in virtually every media type, was frequently featured in *Ebony, Jet*, and *Negro Digest* articles, both during his life and in death. These articles, especially in *Ebony* and *Jet*, were typically complemented by a wide assortment of photographs depicting Malcolm in the various settings associated with his life, work, and death. In one of the most informative and interesting of these full-length *Ebony* articles, the magazine's managing editor, Hans Massaquoi, sought to uncover the "mystery" of Malcolm and reveal to the black reading public exactly who this man was behind his public persona.

Black America wanted to know about Malcolm, and magazines such as *Ebony* clearly helped to give it more than a capsule view of the leader. Moreover, being interviewed by journalists like Massaquoi and featured in African American magazines like *Ebony* conformed to Malcolm's willingness and determination to have his message disseminated to a wider audience than his Muslim* ministry allowed. But the greater exposure most certainly led to an escalation of his problems with internal jealousy within the leadership hierarchy of the Nation of Islam (NOI).* Published in the city where the NOI's national office was located and where the organization and its leader were frequently items of news, it was natural for Johnson's publications to cover the rift that prompted Malcolm's departure from the Black Muslims.* Perplexing, however, given Malcolm's bold message and how he sought to sensitize the world community to the plight of Black America, is the fact that in November 1995, *Ebony*'s fiftieth anniversary edition chose not to include Malcolm X as one of the "pioneers and pathfinders" who "helped create a new racial world." (A picture of Malcolm, however, did make the top fifty photo list.) Ironically, Malcolm's widow, Betty Shabazz,* and Malcolm's protégée and successor to Elijah Muhammad* as head of the NOI, Louis Farrakhan* are among these "fifty-three" history makers.

SELECTED BIBLIOGRAPHY

Adams, 1965; Banks, 1996; *Ebony*, November 1965, November 1995; Hornsby, 1993; *Jet*, May 2, 1976; Johnson, 1993; Massaquoi, 1964; Morrison, 1965; Ploski and Kaiser, eds., 1971; Senna, 1994; Wolseley, 1990.

Robert L. Jenkins

EDELMAN, MARIAN WRIGHT. A graduate of Atlanta's Spelman College and Yale University Law School, Marian Wright Edelman is best known as a civil rights* activist and children's advocate. The first black woman admitted to the Mississippi* Bar during the mid-1960s, she honed her law and administrative skills as director of the National Association for the Advancement of Colored People* Legal Defense and Educational Fund office in Jackson, Mississippi, the state's largest city and central in the period's civil rights struggle. Later, her work took her to Washington, D.C. as the legal counsel to Martin Luther King, Jr.,* who headed the poor people's campaign. It was her interest in children's issues, however, that garnered Edelman national notoriety. In 1973 she founded the Children's Defense Fund, organized to secure funding and to coordinate national activities in support of poor children. Compassionate and indefatigable in her advocacy, Wright remains in the new millennium perhaps the nation's most visible and respected champion for underprivileged causes for children.

Wright's path briefly crossed Malcolm X's, and she was greatly impressed with him. It was while she was in law school that she first encountered Malcolm. Prior to the speech that he delivered on Yale's campus, Malcolm made a special effort to meet Wright personally, who was part of the night's audience. Wright was baffled over how Malcolm knew so much about her before their formal introduction and why he deliberately sought her out. She was, nevertheless, impressed with Malcolm from both the long conversation the two held and the

Children's rights advocate Marian Wright Edelman met Malcolm while she was attending law school. Willie J. Miller Papers, Special Collections Department, Mitchell Memorial Library, Mississippi State University.

"mesmerizing" and "brilliant" speech that he delivered. She marveled over how Malcolm seemed to speak in the voice that expressed the rage of so many young black intellectuals and budding scholars frustrated over the slow pace of black progress. There is no indication that the two significantly crossed paths again, but apparently she followed Malcolm's career long after his Yale appearance. Typical of many who came to regard Malcolm with special reverence, Wright later expressed appreciation for the role that he played in the black rights movement, his audacity, and especially his ability to articulate an alternative view to that of traditional civil rights leaders like Martin Luther King, Jr.

SELECTED BIBLIOGRAPHY

A. Alexander, 1999; Hampton and Fayer with Flynn, 1991; Siegel, 1995.

Robert L. Jenkins

EDMUND PETTUS BRIDGE. On February 4, 1965, at the invitation of the Student Non-Violent Coordinating Committee (SNCC),* Malcolm X spoke at Brown's Chapel A.M.E. Church in Selma, Alabama. Martin Luther King, Jr.,* was in jail at the time of this visit. King's associates felt that Malcolm could possibly instigate the people of Selma to the point that King might lose control of the Selma campaign. It was Malcolm's intention to visit King in jail, but he did not get an opportunity to do so. He sent a message to King, via Mrs. Coretta Scott King,* who had quickly been ushered into the church in an effort to diffuse Malcolm, thinking that he had come to Selma to make King's task difficult. In fact, he came thinking that he could make King's life easier. He stated that white people might be more willing to hear King if they realized that he (Malcolm) was the alternative.

King was attempting to direct the Selma movement from his jail cell. Part of this movement called for a march to the state capital of Montgomery. Marchers would leave Brown's Chapel and walk down Highway 80 (Jefferson Davis Highway), which connected Selma to Montgomery. They would have to cross the Edmund Pettus Bridge. The march had been banned by state and local officials; however, march leaders directed the marchers to proceed with the demonstration.

The march was led by Southern Christian Leadership Conference (SCLC)* officials and King associate Hosea Williams and SNCC's John Lewis.* Once the marchers crossed the bridge, they were confronted by the Alabama Highway Patrol. After issuing a warning to the marchers to turn back and disperse, the troopers charged the crowd, physically attacking the unarmed, peaceful, and nonviolent marchers. Bloodied and tear-gassed, the marchers retreated to Brown's Chapel.

After King halted a second march, many of the more vocal and militant marchers were angry that they were not allowed to continue. James Forman* and other members of SNCC, the group that invited Malcolm X to Selma, withdrew their support from the march.

After days of indecision with the courts, Congress, and the president, and after the death of a clergyman, another march was finally given approval by a federal judge. The march took place more than six weeks after Malcolm X came to Selma to show white people the alternative to Martin Luther King and exactly one month after Malcolm's assassination in New York.

SELECTED BIBLIOGRAPHY

Cone, 1991; Malcolm X (Breitman, ed.), 1970a; J. Williams, 1987.

Mamie Locke

EGYPT. Perhaps no nonblack nation impressed Malcolm X more than did the Middle East* country of Egypt. A student of world history, he knew much about Egypt's contributions to human history, and he marveled over the ancient Egyptians' ability as artisans and builders. In his visits to New York museums of natural history, where he often took school-aged children on tours, he emphasized the wonders of Egypt and talked about the role of black people in the development of Egyptian civilization. In 1959 Malcolm made his first trip to the Middle East, going as the special emissary of Nation of Islam* leader Elijah Muhammad.* During the trip he visited Egypt where he conferred at length with the Egyptian Vice President Muhammad Anwar Al-Sadat.* In the year before his death, during his extended visits to African and Middle Eastern nations, he again visited Egypt, spending time in Cairo, where he gave newspaper interviews, talked to local personalities, and took extensive pictures—still and moving—with the Great Pyramids in the background.

Malcolm strongly supported the position of the nonaligned nations of color and was convinced of their potential to resist the continued exploitation of Western colonial powers. Hence, he was conscious of Egypt's political position in the Middle Eastern world as a real force in the Third World. Much of this support was the result of his respect and fascination with Egypt's President Gamel Nasser.* Indeed, Malcolm thought so highly of Nasser that he named one of his daughters after the Egyptian. Malcolm regarded Nasser as the most important leader in the Middle East, and he was greatly impressed by Nasser's independence and refusal to allow Egypt to be a vassalage state of powerful nations like the United States. He often spoke glowingly, telling the story through lectures and moving pictures to his Organization of Afro-American Unity* audiences about Egypt's political stability and the military might that Egypt under Nasser's leadership had amassed. As occurred in other Muslim* countries where Malcolm traveled, Egypt seemed receptive to Malcolm's visits and recognized his increasing stature as a spokesman for oppressed people throughout the international world.

SELECTED BIBLIOGRAPHY

Collins with Bailey, 1998; DeCaro, 1996; Evanzz, 1992; Malcolm X (Breitman, ed.), 1970a; T'Shaka, 1983.

Robert L. Jenkins

EISENHOWER, DWIGHT DAVID. Dwight David Eisenhower was the thirty-fourth president of the United States and was elected in 1952, taking office in January 1953. A Republican, he served two presidential terms. When he took office, he moved to racially integrate certain facilities and workplaces located in the capital, Washington, D.C. But he was not an exponent of desegregation and had to be pushed to complete the racial integration* of the armed forces, which had started under President Harry S. Truman, a Democrat. Ike, as he was affectionately referred to by his friends, felt that gradual and incremental gains by African Americans would eventually bring about racial integration. But he felt that the government should have a laissez-faire approach to what was considered a sensitive subject at the time, particularly with southerners, who both parties were attempting to woo politically to their own advantage. He did support the right to vote for African Americans, reasoning that such advocacy would open up other doors for blacks once they acquired the ballot.

When Ike took office, he soon thereafter nominated Earl Warren, a Republican and ex-governor of the state of California, for the position of Chief Justice of the U.S. Supreme Court. Later, he regretted his selection and lamented that it was the worst decision that he ever made, for Warren turned out to be liberal and heavily influenced the 1954 *Brown v. Board of Education** Supreme Court decision, which ushered in the era of public school desegregation.

In 1957, the actions of Eisenhower and Governor Orval Faubus of Arkansas grabbed the attention of Malcolm X. Based upon the *Brown* decision, the Little Rock School Board initiated a racial desegregation plan in which nine African Americans were to integrate Central High School. Faubus resisted. Eisenhower invited him to the White House, and they supposedly struck a "gentleman's agreement" in which Faubus would not further obstruct racial integration. But he did, and Eisenhower had to order, against his own philosophy, school integration, with the federal government mobilizing the army against a white lynch mob.

Malcolm maintained that the whole scenario was a travesty enacted by two conservative white politicians to mollify their respective constituencies. He stated that the two politicos gave the appearance of being public enemies but were private friends and that Ike was really sympathetic toward racist southern attitudes.

In point of fact, Eisenhower had taken the unusual step, according to Chief Justice Earl Warren, of lobbying him at a White House function prior to the Court's 1954 *Brown* decision to rule against racial school integration. According to Warren, Eisenhower purportedly stated that white southerners were not bad people; they just did not want their sweet little girls sitting beside some overgrown Negroes. Malcolm argued that the only difference between southern whites and northern whites like Eisenhower was that southerners were more like a wolf, whereas northern whites were more sophisticated with their racism and wily like a fox.

SELECTED BIBLIOGRAPHY

R. Burk, 1984; Carson (Gallen, ed.), 1991; Cross, 1984; Strickland (Greene, ed.), 1994.

Mfanya Donald Tryman

ELECTRONIC MEDIA. Malcolm X is not typically regarded as having been a publicity seeker. Yet few black leaders during the early 1960s were in the public eye more than Malcolm. A controversial figure with a controversial message during a period when the nonviolent civil rights movement* made black Americans internationally newsworthy, Malcolm was also a natural and logical object of the press. While certainly attractive to the print media, Malcolm was equally alluring to the electronics media. On television and radio, his charisma and quick logical mind, combined with a machine gunlike cadence and assertive delivery, gave him an appeal unmatched by anyone except, perhaps, Martin Luther King, Jr.,* when he spoke movingly before large audiences. Whether in Los Angeles, Detroit,* Chicago,* New York, or the national capital, Malcolm

Malcolm attracting the attention of the news
media. Library of Congress.

said things that both alarmed and angered white America, and it often came
across with an effect that could not be as passionately or sensationally captured
by the print press. Almost weekly, especially following his break with the Nation
of Islam (NOI),* he could be found on some aspect of the electronics media,
especially radio, articulating basically the same message: indicting white America for its oppressive treatment of blacks, criticizing the recognized black leadership for their lack of vision, or appealing to his race to seek its own liberation,
regardless of the price to be paid. He could be at his best when on panels, using
his logic to win debates against prominent blacks like Louis Lomax* and James
Farmer* or frustrate through deductive logic and compelling analysis personalities like Joe Pyne,* a notable anti-Malcolm and incendiary television host of
a popular Los Angeles local television talk show.

    While occasionally hosts like Pyne and his audiences sought to antagonize
Malcolm, he always seemed unflappable. Typically, however, when Malcolm
appeared on television or was interviewed on popular local radio shows, he was
treated with great respect, though he was normally asked some of the most
challenging questions. Malcolm understood the power of communications and,

having mastered the art of the spoken word in prison,* utilized his skill brilliantly and eloquently as national emissary for the NOI and self-appointed interpreter for the black-urban alienated. Though the audiences might have been local, these broadcasts, nevertheless, reflected the mass appeal that Malcolm had, and they were important in helping him remain to many the viable alternative voice to the traditional black leadership of the era.

SELECTED BIBLIOGRAPHY

Baldwin, 1963; Carson (Gallen, ed.), 1991; Farmer, 1985; Gallen, ed., 1992; Horne, 1995; Karim with Skutches and Gallen, 1992; Lomax, 1963; Malcolm X with Haley, 1965; Wilkins with Matthews, 1982.

Robert L. Jenkins

ELLINGTON, DUKE. Malcolm Little, as he was known before his Islamic conversion,* was first exposed to the Negro big band sound of blacks in 1940 during a visit with Ella Collins,* his half sister, who lived in Boston. Although introduced to Ella's proud family tradition of middle-class values, the young Malcolm at age fifteen was more impressed with Boston's bright lights, expensive cars, and nightclubs. On a later visit he moved in with Ella and became best friends with "Shorty,"* who frequented Boston's nightlife. Among other things, Shorty was an amateur alto saxophone player. His idol was Johnny Hodges, the talented alto sax player in Duke Ellington's band. Shorty got Malcolm a job as a shoeshine boy at the Roseland State Ballroom,* a popular nightclub for African Americans in Boston. African American bands playing there included those of Ellington, Count Basie,* Lionel Hampton,* Cootie Williams, and Jimmie Lunceford. Because of Malcolm's artistry at dancing the "Lindy Hop,"* one of the era's most popular dances among blacks, many of these band leaders, including Ellington, knew him on a first-name basis.

America became involved in World War II* when Malcolm was seventeen. During one period he worked for the railroad and traveled the Yankee Clipper from Boston to New York.* In New York, he became a part of the African American cultural experience that was Harlem.* In the world's view, Harlem had a reputation as being America's Casbah. Malcolm left the railroad and began working as a waiter at the famous Harlem nightclub Small's Paradise,* which drew large crowds when bands like Ellington's played.

Musicians like Ellington were on the cutting edge of new musical interpretations in Harlem. He opened up for the Cotton Club in 1926 and played there for five years. Musicians of both races met at after-hours spots to "jam" late into the next day. The music, the environment, and the culture of the era were significant influences on what became Malcolm's Harlem hustle.

SELECTED BIBLIOGRAPHY

Goldman, 1979; Malcolm X (Breitman, ed.), 1970a; Malcolm X with Haley, 1965; Parks (Clarke, ed.), 1990; Wolfenstein, 1993.

Otha Burton

EPPS, ARCHIE. Archie Epps edited the three major speeches that Malcolm delivered at Harvard University* from March 1961 to December 1964 that resulted in the book entitled *Malcolm X: Speeches at Harvard.* These programs had different formats and moderators. In at least two programs, there was a question-and-answer format, and the third program included three Harvard professors who reacted as respondents to Malcolm's address. During the question-and-answer period, virtually all of the questions were addressed to Malcolm X. The speeches are actually the second part of the book. The first part of the book examines Malcolm's early life, his speaking style, and his philosophical and religious growth over the years.

Epps first met Malcolm when he visited Boston in the early 1960s, and they had lunch together. Epps recalls that Malcolm chided him for putting cream in his coffee, "integrating" the beverage and making it weaker. Epps was impressed with Malcolm and remembers that Malcolm warned him about becoming a "professional Negro." After their initial meeting, Epps met Malcolm on a number of other occasions when he came to Boston, and he attended Malcolm's first speech at Harvard in 1961. Epps was moved to write about Malcolm in part because he felt that Malcolm was misunderstood but also because the black intellectual movement for liberation that Malcolm advocated was just catching up with the man who boldly and unabashedly advocated it. While Epps did not agree with all that Malcolm said, he had a great deal of respect for him. Epps was the Boston coordinator for the 1963 March on Washington,* which Malcolm ridiculed, and was one of the founders of the *Harvard Journal of Negro Affairs.*

SELECTED BIBLIOGRAPHY

Malcolm X (Epps, ed.), 1991; Sollors, Titcomb, and Underwood, eds., 1993.

Mfanya Donald Tryman

ESKRIDGE, CHAUNCEY. Chauncey Eskridge was a graduate of Tuskegee Institute and John Marshall Law School in Chicago, Illinois.* A prominent civil rights* activist, Eskridge was also a law partner with William R. Ming* in Chicago. The partnership often represented legal matters pertaining to the Nation of Islam (NOI)* in court and particularly tax matters. In addition to being an attorney, Eskridge was an accountant and former Internal Revenue Service agent. Eskridge also represented Elijah Muhammad's* son Wallace Muhammad* when he was convicted for draft evasion and ended up going to prison* rather than fight in the Vietnam conflict.* When Elijah Muhammad heard of an attempt to set up a meeting between Malcolm X and Martin Luther King, Jr.,* with regard to Malcolm's human rights* petition to the United Nations,* he instructed Eskridge to set up a meeting between himself and King in order to minimize the potential of a King-Malcolm alliance. Eskridge was able to set up a long-distance telephone conversation between King and Muhammad. Muhammad was interested in having King attend and sit as guest on the dais with him at the annual Savior's Day Convention* in Chicago in 1965 and instructed Eskridge to arrange this with King. While Eskridge made every attempt to get King to attend the convention, he was not successful in doing so. Because of their busy and conflicting schedules, neither did King and Malcolm ever meet again, their only encounter their chance greeting in Washington, D.C. in 1964 when the Civil Rights Act* was being debated.

Eskridge was a friend of Malcolm's as well as Muhammad Ali* and, along with Eleanor Holmes Norton, represented Ali in his appeal of his conviction of draft evasion for refusing to join the U.S. Army in 1967. Eskridge was associated with perhaps the two most dynamic leaders of the twentieth century in King and Malcolm, as well as one of the greatest heavyweight boxing champions.

SELECTED BIBLIOGRAPHY

Branch, 1988; Evanzz, 1992, 1999.

Mfanya Donald Tryman and Charles Holmes

ESSIEN-UDOM, E. U. E. U. Essien-Udom wrote a firsthand account of the Nation of Islam (NOI)* and black nationalism* and published *Black Nationalism: A Search for an Identity in America*, based upon his research. Along with C. Eric Lincoln's* book *The Black Muslims in America*,* it is one of the two scholarly works initially produced by black academicians on the NOI in the 1960s. The focus is primarily on Malcolm X as the "mover and shaker" in the organization and his role and identity in the NOI.

Essien-Udom had been a Nigerian scholar and doctoral student at the University of Chicago in the 1950s and had spent a decade in the United States before producing this race-oriented work on the Black Muslims.* Because of his strategic location in Chicago,* it was relatively easy for him to gather organizational paraphernalia and related information associated with the Black Muslims in Chicago. He obtained newspaper articles and interviewed followers of Elijah Muhammad,* getting firsthand information on the structure and functions of the organization. Essien-Udom also attended a number of NOI meetings and services, using the observational method to obtain material for his book. He pointed out that the NOI experienced phenomenal growth under the leadership of Malcolm, even during a period of adversity when the Federal Bureau of Investigation* conducted a national negative media blitz. Nevertheless, the NOI went from only fifteen mosques in the early 1950s to fifty mosques in twenty-two states and the District of Columbia in 1959. While the work is an objective account of the NOI, pointing out strengths and weaknesses, it still came under attack by Elijah Muhammad. Muhammad publicly critiqued Essien-Udom's book, arguing that he really did not understand the organization or how it functioned.

Essien-Udom argued that near the end of his life Malcolm was expanding and internationalizing the struggle for independence and linking such indepen-

dence for African Americans with liberation struggles in the Third World involving people of color. As such, Essien-Udom also focused on Malcolm's
transformation from the national spokesman for the NOI to an international
spokesman for people in the Third World, in which Malcolm used the phrase
black revolution in this context.

SELECTED BIBLIOGRAPHY

Essien-Udom, 1962; E.U. and R. Essien-Udom (Clarke, ed.), 1990; Lincoln, 1973; Muhammad, 1994.

Mfanya Donald Tryman

EUROPE. Malcolm spent almost five months of the last year of his life in
Africa and Europe. Theology scholar Michael Eric Dyson suggests that Malcolm's contact with black and "white" African revolutionaries induced him to
revise his worldviews. But Malcolm's contact with European audiences in Paris
in 1964, and particularly in London in 1965, probably also caused him to re-
define some of his views on whites. In Europe, Malcolm confronted racial issues,
ranging from anti-Muslim prejudice in France to anti-immigration laws in Britain. At the time of Malcolm's visit, racist election campaigns toward blacks
were common.

Lebert Bethune, an American black living in Paris, recounts how a small
group of black American students in Paris arranged Malcolm's address at the
Salle de la Mutualite in Paris on November 28, 1964. When Paris's African
American students organized another meeting with Malcolm on February 9,
1965, the French authorities forced him to return to London on the grounds that
he was a danger to public order. Given President de Gaulle's anti-Americanism
and independence, it seems unlikely that American authorities influenced the
French decision. Instead, the students published a telephone interview with Malcolm in a small socialist journal, entitled the *Militant*.* Malcolm, however, presented more speeches and interviews in Britain than he did in France. At the
University of Oxford on December 3, 1964, he debated whether extremism in
the defense of liberty was a vice. In early February 1965, Malcolm was back
in Britain to address student audiences in London and Birmingham and to visit
racially troubled Smethwick.

During his London and Paris visits, Malcolm emphasized that he was neither
a racist nor a segregationist. He informed the *Times* of London that politically
mature students in Britain would play a key role in future change. In a telephone
interview with black students in Paris in February 1965, he suggested that "well
meaning Whites" were welcome in his movement and that violence was to be
used only in self-defense.* At Oxford University he maintained that more whites
would actually be attracted by an uncompromising position. While visiting
Smethwick, he compared the treatment of blacks in the city with Hitler's* treatment of Jews.* And he made it clear that he personally would not wait for
"fascists" in Smethwick to construct gas ovens. But Malcolm's appeal to some

whites did not change his nationalist orientation. He told a London audience that he wanted worldwide black unity similar to what he thought Europeans had created for themselves with the European Common Market. He characterized blacks, particularly West Indians, who aped the English as Uncle Toms,* and he suggested that "Toms" in mixed marriages needed psychoanalysis.

In Europe Malcolm still pictured Martin Luther King, Jr.,* as either a failure or, worse, a betrayer of the black cause. Even though the *London Times* cited his statement of February 4, 1965, that the whites of Selma, Alabama, better accept King's demands, the paper also noted that Malcolm thought King would eventually have to abandon his nonviolent approach. Moreover, in an interview in *Flamingo*, a monthly devoted to London blacks, he scolded King for betraying the cause. His most negative European assessment of King occurred on February 12, 1965, in an interview with the Johannesburg *Sunday Express*, when he concluded that the Nobel Peace Prize winner Chief Albert Lithuli was "a King clone" bent on keeping blacks oppressed.

Malcolm attracted the attention of some European journalists as early as 1964. But most serious assessments of his views were published only after his death. Understandably, the English press devoted more coverage to his speeches than any other European press. Still, the *Times* of London completely ignored Malcolm's visits to Paris and Oxford in late 1964, though the French radio, according to Bethune, announced Malcolm's visit to Paris, who they labeled as one who hated white men. It was in February 1965 that the *Times* sent a special correspondent to interview Malcolm, who was visiting Smethwick. The journalist concluded that Malcolm's activities would not support the racial immigrants and whites in Britain. Moreover, the mayor of Smethwick protested British radio's alleged attempt to turn Smethwick into a Birmingham, Alabama,* and the West Indian student leader of Birmingham, Cedric Taylor, denounced Malcolm's references to gas ovens. After Malcolm returned to the United States, Peter Griffiths attempted to have him barred from future visits to Britain. And several letters from readers published in the journal *New Statesmen* condemned Malcolm for his attacks on King and his attempts to compare blacks' conditions in Britain with those in Alabama.

Two positive accounts of Malcolm's views, which were actually completed before he broke with the Nation of Islam (NOI)* but not published until after his death, appeared in a Parisian and a German journal, respectively. The French journalist Guy Croussy, who visited New York, described how Elijah Muhammad's* lieutenant Malcolm was organizing blacks in Harlem.* He reviewed Malcolm's constructive plans for neighborhood reforms, ranging from improvements in schools and hospitals, but he admitted that most were still in the planning stage. The German journalist Morroe Berger also traveled to the United States in 1964 and interviewed both Muhammad and Malcolm. He offered an intelligent and sympathetic review of the role of Islam* among American blacks, even though he did summarize Elijah's racist views. He described Malcolm as Muhammad's "younger spokesman," and he portrayed him in a positive, nonracist light. He claimed that Malcolm told him that many white stereotypes about Negroes, including their proneness to lethargy, were true.

Immediately after Malcolm's murder the *London Times* described him as "one who was vigorous, tenacious, well-spoken, and competitive." The weekly *Economist*, which had ignored Malcolm's visits to London, argued that his extremism and his call to violence, which appealed to young militant black intellectuals and "Negro criminals," had made him potentially dangerous. But the journal also suggested that orthodox black leaders would soon miss Malcolm because he, unlike civil rights* leaders, was a true revolutionary, not merely a reformer. A more positive assessment appeared in the English journal *New Statesman* by John Morgan, who noted that in London, Malcolm appeared to depart from his usual views by rejecting racial separatism and unprovoked violence. Morgan concluded that Malcolm seemed to be moving closer to King, forming a potentially "formidable force." Another positive account by Murray Kempton, a native southerner writing for the English journal *Spectator*, suggested that Malcolm wanted to trust whites. In fact, according to Kempton, Malcolm had confided to him that genuine white southerners learned about improving race relations. "When you find a white man who is any good at all," Malcolm reportedly said, "you can bet he's a Southerner who has learned something." Three years after Malcolm's death, radical European university students launched a vigorous and often violent attack on the establishment, racism, and remnants of imperialism that would have fulfilled Malcolm's hope in "good-willed whites."

SELECTED BIBLIOGRAPHY

Berger, March 1965, April 1965; Bethune (Clarke, ed.), 1990; Croussy, 1965; *Economist*, February 27, 1965; Kempton, 1965, *London Times*, February 12, 1965, February 26, 1965; Malcolm X (Clark, ed.), 1992; *New Statesman*, February 26, 1965, March 5, 1965.

Johnpeter Horst Grill

EVERS, MEDGAR WYLIE. Medgar Evers was born and reared in Mississippi,* perhaps the South's* most segregated state. Following participation in World War II* and graduation from Alcorn A & M College, he worked as an insurance salesperson. The job enabled him to see firsthand the squalor and misery of black life in his home state, especially the impoverished Delta region. It also enabled him to sell National Association for the Advancement of Colored People (NAACP)* memberships. In 1954 he became the first NAACP field secretary in the state, a job that primarily involved investigating and publicizing injustices. It was a dangerous job since the mere mentioning of the NAACP could get one killed. Working primarily as a loner, Evers opposed the nonviolence philosophy* of Martin Luther King, Jr.,* and the Student Non-Violent Coordinating Committee,* which were organizing in the state. He felt their activities drew unnecessary attention that would result in violence. His activism was most notable in Jackson, where he led a campaign to desegregate public facilities and voter registration. In June 1963, Evers was assassinated, the first ranking civil rights* leader to be murdered. In death, however, he became a national martyr of the civil rights movement.*

Malcolm did not personally know Evers, but he was certainly aware of his work in Mississippi. Although Malcolm longed to tell the "blunt truth" about Evers's death, as a Black Muslim* he was unable officially to say anything while a member of the Nation of Islam.* Occasionally, he privately commented on Evers's senseless death and the climate of white hate pervading the country. One night in heated comments on a program of the Militant Labor Forum,* he raised Evers's name as an example of the suffering blacks endured in the United States. As it had been with his father, he once said it was clearly white racism that killed Medgar.

SELECTED BIBLIOGRAPHY

Evers with Peters, 1967; Lowery and Marszalek, eds., 1992; Malcolm X (Breitman, ed.), 1970a; Malcolm X with Haley, 1965; Rossiter, 1994.

Lawrence H. Williams

EVERS-WILLIAMS, MYRLIE. Myrlie Evers-Williams never knew Malcolm personally, but in a notable way she was vitally associated with a spirit kindred to Malcolm's and his family. Evers-Williams is one of several women from the 1960s whose life was dramatically changed by the assassination of her spouse. She was formerly the wife of Mississippi* civil rights* leader Medgar Evers,* who was murdered in the driveway of his Jackson home in 1962 by avowed white supremacist Byron de la Beckwith. In the years that followed Evers's death, Malcolm, who was most critical of the extent of white violence against blacks in Mississippi, frequently referred to Medgar's murder as an example of the general climate of racial hatred that permeated the nation. In some ways Ever-Williams's experience paralleled that of Malcolm X's wife Betty Shabazz* and her family. Both, of course, were married to nationally known activists, and like Betty, Myrlie was pregnant with a child that her spouse would never see. She and her children, too, witnessed the death of her husband and their father, seeing him lie lifeless in his own pool of blood. Further, controversy would follow in Medgar's death regarding the guilt of the man charged for the murder, as it swirled similarly around those accused in Malcolm's death. Justice would not be meted out to de la Beckwith until more than thirty years later. After Malcolm's murder, Myrlie and Betty became close friends, bonded together out of a shared experience. Like Malcolm's widow, who would earn a doctorate degree and find employment, ironically, at New York's Medgar Evers College, Myrlie also would gain national stature as chairwoman of the National Association for the Advancement of Colored People.* Hence, as it was with Betty, and later Coretta Scott King,* widow of the slain symbol of the modern civil rights movement* Martin Luther King, Jr.,* Myrlie would also work to further her husband's causes.

Myrlie Evers-Williams (left) dedicating Medgar Evers Boulevard in Jackson, Mississippi in 1964, in honor of her slain former husband. Willie J. Miller Papers, Special Collections Department, Mitchell Memorial Library, Mississippi State University.

Malcolm's home after a fire bombing, supposedly by members of the Nation of Islam after his rupture with the group. He was eventually evicted from the house. Library of Congress.

SELECTED BIBLIOGRAPHY

A. Alexander, 1999; Dittmer, 1994; Evers with Peters, 1967; Evers-Williams with Blau, 1999; Salter, 1987.

Robert L. Jenkins

EVICTION. Malcolm X never owned a home in his own name, and the house that he stayed in located at 23-11 97th Street, in the East Elmhurst* area of New York City, was owned by the Nation of Islam (NOI).* On a number of occasions, he had been encouraged to take the legal steps to have the house put in his own name, but he declined every offer. After Malcolm left the NOI and publicly announced the founding of the Muslim Mosque, Inc.* as tensions began to rise between the two parties, the NOI took steps to have him vacate the premises. In a letter dated March 10, 1964, the NOI requested that Malcolm return all property belonging to Temple Number Seven,* transfer car title and insurance from the NOI's name into his own, and that he vacate the property upon receipt of the letter. The letter also demanded that steps would be taken to get legal possession of Malcolm's car if he did not concede and that the utilities at the house in question would no longer be paid by the NOI. Malcolm received the letter shortly before he departed for the Middle East.*

On April 8, 1964, the NOI formally filed eviction proceedings in the Civil Court of New York. Malcolm's lawyer and good friend Percy Sutton,* representing Sutton and Sutton, responded on April 13, 1964, and a hearing on the matter was set for April 17, 1964. On April 18, 1964, the *New York Amsterdam News*,* New York's largest black newspaper, carried an article on page one related to the eviction of Malcolm X from the house owned by the NOI. The hearing scheduled for April 17, 1964, was again postponed, however, because of Malcolm's trip abroad. After two other postponements, the trial was moved to June 15, 1964. While Malcolm ended up on the losing side of the eviction battle and was ordered to vacate the home the following February, he used the witness stand to expose Elijah Muhammad's* alleged adultery and the inner workings of the NOI in front of a press that was at the hearing in full force.

SELECTED BIBLIOGRAPHY

Carson (Gallen, ed.), 1991; Friedly, 1992; Malcolm X (Clark, ed.), 1992; B. Perry, 1991.

Mfanya Donald Tryman

F

FANON, FRANTZ. A renowned West Indian psychiatrist and revolutionary, Fanon is recognized for his writings supporting the liberation of colonial peoples. Born into a middle-class family, Fanon recognized a system of color stratification in his home country similar to many other nations in the world. Although both his parents had white ancestry, he still experienced racism in his native home of Martinque.

After he completed high school, Fanon participated in World War II.* In the war, he helped the Free French liberate the French West Indies. He later fought in Europe* and earned France's highest medal of honor, the Croix de Guerre. In 1947 he began his medical studies, specializing in psychiatry. He was not politically active in medical school, but he allocated time to study philosophy and the political theories of European intellectuals such as Hegel, Mannoni, Sarte, Gobineau, Cesaire, Freud, and Marx.

After obtaining his medical degree with a specialty in psychiatric medicine, he became active with the Algerian rebels. His involvement with Algerian revolutionaries led him to conclude that Western society was corrupt and should not be imitated by colonized peoples. He wrote about his experiences in *A Dying Colonialism* and asserted that it was necessary and beneficial for oppressed people to fight for freedom at all costs.

Fanon examined the problems of blacks in an international context. His writings expressing his views on issues concerning blacks on an international basis influenced Malcolm X. Fanon's first major study, *Black Skin, White Masks* (1952), which presented a psycho-cultural study of racism, reflected his personal frustrations with racism. Fanon encouraged blacks to fight against capitalism* and colonialism as well as racism. Malcolm also experienced frustrations with racism in American society, and he urged resistance to oppression. While Malcolm frequently mentioned the Algerian revolution and held it up as a model for the struggle of blacks to resist colonization and oppression, there is no indication that he ever personally met Fanon.

In 1956, Fanon resigned from practicing psychiatry to devote his time to the independence movement. He quickly acquired a reputation as an outstanding political writer in the cause of Third World liberation. Fanon's publication *The Wretched of the Earth* (1963) urged colonized people to purge themselves of their degradation in a "collective catharsis," a purging that could be achieved by violence against their European oppressors. For black revolutionaries of the late 1960s and 1970s his book and Malcolm's autobiography were regarded as the gospel.

Prior to his death, Malcolm's worldview resembled Fanon's in *The Wretched of the Earth*. He had received this book as a gift while visiting Africa. After reading it, he had concluded that the revolutionary struggle in the world centered around the power to control. Thus, Malcolm aimed to link the black liberation movement in America with the liberation movement in the Third World. Consequently, he held a Pan-Africanist view combined with a Third World socialist view similar to Fanon's.

In 1961, Fanon was diagnosed with cancer. He died in Washington, D.C., at the age of thirty-six, not long before Malcolm's death several years later in 1965 at the young age of thirty-nine. Both men were revolutionaries in their own ways, and they supported a social revolution* to be led by black people. In essence, Malcolm, as did Fanon, examined the problems of blacks in an international context.

SELECTED BIBLIOGRAPHY

Clarke, ed., 1990; Fanon, 1963; Meier, Rudwick, and Bracey, Jr., eds., 1991; A. Smith, 1982; M. F. Wright, 1975.

LaVonne Jackson

FARD, W. D. (Wallace D. Fard; Wallace Dodd Ford; David Ford; David Ford-el; Wali Farrad; Farred Muhammad; F. Muhammad Ali; Professor Ford). The prophet and founder of the Nation of Islam (NOI),* W. D. Fard first appeared in Detroit* in 1930 as a peddler. Some believed he was Pakistani in origin; others, including Malcolm X, believed that he was born in Mecca,* though no evidence has confirmed this. His actual name also was a mystery; he often used Wali Farrad, Professor Ford, Farred Muhammad, F. Muhammad Ali, and W. D. Fard. Some believe that he was actually Arnold Ford, a former Garveyite. Long before his establishment of the NOI, he had acquired an interest in exotic religious sects. During the 1920s he was a member of Noble Drew Ali's Moorish Science Temple,* and when the organization split in the early 1930s, Fard claimed to be Ali reincarnated. Part of Ali's divided following accepted Fard's leadership as founding members of the NOI.

Fard gathered approximately 8,000 people around him, teaching that the so-called Negro originally was a member of the lost tribe of Shabazz,* and by "tricknology" whites had brought them to America. Fard had come to restore their original culture and religion, Islam.* And a written application had to be made in order for African Americans to receive their original names. Fard established a formal organization, consisting of the University of Islam,* Muslim Girls' Training classes,* and the Fruit of Islam,* a paramilitary unit. The organization was placed under the leadership of a minister and a group of assistant ministers who were selected and trained by the prophet. In June 1934, the prophet disappeared and was later deified by Elijah Muhammad,* the NOI's new head. Elijah Muhammad assumed the title of prophet and Messenger of Allah, and Fard was worshiped as Allah* incarnate.

Malcolm X as minister of one of the NOI's largest temples taught his followers about Fard. When he "fished" on the streets for new converts, he talked about Fard's historical role in the founding of the NOI. Moreover, Malcolm supported the concept that an omnipotent Allah certainly manifested himself in the flesh as Elijah Muhammad taught about Fard. He declared that Fard had indeed shown himself to be the "Son of Man." Hence, Malcolm held to the NOI line about the divine nature of Fard, at least until he moved toward acceptance of orthodox Islam, which considered such views as heretical.

SELECTED BIBLIOGRAPHY

Beyon and Cuba, 1990; Brotz, 1970; Collins with Bailey, 1998; DeCaro, 1996; Essien-Udom, 1962; Evanzz, 1999; Lincoln, 1973; Marsh, 1996; Pinkney, 1976.

Lawrence H. Williams

FARMER, JAMES. James Farmer was one of the founders of the Congress of Racial Equality (CORE)* in 1942 and served as its national director from 1953 to 1966. The mission of CORE during Farmer's tenure was to achieve racial integration* in public accommodations through direct but nonviolent actions. This mission placed Farmer and CORE in the vanguard of civil rights* agitation during the early 1960s, as they sponsored many headline-grabbing sit-ins and freedom rides.

At the same time, Malcolm X was rising to national prominence, largely as a result of his criticism of the integrationist civil rights groups and his contrary message of racial separation.* His opposition to integration brought him into a public confrontation with Farmer on a New York radio talk show in 1961, in what Farmer called an impromptu "dialogue." The following year, Malcolm and Farmer agreed to stage a formal debate at Cornell University, in which they could really air their differences through well-prepared arguments. In the Cornell debate, Farmer forced Malcolm to discuss potential solutions to the problem of racial inequality in America rather than the problem itself. Malcolm, normally the attacker and critic, was thus put on the defensive for the first time in his career as a spokesman for the Nation of Islam (NOI),* and Farmer became the only integrationist ever to make Malcolm appear unsure of himself and his

A large man with a robust voice, James Farmer, who once debated Malcolm, often
spoke and wrote kindly of the Muslim
leader. Library of Congress.

message in public. The two held a final televised debate in 1963. Afterward,
both agreed that nothing positive had been accomplished and that they should
therefore cease working against one another and unite for the good of the black
community, which was torn between their conflicting messages.

Thereafter, Malcolm granted Farmer a measure of respect that he never
granted other civil rights leaders. According to Farmer, the two developed a
fairly close friendship that lasted for the remainder of Malcolm's life and included many shared house visits, telephone calls, and postcards. Malcolm's
speeches and interviews after 1963 do not indicate such a close relationship, but
they do reveal Malcolm's respect for Farmer. Although Malcolm's antiwhite
rhetoric softened considerably before his death, he was never completely able
to reconcile his beliefs in racial separation with Farmer's integrationist ideology.
The fact that Farmer had once divorced a black wife to marry a white woman
particularly caused Malcolm consternation. As Malcolm put it, Farmer was now
nearly white. At the very least, it made him no different than whites; he was

similarly guilty of discriminating against black women, for which often he accused the white man.

In one of Malcolm's last speeches before his assassination, he pointed out how Farmer and the other members of the "Big Six" leaders of the civil rights organizations* had used the radicalism of the Black Muslims* to convince white America that integration was a moderate demand. By that time, however, Malcolm himself had begun preaching equality within the United States rather than separatism, indicating that he was moving closer to Farmer's ideology. In demanding equality, "by any means necessary" became Malcolm's new battle cry.

After Malcolm's assassination, Farmer was outspoken in his belief that Malcolm was not murdered by members of the NOI. He stated publicly that he believed the murder could have been a Chinese Communist strike, although he never disclosed the reason. In later years, he indicated that he believed Harlem* drug traffickers had the greatest motive to kill Malcolm, because Malcolm jeopardized their business with his antidrug message. Farmer remained convinced that it was not the Black Muslims who were convicted of the crime that murdered Malcolm. Farmer lived long enough to see some vindication of his views of the murder.

SELECTED BIBLIOGRAPHY

CBS News, 1992; Farmer, 1985; Gallen, ed., 1992; Malcolm X (Perry, ed.), 1989; Meier and Rudwick, 1973.

Thomas Upchurch

FARRAKHAN, LOUIS (Louis Eugene Walcott; Louis X). Louis Farrakhan, a national spokesman and successor to Elijah Muhammad* as leader of the Nation of Islam (NOI),* was born Louis Eugene Walcott on May 11, 1933, in New York City. Ironically, religion played a minor role in the life of young Walcott, although he was raised as an Episcopalian in Boston's Roxbury* community. Instead, he concentrated on improving his musical, oratorical, and singing talents, which he used to make a living in various nightclubs in Harlem,* Boston, and other East Coast cities. Giving up his original name, drugs, and a promising musical career as a Calypso artist, Farrakhan joined the NOI in Harlem in 1955. He studied under Malcolm X and in May 1957, after service as a Captain in the Fruit of Islam,* the Muslims'* paramilitary unit, became the minister of the Boston Mosque, Temple Number Eleven. Initially, Louis and Malcolm were very close friends, and Malcolm sometimes referred to Louis as "my little brother." Malcolm frequently came to Boston to speak at the temple, and the two communicated with each other regularly. However, this close relationship ended when the NOI expelled Malcolm for his controversial comments about John F. Kennedy's* assassination. The ambitious Farrakhan turned against Malcolm in the organization's power struggle, openly criticizing Malcolm and supporting his former mentor's ouster.

Although Farrakhan has never been investigated or even considered by authorities as a suspect in Malcolm's murder, his scathing verbal attacks against Malcolm prior to Malcolm's death continue to provoke heated debates about his role in Malcolm's death. In a three-part series in the former Muslim newspaper *Muhammad Speaks*,* Farrakhan accused Malcolm of being a traitor, a liar, and a hypocrite. As the tensions between Malcolm and the NOI intensified, Farrakhan wrote that Malcolm was "worthy of death" and that he "shall not escape." While these and similar comments certainly do not prove Farrakhan's complicity in Malcolm's assassination, they clearly were instrumental in creating the climate for such an event to take place. To many Malcolm supporters the remarks certainly sanctioned and perhaps predicted Malcolm's murder.

Farrakhan's indirect involvement in Malcolm's murder continues to provide ammunition for those interested in discrediting and embarrassing the popular Muslim minister. While Farrakhan continues to deny vehemently any role in the assassination, his comment that the NOI dealt with Malcolm in a way appropriate for a traitor leads many people to believe otherwise.

Despite the continuing suspicion about Farrakhan's role in Malcolm's death, the Muslim minister attracts large crowds and, ironically, has increased the organization's membership, an organization that Malcolm made known. Farrakhan's excellent oratorical skills and his message of black self-sufficiency and black pride* (aspects of Malcolm's philosophy) are the primary attractions to his speeches. The NOI's alcohol and drug rehabilitation programs enjoy widespread success and command the respect of other groups involved in these kinds of community-based programs.

While Farrakhan's alleged involvement in Malcolm's death continues to make headlines, the minister argues that the federal government and the media deliberately employ this tactic to destroy his popularity among the masses. Whether or not this counteraccusation is true remains to be determined. Nevertheless, Louis Farrakhan and the Nation of Islam now claim Malcolm as one of their own, proof that they have radically changed their attitudes about one of black America's great leaders of the twentieth century.

SELECTED BIBLIOGRAPHY
Friedly, 1992; Gallen, ed., 1992; Gardell, 1996; Goldman, 1979; Magida, 1996.

Curtis Austin

AL-FAYSAL, PRINCE MOHMAED (Prince Faisal). Mohmaed Al-Faysal was the young brother of the Saudi Arabian ruler King Ibn Abdullah Saud Al-Saud. Supposedly King Al-Saud and Malcolm X once scheduled a personal meeting with each other, though the planned meeting never occurred. Malcolm, however, did eventually hold a meeting with Al-Faysal. Saudi Arabia's Crown Prince, Al-Faysal had ascended the country's throne after the Islamic Council removed his brother as king shortly before Malcolm's 1964 Hajj* to Mecca.* By then he was in essence Saudi Arabia's absolute ruler.

During Malcolm X's 1964 visit to the Middle East,* he was honored and humbled by the opportunity to meet and have tea with Prince Al-Faysal. The Saudi press devoted considerable attention to the meeting. Malcolm was struck by the way the prince laid out the "red carpet" for his visit to Saudi Arabia,* in which he was treated as a guest of the state. The Arabic ruler reminded Malcolm, however, that he was merely giving him the standard treatment that one Muslim* gives to another Muslim. Prince Faysal indicated to Malcolm that he had read about the Nation of Islam (NOI)* in the United States, and Malcolm explained the role that he played in the NOI during the last twelve years of his life. Malcolm indicated that his visit to the Middle East was one to learn more about orthodox Islam,* and the prince encouraged him to pursue such a path. Supposedly Al-Faysal was not impressed that as a longtime Muslim Malcolm was not already more familiar with the tenets of the religion. Al-Faysal was struck, however, by Malcolm's quiet demeanor; he was hardly the fire-eating monster that the American press made him out to be. Although Malcolm's meeting with Prince Faysal occupies only three paragraphs in his autobiography, it is clear that this experience was one of the proudest moments of Malcolm's life. When he left Saudi Arabia he left more determined to make his conversion to orthodox Islam complete and was enthused to spread the faith to larger numbers of urban blacks.

SELECTED BIBLIOGRAPHY

Blackside/PBS, 1994; Collins with Bailey, 1998; DeCaro, 1996; Malcolm X with Haley, 1965; Strickland (Greene, ed.), 1994.

Mfanya Donald Tryman, Robert L. Jenkins, and Reginald Colbert

FEDERAL BUREAU OF INVESTIGATION (FBI). The Federal Bureau of Investigation (FBI) began its existence as a subagency under the Department of Justice. It was established in 1919, originally called the General Intelligence Division (GID). A young civil servant, J. Edgar Hoover,* was named to head the new agency. The GID was organized as a direct result of the Red Scare of 1919 when American hysteria reacted to the Bolshevik Revolution in Russia. A series of letter bombs sent through the U.S. mail generated this apprehension. The agency collected and built files on Americans who were suspected as having communist leanings or sympathies, although European immigrants were often the main targets of the investigations. As head of the FBI, Hoover escalated the Bureau's program of domestic surveillance during the 1930s and 1940s. The Bureau was able to blossom under the leadership of Hoover as it prosecuted interstate criminal activities more successfully than local law enforcement agencies. The growing concern over leftist subversives has always been the main focus of the Bureau's activities.

Throughout most of the FBI's existence, its history has been notably intertwined with the life of Hoover. Hardly a friend of the African American, Hoover from the outset demonstrated an intense hostility to all forms of black American militancy. For example, he used his powers against the rising black militancy of the post–World War I era as he actively directed the agency's counterintelligence efforts against Marcus Garvey.* Hoover played a major role in bringing mail fraud charges against Garvey, which led to his conviction and eventual deportation from the United States.

The FBI opened its file on Malcolm Little right after his release from prison in 1953. The Bureau became concerned over the relationship that was developing between Malcolm Little and Elijah Muhammad,* head of the Nation of Islam (NOI).* Malcolm was certainly aware of the FBI methods dealing with black leaders and their organizations, and he was not afraid to criticize them publicly. A letter that Malcolm had written while in prison* in June 1950 suggesting that he identified with some of the ideals of the Communist Party* also grabbed the interest of the FBI. Initially the FBI and the Department of Justice could not agree about the extent of the NOI's subversive tendencies. The FBI regarded the NOI as one of many subversive black militant groups emerging in the nation and in 1952 recommended that it be added to the Attorney General's list of subversive organizations. However, the Justice Department did not view the organization as a serious threat, although it conceded that under certain circumstances the group might become a national security problem. Despite the Muslims'* opposition to the draft and some of its avowed racial views, the Justice Department decided not to prosecute the NOI for conspiring to violate the Selective Service Act. As late as 1959 the Justice Department still did not consider the NOI as subversive, although the FBI was instructed to continue to monitor the organization.

The FBI monitored the activities of Malcolm X throughout the civil rights* era. Malcolm's rise to prominence as a minister of the NOI prompted closer FBI scrutiny because of his outspoken views on racial separatism and his bold antiwhite comments. The FBI collected extensive background information on him, including information about past aliases, his places of employment, prison records, places of residence, and public pronouncements.

The Bureau was successful in placing informants at strategic levels in many of the African American groups and organizations that it monitored. It had well-placed infiltrators in the NOI, Malcolm's Muslim Mosque Inc.,* and the Organization of Afro-American Unity.* The agency was well aware of the internal strife that gripped the NOI and the rift that existed between Malcolm and his former mentor. In 1964, the Bureau sought to capitalize on the problems between Malcolm and the NOI by sending an agent to solicit Malcolm's "cooperation" in gathering information against Elijah Muhammad's organization. Always mistrustful of law enforcement groups, especially the FBI, Malcolm respectfully but adamantly rejected the agency's overtures. Many of Malcolm's followers believed the FBI was involved as a conspirator in Malcolm's murder. This view has not completely disappeared, although no hard evidence substantiates the Bureau's role in the assassination.

SELECTED BIBLIOGRAPHY

Carson (Gallen, ed.), 1991; Friedly, 1992; O'Reilly (Gallen, ed.), 1994.

Lauren Larsen

FEELINGS, MURIEL. Muriel Feelings was one of several women who worked closely with Malcolm X, especially during the last months of his life. Her association with Malcolm began when he was still in good standing with the Nation of Islam (NOI);* she joined the NOI while still in high school. Like many females, it was philosophical position emphasizing the family and its insistence that men play the dominant role in the family that attracted her to the sect. She soon became a staunch supporter of Malcolm and followed him out of the NOI in 1964. She married Tom Feelings, a notable black artist whom Malcolm had met while in Ghana on his 1964 West African tour. A part of Malcolm's inner circle, she, along with a small cadre of others, helped to draft the Organization of Afro-American Unity's* charter. Feelings was in attendance at the Audubon Ballroom* the afternoon of Malcolm's murder and with horror and sadness witnessed the futile efforts of friends and loved ones to revive him. Muriel credited Malcolm with being the one black leader during the 1960s who brought world attention to the African American struggle. Like so many of those who were closely associated with him, in the aftermath of his death she continued to work indefatigably to keep his legacy alive.

SELECTED BIBLIOGRAPHY

T. Davis (Chapnick, ed.), 1993; Strickland (Greene, ed.), 1994.

Robert L. Jenkins

FIELD NEGRO. In a speech entitled "I'm a Field Negro," Malcolm X argued that there were two kinds of black people. The two were distinguished by their status in American society, both during and after slavery. The first kind was the "House Negro."* This is the black man who was more concerned about the well-being of his master than his own or that of other black people. This was the individual who kept other blacks in check for the master. The Field Negro, however, was quite different.

Malcolm provided a historical analysis of the Field Negro. He indicated that these were the slaves who lived in the shacks, ate the worst food, and wore the worst clothes. These were the slaves who worked in the fields from sunup to sundown. They were the ones who most often felt the sting of the master's harsh whip (via the overseer). And because the Field Negro was the one who received the worst treatment, he hated the master, the overseer, and all whites associated with his bondage. Consequently, the Field Negro had nothing to lose in his resentment. They prayed for the master's death if he got sick. They prayed for a strong wind to fuel the flames if the master's house caught fire. The Field Negro was eager to escape from the plantation and supported anyone who wanted to run away.

Malcolm indicated that he was a Field Negro among modern-day blacks. As in the days of black slavery, the Field Negro constituted the masses of black people. He stated that as a Field Negro he would pray for a wind to come along if the master (whites) would not allow blacks to live in the house as human beings. If the master continued to mistreat blacks and became sick, as a Field Negro he would call the doctor and direct him to go in the opposite direction. It would be the responsibility of the Field Negro to demand that black people be treated with dignity and respect and as human beings. If this treatment was not forthcoming, then it would be the responsibility of the Field Negro to rebel against the government that perpetuated their slavery.

In the 1950s and 1960s, the Field Negro was called the "New Negro." This modern-day Field Negro had pride in his blackness and demanded racial separation.* They were the ones in the streets fighting for changes in a white-dominated society. The Field Negro believed strongly in a grassroots movement in the streets and mobilizing the masses. He was part of a revolution* that was sweeping the world where people of color were rising up and throwing off the shackles of bondage. Thus, blacks in the United States were beginning to understand what a "real" revolution involved. According to Malcolm X, a real revolution was not based on loving one's enemy, racial integration,* or sitting at lunch counters with whites. A real revolution was based upon land, which was the basis for independence, freedom, justice, and equality. It was the New Negro or Field Negro who initiated these demands.

SELECTED BIBLIOGRAPHY

Malcolm X (Breitman, ed.), 1965, 1970a; J. White, 1985.

Mamie Locke

FISHING. When Malcolm was released from prison* in August 1952, he went to Detroit* to work in a furniture store as a salesman, where he joined the Nation of Islam (NOI)* and Temple Number One. Malcolm immediately observed that when worship services were held, there were many empty seats. As the assistant minister at the temple, he felt that Minister Lemuel Hassan* was not aggressive enough in seeking new members and recruits. Malcolm decided to seek new recruits on his own, or what he started to refer to as "fishing." Malcolm believed that armed with his knowledge of the streets, his newfound religion, and his ability to cajole people, he should be able to "fish" successfully for new members for the NOI.

By the time Malcolm moved to Harlem* he had perfected the fishing method. Armed with his knowledge of the streets, his charisma, his prison experiences, and Elijah Muhammad's* belief that fishing for the young would attract the old, he was highly successful in building exponentially the membership and temples nationwide. In less than ten years, there were temples in most of the major cities in the United States, and the membership grew from less than 500 to tens of thousands. This growth was assisted by NOI ministers who had been taught how to fish for new members by Malcolm. As minister of Temple Number Seven* in Harlem, the fishing strategy was most obvious in the number of new recruits that joined one of the largest temples under the direction of Malcolm and the NOI. Malcolm would often fish on the busy and bustling street corners of Harlem, and had his ministers do the same, and their efforts were reflected in the explosive growth of Temple Number Seven.

SELECTED BIBLIOGRAPHY

Collins with Bailey, 1998; Karim with Skutches and Gallen, 1992; Lomax, 1963; Malcolm X with Haley, 1965.

Reginald Colbert

FORMAN, JAMES. James Forman was born on October 14, 1928, in Chicago, Illinois,* but was raised on his grandmother's farm in Marshall County, Mississippi.* It was Mississippi to which he would later return as a notable civil rights* activist and play a leading role in improving the plight of blacks in the Magnolia State. A distinguished adjunct professor of anthropology on the faculty of the American University in Washington, D.C., Forman during the 1960s was the executive secretary and director of International Affairs for the Student Non-Violent Coordinating Committee (SNCC).* As such, he played a leading role in the social activism of this crucial period in American history, one of the major leaders of civil rights organizations.* He is the author of six books, the most important being a searing and eloquent memoir of the civil rights movement,* which he entitled *The Making of Black Revolutionaries.*

Forman first met Malcolm X in 1963 in the lobby of the hotel in Washington, D.C. that served as headquarters for Martin Luther King, Jr.'s* March on Washington.* It was a cordial chance encounter where the two exchanged courtesies. Like most of the leaders of the nonviolent civil rights movement, however, Forman initially found little appealing about the life and philosophy of Malcolm X. But paralleling the views of so many of the other young activists of SNCC, Forman grew increasingly disillusioned with the nonviolent movement as the key to black liberation. It had been largely the turn of events in Mississippi, especially the violent deaths of the three civil rights workers during the 1964 Freedom Summer* and the failure of the federal government to protect the activists, that angered and frustrated him. Thereafter, Forman drifted toward militancy, more to the left of his initial civil rights philosophy.

Both Forman and Malcolm were certainly aware of the work and influence of the other. Malcolm, who had met other SNCC workers, including John R. Lewis,* while they were in West Africa on a late 1964 tour that Forman organized, seemed more impressed with the resolve and dedication of these activists in the black struggle than he was with any of the others. Moreover, Forman was not someone from the established civil rights leadership that Malcolm typically referred to in scorn and disrespect. Indeed, after his break with the Nation of Islam (NOI),* Malcolm would comment that he knew Forman as "a friend."

If Forman and Malcolm encountered each other subsequent to their Washington meeting, however, there is no indication of it in their autobiographies.

Like Malcolm, Forman eventually saw the linkage of the African and the African American liberation struggles, especially after Forman's 1964 visit to the African continent. Moreover, by the mid-1960s he had traded in his position on the solution for the African American dilemma from one endorsing civil rights* to one supporting human rights.* An avid student of Malcolm's views who was intellectually indebted to the slain leader by then, he increasingly advocated taking the case of the black American to the United Nations,* an idea that Malcolm and his Organization of Afro-American Unity* were pursuing aggressively in the last days of his life.

SELECTED BIBLIOGRAPHY

Carson, 1981; Forman, 1985; Sales, 1994.

Robert L. Jenkins

FOUNDING FATHERS. Malcolm X often made reference to the "Founding Fathers," those white males who framed the Constitution, and how hypocritical they were in fighting for their own freedom and independence when they owned black slaves. Specifically, he indicated that George Washington, Thomas Jefferson, and others were considered political icons, held in the highest esteem by Americans for their bravery, heroics, and wisdom in the fight for independence and their political philosophy in establishing the U.S. government. Malcolm noted the hypocrisy of the U.S. government in criticizing self-defense* tactics among black Americans when they were attacked by white racists and segregationists, but defending the Founding Fathers for their willingness to employ violence against the British during the American Revolution. Moreover, it was difficult to understand how the United States could deplore violence by people of color in Third World countries seeking their independence when the Founding Fathers used violence for the same ends. He often cited Patrick Henry, and his statement "Give me liberty, or give me death," as a primary example of American heroism worshiped by Americans. American violence, he said, was associated with patriotism when fighting other peoples abroad and glorified in the national anthem, honored in salutes to the American flag, and celebrated on Independence Day. While Malcolm did not openly advocate violence, he made it clear that African Americans should defend themselves against violence, if necessary, just like the Founding Fathers did.

SELECTED BIBLIOGRAPHY

Breitman, 1968; Malcolm X (Breitman, ed.), 1965, 1967; Malcolm X (Clarke, ed.), 1990.

Mfanya Donald Tryman

FOXX, REDD (John Elroy Sanford). Best known for his portrayal as a grouchy junk dealer in Watts (South Central Los Angeles) in the popular 1970s television comedy series *Sanford and Son*, Redd Foxx was raised in a poor family in Chicago,* moved to Harlem* in 1939, and eventually became a successful comedy entertainer.

Foxx, whose real name was John Elroy Sanford, met Malcolm X during the 1940s when both worked at Jimmy's Chicken Shack* in Harlem, an after-hours club that attracted celebrated black talent and large numbers of white patrons. Malcolm and Foxx, respectively known around Harlem as "Detroit Red" and "Chicago Red" because of their light skin and reddish conked hair, sometimes worked together as street hustlers. They once stole a hundred suits from a Harlem cleaners and resold them one by one from a nearby rooftop. Periodically, they went to Communist Party* meetings, not for the political discussions but to consume the free food available at these gatherings. Although Foxx moved to California in 1952 and never actively embraced Malcolm's religious or political beliefs, the two Harlem friends continued to see each other occasionally in the late 1950s and early 1960s.

SELECTED BIBLIOGRAPHY

Malcolm X with Haley, 1965; Price, 1979.

Charles C. Bolton

FRANCIS, REUBEN X. Reuben X Francis was a friend of Malcolm X's and a loyal follower of his Organization of Afro-American Unity.* He was also the leader's security chief, which meant that he was with Malcolm almost everywhere that he went, especially during Malcolm's last months alive. Francis was with Malcolm at the Audubon Ballroom* in New York, where he was assassinated on February 21, 1965.

Malcolm was to speak in a public forum on the evening of his murder. When he came on stage to address the crowd, two men in the audience immediately began to argue with each other. When Malcolm came from behind the podium to calm the audience, several men rose and shot him. Malcolm's security guards returned fire to the source of the shots, and Francis hit one of the men, Talmadge Hayer,* also known as Thomas Hagan, in the leg.

Because he had fired upon the men who fired upon Malcolm X, Francis became a part of the police investigation into the assassination. A grand jury indicted him, along with Thomas Hayer, Norman 3X Butler,* and Thomas 15X Johnson,* in the murder. Hayer, Butler, and Johnson, the latter two confirmed members of Elijah Muhammad's* Nation of Islam (NOI),* were indicted for killing Malcolm X, Francis was indicted on one count of first-degree felonious assault for shooting Hayer, two counts of second-degree assault, and a fourth count of possessing a pistol. Francis was expected to testify for the state in the murder trial, but he was never called. In order to avoid prosecution, Francis reportedly fled to Mexico.

SELECTED BIBLIOGRAPHY

Carson (Gallen, ed.), 1991; Friedly, 1992; Goldman, 1979; Malcolm X with Alex Haley, 1965; Myers, 1993.

Yoshawnda Trotter

"FREEDOM BY ANY MEANS NECESSARY." Malcolm X was an articulate and forceful critic not only of White America but also of the civil rights movement.* Martin Luther King, Jr.'s* philosophies of nonviolence and racial integration,* he said, were incapable of accomplishing substantive political and economic change for blacks. In his view, whites would never allow blacks to achieve full participation in American life as long as blacks renounced violence. Frustrated with continued attacks on black activists in the South,* Malcolm encouraged blacks to take a more militant approach.

On June 28, 1964, Malcolm X delivered a speech to a rally of the Organization of Afro-American Unity,* a group that he had recently founded. In that speech he told the audience that the motto of this new organization was "freedom by any means necessary." This meant, he said, that the time for waiting was over. Blacks must be prepared to use violence, if necessary, if whites continued to resist black efforts to gain equality and political rights.

Malcolm X often stated privately that he was not calling for black guerrilla warfare* against whites. Rather, he said, such statements were exaggerations intended to encourage African Americans to defend themselves and continue the struggle against racial injustice. A student of past and present revolutions, including the American Revolution, Malcolm recognized the power of language to unite and inspire oppressed peoples. In more than one speech, he cited Patrick Henry's famous challenge to the British government, "Give Me Liberty, or Give Me Death."

Precisely what Malcolm X intended by such statements as "freedom by any means necessary" will always be unclear. But what is certain is that he understood that this form of militant rhetoric separated him from the growing numbers of black leaders who were supporting nonviolent protests and marches. He also understood that this kind of militancy appealed to the inner-city blacks who comprised his principal constituency. Years of poverty, crime, and mistreatment at the hands of the police and city officials had left blacks in such areas as Harlem,* Detroit,* and Watts angry and mistrustful of the white political establishment. Many had grown tired of speeches and slogans that told them to be patient or to love the white man. "Freedom by any means necessary" thus became a revolutionary call to arms for urban blacks. Years later, many black and white Americans still, whether rightly or wrongly, consider it the defining statement of Malcolm X's philosophy.

SELECTED BIBLIOGRAPHY

Malcolm X (Breitman, ed.), 1970a; B. Perry, 1991; Sales, 1994.

Phillip A. Gibbs

FREEDOM NOW PARTY (FNP). The Freedom Now Party (FNP) was organized in August 1963 in Detroit, Michigan.* An important though controversial and philosophically fractured branch of the party functioned in New York. One of its founding members, veteran New York civil rights* lawyer Conrad L. Lynn,* notable for his role in the Mississippi* Emmett Till* lynching case, served as its first chairman. Established primarily as an alternative to the Democratic and Republican Parties, founders of the party believed that it would be the vehicle through which blacks might attain and wield larger political power in the northern states. At its establishment, the founders announced that the party would run candidates for office in Connecticut, New York, and California; all of them were soundly defeated. Thereafter, the party concentrated its energy on Michigan. Under the leadership of black Christian nationalist leader Albert Cleage,* the party entered thirty-nine candidates in the 1964 Michigan elections for offices that ranged from Wayne County Drain Commissioner to the U.S. Senate. Party officials realized that their candidates would not likely win, but they were disappointed that they fell far short of garnering the 100,000 to 750,000 votes predicted for the party at the outset of the campaign. By 1966, the party no longer ran candidates for office, its demise hastened by the internal dilemma of whether to allow white participation and the eventual infiltration of the Federal Bureau of Investigation.*

During the last year of Malcolm's life, he and Cleage became close associates, Malcolm even occasionally appearing on programs that the chairman organized in Detroit. The party, trying to capitalize on Malcolm's popularity in the larger Motor City area, reportedly recruited Malcolm to seek one of Michigan's U.S. senatorial seats. In comments made at Wayne State University in October 1963, Malcolm indicated that he favored the establishment of the all-black party. He was impressed with the party's youthful energy, especially its strident and uncompromising views, he would later say, and though he could not endorse the organization, anything was better for blacks than the two traditional parties. Such views likely encouraged Cleage and other party leaders to think that Malcolm would be amenable to the nomination idea. Moreover, he was clearly moving toward a more politically active position and supposedly expressed an interest in seeking political office. Influenced by associates, especially James Shabazz,* one of his closest friends, who warned him of the likelihood of failure in such a race, Malcolm refused to accept the party's nomination overture. As he had been doing for several months, he continued to place his energies in achieving his broader goal of freedom for oppressed people by developing his embryonic Organization of Afro-American Unity.*

SELECTED BIBLIOGRAPHY

Cleage and Breitman, 1968; Cruse, 1967; Lynn, 1979; Malcolm X (Clark, ed.), 1992; Malcolm X (Epps, ed.), 1991; B. Perry, 1991; S. Smith, 1999; Walton, 1972.

Robert L. Jenkins

One of the most well-known images of violent southern resistance to integration is this picture of a burned-out Freedom Riders bus in its effort to desegregate interstate bus terminals. Copyright, Photo by *The Birmingham News*, 2001. All rights reserved. Reprinted with permission.

FREEDOM RIDERS. The term *freedom riders* refers specifically to those individuals who were part of racially integrated groups of bus travelers sent to the South* by civil rights* groups to test the U.S. Supreme Court bans on racially segregated interstate travel and segregated terminal facilities. The most famous freedom ride, the 1961 ride sponsored by the Congress of Racial Equality,* was met with violence, especially in Alabama, and ultimately forced the John F. Kennedy* presidential administration to intervene to guarantee the riders' safety. More generally, however, the term *freedom riders* was used during the 1960s to denote all northerners who came to the South to advance the cause of civil rights.

Malcolm X criticized freedom riders as hypocritical. He pointed out the absurdity of liberal northerners running off to solve the problems of southern blacks when black ghettos in the North remained racially segregated and plagued by numerous ills. He suggested that northerners interested in racial justice put their efforts into fixing conditions in their own backyard. Ironically, southern newspapers, which otherwise ignored Malcolm's message, highlighted his attacks on northern civil rights workers as a way to bolster their claims that the actions of northern civil rights workers originated from something with less-than-noble motives.

SELECTED BIBLIOGRAPHY

Branch, 1988; Malcolm X with Haley, 1965.

Charles C. Bolton

FREEDOM SUMMER. In June 1964 approximately 1,000 volunteers, consisting mainly of northern white college students motivated by the liberal idealism of the early 1960s, traveled to Mississippi* to participate in the Freedom Summer project. Organized by the Student Non-Violent Coordinating Committee (SNCC)* and led by Robert Moses, the project sought to create a black electorate in Mississippi. The volunteers joined with local African Americans to staff freedom schools, where blacks were instructed in their rights as citizens and encouraged to register to vote. A product of these efforts was the creation of the grassroots Mississippi Freedom Democratic Party (MFDP),* which challenged the white regulars at the Democratic National Convention in August 1964. Fannie Lou Hamer,* whom Malcolm met for the first time in New York shortly before his murder, attracted national attention in her capacity as a MFDP convention delegate.

Freedom Summer workers, though trained in nonviolent resistance, were unprepared for the violence they encountered in Mississippi. White supremacists launched a crusade of terror, the most sensational being the Ku Klux Klan* murder of three volunteers—James Earl Chaney, Andrew Goodman, and Michael Schwerner—in Neshoba County. Largely because of its potential for danger to defenseless blacks, Malcolm had disapproved of the civil rights* project. In the project's planning stages he had wired SNCC's James Forman,* volunteering to send some of his followers to Mississippi to give the Klan a dose of its "own medicine," but his gesture was not taken seriously.

Malcolm had long criticized the violence perpetuated against blacks in the southern struggle and by the summer of 1964 had stepped up his call for blacks to arm themselves in self-defense.* In a November 1964 London speech he denounced the murders in the Mississippi summer project and blamed Martin Luther King, Jr.'s* nonviolence philosophy* for the horrible fatal beating that Chaney suffered. Sending blacks unarmed to Mississippi, he said, was a "pink-toed approach;" they simply needed someone to protect them. He lodged similar criticism against the Federal Bureau of Investigation (FBI)* for its failure to bring the Klan to justice in the murders and occasionally used the theme of violence against blacks in the South* in his speeches to rally support for his armed self-defense philosophy.

Freedom Summer and the violence it precipitated spurred the passage of the Voting Rights Act of 1965.* It also caused many SNCC volunteers and other youth to lose faith in nonviolent resistance and embrace the militant doctrines of Malcolm X.

SELECTED BIBLIOGRAPHY

Dittmer, 1994; Goldman, 1979; Malcolm X (Epps, ed.), 1991; McAdam, 1988; Rothschild, 1982.

Charles D. Lowery

FREEMASONRY. Originally a parachurch fraternal group, the Masons are one of the Western world's oldest and most popular fraternal bodies. Like most fraternal groups its appeal has been enhanced by its emphasis on secrecy, rituals, and pomp. Among black Americans the Masons began during the early national period when former slave and Revolutionary War figure Prince Hall overcame initial British discrimination regarding black acceptance and won initiation into the group. In 1787 he was authorized by England's Grand Lodge to establish the first all-black lodge in Boston. Multifunctional in terms of its involvement in the sundry affairs of "brotherhood," the organization has also had a valuable record in the black community in economic and self-improvement* endeavors. Among the untold thousands of blacks who have historically made the group an immensely popular institution in African American communities was Malcolm X's father Earl Little,* who belonged to the organization. So did many early Nation of Islam (NOI)* converts, including Malcolm's mentor Elijah Muhammad,* who had joined the fraternal order in 1924. Indeed, the linkage between the Masons and the NOI was hardly negligible, beginning with the order's Islamic historical roots to the more noticeable Fez, donned with its prominent crescent and stars that Muhammad wore, to the biblical fables and mystical symbolisms for which each organization maintained an attachment. Long before his rise to prominence as the NOI leader, however, Muhammad had ended active participation in the order, though he certainly embraced some of the symbolism and encouraged Masons to join the NOI.

Despite the Islamic connections, Malcolm shared neither his father's nor Muhammad's sentiments about the Masons. The organization fell among the litany of organizations that he occasionally scorned, especially during his conversion and early years in the Muslim* ministry. Perhaps because the group's doctrines in many ways also incorporated Christian ideas, Malcolm could find little commendable about them. Like most of the Christian preachers that he knew, Malcolm regarded Masons, especially those holding the highest level attainable in the body, the thirty-second degree Mason, as being essentially "brain dead." These were the types who attended "ice box" churches ministered by pastors with "frozen mentalities." He held no great respect even for those with whom he shared his own religious faith, black or white. All white Masons, in Malcolm's view, were devils. As Muslims, he said, they could never reach beyond thirty-three degrees of knowledge (when they were no longer Masons but Shriners); hence, they could never attain the full projection of the religion. Although

Two members of the elite security force Fruit of Islam sit in the foreground as their leader Elijah Muhammad addresses an audience. Library of Congress.

Malcolm taught such views as a NOI minister, whether he continued to entertain them privately after his movement into orthodox Islam* is not clear; it is not likely, however, that they were central ideas articulated to audiences in his Muslim Mosque, Inc.,* or the Organization of Afro-American Unity.*

SELECTED BIBLIOGRAPHY

Clegg, 1997; DeCaro, 1996; Franklin and Moss, 2000; Jamal, 1971; Malcolm X with Haley, 1965; B. Perry, 1991; R. Turner, 1997.

Robert L. Jenkins

FRUIT OF ISLAM (FOI). Established as the protective arm of the Nation of Islam (NOI),* the Fruit of Islam (FOI) was the brainchild of NOI founder W. D. Fard* in the early 1930s in Detroit, Michigan.* Along with the Temple of Islam, the spiritual center of the NOI, the Muslim Girls' Training Classes,* composed of the female members of the NOI, and the University of Islam,* whose curriculum was based on the teachings of the Prophet, the FOI was the single most powerful entity of the NOI. Initially, it was under the direction of Elijah Poole, whom W. D. Fard also designated as his First Minister of Islam. Known as The

Messenger of Allah,* Elijah Muhammad* became the spiritual leader of the NOI following the disappearance of Fard, and he named his son-in-law, Raymond Sharrieff,* Supreme Captain of the FOI. Sharrieff was responsible for Muhammad's personal security force, which was composed of several members of the FOI from Chicago's* Temple Number Two, the national headquarters of the NOI. Elijah Muhammad's son, Elijah Muhammad, Jr.,* became the second in command of the FOI and Captain of Temple Number Two's FOI unit.

The FOI is part of every local temple or mosque in the country and composed of the able-bodied male members of the NOI. It has its own separate administrative body, with a military-style structure, based at the national NOI headquarters. All local units took their directions from Sharrieff rather than from their temple spiritual leaders. Hence, Sharrieff was one of the most powerful men in the NOI. It was the exercise of this kind of dual power at New York's mosque, where Malcolm served, that resulted in conflict and controversy between the two men.

The FOI's original purpose was to protect NOI officials and properties from non-Muslims, including the general public and law enforcement personnel. They are most noticeable in the mosque where they search the public and their own membership who attend Black Muslim* meetings or as part of the audience where their officials have been invited to speak. They are instructed and trained to react defensively, not offensively, and to obey legal authorities. Members are given instruction in physical training including body-building, the martial arts, physical hygiene, military drills, and formations as well as the use of firearms. In his autobiography, Malcolm X wrote that FOI members were also instructed in the responsibilities of being a husband and father and head of a household.

Since the era of W. D. Fard, the FOI's functions expanded to include not only security for the NOI from external elements but internal discipline and punishment of members within the movement itself. Discipline, punishment, and sanctions could be incurred for a range of offenses including failing to tithe; moral infractions like adultery; consumption of alcoholic beverages and pork*; and heresy and disobedience to official NOI tenets, which, during the 1960s, could mean participating in civil rights* demonstrations or even in American political life by voting. Sanctions also included the failure of FOI members to sell assigned quotas of the NOI's newspaper *Muhammad Speaks,* which came under the jurisdiction of Sharrieff after Malcolm X left the NOI. After Malcolm left the NOI and others followed him out, many of the defectors* became victims of often violent "discipline" tactics from FOI members.

Internally, the FOI has acted not only as a police force but as a judiciary system with sanctions ranging from suspension and shunning to expulsion. On occasion, physical intimidation and threats have been employed, and there have been, as a result, some documented deaths. There were threats from the FOI against Elijah Muhammad's son and successor, Wallace Deen Muhammad,* and Malcolm X. Allegations have also been made against the FOI in connection with the assassination of Malcolm X. Federal Bureau of Investigation* records also show that Sharrieff threatened Malcolm X, in writing, about making what the NOI considered damaging statements against Elijah Muhammad after Malcolm left the sect. The antagonism resulting from Malcolm's ouster grew more intense between him and FOI officials, and Malcolm frequently commented about the group's skill in being able to conduct deadly missions.

With the death of Elijah Muhammad in 1975, his son, now known as Imam Warith Deen Mohammed, instituted many changes in the NOI and even disbanded the FOI. In 1978, Minister Louis Farrakhan,* once a Malcolm X protégé, took control of Elijah Muhammad's group, resurrected the old NOI, and revived the FOI.

SELECTED BIBLIOGRAPHY

Friedly, 1992; Goldman, 1973; Lincoln, 1961, 1968; Lippy and Williams, eds., 1988.

Nancy-Elizabeth Fitch

G

GALAMISON, MILTON. During the 1950s and 1960s, Milton Galamison was New York's leading civil rights* activist. A Presbyterian minister by profession, he was most noted for his efforts to racially integrate New York's public schools. It was through such broad-based community groups as the Parents Workshop for Equality in New York City Schools and the Citywide Committee for Integration that he largely organized and worked to achieve his goals. Although a leader in the local National Association for the Advancement of Colored People* and the Congress of Racial Equality* branches, Galamison's rhetoric was considerably more outspoken than that of these two national organizations. Hence, their support of his campaigns to eliminate the virtually all-black schools in the city was often lukewarm at best. Still, in February 1964, after bringing together a coalition of city parents, schoolteachers, ministers, civil rights and community organizations, he launched one of the nation's largest demonstrations in support of school integration.

Operating in the same city, it was natural for Malcolm X and Galamison to be acquainted with each other. Their first substantive encounter occurred as a result of their participation in a local television program, where their proposed debate on the questions of nationalism and nonviolence actually focused on Christianity* and Islam.* Philosophically, the two men did not agree about the merits of an integrated society; hence during the period when Malcolm was affiliated with the Nation of Islam (NOI),* for both personal and organizational reasons, he refused to support Galamison's boycotts and other activities to achieve school integration. By 1964, however, with his permanent break with Elijah Muhammad* and the NOI imminent, Malcolm joined Galamison's coalition and gave strong support to the integration movement, though apparently Galamison did not seek his endorsement. This was not done in support of racial integration* but because of Malcolm's continuous opposition to the practices of racial segregation,* always anathema to him because of its dehumanizing effects on black people. Concerned about adversely affecting Galamison's boycott, Malcolm did not, however, actively participate in the demonstrations.

Malcolm considered Galamison his friend and ally, as he was so prone to claim for many people that he established even the most casual of relations with. Militant in his integration views, the fiery pastor was nevertheless easy for Malcolm personally to like. Publically at least, Galamison did not accept Malcolm on equal terms, though he clearly respected him, and on at least one occasion during a local television news interview, he defended Malcolm from apparent detractors. His denial of an ongoing friendship with Malcolm notwithstanding, something beyond a casual relationship between the two men surely existed. Galamison was invited and expected to appear on stage as a speaker in the Audubon Ballroom* the afternoon that Malcolm was slain. Exhaustion from extensive church services during the day of the program, however, prevented Galamison's appearance and perhaps the revelation of a clearer indication of the two men's relationship.

SELECTED BIBLIOGRAPHY

Carson (Gallen, ed.), 1991; Goldman, 1969; Malcolm X (Breitman, ed.), 1970a; Meier and Rudwick, 1973; Meier, Rudwick, and Bracey, eds., 1991; Taylor, 1997.

Robert L. Jenkins

GARVEY, MARCUS MOSIAH. Marcus M. Garvey was a charismatic Jamaican black nationalist with little formal education who in 1914 founded the Universal Negro Improvement Association (UNIA),* a self-help organization whose goal was to promote black economic self-sufficiency and African unity. He moved to New York in 1916 and soon thereafter established a UNIA branch in Harlem,* which became the national headquarters. By 1919 he had established branches in thirty northern cities and claimed a following of 2 million people. Garvey's militant black chauvinism appealed especially to poor ghetto blacks, who, in the pages of the organization's weekly newspaper *Negro World*, read about the past greatness and the future promise of the black race. His program placed great emphasis on black economic self-sufficiency and on African Americans' return to Africa to redeem their homeland. Garvey's influence peaked in 1920 when, at an international convention of delegates from twenty-five countries, he was elected "Provisional President General of Africa." His influence plummeted after 1922 when he was indicted for mail fraud. After serving two years of a five-year prison term, Garvey was deported and died in obscurity.

Malcolm X's father, Earl Little,* had been a Garveyite. Earl's work in the Garvey movement occurred at an early age in Malcolm's life, but it clearly left an impression on him. As an adult, Malcolm recalled with pride the visits he made with his father to various churches and homes doing Garvey missionary work. On a more painful note, he also remembered the problems and eventual murder his father suffered because of his activism. Apparently, Garvey also left

Malcolm's father was a devoted follower of
black nationalist leader Marcus Garvey,
shown here. Library of Congress.

a legacy with Malcolm. He respected the "Black Moses" for his courage and
ideas and occasionally mentioned his name during some of his public pronouncements. An exponent of black nationalism* and black economic self-
sufficiency, Malcolm was a natural choice as a headline speaker for Harlem
organizers of the annual Garvey Day street rallies during the 1960s.

Malcolm, like Garvey, continually articulated great pride in his African roots.
And though he espoused the Black Muslims'* standard line about racial separatism, a view similar to Garvey's, Malcolm was not an ardent advocate of
African Americans' repatriation in Africa as a solution to their American dilemma. Rather, Malcolm's ideas about the African American's return to Africa
involved their "spiritual, philosophical, psychological and cultural" linkage to
the ancestral homeland. Like the American Jews,* whose similar strategic ties

to Israel enhanced their political and economic power in the United States, black Americans did not have to physically remove themselves from the United States to progress. It was a view that admittedly Malcolm had not refined prior to his death, but it was one that he began increasingly to address after his departure from Elijah Muhammad's* fold.

Garvey, through his powerful oratory and uncompromising philosophy, captured the imagination of black urbanites and in later years served as a powerful legacy for Black Power* advocates. Black leaders of his era denounced him because of his philosophy of race pride and separatism. Malcolm, too, was denounced by black leaders of his day, in large measure because his message was similar and, as a powerful legate of Garvey, appealed to the anger and frustrations of millions of ghetto blacks about their proper place in America.

SELECTED BIBLIOGRAPHY

Cronon, 1995; E. U. and R. Essien-Udom (Clarke, ed.), 1993; Fax, 1972; Malcolm X with Haley, 1965; *New York Amsterdam News*, August 10, 1957, May 23, 1964; Vincent, 1971.

Charles D. Lowery

GIOVANNI, NIKKI. Nikki Giovanni was born on July 7, 1943, in Knoxville, Tennessee. Giovanni is a prominent American poet and author of nearly twenty books. Her works celebrate black consciousness, women, men, family, and the concept of self-realization. Giovanni graduated from Fisk University with honors, earning a baccalaureate degree in history. As a college student during the height of the civil rights movement,* she became involved with the black struggle through the Student Non-Violent Coordinating Committee (SNCC).* SNCC also became the platform that launched her activist role in the African American community.

Giovanni's early poetry reflects a deep commitment to the black consciousness movement, its goals, and its leaders. Giovanni apparently never personally knew Malcolm, but like so many young black activists of her college life, especially those affiliated with SNCC, she was obviously influenced by him. Her early poems focused on her work with black cultural nationalists to promote the ideal of a black struggle for democracy and self-determination, as espoused by Malcolm X. The genius of Giovanni is the political force inherent in her cultural nationalism that unifies with Malcolm's call for black self-determination. In this vein, Giovanni views Malcolm as the embodiment of black aspirations for transformation and redemption. Giovanni admires Malcolm as a nation-builder of the Nation of Islam (NOI)* and the black nationalist movement, a statesman of Pan-Africanism,* a fighter for his own dignity as a black man, and a skillful warrior in the struggle for justice and liberty for all African Americans.

Like notable black literary giant Amiri Baraka,* Giovanni was one of several major intellectual voices that criticized filmmaker Spike Lee* and his 1993 epic of Malcolm's life. In Giovanni's view, Lee's production trivialized Malcolm's life, sending the wrong message about the real Malcolm and his greatness as a strident voice of black American protest.

SELECTED BIBLIOGRAPHY

Giovanni, 1970, 1994.

Lehlohonolo Tlou

GIRLFRIENDS. Like many youth of his age, it was not unusual for Malcolm to have many girlfriends. At the age of sixteen, Malcolm moved to Boston to live with his half sister Ella Collins.* It was in Boston's nightlife that Malcolm gained a reputation as a ladies' man and interacted with numerous women. Tall, strikingly handsome, a good dancer, and flashy dresser, Malcolm attracted the attention of women from both inside and outside of Boston's black hipster culture. According to one biographer, he was particularly taken with a fair-skinned girl named Gloria Strother,* from the more affluent "Hills" section of Boston's Roxbury* community. Little came of the relationship, although the two kept in contact with each other, Gloria even visiting and writing Malcolm when he was imprisoned. "Heather,"* whom he met while in prison,* was also close to Malcolm, and following his release from jail, the two contemplated marriage. Laura and Sophia, however, were girls who had a profound effect on Malcolm. He also affected their lives considerably, though in a negative way.

Malcolm met Laura at the Townsend Drug Store where he worked as a soda fountain clerk. She impressed young Malcolm as friendly, natural, and unpretentious. They eventually became dancing partners, Malcolm's "perfect" Lindy Hop* partner. Young Laura lived a protected life in the custody of her grandmother until she met Malcolm. She was a nonsmoker, nondrinker, and diligent high school student who had planned to attend college. However, these plans changed after meeting Malcolm, who introduced her to the nightlife. Laura started defying her grandmother, drinking liquor, using drugs, and eventually became a prostitute. Malcolm, however, felt responsible for her eventual fate.

Sophia (actually Beatrice Caragulian Bazarian*), a white girl, met Malcolm on the dance floor at the Roseland Ballroom.* Their developing relationship soon drove a wedge between Malcolm and Laura. Malcolm described her as a very attractive woman. Sophia lavished money on Malcolm and gave him status among his friends. They developed a lasting relationship that continued even after her marriage to another man. Sophia and her sister Ruby became crime partners with Malcolm and his namesake, Malcolm "Shorty"* Jarvis, and burglarized houses in rich, white neighborhoods.

On February 23, 1944, Malcolm was sentenced to a ten-year prison term for burglary. This was a blessing in disguise, which eventually led to his Islamic conversion.* Thereafter, he seemed consumed by his religion and what would be his life's work in the cause of black progress. Until his decision to marry Betty Sanders, Malcolm seemed only to have a fleeting interest in women after his release from prison.

SELECTED BIBLIOGRAPHY

Goldman, 1992; Malcolm X with Haley, 1965; B. Perry, 1991; Rummel, 1989; Strickland (Greene, ed.), 1994.

Morgan Ero

GOHANNA FAMILY. Mabel and Thornton Gohanna of Lansing, Michigan,* were foster parents to Malcolm Little. Following his father's death, young Malcolm helped to provide for his mother and siblings by running errands, shooting rabbits, and catching frogs to sell to neighbors as well as by stealing. However, these activities failed to provide the income to keep the Little family intact, and Malcolm and his younger sisters and brothers soon became responsibilities of the state of Michigan. Wards of the court, such as Malcolm, were regularly placed in family homes such as the Gohannas, who were noted for feeding and taking care of homeless children, ex-convicts, and other people in need. Malcolm's arrival at the Gohannas in 1937 marked the beginning of the final dissolution of the Little family, preceding his mother's hospitalization in 1938. Later in life, Malcolm described the Gohannas as very religious people who also loved to hunt and fish. Despite the attention lavished upon their thirteen-year-old ward, Malcolm seriously doubted that they truly liked him. Malcolm's school deportment problem caused his final expulsion from the Lansing school system and his removal from the Gohanna family. He was placed in a white detention home in Mason, Michigan.*

SELECTED BIBLIOGRAPHY

Malcolm X with Haley, 1965; B. Perry, 1991; Wolfenstein, 1981.

Thaddeus M. Smith

GOLDMAN, PETER. Peter Louis Goldman, a white liberal journalist and later a senior editor for *Newsweek*, worked on survey data in the 1960s that examined critical issues concerning African Americans. In 1969 Goldman was assigned the task of interpreting the data from the third major survey that appeared as *Report from Black America*. However, Goldman's best-known work is his highly praised biography *The Death and Life of Malcolm X* (1973), which documents the rise to fame and the untimely death of Malcolm X. One of the first major biographies to appear following the assassination of Malcolm X, Goldman's study is a sensitive but critical appraisal based on his personal three-year acquaintance with Malcolm, extensive interviews, and documentary sources. (Goldman knew Malcolm relatively well before his death but once commented that their philosophical differences meant they could not be real friends.) It is not just a simplistic portrayal that argues that Malcolm was the product or the essence of one particular ideology. Rather, it captures the complexities and contradictions of Malcolm's life and the tragedy of his death. Unusual for the time, Goldman rejected the conspiracy theories about Malcolm's death, though he has modified his position over time. Goldman concludes that Malcolm's purpose as a black spokesman was to educate White America about the depth of black grievances against them. No one was more effective than Malcolm in using the media to this end, Goldman said.

SELECTED BIBLIOGRAPHY

CBS News, 1992; Evanzz, 1992; Goldman, 1969, 1973; Goldman (Franklin and Meier, eds.), 1982; B. Perry, 1991.

Thaddeus M. Smith

GOLDWATER, BARRY. A U.S. senator from Arizona, Barry Goldwater was one of the most notable Republican Party* leaders in the 1960s. A thirty-year veteran of Congress, he served on several powerful Senate committees, including the Armed Services and the Select Committee on Intelligence. Considered to be the father of the national political conservative movement since 1970, in 1964 Goldwater ran for the presidency against Democrat Lyndon B. Johnson.* Candid and prone to make off-the-cuff remarks, Goldwater appealed, nevertheless, to many whites because of his strong anticommunist rhetoric and fiscal conservatism. It was during this campaign that Goldwater first became a part of Malcolm's consciousness.

Although Malcolm X was beginning to assume a greater role in political advocacy, he had not totally abandoned the position that Muslims* under the Nation of Islam* took in refusing to vote or participate in the political process. In his opinion, however, black voters had a simple decision to make of choosing between the wolf (Goldwater) and the fox (Johnson). While he mistrusted all professional white politicians, he was decidedly anti-Johnson and chided blacks for being too predictable in supporting the Democrats, a party that never kept its promises to them. Although Malcolm lambasted Johnson as a southern Klansman, he clearly did not find the ultraconservative Goldwater and the Republicans any more appealing. To be sure, Malcolm regarded Goldwater as a racist, as did most blacks, but, Malcolm remarked, he simply was "not a leading racist." Still, he said, the popular Goldwater was at least honest in letting black people know that he did not care for them and that they should expect little from the Republican candidate if he won the presidency. As Malcolm predicted, however, in the wake of a large monolithic black Democratic vote, Goldwater, whom Malcolm claimed was made by devious and ardent Johnson supporters to look like a "wolf" to blacks and the international community, lost the election in a landslide.

SELECTED BIBLIOGRAPHY

Bacon, Davidson, and Keller, eds., 1995; Brink and Harris, 1964; Malcolm X (Breitman, ed.), 1970a; *Militant*, December 7, 1964.

Robert L. Jenkins

GRAHAM, BILLY. During the late 1950s and early 1960s Billy Graham came of age as the United States' foremost evangelical minister. His charismatic

Arizona Republican Senator Barry Goldwater, whom Malcolm preferred for president over Democrat Lyndon B. Johnson in 1964. Mississippi Republican Party Papers, Special Collections Department, Mitchell Memorial Library, Mississippi State University.

speaking style and youthful exhilaration left audiences spellbound and moved thousands of them to dedicate their lives to Jesus Christ. Malcolm X, who came of age as a minister in the Nation of Islam (NOI)* during these same years, studied Graham's mannerisms and precise diction. Although the two men never met, Malcolm sometimes quoted Graham. In his speeches before both whites and blacks, Malcolm combined Graham's oratorical techniques with his own, including direct eye contact with the audience. Soon after he separated from the NOI, Malcolm founded the Muslim Mosque, Inc.,* an organization that was similar to Billy Graham's evangelical crusade. Malcolm maintained that Graham's organization did not foster jealousy among other ministers, yet spread white nationalism. On the contrary, Graham told people to join whatever church taught the Gospel of Christ. Malcolm believed that this same strategy could be used in bringing black people together. Malcolm did not believe that blacks had to follow him. Rather, what was important was for them to affiliate with any group that advocated black nationalism.* Graham's approach was, in Malcolm's view, useful in furthering the goals of the black liberation movement.

SELECTED BIBLIOGRAPHY

DeCaro, 1998; Goldman, 1973; B. Perry, 1991.

Phillip A. Gibbs

GRANT, EARL. Earl Grant was one of approximately twenty Muslim* followers of Malcolm X who had rushed to Malcolm's home after suspecting foul play during the winter of 1964–65. They had tried to telephone Malcolm at home but kept getting a recording stating that his phone had been disconnected. Malcolm had received a number of death threats. When Grant and others arrived at Malcolm's home, they found that he was safe after he answered the door.

After an Organization of Afro-American Unity* meeting five days before Malcolm's assassination on February 21, 1965, Grant suggested that Malcolm spend the night at his home for security reasons. However, Malcolm refused, stating that Grant had a family and that he did not want to jeopardize anyone else's life because of his own predicament. It was Grant who suggested to Malcolm that he cancel his speaking engagement on that fateful day at the Audubon Ballroom* in February 1965. Grant had realized how upset and nervous Malcolm was backstage before Grant made his final opening speech for Malcolm. Malcolm had told Grant that something was not right, perhaps sensing his own death at the hands of the assassins. As a close associate of Malcolm's, Grant spent the last hour of Malcolm's life with him.

SELECTED BIBLIOGRAPHY

Gallen, ed., 1992; Grant (Clarke, ed.), 1990; Malcolm X (Karim, ed.), 1971; B. Perry, 1991.

Mfanya Donald Tryman

GRAVITTS, (CAPTAIN) JOSEPH X (Yusuf Shah). In the litany of Nation of Islam (NOI)* leaders who turned against Malcolm X two years before his death, none was more determined to see him discredited than Captain Joseph. One of a number in Elijah Muhammad's* inner circle, Joseph served as a Captain of the Fruit of Islam (FOI)* in Harlem's* Temple Number Seven* where Malcolm was the minister. As a temple leader, he had acquired a reputation for a propensity to violence and strong-armed approaches to resolving problems in the temple among NOI members. The tactics did not always please Malcolm, but as a Captain answerable only to the FOI Supreme Commander in Chicago,* Joseph's power was essentially equal to that of Malcolm's and there was little Malcolm could do to discipline him. Joseph's loyalty to Elijah Muhammad and the NOI, however, was unswerving.

Prior to Malcolm's troubles with Elijah Muhammad, the relationship between

A former friend, Captain Joseph (left) eventually became one of Malcolm's most bitter
foes. Library of Congress.

Malcolm and Captain Joseph had been a good one, or so Malcolm thought.
There was certainly nothing on the surface to directly indicate an impending
breach between the two of them. According to Malcolm's nephew, Rodnell
Collins,* and Malcolm himself, Malcolm had personally recruited Joseph into
the NOI from the Detroit* gutter in 1952. Joseph was impressed with Malcolm
from the beginning of their association. Long after Malcolm's death Joseph
acknowledged Malcolm as the most brilliant man he had ever known. Joseph,
whose pre-NOI name was Joseph Gravitts (before his death, he would call himself Yusuf Shah), was a dope addict, alcoholic, and wife abuser, and Malcolm
had cleaned him up through a model self-improvement* and rehabilitation program. The improvement had been so thorough with Joseph and others similar
to him that Malcolm had "fished" into the NOI, Collins claimed, that an unsuccessful proposal was made to New York social services officials to consider
adopting the program to help others.

    Apparently Joseph's rise in Temple Number Seven was rapid, and Malcolm
certainly trusted him. When Malcolm learned in greater detail about Elijah Mu-

hammad's sexual improprieties with several of Muhammad's personal secretaries, he informed Joseph and a number of other Muslim* leaders about it, including Boston temple minister Louis X Farrakhan.* In part, this influenced Malcolm's undoing in the NOI. Joseph, who was supposedly smarting over a failure to receive a higher position in the Chicago headquarters and blaming Malcolm for it, quickly reported to John Ali,* one of Muhammad's closest lieutenants, that it was Malcolm who was spreading rumors about the NOI leader's sexual peccadilloes and paternity problems. Thereafter, the breach widened considerably between Malcolm and Muhammad, and between Malcolm and Captain Joseph. Malcolm correctly blamed Joseph for working with John Ali, Muhammad's son-in-law and Supreme FOI Commander, Raymond Sharrieff,* and other envious NOI insiders to intensify the discord between himself and his mentor. He sought to remove Joseph from his post, but Muhammad denied the request, and in the end, there was little that he could do to stop the tempest that was swirling around him.

Essentially a spy close to the center of Temple Number Seven authority, Joseph, "the fat one," as Malcolm pejoratively referred to him, kept Elijah Muhammad informed about Malcolm's activities and comments. When Malcolm was permanently relieved of his duties in the temple, Joseph, as a major player in the turn of events, saw his responsibilities in the temple expand immensely. Accordingly, his criticisms of Malcolm became more threatening and more frequent. It was, Joseph, for example, who roundly blamed Malcolm for setting a middle-of-the-night fire to his own home in February 1965. According to one historian who chronicled a study of the conspiracy theories of the assassination of Malcolm X,* it was Joseph who issued one of the initial death orders against Malcolm, organized an assassin team from Newark, New Jersey, and predicted the day before the assassination that Malcolm's murder was imminent.

Historian Zak Kondo claims that Joseph "dropped seeds" that led to Malcolm's murder. Indeed, at one time Malcolm himself would say that it was Joseph who was the most decisive in planning his assassination. In 1991 interview with Spike Lee,* Joseph refused to answer the question if someone had given him orders to kill Malcolm. But how crucial Joseph's role actually was in the death is still open to speculation. To be sure, there is every indication that Joseph acquired an intense dislike for Malcolm, and Malcolm in turn for him. But by the time that Malcolm was killed, the climate of bitterness between him and other loyal Muhammad supporters was so strong that threats and rumors came from many NOI quarters. That Joseph helped to charge the atmosphere is undeniable, and in this respect he was hardly an innocent bystander who believed that he had nothing to gain from Malcolm's death. Apparently time never tempered Joseph's intense dislike for Malcolm, and long after Malcolm's death Joseph refused to acknowledge any remorse over the assassination. As he had in 1964 and 1965, during the 1990s Joseph still referred to Malcolm X as a "Benedict Arnold."

SELECTED BIBLIOGRAPHY

Blackside/PBS, 1994; CBS News, 1992; Clegg, 1997; Collins with Bailey, 1998; Friedly, 1992; Goldman, 1979; Kondo, 1993; Lee with Wiley, 1992; Malcolm X (Clark, ed.), 1992.

Robert L. Jenkins

GRAY, JESSE. Jesse Gray was a friend of Malcolm X and the leader and organizer of a rent strike and housing movement in Harlem.* Like Malcolm, in the early 1960s Gray was considered a radical and on the periphery of the civil rights movement,* which was concentrated in southern states and cities. While racial segregation* and white supremacy in the South* were considered to be important issues, the movement did not address problems in the North that were just as complex and intractable. These included dilapidated housing, roach-infested tenement buildings, rats that were biting babies in urban dwellings, and general disrepair of apartment and housing residences. Gray, like Malcolm in the wider political arena regarding human rights,* contended that there must be a quid pro quo between landlords and tenants. Simply collecting rent every month, while ignoring the problems that tenants related to their dwellings, was unacceptable based upon Gray's movement philosophy. Malcolm maintained that the civil rights movement preaching nonviolence in the face of violence was just as unacceptable.

Once Malcolm established the Organization of Afro-American Unity,* he increasingly reached out to Gray as part of a coalition-building process in addressing issues of mutual concern. Just as Malcolm had a militant image created and perpetuated by the media, Gray was considered a "militant civil rights activist." Malcolm publicly supported Gray and spoke at a number of rallies sponsored by the Community Council on Housing headed by Gray. Likewise, Gray supported Malcolm's efforts in political liberation and human rights and spoke on Malcolm's platform on more than one occasion. Both Gray and Malcolm were critical of Police Commissioner Michael J. Murphy for police treatment of race-related police incidents, and their unfavorable comments often appeared in New York City newspapers. When Malcolm was assassinated, Gray came under the scrutiny of the Federal Bureau of Investigation* for advocating a picket line and boycott of retail merchants on 125th Street in Harlem who did not close their stores out of respect for the slain leader.

SELECTED BIBLIOGRAPHY

Carson (Gallen, ed.), 1991; Cone, 1991; Sales, 1994; Walker, 1965.

Mfanya Donald Tryman

GREAT DEPRESSION. Symbolic of the beginning of the Great Depression was the October 29, 1929 crash of the New York Stock Market. Until the nation's entry into World War II* ended it, the Great Depression marked the worst economic upheaval in America's history. The Great Depression was a significant period for the origin of a number of movements and the founding of organizations. It was in Detroit, Michigan,* in 1931 during the Great Depression that the Nation of Islam* was founded, an organization Malcolm eventually joined and arguably became its most recognized member.

Malcolm X was born four years before the Stock Market crash. As a youth growing up in the 1930s, he was profoundly affected by the economic deprivation that his family endured. Malcolm often reflected upon how his mother, Louise Little,* boiled dandelion greens to feed the eleven children that made up the family and how he and his brothers would go out at night to steal whatever they could to satisfy their hunger. Living in the rural area in Lansing, Michigan,* at the time of the depression, Malcolm recalls he also often went into town after school and tried to steal fruit to alleviate his hunger. Occasionally, he also would show up at some of his parents' friends' houses around dinnertime, knowing that they would offer him dinner as well. The poverty and hunger of the Little family worsened after the death of Malcolm's father, who had been the breadwinner for the family. Malcolm referred to this depressed economic era as an example of how already deprived people, especially African Americans, were further negatively impacted by the turn of events.

Having a large number of brothers and sisters and no father, the Littles survived, in part, on handouts from other families and state relief. Malcolm's mother attempted to hold the family together economically by taking a part-time job as a seamstress and doing domestic work. Although very light in complexion, employers eventually found out that she had black blood. Consequently, she was fired and returned home, attempting to hold back tears in front of her children. It was during the depression that Malcolm's family reached the nadir, and the state welfare agency broke the Littles up because they felt that Malcolm's widowed mother could no longer take care of them.

SELECTED BIBLIOGRAPHY

Lomax, 1963; Malcolm X with Haley, 1965; B. Perry, 1991.

Mfanya Donald Tryman

GREGORY, DICK (Richard Claxton Gregory). Richard Claxton "Dick" Gregory was born in 1932 in St. Louis, Missouri. He grew up in poverty during the Great Depression.* He ran track while in high school and received an athletic scholarship to Southern Illinois University. After serving in the U.S. Army and holding several jobs, he began a career as a comedian performing in black nightclubs. His big break in show business came in 1961 when he replaced another comedian unable to fulfill his booking at Chicago's* Playboy Club. He became an instant success. Thereafter, television appearances and coverage by *Time* magazine helped to propel him to fame as a black entertainer.

Gregory had a genuine concern for political and social issues and a commitment to civil rights.* His civil rights activism began in high school when he led a march on the St. Louis, Missouri, school board in protest of a policy that

Comedian Dick Gregory, a friend of Malcolm and noted civil rights activist, is led into a police paddy wagon by Birmingham policemen during a street demonstration. Copyright, Photo by *The Birmingham News*, 2001. All rights reserved. Reprinted with permission.

excluded black high school sports records from recognition in the city's official sports record books. Later in life he participated in numerous civil rights demonstrations in the South* and performed benefits for organizations such as the Congress of Racial Equality (CORE)* and the Student Non-Violent Coordinating Committee (SNCC).*

Gregory met Malcolm X in the early 1960s. Despite his association with the nonviolent protest movement, Gregory and Malcolm developed a close friendship. Occasionally the two met and fraternized at a popular Harlem* café. The two held mutual respect and appreciation for each other—Gregory for Malcolm's courage and strong sense of morality, Malcolm for Gregory's comedy talent, bluntness, and social activism. At the height of Malcolm's disillusionment with Elijah Muhammad,* a negative remark from Gregory in his Apollo Theatre* dressing room about Muhammad's paternity problems briefly angered Malcolm. But the two were never estranged. Prior to Malcolm's death, when he was beginning to contemplate movement into a larger civil rights role, Gregory praised Malcolm and predicted that the Islamic leader would play a leading role in the Black Revolt. Malcolm's addition, he said, would be "a solid gain for the struggle." In one of Malcolm's last public speeches, he invited Gregory to speak to the audience and afterward praised the comedian as a "freedom fighter," a true revolutionist.

SELECTED BIBLIOGRAPHY

Breitman, 1967; DeCaro, 1996; Gregory with Lipsyte, 1972; Gregory with McGraw, 1976; Malcolm X with Haley, 1965; *Militant*, April 20, 1964.

Lauren Larsen and Robert L. Jenkins

GUERRILLA WARFARE. Malcolm X vehemently disagreed with Dr. Martin Luther King, Jr.'s* concept of nonviolence, advocating armed-self-defense* instead when necessary for black freedom. Malcolm maintained that there are no revolutions that are nonviolent. At the global level, he supported revolutionary violence in support of liberation movements. Malcolm believed that guerrilla warfare was effective in neutralizing the power of the colonial state. Accordingly, he recognized the possible utility of guerrilla warfare in the United States to offset the government's use of military* power to buttress institutional racism. In his "The Ballot or the Bullet"* speech given on April 3, 1964, Malcolm observed that dark-skinned people invariably had defeated whites in guerrilla warfare, the prevailing military mode throughout the world.

Nevertheless, Malcolm held out some hope for the reformist strategies of the civil rights movement.* His phrase "the ballot or the bullet" implied that unless electoral politics brought genuine empowerment to blacks, including control of their own communities, then urban guerrilla warfare would be the natural alternative. In addition, Malcolm contended that the fear that guerrilla warfare evoked in whites might help break the back of white racism.

SELECTED BIBLIOGRAPHY

Bracey, Meier, and Rudwick, eds., 1970; Malcolm X (Breitman, ed.), 1965.

Monte Piliawsky

GUEVARA, ERNESTO "CHE." Reared in a middle-class family, Che Guevara earned a medical degree at the age of twenty-five. However, his genuine concern for the impoverished convinced him of the need for a global socialist revolution. Guevara developed the *foco* theory of guerrilla warfare* that deployed a mobile jungle base.

Guevara was Fidel Castro's most trusted military* strategist during the Cuban Revolution (1956–59). In the early 1960s, serving as Minister of Industries, he reoriented the Cuban economy toward socialism. Guevara was killed in 1967 while leading a guerrilla band in Bolivia.

Guevara's role as a symbol of revolutionary commitment and heroism for white new leftists in the late 1960s paralleled Malcolm X's inspirational role as an apostle of black liberation for African Americans. Although Malcolm never

met Che, he did confer for two hours with Che's confidant and friend Fidel
Castro* at Harlem's* Hotel Theresa* in September 1960 during Castro's visit
to the United States.

Malcolm viewed black nationalism* in an international perspective as part of
a larger revolutionary reaction to white racist oppression. Malcolm offered rhetorical support for guerrilla warfare in the United States. Both Guevara and
Malcolm toured Africa in the mid-1960s, opposing imperialism and neocolonialism. Both men fueled Third World consciousness, resulting in a subsequent
powerful nonaligned movement of developing nations. Guevara exported revolution to other countries. Malcolm attempted to start a revolution in the United
States. Shortly before his death, Malcolm had invited Che to speak at one of
his Harlem rallies, but the international revolutionary could not make it because
of other commitments. Malcolm proudly read Che's message apologizing for
his absence and filled with warm words of encouragement to the Organization
of Afro-American Unity* gathering.

SELECTED BIBLIOGRAPHY

Anderson, 1997; Guevara, 1968; Malcolm X (Breitman, ed.), 1965; Sinclair, 1970.

Monte Piliawsky

H

HAGGINS, ROBERT. Malcolm X's life as a black leader centered around the media. Besides Martin Luther King, Jr.,* no African American commanded the attention that he did from either the printed or the electronic media.* Malcolm's world was also photographically centered. He personally loved the camera, being behind the camera as well as being the subject of photography. Hence, with his being a popular subject for media interviews, he was also one of the nation's most photographed personalities. Few did as much to preserve Malcolm in photographic image than did Robert Haggins, a photographer and reporter for the radical *New York Citizen Call,* a black tabloid.

Haggins first met Malcolm in a 1960 interview assignment. From the outset, Malcolm impressed him. Specifically, what Haggins found so informative and intriguing was Malcolm's explanation about the meaning of the "X"* in his name and the importance of black people not identifying with their former slave masters by continuing to carry their last name. Malcolm had awakened something in Haggins that no one else had done before. It was in this meeting, Haggins would later say, that he became a Muslim,* though it was not something he was aware of at the time. Apparently, Malcolm was mutually impressed with Haggins and, seeking an alternative to the white press's portrayal of him as a violent ogre, designated Haggins as his personal photographer. Thereafter, Haggins was almost a constant companion of Malcolm's, traveling widely with him in his new photographic capacity. At Malcolm's, urging, Haggins's work sought primarily to capture the human side of Malcolm, and many of the best photographs of the Muslim leader, whether in personal conversation with someone, in a family setting, or simply in intellectual contemplation, depicted Malcolm's quiet, compassionate, and soft demeanor, a side that Malcolm seldom revealed to the public. Understandably, the two men grew close in their relationship, and Haggins became a devoted Malcolm friend and follower in both the Nation of Islam (NOI)* and after Malcolm's break with the organization. It was Malcolm, Haggins would later say, who taught him so much about life. As a display of his admiration for his friend, Malcolm, upon his return from Mecca,* would give his personal clothing bag and personal camera as gifts to Haggins. Haggins was in the Audubon Ballroom* the evening that Malcolm was murdered. It was Haggins who supposedly tripped Talmadge Hayer,* one of the men convicted of killing Malcolm as he sought to escape the shooting scene.

Although photographers such as Gordon Parks,* Eve Arnold, Bob Adelman, staff camera personnel from United Press International, the Associated Press, and a host of other media-connected people took literally thousands of surviving photos of Malcolm, none seem to capture the public and private Malcolm more forcefully and humanely than do those taken by Haggins. What they captured remain some of the most enduring aspects of the Malcolm X legacy. Haggins continues to hold the negatives, and hence photographic rights, to hundreds of the pictures taken of the NOI and Malcolm, including one of Malcolm lying dead at the murder scene.

SELECTED BIBLIOGRAPHY

T. Davis (Chapnick, ed.), 1993; Gallen, ed., 1992; Lee with Wiley, 1992.

Robert L. Jenkins

HAJJ. By January 1964 Malcolm X had already come to realize that his break with the Nation of Islam (NOI)* would be permanent. He lamented the disassociation, for on numerous occasions he expressed what most had long known: His bond with Elijah Muhammad,* head of the sect, had always been strong and genuine. Despite the problem that led to the ruptured relationship, the break would be difficult. It had, after all, been Muhammad who was responsible for the opportunity that made Malcolm a nationally recognized leader, but more important, he was an integral force in Malcolm's life, the one person whom Malcolm credited as guiding and inspiring his redemption from a purposeless and dishonorable life. Although he could hardly predict it at the time, however, Malcolm's departure from the NOI and Muhammad proved beneficial in his development politically, philosophically, and spiritually. It was particularly his spiritual growth and maturity that many took notice of within months of his independent course and that invariably influenced a reshaping of his political thought. This change occurred as a direct result of his conversion to orthodox Islam* and his Hajj in the spring of 1964 to Mecca.* As required by the religion, every Muslim,* if possible, was expected to make the pilgrimage to Islam's holiest city at least once in their lifetime. Malcolm's half sister Ella Collins,* who had played an important role in his early life, herself a Muslim,* financed Malcolm's Hajj.

If Malcolm had a major interest in making the pilgrimage previously, it never manifested itself. To be sure, he had visited Saudi Arabia* in 1959, sent by his mentor to the Middle East* on a fact-finding mission, but the Hajj was not a part of his itinerary. Once he made the decision to pursue the pilgrimage in

1964, however, he worked diligently to fulfill the necessary requirements of his conversion, studiously applying himself to learn the most fundamental precepts of the religion. After considerable consultations and preparation by orthodox Muslim leaders in New York, Islamic officials in Saudi Arabia granted him permission to enter the city. It was literally an eye-opening life experience for Malcolm, accustomed to only the narrow, racially oriented version of Islam as taught and practiced by Elijah Muhammad and the NOI. On the Hajj, Malcolm saw people of various cultures and racial stock worshiping together in equality. Despite their often color differences, he learned of their acceptance of each other in true Islamic brotherhood, and it inspired him to give to other blacks a greater appreciation for the religion. While in Mecca he visited many major holy sites. He was treated like a dignitary, even honored by the country's monarch. He followed his initial trip to Mecca with a second one, the Omra, several months later.

Malcolm readily acknowledged the personal spiritual development that he derived from the Hajj. But it was the modification of his racial politics and philosophy that was most affected. The Hajj clearly influenced him to abandon his blanket condemnation of all whites as insincere in their relationship with blacks. Even interracial marriage,* an institution that Malcolm often expressed a dislike for in the most strident rhetoric, became more tolerable to him. After his return to the United States, he developed genuine relationships with numerous whites, persons whom he came to like, trust, and truly respect. And they felt similarly about him, some appreciating more than ever before his sincerity and commitment to fight racism and help liberate the black masses. Although Malcolm returned from the Hajj with a new component to his name, El-Hajj Malik El-Shabazz* (long before his Hajj, Malcolm referred to himself by the name of Malik Shabazz), and a modified belief in the possibilities of black and white relations, he never completely veered from his general mistrust of whites or his opposition to racial integration* as a viable solution to the black plight in the Western world. He had made, nevertheless, significant movement from where he had been only several months before.

SELECTED BIBLIOGRAPHY

Carson (Gallen, ed.,), 1991; Clegg, 1997; DeCaro, 1996; Goldman, 1979; Malcolm X with Haley, 1965; B. Perry, 1991; Strickland (Greene, ed.), 1994.

Robert L. Jenkins

HALEY, ALEX PALMER. Journalist Alex Haley had a relatively undistinguished career until his recognition as the moving force behind the completion of *The Autobiography of Malcolm X** in 1965. Just as that work became one of the most influential books of the 1960s, so did Haley's Pulitzer Prize–winning *Roots* in the following decade, which later also won acclaim as a multipart miniseries on national television. Prior to his unexpected death in 1992, Haley was widely saluted as one of America's pivotal forces in restoring pride in the black heritage.

Although born in Ithaca, New York, while his father pursued a master's degree at Cornell University, Alex Haley spent his early years in his mother's ancestral home of Henning, Tennessee, where his father assumed control of the Palmer family's lumber business. Later, Haley's father moved the family to various southern cities as he pursued a teaching career in agriculture. Throughout his life, Alex Haley would credit his father's rise from humble beginnings to college teacher as the "bootstrapping" that had influenced him doggedly to pursue success. Haley attended Elizabeth City Teachers College in North Carolina from 1937 to 1939, after which he joined the U.S. Coast Guard; he retired from the service in 1959 at the rank of chief journalist, a dramatic leap from his entry position as mess boy.

Haley remained a relatively obscure journalist until he interviewed Black Muslim* leader Malcolm X in 1963 for *Playboy*. Initially Malcolm mistrusted Haley, calling him a tool of whites who came to spy on the Muslims.* Malcolm soon overcame his suspicion of Haley, however. The interview resulted in a close collaboration between Haley and Malcolm X and eventually to the publication of *The Autobiography of Malcolm X* in 1965. During the course of the book project the two men grew even closer as Malcolm revealed much about himself and the life that he had. Haley disagreed with many of Malcolm's views, but he respected him as a leader immensely. His epilogue in the autobiography is revealing and compassionate. Although Malcolm had worked closely with Haley during the interviewing stages of the book, he never had the opportunity to read the final work because of his assassination only weeks prior to the book's release. Reportedly, 6 million copies in eight languages of Malcolm's life story had been sold by the time Haley's next major work, *Roots: The Saga of an American Family*, exploded on the scene in the mid-1970s.

SELECTED BIBLIOGRAPHY

Cloyd, ed., 1990; Malcolm X with Haley, 1965; Moritz, 1977; *New York Times*, February 11, 1992.

Irvin D. Solomon

HAMER, FANNIE LOU. Fannie Lou Hamer was a former Mississippi* sharecropper who gained national prominence as a Student Non-Violent Coordinating Committee (SNCC),* civil rights,* and political activist. She was once described as one of the angriest women in Mississippi. Yet it was that anger that gave her the tenacity and determination to seek change in America.

Malcolm X described Hamer as one of the country's foremost freedom fighters in the forefront of the Mississippi black rights struggle. Hamer's desire to become involved in the civil rights movement* was motivated by the harsh life her parents were forced to live. It was also driven by a racist and violent system that victimized blacks. Her belief in the tenets of democracy caused her to

Malcolm admired Mississippi grassroots civil rights leader Fannie Lou Hamer. Library of Congress.

always pose the question "Is this America?" when it came to the treatment of blacks.

As a prominent force in the civil rights movement, she challenged the president and the national Democratic Party* to do more for blacks. She was a founding member of the Mississippi Freedom Democratic Party (MFDP)* and played a key role in mobilizing the community around the civil rights movement.

Malcolm first met Hamer in December 1964 when she came to Harlem* to solicit support for the MFDP's effort to unseat the regular white Democratic congressional delegation. The two shared a speaking platform at the church where she spoke. This occurred after Hamer, in a racially integrated delegation, tried to unseat the segregated, white Mississippi delegation to the 1964 Democratic National Convention in Atlantic City, New Jersey.

Malcolm learned much about Hamer and what she and other blacks endured in SNCC's Mississippi campaign. He was touched by Hamer's personal struggles with Mississippi whites and, when he spoke, broached the prospect of a Mau Mau*–type uprising in Mississippi if whites failed to grant concessions.

Malcolm was so impressed with Hamer's speech that he invited her to an Organization of Afro-American Unity (OAAU)* meeting scheduled for the same night. During the course of his speech he promised her the support of the OAAU in whatever ways they were needed in Mississippi's civil rights struggle. Malcolm told the crowd that either white Mississippi would have to deal with Hamer's party or face the prospects of dealing with him and more violent alternatives. A woman with a fighting and God-fearing spirit, Hamer became a symbol of strength, courage, and perseverance for all.

SELECTED BIBLIOGRAPHY

Branch, 1998; Carson (Gallen, ed.), 1991; Crawford et al., 1990; Malcolm X (Breitman, ed.), 1965; K. Mills, 1993.

LaVerne Gyant

HAMPTON, LIONEL. Lionel Hampton was a major figure during the big band, jazz-Swing era who played, like many other noted jazz musicians, at Boston's Roseland Ballroom.* As young "Detroit Red," Malcolm X hustled and shined shoes at the Roseland for Hampton, Duke Ellington,* Count Basie,* and other black big band entertainers of that day. Hampton became famous for his musical improvisations on the "vibes." Hampton's skills were recognized by the major white Swing-era jazzman Benny Goodman, who hired him to play in (thus desegregating) his quartet. This type of jazz became the cultural and social context through which Malcolm X learned that life was a "hustle." Malcolm was enthralled by this music and developed his own musical innovation by popping his shoeshine rag to the beat of the musician's recordings.

Hampton knew Malcolm on a first-name basis, and the two frequently encountered each other in the ballrooms and clubs that catered to black nightlife. It was at some of these clubs that Malcolm made a name for himself because of his dancing ability. Malcolm had considerable respect for Hampton, not only as a musician but also as a businessman. Hampton uniquely found ways to earn greater salaries than most music entertainers by contracting with ballroom owners for a share of the gate receipts.

Jazz, for many Black Muslims,* retained its importance after they left the hustling, sporting life of the Roseland and other ballrooms. This music is played in the temples before religious teaching begins.

SELECTED BIBLIOGRAPHY

Hampton with Haskins, 1989; Malcolm X with Haley, 1965; Tirro, 1993.

Malik Simba

HANDLER, M. S. M. S. "Mike" Handler was a journalist for the *New York Times** whose experience with the press had spanned more than thirty years by the 1960s. Handler spent much of his early career in western and eastern Europe,* where he reported on a variety of social and political issues for the *Times* before being reassigned to New York. Primarily the *Times* obituary writer before moving to the night editor's desk, Handler was soon attracted to issues relative to the restlessness in black America. He found the Nation of Islam (NOI)* and Malcolm X interesting copy; hence, he followed their activities closely and authored numerous articles about them and their activities for the paper. It was largely his interest in reporting on the NOI and tensions in the black community during the 1960s that led him directly to Malcolm X. Their first encounter occurred in 1963 in the Temple Number Seven Restaurant,* Malcolm's normal meeting place on Lennox Avenue in Harlem* for interviews with the press. The two talked for more than three hours, Handler largely listening as Malcolm expounded his normal criticism of whites, the effect of racism on black people, and NOI doctrine. Numerous other meetings would follow between the two men, some of them little more than a simple walk with Malcolm down the sidewalks of Harlem. In short order, there developed a warm and genuine friendship between Handler and Malcolm. On occasions, Handler even entertained Malcolm in his home. Unusual for Malcolm in his relationship with whites, in a personal letter to Handler from Egypt during his second 1964 trip to Africa, he confided some of his deepest and most critical thoughts about his mentor, Elijah Muhammad.*

Malcolm greatly impressed the New York journalist with his intelligence and leadership ability. To the chagrin of Muhammad, Handler gave Malcolm the credit for the increasing popularity of black nationalism* among urban blacks and, long before the break with Muhammad's sect, declared Malcolm as the real head of the NOI. He contended that Malcolm's status as a beloved figure among urban blacks was well deserved. Malcolm, he wrote, was brutally honest with the black masses and had the ability not only to articulate their concerns and aspirations but also to embolden them in their demands. Unlike many whites, especially among the press corp, Handler understood much about what Malcolm sought to achieve for black people. Perhaps his experience as an international reporter gave him the ability to look beyond the charisma and rhetoric of the political Malcolm to see a "remarkable" leader who in the last days of his life was in the process of redefining himself and fashioning an operational program for the African American dilemma in the United States.

SELECTED BIBLIOGRAPHY

Branch, 1998; Davis and Dee, 1998; DeCaro, 1996; Friedly, 1992; Malcolm X with Haley, 1965; *New York Times*, April 20, 1963.

Robert L. Jenkins

HANSBERRY, LORRAINE. Although her career was brief, native Chicagoan Lorraine Hansberry was one of twentieth-century Black America's most gifted literary figures and playwrights. Her most accomplished production, which was also her first, was *A Raisin in the Sun*, which opened on Broadway in 1959. The critically acclaimed and award-winning play about the middle-class aspirations of a poverty-stricken black family was eventually made into a Hollywood movie. By nature a challenging and outspoken personality, these traits were characteristic of her work and were particularly visible in how she dramatized biting social issues. Among the luminaries in the arts, Hansberry was clearly one of the era's prominent champions of black uplift. Despite her support of racial integration,* she could and often did pursue causes aggressively and was closely identified with a group of Harlem* intellectuals associated with black nationalism.*

Like Malcolm X, Hansberry was a critic of United Nations* Under Secretary Dr. Ralph Bunche* and mirrored Malcolm's condemnation of the murder of African leader Patrice Lumumba.* Nevertheless, as a prominent New Yorker whose associations crossed diverse racial and class lines, Hansberry became an easy target for Malcolm X's criticisms. It was her interracial marriage* that subjected her most to Malcolm's scorn. In the early 1960s, Malcolm frequently called negative attention to the tendency of well-known blacks in the entertainment industry to marry whites. In his view this was a serious personal flaw, but more important, Malcolm regarded any form of racial integration* as potentially destructive to the race. Hansberry resented the frequent references to her marriage, and when she had a chance to meet Malcolm, she told him so in no uncertain terms. By then, however, Malcolm had already moderated his views on interracial marriage, if not total racial integration, the effect of his eye-opening 1964 pilgrimage to Mecca.* Apparently, Malcolm found a way to win Hansberry over, and the two became fast friends and great admirers of each other. A reflection of how much the relationship between the two had grown was further amplified when, in January 1965, slightly more than a month before his assassination, Malcolm was part of a large turnout at Hansberry's funeral. At her death, Hansberry was only thirty-five years old.

SELECTED BIBLIOGRAPHY

A. Alexander, 1999; Branch, 1988; Cruse, 1967; Evanzz, 1992; Goldman, 1977; Hansberry, 1964.

Robert L. Jenkins

HARLEM. During the 1960s, Harlem, New York, known as the black Mecca,* had the largest concentration of African Americans of any other black American community. It became well known when many blacks migrated to the city in the early twentieth century. This migration, in part, influenced the Harlem Renaissance, which represented a flowering of intellectual, cultural, and social activity in the black community. Harlem represented the ideal city for black America. It offered opportunities and excitement at its famous entertainment spots such as the Cotton Club, Connie's Inn, and the Apollo Theatre.* The best black entertainment could be found at these establishments. Life for blacks appeared very exciting in Harlem. As a result, it attracted African Americans like Malcolm X, who eventually ventured there from Boston in 1942.

Several civil rights leaders including Andrew Young (second from left), James Farmer (fourth from left), and John Lewis (on right), on platform in Harlem. Lawyer Percy Sutton and black nationalist bookstore owner Lewis Michaux sit in the background. Library of Congress.

Harlem's exciting social and cultural activities intrigued Malcolm, and he quickly established a name among Harlemites. He made numerous friends and enjoyed the good life. As a result of too much time spent in the streets having a good time, Malcolm lost his job as a cook in Boston, where he lived, because he would not report to work as required; Harlem was consuming him.

After Malcolm lost his job, he moved permanently to Harlem without any money or employment. He soon acquired a job as a waiter in the famous night-club Small's Paradise Club.* In 1943, an army spy had visited Small's and reported Malcolm to the police for attempting to set him up with a prostitute. Malcolm did not have a police record, so he was released. However, he lost his job at Small's and was barred from entering the club again. This incident led to Malcolm's life as a cocaine addict and hustler. He also engaged in other forms of criminal activity in Harlem. Malcolm's criminal activity eventually caught up with him in Boston and led to his conviction for stolen jewelry.

In 1952, after spending six and a half years in Massachusetts prisons, Malcolm joined the Nation of Islam (NOI)* under leader Elijah Muhammad.* In 1954 Muhammad assigned Malcolm to the mosque in Harlem. He became chief minister of New York Temple Number Seven* and assumed responsibility for delivering the word from Allah,* recruiting members, and making the temple more visible in the black community. Of course, Malcolm had to compete with other religious groups in Harlem. Malcolm distributed information about the teachings of Muhammad to attract people to the temple. He had his greatest success among members of the Christian denominations. Many would come to hear his teachings about Allah and how Christianity* had failed black people. Muslim* membership at Temple Number Seven gradually increased, where Malcolm served as minister until March 1964.

Due to Malcolm's efforts, the NOI increased its membership in Harlem and other major cities. He preached Islam* to thousands of converts, and his congregation became the most well known in the Black Muslim* community. As he became more powerful, conflict developed between Malcolm and Elijah Muhammad. Malcolm felt that the NOI should take a more activist position and assist non-Muslim blacks in the struggle for civil rights.*

In 1964, Malcolm broke away from the NOI and started his own religious group, the Muslim Mosque, Inc.* Soon thereafter, he began the Harlem-based Organization for Afro-American Unity* to address black political and human rights* issues. Malcolm had evidence to prove that a high percentage of New York City's blacks responded to his teachings in both the spiritual and political arenas. On February 21, 1965, Malcolm was assassinated at the Audubon Ballroom* in Harlem. His death, however, did not end an identity that blacks had long maintained with Black Harlem.

SELECTED BIBLIOGRAPHY

Davies, 1990; Malcolm X with Haley, 1965; Myers, 1993; A. Smith, 1982.

LaVonne Jackson

HARLEM RENT STRIKE. The Harlem Rent Strike was an organized protest in Harlem,* New York, initiated in February 1965 by local black activists under the leadership of Jesse Gray,* a close friend of Malcolm's. The protest was aimed at mostly white slum landlords who refused to make necessary housing and apartment repairs, yet insisted on collecting rent every month from black tenants. The problems included dilapidated housing, uncontrolled rats and mice that were biting babies and children, defective plumbing, faulty electrical wiring and systems, and related problems of maintenance. Gray headed the Community Council on Housing, a neighborhood organization that advocated residential reforms in the Harlem area.

Malcolm supported the Harlem Rent Strike verbally but would not march or participate in nonviolent protest. He reasoned that there would not be any guarantee that those in opposition to nonviolent protest marches in support of the Harlem Rent Strike would also be nonviolent. Given his philosophy of self-defense,* he argued that he would only be as nonviolent as the opposition. Nevertheless, when Malcolm founded the Organization of Afro-American Unity,* he supported a two-pronged attack on housing problems. He argued for a self-improvement* housing program as well as a housing rent strike. In fact, he proposed a rent strike that would include all of Harlem, not just one particular block or area. Essentially, though, he felt that no outsider could clean up their own houses and neighborhoods better than the people who lived in them. Malcolm felt that slum housing conditions were just one among a number of factors that might lead to long hot summers* in big cities and that the Harlem Rent Strike was just a precursor of things to come.

SELECTED BIBLIOGRAPHY

Cone, 1991; Malcolm X (Breitman, ed.), 1970a; Sales, 1994; Walker, 1965.

Mfanya Donald Tryman

HARLEM STREET CORNER INTELLECTUALS. As minister of Temple Number Seven* in Harlem* starting in 1954, Malcolm was exposed to, and participated as one of, the "Harlem Street Corner Intellectuals" at the corner of 125th and Seventh Avenue. It was at this corner that a bookstore existed, owned and operated by Lewis Michaux,* known as the National Memorial African Bookstore—"The House of Common Sense and Home of Proper Propaganda." The corner and bookstore represented a hotbed of black nationalism* in Harlem, and it was relatively easy for debaters of issues or lone speakers to attract a crowd, for people in Harlem were already among the most destitute, and having someone to vent their anger at and blame for their segregated conditions was a natural attraction for speakers and debaters. Lone speakers were literally seen on a portable soapbox alternatively lecturing, haranguing, admonishing, criticizing, and informing listening audiences and passersby about black nationalism and various issues related to race relations, black history,* and the coming race war in America.

While initially laboring in obscurity in what Malcolm referred to as "fishing"*
for new recruits, he gradually became a regular and increasingly popular figure
at these rallies and debates. Fishing meant mingling among the crowd and encouraging people to attend the Nation of Islam (NOI)* meetings at the local
temple. But as his popularity grew, it became increasingly common to see Malcolm on a dais debating or sharing the podium with Pan-Africanists, Garveyites,
and black nationalists—including Michaux, Elombe Braath,* Ahmed Basheer,
George Reed, Carlos Cooks,* Josef Ben Jochannan, James Lawson,* and Eddie
"Pork Chop" Davis. Given Malcolm's charisma, debating skills, and oratorical
ability, it was relatively easy for him and his quixotic adversaries to attract an
audience that sometimes swelled into the thousands.

Malcolm was more formal and structured in preparation and delivery than
other black nationalists that occupied the scene. Rather than stand on a soapbox,
he was more prone to have a dais that could accommodate several guest speakers
or debaters, with bunting, microphones, and posters. In addition, he would often
stand in the crowd and observe his assistant ministers of Temple Seven speak
to and lecture crowds on Islam* and other topics. Malcolm was, of course,
almost invariably dressed in the traditional NOI dark suit and bow tie, the latter
a trademark of the sect. But as the national spokesman for the NOI, his designated title, he also enjoyed "one on one" political and historical arguments with
Michaux and other black nationalists in the backroom of Michaux's bookstore,
where there was no audience to sway and even less formality.

SELECTED BIBLIOGRAPHY

Goldman, 1979; Karim, with Skutches and Gallen, 1992; Sales, 1994.

Mfanya Donald Tryman

HARLEM STREET RALLIES. Almost from the start of Harlem's* beginnings as a black ghetto, street rallies became a common feature of the landscape.
The varied special interest groups and individual leaders, however radical or
mainstream, who called the community home could readily find an audience to
espouse their views. From a makeshift stage or elevated platform in front of
well-known landmarks such as the Hotel Theresa,* Lewis Michaux's* National
Memorial African Bookstore, or any street corner busy with street traffic, the
rallies were an important conduit through which advocates and community leaders could convey their messages to interested and affected constituencies. Sometimes these rallies were announced far in advance and were well organized with
a slate of known and unknown speakers; at other times they might be more
spontaneous. Saturdays and Sundays were especially popular days to host them,
often making Harlem a beehive of activities with more than one occurring simultaneously. By the time of Malcolm X's emergence as a Nation of Islam
(NOI)* leader, these rallies were already legendary, but few could attract the
crowds that he could. Malcolm knew how to work a crowd, and he used this
ability with telling effect. Witnesses maintain that only a few who heard him

speak could not feel the electriclike charge that flowed from his words and emotions. As much a reflection of his popularity as they were opportunities to espouse his views about black self-improvement,* black nationalism,* and racial solidarity, civil rights,* the evils of white racism, the philosophy of Elijah Muhammad* and the NOI, the rallies soon became a source of major concern to Muhammad and the NOI inner circle. Jealous of his charismatic appeal and escalating international prominence, the NOI's Chicago, Illinois* headquarters instructed Malcolm to discontinue the rallies, but he persisted and their size, frequency, and popularity grew exponentially. After his expulsion from the NOI and the founding of his own Organization of Afro-American Unity,* Malcolm's street rallies became as important a source for expounding his message to the disaffected black urban dwellers as was the press to a larger, often more sophisticated and racially diverse audience.

SELECTED BIBLIOGRAPHY

T. Davis (Chapnick, ed.), 1993; Hampton and Fayer with Flynn, eds., 1991; Myers, 1993; Osofsky, 1971; Sales, 1994; Strickland (Greene, ed.), 1994.

Robert L. Jenkins

HARRIS, DONALD. Donald Harris was a Student Non-Violent Coordinating Committee (SNCC)* staffer whose civil rights* work involved him in numerous southern campaigns. During the 1963 Georgia movement, he was arrested on a spurious charge of seditious conspiracy in Americus, a capital offense in the state, and for several months faced a possible death penalty for the offense if found guilty. Like several other members of SNCC in the mid-1960s, Harris and Malcolm established personal contact with each other, though the relationship never had the opportunity to blossom into something more significant. Increasingly, SNCC staffers, frustrated by the slow gains of the civil rights era and the constant personal danger from southern white provocateurs, came under Malcolm X's influence in the months before his death.

   During the summer of 1964 Malcolm began an extensive trip to Africa and the Middle East.* East African nations such as Ethiopia, Kenya, and Tanzania and West Africa's Nigeria* and French West Africa (now Guinea) welcomed the black American leader in a manner befitting a world-renowned celebrity. Malcolm's visit occurred during a time when black nations on the continent were a popular place for African Americans to visit. Many travelers visited simply to satisfy their curiosity about developments there; others made the tour to establish closer political, cultural, and spiritual links with leaders of these countries. It was for this latter reason that Donald Harris found his way to Africa. At the time that Malcolm was on his second tour, a small contingent of activists from SNCC were also touring the continent. Financed by a gift from longtime SNCC champion and Hollywood entertainment giant Harry Belafonte, the SNCC group included other well-known veteran activists such as John Lewis,* Fannie Lou Hamer,* James Forman,* and Julian Bond. It was Harris, along with

John Lewis, who had a chance encounter with Malcolm in the lobby of a hotel in Nairobi, Kenya, on the first day of their arrival in the city. Malcolm knew neither man prior to the meeting, but they were certainly familiar with his militant message, particularly his position on armed self-defense* and Pan-Africanism.*

In a report the two submitted to SNCC, Harris indicated that over the course of two days of periodic meetings there was ample opportunity for them to move beyond formalities and talk extensively about views they shared in common. In their conversations, Malcolm talked much about what he had learned on the trip. He was particularly impressed with the African leaders' support of the black rights struggle in the United States. Harris and other SNCC staffers were steadfastly moving toward Malcolm's position of seeking a more global alignment in solving black problems. Harris indicated that Africa had opened its doors to Malcolm. The Muslim* leader already had a loyal African following and had left a significant influence on the people wherever he visited on the continent. Accordingly, Harris reported that Malcolm's views of domestic and international affairs were the yardstick by which African leaders judged him and SNCC's touring delegation. Harris and Lewis's account of their African tour and meeting with Malcolm found its way into several black newspapers after their return. It is largely the result of what they reported that adds to the understanding of Malcolm's growing influence in Africa and how the continent embraced him during the last months of his life.

SELECTED BIBLIOGRAPHY

Carson, 1981; Lewis and D'Orso, 1998; *Militant*, April 5, 1965.

Robert L. Jenkins

HARVARD UNIVERSITY. The five-part television documentary "The Hate That Hate Produced"* promoted Malcolm X and the Nation of Islam (NOI)* into national prominence. Over the next two years numerous invitations from black and white colleges and universities arrived at the NOI headquarters. Always in need of funds, the NOI encouraged Malcolm to accept the invitations. One biographer, Bruce Perry,* suggested that Malcolm's appeal was based on his oratorical techniques. However, Malcolm never felt at ease among the highly educated, and a few observers noted that at his first appearance at Harvard, he was visibly nervous. However, nervousness was something that he would overcome with time and numerous stage appearances. Malcolm's addresses to college audiences often aroused extreme reactions, from indignation, rage, and hostility to uncontrollable enthusiasm. One admirer noted that his debates were controversial but interesting.

On March 24, 1961, he appeared on a panel debating "The American Negro: Problems and Solutions" at the Harvard Law School Forum. Malcolm argued in favor of complete racial separation* as a solution to America's race problem, while Walter Carrington, a black Harvard graduate, advocated racial integration* as a viable solution. Carrington was a member of the National Association for the Advancement of Colored People (NAACP)* and the Massachusetts State Commission against Discrimination; these organizations favorably compared to what many viewed as Malcolm's questionable credentials as a leader in the NOI. Intentional or not, Carrington's role at the debate was that of foil to Malcolm. Apparently, a popular draw and a favorite among Harvard's intellectual elite, Malcolm spoke at the prestigious campus on two other occasions: in March 1964 shortly after his break with Elijah Muhammad* and in December 1964 following his return from Africa. In these subsequent speeches, Malcolm's presentations centered on issues of black nationalism* and the linking of the black American struggle to the human rights* of blacks in the international arena. In many ways, what Malcolm had to say at Harvard documents his evolution as a little known black spokesman to a major international figure with worldwide influence and appeal. Malcolm's remarks, carefully selected for his college audience, emphasized the theological nature of the NOI rather than a particular political point of view.

The significance of the Harvard Law School Forum was not the subject of the debate or its outcome. According to Malcolm, the events at the forum signaled his spiritual awareness that the religion of Islam* had elevated him from the gutter as Detroit Red.* At this point Malcolm began to distinguish between Allah* and his Messenger, Elijah Muhammad. He was still willing to die to protect Muhammad, but his deliverance he owed to the religion of Islam and Allah. Malcolm's spiritual awareness also marked the beginning of his intellectual and activist development as a political ideologue outside the tenets of NOI. Theology scholar James Cone pointed out in his study *Martin & Malcolm & America* (1991), that as a popular speaker and debater with white and black intellectuals, because Malcolm asked more questions than Elijah Muhammad, he also demanded more answers. Malcolm's appearances at elite institutions like Harvard were his first step towards secular black nationalism and his ultimate break with Elijah Muhammad.

SELECTED BIBLIOGRAPHY

Carson (Gallen, ed.), 1991; Cone, 1991; Gallen, ed., 1992; Karim with Skutches and Gallen, 1992; Lincoln, 1994; Malcolm X (Epps, ed.), 1991; Malcolm with Haley, 1965; B. Perry, 1991; Sales, 1994; Wolfenstein, 1981.

Thaddeus M. Smith

HASSAN, LEMUEL. Lemuel Hassan served as minister at Temple Number One in Detroit, Michigan.* After Malcolm was released from prison* in Massachusetts in 1952, his siblings Hilda* and Wilfred* (Little) convinced him to come to Detroit and devote himself to the Muslims.* With his family's support and Minister Lemuel Hassan's direction, Malcolm learned and absorbed the teachings of Nation of Islam (NOI)* leader Elijah Muhammad,* the Messenger of Allah.* As temple leader, Hassan charted out the connections between Christianity* and black suffering, enslavement, and death. Malcolm quickly came to understand this connection: The Cross symbolized the lynching of the black man, whereas the Muslim flag (crescent and star on a red background) emphasized that the teachings of Elijah Muhammad were the keys leading the black man to freedom, justice, and equality. However, the fact that the temple had so few members bothered Malcolm. With Minister Hassan's full support, whom Malcolm liked superficially, he began to proselytize in the streets, pool halls, bars, and any other place he found his politically and religiously blind brothers. In the fall of 1952, with the encouragement of Elijah Muhammad and Minister Hassan, Malcolm gave "extemporaneous lectures" at Temple Number One. Malcolm's activities, "fishing"* in the streets and at the temple, were so successful that the congregation tripled. For his efforts, Malcolm was named assistant minister of Temple Number One by the summer of 1953.

Malcolm publicly praised his former mentor, but by 1957 there were differences between him and Hassan. Privately, Malcolm, who by then supervised most of the NOI temples, including Detroit's, criticized Hassan for his lack of leadership. Consequently, Muhammad removed Hassan as temple minister. Malcolm temporarily replaced him and was subsequently succeeded by his older brother Wilfred.

SELECTED BIBLIOGRAPHY

Malcolm X with Haley, 1965; B. Perry, 1991; Wolfenstein, 1981.

Malik Simba

HASSOUN, SHEIK AHMED. The Muslim Mosque, Inc.,* the new organization founded by Malcolm X, became the primary site for teaching orthodox Islam.* Sheik Ahmed Hassoun, a spiritual adviser and grandfatherlike figure to Malcolm X, was a short, slightly built, dark-skinned elderly man who taught classes on a regular basis at the Muslim Mosque in Harlem.* Sheik Ahmed was from Mecca,* Saudi Arabia,* the holiest of all Islamic places. He purportedly was selected by the secretary general of the Muslim World League,* Grand Sheik Muhammad Sarur Al-Sabban, to assist Malcolm in correcting the many distortions of true Islam by religious sects in the United States. His appearance belied his astute and sharp mind. He often was seen walking leisurely with his cane, if slowly, in Harlem* with his traditional garb on.

But Sheik Ahmed was very alert and his perspicacity made him often advise Malcolm to be cautious of those who surrounded him. He counseled Malcolm on his reckless disregard for his own safety, given Malcolm's controversial persona, but to no avail. Sheik Ahmed maintained that every person who came to the Organization of Afro-American Unity (OAAU)* offices or meetings should be searched, regardless of what Malcolm wanted. Sheik Ahmed prepared Malcolm's body for a Muslim* funeral after his death but quickly exited the United States after the funeral. He had become disenchanted with the threats, violence, conflict, and discord between the Muslim Mosque and the OAAU in the wake of Malcolm's death. Malcolm's cousin and wife arranged for Sheik Ahmed's return to his native country.

SELECTED BIBLIOGRAPHY

Collins with Bailey, 1998; Gallen, ed., 1992.

Mfanya Donald Tryman

"**THE HATE THAT HATE PRODUCED.**" In July 1959, reporter Mike Wallace* produced a five-part report on the Black Muslim* movement entitled "The Hate That Hate Produced" for the CBS news show *News Beat*. Malcolm X was one of the Muslims* featured in the series. "The Hate That Hate Produced" revealed, in part, Malcolm's political and social views. This media exposure not only made the general American public aware of the Black Muslims, but it also secured Malcolm's position as the organization's leading spokesman.

The report, however, was more than just a television documentary; it was part of a political philosophy that the Black Muslim leader espoused almost until his assassination. As Malcolm stated at a London School of Economics lecture in February 1965, white Americans had taught African Americans to hate their features, blood, and who they were as a race. Consistent with Elijah Muhammad's* teaching that the real serpent in the Bible's* Adam and Eve story was the white man. Whites had to be destroyed, he said, because they were incapable of doing good. For this reason, Malcolm said he was teaching blacks to hate their white oppressors and hate groups such as the Ku Klux Klan,* who were responsible for black self-hatred.

Once he had explained the hate that hate produced, Malcolm X encouraged blacks to take a stand against their white oppressors if they were physically threatened. Blacks, in other words, had a right to defend themselves against hostile whites because these oppressors produced a hateful and harmful society for blacks.

SELECTED BIBLIOGRAPHY

Gallen, ed., 1994; Lomax, 1963; Malcolm X (Breitman, ed.), 1970a; *Newsweek*, March 23, 1964.

Craig S. Piper

HAYER, TALMADGE (John Hagan; Thomas Hagan; Mujahi Abdul Halim). On February 21, 1965, nearly nineteen years to the day after receiving a ten-year prison sentence that eventually led to his conversion to the Nation of Islam (NOI),* Malcolm X was brutally murdered. This horrific event took place in front of his wife and children who were seated less than twenty-five feet away from where he fell.

Talmadge Hayer (also known variously as John or Thomas Hagan and Mujahi Abdul Halim), from Paterson, New Jersey, a member of the Newark Mosque* and reportedly a member of the Fruit of Islam (FOI),* was one of three men indicted and convicted of Malcolm's assassination. At the scene of the murder, New York's Audubon Ballroom,* Hayer was shot in the hip and mobbed by Malcolm X loyalists in his attempt to escape. Hayer was rescued by the police, found with a 45-caliber clip and four rounds of ammunition on his person. Hayer initially testified that he was not a member of the NOI, had never practiced karate, and did not have a gun at the Audubon Ballroom the day that Malcolm was murdered. A Federal Bureau of Investigation* informant, however, identified Hayer as a member of the FOI who performed searches of attendees at NOI meetings in Newark and Paterson, New Jersey, and in Philadelphia. In addition, Hayer once served as part of the security force for Elijah Muhammad* in Chicago.* At the assassination trial a photograph was produced showing Hayer as a member of a karate group. Exactly one year after the assassination, on February 21, 1966, Hayer was linked by ballistic experts to one of the weapons used to murder Malcolm. Hayer finally admitted that he and three others were hired to kill Malcolm, though he denied that the other two men charged and tried with him were involved. The three men were nevertheless convicted of first-degree murder on March 11, 1966, and sentenced to life imprisonment. All three eventually won parole.

Although Hayer and his accomplices were convicted, many questions remain unanswered about the complicity of the law enforcement and intelligence communities in Malcolm's murder. Motive, means, and opportunity are three factors that have been raised regarding the assassination. It is clear that other entities besides the Nation of Islam fall under the umbrella of those three variables with regard to the assassination.

SELECTED BIBLIOGRAPHY

Carson (Gallen, ed.), 1991; Evanzz, 1992; Karim with Skutches and Gallen, 1992; Lomax, 1968; Malcolm X with Haley, 1965.

Horace Huntley

HEATHER. Heather is a pseudonym for a young woman who was one of Malcolm's ex-girlfriends and who became one of Elijah Muhammad's* lovers. She is described as a Muslim* woman with expressive eyes who had once visited Malcolm at Charlestown Prison. She wrote to Malcolm because she was impressed with his conversion. Malcolm eventually moved to Boston, where Heather lived with her guardian. During the time while Malcolm was in Boston, he became close to Heather, and they became engaged. Malcolm, however, left Boston in March 1954 without telling her. When she finally reached him, he reneged and expressed his noncommitment to marriage at that time. Because of his obligation to the Nation of Islam (NOI),* he had to travel constantly for the organization.

Heather eventually moved to Chicago, Illinois,* and began to work for Elijah Muhammad as a secretary. Elijah Muhammad is said to have told Heather that it was prophesied that he should sleep with virgins and bear offspring with them.

Heather had several children for Elijah Muhammad. When she finally left Chicago for Los Angeles, she moved in with another of Elijah Muhammad's former secretaries, Robin. Robin also bore children out of wedlock for Muhammad. Malcolm, who had discounted the rumors of Muhammad's adulterous relationships for years, found out about Heather and Robin and encouraged them to file paternity suits against Elijah Muhammad. When Malcolm finally became aware of the truth of his former mentor's sexual behavior, he grew more disillusioned with him. It also made more certain his break from the NOI. Moreover, it was Muhammad's concern over the paternity issue that strained his relationship even more with Malcolm.

SELECTED BIBLIOGRAPHY

Goldman, 1979; Malcolm X (Clark, ed.), 1992; B. Perry, 1991.

Sharron Y. Herron

HENRY, MILTON (Brother Gaidi Obadele). In 1963, Milton Henry had tried, unsuccessfully, to persuade Malcolm to run for a seat on the New York City Council. When Malcolm declined the offer, Henry ran for the seat and won it. Henry later became a practicing attorney in Detroit, Michigan,* and was a close friend of Malcolm X's. Henry accompanied Malcolm on one of his trips to Africa during the summer of 1964. While touring African nations, Malcolm became violently sick after dining with Henry in a restaurant in Cairo, Egypt.* He was rushed to a hospital and his stomach was pumped, and Malcolm's life was saved. After the death of Malcolm in February 1965, Henry wrote a story in the *New York Amsterdam News,** a black newspaper in Harlem,* New York, arguing that the Central Intelligence Agency* had attempted to assassinate Malcolm by putting poison in his food.

Henry had been deeply influenced by two of Malcolm's speeches—"Message to the Grass Roots"* and "The Ballot or the Bullet."* Before Malcolm had died, he had delivered these speeches, which addressed the question of land and revolution* for African Americans. These two speeches were the catalyst for Henry, along with his brother Richard Henry,* in setting up a "shadow government," the Republic of New Africa (RNA),* in 1968 in five states in the Deep South that constitutes what is commonly known as the Black Belt. A confrontation with Mississippi* law officials, however, in the early 1970s ended Henry's and the RNA's quest for a separate black nation within the United States.

Henry argues that the genius of Malcolm X's life lay ultimately in his ability as an evangelist. This viewpoint differs from others who have emphasized the organizational skills of Malcolm. Henry stated, however, that Malcolm's evangelical appeal was greater and more significant than his organizational abilities.

SELECTED BIBLIOGRAPHY

Bracey, Meier, and Rudwick, eds., 1970; Evanzz, 1992; Friedly, 1992; Van Deburg, 1992.

Franklin Jones and Mfanya Donald Tryman

HENRY, RICHARD B. (Brother Imari Abubakari Obadele). Richard B. Henry was a friend of Malcolm X and the brother of Ajay and Milton Henry,* the latter a practicing attorney in Detroit, Michigan.* Richard, also known by the African name of Imari Abubakari Obadele, was active in the black nationalist movement in Detroit, Michigan,* in the 1960s.

Not long after the death of Malcolm X, Richard, who by then had changed his name to Imari, wrote *War in America: The Malcolm X Doctrine.* The book became the blueprint for carrying out and implementing the ideology of Malcolm X and the basis upon which the Republic of New Africa (RNA)* was established in 1968. The RNA constituted the five southern states of Alabama, Georgia, Louisiana, Mississippi,* and South Carolina. Malcolm had often talked about the need for African Americans to have their own land, separate from whites, since history had shown that whites were incapable of treating blacks fairly or justly. The only solution, Malcolm argued, was racial separation.*

The RNA that Imari helped establish did not escape the notice of the U.S. government and the Federal Bureau of Investigation (FBI),* and the RNA was soon listed as a "key extremist group." Imari had written that the international alliances with the Afro-Asian bloc* of nations, Third World countries whose causes Malcolm often championed, would be the key to protecting the new republic from interference from the U.S. government. The FBI, determined to prevent such an alliance, launched a campaign to disrupt, discredit, and neutralize the organization. In 1971, as the result of a police raid on the RNA in Mississippi, eleven members of the group were arrested and imprisoned for "assaulting" police officers, in which one was killed and two were injured. Several RNA members, including Imari Obadele, served from three to ten years in prison* as a result.

The failure of the RNA in Mississippi, however, all but ended substantive efforts by the RNA and other ideologically similar black groups to advance this aspect of Malcolm's philosophy.

SELECTED BIBLIOGRAPHY
Imari, 1966; Malcolm X (Breitman, ed.), 1965; Obadele, 1993.
                                            Franklin Jones and Mfanya Donald Tryman

HICKS, JAMES (JIMMY). As chief spokesperson and minister for the Nation of Islam (NOI),* Malcolm X periodically gave interviews to the media. One of his interviewers was James Hicks, editor of the African American newspaper the *New York Amsterdam News,** who eventually became one of his good friends. Hicks's first significant exposure to Malcolm came as a result of the New York police's brutal beating of Black Muslim* Hinton Johnson* in 1957. Hicks wrote about the incident and Malcolm's role in insisting that police seek medical care for Malcolm's injured fellow parishioner. During the Johnson affair Malcolm had shown the gift of his leadership and his ability to exercise power by averting a riot in front of the police precinct. Hicks was so impressed by the leader's Islamic teachings and the compelling influence that he had on other Black Muslims that he recruited him to write a column for the paper on a permanent basis. Malcolm's column was immensely popular among many blacks because of his persuasive illumination of issues that provided an understanding about how whites continually oppressed blacks. However, the column may have contributed to the problems that Malcolm later had with Elijah Muhammad,* the head of the NOI.

Accordingly, Malcolm expressed to Hicks the belief that the Messenger wanted to write the column himself, because Elijah believed that Malcolm was becoming too powerful in New York. Consequently, he asked Hicks to allow Muhammad to pen the column, though Hicks thought that Muhammad was hardly Malcolm's equal as a writer.

By the time of Malcolm's death in 1965, he and Hicks were close friends. Because of the friendship, Hicks was deeply grieved over Malcolm's assassination. He wrote about the loss of his friend in his newspaper and concluded that while he did not agree with the NOI's advocation of a separate state, Malcolm had done a tremendous job of rehabilitating many ex-cons and drug addicts while he was in the NOI. Hicks did not speak about the independent Malcolm X and his political platform; nevertheless, he hoped that his friend's goal of rehabilitating wayward people would not die with him.

SELECTED BIBLIOGRAPHY

Cone, 1991; DeCaro, 1996; Goldman, 1979; Malcolm X with Haley, 1965; Myers, 1993.

Yoshawnda Trotter

HIMES, CHESTER BOMAR. Before his death in 1984, Chester Himes was one of the most prolific and popular black novelists in the twentieth century. A number of his works, including *If He Hollers Let Him Go*, one of his most acclaimed, were in part social commentaries on the American racial order. His most notable publications, however, were entertaining detective stories centering on Harlem* and featuring two main characters, Coffin Ed Johnson and Grave Digger Jones. A popular 1970s movie bearing the same name and another popular Himes novel, *Cotton Comes to Harlem*, spotlighted the detective characters and starred longtime Malcolm X friend comedian Redd Foxx.* Like many of the other popular black literary giants of his era, Himes too lived a part of his life in the black expatriate community that resided in Paris, France. Malcolm first became acquainted with Himes's work while he was incarcerated. In prison,* he read *If He Hollers Let Him Go*, a violent and angry novel that Himes hoped would shock white America from its lethargy in trying to fix the race problem. In some ways, Malcolm's life paralleled that of Himes's; as a youth, Himes had also spent time in prison for robbery. Like Malcolm, it was while he was incarcerated that Himes made a conscious effort for self-improvement* and began to write.

Apparently, the two men first met in 1962. Himes was in Harlem* acting as a translator for a French television news crew filming a documentary. The crew established their headquarters across the street from the Hotel Theresa* in the bookstore owned by Malcolm's friend Lewis Michaux.* In an interview shortly before his death, Himes claimed Malcolm as a good friend, though he admitted not having known him extremely well. He claimed no affinity for Malcolm's religious views. Yet it was Malcolm and the Black Muslims'* political philosophy that Himes declared that he preferred over that of the less militant civil rights* leaders. Indeed, Himes professed himself as not being the "conventional" African American of that day; he was, he wrote, very much a Malcolm X in his beliefs about black and white relations and claimed a general mistrust of whites. In this respect, he was not unlike many of the era's other prominent black men of letters, though he was hardly a "movement" activist like some of them. Still, there is much that was ambiguous about Himes's expressions, considering the intimate interracial relationships he had with numerous European white women and his eventual marriage to a white Englishwoman.

When Malcolm went to Paris on a speaking engagement in 1964, he and Himes visited extensively with each other. The visit seemed to please Himes immensely, and he continued to maintain a healthy respect for Malcolm as an effective leader in the international community. Indeed, it was largely because of Malcolm's meaningful work in this regard, Himes maintained, that prompted his murder. It was not the Black Muslims, he claimed, that acted alone in Malcolm's death; they were simply the trigger men. Rather, it was the Central Intelligence Agency (CIA),* which had been monitoring Malcolm and his followers in France, who organized the assassination and found a readily available alibi in the estrangement that existed between Malcolm and his former organization. The American agency, Himes asserted, had organized other assassinations in foreign countries, and there was nothing to convince him that the CIA's concern about Malcolm being an international danger to American interests did not encourage them to arrest Malcolm's growing prestige and influence. Indeed, he claimed, French authorities had detected the plot to kill Malcolm prior to his second visit to Paris, prompting France to deny Malcolm's entry into the historic city. Of course Himes offered no evidence in implicating the CIA's involvement in Malcolm's death. Nevertheless, it is a view that many in contemporary America even now refuse to discount.

SELECTED BIBLIOGRAPHY

Fabre and Skinner, eds., 1995; Himes, 1972, 1976; Stovall, 1996.

Robert L. Jenkins

HITLER, ADOLF, AND THE NAZIS. In the generation following World War II* no name was more internationally recognizable than that of Adolf Hitler. In 1939, the ambitious dictator of the Nazi Germany regime deliberately set in motion what became history's most deadly war. More sinister was his ideological extremism in support of Aryan purity that took an unparalleled toll on death and suffering for millions of Europe's* civilian racial and ethnic minorities, especially the Jews.* During the 1960s, some Americans sought to equate the Nation of Islam (NOI)* and its black supremacy views with that of Hitler and the Nazis. Understandably, Malcolm X was quick to rebut any semblance of NOI similarity to Nazism. Indeed, Malcolm remarked, it was the United States that came closer to Nazism than the Black Muslims.* Historically, the country had practiced racism against black people since their arrival on American shores; it certainly was mistreating them long before Hitler's birth, he added. Repeating an often made statement found in the World War II black press, Malcolm said that Hitler had, in fact, learned much of his virulent racism from the United States. In his characteristic emotional speaking style, Malcolm could raise Hitler and the Nazis in symbolic ways to blast the government for its official discrimination against black people and against those black civil rights* leaders whom he had always blamed for doing white bidding. Had it not been for Hitler's emergence and the need for black labor during the war, the national government would never have made concessions to hire them in the industrial plants, he said. Hence, their improved status in the national workforce came not from the goodwill of the national government to treat black people like first-class citizens but as a necessity to defeat Hitler.

Similarly, the same rationale prevailed for their direct participation in the war. Prior to the Nazi leader's ascendancy, blacks were hardly even allowed in the military,* he asserted. For those race leaders who pushed the government for inclusion, he expressed nothing but scorn, for it had been through their insistence that black boys were drafted and allowed to die on the battlefield the same as whites that were responsible for the deaths of so many blacks during the conflict. While it is doubtful that Malcolm truly believed it, he could nevertheless say with telling effect to the audiences that he addressed that America was just as capable as Hitler's Germany of building gas ovens to deal with its own racial problems. Such messages, of course, had no national boundaries when blacks were subject to white racism. To those blacks who were being mistreated in the racially torn town of Smethwick, in England, Malcolm could find rhetorical parallels with the Nazi's mistreatment of Jews and suggested to them not to wait until the town's "fascist element . . . erect gas ovens" before they acted in their own self-defense.*

It was especially the white South,* Malcolm reasoned, that the most striking parallels to Nazi racial policies existed. In the region, criminal acts in support of white supremacy had caused undue physical harm and death to blacks historically, and the South's political leaders had always given unqualified support to the practices. Hence, because of their strident antiblack views, Malcolm readily condemned leaders like Mississippi* U.S. senator James Eastland and Governor Ross Barnett, along with organizations like the White Citizen's Council* and the Ku Klux Klan* as "Nazis."

Of course, American versions of Hitler-like organizations swirled in Malcolm's world. Malcolm, along with several other top NOI officials, had once

briefly consorted with the Klan in Atlanta about mutual interest in racial segregation.* In 1961 Malcolm spoke at a large NOI gathering in Washington, D.C.
with American Nazi Party* members and party chieftain George Lincoln Rockwell* in the audience. But there is nothing to indicate that Malcolm ever had a
modicum of affinity for these groups. He never wavered from his criticism of
their racism and violent nature toward blacks, and after breaking with the NOI,
he publically condemned the sect and his mentor for flirting with them.

SELECTED BIBLIOGRAPHY

Grill and Jenkins, 1992; Malcolm X (Clark, ed.), 1992; Malcolm X (Epps, ed.), 1991;
Samuels (Meier, Rudwick, and Bracey, eds.), 1991; *Times* (London), February 12, 1965.
                                                                    Robert L. Jenkins

HOLIDAY, BILLIE J. (Eleanora Fagan; "Lady Day"). The world of Malcolm X in his years of early adulthood, the 1940s, was centered in the street
life of Boston and New York. In the ghettos of these cities, nightclubs such as
the Roseland Ballroom,* Wallys, the Savoy,* the Apollo,* the Onyx, and
Small's Paradise Club* attracted some of the nation's giants of jazz and big
band orchestras. Malcolm, a popular and frequent patron of these clubs, came
to know many of them personally. One of the truly legendary black celebrities*
who Malcolm met and established a friendly relationship with was jazz singer
Billie Holiday. Known affectionately by her wide and loyal following as "Lady
Day," Holiday, actually Eleanora Fagan, the daughter of standout rhythm gui-
tarist Clarence Holiday, was born and raised in Baltimore, Maryland, during the
1920s when the city was noted for its early jazz artists. By age fifteen, her
musical talents were already manifest. Possessing a unique sensuous voice and
an impressive style, Holiday cut her first record in 1933 at age eighteen.
Thereafter, her rise on the blues and jazz circuit was mercurial. At the height
of her career she became a featured singer with greats such as William "Count"
Basie* and Artie Shaw, eventually established her own band, recorded dozens
of future classic songs and albums under titles that included "Loveless Love,"
"Ain't Nobody's Business If I Do," "Good Morning, Heartache," "God Bless
the Child," and "Lady in Satin," and performed sold-out concerts at such prestigious places as Carnegie Hall and Philadelphia's Academy of Music.

    Malcolm was an admiring fan of Holiday's. His favorite Holiday song, which
according to Malcolm she was aware of, was "You Don't Know What Love
Is," and she apparently included it in her act whenever Malcolm attended her
shows. Occasionally, when Holiday was in New York performing, the two
shared personal moments together. During the period, Malcolm and Holiday
also shared a penchant for illicit drugs, though Malcolm was never addicted to
the more dangerous hard-core heroin like Holiday. Malcolm, who as a dealer
frequently supplied some of the musicians of the day with their drug of choice,
makes no mention of procuring drugs for Holiday, however. Eventually, Holiday
was consumed by her habit, and she gradually experienced a deterioration of

"Lady Day" Billie Holiday, one of Malcolm's favorite singers in the early 1940s. © Bradley Smith/CORBIS.

the skills that denoted her uniqueness as "The First Lady of Song." Occasionally jailed and hospitalized because of her usage, Holiday died in 1957. In his autobiography, Malcolm lamented her death as the tragic loss of a talented artist with a big heart. In Malcolm's opinion, racism prevented America from truly appreciating just how great a talent Holiday was.

SELECTED BIBLIOGRAPHY

A. Alexander, 1999; L. Brown (Perry, ed.), 1996; Malcolm X with Haley, 1965; O'Meally, 1991.

Robert L. Jenkins

HOLMAN, BENJAMIN. Benjamin Holman was a black reporter for the *Chicago Sun Times*. He infiltrated the Nation of Islam (NOI)* and became a member. However, his objectives were less than noble. He gained membership as part of an assignment for the newspaper he worked for, which was to write about the NOI from an insider's rather than outsider's perspective. Consequently, he wrote a series of articles about the NOI and its most public leader, Malcolm X, as well as Elijah Muhammad,* the organization's leader.

On May 13, 1963, Malcolm and a number of other speakers addressed an antisegregation rally outside the Hotel Theresa* in Harlem.* A. D. King, the younger brother of Martin Luther King, Jr.,* was the last speaker to address the crowd and was roundly booed by the crowd of 3,000 for advocating nonviolence in order to achieve civil rights* goals. Chants of "We want Malcolm" continued to emanate from the crowd. As King was leaving the stage, Holman, who was identified in the crowd, was attacked by roughly six Black Muslims* and beaten severely. With blood coming from a head wound, Holman retreated into the Hotel Theresa and sought medical care.

Almost two years later, at the annual NOI Savior's Day Convention* in Chicago* in February 1965, speaker after speaker gloated over the death of Malcolm X, which had occurred five days earlier on February 21, 1965. Louis Farrakhan,* when it was his time to speak, whipped the audience into a frenzy as he railed against Malcolm X. Suddenly, Farrakhan spotted Holman in the audience, who was covering the convention for the CBS television network, and fingered him for the audience to see. As he continued to instigate, hundreds of Black Muslims surrounded Holman as the audience incited the Muslims* on with shouts of "kill him" and other terms of agitation. Finally, Elijah Muhammad, Jr.,* arose and demanded that the crowd back off of Holman. He was quickly escorted from the hostile auditorium crowd by security guards. Holman's risky fraternization with Malcolm X and the Black Muslims turned out to be a dangerous venture on more than one occasion, and his newspaper series on the NOI carried a heavy personal price tag.

SELECTED BIBLIOGRAPHY
Evanzz, 1992, 1999; Magida, 1996.

Mfanya Donald Tryman

HOLY QU'RAN. The Holy Qu'ran is considered the last Book of Revelation for every orthodox Muslim* from Almighty God and represents guidance and spirituality for every aspect of a Muslim's life. The Five Pillars of Islam,* which every orthodox Muslim must adhere to, are to believe that there is only one God (Allah)* and that the Prophet Muhammad* is his messenger; to pray five times a day; to pay a portion of one's earnings to the less fortunate; to fast during the month of Ramadan; and to make the Hajj* (trip) to Mecca* in Saudi Arabia,* the holiest of all Islamic places and the home of the Prophet Muhammad. The Holy Qu'ran is considered to be the divine word of Allah as given directly to the Prophet Muhammad. The Hajj must be taken during a Muslim's lifetime (if one can afford the trip).

Malcolm X formally became a Sunni Muslim after making the Hajj in 1964. At this point he publicly converted to orthodox Islam from "Black Islam" and the Nation of Islam (NOI)* taught by Elijah Muhammad.* He stated that he no longer believed that all whites were devils as taught by black Islam. He condemned selective references to the Holy Qu'ran by Elijah Muhammad as blasphemy. He stated that the Holy Qu'ran does not recognize color and that he met and saw numerous whites in Mecca who also had made the Hajj. But Malcolm began teaching about the Holy Qu'ran much earlier, after making a trip to the Middle East* and the University of Al-Azhar in Cairo, Egypt.* The university is considered the academic center for the study of Islam and the Holy Qu'ran. Malcolm's teaching began with a selective audience of prudently chosen NOI members in New York, Los Angeles, and Washington, D.C. When Malcolm was assassinated, he was administered last rites in the orthodox Islamic tradition based upon the Holy Qu'ran.

SELECTED BIBLIOGRAPHY
Hitti, 1970; M. Lee, 1996.

Mfanya Donald Tryman and Abdul Al-Barrak

"THE HONORABLE ELIJAH MUHAMMAD TEACHES US." Malcolm X readily and consistently acknowledged Elijah Muhammad* for literally turning around his life. Before his conversion to Islam* and membership in the Nation of Islam (NOI),* Malcolm had renounced religion and involved himself in petty crime. While in prison* Malcolm disavowed any intention of returning to his former life and committed himself to both his new religion and furthering the work of Elijah Muhammad. Until his break in 1964 from the NOI, Malcolm considered Muhammad more than a mere mentor, he was virtually a father figure to him, someone for whom he was willing to kill. In the speeches and public comments that Malcolm made as Muhammad's chief emissary, he was careful to prefix his comments in mantra-like fashion with the words, "the honorable Elijah Muhammad teaches us." The phrase was hardly an admission that Malcolm could not think for himself, for indeed he was one of black America's most brilliant minds. Nor was it, as Malcolm's comedian friend Dick Gregory* thought, part of some kind of game that Malcolm was playing on Elijah Muhammad. Rather, it was Malcolm's recognition of the wisdom that Muhammad imparted to him and other Muslim* followers as the Messenger of Allah.* No black man, in Malcolm's view, was more intelligent than Muhammad or, like Muhammad, had the keys to elevating black people and thus resolving the "so-called Negro"* problem in America. Malcolm was unequivocally convinced of this and he felt bound to tell his listener so.

In the initial stages of Malcolm's national notoriety, many people who heard him constantly preface his remarks with "the honorable Elijah Muhammad teaches us" refused to accept his often repeated acknowledgment of Muhammad's influence in his life or failed to understand the special relationship that Malcolm had with the NOI leader. It was a devotion that Malcolm found hard to abandon, even in the early weeks of his rupture with the NOI.

SELECTED BIBLIOGRAPHY

Gregory, 1976; Library Distributors of America, 1993; Malcolm X with Haley, 1965.

Robert L. Jenkins

HOOVER, J. EDGAR. J. Edgar Hoover was the director of the Federal Bureau of Investigation (FBI),* a position to which he was first appointed in 1920 as the Justice Department's Bureau of Investigation. The FBI spent time gathering files and information on any organization and person that was affiliated with the civil rights movement* as well as black nationalists like Malcolm X. Hoover is said to have been paranoid about the possibility of communist infiltration into groups that were considered subversive or black nationalist hate groups. Although officially he considered Malcolm less of a threat than Martin Luther King, Jr.,* he maintained, nevertheless, a large surveillance file on Malcolm. Many believed that Hoover and the FBI aided in the assassination of Malcolm X through a counterintelligence operation that eventually became called COIN-TELPRO.*

Hoover and the FBI knew about the friction between Malcolm X and Elijah Muhammad* long before it hit the press, because information about their relationship was supplied by informants from within the Nation of Islam.* Hoover's agency was instrumental in spreading rumors regarding the adulterous behavior of Elijah Muhammad. It was a tactic that Hoover employed with telling effect; there were many other instances when his bureau sought to discredit individuals that he labeled as dangerous to national interests. Hoover also sought to ruin Malcolm by encouraging the Justice Department to pursue legal proceedings against Malcolm for violating the Smith Act, a measure that made it illegal to teach or advocate ideas calling for the overthrow of the federal government. The Justice Department, however, could find little evidence to support Hoover's claims.

SELECTED BIBLIOGRAPHY

Friedly, 1992; Goldman 1979; Malcolm X (Clark, ed.), 1992; Malcolm X with Haley, 1965; B. Perry, 1991.

Sharron Y. Herron

HOTEL THERESA. The Hotel Theresa is a famous hotel located in the heart of Harlem* at 125th Street and 7th Avenue. Fidel Castro,* the controversial communist political leader of Cuba,* visited the United States in September 1960 while attending a General Assembly meeting of the United Nations.* He decided to stay at the Hotel Theresa after experiencing discriminatory treatment from other hotels, being denied patronage because of his politics. Castro's stay was only part of the hotel's varied history. Built in 1916 by nickel cigar manufacturer Gustav Seidenberg, it was named in honor of his wife Theresa. Until blacks took over the former white community of Harlem, African Americans were not allowed to stay in the hotel. During World War II,* the swanky establishment was taken over by the U.S. Army and utilized as a distribution center to house combat-weary soldiers returning from overseas duty. By then, it was already regarded as the "Waldorf of Harlem," prominent for lodging some of black America's most well-known personalities. Its bar was once regarded as Harlem's social center. During the 1970s, long after its heyday as black America's classiest hotel, National Basketball Association great Wilt Chamberlain purchased the structure.

Many Harlemites were delighted to have the controversial Castro residing in the hotel. While he was there large crowds frequently gathered nearby hoping to catch a glimpse of the legendary revolutionary. Malcolm X arranged a meeting with Castro at the hotel, along with several Muslim* members and two men from the black press, as a part of a Harlem welcoming committee for Third World dignitaries. The meeting lasted approximately one-half hour, an informal affair as the two men conversed while sitting on the bed in the hotel room. Malcolm, subsequently, was accused of supporting communism by members of the media. Unfortunately Lowe B. Woods, the elderly proprietor of the hotel, suffered scathing criticism from some black leaders and anti-Castro forces for his refusal to deny the communist leader lodging in the hotel. Even pressure from the federal government, however, did not move Wood to change his course.

The Hotel Theresa often served as a gathering point for outside meetings. Malcolm occasionally spoke to large crowds regarding issues that affected African Americans in front of the landmark structure. Well-known African dignitaries and leaders such as Kenneth Kaunda of Zambia and Kwame Nkrumah* of Ghana had the opportunity to address rallies in front of the Theresa as well. It was at the Hotel Theresa that Malcolm located his fledgling new organization, the Muslim Mosque, Inc.,* and headquartered his Organization of Afro-American Unity.*

SELECTED BIBLIOGRAPHY

Blount, 1946; *Dallas Express*, September 23, 1944; Evanzz, 1992; Myers, 1993; *New York Times*, May 15, 1963; *Washington Daily News*, September 21, 1944.

Mfanya Donald Tryman and Robert L. Jenkins

HOUSE NEGRO. The *House Negro* is a term frequently used to describe the slave who lived a better life than the Field Negro.* He had better food, wore better clothes, and had better living conditions. Malcolm X pointed out that the House Negro was the one who lived close to the master, in the attic or basement, and was at the master's beck and call. The distinction between the House Negro and the Field Negro was simple, according to Malcolm. The House Negro defended his master and his master's property more than the master did himself and had an undying love for him. Whenever the master referenced "we" the House Negro would also say "we." In essence, the House Negro was the master's alter ego. Because the House Negro was so brainwashed, he had no desire to run away since he felt that there was no better life than the one he had.

Malcolm stated that the House Negro's mentality survived in the contemporary Negro.

The modern Negro, Malcolm derisively noted, did not differ that much from the House Negro of slavery times. His identity was closely connected to that of the white man. He wanted to live near the master and proudly proclaim that he had a special status if he was the only Negro who lived in the neighborhood. He also wanted to be the only Negro at his job and in the schools with whites.

As in the past, the "slave master" continued to use the House Negro to keep the Field Negro in check. Malcolm called the modern House Negro an Uncle Tom.* His job was to keep blacks in check for whites. That meant keeping blacks under control and passive through the nonviolent peaceful protest movement of the early 1960s. The job of the modern House Negro was to teach black people how to suffer peacefully when attacked by white authorities during demonstrations. The same strategy that was used in slavery, Malcolm said, was used during the civil rights movements* by the same white man. He took a Negro, made him prominent, publicized him, then made this Negro the spokesman for all other Negroes. This Negro was identified as the leader but was accommodating, peaceable, and self-serving.

Malcolm used as an example of his views about the House Negroes the gathering at the March on Washington.* He called it a demonstration of House Negroes and whites liberal,* not the Field Blacks. However, according to Malcolm X, the initial Washington March was thought of by Field Negroes before the civil rights' leadership took charge of it and lessened the militant atmosphere.

SELECTED BIBLIOGRAPHY

Malcolm X (Breitman, ed.), 1965; J. White, 1985; Xenon, 1991.

Mamie Locke

HOUSE UN-AMERICAN ACTIVITIES COMMITTEE (HUAC). The House Un-American Activities Committee (HUAC) was a special committee set up in the U.S. House of Representatives designed to investigate leaders and groups that were considered subversive to the interests of the American government. HUAC threatened or destroyed the careers of many Americans and particularly of a number of black American leaders, artists, and intellectuals, including W.E.B. Du Bois,* Langston Hughes, and Paul Robeson.* Robeson was stripped of his passport as a result of a HUAC investigation. Du Bois, at the time in his eighties, was malevolently attacked and charged in federal court with being an unregistered agent of another government. Civil rights organizations* came under attack as well.

Neither Malcolm nor the Nation of Islam (NOI)* were ever formally investigated by the committee. However, in August 1962, when Malcolm was the national spokesman for the NOI, the committee chairman announced that he would seek an extensive investigation of the sect. Malcolm and Elijah Muhammad* were both issued subpoenas to appear before HUAC in Washington. Once this was known publically, civil rights organizations and individual citizens protested and wrote numerous letters to Congress. Muhammad ordered Malcolm to cancel all of his campus speaking invitations. The hearings moved ahead, but black congressmen, including Charles C. Diggs, Adam Clayton Powell, Jr.,* and Robert Nix, criticized the hearings as a waste of money. After only a few hours of testimony, HUAC closed down the hearings, in part because they were racially divisive since the NOI had been considered a legitimate religious group by a lower federal court. Consequently, Malcolm and the NOI were never thrust into what for many was the humiliating national arena of bright lights, flashing light bulbs, television cameras, and hostile questioning for which HUAC was well known.

SELECTED BIBLIOGRAPHY

Clegg, 1997; Evanzz, 1999; Goldfield, 1997; Woodard, 1999.

Mfanya Donald Tryman

HOWARD UNIVERSITY. Located in Washington, D.C., Howard University is one of the oldest institutions of higher learning established for the education of African Americans, though it has become one of the most culturally diverse colleges in the nation. Founded in 1867 shortly after the end of the Civil War, it was named after Union General Oliver O. Howard, who headed the Freedmen's Bureau and who played a key role in Howard's establishment and early development. The college, with its comprehensive curriculum and several professional schools, including Law, Medical, and Dental Schools, has played an important role in educating some of the nation's most gifted and prominent black leaders. Its historical faculty listing is a veritable "who's who" of black intellectuals of the twentieth century and includes the names of personage such as historians Charles Wesley, Rayford Logan, and John Hope Franklin, sociologists Kelley Miller and E. Franklin Frazier, economist Abraham Lincoln Harris, biologist Ernest E. Just, medical researcher Charles Drew, law professors Charles H. Houston and James M. Nabrit, literary scholar Alain Locke, and former college president and internationally known educator Mordecai Johnson.

The college has a strong heritage of social concerns and involvement in black uplift endeavors. Hence, throughout the twentieth century notable leaders from the world stage, including international revolutionary figures as well as veteran leaders of the black rights struggle, spoke frequently on the campus. Howard during the 1960s was clearly an intellectually exciting place to be and seemed fitting for someone like Malcolm X to appear. Accordingly, Malcolm became one of the earliest controversial black leaders of the 1960s associated with the college. This occurred as a direct result of an invitation extended to Malcolm in October 1961 by activist Tom Kahn* and future Student Non-Violent Coordinating Committee (SNCC)* leaders Stokley Carmichael* and Courtland Cox to accept a speaking engagement at Howard. Though Malcolm had hardly

Malcolm X with civil rights activist Bayard Rustin (left) and a student leader at Howard University in 1961, in one of the many appearances that he would make at predominantly black colleges. Courtesy of the Moorland-Spingarn Research Center, Howard University Archives.

achieved the international status that he would a couple of years later, and Howard's mostly middle-class student body knew little about Malcolm, his views about separatism and self-defense* were not widely muted; they were exotic enough to attract considerable interest from the notable intellectually challenging environment at the college.

It was precisely because of his membership in the controversial Nation of Islam* and his militancy, however, that university officials were lukewarm to the idea of Malcolm's appearance. Student leaders of the National Association for the Advancement of Colored People (NAACP)* had, in fact, sought to bring Malcolm to the campus several months earlier, but the administration refused to sanction it. Presumably they were concerned over how Congress, which was responsible for the university's funding, might react to Malcolm's presence. Even an attempt to move the engagement off the campus to a local church failed because of NAACP opposition. To some extent, Malcolm seemed to relish the controversy over his preempted appearance at the premier black school because he knew that it would stimulate a greater interest in his message. He was right. When Malcolm did appear at the college it was before a large and attentive audience.

Malcolm appeared on the program in debate format with Bayard Rustin,* one of the civil rights movement's* most recognizable names. An organizer of the Congress of Racial Equality (CORE)* and veteran leader in the NAACP, he was also a close associate and adviser to Martin Luther King, Jr.* Rustin had himself lobbied for Malcolm's appearance because he believed in Malcolm's right to be heard. He also favored the debate format, not only hopeful of exposing Howard students to alternative strategies about the course of the black struggle but also determined to show the danger and bankruptcy of Malcolm's and the NOI's support of separatist ideas and opposition to nonviolent activism.

A charismatic speaker, Malcolm had long proved himself a talented orator, and though the scholarly Rustin had a widespread reputation as an eloquent speaker himself, he got more than he bargained for in Malcolm. Both men presented their standard views about the merits of racial integration* versus racial separation,* and Malcolm talked at length about his support of black nationalism.* In no uncertain language Malcolm gave a manly accounting of his views on self-defense* against white racism, saying things in the bold ways that the black middle-class* audience was unaccustomed to hearing. With his sharp mind and analytical thinking, Rustin also apparently did well. By all accounts, however, Malcolm won over the audience, acquiring a significant amount of support from the college audience that would continue to pay dividends in support of his views from elements of similar young people groups in the months that followed.

The debate at Howard was not the last time that Malcolm would best an opponent in public debate over contemporary issues that affected black people. It was, however, precisely because of his acumen as a debater, his sharp wit, and his logical mind that many prominent black and white leaders were always apprehensive over the prospect of matching words with him in any kind of public venue.

SELECTED BIBLIOGRAPHY

J. Anderson, 1997; DeCaro, 1996; W. Dyson, 1941; D. Levine, 2000; Logan, 1969; Meier, 1992; Rustin, 1971.

Robert L. Jenkins

HUMAN RIGHTS. Malcolm X maintained that the struggle for civil rights* was misguided. Martin Luther King, Jr.'s* strategy of nonviolent civil disobedience, he argued, had little chance of ending white subjugation of African Americans. He further asserted that African American efforts to receive justice from the American political system were futile. The U.S. government, which was controlled at all levels by white men, said Malcolm, would never protect the lives and property of its black citizens. Convinced that the struggle for civil rights must be transformed into a struggle for human rights, Malcolm appealed to the newly independent African nations to present a resolution to the United Nations* that would condemn the United States for its brutal oppression of African Americans. The resolution that Malcolm and his supporters drafted asserted that the United States' treatment of African Americans violated the United Nations Charter on Human Rights.

Malcolm felt that the plight of black Americans would have a more respective audience in a wider political arena if these concerns were couched in human rights violations. One of the primary goals of his newly formed Organization of Afro-American Unity* was to serve as a vehicle to bring such charges. Unfortunately, his untimely death aborted this effort, to which Malcolm devoted the last months of his life.

SELECTED BIBLIOGRAPHY

Goldman, 1973; Malcolm X (Breitman, ed.), 1965; Sales, 1994.

Phillip A. Gibbs

HUSTLING. As a teenager, in the streets of Roxbury,* a historic African American section of Boston, Malcolm learned that everything in the world was a hustle. Against the wishes of his half sister Ella Collins,* Malcolm rejected middle-class notions and chose to refine himself in the art of hustling. While working as a clandestine shoe shiner at Boston's Roseland Ballroom,* Malcolm sold liquor and marijuana, and this led him to other hustles. At the age of sixteen, he found work on the New Haven railroad, which ran between Boston and New York City; it was during this period of Malcolm's life in 1942 that he was introduced to hustling, Harlem-style. Moving from porter to waiter at Harlem's* Small's Paradise Club,* Malcolm was in the heart of the nightlife. He listened intensely to his customers' stories about hustling and how they made fast money. Soon he was fully initiated into the hustling society. With such teachers as the numbers runner* West Indian Archie* and Sammy the Pimp,* Malcolm learned to adhere to the rules of the hustling society. Malcolm was extremely diversified and skilled in the hustling arena. He participated in burglary, the selling of narcotics, and even guided customers to Harlem's bawdy houses. Ultimately it was the hustling life that led to Malcolm's imprisonment.

SELECTED BIBLIOGRAPHY

Malcolm X (Epps, ed.), 1991; Malcolm X with Haley, 1965; B. Perry, 1991.

Nancy J. Dawson

I

INTERRACIAL MARRIAGE. In his younger days as a hipster in Boston and New York, Malcolm X experienced occasional flirtations with white women. During most of his public career, however, no issue seemed to evoke as much emotion from him than that dealing with the intermingling of the races. As a member of Elijah Muhammad's* Nation of Islam (NOI),* he held the sect's doctrinal line on matters of racial separation* and was especially vocal against mixed marriages between black and whites. In no uncertain language, Malcolm denounced interracial marriages as something most appealing to black celebrities.* According to Malcolm, these elements were among the deluded modern-day "Uncle Toms"* and "integrationists" who fell for the white line of racial superiority and sought uppermost to force themselves into a white world where they were not really wanted. Many of these were Hollywood entertainers—movies stars and singers—involved in these interracial marriages, Malcolm claimed. The singers, he said, had once been popular figures in the black community, where their records were among the favorite jukebox tunes, but in the mid-1960s the black masses neither trusted nor respected them, and hence they were being summarily rejected for crossing the color line. Malcolm claimed bewilderment about what some of these blacks sought to prove, because they could never be truly accepted in a white world; he concluded that many of them were in obvious need of psychoanalysis.

While there is little doubt that Malcolm's criticism of mixed marriages once reflected his true sentiments, by the end of his life he was beginning to reject blanket condemnation of the practice. The change became notable after his return from the pilgrimage in the summer of 1964. In the holy city, he was exposed to orthodox Islam* with its attendant belief in the brotherhood of man, regardless of race and color, and he soon endorsed its merits. When one accepted the humanity of all people, Malcolm would say, then the matter of interracial marriage had little significance. Malcolm's post-Hajj* views were clearly a departure from his earlier position, yet he would not abandon his basic belief that mixed marriages could never be truly countenanced in America because white society would never accept black people as equals.

SELECTED BIBLIOGRAPHY

Goldman, 1979; Malcolm X (Breitman, ed.), 1965; Malcolm X (Perry, ed.), 1989; Malcolm X with Haley, 1965.

Robert L. Jenkins

ISLAM. Malcolm X accepted the religion of Islam while incarcerated. He was exposed to it by his brothers who practiced the religion and through his correspondence with Elijah Muhammad,* the leader of the Nation of Islam (NOI).* Malcolm perceived Muhammad's brand of Islam as the religion for black people. Based on its teachings that black people are God's chosen people, that Allah* is a black man, and that Islam as a religion stood for justice, freedom, and equality, it certainly seemed an acceptable religion for him to follow.

Islam is one of the world's largest religions. It was started in A.D. 622 by the Prophet Muhammad.* The basic beliefs of Muslims* practicing Islam are that there is no God but Allah whose prophet was Muhammad. They believe there is a heaven and hell. Their Bible* is the Holy Koran (Holy Qu'ran*). Muslims do not eat pork,* drink alcohol, or gamble. During the month of Ramadan every Muslim is expected to fast. They are required to pray five times daily, and they worship primarily at mosques. Being charitable is a cornerstone of their religious duty. Taking a pilgrimage to Mecca,* the Hajj,* at least once in their lives is a goal of all Muslims. Malcolm made the historic pilgrimage to Mecca, and it had a dramatic impact on his life. This represented his ultimate dedication to the religion and symbolized his break from the NOI.

Islam is the youngest of the other two major religions practiced in the West: Judaism* and Christianity.* However, it is the most widely practiced religion among the peoples of Africa and Asia. In the Islamic tradition, God can never be represented, nor is he ever incarnated in any human or superhuman force. To portray an image of God is to place human limitations upon him according to Islamic tradition; therefore, Allah has to be placed above all human identifications. In addition, Allah is perceived as universal. Malcolm detected contradictions in these religious tenets as practiced by the NOI. Hence, later in his life he rejected the NOI's teachings that God was incarnated in the person of a half-white, half-black man named W. D. Fard,* and he warned of the dangers of deifying a human.

After visiting Mecca, Malcolm had concluded that the NOI did not practice traditional Islam; thus, he rejected its teachings. Malcolm soon realized that blacks' oppression had more to do with European America's history and culture rather than the biological traits of white people as taught by the Black Muslims.*

SELECTED BIBLIOGRAPHY

Davies, 1990; Karenga, 1982; Malcolm X with Haley, 1965; Myers, 1993; Rashad, 1991; A. Smith, 1982; R. Turner, 1997.

LaVonne Jackson

ISLAMIC CONVERSION. On February 23, 1946, Malcolm Little received a ten-year prison* sentence for his involvement in a Boston house burglary ring. He spent the first two years of his sentence in Boston's Charlestown State Prison before being transferred to the Norfolk Prison Colony. Anger and contentious behavior seemingly consumed his initial prison years, but his conversion to a brand of Islam* promoted by Elijah Muhammad,* head of a small sect known as the Nation of Islam (NOI),* transformed his life.

There was little in Malcolm's background that might suggest his acceptance and later devotion to Islam. To be sure, he had come from a home where religion held a prominent place and where some of Elijah Muhammad's philosophy paralleled that of his father, J. Earl Little.* Malcolm's father, a follower of Marcus Garvey,* had been a Protestant preacher prior to his tragic death in Michigan, although he never served in a permanent pastorate. Long before Malcolm had reached adulthood, however, he had rejected organized religion and moral virtue, substituting in their place a creed guided by a devotion to street hustling* and crime. Malcolm's half sister Ella Collins* and brothers Wilfred Little* and Philbert Little,* the latter a devout member of the NOI, wrote and visited him frequently in prison and encouraged him to abandon his old habits and ways of thinking. It was Philbert who suggested that Malcolm follow the teachings of the Islamic leader Elijah Muhammad.

Malcolm easily stopped smoking cigarettes and eating pork,* the initial steps in his conversion. It was with greater difficulty, however, that he learned to accept the Muslim* prayer practices. His siblings readily provided him the information he needed to learn about the teaching and philosophy of Elijah Muhammad. "The truth," as taught by the black Messenger, included an ordered refutation of the lowly place assigned blacks in American history and an analysis of how Christianity,* "the White man's religion," helped to perpetuate the black man's oppression. An account of Yacub's* history, central to understanding Nation of Islam views about whites, introduced Malcolm to Muhammad's teachings about how and why white men came to be the "white devils"* that the Black Muslims* so readily claimed they were.

For Malcolm, the religion's explanation of the cause of black oppression and the role of white men in influencing the self-destructive paths on which blacks often found themselves seemed logical. The more he learned of Elijah Muhammad and the NOI's doctrines, the more he accepted their philosophy as a way of self-improvement.* The process of his redemption became both spiritual and intellectual.

Elijah Muhammad was always at the center of his Islamic conversion, for in many ways Malcolm found it difficult to separate the religion from the man who carried its message. A constant flow of correspondence between the two soon became more than proselytizing exchanges but was the budding of a relationship—a bond that proved mutually beneficial to both men once Malcolm was paroled from prison. For Malcolm, the radical religious transformation set the stage for him to become one of the most recognized, though often misunderstood, leaders of his time.

SELECTED BIBLIOGRAPHY

Goldman (Franklin and Meier, eds.), 1982; Malcolm X with Haley, 1965; Rummel, 1989.

Robert L. Jenkins and Mfanya Donald Tryman

J

JAABER, IMAM HESHAAM. Imam (a spiritual leader) Heshaam Jaaber was part of a small community of black orthodox Muslims* that lived in the New York and New Jersey area. A native-born American, Jaaber was a recognized leader in the "Addeynu Allahu"—the Universal Arabic Association, Inc. Founded in Brooklyn, New York, in the 1930s by Professor Muhammad Elzadeen, the association was one of the nation's oldest Sunni Islamic groups; Jaaber served as one of its national Imams. It was Jaaber and a small group of his New Jersey followers who went to the Brooklyn Police station the day following Malcolm's murder to claim the body.

Even in death, controversy and fear remained closely associated with Malcolm. In the aftermath of the assassination, issues emerged about the autopsy, who would be responsible for his body, the final arrangements, and where funeral services were to be held. These concerns soon abated, though resolution of the latter proved more difficult because violent threats from perceived murder conspirators scared potential churches away from scheduling the service in their sanctuary. Indeed, it was the fear of violent retribution and potential problems with federal authorities that supposedly prevented New York's Muslims, many of whom where foreigners, from taking a more active role in Malcolm's formal funeral rites.

Shortly after his departure from the Nation of Islam,* Malcolm took the "declaration of faith," one of the five pillars of Islam,* and accepted orthodox beliefs as a Sunni Muslim.* As an orthodox Muslim, who had also made the all-important Hajj,* the required pilgrimage to Mecca,* in death Malcolm was entitled to the traditional Islamic ritual before his burial.

It was Jaaber who assumed the responsibility of performing the Islamic funeral rituals for Malcolm, whom the Arabic association officially considered "a martyr." Jaaber, whose relationship with Malcolm went back as far as Malcolm's stay in Roxbury,* held great respect for him. He insisted that the rituals be publically administered as an Islamic duty, although some of his coreligionists disagreed with his views about the obligation. Prior to the Janaza (funeral), Sheik Ahmed Hassoun,* an elderly Sudanese scholar who had befriended and mentored Malcolm, prepared the body, washing it according to Islamic practice, and then shrouded it head to toe in traditional white Arabic burial attire. A booklet was prepared for non-Muslims to understand the rituals. But it was Jaaber who performed the most important parts of the services, managing the sequence of affairs and supervising the rituals. After two eulogies, one by Hassoun, the second, a moving presentation by actor Ossie Davis,* Jaaber began his role. Dressed in full Shaykh Al-Arabic regalia, he descended from a balcony before the large gathering of family and notables and took his position alongside other Muslim participants next to Malcolm's glass-topped, sealed coffin. In a ceremony that lasted several minutes, Jaaber then led the Muslims in the most sacred portion of the rituals: the Janaza Salat (funeral prayers), a recitation of four formal and expressive prayers delivered as the participants face the direction of Mecca. Jaaber gave additional supplications at the Hartsdale, New York, burial site before the crowd dispersed and allowed the black apostle of armed self-defense* to "rest in peace."

SELECTED BIBLIOGRAPHY

Collins with Bailey, 1998; Jaaber, 1992; *Militant*, March 8, 1965.

Robert L. Jenkins

JACK, HULAN E. A native of St. Lucia, British West Indies, Hulan Jack moved from Barbados in 1923 to New York City and by 1932 was heavily involved in local politics. Between the 1940s and 1970s, he was one of the city's most recognizable black political leaders. He first gained national attention in 1940 when, as a Democrat, he was elected to the New York state assembly, the first African American to sit in that body. He served continuously in the legislature until 1953 and an additional term from 1968 to 1972. During his tenure as a legislator, he championed human rights* and antidiscrimination causes. Highly regarded in the Harlem* community during the mid- and late 1950s, his work received recognition primarily from his local leadership position as the Manhattan Borough president, the first black so elected. The borough was one of the wealthiest and most densely populated in the country, and with the office came considerable opportunity to mingle with important people from all levels. As borough president, he knew and worked with many of black New York's prominent leadership, including Adam Clayton Powell Jr.,* Jackie Robinson,* Roy Wilkins,* James Lawson,* and of course, Malcolm X. Although he was not a Muslim* and did not frequently agree with them (nor they with him), Jack, nevertheless, admired the work that the Nation of Islam (NOI)* was doing in the city, and unlike some of the more conservative national and local black leaders, he had no problem associating with leaders like Malcolm and Elijah Muhammad.* He appeared on programs with Malcolm, consulted with him on issues of mutual interest, and greeted alongside the Muslim minister important dignitaries, such as Ghanaian President Kwame Nkrumah,* when they visited New York. Similar to Malcolm and other black leaders sensitized to the socioeconomic and political plight of blacks in America, Jack denounced the deplorable conditions in the urban ghettos and white racism, which he blamed in part for them. Although controversies growing out of numerous local fights with other black New York leaders frequently swirled around Jack, he remained a popular political figure in the Manhattan Borough throughout his career because he was willing to take bold stands on issues that he believed in.

SELECTED BIBLIOGRAPHY

Evanzz, 1992; Hamilton, 1991; Jack, 1982; Klein (Saltzman, Smith, and West, eds.), 1996; Lincoln, 1994; B. Perry, 1991.

Robert L. Jenkins

JACKO, EDWARD W. Despite the fact that Malcolm X was not a notable exponent of the civil rights movement,* during his career with the Nation of Islam (NOI),* his life was filled with persons associated with the movement. One of these persons with whom Malcolm worked closely in the early 1960s was New York City attorney Edward Jacko. Jacko, who maintained a legal partnership with Jawn Sandifer,* an associate of Malcolm in his prison* ministry, worked with the National Association for the Advancement of Colored People* and Martin Luther King, Jr.,* and also did considerable legal work for the NOI. Malcolm's ties with Jacko began in 1957 with legal matters growing out of the Hinton X Johnson* case. Malcolm and the NOI retained Jacko to represent Johnson, who had been brutally beaten by a New York City police officer. The bold stance that Malcolm had taken in the affair had enhanced his reputation among law enforcement authorities in New York and helped to make him and the NOI in Harlem* familiar names among Harlem residents. Because he was falsely arrested and sustained severe permanent physical damage from the beating, Jacko sued the city of New York on behalf of Johnson, eventually winning a settlement of $75,000; it was believed to be at the time the largest damage settlement suit ever. It was Jacko who also represented Malcolm in one of his own suits against the New York City police department for its raid on an apartment that Malcolm and his wife Betty Shabazz* shared with three other couples. The raid had occurred at the wrong address, but the incident, which involved the police firing their weapons in the apartment, was potentially a dangerous one and understandably angered both Malcolm, who was not home at the time, and Elijah Muhammad.*

Subsequently, Malcolm and Jacko continued their association, Jacko, for example, doing the legal work on behalf of the establishment of Malcolm's Muslim Mosque, Inc.* Malcolm and Jacko, along with Sandifer, also teamed up to address additional police brutality matters on behalf of New York City blacks.

Long after Malcolm's death, however, Jacko maintained an important legal association with Elijah Muhammad and the NOI.

SELECTED BIBLIOGRAPHY

Carson (Gallen, ed.), 1991; DeCaro, 1998; Evanzz, 1999; Goldman, 1979; Karim with Skutches and Gallen, 1992; Malcolm X (Clark, ed.), 1992.

Robert L. Jenkins

JAMAL, HAKIM A. (Allen Donaldson). Hakim Jamal, formerly known as Allen Donaldson, was purportedly a cousin of Malcolm X and a close friend. After Malcolm officially and publicly left the Nation of Islam (NOI),* Jamal followed Malcolm and also left. In January of 1965 Malcolm's plane was scheduled to arrive at Los Angeles International Airport from New York, where Jamal and Edward Bradley* arranged to pick him up. Malcolm was coming to town to meet with two of Elijah Muhammad's* former secretaries. Jamal recognized a member from the NOI also waiting in the airport and through airport authorities had Malcolm's plane diverted to another terminal. Only seven people close to Malcolm were supposed to know of his arrival, and the Black Muslims* that Jamal recognized were ominous in nature. In 1971, Jamal wrote a book entitled *From the Dead Level: Malcolm and Me*, which included an account of this incident in which he alleged that this may have been a planned assassination attempt on Malcolm. In addition, Jamal's work chronicled the life and times of Malcolm, the experiences he shared with him, and the influence of Malcolm on Jamal, including allegations Jamal makes against Elijah Muhammad similar to those made by Malcolm in late 1964.

Like Malcolm, Jamal was slain in a hail of bullets by suspected Black Muslim assassins in front of his wife and children in Boston in 1973. After Malcolm's death in 1965, Jamal had increasingly become a vocal critic of Muhammad and the NOI. It was initially suspected that his assassination was the result of such verbal attacks on Muhammad.

SELECTED BIBLIOGRAPHY

Friedly, 1992; Jamal, 1971; *New York Times*, May 3, 1976.

Mfanya Donald Tryman

JEREMIAH X (Jeremiah Shabazz; Jeremiah Pugh). According to C. Eric Lincoln's *The Black Muslims in America*,* Louis X (Farrakhan)* of Boston and Jeremiah X of Atlanta were two of Malcolm's young handpicked ministers. Jeremiah replaced a very popular James X. Speculation has it that under James's direction, the Atlanta mosque failed to realize any significant increase in membership and that he was too closely associated with the non-Muslim and middle-class black community. Jeremiah increased the numbers in the mosque and concentrated on the most depressed segment of Atlanta. In his capacity as regional representative in the Southeast, Jeremiah X oversaw the operation of mosques in Chattanooga, Birmingham, Miami, Jacksonville, and other south-eastern cities and reported directly to Malcolm. He also was involved with land negotiations of the Nation of Islam (NOI).*

In May 1963 there were rumors that Malcolm had been invited to Birmingham by Jeremiah during the civil rights* demonstrations. Malcolm did not appear in Birmingham, he said, because Jeremiah did not invite him. But Malcolm, who exercised official jurisdiction over Jeremiah and the Birmingham mosque, needed no special invite from Minister Jeremiah; by his authority alone, unless prohibited by orders from the Messenger, he had the right to be in the city. Apparently, Elijah Muhammad* did not approve. Though Malcolm did not go to Birmingham, Jeremiah certainly made himself visible during the campaign. On one occasion Martin Luther King, Jr.,* embraced the Muslim* leader, show-ing his affection for him. But King was quick to point out that he and his supporters had as much disdain for Jeremiah's philosophy, "Black supremacy," as they did for "White supremacy."

Although Louis and Jeremiah had been handpicked by Malcolm, after his expulsion from the NOI, his two prodigies wrote critically inflammatory and derisive articles about his "hypocrisy."

SELECTED BIBLIOGRAPHY
Eskew, 1997; Evanzz, 1992; Lincoln, 1961; Malcolm X (Clark, ed.), 1992.

Horace Huntley

JEWS. Despite the anti-Semitic views he expressed, Malcolm X's feelings to-ward Jews were ambivalent and complex. On the one hand, he recognized the legacy of oppression and persecution that Jewish people shared with those of African descent. He envied the Jewish heritage of education and intellectual achievement. In addition, his pro-Arab alliances did not prevent him from ad-miring the fact that Jews had a homeland in the state of Israel. On the other hand, he used shockingly anti-Semitic terms like "yids" and denounced Jews for exploiting black people.

Malcolm X's views on Jewish people were informed by a variety of factors. For instance, as the journalist James Baldwin* pointed out, the anti-Semitism of many African Americans is rooted in their antiwhite feelings. Most American Jews are white and therefore benefit from their "in-group" status. Also, daily encounters reinforced black resentment of Jewish people. Malcolm X was chief among those who pointed out that many Jews owned real estate and profitable businesses in Harlem* and other black areas that allowed them to live com-fortably in the suburbs, areas that excluded black people. Living far from the areas where they exploited blacks, they simply showed a disregard for the black plight.

Malcolm was particularly critical of the Jews because of their involvement in the civil rights movement.* While he did not claim all Jews were insincere about their support of black justice, he regarded Jewish participation as largely self-serving. Jews, he said, only sought to deflect attention from anti-Semitism to discrimination against blacks.

Baldwin also pointed out that while Jewish immigration across the Atlantic had resulted in their freedom from a kind of slavery and oppression, for people of African descent who were brought to America, it was a house of bondage. By the time Malcolm X emerged as a public figure, Americans of European descent began to recognize the profound Jewish anguish and their resistance to oppression in Europe.* Concurrently, White America denounced the struggle led by Malcolm X that exposed and condemned the pain and misery that the descendants of Africans suffered in America. In his last year, Malcolm's interest in working with people of all races and both genders for human rights* deepened. His experience in Mecca* with fair-skinned Arabs and people who would be considered white in America loosened the reactionary racism that had dominated so much of his life. This contributed to a new willingness to reexamine his position on Jews. Until his death, Malcolm began to try to mend fences with sympathetic Jewish people who shared his commitment to promoting human rights.

SELECTED BIBLIOGRAPHY

Baldwin (Hentoff, ed.), 1969; Myers, 1993; B. Perry, 1991; Rodgers and Rogers, 1983.
Carolyn Williams

JIMMY'S CHICKEN SHACK. Jimmy's Chicken Shack was not a shack, nor was it a place that simply served chicken. Rather, it was a nightclub in Harlem* and well known for the white and black celebrities* that visited the club as customers. In addition, black entertainers such as blues singer Billie Holiday* were often star attractions. After the more traditional nightclubs that whites frequented downtown closed for the night, taxis and limousines carrying white patrons would visit after-hours black nightclubs in Harlem known for their entertainment as well as good food. At one time Malcolm worked the streets as a "steerer," guiding whites to such clubs and other forms of more nontraditional "entertainment" in Harlem after clubs in downtown New York had closed.

It was at Jimmy's Chicken Shack that Malcolm and Redd Foxx* worked together. Malcolm was a waiter; he and Foxx, who became one of the best-known black comedians in the United States, worked together as dishwashers at one point. This was in the 1940s, a time when Harlem was still bustling with activity well into the next morning. Malcolm described Jimmy's at 4:30 in the morning as a place where one's eyes would hurt because the smoke was so thick; very drunk white women and men would start hugging blacks, stating that they thought that blacks were just as human as they were; and whites would be slapping on each other's backs and laughing uncontrollably. The club would be jampacked, wall to wall, and patrons would be eating chicken and sipping whiskey out of coffee cups (presumably to give the police the impression that they were simply sobering up by drinking coffee if there was a surprise "bust").

Jimmy's Chicken Shack was part of a world that Malcolm enjoyed in his youth but held little fascination for him as a Muslim* leader.

SELECTED BIBLIOGRAPHY

Lomax, 1963; Malcolm X with Haley, 1965.

Mfanya Donald Tryman

JOHNSON, HINTON (Hinton X). On April 14, 1957, an incident occurred in Harlem* that brought Malcolm X and the Nation of Islam (NOI)* to the attention of the general public. The incident began when an intoxicated man named Reese Poe, who had been fighting with his female companion, was stopped by a white police officer. According to the police report, the drunk bit the officer, pushed him into a wall, and gripped him with a firm bear hug. At this time a second officer intervened, grabbing the drunk, and struck him in the chest. The officer hit the heavily built black man continuously, although it appeared the blows had no effect on the intoxicated aggressor. Eventually, the black man was subdued and placed on the ground by the two officers. As a result of the beating, the victim had his head and clothing covered with blood.

One observer of the incident was a Black Muslim* named Hinton Johnson, Brother Hinton X as he was known in the NOI. Johnson, along with another onlooker, shouted to the two officers that this was New York, not the South.* The officers then instructed Johnson to move away. Hinton refused, and the officers began clubbing him. The blows from the nightstick struck Johnson viciously about the head. He was able to protect himself only by occasionally holding on to the nightstick.

There remains much controversy regarding how the incident actually began. Johnson stated that as he was leaving the scene, the officer spun him around and then struck him. The officer claimed, however, that he struck Johnson after he accidentally backed into Johnson, and Johnson grabbed him by the throat.

Bleeding and handcuffed, Johnson, who had never before had encounters with the police, was taken to the Twenty-eighth Precinct Station House. Hinton, because of the extensive injuries received, laid on the jail cell floor moaning and praying. According to him, he was struck in the mouth and pushed against a wall with such force that he blacked out while in police custody.

In less than half an hour after the arrest, Malcolm was notified at Temple Number Seven* that Johnson had been beaten and jailed; shortly thereafter, about fifty Muslims* from Malcolm's temple appeared outside the 123rd Street police station. Standing in rank formation, along the sidewalk and curb, the contingent awaited Malcolm's arrival.

Upon arrival Malcolm asked to see Johnson but was told that Johnson was not there. However, after Malcolm learned that Johnson was in fact there, he refused to leave without seeing him to determine if he needed medical assistance, noting that his men would remain as well.

By this time the crowd had grown to nearly 3,000 people, including a large number of women. The police realized that they had a potential riot on their hands and quickly summoned a number of influential citizens for assistance. One such citizen was James Hicks,* editor of the *New York Amsterdam News*,* the city's most prominent black newspaper.

Hicks was Malcolm X's friend and was therefore requested to arrange a meeting at his office with Malcolm and members of the police department. Upon arrival at Hicks's office, he was confronted by the white Deputy Police Commissioner Walter Arm, who blatantly informed Malcolm that he wanted the demonstrators removed. Arm prefaced his remarks by stating that he was telling Malcolm and not begging him. Malcolm responded by immediately walking out of Hicks's office. And he only returned at Hicks's personal request.

Malcolm then began to utilize his new bargaining position. He was given reassurance that if Johnson required medical treatment, he would be transported to the hospital. Malcolm acknowledged that if this was the case, he would, in turn, remove his people from the streets.

At the precinct station, Malcolm had to contain himself when he saw Johnson's condition. Johnson was semiconscious, and his skull was cracked. Malcolm demanded that Johnson be taken immediately by ambulance to the hospital. He was immediately transported to the Harlem hospital. Malcolm then complied with the police request to take the responsibility of sending his people home. With one gesture of his hand, Malcolm had all of his followers disperse. This represented a great display of power that police officers found difficult to understand, especially emanating from a black man.

Although Hinton Johnson survived the ordeal, it was not without permanent physical damage. A legal suit against the police department resulted in an eventual award of $70,000.

The Hinton Johnson incident allowed Malcolm to rescue Johnson from what many in the black community considered a dangerous adversary. The episode elevated Malcolm X to the status of a hero in Harlem.* One result was almost immediate: Temple Seven's membership increased immensely as a result of this incident.

This incident proved that Malcolm could, in fact, influence those who many considered unresponsive to the black community. Malcolm could wield real power in the black community vis-à-vis white police force.

SELECTED BIBLIOGRAPHY

Friedly, 1992; Goldman, 1973; *New York Amsterdam News*, January 26, 1963; B. Perry, 1991.

Ronnie Tucker and Mfanya Donald Tryman

JOHNSON, LYNDON B. In 1964 Lyndon B. Johnson and Barry Goldwater* vied for the presidency of the United States. At that time, Malcolm X was one of the most sought-after speakers in America, and he was consistently asked which of the two men would be best for African Americans. His reply was characteristic of his militancy and desire to highlight the similarities between the Republican* and Democratic* Parties. According to Malcolm, the differences in Johnson and Goldwater were minuscule. In fact, Malcolm thought the conservative Goldwater was more reputable than the liberal Johnson, because the former was at least truthful about his disdain for black people.

Malcolm often used analogies in his speeches to make a point. In this case, he used the wolf and fox analogy. The wolf is straightforward, and his adversary understands the danger at hand. Conversely, the fox is devious and will pretend to be something he is not, lulling his victim to sleep to gain an advantage while that victim is anesthetized. Malcolm suggested that the liberal Johnson was more detrimental to black achievement than the conservative Goldwater. He pointed to the progress of black southerners and the lack of such progress for black northerners, based upon his reference to the canine analogy. Therefore, Malcolm said he would vote for neither candidate, nor would he recommend either to other blacks. He frequently criticized Johnson, because of the Texan's close friendship to many leading anti–civil rights politicians from the South.* For Malcolm, it was clear that Johnson's relationship with many of these leaders existed because they shared similar views about African American progress.

SELECTED BIBLIOGRAPHY

Geyelin, 1966; Malcolm X with Haley, 1965; *Militant*, June 1, 1964; Reedy, 1982.

Horace Huntley

JOHNSON, THOMAS 15X (Khalil Islam). Thomas 15X Johnson joined the Nation of Islam (NOI)* in 1960 and quickly found his place in the local Fruit of Islam (FOI),* the organization's paramilitary body. Like so many of those who were early members of Harlem's* mosque, it was Malcolm X that captured Johnson's imagination and eventually his allegiance to the NOI. Johnson first learned about Malcolm and his ideas from Malcolm's frequent radio and television appearances. Admittedly, Malcolm impressed Johnson. A former drug addict, Johnson was typical of numerous members of Temple Number Seven,* a testimonial to the many successes that Malcolm achieved fishing* men from the gutter and rehabilitating their lives. As a member of the FOI, Johnson spent a considerable amount of his temple responsibility guarding Malcolm, although he and Malcolm were apparently not closely associated. Yet Johnson rose quickly through the ranks of the FOI, eventually becoming a lieutenant in the body.

Finding it difficult to understand the rift between Malcolm and Elijah Muhammad,* Johnson refused to side with Malcolm when he broke away from the Messenger and the NOI. In 1965 he became one of a trio of NOI members tried for Malcolm's murder. Arrested several days after the slaying, he was tried along with Talmadge Hayer* and Norman 3X Butler* for the crime. Just prior to his arrest, Johnson, Butler, and another former member of the Harlem temple were out of jail on bail, accused in the shooting of Benjamin Brown,* an NOI defector;* it was this incident that led New York City police officials to connect both Johnson and Butler to Malcolm's murder. Although identified as one of the assassins by Cary Thomas,* one of Malcolm's bodyguards, the evidence against Johnson was considerably less creditable than it was against both Hayer and Butler. Establishing a motive by the prosecution was no less dubious. All of this became more obvious during the assassination trial* when Thomas, the prosecution's star witness, gave vague and equivocating testimony, and Hayer confessed to the murder before disclaiming both Johnson's and Butler's involvement.

Johnson consistently denied implication in the slaying. Moreover, there was little substantive evidence to prove that he was even present in the Audubon Ballroom* the evening of Malcolm's murder. New York legal officials, however, were determined to pursue the prosecution and, despite all of the discrepancies in their case, acquired the sought-after conviction. Johnson served fourteen years of his life sentence for the conviction. In prison,* Johnson, like the other two men convicted of Malcolm's slaying, would adopt a formal Arabic name; Johnson became Khalil Islam. After his parole, Khalil Islam faded into obscurity.

SELECTED BIBLIOGRAPHY

Friedly, 1992; Breitman, Porter, and Smith (Miah, ed.), 1976; Karim with Skutches and Gallen, 1992.

Robert L. Jenkins

JONES, CLARENCE. Clarence Jones was a civil rights* activist in the 1960s and practicing attorney in New York City. He represented Martin Luther King, Jr.,* as well in legal matters, and King sought his advice on civil rights demonstrations and related matters of civil disobedience. Jones was responsible for trying to set a meeting up between King and Malcolm X. He had served as a liaison between the two leaders since March 1964 when they initially and briefly met in Washington, D.C. during congressional debate on the 1964 Civil Rights bill. The purpose of the meeting was to show that King was interested in supporting Malcolm X's petition to the United Nations* with regard to the violation of the human rights* of black Americans. According to Jones, King's support would involve a degree of reciprocity on the part of Malcolm, in which he would support King's northern campaigns and King would support Malcolm's ventures in the South.* While Jones was successful in getting the two leaders connected by long-distance telephone on several occasions, he was never able to get the two leaders together for what may have been the strongest black coalition in the 1960s. Jones's efforts were complicated by King's associates, who thought that such a meeting would hurt his reputation with white liberals,* and scheduling conflicts of two of the most sought-after speakers during this period.

SELECTED BIBLIOGRAPHY
Branch, 1998; Evanzz, 1992, 1999.

Mfanya Donald Tryman

JUDAISM. Judaism is one of the major religions of the world. The Torah is the Five Books of Moses (which is the beginning of the Hebrew and Christian Bibles) and states that the Hebrews are descendants of Abraham. God formed covenants (agreements) with Abraham, Moses,* and Noah, but it was with Abraham, as recorded in Genesis, that God formed the covenant in which Jews would be God's "Chosen People," in which God would establish a homeland for Abraham's descendants in return for their complete obedience to him. Jews in the Middle East* see that "great nation" in Israel, established in 1948. Judaism is, nevertheless, a community-based religion and Jews,* like Christians, believe in the Ten Commandments. Judaism puts great emphasis upon monotheism, the idea that there is only one God.

Throughout Malcolm X's short career as spokesman for the Nation of Islam (NOI),* he was constantly accused by the mainstream media of being anti-Semitic. Historically, many blacks, particularly in northern urban areas, have harbored strong anti-Semitic feelings. Despite this fact, however, Malcolm X did not fit into this category. While many of his opinions about Judaism and Jews were less than congenial, Malcolm made it clear that people had a right to choose their own religion. For one to begin to understand Malcolm's attitude toward Judaism, it is important to first understand his experiences with Christianity,* a religion he thought was closely linked to Judaism.

His father's itinerant Baptist ministry notwithstanding, Malcolm's alienation from Christianity began when he was quite young. His experiences with violence and humiliation at the hands of so-called Christian whites in Omaha, Nebraska,* and Lansing, Michigan,* proved to him that there was a contradiction between what whites said about Christian love and what they practiced. Malcolm was also well aware of the many black lynchings that southern white Christians took part in. Living the life of a hustler, pimp,* and burglar, Malcolm saw no merit in believing in the Christian concept of Jesus as someone divine.

Malcolm's rejection of Christianity became official as his life was radically transformed through the teachings of Elijah Muhammad,* who informed Malcolm that for centuries whites had used Old Testament (the Jewish Torah) scriptures to justify black slavery.* He taught Malcolm that Christ did not die on the cross but was merely in a chemically induced coma when the Roman soldiers removed him. Thus, he only appeared to arise from the dead, after which he traveled to Asia, fathered many children, and died in his seventies. These teachings forced Malcolm to change his views on suffering and redemption. Muhammad taught Malcolm that Jesus had survived his ordeal and thus gave him, and other blacks, a new sense of hope for an end to their own suffering.

Armed with these teachings, Malcolm set out to spread the word to other blacks. Explaining to blacks that they had been duped into believing white interpretations of the Bible,* Malcolm attempted to convince blacks that Islam* was their real religion. As a result of this and a host of other reasons, establishment Jews picked up on Malcolm's statements and proceeded to label him anti-Semitic. Consequently, Malcolm spent an enormous amount of time trying to prove that he was not anti-Semitic.

When Malcolm became a nationally known Muslim* minister, he sometimes spoke about the dubious and often antagonistic relationship between blacks and Jews. His customary response to accusations of anti-Semitism often made it appear that he partially blamed the Jews for black suffering. For example, Malcolm often intoned that the Black Muslims* were not "anti-anything." In fact, he said, they were simply "anti-wrong," and this meant "anti-exploitation, and anti-oppression." In a June 1963 interview with Kenneth Clark,* City College of New York psychology professor and local black activist, Malcolm explained that many Jews harbored a guilty conscience if anyone mentioned that exploitation dominated their business affairs in black communities. Hence, Jews derived considerably more economic benefit from their relationship with blacks than blacks did with Jews. Malcolm concluded his remarks by adding that most Jews, when black exploitation is mentioned, accused blacks of being anti-Semitic to hide their own guilt in exploiting blacks.

Consequently, Malcolm's disdain for Jewish merchants can be easily construed as anti-Semitism. While Malcolm continued to deny accusations of anti-Semitism, he sometimes worsened matters by claiming that Jewish merchants and plantation owners actually financed the slave trade. Again, Malcolm was not attacking Judaism, but he left very little room for Jews to wonder what he thought about their religion.

Paradoxically, Malcolm often admonished blacks to learn from the Jews' examples of thrift and community solidarity. He taught blacks that Jews never lost their pride, manhood, or sense of value. These things, he said, enabled Jews to think and act independently, something necessary for blacks to do to acquire real freedom.

Despite these admonishments, however, Malcolm still seemed to make anti-Semitic accusations more plausible by comparing the plight of the 6 million Jews in World War II* Europe* with the plight of blacks during the African slave trade. In not so covert terms, Malcolm seemed to minimize the Jews' suffering in comparison to the tragedy that Africans experienced in the Americas. For example, when asked about Jews and their fate under Adolf Hitler and the Nazis,* Malcolm complained that everybody talked about the Jewish plight under Nazism, but no one said anything about the 100 million blacks who were "kidnapped" and transported to the Americas as slaves. He condescendingly added that everyone "was teary-eyed for Jews who were responsible for their own plight," but there was no concern over the enormous losses incurred by blacks. While one might assume that Malcolm used this technique, in part, to arouse his audience, it is clear that his feelings about Jews were less than affectionate and, from this comment, very close to being anti-Semitic.

SELECTED BIBLIOGRAPHY

Borowitz, 1984; Cone, 1991; Gallen, ed., 1992; Goldman, 1979; Neusner, 1987; Salzman et al., 1992.

Curtis Austin

K

KAHN, TOM. Tom Kahn was a noted labor activist and critic of Malcolm X who coauthored with Bayard Rustin* the anti–Malcolm X article "The Mark of Oppression." Kahn graduated from Howard University* in 1963 and began his involvement in the civil rights movement* with service on the Committee to Defend Martin Luther King, Jr.* In 1963 he helped to coordinate the March on Washington.* Kahn's activism became more mainstream when he became the chief speechwriter for Senator Henry M. Jackson in the early 1970s. He eventually became editor of the AFL-CIO *Free Trade Union News* and served on the board of the A. Philip Randolph* Institute. In the spring 1965 edition of *Dissent*, the article by Kahn and Rustin was reprinted as "The Ambiguous Legacy of Malcolm X."

The article attacked attempts to eulogize Malcolm as a great and charismatic leader. According to Kahn and Rustin, although Malcolm's eloquence revealed racism's evil, the slain leader did not develop a viable program to combat this evil. In fact, they claimed, Malcolm's fiery rhetoric "frightened and worried white liberals"* who supported the civil rights movement and "let off the hook" whites who were hostile and indifferent to black progress and, therefore, used Malcolm's words to solidify their own political inertia. Kahn and Rustin grudgingly alluded to the change in Malcolm's political and religious positions after the split with the Nation of Islam (NOI)* but argued that uncertainty still clouded his actions. The authors noted that even though Malcolm succeeded in resurrecting a sense of black manhood* in the ghetto, he failed to look beyond the ghetto, unaware that the national economy was creating technological conditions that would eventually require a strategy for social change that could and should result in the ghetto's destruction.

SELECTED BIBLIOGRAPHY
Kahn and Rustin, 1965; Malcolm X (Breitman, ed.), 1967.

Malik Simba

KAID, TAHER. Taher Kaid was the Algerian ambassador to the Republic of Ghana* during the early 1960s. It was Kaid, an orthodox Muslim,* with whom Malcolm had a major discussion during his 1964 visit to the Ghanaian Republic, that helped to reshape Malcolm's thinking about black nationalism,* Islam,* and whites. During the visit, Malcolm, who was en route to the United States following his Hajj,* was basking in the attention that he received from many of the revolutionary Third World figures officially associated with Ghana. Malcolm and Kaid were kindred spirits not only in their adherence to Islam but also in their support of national liberation struggles. Indeed, Malcolm would later describe Kaid as "extremely militant" in his position on nationalism and a revolutionary in the truest sense. Apparently, however, Malcolm gave little thought to exactly how much the two men had in common. At the time of the meeting, Malcolm was still emphatically race conscious in his views about whites, especially his mistrust of them. Moreover, he had not abandoned his separatist views regarding nationalism, though he was clearly searching for redefinition of his philosophy on several subjects, including black nationalism. During the course of their conversation, Kaid, inquired of Malcolm about where, as a Caucasian, but also as an African, a fellow Muslim, and a revolutionary, did he fit into Malcolm's views about Islamic brotherhood and his goal of black nationalism. Malcolm did not indicate how he responded to the question, but the impact of it weighed heavily on him, admittedly influencing him to reappraise his position on the subject. Apparently, Malcolm's lack of an unqualified answer to Kaid did little to lessen the Algerian's respect for him. Indeed, Kaid thought so highly of Malcolm that he and an entourage of foreign diplomats accompanied a contingent of Ghanaian officials to the airport with Malcolm to bid the black American farewell from Africa.

On the Hajj, Malcolm had already learned that true Islam did not distinguish between skin color in defining brotherhood. After his visit with Kaid, he reasoned further that the black American struggle for liberation did not automatically exclude the assistance of sincere whites, an important move in garnering a broader base of support from nonblack Third World Muslims. While Malcolm never completely abandoned his general mistrust of whites, it was certainly not long after his encounter with Kaid that Malcolm showed that his thoughts on black nationalism as the panacea for the so-called Negro problem were evolving from their purely separatist framework based on skin color. He lessened his heretofore restrictive usage of the term and increasingly moved toward an interpretation that emphasized black management of the social institutions and the politics and economic affairs of their communities.

SELECTED BIBLIOGRAPHY

Cone, 1991; Goldman, 1979; Malcolm X (Breitman, ed.), 1965; Sales, 1994.

Robert L. Jenkins

KARENGA, MAULANA RON. Malcolm X's black nationalism* legacy developed in numerous ways. One was the development of individuals who advocated cultural nationalism as a means of liberating the American Negro from white racist oppression. Using Malcolm's analysis, these advocates argued that black's dependence on Western (white) cultural values solidified the chains of oppression that bound blacks. Perhaps no one has been a more articulate spokesman for this view than Ron Karenga, a Black Studies scholar who teaches in the University of California system and leader of the cultural nationalists organization called US.* Like many blacks whose activism of the 1960s and 1970s advocated a militant position, Karenga admired Malcolm and considered himself an heir to many of Malcolm's ideas.

By the early 1970s Karenga had developed an alternative cultural value system named the Nguzo Saba, using the African language of Kiswahili. The Nguzo Saba, or the Seven Principles, seeks to convey unitary values for all black people. These principles are based, in part, on Malcolm's vision of Pan-Africanism* and a wider vision of black unity. These principles are Umoja (unity), Kujichaguilia (self-determination), Ujima (collective work and responsibility), Ujamaa (cooperative economics), Nia (purpose), Kuumba (creativity), and Imani (faith). These seven principles, practiced throughout one's life, were to be officially observed every year from December 24 through January 1 in the celebration of Kwanzaa, representing an African season of harvest and celebration. Each principle is highlighted, examined, and practiced by all participating blacks during these seven holy days. Karenga and most cultural nationalists hoped that the adoption of these African values would liberate blacks from the sense of personal and collective inferiority imposed upon them by Western hegemony.

SELECTED BIBLIOGRAPHY
Karenga, 1980; Sales, 1994.

Malik Simba

KARIM, BENJAMIN (Benjamin Goodman; Benjamin 2X; Benjamin K). One of Malcolm X's chief aides, at Harlem* Temple Number Seven* and later at the Muslim Mosque, Inc.,* Benjamin Karim, née Goodman, was raised in Virginia. Trained as a radar man in the U.S. Air Force and unable to find a similar job at a commercial airport, because he felt he was discriminated against, he came to Harlem. Acquaintances, who had heard about the Nation of Islam (NOI)* and were captivated by Malcolm X, told Karim about the new temple being established. Impressed by the NOI's focus on love, brotherhood, and unity among black people, he became a Muslim* and was variously known as Benjamin K and Benjamin 2X.

Karim eventually became an assistant minister to Malcolm at Temple Number Seven and assisted him in establishing other mosques throughout the country. When Malcolm left the NOI, Karim left as well, and when Malcolm made his Hajj* to Mecca* and later toured African and Arab countries in 1964, Karim was the interim leader of Malcolm's fledgling Organization of Afro-American Unity.*

Benjamin Karim was usually the warm-up speaker for Minister Malcolm and often substituted for him when he was unable to fulfill speaking engagements. Karim had just introduced him on February 21, 1965, at the Audubon Ballroom* when Malcolm was assassinated. In 1992 he wrote *Remembering Malcolm*, a book about his life and work with Malcolm. Indeed, much of what the American public in general and scholars specifically have learned about Malcolm since his death has been gleaned from the writings on Malcolm that Karim authored.

SELECTED BIBLIOGRAPHY

Friedly, 1992; Goldman, 1973; Karim with Skutches and Gallen, 1992.

Nancy-Elizabeth Fitch

KENNEDY, JOHN FITZGERALD. With the possible exception of Martin Luther King, Jr.,* no other public figure of his day was as frequent a target of criticism by Malcolm X as was John F. Kennedy. Malcolm thought that Kennedy, a Massachusetts Democrat elected in 1960 as president, was especially ambiguous on the issue of civil rights.* Although he campaigned in favor of sweeping civil rights changes, once elected, Kennedy failed to move with "all deliberate speed" to implement such reforms. Malcolm often criticized Kennedy's reluctance to sign even a simple executive order prohibiting racial discrimination in federally financed housing. For his reluctance to exercise even the most moderate civil rights stance, Malcolm repeatedly labeled Kennedy as "a segregationist." To Malcolm, Kennedy was more interested in dismantling the Berlin Wall than the "Alabama Wall." The Kennedy strategy, Malcolm insisted, was quite simple, and that was to promote a false sense of racial progress. All three of the Kennedy brothers—John, Robert,* attorney general, and Teddy, a U.S. senator—were vilified by Malcolm, and he referred to them collectively as the "K.K.K."

According to one historian, Malcolm sought acceptance, and he anguished over the fact that the president never included him in his talks with other black leaders at the White House. Understandably, Kennedy did not view Malcolm positively, either. He found Malcolm's rhetoric dangerous, a real threat to national security, although on the eve of his death the president still had no evidence that Malcolm and the Nation of Islam (NOI)* were doing things to violate federal law, a view contrary to that of Federal Bureau of Investigation* Director J. Edgar Hoover.*

Upon hearing of President Kennedy's assassination, Malcolm gleefully responded in private about "the old devil['s]" death. In a speech in Harlem's Temple Number Seven* on the night of the assassination, Malcolm was rather subdued on the Kennedy tragedy, but nevertheless contented himself with an oblique reference to the punishment of God and people reaping what they sow. With his normally caustic style and vitriolic views, Malcolm could have been more inhumane with his statement, but undoubtedly his demeanor was influenced by the directives of Elijah Muhammad* instructing NOI ministers not to comment on the Kennedy assassination. The directives were issued because it was felt that any public utterances, especially those of a pejorative nature, about the slain president were certain to offend blacks who idolized him.

Malcolm's silence and restraint, however, seemed to have been broken some nine days after the assassination on December 1, 1963, when he spoke to a gathering at the Manhattan Center. In the text of the speech, he criticized the slain president for delaying his response to the turbulent Birmingham, Alabama,* campaign until blacks had become the direct targets of violence, as they were in Birmingham's Sixteenth Street Baptist Church bombing* that killed four young black children. Malcolm further accused the late chief executive of attempting to undermine the original design of the March on Washington* or, at the very least, to orchestrate it by offering large sums of money to its organizers. But Malcolm's most telling comments came during the question-and-answer period. When asked about the assassination, he departed from the restraint and discipline of his formal address and responded by saying it was a case of "the chickens coming home to roost."* He even compared it to the assassinations of African leader Patrice Lumumba* and Vietnamese leaders Ngo Dinh Diem and Ngo Dinh Nhu, all of whom died in coups that the Kennedy administration condoned.

In the weeks and months that followed the speech, Muhammad silenced Malcolm indefinitely and ultimately relieved him of his duties as both National Representative of the NOI and minister of Temple Number Seven. This turn of events would leave Malcolm dejected and in emotional shock. Malcolm sought a medical explanation of how he was feeling but was told it was not physiological. It truly represented one of the lowest points of Malcolm's life and accelerated his alienation from, and eventual break with, the NOI.

SELECTED BIBLIOGRAPHY

Clegg, 1997; Farmer, 1985; Myers, 1993; B. Perry, 1991; Young, 1996.

                                                                    Saul Dorsey

KENNEDY, ROBERT (BOBBY) F. Robert Kennedy, also known as Bobby Kennedy, was a younger brother of President John F. Kennedy.* He was one of three sons reared for public service by his father, wealthy Massachusetts businessman and political leader Joseph P. Kennedy. A graduate of Harvard University* and the University of Virginia Law School, Robert's greatest challenge began in 1961 when, at age thirty-six, he accepted an appointment in his brother's cabinet as attorney general. As such, during the 1960s he played a central role in the era's civil rights* activities. An acquaintance of the leading civil rights leaders, he often acted as broker between those who sought substantive social change and those who opposed them.

It was during this crucial period that Malcolm X and Robert Kennedy's paths crossed. Malcolm never personally met Bobby Kennedy, but as the nation's chief law enforcement officer Bobby influenced Malcolm's views about the state of America's race relations. Malcolm disliked President Kennedy immensely, regarding him as a southern sympathizer, a "Dixiecrat."* It was Kennedy and the Democrats' unwillingness to protect southern blacks from racial violence and their steadfast refusal to recognize the African American quest for equality that most angered Malcolm. Malcolm frequently remarked that President Kennedy and the Democrats simply never lived up to their campaign promise to black people. As a member of the president's inner circle, Bobby was a natural target of Malcolm's wrath, though his direct references to the attorney general were infrequent. A master at using clever descriptions for people whom he held in disdain, Malcolm disparagingly referred to Bobby and the other two Kennedy brothers as the "K.K.K." He lambasted Robert for his secret work with Mississippi* Governor Ross Barnett in the James Meredith* 1962 Ole Mississippi desegregation imbroglio. In Malcolm's opinion, it was for political purposes that Bobby placated both the forces of racial integration* and racial segregation* in "a deal" when Barnett abandoned his public position of physically blocking Meredith's admission in the presence of federal marshals. Blacks were duped by the affair, Malcolm said, because the Kennedys claimed to be racial liberals, a group that Malcolm held in great contempt. All that occurred, Malcolm would later say, was simply the admission of one lone black student. This was tokenism, and coming from the support of liberals like Bobby Kennedy, tokenism was the same as hypocrisy. Neither Bobby nor the president, he said, deserved credibility in the black community.

There is little to indicate that the attorney general had much to say publically in response to any of Malcolm's criticisms. To be sure, Bobby Kennedy was aware of the black disenchanted for whom Malcolm so eloquently spoke. That he understood the potential threat that Malcolm posed to the country's established order is clear, for it was the attorney general who gave the Federal Bureau of Investigation* the authorization to scrutinize the black leader more closely through the use of the wire tap. Malcolm and the group for whom he spoke, Kennedy informed newsmen, needed to be watched very carefully. Nevertheless, Bobby continued to enjoy immense popularity among black Americans and was assured of their solid support in his own presidential bid in 1968, had he not been assassinated during the Democratic Party's* nomination campaign.

SELECTED BIBLIOGRAPHY

Malcolm X (Clark, ed.), 1991, 1992; Malcolm X (Perry, ed.), 1989; B. Perry, 1991; Schlesinger, 1978; Xenon Studio, 1991.

Robert L. Jenkins

KENYATTA, CHARLES (Charles 37X Morris). Charles Kenyatta, also known as Charles 37X Morris, described by the Federal Bureau of Investigation (FBI)* as a "militant black nationalist," and one of the men standing guard at Malcolm X's assassination, was recruited into the Nation of Islam (NOI)* by Malcolm in the early 1950s in Detroit, Michigan,* where both worked at a construction site. Malcolm spent his evenings teaching at Detroit Temple Number One where Charles was greatly influenced by one of his lectures. Over the next decade Charles became a devoted admirer and one of the few close confidants and aides of Malcolm X. Because of their similar backgrounds, Malcolm and Charles formed a natural alliance. He was often referred to as Malcolm's one-man intelligence within the NOI. Like Malcolm, Charles was street educated and had a strong distrust of intellectuals. The distrust, coupled with sometimes bitter rivalry between Malcolm's other close associates, created petty squabbling within the ranks of the Organization of Afro-American Unity (OAAU)* that Malcolm headed. Malcolm's influence on Charles was profound. For example, after Malcolm's return from Mecca* and a tour of Africa, he suggested that Charles change his last name to Kenyatta, in honor of Jomo Kenyatta, a former African revolutionary and prime minister whom Malcolm greatly respected. Apparently, Charles accepted Malcolm's suggestion. He also grew a beard like Malcolm's. Kenyatta found it difficult to accept Malcolm's changing philosophy about whites, but he remained Malcolm's friend and confidant.

Following Malcolm's assassination, Kenyatta testified against the accused Norman 3X Butler* and Thomas 15X Johnson,* both of whom received life sentences. In 1967, Kenyatta was one of the speakers at a memorial march where he lavished praise upon the late charismatic leader of the OAAU. Two years later Kenyatta survived an assassination attempt in the rash of post–Malcolm X assassinations perpetrated against former confidants of the fallen leader.

SELECTED BIBLIOGRAPHY

Carson (Gallen, ed.), 1991; Evanzz, 1992; Friedly, 1992; Gallen, ed., 1992; Goldman, 1979; Malcolm X with Haley, 1965; B. Perry, 1991.

Thaddeus M. Smith and L. Henry Whelchel

KHAALIS, HAMAAS ABDUL (Ernest T. 2X McGee). Hamaas Abdul Khaalis, previously known as Ernest T. 2X McGee, was the national secretary for the Nation of Islam (NOI)* until 1957. He had joined the Black Muslims* in 1950 and was a part of Elijah Muhammad's* designated team, which included Malcolm X, selected to expand the organization nationwide. In 1957, he was demoted by Malcolm X in favor of John Ali,* who became closely associated with Malcolm until Malcolm's expulsion from the Black Muslims in 1963. After his demotion, McGee left the NOI in favor of an orthodox Islamic sect that became known as the Hanafi and changed his name to Hamaas Abdul Khaalis. The headquarters of the Hanafi was located in Washington, D.C. in a home that had been purchased by Lew Alcindor, who had been a star center at the University of California at Los Angeles and went on to excel in the National Basketball Association. Alcindor joined the Hanafi and subsequently changed his name to Kareem Abdul-Jabbar.

In January of 1973 Khaalis wrote a scathing three-page letter denouncing Elijah Muhammad* as a fraud and questioning the legitimacy of the NOI and its founding by W. D. Fard* supposedly based upon the Holy Qu'ran.* He also claimed that the NOI was stealing money from members and preparing them for hell. The letter came in the wake of a number of rival assassinations and shootings between the Black Muslims and opposing groups.

Less than two weeks after the letter, which was dated January 5, 1973, eight Black Muslims drove in two cars from the Philadelphia mosque to Washington, D.C., where they plotted the assassination of Khaalis. The next day, after an elaborate plan of deception to gain entrance into his home, they shot in the head and killed at point-blank range adults and children of his family and drowned three infants as they quietly slept. Khaalis, who was not at home at the time of the murders, luckily escaped harm.

Minister Louis X Farrakhan,* who had been making veiled threats against anyone speaking ill of the NOI or Muhammad right before these murders, reminded his listening audience in a radio broadcast after the murders that hypocrites like Malcolm X deserved to die. He refused to apologize for the gross murders in Washington, D.C. Khaalis maintained that although he originally blamed Malcolm for his demise in the NOI, the two had "mended fences" after Malcolm's ouster in 1964.

SELECTED BIBLIOGRAPHY

Evanzz, 1992, 1999; Marable, 1991.

Mfanya Donald Tryman and Yoshawnda Trotter

KILLENS, JOHN OLIVER. Although he grew up in the shadow of Richard Wright,* unlike Wright, Georgia-born African American novelist John Oliver Killens never became an expatriate. He remained in America, adding his voice to the activities of the political Left from the mid-1940s to the mid-1950s, specifically by organizing black and white workers for the Congress of Industrial Organizations (CIO)* and through his activities in the Progressive Party. Between 1951 and 1955, he wrote for *Freedom*, a newspaper ideologically rooted in communism,* thoroughly convinced of the potential power of organized black labor.

Firmly committed to the concept of writing as a vehicle for social protest, Killens made a major impact on the African American literary tradition throughout the 1960s and 1970s. Through his emphasis on the effects of violence and race on the black family, he continued and contributed to the "protest tradition" most often associated with Wright. Beginning with the publication of his first novel, *Youngblood*, in 1954, Killens authored four novels, two children's books, a collection of essays, three plays, and two screenplays. His work appeared in such popular magazines and journals as the *Saturday Evening Post*, the *New York Times Magazine, Ebony,* *The Black Scholar*, and *Black World*. The Howard University* graduate, a recognizable figure in Harlem's* intelligentsia, was among the founders of the Harlem Writer's Guild, a forum that enhanced the early careers of many of contemporary America's better-known writers, including Paule Marshall, Maya Angelou,* and Ossie Davis.*

Killens was philosophically opposed to the concept of nonviolence promoted by Dr. Martin L. King, Jr.* Although he actively participated in the civil rights movement* from 1954 through 1970, he did not believe nonviolence was a good vehicle through which black liberation could be achieved. His shift from a socialist philosophy to black nationalism* is closely aligned with his friendship with Malcolm X. Killens, whose alliance with Malcolm began in the late 1950s, long before it had become fashionable for black celebrities* to befriend him, often met with Malcolm for discussions on various issues that the two found of mutual interest, especially the plight of black Americans. He was also a key figure in the founding of the Organization of Afro-American Unity (OAAU)* in 1964. The OAAU was determined, as noted in its charter, to solidify black Americans in their quest for human rights.* It was a goal to which Killens had philosophically and actively devoted his life to make possible.

SELECTED BIBLIOGRAPHY

Angelou, 1986; Goldman, 1979; Sales, 1994.

Wilfred D. Samuels

KING, CORETTA SCOTT. Educated at Antioch College and the prestigious New England Conservatory of Music, Coretta Scott King's life through marriage and family moved her far from the music career for which she prepared. The wife of Martin Luther King, Jr.,* symbol of the modern civil rights movement,* Coretta would emerge as a prominent and effective spokesperson for black causes in her own right after the 1968 assassination of her husband. Although she was seldom in the spotlight during King's activism, she could often be found by his side in the demonstrations and marches that he led.

Like her husband, Coretta was committed to nonviolent tactics as the key to effective social change. Nevertheless, she, as did her husband, held a healthy respect for Malcolm X and what he ultimately sought to achieve for black people. Coretta, like Martin, only encountered Malcolm once, this during the 1965 Selma, Alabama, voting rights campaign. Activists from the Student Non-Violent Coordinating Committee (SNCC),* becoming increasingly disillusioned with the nonviolent strategy, invited Malcolm to speak at a planned rally in the local Brown's Chapel A.M.E. Church. At the time, King was in a Selma jail for his role in leading the protest, and King's aides were alarmed by Malcolm's presence in the city. Worried that his rhetoric might intensify an already charged atmosphere and ultimately lead to violence, they succeeded in having Coretta speak to the gathering before Malcolm. Coretta gave a brief but inspiring speech in the spirit of nonviolence, after which she formally met Malcolm. Malcolm told Coretta that he had tried to visit Martin in jail but had been unable to see him; his travel itinerary after the program would not permit him to make another effort. More significantly, during the course of their small talk, Malcolm told

Coretta that he had not come to the city to cause trouble for Martin's campaign. Indeed, he said, he hoped to convey to recalcitrant whites that it was in their best interest to concede to Martin's demands rather than face the alternative that he, Malcolm, and his followers presented.

Malcolm's words were veiled references to his philosophy of addressing violence with violence. And Coretta clearly understood it as such. Yet King came away from her encounter with Malcolm convinced that he and her husband had more in common than many believed; they especially shared views about black pride* and the "connectedness" to Africa. Martin, she claimed, truly respected Malcolm, and had Malcolm not been murdered, the two would likely have established a closer relationship. The result, she said, would have been a formidable combination in the black liberation struggle.

Coretta maintains that the black firebrand impressed her with his intelligence and gentle nature. Apparently, as he had done with so many others who condemned him before meeting him personally, Malcolm found a way to charm Coretta. She would later become a close friend of his wife, Betty Sanders Shabazz,* personally understanding the agony that Malcolm's widow endured when Martin would also be felled by an assassin's bullet.

SELECTED BIBLIOGRAPHY

Hampton and Fayer with Flynn, eds., 1991; C. King, 1969; Lowery and Marszalek, eds., 1992; Young, 1996.

Robert L. Jenkins

KING, MARTIN LUTHER, JR. Perhaps no other black leader in American history is more revered than Martin Luther King, Jr. The son of a prominent Atlanta Baptist minister and a graduate of Boston University's prestigious School of Theology, King worked tirelessly during the 1950s and 1960s to eliminate racial injustice in America. But King's goal of racial integration* through nonviolent resistance to oppression placed him squarely at odds with Malcolm X and the Nation of Islam (NOI).* Convinced that King was little more than a twentieth-century Uncle Tom,* Malcolm X encouraged blacks to eschew integration and to embrace a philosophy of self-improvement* and racial separation.* King, however, rejected Malcolm's separatist philosophy and argued that neither blacks nor whites would ever realize the full promise of American democracy in a racially divided nation.

King was born in Atlanta, Georgia. His parents, Alberta Christine Williams and Martin Luther King, Sr., were educated and well-respected members of Atlanta's prosperous black middle class. King and his family lived in an affluent black neighborhood and wore fashionable clothes, and his father, the pastor of Ebenezer Baptist Church, often drove a new car. But the Atlanta of King's youth was segregated. Blacks attended separate schools, ate in separate restaurants, drank from separate water fountains, and rode in the back of the city buses.

Civil rights leader Martin Luther King, Jr., Malcolm X's greatest rival for the support of urban black Americans during the 1960s. Library of Congress.

Wealth and education, King soon learned, made little difference in a society in which skin color determined a man's worth.

The racial indignities of racial segregation,* however, did not deter young King from a love of books and knowledge. He read voraciously and excelled in all of his studies. At the age of fifteen he gained admission to Morehouse College. After graduating from Morehouse with a degree in sociology, King pursued a divinity degree at Crozier Seminary in Pennsylvania. After finishing at Crozier, he entered the Ph.D. program in theology at Boston University.

At Crozier and at Boston University, King threw himself into his studies, reading philosophy, history, and a multitude of religious courses. But King also enjoyed an active social life in which he made many white friends. Although initially suspicious of white people, he realized that not all whites held the same attitudes with regard to race. He now believed that it was possible for whites and blacks to live and work together in Christian brotherhood.

It was during this same period that King began formulating the moral and philosophical principles that he would later adopt in the civil rights movement.* Inspired by the theology of Walter Rauschenbusch and Reinhold Niebuhr, King concluded that Christians had an obligation to combat evil and injustice in society. But the man who would have the most profound impact on his philosophy about civil rights* strategy was neither a Christian nor a theologian. On the contrary, he was Mahatma Gandhi, an Indian lawyer turned holy man, who used nonviolent resistance to challenge British imperialism in India during the 1930s and 1940s. According to Gandhi, people must never meet oppression with hatred. Hatred, he noted, only led to bitterness and bloodshed. The moral and spiritual power of love, said Gandhi, would redeem the oppressor and the oppressed from the evil of injustice.

King employed Gandhi's philosophy of nonviolent resistance in the Montgomery Bus Boycott of 1955–56 and in subsequent struggles against segregation and black disenfranchisement in the South.* King believed not only that nonviolence was the appropriate moral or Christian course but also that it was the only practical way that blacks could ever achieve meaningful change in America. Violence, he argued, would frighten whites and give the authorities an excuse for killing blacks and continuing the system of racial oppression. If blacks were going to break down the barrier of discrimination, they would have to convince whites that they simply wanted to share in the American promise of freedom and equality. The "soul force" of brotherly love and nonviolent resistance would ultimately shame whites into ending racism.

Malcolm X rejected King's approach. He and the NOI argued that King's message of brotherhood and nonviolent resistance had little chance of improving the lives of black Americans. Malcolm X found King's emphasis on nonviolence to be unrealistic. After seeing young children attacked by police dogs and blasted with water cannons in the streets of Birmingham, Alabama,* he raised his level of criticism of the civil rights leader. King, in his view, was the white man's best friend. As long as King told blacks to refrain from violence, whites would continue to brutalize them. The only way blacks would ever gain dignity and control of their lives was through self-defense,* self-help, and separation from whites, Malcolm contended.

During all the years of their activism, King and Malcolm encountered each other only twice. After years of verbal sparring against each other, a chance meeting between them occurred in 1964 during the U.S. Senate debate over the 1964 Civil Rights bill. It was a polite meeting, the two respectfully greeting each other, shaking hands, and posing for photographs before an interested but dismayed crowd. A second brief meeting happened in late 1964 when King was in New York. Although the media had consistently described Malcolm and Martin as true adversaries, no animosity really existed between the two leaders. Each respected the work that the other was doing in the liberation of black people. Indeed, Martin agreed with Malcolm's views about black racial pride and supported much of Malcolm's Pan-Africanism* regarding the important cultural nexus black Americans and Africans should strengthen. And Malcolm even vowed to come to Martin's aid on one occasion, when he was threatened by a white supremacist.

Unaware of the Federal Bureau of Investigation's* longtime scrutiny of nearly every one of King's moves, Malcolm joked during the coincidental meeting that the handshake and cordial greetings would surely provoke the agency's investigation of King. In a later response to the media's criticism about his exchange of niceties with the man touted as an opponent, King quipped that he would have had no trouble similarly greeting staunch segregationist governors George Wallace* of Alabama and Ross Barnett of Mississippi,* men whose views he had spent years demonstrating against. To King, the matter was simple: It was not the man who he disagreed with; it was his ideas about separatism and violence.

By the time of his death, however, Malcolm X had begun to temper his criticism of King and the civil rights movement. During a pilgrimage to Mecca,* he saw white and black Muslims* worshiping together in a spirit of brotherhood, and he believed that such cooperation was also possible in America. He now rejected separation as the only course for black Americans. This, together with revelations about the illicit activities of NOI leader Elijah Muhammad,* led Malcolm X to question some of his and the NOI's earlier positions. Indeed, there is much to indicate that Malcolm was moving toward playing a greater, more visible role in the very social movement that he had so frequently railed against. He would never, however, abandon his idea of employing violence in self-defense to achieve black justice.

King, however, never wavered in his commitment to racial integration through nonviolence. His bold and thoughtful leadership of numerous marches, sit-ins, and boycotts throughout the South* was one of the factors that forced the federal government to accelerate the desegregation of public schools, restaurants, and hotels. His efforts also helped achieve federal protection for those black citizens seeking to register to vote in the South. Yet by the time of his assassination in

1968, the movement that he helped to found began to splinter. Disillusioned and restless with the progress of the movement, many young urban blacks echoed the concerns of Malcolm X and called for Black Power.*

SELECTED BIBLIOGRAPHY

Branch, 1988, 1998; Cone, 1991; Garrow, 1986; M. King (Carson, ed.), 1998; Oates, 1982; B. Perry, 1991.

Phillip A. Gibbs

KLAN IN OMAHA. The Ku Klux Klan (KKK) during the years of Malcolm's youth constituted the second Klan movement in the United States. No longer confined to the South,* as in the Reconstruction era, the Klan of the 1920s was particularly strong in midwestern cities such as Omaha, Nebraska.* Indeed, it was in Omaha where the group established its first "klavern" in the state in the early 1920s. Strongly anti-Catholic in this midwestern milieu, it also maintained its strong historical opposition to black American advancement. The KKK was a negative recollection in Malcolm X's life. Malcolm's early childhood memories included the violent acts of the Klan that affected his family. Malcolm's father, the Reverend Earl Little,* battled with the Klan, because the organization disapproved of his activities on behalf of Marcus Garvey's* Universal Negro Improvement Association.* On one occasion, mounted Klansmen looking to harm Malcolm's father surrounded the Little home, brandishing firearms, waving torches, and shattering the window panes. Away from home at the time, Reverend Little escaped their vengeance, but violent acts by the Omaha Klan occasionally disrupted life in the Littles' household. The Klan's activity eventually influenced the Little family to flee Omaha for Milwaukee, Wisconsin. Throughout his life Malcolm would be vehement in his anti-Klan views.

SELECTED BIBLIOGRAPHY

Chalmers, 1965; Malcolm X with Haley, 1965; B. Perry, 1991.

Phyllis Gray-Ray

KLUNDER, REVEREND BRUCE. The Reverend Bruce Klunder was a charter member of the Cleveland, Ohio, branch of the Congress of Racial Equality (CORE)* in the early 1960s. A graduate of Yale Divinity school, Klunder, who was white, sought to educate his congregation to the need to end social injustice, particularly toward African Americans. In 1964, Reverend Klunder joined protests against the construction of segregated schools in Cleveland's inner city. At one point, Klunder laid down near a bulldozer that was preparing the ground for one such school. The bulldozer crushed him to death, the incident ruled to be an accidental homicide. The anger in Cleveland's black community over this incident was a factor in the African American Carl Stokes's unsuccessful run for the mayor's office in 1965 (he succeeded upon a second try in 1967, making him the first elected black mayor of a major American city). Following a speech entitled "The Black Revolution" in New York City on April 8, 1964, Malcolm X was asked his opinion on Klunder's death by James Wechsler* of the *New York Post*. Malcolm shocked the largely white audience by stating that blacks would not applaud the death of one white person while "22 million Negroes are dying every day." The statement prompted a journalistic tempest, with the liberal white Wechsler leading the protest against Malcolm for what was viewed as an impolitic, if not insensitive, comment. Malcolm disliked white liberals,* and he left in the exchange with Weschler no doubt about how he regarded the insincerity of liberals in general and Weschler specifically. Malcolm sought to explain in greater detail exactly what he meant about the comment, but he never apologized for it. Had this incident occurred after he made the Hajj,* Malcolm likely would have moderated his comments considerably.

SELECTED BIBLIOGRAPHY

Bullard, 1989; Hampton and Fayer with Flynn, eds., 1991; Malcolm X (Breitman, ed.), 1970a.

Damon Fordham

KOCHIYAMA, YURI. Yuri Kochiyama was a longtime Nisei Japanese community activist who lived in Harlem* during the 1960s. Impressed with Malcolm X's work on behalf of black justice, Kochiyama sought Malcolm out, finally meeting him personally in the fall of 1963 in the Brooklyn, New York, criminal courthouse. During the brief meeting, she told Malcolm that while she admired his forthright stand on numerous issues, she disagreed with his views opposing racial integration.* Malcolm invited her personally to meet and talk with him at length about the issue, but his travels precluded it, and it would be nearly a year before the two had an opportunity to come together. The two finally met at Kochiyama's apartment, where Malcolm had gone at Kochiyama's invitation to meet several of her friends in a Hiroshima-Nagasaki Peace Study Mission reception. Thereafter the association grew, influenced by Malcolm's frequent patronage of the Thomford Ice Cream Parlor near his Organization of Afro-American Unity (OAAU)* headquarters, where Kochiyama worked as a waitress. (Ice cream was one of Malcolm's favorite foods, which he ate frequently.) Malcolm visited Kochiyama's home often, especially during the period when he was establishing the OAAU. There he met with other OAAU supporters and networked with Kochiyama and her Japanese friends, many of whom had come to admire Malcolm and his uncompromising stand on human rights.* Malcolm reportedly impressed his Japanese admirers with his understanding of Japanese and Far East history, an affirmation of the multidimensional aspects of his international interests and knowledge. To Kochiyama, Malcolm's message was universal to all people suffering from oppression. What Malcolm said about blacks learning about themselves and their past before determining which direction the race should go in, she said, was no less significant for Asians.

Along with her young son, Kochiyama was in the audience of the Audubon Ballroom* to hear Malcolm speak on the fateful Sunday afternoon of February 21, 1965. Sitting near the scene of the disturbance that preceded the shooting, she was hardly prepared for what transpired but recognized almost immediately that the shots had felled Malcolm. Determined to be near her dying friend, she rushed to the stage where she cuddled his head in her lap before she moved to assist Malcolm's youngest child.

In the years after his death, Kochiyama remembered Malcolm as not only an associate but a close friend, one who thought well enough of her to send numerous postcards during his busy travel schedule in Africa in 1964. For many years, she honored that memory, along with other Malcolm friends and supporters, with an annual May 19 pilgrimage, Malcolm's birthday, to his New York gravesite.

SELECTED BIBLIOGRAPHY

Blackside/PBS, 1994; Gallen, ed., 1992; Sales, 1994; Strickland (Greene, ed.), 1994.

Robert L. Jenkins

KOREA. While still in prison,* Malcolm in 1950 wrote an acerbic letter to President Harry Truman regarding the entry of the United States into the Korean War. Paul Robeson,* a popular entertainer and political activist who was an avowed communist and hero of Malcolm, exhorted black Americans to resist the war effort, arguing that the fight for freedom for black Americans was here in the United States. In Malcolm's letter he stated that he was a communist as well and had tried to enlist in the Japanese military during World War II.* Malcolm was reprimanded by Elijah Muhammad,* who felt that Malcolm's letter may have led to a focus by the Federal Bureau of Investigation* on the Nation of Islam* mosque in San Diego, in which several members, including the lead minister, were charged in 1951 with violation of the Selective Service Act of 1948.

Malcolm made reference to Korea after the death of Emmett Till,* a fifteen-year-old youngster who had gone to Money, Mississippi, from Chicago* in the summer of 1955 to visit his grandparents. For allegedly whistling at a white woman in a country store, Till was brutally murdered and his body weighted and dumped in the Tallahatchie River in Mississippi* by the woman's white husband and another white man. Malcolm noted that the U.S. government wanted blacks to fight in foreign wars like Korea but did not want to provide them justice at home. Both of the white men tried in the Till case were found not guilty after a two-week trial. Malcolm pointed out in speeches that the U.S. government was often violent abroad in countries like Korea, but when it came to black Americans seeking their freedom at home in violent environments, the government wanted them to be nonviolent. It was a theme that Malcolm raised frequently.

SELECTED BIBLIOGRAPHY

Evanzz, 1992; Hacker, 1992; Malcolm X (Clark, ed.), 1992.

Mfanya Donald Tryman

KU KLUX KLAN (KKK). The Ku Klux Klan (KKK) was founded by six Confederate veterans in Pulaski, Tennessee, in December 1865. Originally a fraternal organization, it quickly became an instrument used to overthrow the hated Republican Reconstruction governments in the South.* It legitimated its existence through intimidation and violence in order to maintain "White Supremacy."

During the 1920s, the Klan reappeared, expanding into a national movement. After World War I, the Klan put a greater emphasis on violence, and its ideology shifted to include a broader-based racism, opposition to anything not "one hundred percent Americanism." Hence, this second Klan movement in the post–World War I era was anti-Catholic, anti-Semitic, and violently antiblack. It was particularly prominent in the Midwest, where it established a real presence in the political arena and sought to keep blacks subservient. Malcolm X's earliest memories of the Klan and Klan-like organizations occurred at a young age in Omaha, Nebraska,* and Milwaukee, Wisconsin. In these cities, Malcolm's family was frequently subjected to Klan outrages. During the 1960s the KKK strengthened, primarily in the American South as a vanguard organization opposed to the black civil rights* struggle. It escalated its activities with lynchings, bombings, and other acts of terrorism. Its violent acts were so rampant that it became a target for infiltration and disruption by the Federal Bureau of Investigation.*

As a national figure, Malcolm X was a constant critic of the Klan. He lashed out at the KKK's racism and violence and frequently vowed to fight fire with fire when it came to the organization. To Malcolm, it mattered little if it was the Klan that was directly responsible for some of the atrocities blacks confronted in the South; all white racism was synonymous to Ku Klux Klanism. Nevertheless, in 1961, at the direction of the Nation of Islam (NOI)* leader Elijah Muhammad,* Malcolm met with the Imperial Wizard of the Ku Klux Klan in Atlanta, Georgia. Since the Klan and the NOI held similar beliefs about racemixing and racial separation,* the discussion centered on ways and means that would facilitate these racial views and make physical separation more expedient. Malcolm, however, was embarrassed by the secret meeting and later sought to expose Muhammad for the debacle.

SELECTED BIBLIOGRAPHY

Bullard, 1988; B. Perry, 1991; Schmaltz, 1999.

Phyllis Gray-Ray

KUNTSLER, WILLIAM. William Kuntsler was a New York attorney who specialized in defending controversial public figures. During the 1960s, he was

Two heavily armed Ku Klux Klansmen prepare for a rally during the turbulence of Alabama's civil rights strife. Birmingham Public Library, Department of Archives and Manuscripts (Catalog Number BPH2).

known especially for defending radical protest groups including the Black Panther Party for Self-Defense.* In addition, he has been involved with civil rights organizations* such as the Southern Christian Leadership Conference* and the American Indian Movement (AIM).

Kuntsler first interviewed Malcolm on radio station WMCA in New York in 1960. Over several years they became fairly good friends, although Kuntsler notes that this was a period when Malcolm was referring to all whites as "devils." Nevertheless, Kuntsler had a great deal of admiration for Malcolm. He asserted that Malcolm was on the cutting edge of history and that he was engaged in an ongoing battle to win the minds of black Americans and free them from the legacy of slavery and the mental shackles that still bound them. Kuntsler maintains that the firebombing of Malcolm's house the same evening that Martin Luther King, Jr.,* and Malcolm had a conversation about building a loose coalition, and Malcolm's murder one week later, may have been related to that dialogue. Kuntsler maintains that while the Federal Bureau of Investigation* may not have been directly involved in Malcolm's ultimate demise, the agency contributed to the climate of violence that ended the life of the black nationalist leader.

It was Kuntsler who also handled the attempt by Talmadge Hayer,* a convicted assassin of Malcolm X, to have the Malcolm X case reopened by filing an affidavit with the New York Supreme Court. However, the motion failed, with a judge on the Supreme Court refusing to nullify the convictions of Norman 3X Butler* and Thomas 15X Johnson.* Hayer had maintained in his affidavit that Butler and Thomas had no role in the assassination of Malcolm X.* Once the legal process failed him, Kuntsler turned to a political strategy. He got in touch with the Congressional Black Caucus and Congressman Charles Rangel, a Democrat representing Harlem* where Malcolm mostly worked. But Rangel's efforts failed to have the Malcolm X case reopened as well. In 1981, Kuntsler was interviewed on *60 Minutes* by Mike Wallace* and received nationwide publicity for his legal argument in support of Butler and Johnson. Butler and Johnson won parole in the mid-1980s.

SELECTED BIBLIOGRAPHY
Carson (Gallen, ed.), 1991; Friedly, 1992; Gallen, ed., 1992; Wicker, 1975.

Mfanya Donald Tryman

KUPCINET, IRV. Irv Kupcinet worked as a journalist for the *Chicago Sun-Times* but acquired his real prominence as a local television personality in the "Windy City." His long-running weekly syndicated talk show *At Random* began in 1958 with an open-ended format that started at Saturday midnight and often ran for hours. In the early 1960s it was reformatted and renamed *Kup's Show*. In many ways the changes made it a forerunner to the popular format of the daily television discussion shows of the 1990s. Kupcinet included on his guest list not only well-known figures of American popular culture but also prominent political leaders and controversial figures such as the American Nazi Party* leader George Lincoln Rockwell.* Malcolm X, who was a frequent subject of Kupcinet's newspaper articles during the impending split from Elijah Muhammad,* was also one of the most popular guests on "Kup's" television show. Militant, articulate, and well known as a spokesman for the disillusioned black urban dweller, Malcolm was a natural in attracting a sizable viewing audience for the show. Indeed, Kupcinet acquired considerable mileage from the controversy that surrounded Malcolm, making him a subject of conversation even when Malcolm was not a guest on the show. Likewise, Malcolm increased the popularity for the New York–based David Susskind* when he made appearances on his *Open End* syndicated talk program.

Apparently, Kupcinet held Malcolm in great respect. Kupcinet refused to regard Malcolm as a simple hatemonger seeking to terrorize whites; rather, Malcolm was a genuine revolutionary committed to a real cause. As he always had a tendency to do, Malcolm was forthright in answering Kupcinet's questions. During one of his appearances, Malcolm told the columnist-television host that he no longer demonized all whites, but he refused to apologize for any of his past views. Kupcinet was not only willing to write about and interview Malcolm, but he also moderated a debate between the fiery Muslim* and Louis Lomax,* the journalist who first exposed Malcolm and the Black Muslims* to a national television audience in 1959. In the last year of his life, estranged from the Nation of Islam* sect, Malcolm made other appearances on "Kup's" Chicago* show, surely agitating Muslim* leader Elijah Muhammad and his anti-Malcolm camp. Occasionally, Malcolm was the lone interview for Kupcinet; at other times, he was part of a group of black leaders and spokespersons who debated the day's relevant racial issues and the finer points that propelled the period's black revolution.

SELECTED BIBLIOGRAPHY

Branch, 1998; L. Brown, 1977; Carson (Gallen, ed.), 1991; Evanzz, 1992; Goldman, 1979; Malcolm X (Clark, ed.), 1992.

Robert L. Jenkins

L

LANSING, MICHIGAN. Lansing, Michigan, was the home of Malcolm Little in his early formative years. The Little family moved there in July 1929 after a brief residency in Milwaukee, Wisconsin. Malcolm attended the Pleasant Grove Elementary School about two miles outside of Lansing.

Lansing had a very tight-knit black community. The black middle class consisted of those who worked at semiskilled jobs. Earl Little,* Malcolm's father, tried to fit in but was not altogether successful doing so. Most of the African Americans of Lansing lived on the west side; the Littles lived in a farmhouse near the city limits.

When it was discovered that the home the Littles lived in had a restrictive covenant clause prohibiting the sale of the property to blacks, they were ordered to vacate the premises. The home mysteriously went up in flames in November 1929. The Littles then moved closer to the city in what is now considered East Lansing, but they were stoned by white neighbors. They then moved south to the outskirts of Lansing on a six-acre plot of farmland in a mainly white section. Here Malcolm made friends with young whites and attended school.

In his autobiography, Malcolm displayed a bitterness toward the black people of Lansing, especially the middle-class blacks.* Many of these blacks were turned off by the Littles' advocacy of Garveyism. Malcolm's family hardly received community compassion and concern from Lansing's blacks after his father's tragic death. Some regarded the Littles as simply too independent and sought to let their independence and pride get them through their ordeal; others withheld economic assistance because they feared that a white response to their effort might prove violent. Of course, Malcolm held his most lasting contempt for Lansing because the white welfare system broke up his family after his mother was committed to a mental institution. A negative memory of Lansing notwithstanding, Malcolm recounted with some fondness his early life in Lansing, especially the part when he accompanied his father on road trips as he went around preaching Garveyism.

SELECTED BIBLIOGRAPHY
Collins with Bailey, 1998; Malcolm X with Haley, 1965; B. Perry, 1991.

Charles Pete Banner-Haley

LAVISCOUNT, REVEREND SAMUEL. During his teenage years in Boston, Massachusetts, Malcolm X attended St. Mark's Congregational Church in Roxbury.* Samuel Laviscount, a West Indian immigrant who had studied at Atlantic Union College and the School of Religion at Howard University,* served as the church's pastor. Laviscount was known to be a sincere man who struggled to improve the social and spiritual lives of African Americans in the Roxbury community. At St. Mark's church, for example, he often conducted public forums to discuss significant social and political issues facing African Americans. Malcolm not only attended these forums, but he also participated in the question-and-answer sessions. Yet despite his interest in the public forums and his apparent affection for Laviscount, Malcolm never became an active member of the church. After Malcolm left Boston, he did, however, seek to make contact with Laviscount. Shortly following his conversion to Islam,* Malcolm wrote Laviscount a long letter in which he dismissed Christian doctrine as mere fantasy. Malcolm's letter concluded that Elijah Muhammad* and the Nation of Islam* were the only true salvation for a black man. Whether or not Malcolm and Laviscount maintained a strong relationship once Malcolm obtained national stature is difficult to determine.

SELECTED BIBLIOGRAPHY
DeCaro, 1996, 1998.

Phillip A. Gibbs

LAWSON, JAMES. James Lawson was a New York public relations man who directed a small but active black nationalist organization known as the United African Nationalist Movement (UANM). A Garvey*-inspired supporter of African independence, Lawson traveled to a number of African countries during the 1950s. Over the course of his travels, he cultivated friendships with many African leaders and dignitaries, including the emperor of Ethiopia, Haile Selassie.

Although Lawson was a member of the Ethiopian Orthodox Church, he initially supported Elijah Muhammad's* Nation of Islam (NOI)* because of its emphasis on black separatism. Like Muhammad, Lawson believed that racial integration* would only hinder black Americans' efforts to gain freedom and independence. But Lawson's support for the NOI wavered in the early 1960s as he joined forces with Talib Dawud,* leader of a rival black Islamic group in

New York who opposed Muhammad's version of Islam* doctrine. Initially, because Malcolm was such a strong and positive voice in support of Muhammad, it is unlikely that he viewed Lawson's competition with the NOI favorably, though there is little to indicate any personal enmity between the two. Indeed, the two often joined other black nationalists in debates and in discussions in Harlem* street rallies and supported each other in various other ways in the early 1960s. The growing popularity of Malcolm X, the nation's most dynamic and angry spokesperson for blacks, however, posed a threat to Lawson's organization and to his leadership of Harlem's black community. Lawson's fears were well founded. By the mid-1960s, Lawson and the UANM had already faded into obscurity.

SELECTED BIBLIOGRAPHY

DeCaro, 1996; Essien-Udom, 1962; Hall, 1978; Lincoln, 1994; *New York Times*, January 25, 1960.

Phillip A. Gibbs

LEAGUE OF REVOLUTIONARY BLACK WORKERS. The League of Revolutionary Black Workers was one of several organizations that emerged after the death of Malcolm X. In one sense, this entity was a reflection of his thinking before he was assassinated. Building on Malcolm's philosophy of black nationalism,* the League represented a codification of street people and industrial workers. It was the former that Malcolm had predicted would revolt in large cities, which actually began to happen in the summer of 1963 and continuously every summer through 1968.

In 1968, the League actually took on the form of an organization. Ideologically, the League felt that some of the very street people in the early and mid-1960s that represented revolutionary potential were now factory workers and laborers on assembly lines in car plants such as Detroit.* Hence, the core of the League was found in the automobile industry, committed to a world revolution* and an unending struggle against imperialism, racism, and capitalism.*

The League had a number of things in common with Malcolm. Malcolm, like the League, originated in the Detroit area, and early on as a minister in the Nation of Islam (NOI),* Malcolm had recruited members from the assembly lines for the NOI, when he worked there in the early 1950s in a truck factory. Some of Malcolm's most important speeches, such as "Message to the Grass Roots," were delivered in Detroit where the League was situated. And Malcolm had a working-class background like almost all League workers.

SELECTED BIBLIOGRAPHY

Boggs, 1970; Breitman, 1967; Malcolm X (Breitman, ed.), 1965; Sales, 1994.

Mfanya Donald Tryman

LEAKS, SYLVESTER. A native of Macon, Georgia, Sylvester Leaks became a part of a small cadre of New York's black intelligentsia that associated with

Malcolm X during the 1960s. This Harlem* inner circle of famed literary and cultural personalities included James Baldwin,* John O. Killens,* John Henrik Clarke,* and Ossie Davis,* all of whom were also influenced by Malcolm. During the period, Leaks worked with New York youths in creative writing workshops and served as the president of the influential Harlem Writer's Guild. His relationship with Malcolm began during the late 1950s while Malcolm was a member of the Nation of Islam (NOI).* Apparently, though uncharacteristic of Malcolm at the time because of his mistrust of most educated blacks, Malcolm thought enough of Leaks to seek his assistance in starting and running the NOI's newspaper, *Muhammad Speaks*.* Perhaps it was the two men's mutual interest in African and African American history and culture that brought them together; Leaks lectured extensively on the subject. Malcolm tabbed Leaks, who was beginning to establish himself as a reputable novelist and author of short stories, to edit the New York edition of the Muslim* newspaper. Collectively, Malcolm and Leaks shaped the paper into one of the country's highest circulated newspapers and the financial centerpiece of NOI business enterprises.

SELECTED BIBLIOGRAPHY

Bush, 1999; Cruse, 1967; Hughes, 1967; Sales, 1994.

Robert L. Jenkins

LEAVELL, BALM. Balm Leavell was the publisher of *The New Crusader*, a black newspaper in Chicago* that reported primarily on black events, issues, and personalities. Leavell was one of the first people outside of federal government service to obtain information about how high-level officials in the Nation of Islam (NOI)* were actually functioning as Federal Bureau of Investigation (FBI)* informants or agents. This did not include Malcolm X. In fact, a number of Black Muslims* who had made the conversion to Islam* confessed to Malcolm that they were policemen who had the assignment of infiltrating the black organization. Leavell, utilizing his newspaper, was one of the few black journalists or media professionals to criticize the NOI in the late 1950s. In fact, he questioned the legitimacy of Elijah Muhammad* as the Messenger of Islam, as Malcolm would later do, and wrote a series of articles in the paper "exposing" Muhammad. It was clear to anyone who read the newspaper that it was an anti–Black Muslim publication at one time. On racial matters, however, the paper had views parallel to those of Muhammad and Malcolm and exhorted blacks to rise up and destroy the notion of white supremacy. This was an underlying theme in many of Malcolm's speeches and sermons.

Leavell soon abandoned his negative views of the NOI, and the paper began to run a column in its publication on a regular basis that Elijah Muhammad wrote. For his altruistic outreach toward Elijah Muhammad, Leavell was investigated by the FBI. Subsequently, the FBI began to make routine visits to the publisher's office, questioning him about his relationship with Elijah Muhammad. Like Leavell, Malcolm would be visited by the FBI and interrogated. In the case of Malcolm, however, it was with regard to the activities of the NOI.

SELECTED BIBLIOGRAPHY

Evanzz, 1992; Malcolm X (Breitman, ed.), 1965; *New Crusader* (Chicago), August 1, 15, 22, 29, 1959.

Mfanya Donald Tryman

LEE, SPIKE. Shelton Jackson (Spike) Lee is a prolific and important independent African American filmmaker. The eldest of five children, he is the son of William James Edwards Lee III and the late Jacquelyn Shelton Lee. His paternal grandfather and father were graduates of Morehouse College; and his maternal grandmother and mother were graduates of Spelman College. Lee graduated from Morehouse in 1979 and from New York University with a Masters of Fine Arts degree in the early 1980s. His first film was *The Messenger* (1984). He has made ten films and has also directed music videos and products and political commercials.

He began his seventh film, *Malcolm X,** in New York City in September 1991. The controversy surrounding Lee's making of the bio-picture was intense. In the summer of 1991 at a Harlem* rally, poet Amiri Baraka* publicly admonished Lee not to cheapen Malcolm's life. Producer Marvin Worth, who had secured the film rights to Malcolm's life in 1968, assigned the project to Norman Jewison, a white director. Worth later relented under Lee's persistence, however, that a black director was needed. Lee charged the studio with racism and fought over money as well as the length of the film. He reminded the studio that David Fincher had a budget of $50 million for *Alien* and that Oliver Stone's *JFK* had a running time of three hours and eight minutes. Lee articulated his views about *Malcolm X*, the movie, and how the former Nation of Islam (NOI)* leader has impacted his life in his 1992 book *By Any Means Necessary: The Trials and Tribulations of the Making of Malcolm X.*

Lee's *Malcolm X* opened on November 18, 1992. Fan anticipation for Lee's film was high nationwide. Media attention was widespread and helped to make the commercialization of Malcolm's name through the sale of clothing, hats, and other products a tremendous economic success. Based on the book, *The Autobiography of Malcolm X,** the movie opened to large audiences across the nation, attracting both black and white moviegoers. Though not a "blockbuster" in the traditional Hollywood meaning of the term, the movie made a considerable profit and helped to cement Lee's position as a serious and talented moviemaker.

SELECTED BIBLIOGRAPHY

Corliss, 1992; Cloyd, ed., 1994–1995; Hawkins, 1992; Lee with Wiley, 1992; *New York Times*, November 18, 1992; Wiley, 1992.

Fon Louise Gordon

LEWIS, CLAUDE. As a leader among the Black Muslims,* journalists frequently looked to Malcolm X to voice the goals and the ideals of the group. Claude Lewis, an African American syndicated columnist for the *Philadelphia Inquirer*, knew Malcolm well; the two men occasionally met over coffee in local restaurants that Malcolm frequented. Lewis had several interviews with him, in which he discussed his favorite subject, white liberal hypocrisy. However, Lewis's most notable interview with Malcolm occurred in late December 1964 when he was a reporter for the *New York Post*. (Lewis had also interviewed Malcolm as a reporter for the *New York Herald Tribune*.) Giving interviews was Malcolm's way of getting his thoughts on record, but the opportunity also gave credibility to his leadership.

In the December 1964 interview, Malcolm X reflected on many concerns, including his image, his organization, and his public stance. The outspoken leader told Lewis that having a sense of humor was an important means of keeping one's sanity. He recounted that America was a hypocritically paradoxical society and that if one did not laugh, it would be easy to "crack up." In retrospect, it seemed to Lewis as if Malcolm sensed, like Martin Luther King, Jr.,* would sense in 1968, that he might die. Malcolm told Lewis that few people spoke out as he did about so many controversial things and lived to get old. Malcolm also spoke of blacks achieving their due rights "by any means necessary" and talked of his love and respect for his people on the streets when they seemed to be progressing. Lewis observed, however, that instead of Malcolm's usual interplay of fire and wit during an interview, he seemed tired and worn down. Clearly, the problems that Malcolm were encountering because of his break with Elijah Muhammad* were taking their toll. Within two months, Malcolm's prophetic vision about dying came true.

Lewis published his interview with Malcolm in a special report in the *National Leader* on June 2, 1983. He contemplated that the Black Muslim leader altered his views from those he held when he was part of Elijah Muhammad's Nation of Islam.* Yet Malcolm's change was rarely reflected in the daily press.

SELECTED BIBLIOGRAPHY

Cone, 1991; Gallen, ed., 1992; Goldman, 1979; Myers, 1993; B. Perry, 1991.

Yoshawnda Trotter

LEWIS, JOHN. Born to a sharecropping family in Troy, Alabama, John Lewis was raised on a farm and after graduating from high school attended Nashville's American Baptist Theological Seminary, where he received a bachelor's degree in 1961. In 1967 he also earned a bachelor's degree from Fisk University, where he studied religion and philosophy.

During Lewis's college years, he was deeply involved in the civil rights movement.* He organized and led sit-ins and freedom ride demonstrations. He was also a founding member and eventual chairman of the Student Non-Violent Coordinating Committee (SNCC),* one of the movement's elite civil rights or-

John Lewis was one of a number of SNCC
leaders whom Malcolm met and came to admire. Library of Congress.

ganizations.* John Lewis represented SNCC at the March on Washington,*
where he delivered a modified speech of the original that seemed influenced by
the angry tones of Malcolm X. Indeed, Malcolm had been so impressed with
the speech that Lewis was prevented from delivering that Malcolm had one of
his female protégées, Almina (Sharon 10X) Rahman,* deliver it before a large
street rally in Harlem,* New York, several days later.

Lewis first encountered Malcolm in the lobby of his Washington hotel and
was shocked to see the Muslim* leader there. Lewis claimed that Malcolm's
presence was a little unsettling because of the great fear that March leaders like
Roy Willkins* and A. Philip Randolph* had about the potential for violence
during the affair. Lewis met Malcolm personally, and they talked briefly. In
Nairobi, Kenya, in 1964, when Malcolm was on his second Africa tour, Lewis
was on the continent for a SNCC fact-finding mission. In a report to SNCC,
Lewis told of the positive efforts that Malcolm was having in Africa.

Lewis was impressed by Malcolm, especially with Malcolm's ability to articulate the frustrations of black America. He was encouraged over Malcolm's

evolving views about whites and that Malcolm was moving toward a worldview of the black struggle in America and Africa. Malcolm no longer seemed "angry" and brooding as Lewis had typically regarded him. Lewis respected Malcolm, and Malcolm liked Lewis and the work that he and SNCC were doing. But Lewis never considered Malcolm a civil rights* leader and claimed that he could never accept Malcolm's ideas about black freedom using whatever methods were necessary to achieve gains. Hence, Lewis adhered to the nonviolence philosophy* of Martin Luther King, Jr.,* even as SNCC was becoming more militant and was trying to find ways to incorporate Malcolm's teachings in the organization.

Lewis left SNCC when the more militant Stokely Carmichael* assumed its leadership, but he continued to be active in civil rights activities. In 1986 he ran for Georgia's Fifth Congressional seat, facing his former SNCC colleague Julian Bond in the primary. In 1987, a victorious Lewis took his seat in the U.S. Congress.

SELECTED BIBLIOGRAPHY

Branch, 1988; J. Lewis with D'Orso, 1998; Pearson, 1994; Sales, 1994; Strickland (Greene, ed.), 1994; J. Williams, 1987.

Charles Pete Banner-Haley

LIBERATOR. The *Liberator* was one of several black informational magazines that gained considerable notoriety during the black civil rights* revolution of the 1960s. Published in New York City in 1961, the magazine was established in the wake of former Congo* leader Patrice Lumumba's* death in Zaire. (Lumumba was a popular symbol of the African freedom struggle for African American nationalists.) The journal was founded by the Liberation Committee for Africa, a group of black intellectuals whose interest ran the gamut of black liberation issues, including questions relative to Pan-Africanism,* nationalism, and colonialism. Actor, playwright, and director Ossie Davis,* who served on the *Liberator*'s advisory board, proclaimed the magazine as America's "most important Black nationalist" journal. Noted novelist James Baldwin* also served on the advisory board before a rift over the journal's anti-Semitic bent eventually influenced both his and Davis's resignation. With a distribution found primarily in Harlem* and in several other large black communities, the journal's circulation peaked in Malcolm X's lifetime at approximately 1,200 copies monthly, but before its demise in 1970, it would eventually achieve a circulation of 20,000 copies. Its only editor in chief was founder Daniel H. Watts,* an architect by profession and an occasional college campus speaker, regarded by a congressional investigative committee as one of the New Left's "radical rhetoricians."

The journal published articles by a number of black literary luminaries, many of whom would become familiar names associated with freedom struggle issues throughout the black world. These included such people as LeRoi Jones (Amiri Baraka),* Nathan Hare, Eldridge Cleaver,* Harold Cruse, Addison Gayle, Jr., and Toni Cade. In many ways, the journal was a vanguard in the movement to involve the arts as political weapons in the black freedom struggles of the era. Malcolm X, one of the nation's premier militants, would also be published in the journal. Before his death he wrote occasional editorials for the *Liberator*, though he had wanted to publish a regular monthly column for the journal. More frequently, his voice and philosophy as Black America's most visible revolutionary found a prominent place in the editorials and articles that others published in the journal. Upon his murder, editor Watts, who knew Malcolm well, wrote passionately about Malcolm, lamenting, as so many other supporters did, his death and assessing the influence that Malcolm had on the freedom struggles of the period.

SELECTED BIBLIOGRAPHY

Cruse, 1967; Daniels, ed., 1982; Goldman, 1979; Leeming, 1994; Wolseley, 1990.

Robert L. Jenkins

LINCOLN, C.(HARLES) ERIC. C. Eric Lincoln was a prominent scholar and theologian of African American religion at Duke University. Lincoln was the author of the seminal text on the Black Muslims,* *The Black Muslims in America** (1961, revised in 1971 and reprinted in 1991). Lincoln was also a novelist, minister, and social critic of African American affairs. The strength of his work, however, lies in his studies of African American religious faith in all its varieties.

Lincoln was born in Athens, Alabama. He was educated at LeMoyne College in Tennessee and Fisk University. Ordained as a Methodist minister, Lincoln held the pastorate of several churches in the South.* In 1956, he completed his Bachelor of Divinity degree at the University of Chicago and a Ph.D. from Boston University in 1960.

Professor Lincoln was very active in the civil rights movement,* especially as a member of the National Association for the Advancement of Colored People (NAACP).* In 1961, *The Black Muslims in America* was published in the midst of national attention on the Nation of Islam's (NOI)* major spokesperson Malcolm X. The book grew out of Lincoln's doctoral dissertation. Lincoln's serious academic yet accessible study of the NOI afforded readers with the most in-depth coverage of that movement to date. According to journalist Peter Goldman,* a major Malcolm X biographer, it was Lincoln who coined the term "Black Muslim." Within the work was a groundbreaking interview with Elijah Muhammad.*

Lincoln first met Malcolm when Malcolm wandered into the offices of the Black *Atlanta Daily World* where Lincoln was employed. It was the beginning of a long and "mutually rewarding friendship." Lincoln would later invite Malcolm to speak at Boston University, his first public appearance, and he arranged for Malcolm to make speaking appearances at other places doing their relationship. Along with Louis Lomax,* who was writing a book on the NOI about the same time that Lincoln was preparing his manuscript, Lincoln helped Malcolm

establish the organization's newspaper, *Muhammad Speaks*.* One of the few
intellectuals that Malcolm respected, Lincoln remained close to Malcolm until
his death in 1965. In the years following Malcolm's death he continued his
analysis of Malcolm's life, helping Americans to understand his meaning and
legacy as a revolutionary spirit. Professor Lincoln also remained close friends
with other prominent members of the NOI, including Minister Louis Farrakhan.*
With regard to Malcolm X, Professor Lincoln's enduring contribution is *The
Black Muslims in America*, wherein he discusses NOI's theology as Malcolm
dispensed it to those African Americans receptive to its teachings. Lincoln died
in 2000 after an extended illness.

SELECTED BIBLIOGRAPHY

Dyson, 1994; Gates, 1996; Goldman, 1979; Lincoln (Clarke, ed.), 1990; M. Williams,
ed., 1992.

Charles Pete Banner-Haley

LINDY HOP. During the 1920s several dances were introduced in the big
ballrooms of Harlem,* New York. One of the dances made popular at the Savoy
Ballroom* was the Lindy Hop. The Lindy Hop involved improvisation and
acrobatics. Couples performed floor steps and "air steps" to the delight and
entertainment of spectators. As a young man, during his "hipster" days Malcolm
danced the Lindy in full costume with wide-brim hat, long chains, and zoot
suits.* In his autobiography, Malcolm X recalls Lindying to Count Basie's*
band at the Roseland Ballroom* in Boston in 1941. Many of the big band
leaders, including Basie, knew him personally because of his dancing ability.
Malcolm describes the technique, the competitiveness, and the excitement that
surrounded this particular dance craze of the 1940s. According to Malcolm, a
girl named Laura was his favorite Lindy-dancing partner because she was light
on her feet and easy to guide on the dance floor. The Lindy Hop was an important link in black dance, but for Malcolm dancing the Lindy was simply an
enjoyable way to express himself and acquire notoriety in Boston's and New
York's hipster culture nightlife.

SELECTED BIBLIOGRAPHY

Emery, 1988; Hazzard-Gordon, 1990; Malcolm X with Haley, 1965.

Gerald L. Smith

LITTLE, HILDA. Three years older than Malcolm, Hilda was the oldest of
Malcolm X's two sisters born to the union of Earl* and Louise* Little. Only
nine years old at the time of her father's murder, Hilda, like Malcolm, was
traumatized by his death. Long before her mother was institutionalized in a
mental facility, Hilda began to play a mature role helping to sustain the Little
household by watching the children and doing most of the cooking and other
chores. Understandably, it was not an easy situation for her having to assume

so much responsibility at an early age, and Malcolm and the younger siblings made it worse because they were often disobedient and difficult to manage. After her mother's departure, she, along with Wilfred Little,* their eldest brother, worked harder but unsuccessfully to keep the family together. By the time that Malcolm left his Michigan foster home to live with his half sister Ella Collins* in Boston in 1940, Hilda was nearly grown and hence was able to care for herself. She finished high school in 1941 and several years later followed her brothers into the Nation of Islam (NOI).* Committed to the NOI early on, she worked in the women's training classes and assisted her brothers in recruiting new members into the organization, including Malcolm with whom she corresponded and had a long visit when he was imprisoned. In fact, it was Hilda who did the most to familiarize Malcolm with the NOI's historical and religious doctrine, especially their views about Yacub,* "the big-head mad scientist" who created the so-called white devil* race and, the divinity of founder W. D. Fard,* regarded by the sect as Allah* in human form.

As he did about his other siblings, an older Malcolm spoke affectionately about Hilda, expressing considerable appreciation for the work that she did in their parentless home and in helping to facilitate his conversion to Islam.* During Malcolm's estrangement from the NOI, Wilfred abandoned Malcolm in support of Elijah Muhammad.* The record is not readily clear, however, whether Hilda also took an uncompromising position in support of the NOI leader.

SELECTED BIBLIOGRAPHY

Collins with Bailey, 1998; DeCaro, 1996; Malcolm X with Haley, 1965; B. Perry, 1991; Wolfenstein, 1993.

Robert L. Jenkins

LITTLE, J. EARL, JR. Earl Little, Jr., was the half brother of Malcolm, the eldest of Earl Little's* ten children, and one of three children by his first wife. An entertainer who sang in Boston nightclubs in the 1940s, Little went by the stage name of Jimmy Carlton. Earl was born in Reynolds, Georgia, and was part of the migration northward by blacks in the 1920s and 1930s with his family settling in Boston. While still in his early teens, Earl worked in his mother's store in Boston. Because of his desire to be an entertainer, as he got older he typically worked there during the day and sang in nightclubs at night.

Like Malcolm, as a youngster growing up he stayed in trouble with the law and spent time in reform school as well as prison* for burglary and related crimes. He often provided Malcolm with front row seats at his performances, which Malcolm cherished. Although Malcolm's senior by eight years, they were very close to each other. Like Malcolm, he was also tall, standing six feet and two and a half inches. Earl Little died very young in 1941 of tuberculosis. Malcolm took his death very hard.

SELECTED BIBLIOGRAPHY

Collins with Bailey, 1998; B. Perry, 1991.

Mfanya Donald Tryman

LITTLE, J. EARL, SR. J. Earl Little was born in 1890 in Reynolds, Georgia, the son of a farmer. After a youthful marriage that resulted in three children, he left his wife and family for Montreal, Canada. Eventually his wanderlust carried him to Philadelphia and to several cities in the Midwest, including Omaha, Nebraska,* Milwaukee, and Lansing, Michigan.* Nearly illiterate, he apparently provided for what became a large family with his second wife, Louise Little,* by working odd jobs. Although Malcolm claimed his father was a self-ordained Christian minister who frequently guest-preached in local churches, Little himself made no claims to be a minister. Little was also notable in the communities where he lived as an enthusiastic organizer for the popular urban black nationalist Marcus Garvey.* Apparently, he used the pulpits of the churches where he spoke to spread the nationalist ideas of Garvey. As a follower of Garvey, Little imbued his children, including Malcolm, with the tenets of black nationalism.*

Although Earl died when Malcolm was only six years old, he significantly influenced Malcolm's political education. Earl and his family moved to Omaha, Nebraska, around 1920, where his United Negro Improvement Association (UNIA)* activities led to a Ku Klux Klan* attack on his house. In Omaha, Earl served as branch president of the UNIA. Earl continued his Garveyite activities in Milwaukee and Lansing, where Malcolm remembered the most about his father's involvement with the organization.

Earl Little was killed by a streetcar in Lansing, but Malcolm always believed that his father had been murdered for his nationalist beliefs. Like Mississippi* civil rights* leader Medgar Evers* and Congolese leader Patrice Lumumba,* Malcolm once said in a speech that racism had also caused the death of his father. As an adult, Malcolm seldom talked about his father, though he recalled the severe beatings his father gave to his brothers and sisters. Malcolm believed that he escaped these harsh punishments because his father was color-struck, favoring Malcolm over his darker siblings. Malcolm saw this favoritism as a weakness in his father, but he still admired his toughness and manhood in raising and protecting his family.

SELECTED BIBLIOGRAPHY

DeCaro, 1996; Malcolm X with Haley, 1965; B. Perry, 1991; Vincent, 1989; Wolfenstein, 1993.

David T. Gleeson

LITTLE, LOUISE NORTON (Louisa Little). Louise Norton Little, the mother of Malcolm X, was born on the Caribbean Island of Grenada. Seeking opportunity in North America, Louise immigrated to Canada in 1917. Louise soon realized, however, that North Americans drew an absolute line between black and white. Prohibited from enjoying the same rights and opportunities as white citizens, Louise came to embrace the philosophy of Marcus Garvey,* the Jamaican-born black nationalist who headed the Universal Negro Improvement Association (UNIA).* Louise was an active member of the UNIA, serving at times as a reporter for the organization's publications. It was at a UNIA convention in Montreal that Louise met and later married Earl Little, Sr.* Soon after their marriage, Louise and Earl moved to the midwestern United States in search of a suitable home. White residents, however, did not welcome Earl and Louise's outspoken views on black equality, and the couple was often forced to flee.

Although the Littles had limited funds and were often on the road, Louise sought to provide a stable home for her growing family. But Earl was given to violent outbursts and frequently beat Louise. Despite Earl's violent rages, Louise never hesitated to whip her children. Malcolm claimed at times that he received more than his share of his mother's whippings because of his light skin. According to one biographer, Malcolm's claim may contain some element of truth. Louise, a light-skinned woman who often passed for white, was the out-of-wedlock daughter of a Scotsman and a Black West Indian. Given the circumstances of her own birth, it is quite possible that Louise saw Malcolm as a constant reminder of her own illegitimacy. Whatever the case, Malcolm did not, by most accounts, have a close and loving relationship with Louise. Nevertheless, it is clear that she gave him a strong appreciation of both learning and spirituality.

Unlike Earl, who had received a rudimentary education in his native Georgia, Louise had been educated in the Anglican schools of Grenada. There she had developed a broad vocabulary and learned to speak English with a slight British accent. An inquisitive and deeply spiritual woman, Louise encouraged Malcolm and his brothers and sisters to avoid strict religious orthodoxy and cultivate a personal relationship with God. As a result, Louise sought to expose her family to a variety of Christian denominations and faiths, including the Baptists, Methodists, Pentecostals, and the Seventh Day Adventists. Although Malcolm admired his mother's open-minded approach to spirituality, he would later abandon her caution against religious orthodoxy when he converted to Islam.*

Following Earl's death in 1931 in East Lansing, Michigan, Louise found less and less time for the spiritual and educational needs of her children. The pressures of providing for a family of seven required Louise to work at a variety of domestic jobs. But sewing and cleaning did not pay enough to sustain the family, and Louise was forced to accept welfare. By now she had also given birth to an illegitimate son and was exhibiting the signs of a mental disorder. Convinced that Louise was incapable of taking care of the children, the state welfare agency sent Malcolm and his brothers and sisters to live in foster homes. Malcolm later maintained in his autobiography that meddling welfare workers had broken up his family and contributed to the mental breakdown of his mother. After the removal of Malcolm and his brothers and sisters, the state placed Louise in the Kalamazoo asylum. Although Malcolm would go to Boston to live with his older half sister Ella Collins,* he did visit his mother whenever possible. In 1963 Malcolm and his brother Wilfred moved Louise to their sister's home in Lansing, Michigan,* where she lived until her death in 1991.

SELECTED BIBLIOGRAPHY

Carew, 1994; DeCaro, 1998; Malcolm X with Haley, 1965; B. Perry, 1991.

Phillip A. Gibbs

LITTLE, PHILBERT (Philbert X; Abdul Aziz Omar). Malcolm's older brother Philbert was closest to him in age. From an early age they developed a sibling rivalry. As a child, Malcolm had envied Philbert's boxing prowess, and they competed constantly. In 1937, after their father's death and the committal of their mother to the state mental institution, the social services agency in Lansing, Michigan,* broke the boys up; when Malcolm subsequently moved to Boston, they grew apart. While Malcolm lived his life as "Detroit Red" in the streets of Boston and New York, Philbert joined the Nation of Islam (NOI)* and became Philbert X. Philbert wrote to Malcolm when Malcolm went to prison,* but the future Muslim* was not ready to convert. When Malcolm finally joined his brother in the NOI, he often worked closely with Philbert, the leader of Elijah Muhammad's* followers in East Lansing, Michigan. Despite the renewed friendship, Philbert sided with Elijah Muhammad when Malcolm broke with the NOI. He gave a news conference to denounce his younger brother. In an interview long after Malcolm's death, Philbert, who had changed his name to Abdul Aziz Omar, stated that his personal attack on Malcolm was written by the NOI, and he read this script to help reinforce the NOI and not to destroy his brother.

SELECTED BIBLIOGRAPHY

Malcolm X with Haley, 1965; Strickland (Greene, ed.), 1994; Wolfenstein, 1993.

David T. Gleeson

LITTLE, REGINALD. Reginald was the fifth born of the eight children of the union between Earl* and Louisa Little.* He was the immediate younger brother of Malcolm, born in 1927 in Milwaukee, Wisconsin, just prior to the family's move to Lansing, Michigan.* As youngsters, Reginald and Malcolm were reasonably close. Reginald held Malcolm in extreme admiration, that is, until older brother Philbert* began competing and enjoying some success in Golden Gloves boxing competition. Malcolm, in an effort to recoup Reginald's admiration, briefly entered boxing. The experience was disastrous and humiliating for Malcolm. As a result, Malcolm actually lost more esteem in Reginald's eyes.

Reginald would eventually join the merchant marines, from which he later resigned at the urging of Malcolm to become a hustler. Although Malcolm apparently thought the two were once again close, this was not the case, according to Reginald, who felt his older brother was too resentful of personal questions.

While Malcolm was in prison* and making the conversion to the Nation of Islam (NOI),* Reginald, already a Muslim,* was isolated by Elijah Muhammad* for an extramarital affair. Malcolm appealed to Muhammad on Reginald's behalf, but to no avail. Reginald became itinerant after his isolation, even attempting to start a rival Islamic movement, which never showed any promise. Ultimately, he would spend several stints in mental institutions but generally languished between the worlds of reality and make-believe. Malcolm felt partly responsible for Reginald's illness, although he knew it was probably caused by the family's rejection of him as ordered by Muhammad. His lament notwithstanding, Malcolm's death ended all possibility that he and Reginald would ever have the opportunity to rebuild their brotherly relations.

SELECTED BIBLIOGRAPHY

Breitman, 1967; Goldman, 1973; Malcolm X with Haley, 1965; Norden, 1967; B. Perry, 1991.

Dernoral Davis

LITTLE, ROBERT. Robert Little was Malcolm X's half brother, the youngest child born to his mother Louisa Little* and a male suitor seven years after the death of her husband, J. Earl Little.* Malcolm was thirteen years older than Robert, and because he was away from East Lansing, Michigan,* living in Boston with his half sister Ella Collins* when Robert was growing up, the two hardly spent much time with each other during their childhood. Indeed, Robert was a baby when the family was broken up after their mother's committal to a mental facility; Robert along with older sister Yvonne Little* were placed with a West Indian foster family.

Apparently, Robert had little opportunity to visit Malcolm during his incarceration. Hence, it was after Malcolm's release from prison* and brief return to Detroit, Michigan* in the early 1950s that he and Robert renewed their family ties. Robert remembered his later relationship with Malcolm with great affection, recalling one of the most memorable experiences of his life, when Malcolm took him and a group of school-aged youth to a natural history museum and explained authoritatively aspects of African history. It was, he said, "probably the most informative day of my life."

Apparently there were major periods when Malcolm and Robert did not see each other, though Robert was aware of the impact that Malcolm was making as a Muslim* leader. The two had a chance for a much sought after reunion in January 1963 when Malcolm spoke at Michigan State University, where Robert was doing post-graduate work in psychology. Unlike his other male siblings, Robert did not become a member of the Nation of Islam,* devoting much of his life to work in social work. After a long career working with the Michigan

Department of Social Services, he died on November 23, 1999, of complications from lymphoma.

SELECTED BIBLIOGRAPHY

Collins with Bailey, 1998; DeCaro, 1996; *Detroit News*, November 28, 1999; Evanzz, 1992; Lee with Wiley, 1992; Malcolm X with Haley, 1965; Richardson and Turner (T. Perry, ed.), 1996.

Robert L. Jenkins

LITTLE, WESLEY. Born in 1928, three years after Malcolm, Wesley Little was Malcolm X's youngest full brother. While Malcolm indicated that he maintained a close relationship with his siblings during his childhood, it appears that he had a stronger relationship with both Philbert* and Reginald,* the former born two years before him, the latter nearly two years before that. Though Wesley is seldom mentioned in Malcolm's autobiography, apparently the two grew closer, especially after Malcolm's imprisonment and conversion to Islam.* At some point between 1947 and 1950, Wesley, along with his brothers and older sister, joined the Nation of Islam (NOI),* and with them he visited Malcolm regularly in prison* and helped to convert him to Islam. After Malcolm was released from prison, he lived briefly in Boston, eventually returned to the city from Detroit* to establish a Black Muslim* temple, and thereafter traveled there frequently on behalf of the NOI. These were times when Malcolm renewed stronger ties with family members and friends. During some of this period, Wesley, who usually resided in Michigan, spent considerable time in Boston as well. According to Malcolm's nephew Rodnell Collins,* Wesley and Malcolm once dated the same woman. The woman was someone, he said, to whom Malcolm was formerly engaged shortly after his release on parole. The relationship did not work out well for Wesley either, but evidently it caused no strain between the brothers. Similarly, unlike the hostility against Malcolm that his other brothers displayed in the conflict with Elijah Muhammad* and the NOI, apparently no estrangement between Wesley and Malcolm existed. Still, the true nature of their relationship during these difficult times is not completely clear. Like his other siblings, Wesley, perhaps also concerned about own his personal safety, did not attend Malcolm's funeral.*

SELECTED BIBLIOGRAPHY

Collins with Bailey, 1998; Malcolm X with Haley, 1965; B. Perry, 1991.

Robert L. Jenkins

LITTLE, WILFRED. Wilfred was the oldest of the eight offspring of Earl* and Louisa Little* and the eldest brother of Malcolm. Following the death of their father and the institutionalization of their mother, Wilfred endeavored to keep his siblings together despite the absence of both parents. The children were eventually split up, in spite of Wilfred's attempts to avert precisely that.

Wilfred was the first of the Little children to join the Nation of Islam (NOI).*

In fact, Wilfred was partly responsible for the conversion of Malcolm, whom he visited and wrote to while in prison.* Wilfred was generally regarded as the titular head of the family and highly respected by most, if not all, of his siblings, including Malcolm. When their half sister Ella Collins* fell ill, it was Malcolm who suggested that her son be allowed to live with Wilfred. Wilfred eventually became minister of Temple Number One in Detroit,* a key mosque of the NOI, and for a while Malcolm was an assistant minister there, though before Wilfred was in charge. Philbert,* another brother, was minister of the temples in Lansing,* Grand Rapids, Flint, and Saginaw, Michigan.

In 1963, when a controversy emerged over rumors that Malcolm planned to take control of the NOI following Elijah Muhammad's* death, the three brothers talked of the need to coalesce if either was threatened. However, as Malcolm's difficulties with the NOI began mounting toward the end of 1963 and afterward, there is little to suggest that Wilfred rushed to his aid. Wilfred was more reserved and nonverbal. He apparently admired Malcolm's drive, ambition, and resulting public persona, although he felt his brother's manipulation of the media did not always serve him well. Whether Wilfred was supportive of Malcolm in his break with the NOI is less clear, though he certainly made no public utterances of denunciation. Upon Malcolm's death, he stated the obvious, that his brother was dead, and along with all the other siblings, he refused to attend the funeral. The lone exception was the half sister Ella Collins.

SELECTED BIBLIOGRAPHY

Goldman, 1973; Lincoln, 1973; Malcolm X with Haley, 1965; B. Perry, 1991.

Dernoral Davis

LOMAX, LOUIS. Louis Lomax was a black writer and television news reporter during the peak years of the modern civil rights movement.* He was a news analyst for KITV in Los Angeles and a news writer for the CBS Mike Wallace* television show.

In 1959, Lomax was in Harlem* researching a documentary on black nationalism.* After learning about Malcolm X and the Nation of Islam (NOI),* Lomax aired a weeklong report on the Mike Wallace Show entitled "The Hate That Hate Produced."* The show sparked the beginning of a strong relationship between the two men. Malcolm regarded Lomax as a sincere man, and he respected both the man and his journalistic ability immensely. He was one of only a few men associated with the media that Malcolm X trusted. Lomax's feelings toward Malcolm were mutual. Later, Lomax assisted Malcolm's effort in founding the NOI's newspaper, *Muhammad Speaks.** Malcolm often spoke candidly with Lomax about the Muslims* and his relationship with Elijah Muhammad.* In 1963 Lomax published a book entitled *When the Word Is Given,** which included five of Malcolm's speeches and one from Elijah Muhammad. Malcolm's picture appeared on the front cover with Elijah Muhammad's on the back, an act that supposedly angered Muhammad. In 1968 Lomax published a more biographical, though hardly critical, account of Malcolm's life in *To Kill a Black Man*. Like his friend, Lomax died a tragic death when the brakes failed on his car in July of 1970.

SELECTED BIBLIOGRAPHY

Lomax, 1963, 1968; Page, comp., 1977; B. Perry, 1991; Wolfenstein, 1993.

Gerald L. Smith

"LONG HOT SUMMERS." *See* Theme Essay "Malcolm X and the 'Long Hot Summers.' "

LOS ANGELES HERALD-DISPATCH. The *New York Amsterdam News,** would, for many years, publish considerable news relative to the Nation of Islam (NOI),* especially dealing with issues centering around Malcolm and his New York following. But it was a California journal, the *Los Angeles Herald-Dispatch*, that, at least briefly, would be most closely identified with the NOI. Before Malcolm X started *Muhammad Speaks** in May 1960, the new unofficial "official" organ of the NOI became the *Herald-Dispatch*. Largely as a result of its influence with the NOI, the paper published a regional edition that circulated in the organization's headquarters city of Chicago* and other major American cities.

Founded in 1952, the *Herald-Dispatch* was one of three black newspapers published in California's largest urban center during the 1960s. With a circulation of only about 3,000 at its peak before association with the NOI pushed its circulation upward, the *Herald-Dispatch* established an early reputation for its antiestablishment position. Not long after its appearance, it started a roller-coaster relationship with the NOI when it became a major carrier of NOI news. Malcolm had initiated the NOI's first significant contact with the paper in 1957 while in Los Angeles to organize the city's first Black Muslim* mosque. While there, he began a weekly column entitled "God's Angry Men" and visited the office regularly to learn the details of newspaper publishing from one of the paper's executives. Addresses by both Malcolm and Elijah Muhammad* regularly appeared in its column. Its editor-owner, Sanford Alexander, though not a member of the NOI, was clearly in tune with many of the NOI's views. The paper criticized some of the more recognizable "Establishment" black leaders, who frequently came under attack from Malcolm. Roy Wilkins,* Whitney Young,* and Ralph Bunche* were derisively labeled as "Uncle Toms"* and too conservative to influence black progress. The paper also indicted the United States as a kind of Nazi Germany—a perverse Christian nation—for its use of the atom bomb on Japan. But the paper was hardly a friend of Judaism;* Jews* were condemned for their supposed infiltration of the National Association for the Advancement of Colored People (NAACP),* and the paper occasionally railed at Israel for its treatment of the Palestinians. At the same time, it extolled the virtues of Muhammad and the NOI's racial objective of racial unity as the

Joe Louis, a favorite of Malcolm's, in one of his many heavyweight fights. Library of Congress.

only salvation for Black America. It was largely for these positions that Malcolm X praised the Los Angeles paper. No black paper in the nation, Malcolm proclaimed, was "Blacker" than the *Herald-Dispatch*. Such views, however, would also subject the paper's owner to a Federal Bureau of Investigation* probe.

SELECTED BIBLIOGRAPHY

Evanzz, 1999; Lincoln, 1994; Myers, 1993; B. Perry, 1991; Wolseley, 1990.

Robert L. Jenkins

LOUIS, JOE (Joe Louis Barrow). Malcolm X always remembered the eruption of race pride that swept through Black America after Joe Louis knocked out James J. Braddock on June 22, 1937, to become heavyweight boxing's world champion. Exactly a year later, Louis knocked out, in one round, Max Schmeling of Germany, claiming revenge for a defeat in 1936 and defeating the pugilist of Adolf Hitler's* "master race." African American boys everywhere dreamed of being the next "Brown Bomber."

Malcolm's initial response to Louis's success was to become a boxer. His brother Philbert* was a natural boxer, and Malcolm entered novice competition in Lansing, Michigan.* He was twice defeated by the same boy, Bill Peterson, who was white, and he subsequently gave up boxing. However, through his incarceration at Norfolk Prison, Malcolm continued to follow Louis. Yet, by late 1963, after having risen to prominence in the Nation of Islam (NOI),* Malcolm referred to Louis as a stooge for White America. What led to this characterization is not clear, thought it might have been influenced by a negative comment about Malcolm and the NOI attributed to Louis. Toward the end of his life, Malcolm's tone regarding Louis changed again. He began to see himself as an "oratorical" Joe Louis and used boxing images and analogies in his speeches. One of Malcolm's foremost goals was to build black pride,* something he credited Joe Louis's victories with doing in the 1930s.

SELECTED BIBLIOGRAPHY

Bak, 1996; Gallen, ed., 1992; Malcolm X with Haley, 1965; B. Perry, 1991.

Alan Scot Willis

LUMUMBA, PATRICE. Patrice Lumumba was prime minister of the Belgian Congo* (subsequently named the Republic of Zaire). He was a contemporary of Ghana's Kwame Nkrumah,* Gamal Nasser* of Egypt,* and other Pan-Africanist leaders of the African continent. In June 1960, Lumumba took office as the Congo's first democratically elected leader.

Like many other Pan-Africanists in the United States, Malcolm became a champion of Lumumba, perhaps respecting the African revolutionary most for his support of a united Africa and his fierce and outspoken criticism of colonialism. Malcolm, however, was not personally well acquainted with Lumumba. He had met and talked with him only once, when Lumumba came to the United States in 1960 to speak in Washington, D.C. at Howard University.* Malcolm wrote or said little about this meeting. Apparently, however, it so impressed him that he sought and received Elijah Muhammad's* permission to invite Lumumba to a special gathering of African, Arab, and Asian leaders that he, Malcolm, planned to host in conjunction with Lumumba's scheduled speaking engagement the following year at Harlem's* Abbyssinian Baptist Church. Before the New York visit occurred, however, rival forces led by Colonel Joseph-Desiore Mobutu overthrew the regime; Lumumba was assassinated several months later.

Lumumba's murder enraged Malcolm and other black nationalists in the United States. In the months following Lumumba's death, Malcolm spoke harshly about the U.S. government's role in Congo affairs. He implicated the Central Intelligence Agency (CIA)* in the assassination and condemned the United States for establishing a virtual puppet regime in the country with its support of Moise Tshombe,* one of Lumumba's bitterest enemies and successor as premier. In no uncertain terms, Malcolm said, Tshombe was an Uncle Tom,* "an international murderer" hired by the United States. He linked Lumumba's murder to the lynching of Mississippians Mack Charles Parker and Medgar

Evers* and his own father, Earl Little,* declaring that it was time for white people to start dying in the name of revolutions. Understandably, many believed that Malcolm was behind a demonstration of black nationalists protesting the Lumumba murder that turned violent at the United Nations* headquarters. Malcolm, however, denied his and the Nation of Islam's* involvement.

Malcolm's affection and respect for Lumumba was so great that he vowed to name his firstborn son after the slain leader. He and his wife never produced one, but they named their last child, a girl, Gamilah Lumumba, in honor of Egypt's* Gamal Nasser* and Lumumba.

SELECTED BIBLIOGRAPHY

Carson (Gallen, ed.), 1991; Clarke, ed., 1990; Evanzz, 1992; Malcolm X (Breitman, ed.), 1965; Malcolm X (Perry, ed.), 1989; Malcolm X with Haley, 1965; Myers, 1993.

Akwasi B. Assensoh and Yvette Alex-Assensoh

LUQMAN, ANAS M. (BROTHER). Anas Luqman, referred to affectionately by those close to him as Brother Luqman, was a Black Muslim* and belonged to the Nation of Islam (NOI).* He was also a member of the Fruit of Islam (FOI),* the paramilitary unit responsible for defending members of the NOI. When Fidel Castro,* the leader of Cuba,* made his historic visit to the United States and stayed in Harlem* because he had a hard time getting lodging elsewhere, Luqman was responsible for working out security arrangements at the hotel where Castro stayed. Luqman was a Vietnam conflict* veteran and had specialized in explosives. When the rift developed between Elijah Muhammad* and Malcolm X, Luqman was a member of Temple Number Seven* in New York, which Malcolm had been the minister over before his suspension.

As the Savior's Day Convention* neared in 1964, a day when members of the NOI gather in Chicago* for their annual convention, Luqman was approached by Captain Joseph,* commander over the FOI, who instructed Luqman to plant a bomb under Malcolm's car, which would detonate when the ignition was turned on. Luqman not only refused to do so and immediately quit the NOI but informed Malcolm of the lethal scheme. In addition, Luqman quickly informed the *New York Amsterdam News*,* the largest black newspaper circulating in the largest city in the United States.

In early February 1965, shortly before Malcolm was assassinated, Luqman, along with twenty of his Muslim* brothers, rushed to Malcolm's house in East Elmhurst,* Queens, from another part of New York City when no one would answer the phone at his residence. They feared that he may have been killed at that point. When Malcolm was assassinated later in that same month, Luqman was part of the security detail at the Audubon Ballroom.* He ended up with a bullet hole in his coat when he tried to stop one of the assassins from fleeing after the assassination.

SELECTED BIBLIOGRAPHY

Bush, 1999; Evanzz, 1999; Karim with Skutches and Gallen, 1992.

Mfanya Donald Tryman

LYNN, CONRAD. Conrad Lynn was considered a radical lawyer who represented and defended a number of controversial leftist causes and political figures and became a chief legal representative of the Black Muslims* in Harlem.* He initially had disdain for them but became impressed with the ability of the Nation of Islam (NOI)* to convert convicts and ex-convicts as well as drug addicts, prostitutes, alcoholics, and other social outcasts into upstanding, law-abiding Muslims* associated with the NOI.

It was Malcolm X who influenced Lynn to examine more critically the role of the NOI in big cities, where so many social pathologies exist among African Americans in black ghettos. Lynn initially felt that their case was hopeless. Once Lynn became convinced that Malcolm and the NOI represented a good cause, he joined them on picket lines and in other political protests. Lynn shared the dais in political forums with Malcolm in New York City and felt that Malcolm was one of the great orators of our time, who not only was a great speaker but who had the ability to combine humor with sarcasm in attacking the injustices against blacks in the American political system. Malcolm's ability to combine thought with passion and emotion, Lynn felt, put him in a category by himself and created the basis for the political schism that developed between Malcolm and Elijah Muhammad,* which was exacerbated by Malcolm's founding of the Organization of Afro-American Unity (OAAU).*

Malcolm's death, Lynn felt, had an incalculable effect upon the black movement for political liberation at a time when Martin Luther King, Jr.,* was losing influence among blacks, particularly black youth. In life, Malcolm had a great influence on Lynn and inspired him as a political activist. But Lynn was not convinced that Malcolm's death was due just to a feud between him and the NOI, suggesting that a third, unknown party may have played a greater role.

SELECTED BIBLIOGRAPHY

DeCaro, 1998; Lynn, 1979; Sales, 1994.

Mfanya Donald Tryman

M

MAFIA. Since his death in 1965 numerous rumors have emerged suggesting a possible link between Malcolm X and the Mafia. It is possible that Malcolm had dealings with the Mafia during his underworld days. For example, in his autobiography and in several of his early speeches, Malcolm claimed to have sold reefer* and other illicit drugs to policemen while he continued to work as a thief and a numbers runner.* The insinuation is that Malcolm was able to continue this illicit affair because of the protection of organized crime. It is widely known that the Mafia or members of that group during Malcolm's street hustling* days in the early 1940s controlled the numbers games and drug trade in Harlem* and in other northern ghettos.

A case in point is the example of Dutch Schultz, formerly a well-known and highly respected New York mobster. Schultz began his takeover of the Harlem ghetto in the 1930s, and by the time that Malcolm had come of age, the Schultz mob was in complete control of Harlem's numbers racket. Malcolm points out in his autobiography that he heard numerous accounts about the violent and strong-armed tactics Schultz's gang employed to maintain its kingpin status. Nevertheless, however tenuous the speculation might be, neither Malcolm nor the sources make mention of a Mafia-Malcolm relationship, either before his incarceration or after his prison* transformation to Islam* in 1947.

Moreover, the Federal Bureau of Investigation (FBI)* and Central Intelligence Agency (CIA)* hawked nearly every move Malcolm made soon after his prison release. Certainly these agencies would have leaked a Mafia connection to one of their many "friendly" media operatives. In addition, one can probably conclude that since Malcolm and his family were nearly destitute after the split with the Nation of Islam,* Mafia connections were highly unlikely.

There has also been conjecture about Mafia involvement in Malcolm's assassination. This theory was first advanced by James Farmer,* a few days after Malcolm's murder, when he intimated that the death of Malcolm may have had

"international implications." He was alluding to the fact that Malcolm was causing international drug traffickers to lose enormous amounts of money in the
ghetto. The Muslims'* drug rehabilitation programs and their efforts to rid some
black neighborhoods of drugs caused an increasing loss of revenue for whom-
ever was responsible for the Mafia's drug trade in those areas. This theory
looked even more plausible when Talmadge Hayer,* the man who admitted he
was paid "handsomely" by "someone" for murdering Malcolm, was represented
in his appeal by Edward Bennett Williams, a well-known lawyer who represented dozens of men with ties to organized crime. While some people continue
to accept this theory regarding Malcolm's death, Farmer, for a number of reasons, later dropped it.

For those who continued to believe the Mafia link to Malcolm's murder,
formerly secret information about the Mafia that various scholars published under the Freedom of Information Act proved quite timely. While this information
did not explicitly state that the Mafia murdered Malcolm, it did indicate that
there was a Mafia and government conspiracy to murder enemies of the United
States, a category in which Malcolm easily fit. Baba Zak A. Kondo, author of
CONSPIRACYS: Unraveling the Assassination of Malcolm X, points out that
FBI Director J. Edgar Hoover,* after learning of a CIA-Mafia plot to kill Fidel
Castro,* informed Attorney General Robert Kennedy* that a bureau agent could
arrange to kill Castro. He added that Michael Milan (an alias), a former assassin
and a Mafia hit man who Hoover personally recruited, and others were part of
a clandestine squad established to resolve sensitive national security problems.
Milan claimed that the squad "regularly" conducted Hoover-ordered assassinations. For many, this information certainly gave further credence to the idea that
Malcolm might have been a target of one or several of these alleged clandestine
activities.

While none of these theories can be proven in their entirety, one does not
have to have an active imagination to conclude that Malcolm and the work he
was doing, at the very least, perturbed both the federal government and the
Mafia. In many of his speeches, Malcolm pointed out national, state, and local
complicity in Mafia dealings. He argued that if the U.S. government was really
interested in eliminating the Mafia, it certainly had the money, power, and personnel to succeed. He sometimes insisted that American imperialism and capitalism* were so inextricably linked that it was becoming increasingly difficult
to differentiate between legitimate business enterprises and Mafia-front organizations. One can infer from Malcolm's anticrime stance and his obvious influence in black and other minority communities that criminals (especially
professionally organized criminals) had nothing to lose and much to gain from
Malcolm's silence.

While it is not enough to simply speculate on what is significant in the life
of such an important person like Malcolm, speculation often helps to lead to
what some consider the ultimate truth. Speculation about Malcolm's connection
to the Mafia has and will continue to spur research and create dialogue, the two

necessary elements in the search for truth and objectivity. What is known is that Malcolm X, the acknowledged leader and spokesman of many ghetto disenchanted residents, viewed the Mafia as one of the barriers to the liberation of black people everywhere. He also made it clear that until black people united behind the common causes of freedom and justice, the Mafia and similar organizations would continue to control their neighborhoods and communities.

SELECTED BIBLIOGRAPHY

Evanzz, 1992; Gage, 1971; Malcolm X with Haley, 1965.

Curtis Austin

"MAKE IT PLAIN, MALCOLM." Speaking and debate techniques that Malcolm X acquired while in prison* proved useful to him in his ministry as a Muslim.* By the time he was paroled, he had become a master orator. Although many disagreed with some of his views, few could hear him speak without being moved. Even the most unflappable, according to one of his former associates, Almina Rahman,* could not listen to Malcolm and not be mesmerized, occasionally moved to tears or inspired to riot. It was on the Harlem* street corners before large gatherings and a carnival-like atmosphere, where he gave many of his speeches as the minister of Muslim Temple Number Seven,* that he seemed most effective in touching the emotions and stirring the intellect of his audiences. Malcolm lectured and proselytized among many of these Harlemites, who by religious orientation were Christians. Customarily, during their church services, many of these same people would likely have participated in the "call and response" practices characteristic of black churches since the days of slavery. In some ways, this practice was similarly characteristic of those who heard Malcolm preach and lecture. A typical reaction to what the audience interpreted as a significant idea or major point that Malcolm made was a simple, "Make it plain, Brother Malcolm! Make it plain." Caught up in the rhythm and cadence of his messages, which were filled with metaphors, clichés and simple logic in denouncing white racism, or criticizing political and civil rights* leaders and the American government, the crowd would urge him on—"Speak, Brother Malcolm" and "Make it clear." Interspersed with these and similar remarks was applause, a greater acknowledgment of the crowd's agreement with Malcolm, and a display of appreciation for his courage to take bold stands and speak even bolder truths.

SELECTED BIBLIOGRAPHY

Lomax, 1963, 1968; Strickland (Greene, ed.), 1994; M. White (Leeman, ed.), 1996.

Robert L. Jenkins

MALCOLM AS A DEBATER. Malcolm's oratorical and debating skills were seldom matched by those who encountered him in public forums. While still in Norfolk prison,* Malcolm joined the debating team. Debating and public speaking seemed to come naturally to him, and he enthusiastically matched wits with debating teams that came from Harvard* and Yale for argumentative encounters. As would happen when he became a public figure and national spokesman for the Nation of Islam,* he debated the critical issues of the day in these skirmishes. Malcolm also learned to master a number of debating techniques that served him well in the heat of what he referred to as "verbal bullets." This included answering a difficult question with an equally difficult question, redefining an issue framed by his opposition, rephrasing an opponent's question to suit his answer, ansking the loaded question, and giving unresponsive stock answers. He was known for his meticulous preparation for debates, which included, among other things, rehearsing as he drove in a car, reviewing television and radio playbacks of his performances, and putting himself in his opponents' shoes.

He debated well-known public figures at black and white colleges and universities as well as on "live" radio and television talk shows. While many, if not most, of his adversaries in this arena had college degrees, Malcolm, as part of his introductory remarks, often pointed out such discrepancies, reminding the audience that he was an eighth-grade dropout. But he was neither intimidated nor deterred by such educational disparities, and more than rose to the occasion during most verbal exchanges. He invited a number of his critics, particularly black leaders in the civil rights movement,* to debate him in public forums. He had few takers, for even his critics acknowledged his considerable talent in debating and avoided such a confrontation in this arena.

His speaking and debating skills made him one of the most sought-after public figures on college campuses and on television and radio in the early 1960s. This included some of the most prestigious universities in the country, including Ivy League schools. In the case of Harvard University, he spoke and debated on three different occasions reknown professors and public figures in their respective domains of influence and expertise. At Oxford University in England, he received a standing ovation from the audience for his debate and appearance.

SELECTED BIBLIOGRAPHY

Clarke, ed., 1990; Collins with Bailey, 1998; Flick and Powell, 1988; B. Perry, 1991.

Mfanya Donald Tryman

MALCOLM AS A FAMILY MAN. Within a year of their marriage, Malcolm X and his wife, Betty Sanders Shabazz,* had already begun a family. Malcolm and Betty's marriage would last for only seven years before it was cut tragically short by his assassination in 1965, but they would produce six children, all girls, together. Two of his children, twins Malaak and Malikah, were born after his death. According to Betty, each of the pregnancies was planned. Although he and his wife talked about the prospect of having a son, he never belabored the idea, grateful that his family of girls was born healthy.

Malcolm was a major force in shaping the Nation of Islam (NOI)* during the 1960s and subsequently his own organizations. Consequently, his frequent absences from the home in their behalf understandably made Betty's task as homemaker and chief child rearer difficult ones. His absences were something that he always felt guilty about. Throughout his association with Elijah Muhammad,* Malcolm left no doubt about how strong his affection was for the leader of the NOI. Yet there is every indication that Malcolm's love and dedication to Muhammad and the causes that he championed himself were exceeded only by his love and deeper commitment to Betty and his family. As a Muslim,* Malcolm hardly practiced democracy in the home. He believed that there were decided roles for men and women to play in the home as husband, wife, father and mother, and at times his adherence to this philosophy caused strains in the family. On at least three occasions, Betty briefly left him and their home. Yet their resolve to keep their family intact only seemed to harden. During his most stressful time with the NOI, Malcolm's family suffered with him the concern over stalkers, threatening phone calls, legal challenges, and a serious bombing of their home. With all that he had specifically put Betty through during their life together, he once said, he could do nothing else but "love this woman."

The strong relationship naturally carried over to his relationship with his children. It only took the birth of his first child to realize that he truly liked being a father. Friends and admirers related how Malcolm, like many doting fathers, carried pictures of his children in his wallet and proudly showed them off. Affable and humorous by nature, Malcolm in his private time, according to Betty, was comfortable as a husband and father and found it easy to spend playful time with them. One of his favorite foods was ice cream, and his family was quick to indulge him with it at mealtime. He was great at teasing, though Betty was not always accepting of it. His wife claimed that Malcolm could be gentle and affectionate in his relationship with his children, but he also knew how to be strict as a disciplinarian. Rearing children was a new experience for them both, but Malcolm's philosophy about the responsibility demanded proper supervision and training to ensure that they were well behaved, considerate of each other, educationally prepared to take care of themselves, moral in their actions, and spiritual in their beliefs. One of the things that he clearly wanted to avoid was for his daughters to grow up "wild," which characterized his own youth.

Although Malcolm and his family never suffered materially for the necessities of life, there was seldom a great amount of money in the household. Salaried by the NOI, Malcolm nevertheless worked tirelessly to enhance financially Muhammad's family and the NOI, sacrificing considerable potential income for himself and his own family. Once he separated from the group, much of the family income derived from his frequent lectures and speaking engagements, loans from his half sister Ella Collins,* advances from his writings, and the generous contributions of friends and followers. At his death, friends and well-wishers worked to raise sufficient money to bury him and help sustain his bereaved family. However, he left Betty and his family the prospects of considerable financial gain from a book contract, his autobiography, a book that eventually turned out to be more lucrative than he ever could have imagined.

(Unfortunately, Malcolm's family ultimately benefitted little financially from the sales.) And supposedly after his death many of his Arab admirers contributed generously to the family.

Like Betty, Malcolm's four children sat in the audience of the Audubon Ballroom,* where they heard his last words at the podium before his murder. Even though his family was very young at the time (only Attallah, the eldest, has any real memory of her father), the trauma from the experience affected them well into their later years. For the most part, Betty once wrote, the family dwelled on only the happy times that the family shared with Malcolm as a husband and father.

SELECTED BIBLIOGRAPHY

Angelou, 1986; Blackside/PBS, 1994; Evanzz, 1999; Gallen, ed., 1992; Karim with Skutches and Gallen, 1992; Malcolm X with Haley, 1965; A. Shabazz, 1997; B. Shabazz, 1969, 1995; B. Shabazz as told to Taylor and Edwards, 1992; B. Shabazz (Clarke, ed.), 1990.

Robert L. Jenkins

MALCOLM AS A FUND-RAISER. When it came to raising funds, particularly for the Nation of Islam (NOI),* Malcolm rose to the task. He had no equal among rival Black Muslim ministers across the country. This was also true in generating monies for the annual Savior's Day Convention* in Chicago. Money, of course, is the lifeblood of any organization, for, generally speaking, without money it is difficult to achieve organizational goals. But Malcolm's ability to generate funds for the NOI only incited the envy and jealousy that already existed among other ministers and mosques who thought that Malcolm already was receiving too much attention. Malcolm's oratorical skills and charisma were important assets in raising money. His exhortations and preaching of economic black nationalism* had a magnetic effect on his remunerative goals.

Since Malcolm was the most popular and visible figure associated with the NOI, African Americans as well as Black Muslims* in Temple Number Seven* that he headed were more than happy to contribute funds for what were considered worthy efforts. While Malcolm raised millions of dollars for the NOI, he never kept a cent for himself. It was Malcolm who suggested that Elijah Muhammad's* children be given administrative jobs in the organization. At the time, they all were performing menial jobs for menial pay, working primarily for whites, the same people that they disdained. Consequently, Malcolm almost single-handedly began to raise funds in the early 1960s so that Muhammad's children could take over administrative positions. This created a political and economic power base for them that would, ironically, later be used against Malcolm.

SELECTED BIBLIOGRAPHY

Draper, 1971; Karim with Skutches and Gallen, 1992; B. Shabazz (Clarke, ed.), 1990.

Mfanya Donald Tryman

The New York headquarters of the Nation of Islam newspaper *Muhammad Speaks*, first established by Malcolm in the basement of his home. Library of Congress.

MALCOLM AS A JOURNALIST. Malcolm X possessed considerable journalistic skills, although he had no formal school training or expertise in the area. However, he did develop on-the-job training at the *Los Angeles Herald-Dispatch*,* a leftist-oriented newspaper in California's largest city. Malcolm, while the chief minister of the New York mosque and overseer of a number of others, was sent to Los Angeles in 1957 by Elijah Muhammad* to supervise the momentous growth the mosque experienced under his direction.

As a journalist with considerable media savvy, Malcolm realized the power of the mass media as well as the printed word. He knew that the media had the ability to twist and interpret events to sell or gain publicity, often sacrificing the truth for profit motives, or, as Malcolm said, to make the innocent look guilty and the guilty look innocent. While with the *Herald-Dispatch*, he had learned as much as possible about the publishing business, and that experience benefited him. The *Herald-Dispatch* published a weekly commentary by Malcolm entitled "God's Angry Men." Perhaps this is what motivated Malcolm, assisted by his friend and journalist Louis Lomax,* in starting *Muhammad Speaks** in 1960, the official newspaper of the Nation of Islam (NOI)* that had a national circulation, after his "internship" with the *Herald-Dispatch*. At its peak, *Muhammad Speaks* had a circulation of 500,000. In addition, Malcolm wrote a weekly column in the *New York Amsterdam News** that had a wide circulation in the New York City area. Malcolm also started a magazine called *The Messenger** in the New York area, but it quickly collapsed.

Ominous signs suggested that Malcolm's journalistic endeavors would be temporal in nature. In the early 1960s, Malcolm's New York column was taken over by Elijah Muhammad. Not long thereafter, Muhammad also took over his column in the *Herald-Dispatch*, and Malcolm received less coverage in the newspaper that he started. Ironically, *Muhammad Speaks* was used as the primary instrument to propagate to NOI members Malcolm's misdeeds in the eyes of Elijah Muhammad, Louis Farrakhan,* and others in the sect's leadership cadre. In short, commentaries in *Muhammad Speaks* would make the political climate toward Malcolm vindictive and ugly.

SELECTED BIBLIOGRAPHY
Carson (Gallen, ed.), 1991; Gallen, ed., 1994; B. Perry, 1991.
                                        Mfanya Donald Tryman and Keith O. Hilton

MALCOLM AS A SPEAKER. Malcolm X possessed a number of talents. He was an outstanding debater, had good journalistic skills, and was exceptionally bright. In prison,* he had studied and memorized words in the dictionary. But one of his talents that stood out the most was his speaking ability. Possessing a charismatic and charming persona, his speaking ability was second to none, even though much of what he said as a member of the Nation of Islam* was antiwhite and anti-American. He was one of the most sought-after speakers on college campuses in the last years of his life. This was true of elite Ivy League schools as well as historically black schools like Howard University* and Morgan State College (now University).

His oratory could be spell-binding. He was bold and provocative, but he had the sophistication and refinement of an artisan. Malcolm was a master in the use of hyperbole, metaphors, similes, analogies, and other linguistic gymnastics that helped to drive points home or to provide examples of hypocritical American domestic and foreign policies. His rhetorical skills, combined with his self-taught knowledge of history and the social sciences, made him a formidable orator. Though much of his speaking ability was innate and self-taught, it was enhanced while he was a member of a prison inmate debating team. Although he often prefaced his statements, and particularly his introductory statements, with "The Honorable Elijah Muhammad,"* the media and invitations for speaking engagements rarely sought Elijah Muhammad out, and Muhammad only occasionally accepted such invitations. The popular speaker in demand was Malcolm X. And it was his speeches, quotes, citations, and remarks that were referenced by the mass media. However, Malcolm's oratorical skills and related leadership ability would also get him in trouble, since he, rather than Elijah

Muhammad, the leader of the Nation of Islam, always received the publicity and was the one that a large segment of the public most revered.

SELECTED BIBLIOGRAPHY

Clegg, 1997; Malcolm X (Breitman, ed.), 1965; Malcolm X (Clark, ed.), 1992; M. White (Leeman, ed.), 1996.

Mfanya Donald Tryman

MALCOLM AT THE WHITE COLLEGES. During his life as an activist, Malcolm X spoke across the nation taking the message of Elijah Muhammad* and the Nation of Islam (NOI)* and eventually his own through the Organization of Afro-American Unity* to many different forums. A popular speaker because of his fiery though unorthodox message for both black and white America, Malcolm found the college campus perhaps his most accessible medium. He was particularly in demand on the white campuses and lectured constantly at such institutions as the University of California at Berkeley, Michigan State University, the University of Chicago, Wayne State University, Barnard University, and Boston University. But it was on the Ivy League campuses of Harvard,* Yale, Columbia, Cornell, Brown, Dartmouth, and the University of Pennsylvania that Malcolm seemed to attract the greatest attention. At Harvard University alone, Malcolm spoke on three separate occasions, in 1961 and twice in 1964. As one would expect, especially when he was in good standing with the NOI, the local membership came to hear him speak in great numbers. Frequently, however, these programs were organized by scholars and filled with audiences of the middle class and intellectuals, both black and white, groups that he often collectively criticized. They were also great attractions for young people, whom Malcolm often challenged to think for themselves.

Frequently during these programs, someone from the university community spoke in opposition to Malcolm's ideas, and question-and-answer sessions routinely followed. These engagements revealed much not only about Malcolm's thinking about contemporary world issues but also about the evolution of his thought on race relations and the place of blacks in American society. Often spirited affairs where he held his own against some of the most prominent scholars in their field, something that Malcolm himself marveled over, the appearances came under increasing attack by Elijah Muhammad* and the cabal of Malcolm detractors around him. Consequently, Muhammad would order him to end his acceptances of the engagements on white campuses. Muhammad justified his decision on the grounds that Malcolm's comments unnecessarily subjected the NOI to negative press attacks and that the engagements did little to attract new recruits from the predominantly white audiences. Malcolm acceded to the Muslim* leader's demand, but by the time he had fulfilled the engagements previously accepted, the break with his former mentor had already become irrevocably complete, and he naturally disregarded the agreement. Thus, during the last months of his life Malcolm continued to be a popular draw for white colleges, even overseas, and under the direction of his friend, divinity scholar C. Eric Lincoln,* who had arranged for Malcolm's first speaking engagement at a predominantly white college in 1960, Malcolm was outlining a national speaking tour for the many white campuses that had made him the most sought-after speaker on the lecture circuit.

SELECTED BIBLIOGRAPHY

Branch, 1998; Cone, 1992; Gallen, ed., 1992, 1994; Lincoln, 1994; Lomax, 1963; Malcolm X (Epps, ed.), 1991.

Robert L. Jenkins

MALCOLM ON EDUCATION. As a youth, Malcolm X was a good student. Fellow students and classroom teachers alike in the schools of Lansing, Michigan,* recognized his ability, though one of his teachers, a Mr. Ostrowski,* deliberately sought to diminish Malcolm's aspirations to become a lawyer by casting doubt on his intellect simply because of his color. Disillusioned with his life in a white environment, Malcolm, however, left the public schools of Lansing for the street life of Boston, terminating his formal education at the eighth grade. His subsequent intellectual development occurred through self-teaching. In prison,* and later as one of the world's most recognized black nationalist leaders, Malcolm, through his own initiative, improved himself intellectually so greatly that few could compete with his sharp mind and his wide-ranging knowledge. A lifelong learner who read incessantly, he felt vindicated by his own self-education when important radio and television personalities such as Irv Kupcinet,* Barry Gray, and Mike Wallace* sought out his views on issues other than race. Moreover, Malcolm spoke and debated at prestigious universities like Harvard,* Yale, and Howard.* Perhaps it was because of his own lack of a formal education that he often expressed suspicion about highly educated blacks. Nevertheless, he could extol the value of his incarceration because, as he said, it provided him with far more opportunity to educate himself, while at the same time lament not having gone to college to formally pursue one of his interests, either in law or languages. Indeed, he wrote in his autobiography, that he would feel no shame even as an adult returning to the public schools of New York to acquire his high school diploma.

Malcolm spoke widely about the importance of education and expressed pronounced views about it. He excoriated white racists for their violent opposition to the admission of James Meredith* to the University of Mississippi and labeled the desegregation effort as a poor way for Mississippi* to make up for its historical denial of educational opportunity to its black citizens. He roundly criticized the deplorable state of education in the northern ghettos, remarking that they were as essentially segregated as those in the American South.* Not a street activist in terms of changing the nation's social order, he could nevertheless support the efforts of Harlem* leaders such as the Reverend Milton Galamison* and other demonstrators to improve the quality of public education in the black community. As a member of the Nation of Islam* and a black nationalist, Malcolm did not philosophically support integrated schools. He was, for example, particularly critical of the 1954 *Brown v. Board of Education of Topeka, Kansas** U.S. Supreme Court decision, which called for the desegregation of American schools, not because he supported the concept but because he regarded it as the misguided consequences of the goals of white liberals,* middle-class blacks,* and the civil rights* community. Black integrationists, he often said, were actually Uncle Toms* who believed that whites were superior to African Americans and who were ashamed of their own race.

As a black nationalist, Malcolm strongly felt that black children would benefit more from the leadership of African American principals and teachers and learning from textbooks, especially history textbooks, written by and for black Americans. This instruction would teach blacks how to survive in a predominantly white world and also to be aware of and proud of their African American heritage. There was greatness in the black past, he said, and black children were being systematically denied knowledge of it. Since little was being done by uncaring whites to raise the standards of black schools, Malcolm hoped to use his Organization of Afro-American Unity* as a potent force to improve their quality. Accordingly, the organization would seek to find qualified African Americans to serve as principals and teachers of black schools, recommend qualified blacks as appointees to school boards, push vigorously for Afrocentric textbooks and curricula, and encourage greater black parental involvement in the school life of their children. But he also sought to impact on children's education more directly. Hence, he was not opposed to visiting the schools to talk to individual classes and could occasionally be found leading groups of young schoolchildren on field trips to historical and natural history museums.

Malcolm X was a master teacher in his own right. Although his classroom was essentially the streets of black America, he nevertheless understood the role of formal academic training in human progress. Since his death, a number of children's books on Malcolm's life and views have been published as an educational tool explaining his role in black history.* Like many black leaders before, during, and after his life and times, he correctly saw quality education as the key to the black future and felt bound to encourage it as the bridge to black liberation, its acquisition important for safeguarding all people's human rights.*

SELECTED BIBLIOGRAPHY

Karim with Skutches and Gallen, 1992; Malcolm X (Breitman, ed.), 1970b; Malcolm X (Clark, ed.), 1992; Malcolm X (Perry, ed.), 1989; Malcolm X with Haley, 1965; T. Perry, ed., 1996; Smallwood (Conyers, ed.), 1999.

William A. Person

MALCOLM ON VIDEO. Perhaps nothing has done more to familiarize Malcolm X to the American people since his death than depictions of his life and work through television documentaries and videos. The benefits from this media form have especially influenced knowledge about Malcolm for a generation of young people, products of the television age, attending the nation's schools and colleges. America's fascination with learning about Malcolm X through the visual genre began in 1959 with television personality Mike Wallace's* exposé of Malcolm X and the Black Muslim* sect in the series "The Hate That Hate Produced."* In death, however, video-formatted histories of Malcolm's life and ideas have not emphasized the negative aspects of Malcolm's life found in this early documentary. Indeed, in nearly all cases these visuals have portrayed Malcolm's life, including his youth, sympathetically while analyzing the evolution of his work and thought critically and with considerable balance. Notable representation of this kind of objectivity, for example, can be found in the CBS News–produced *The Real Malcolm X, an Intimate Portrait of the Man*, the Blackside/Public Broadcast System's devotion of one of its segments to Malcolm in the award-winning documentary series *Eyes on the Prize*, Blackside/ PBS's more focused *Malcolm X: Make It Plain*, and A&E Television's *Malcolm X Biography*, all of which were aired as major media events on national television prior to their release for public sale. Like these major portrayals, most of the other accounts have simply sought to reveal the international environment, especially the American environment, that produced Malcolm and the character, work, and ideas of one of Black America's most revered and controversial figures. Interviews of a diverse group of personalities, including relatives and intimate friends of Malcolm, do much to enhance the videos and shed light on his development and growth as a man and leader.

More than a dozen major video-formatted documentaries and biographies have been made about Malcolm X, clearly rivaling the interest that America has shown in Malcolm's most notable challenger during the height of his popularity, Martin Luther King, Jr.*As such, these videos show the continuing fascination Malcolm's life elicits from a wide range of the worldwide public.

SELECTED BIBLIOGRAPHY

A&E Entertainment, 1995; Blackside/PBS, 1987, 1994; CBS News, 1992; Films for the Humanities, 1998; Greaves, 1990; Library Distributors of America, 1993; Schlessinger Video Productions, 1992; Simitar Videos, 1994; United American Videos, 1998; Warner Studio, 1972; Xenon Studios, 1991.

Robert L. Jenkins

MALCOLM'S EDUCATION. When his life is examined, there is a significant difference between Malcolm X and other black leaders of the twentieth century: his educational background. Research on African American leadership in the twentieth century shows that in many instances these individuals received a high school, if not college, education. Malcolm X's highest level of formal educational attainment was the completion of the eighth grade. Thus, the nonformal educational attainment Malcolm X gained through his life experiences would eventually prepare him for his role as a black leader. Malcolm's lack of formal education during the 1930s was indicative of the existing social barriers African Americans faced. This required them to go outside of the formal system of public education and seek nonformal educational opportunities provided by African American organizations. This further underscores the importance of black organizations providing black adults with nonformal education (learning outside of a traditional school setting).

Malcolm transformed himself from a poor student in elementary school into an academically and socially successful student, being voted president of his eighth-grade class. Yet the reality of racism directly impeded his academic and career aspirations because he was discouraged from pursuing a law career by his English teacher.

Witnessing white students of lesser academic achievement being encouraged to pursue professional career paths greatly disturbed Malcolm, and he became apathetic and withdrew socially from his white classmates. In recalling this incident in his autobiography, he wondered what he might have been with encouragement from his middle school teacher. This experience marks a turning point in Malcolm X's participation in formal education, as he would drop out of public school after the eighth grade. As a teenager, Malcolm's nonformal education would come from life experiences in the black community in Boston, Massachusetts, and Harlem,* New York, where his life experiences provided a basis for his social growth. He became a self-proclaimed "hustler" and petty criminal and later a prisoner in the Massachusetts penal system. While in prison,* Malcolm engaged in nonformal self-directed learning.

Malcolm X's self-directed learning began during his incarceration in the Massachusetts penal system during the 1940s. While at the Charlestown State Prison, Malcolm met a fellow inmate named John Elton Bembry (Bimbi).* Malcolm stated in his autobiography that Bimbi was the first man who gained his total respect by his use of words and thoughts; Bimbi had a dramatic effect on the entire prison, and he identified Bimbi as the inspiration for his self-directed learning.

Malcolm was later transferred to the Norfolk Prison Colony in Norfolk, Massachusetts, in late 1948, where he participated in a radical form of adult education classes available to the prison population at that time and which also had an extensive library system. It was during the same period that Malcolm X was introduced to the Nation of Islam (NOI)* by his siblings as a way to bring the family back together and provide him with direction. What is significant here is that Malcolm's self-directed learning intensified after hearing about the teachings of Elijah Muhammad.* It was at this point that Malcolm X's self-study increased as he read books on history, philosophy, biology, and religion to verify the accuracy of some of Elijah Muhammad's teachings about history and race relations.

Malcolm X used his self-directed study and analysis to discuss conditions about black life in such a way that black and white people were drawn to his message. Malcolm's public discourse on African American life and society gave him the role of a nonformal educator who developed an ideology and praxis for educating African Americans. It was his intellectual curiosity and exploration that made him a student of life and black history.* This became an important asset that he utilized in his meteoric rise in the NOI's leadership hierarchy and led him to eventually become an international spokesman on the issues of racial justice and human rights.* But because of jeolousy, his education and intelligence also led to his demise.

SELECTED BIBLIOGRAPHY

Branham, 1995; Goldman (Franklin and Meier, eds.), 1982; Malcolm X with Haley, 1965; Merriam and Caffarella, 1991; B. Perry, 1991; Strickland (Greene, ed.), 1994.

Andrew P. Smallwood

MALCOLM'S FUNERAL. Malcolm X's murder sent shock waves throughout the national African American community. Followers of all different races and creeds descended on Harlem* to pay their respects to the fallen leader. His body lay on public display from February 22 to February 26 at the Unity Funeral Home on Harlem's east side.

Malcolm's funeral was held on Saturday, February 27, 1965, in Harlem's Faith Temple Church of God in Christ. Several other local churches had refused to allow Malcolm to be funeralized in their sanctuary, fearful over the death threats and potential danger from angry Muslims* and anti-Malcolm foes. Indeed, Bishop Alvin A. Childs, Faith Temple's pastor, and his wife received numerous death threats before and after the funeral services, the sources of which were never revealed. Malcolm was virtually financially broke at his death, so the cost of the funeral was paid by his friends, who contributed to a fund spearheaded by his lawyer and friend Percy Sutton.* With the funds, Betty Shabazz,* his wife, purchased a nine-inch-thick bronze casket lined with eggshell velvet cloth and encased in a glass shield. Malcolm's body was dressed in a dark business suit with a white shirt and dark tie. The remains were wrapped in seven white linen shrouds, an Islamic custom. New Jersey Sunni Islam* Iman Heshaam Jaaber* performed the orthodox Islamic funeral rituals, including the Janaza Salat (funeral prayer). More than 2,000 followers, admirers, onlookers, and adversaries reportedly attended the service, though most had to stand outside of the church itself. The actor Ossie Davis* delivered a stirring eulogy of the man whom he had known for many years and whom he greatly admired. Davis considered Malcolm, who had visited his home in New York on numerous occasions, the true embodiment of "Black manhood."* He told his audience that Malcolm was for black Americans their "Shining Prince."

Ella Collins,* Malcolm's half sister, was the only one of his siblings to attend the funeral. Wilfred,* Malcolm's oldest sibling, who headed the Detroit Temple, refused to mourn his brother's death. It made little "sense," he reportedly said, in getting emotional over his brother's death. According to Wilfred, Malcolm was dead, and he was better off because of it. Wilfred and Philbert,* another brother, on the day of the funeral attended the Nation of Islam's* Savior's Day Convention* held in Chicago, Illinois,* where they both publicly denounced Malcolm as a traitor to Elijah Muhammad.*

Malcolm had predicted that his death would precede the Savior's Day Convention, and his prediction had proved true. The large gathering at his funeral was representative of the many lives that he had touched.

SELECTED BIBLIOGRAPHY

Gallen, ed., 1992; Jaaber, 1992; Malcolm X (Breitman, ed.), 1967; Wood, ed., 1992.

Bridgette Stasher

MALCOLM'S INFLUENCE ON THE INCARCERATED. For Malcolm X, nothing did more to redeem him from the depths to which street life had lowered him than his conversion to Islam.* In prison,* his siblings' letters and visitations introduced him to the views of Elijah Muhammad,* leader of the Nation of Islam (NOI).* Thereafter, little of Malcolm's former life had much more than symbolic meaning to him. In the years after his release from prison, even during the period of his national stature, Malcolm never forgot how the redemptive force he found inherent in the NOI transformed his life. Hence, it was with great compassion that he "fished" among fallen blacks, especially on the streets, not just to increase the size of the NOI but as a way to rehabilitate and reform the broken lives of black men who were trapped in crime and vice, as he once was. This mission naturally took him into the prison system where he sought to promote Elijah Muhammad's brand of Islam. During his own incarceration as a young man, he had already enjoyed a modicum of success in converting several of his friends to Islam.

This prison experience, however, proved more difficult. In the beginning he had problems convincing state prison officials to sanction his work among the inmates because they feared his acerbic messages as potentially harmful to prison order. Largely through the efforts of former NOI attorneys Jawn Sandifer* and Edward Jacko,* however, he soon gained widespread access to New York's prisons, including those inmates held in maximum security institutions.

Concentrating most of his energies on those who had professed no set religious allegiance when they first entered prison, apparently so as not to offend the more traditional Christian and Jewish prison ministry, Malcolm's outreach work quickly won influence among the population. Although he sought to convey his messages to the incarcerated as an extension of Muhammad, it was clearly Malcolm who left the greatest impression on the lives of those he encountered. As others outside of the prison walls frequently did, the men found him mesmerizing and his preachments, both the religious and secular ones, difficult to resist and easy to digest. With combined emphasis on the importance of submission to Allah,* the teachings of Allah's Messenger, the importance of self-improvement* and racial pride, Sandifer, who had considerable personal knowledge of Malcolm's prison ministry, claims that Malcolm helped many of these men reclaim their dignity. Understandably, then, when many of them won their release from prison, they became supporters of Malcolm's ministry at Harlem's* Temple Number Seven.*

Malcolm became so successful at this work that journalist and friend Louis Lomax* in 1963 called him the Muslim* movement's "St. Paul." Even before Malcolm's work among inmates, however, the NOI was involved in proselytizing in the prisons. But it was Malcolm who did more than any other "evangelist" in elevating inmate interest in the NOI. Indeed, this incarcerated class constituted no insignificant component of their total membership, though in the 1960s no one outside the NOI's inner circle ever knew the exact number of adherents to the group, and they refused to divulge the count. It was largely because of their success in converting prison inmates, their biting criticism of whites and the conservative black leadership, and the general mysticism surrounding them that many nonsupporters gave the organization little respect. Malcolm's views also won many prison converts whose lives he never personally encountered. In the aftermath of his fight with his former mentor, many of these men continued to regard him as their champion and, rather than side with Muhammad, remained loyal Malcolm X supporters. For these supporters, it was both Malcolm the man and the message that sustained his appeal among them.

SELECTED BIBLIOGRAPHY

Cleaver (Scheer, ed.), 1969; DeCaro, 1998; Evanzz, 1992; Lomax, 1963; Malcolm X (Clark, ed.), 1992; Strickland (Greene, ed.), 1994, Yakubu (T. Perry ed.,) 1996.

Robert L. Jenkins

MALCOLM'S MUSICAL WORLD. Within a matter of months after his permanent move from Mason, Michigan,* to Boston's Roxbury* community, Malcolm X transformed himself from a "country bumpkin" to a "city slicker." These were the years of Malcolm's adolescence and early adulthood when music seemed to shape much of his world. While there was much in the streets of Roxbury and later Harlem* that helped to influence this part of his life, nothing seemed to give him more satisfaction than listening to and being around some of the greatest music and black artists of the twentieth century. This period of Malcolm's life coincided with the big band era of the late 1930s and 1940s when entertainers like Duke Ellington,* Lionel Hampton,* Billy Holiday,* Count Basie,* and Dinah Washington* were virtually household names. These musicians were among Malcolm's favorites. He knew some of the numerous black celebrities* on a personal basis, but he also admired and listened to music of great white artists like Tommy Dorsey and Benny Goodman. Malcolm "Shorty" Jarvis,* Malcolm X's closest friend at the time, said that he and Malcolm could be found anywhere there was good live music being played, though Malcolm claimed that Shorty, who was interested in becoming a band leader himself, seldom went to the ballrooms to hear these musicians. Artists like

Hampton and Holiday knew Malcolm's favorite songs and readily played them, often on request. These people, Malcolm said, played the kind of music that made him want to dance, a kind of music that "just wound me up."

Malcolm lamented that he never learned how to play some kind of musical instrument himself. Typical of most contemporary youths, he nevertheless got considerable fulfillment from listening to the music of others. And though he left no personal musical legacy for future generations to marvel over, his strength of character, intelligence, anger, and display of black manhood* and black pride* has certainly influenced the evolution and development of Rap music* and its performers, one of the contemporary world's most popular music genres.

SELECTED BIBLIOGRAPHY

CBS News, 1992; Malcolm X with Haley, 1965.

Robert L. Jenkins

MALCOLM'S PHOTOGRAPHIC WORLD. During the early 1960s, perhaps with the exception of Martin Luther King, Jr.,* no black American was in the national media spotlight more than Malcolm X. Not only was he the source of considerable attention in the print press; he was also constantly photographed. Professional and amateur photographers captured him during some of his angriest moments, "exhorting" before large and attentive street crowds, in contemplative solitude, in his family setting, and during the most anguished period of his life just prior to his murder, the troubled times with his mentor, Elijah Muhammad.* The interest that Malcolm generated from behind the camera prompted him to contract his own personal photographer, Robert Haggins,* whose work Malcolm greatly respected and whose close-working relationship with him blossomed into a trusting friendship. Malcolm gave most of his photographic equipment to Haggins prior to his murder.

Although one former associate said that Malcolm was not particularly good at it, Malcolm was himself an amateur photographer and could often be seen with a camera in his possession. This was especially true when he made trips abroad, where an apparent obsession with photography exceeded typical tourist impulses. His photographic interest included both still and moving pictures. It was the moving pictures that he took abroad that occasionally embellished his Muslim Mosque, Inc.,* and Organization of Afro-American Unity* lectures in the Audubon Ballroom* about the Hajj* and Africa. He was proudest of his own work taken in Egypt* in 1964, where he filmed activities of the heads of states of the Republic of Ghana* and Ethiopia and the massive military might on parade amassed by President Gamal Abdel Nasser,* whom he regarded as a personal friend. Malcolm believed that showing to his black followers what Nasser had achieved not only could serve informational purposes about the international world but also could work to help them understand why the Egyptian leader could boldly seek and maintain a nationalistic course for his country free of American domination.

Images that Malcolm photographed do not readily appear in printed sources to validate his interest in personal photography. News entities such as UPI/ Bettmann, AP/Wide World, *Look* and *Life* magazines, and a host of individual professional photographers like Gordon Parks,* Eve Arnold, John Launois, and Robert Haggins, however, have done much to preserve the visual images of Malcolm the man and helped in many ways to make him seem bigger in death than he was in life.

SELECTED BIBLIOGRAPHY

T. Davis (Chapnick, ed.), 1993; Gallen, ed., 1992; Goldman, 1979; Malcolm X (Clark, ed.), 1992.

Robert L. Jenkins

MALCOLM'S SPLIT WITH THE NATION OF ISLAM. Malcolm X and Elijah Muhammad* were very close, so close that Malcolm was often referred to as Muhammad's son and heir apparent. However, their relationship would become strained. There are many reasons given for the split between Malcolm X and the Nation of Islam (NOI).* The official explanation given by Elijah Muhammad and his spokesmen was that Malcolm had disobeyed directives regarding the assassination of President John F. Kennedy.* Addressing a rally in New York nine days after the assassination, Malcolm was asked to comment on the death of the president. Malcolm stated, within the context of commenting on the deaths of leaders in Vietnam* and black leaders in the United States and Africa, that Kennedy's death was an instance of "chickens coming home to roost."* The media indicated that Malcolm had dismissed the significance of the president's assassination with his unkind comment. More significant, his statement came in direct conflict with a directive from Chicago,* that NOI ministers were not to comment on the tragedy.

Malcolm went to Chicago the day after the speech for his monthly visit with Elijah Muhammad. At this meeting, Muhammad reminded Malcolm that all ministers were under strict orders not to comment on the assassination of President Kennedy. After telling Malcolm that his comment was ill-timed, Muhammad "silenced" him for ninety days as punishment for his disobedience. This meant that Malcolm could not make any public statements on any subject during this period. To Malcolm X, this was the worst possible disciplinary measure that he could suffer. However, he willingly accepted the punishment.

The ninety days' suspension set in motion the termination of the association between Malcolm X, Elijah Muhammad, and the NOI. However, the actual split began earlier in 1963 with Malcolm's suspicion that Elijah Muhammad had not adhered to the NOI's strict sexual code that he preached to his followers. Upon confronting Muhammad over the allegations of fathering children with several of his young secretaries, and Muhammad not denying the fact, Malcolm became more disillusioned with Muhammad and lost respect for both his mentor and the movement. Further, he was disenchanted with the political conservatism of Muhammad and his persistent refusal to allow the NOI to became involved with the civil rights movement.*

Malcolm X had come to identify more and more with the black masses. He felt that the NOI would be a tremendous force in the overall struggle, if the organization would engage in less talk and more action. He felt that Muhammad needed to, at the very least, relax the nonengagement policy. On the one hand, the image of the NOI in the public arena was one in which the Muslims* talked tough but did not actually do anything. On the other hand, the leaders of the civil rights movement were actively involved in initiating and bringing about change for the masses of black people.

The ninety-day period of silence did not actually end Malcolm's suspension; Elijah Muhammad did not make contact with Malcolm to lift it. Malcolm X felt that his suspension was actually an effort to curb his influence as his ideas and political philosophy began to diverge from Muhammad's. According to Malcolm and Wallace Muhammad,* Elijah's son, who also split from the NOI, the Chicago officials were jealous of Malcolm's popularity. Because he was so close to Muhammad, these individuals began to plant seeds of doubt and suspicion in Muhammad's mind about Malcolm. One Chicago official, Henry X, stated that Muhammad was concerned about Malcolm abandoning religion for what he called "political sociology." Malcolm's emphasis on black nationalism* was drawing the NOI into conflict with the white power structure and into both national and international politics. This went against the official NOI policy of nonengagement.

On March 8, 1964, after a number of attempts to contact Muhammad for reinstatement, Malcolm X announced that he was leaving the NOI and would start a new movement. He would remain a Muslim, but he would engage in a struggle for many of the objectives from which the NOI had abstained. He indicated that internal differences within the NOI had forced him out and that he did not leave on his own free will. He also stated that since he was no longer tied to the NOI, he was going to take advantage of having more independence and engagement in political action.

His method for doing this was through the establishment of new organizations called the Muslim Mosque, Inc.* and a more politically oriented organization called the Organization of Afro-American Unity.*

SELECTED BIBLIOGRAPHY

Brisbane, 1970; Cone, 1991; Malcolm X with Haley, 1965; Malcolm X (Breitmen, ed.), 1965; J. White, 1985.

Mamie Locke

MALCOLM X AND THE EMERGENCE OF RAP. When examining the black urban social movements, Malcolm X's leadership represented the catalyst for community organizing in the 1950s and 1960s exploring the possibility of social change through community empowerment. Malcolm X's ideology and public statements influenced a later generation of black artists in the genre of rap music seeking an outlet for creative expression in an African American community context. Malcolm X as an advocate for the study of black history* and culture laid a foundation of uncompromising black cultural expression for black people to follow. Through his speeches and autobiography, Malcolm X became a significant influence on the Black Arts movement of the late 1960s with regard to black pride,* black manhood,* white racism, and issues of social inequality.

Celebrating a new outlet for artistic expression, young African American males in New York City and other black urban communities developed rap music during the economic blight of the 1970s. The legacy of rap music has roots in the oral tradition found in various precolonial African societies and the vocal artistry found in the modern music of jazz and rhythm and blues artists who used their vocal skills to communicate the various moods that encompass the black experience. The early pioneers of rap music (for example, D. J. Kool Herc and D. J. Grandmaster Flash and Afrika Bambaataa) as children of the 1960s in New York City were influenced musically and culturally by the Black Arts movement and the cultural nationalist movements. During this same period Black soul (James Brown, Otis Redding, and Marvin Gaye) represented a new form of modern musical expression centered in the African American experience. Thus, with the genesis of rap music in the mid-1970s in New York City, one finds urban-based African American males offering social criticism and insight into the growing problems of black communities in the United States. With the more politically conscious rap music a search for symbols of black manhood and success occurred, and these symbols eventually embodied themselves in living figures such as Louis Farrakhan* and Jesse Jackson and in historical figures such as Malcolm X.

Malcolm X's struggle in urban America in the 1940s, his later success, and then his tragic death represent both the problems and possibilities of the black male experience in American cities. Malcolm's position on cultural identification and pride was embraced during a time of economic crisis and black artistic decline in many inner cities during the late 1970s and 1980s and served to influence a new generation of black youth. Some researchers discuss African American rap artists' sampling of excerpts from Malcolm X's speeches and utilization of themes he popularized, such as the life of the "Hustler," cultural identification and linkage to Africa, issues of crime and violence in black ghettos, and the exploration of Islamic faith. These themes were strongly identified with Malcolm X and effectively communicated in his charismatic and rhetorical style. Malcolm X was well known for his use of analogies and metaphors in public speeches, and in some instances he drew comparisons with historical events such as the lynching of black men to the current psychological state of black suffering, noting that both represented the negative effects of racial prejudice.

Malcolm X as a cultural advocate taught black rap artists to identify with their African cultural heritage, to be politically empowered through identification with cultural nationalism, and ultimately to communicate with black people and society about the black experience in America. These artists, such as Grandmaster Flash and the Furious Five, Public Enemy, KRS-One, Poor Righteous Teachers, and X-Clan, placed African American life and culture at the center of their artistic expression. They aligned themselves to the "committed school" of artistic expression seeking to be functional, by representing the black masses, committed to the process of black liberation from social oppression. Malcolm X's support of black people leaves a legacy that manifested itself in black cultural pride.

SELECTED BIBLIOGRAPHY

Branham, 1995; Goldman, 1979; Neal, 1989; Sales, 1994.

Andrew P. Smallwood

MALCOLM X AND HUMOR. As a black leader, Malcolm X established a reputation as a serious analyst and critic of America's treatment of its black minority population. Few people were able to match his knowledge, understanding, wit, and logical conclusions about the country's racial order. He frequently used his own troubled background as an example to show the effects of a lack of knowledge, anger, and disillusionment and could condemn in the most scathing rhetoric, effectively moving between the employment of parables, fables, and invective to impart wisdom. Hence, in his frequent lectures, debates, and encounters with the media he revealed a side of himself that was often intimidating. But there was another side to Malcolm that showed that he was actually approachable, fun loving, and especially humorous. He could and often did show this "human side" of himself.

Malcolm loved to laugh and was proud of the ties that he established with comedians like Redd Foxx* and Dick Gregory.* Gregory claimed that whenever Malcolm came to one of his shows in New York, he simply "laughed all over" from his routine. More telling, however, was Malcolm's use of humor in his own commentary. A master at moving a crowd or simply making one think, he often interspersed humor (normally wry humor) in his presentations to stress a point or to make some idea more logical to his audiences. Hence, he could amuse his audiences with funny caricatures of black leaders, depicting them as a "Rev. Dr. Chickenwing" or a "Whitey Young," with comparisons of the house Negro* and the field Negro* or condemnation of whites as "nothing but an old pale thing." Predictably his listeners responded with laughter and/or deeper contemplation.

Malcolm had a magnetic smile and an affable personality that made it difficult for anyone who knew him well to truly dislike him. In many ways his sense of humor embellished these traits. Only after he was consumed by the stress from his ordeal with Elijah Muhammad* and the Nation of Islam* did he become more jaded, publically and privately, and understandably seemed to lose this part of his demeanor.

SELECTED BIBLIOGRAPHY

Angelou, 1986; CBS News, 1992; Gregory with McGraw, 1976; Malcolm X with Haley, 1965.

Robert L. Jenkins

MALCOLM X AND SEX. During his youth, especially when he lived in Boston, Malcolm X acquired a reputation as a "ladies' man." Already displaying the magnetic personality and charisma that would endear him to many followers when he became a Muslim* minister, Malcolm enjoyed an immense popularity among many of the young women who frequented the night spots that he patronized. Looking older than his age, according to one of his relatives, even much older women from his Roxbury* neighborhood seduced him. The fact that he was tall, thin, strikingly handsome, a good dresser, and an even better dancer enhanced his allurement, characteristics that made many of his male friends envious of the attraction that women had to him. Except for a few subtle passages in his autobiography, however, Malcolm made very little of the personal successes that he experienced sexually with women. Any further opportunity to associate with women sexually ended for him for the next six years once he was imprisoned in 1946.

A morally upstanding man after his Islamic conversion,* from the time of his parole in 1952 to his marriage to Betty Sanders Shabazz* in 1958, Malcolm refrained from any sexual activity. Female members of the Harlem* temple where he ministered had, of course, found him attractive and often raved over the prospects of his "availability." But since his acceptance of Islam,* Malcolm had frowned on sexual activity outside of marriage and taught his followers about the evils of violating Islamic tenets regarding adultery and fornication. Indeed, Malcolm taught so strongly against this form of moral weakness that he claimed many thought he was "anti-woman." His message was in many ways the message that he and others heard often from Elijah Muhammad* himself. Moreover, perhaps Malcolm's abstinence was influenced by his experience with many of the women with whom he associated before his imprisonment; he certainly had a general mistrust of their motives that can be traced to that period.

Regardless, until he wedded Betty, he chose to focus all of his energies unswervingly on furthering the goals and program of the Nation of Islam (NOI).* In the process, with his constant worldwide travels and opportunities to meet and socialize with numerous women, the temptations must have been great. Yet his resolve remained unshakable. "We gain strength from the temptations that we resist," he once said. Hence, Malcolm's commitment to celibacy and later fidelity in his marriage were calculated decisions, borne of several factors that collectively influenced his value system about sex.

By the time Malcolm was writing his life's story in 1964 and 1965, he was still reeling from the sex revelations and paternity problems of Elijah Muhammad, revelations that shook Malcolm's faith in Muhammad as a righteous man and that essentially ended his relationship with his mentor and the NOI. Malcolm paid the ultimate price for his role in helping to disclose the Messenger's hypocrisy about adultery, but given how he had formulated his own value system about sex, he could not have remained true to his beliefs and ideals by disregarding his mentor's sexual peccadilloes and moral weakness.

SELECTED BIBLIOGRAPHY

Angelou, 1986; CBS News, 1992; Collins with Bailey, 1998; Malcolm X with Haley, 1965; B. Perry, 1991; Wood, ed., 1992.

Robert L. Jenkins

MALCOLM X COLLEGE. Influenced by a surging national political and cultural movement to empower black people, Malcolm X's popularity grew enormously in the years after his death. In some urban areas where awareness of the slain icon once seldom extended beyond his militant antiwhite rhetoric, many "mainstream" black leaders increasingly endorsed his philosophy of self-help and racial pride. In Chicago,* location of the Nation of Islam* headquarters, many blacks certainly rejected the sect's harsh view of Malcolm, embracing him instead as a bona fide freedom fighter. Such views in Chicago coalesced with student protests that closed several city colleges over inadequately addressed civil rights* issues to push for a campus named in Malcolm's honor. Meeting in 1969 with state, local, and college officials, a contingent of blacks from student, political, and community groups succeeded in renaming Herzl Junior College (formerly Crane Jr. College), one of the city's oldest colleges, Malcolm X Shabazz Community College. In 1971 Chicago officially established a new campus with imposing buildings.

From the outset, the two-year college did much to remind students and community supporters about the man for which it was named. Although not technically a "black college," leaders sought to make it a real community-oriented institution but with clear ties to the black nationalist tradition of Malcolm X and his predecessors. Opening ceremonies of the new campus featured singer Harry Belafonte leading "Lift Every Voice and Sing," the so-called Negro national anthem, and raising the red, black, and green flag, symbolic of the cause of black liberation first flown by Marcus Garvey's* Universal Negro Improvement Association.* Academic programs catered to traditional students seeking a closer identity with Malcolm's black nationalist views. Extensive core courses in a Black Studies* curriculum highlighted the program designed to prepare students to become a force in liberation causes. Also included were special

services for the downtrodden: high school dropouts, drug addicts, and prison*
parolees—those whom Malcolm often championed.

During its annual Black Awareness Month celebrations, special attention is
still focused on the life and work of Malcolm X. A permanent display exists in
the school library containing numerous items, including books and articles, relating to Malcolm's life. And before her death, Malcolm's wife and children
each spoke during campus ceremonies. Perhaps the most poignant physical reminder of Malcolm's life and his linkage to the college, however, is the automobile that the black leader drove prior to his assassination that sits on
permanent display at the school's entrance.

SELECTED BIBLIOGRAPHY

Bush, 1999; Chicago Community College Website; Malcolm X College, 1997; Pinkney,
1976; Van Deburg, 1992.

Robert L. Jenkins

MALCOLM X FOUNDATION. After Malcolm X's death in February 1965,
African Americans around the country used various means to commemorate one
of the most dynamic and charismatic leaders of the twentieth century. In Los
Angeles, his cousin Hakim Jamal* attempted to establish the Malcolm X Foundation as a means to remember Malcolm through black history,* culture, and
other areas, emphasizing Malcolm's teaching as a legacy for blacks. But Jamal
was killed in a hail of bullets in 1973 by members of the Nation of Islam,* and
the Foundation under his auspices never really got off the ground.

In Omaha, Nebraska,* Rowena Moore was successful in establishing the Malcolm X Foundation, which had as its primary goals the acquisition of the home-
site where Malcolm lived as a child with his family and the establishment of a
Visitors Center and historical monument dedicated to his memory. After Moore
died in the early 1990s, a legal dispute developed between her estate and the
Foundation over the property title. It was resolved and the Foundation was given
the title to the land. In order to fund the Visitors Center, the Foundation had to
raise $1.5 million. The Malcolm X Foundation and the property, which no
longer contains a house, is listed on the National Historical Register. The Foundation has a Board of Trustees, and Johnny Rogers, former football player with
the University of Nebraska, is the board's chief executive officer.

The Foundation has an annual celebration around the birthday of Malcolm X
with numerous activities and events, including speakers. Maulana Karenga,*
Gwendolyn Brooks, Sonia Sanchez,* and Dick Gregory* have been some of the
invited speakers. Over the last five years, Malcolm's siblings have participated
in a panel discussion around the life of Malcolm X. Malcolm X Park, named
after Malcolm, has also been the host of various events in the celebration of the
life and times of the black leader.

SELECTED BIBLIOGRAPHY

Evanzz, 1999; Jamal, 1971; Sales, 1994; Tryman interview with Council, July 25, 2000.
                                                            Mfanya Donald Tryman

MALCOLM X LIBERATION UNIVERSITY. In the years after his death, Malcolm X's influence reached into many areas of Black America. Simply evoking his name for many meant an adherence to his views and a conscious statement that what he taught was important enough for the world not to forget. Newborn children were named after him, documentaries were filmed that highlighted his life and beliefs, schools were named in his honor, and institutions and organizations emerged that capitalized on his memory and memorialized his philosophy by also adopting one version or another of his name and ideas. One such institution was the Malcolm X Liberation University. The school was founded in 1969 in Durham, North Carolina, once the location of one of America's major black economic meccas, after students disagreed with Duke administrators over issues related to a proposed Black Studies* Department. A year later, however, it moved to Greensboro as a separate and independent entity, beginning classes "in an abandoned warehouse" with fifty-nine students. A branch of the college, however, remained in Durham. Howard L. Fuller, a popular figure among black nationalists, was one of the university's founders and served as its director. The college recruited its clientele from disaffected black students looking for an alternative form of university education.

Malcolm, whose formal education was greatly limited, valued education and was a constant source of encouragement to students, regardless of the level of their pursuit. Malcolm X Liberation University fell within the parameters of what Malcolm often taught black people about doing for themselves before seeking help from whites. Foremost with Malcolm was his espousal of a strident economic, social, and political consciousness that largely defined him, and it was the university's militancy, its commitment to black nationalism,* and its focus on black social consciousness that similarly constituted its uniqueness. The college geared its program to educate students who would address black community needs and to prepare them for struggles in the cause of black liberation. With courses in Swahili, African Civilization, Colonialism, Neo-Colonialism, Slavery, and the Independent African World, and curricula that included majors in land development, ideological systems, engineering, communications, biomedicine, and teacher education, the university offered students a challenging learning environment on the college campus. There were also study opportunities abroad because every student was required to spend a part of their university enrollment matriculating in Africa. Malcolm learned much from his visits to the African continent; hence students were also expected to learn from their matriculation there. Graduates did not receive degrees but were expected to put their learning and experiences to work, helping to elevate the masses in African or African American communities and inspiring their struggle for peace, justice, and equality.

Like a number of other black nationalist organizations that appeared in the late 1960s and early 1970s, Malcolm X University sought to respond to Malcolm's message by making black education relevant to community needs and the black freedom struggle. These features paralleled Malcolm's views and made the university appealing to many among the black disenchanted. Despite the great optimism about the future of the university (Malcolm's widow Betty Shabazz* highlighted the school's opening ceremonies and remained a strong supporter), Malcolm X University fell victim to the same problem that hurt numerous other black colleges during the last quarter of the twentieth century: a lack of funding. By 1976 it no longer functioned.

SELECTED BIBLIOGRAPHY

Ballard, 1973; Bush, 1999; Hopson, 1970; *New York Times*, October 28, 1969; Pinkney, 1976.

Robert L. Jenkins

MALCOLM X SOCIETY. In the wake of the death of Malcolm X, Milton Henry (Brother Gaidi Obadele)* and Richard Henry (Brother Imari Obadele),* siblings who had been close to Malcolm, became discontent with the objectives of civil rights organizations* in Detroit, Michigan,* considering them too reform oriented and moderate. Alternatively, they decided to help found an organization, the Malcolm X Society, that was more congruent with their ideological orientations. Milton and Richard did not feel that racial integration* was a realistic goal worth pursuing for blacks and noted that blacks in Detroit had not been very successful in their fight against police brutality.* The Malcolm X Society emphasized self-defense* and self-determination and felt that the black struggle in the United States had to be internationalized with that of the Third World liberation movement. The Society demanded that land in the South* be turned over to African Americans independently in order for blacks to start their own government. Beginning in earnest in late 1967, Imari and Gaidi put much more time in the Society to achieve its goals. It was at this time that the brothers, like Malcolm had earlier, dropped their "slave" names and adopted names related to their African ancestry. Brother Imari quit his U.S. Army civilian job and wrote *War in America: The Malcolm X Doctrine*, which demanded five southern states with the heaviest black populations for a nation–state and as part of a reparations* package for hundreds of years of slavery and oppression. Brother Gaidi maintained his law practice. The Malcolm X Society served as the forerunner to the Republic of New Africa (RNA),* established in 1968, with Robert F. Williams* as the provisional president. The RNA would have some of the same goals as the old Malcolm X Society but a short existence.

SELECTED BIBLIOGRAPHY

Hall, 1978; Van Deburg, 1992.

Mfanya Donald Tryman

***MALCOLM X*: THE MOVIE.** In the years after his death, many of those who were close to Malcolm X and who understood and appreciated what he sought to achieve for black people strove to perpetuate the memory of his life and work. Through scholarly studies, popular literature, and poetry, through special programs and ceremonies, and through documentaries, a plethora of Malcolm materials flooded the nation, analyzing the life of one of America's bravest and most committed but misunderstood black leaders. As Malcolm's popularity grew widely in death, Hollywood almost naturally acquired a commercial interest in him. Getting Malcolm to the big screen, however, was both a long, arduous, and controversial process. Soon after his death, Malcolm followers and supporters had expressed an interest in the film genre to tell the story of his life, but competing interests and different views about how the story should be told ultimately affected the effort. Novelist, civil rights* activist, and close associate of Malcolm X James Baldwin* contracted with Columbia Pictures in 1968 to write a screenplay on Malcolm's life, based largely on Malcolm's autobiography. A disagreement with the studio over starring roles, and Baldwin's refusal to alter the script for a more sanitized version of Malcolm's life, however, soon jettisoned the project. Subsequently, Baldwin published the highly criticized screenplay in 1973 over the title *One Day, When I Was Lost.* Other screenwriters, including David Bradley and Charles Fuller, were hired and fired for reasons similar to Baldwin's departure from the cinema project.

Not until noted veteran black filmwriter, actor, producer, and director Spike Lee,* a great admirer of Malcolm X, acquired the rights to film and direct the movie for Warner Brothers did longtime supporters of the popular project become optimistic about its completion. Still, the effort generated considerable controversy; black militants were concerned about the movie falsely depicting Malcolm's life, perhaps softened in order to assuage black and white middle-class sensibilities, while the studio and Lee battled over production costs. Only with Lee's shrewd maneuvering of the studio, and the timely investment of a number of prominent and wealthy black personalities, was the movie finished.

Closely paralleling the autobiography, *Malcolm X* was released in 1992 in the midst of one of the greatest advertising and media blitzes in cinema history. Costing more than $34 million, the movie was a true epic, three hours and twenty-one minutes in duration and starring some of Hollywood's most talented and popular actors, including Denzel Washington, Angela Basset, and Al Freeman. Generally well received by the movie critics, the film's dramatic moments—from Malcolm's hair conking episode, to his prison* experience, to his acrid white devils* rhetoric, to his Mecca* transformation and death—were brilliantly performed by its bevy of stars. Despite criticisms from both those who regarded Malcolm as a hero and those who never accepted his politics, the movie remained largely true to Malcolm's life, capturing his politics and consciousness as embodied in his own words, "by any means necessary."

Malcolm X was a source of great pride to that part of Black America who had come to appreciate Malcolm and an eye-opening experience for those who knew little about him. Just as significantly, it proved to be one of the most successful films of the 1990s. It generated millions of dollars in profits at the box office and set off a marketing bonanza with a diversity of "X"-labeled products that enhanced his cultural hero status and, ironically, made him a popular figure among many white youth.

SELECTED BIBLIOGRAPHY

Baldwin, 1973; Guerrero, 1993; Lee with Wiley, 1992; Leeming, 1994; Standley and Pratt, eds., 1989.

Robert L. Jenkins

MARCH ON WASHINGTON. On August 28, 1963, more than 200,000 people participated in the March on Washington for Jobs and Freedom. The march was a result of a long movement organized by civil rights* activist Asa Philip Randolph.* In 1941 Randolph publicly announced that he would lead African Americans in a march on the nation's capital to protest the government's exclusionary employment policies in the defense industry and the policy of racial segregation in the armed forces. Only six days before the march was to take place, President Franklin D. Roosevelt issued Executive Order 8802, barring discrimination in defense work and creating the Fair Employment Practice Committee to oversee the policy. Consequently, Randolph canceled the march. Twenty-two years later, Randolph reinstituted his plans with the help of several prominent civil rights leaders, including Martin Luther King, Jr.,* John Lewis,* James Farmer,* Whitney Young, Jr.,* Roy Wilkins,* and Bayard Rustin.*

Malcolm was one of the few leaders to publicly criticize the march that he labeled "The Farce on Washington." Though not invited, Malcolm attended the historic occasion to be a thorn in the side of the American government and to be the conscience of the civil rights leadership. The night before the march, he participated in a news conference outside of the hotel where the demonstrators were meeting. He told reporters that night that although he did not agree with the march, he was there to support black people. Malcolm denounced the leadership of the march, who he argued were coopted by Euro-American philanthropists and the Kennedy administration, who, he said, endorsed the march in order to control it. Malcolm explained in his *Autobiography* that the "angry black man march" had been taken over by integrationists, whites, and the middle- to upper-income African Americans who had previously deplored the concept of a march.

In subsequent speeches, Malcolm continued to condemn the march. In his speech "Message to the Grassroots," Malcolm called the march a "circus and a picnic" and attacked the march's leadership for the inclusion of Euro-American leaders. Malcolm was referring to Ministers Matthew Ahmann and Eugene Carson Blake, Rabbi Joachim Prinz, and labor leader Walter P. Reuther, who were all part of the organizing committee assembled by Randolph and other civil rights leaders. Malcolm believed that by including Euro-Americans in the leadership, the march lost its militancy and was ineffective in changing the prejudiced views of white politicians.

Just as Malcolm criticized civil rights leaders, they in turn criticized him for his failure to register any concrete political gains. It would have been difficult for Malcolm to actually participate in any march, since Elijah Muhammad* had strict policies for his members regarding political involvement. There is evidence, however, to suggest that Malcolm pressed Elijah Muhammad for permission to engage in demonstrations.

Malcolm's presence at the march created a needed counterbalance. In retrospect, many scholars and former civil rights leaders believe that the nonviolent segment of the civil rights movement* was more widely accepted by the government and whites in general because they feared leaders such as Malcolm.

SELECTED BIBLIOGRAPHY

Goldman, 1979; Hampton and Fayer with Flynn, eds., 1990; Malcolm X (Breitman, ed.), 1965; Malcolm X with Haley, 1965; B. Perry, 1991; Pfeffer, 1990; Strickland (Lowery and Marszalek, eds.), 1992.

Nancy J. Dawson

MARKS, CHARLES. Charles Marks was the presiding judge in the trial of the three defendants, Thomas 15X Johnson,* Talmadge Hayer,* and Norman 3X Butler,* who were accused of murdering Malcolm X. The trial began on January 12, 1966, in a New York City courtroom. Marks consistently overruled objections from the six lawyers for the defendants during the trial and sustained objections for the prosecution. In many instances, Marks did this in a perfunctory and arbitrary manner, not pausing to hear the lawyers for the defense explain their reason or reasons for their objection and cutting them off before they could complete their rationale for the objection. This apparent pattern led to a number of confrontations between Judge Marks and Peter Sabbatino,* the most vocal of the lawyers for the defense. In addition, Marks on more than one occasion did not allow the defense the opportunity to examine documents before the items were put into evidence by the prosecution.

Perhaps the most dramatic moment in the trial occurred as Betty Shabazz,* the wife of Malcolm X, was leaving the witness stand, where she had just completed empathic but calm testimony. As she passed the defense table, however, she began to shout that the defendants had murdered her husband and moved toward the defendants with her fists balled. She was restrained by court personnel, and as she was led out of the courtroom, she continued to yell that they had murdered her husband. The defense lawyers immediately asked Judge Marks for a mistrial, which he again overruled. Marks simply instructed the jury to disregard the emotional outburst and noted that Malcolm's widow did not physically point a finger at anyone.

The jury came in with a verdict of guilty of first-degree murder for the three defendants. On April 14, 1966, Marks sentenced each of the three defendants

Like many of the 1960s black leaders, Thurgood Marshall, the first African American to sit on the U.S. Supreme Court, found little about Malcolm X and his views that was consistent with traditional civil rights goals. Library of Congress.

to terms of life imprisonment. The case was appealed by the defense, based upon a controversial ruling by Judge Marks that allowed a key witness to testify privately because of a fear for his life. On April 16, 1969, the state Supreme Court of New York upheld Marks's controversial ruling.

SELECTED BIBLIOGRAPHY

Breitman, Porter, and Smith (Miah, ed.), 1976; Friedly, 1992; Goldman, 1979.

Mfanya Donald Tryman

MARSHALL, THURGOOD. Malcolm X had few friends in the civil right movement.* He was sharply critical of, and made no effort to cultivate friends within, the movement. Conversely, there were some in the civil rights movement who criticized if not Malcolm specifically, then certainly the Nation of Islam (NOI).*

Thurgood Marshall, the former chief National Association for the Advancement of Colored People* attorney, lead counsel in the *Brown v. Board of Education, Topeka, Kansas** case, and the first African American Supreme Court justice, was an early and outspoken critic of the NOI. He seemed convinced that Elijah Muhammad* was a charlatan, if not a complete fraud. In fact, Marshall often referred to the Muslims* as a group of former penitentiary thugs and perhaps financed by a militant Arab organization. Such an indictment, according to Alex Haley* who helped Malcolm write his autobiography, angered Malcolm deeply, and he often "spat fire" in response to it.

With respect to Malcolm specifically, Marshall, prior to his death, is reported to have concluded that he did little beyond talk. Malcolm was never quoted as having made a personal attack or negative comment about Justice Marshall. Nevertheless, neither clearly held the other in high esteem. As a lifelong advocate of racial integration,* Marshall had neither appreciation nor tolerance for the views of Malcolm and the NOI, particularly those that emphasized racial separation* and balkanization. Marshall's intolerance may even have been sufficient to cause him to regard the Muslims as subversive. For his part, Malcolm viewed Marshall, as he did essentially all black civil rights* leaders, as an "Uncle Tom."* Furthermore, Marshall and other civil rights leaders, in Malcolm's estimation, were proposing the very thing that would contribute to the demise of blacks—racial integration. The ideological postures Malcolm and Marshall assumed served to divide them. Each so thoroughly internalized their stance that neither could fully appreciate the merits of the other's position. And yet ironically enough, both fought for the same noble cause, black liberation, albeit under different ideological battle flags.

SELECTED BIBLIOGRAPHY

R. Franklin, 1990; Gallen, ed., 1992; Kly, 1986; Malcolm X with Haley, 1965; Wolfenstein, 1981; Wood, ed., 1992.

Dernoral Davis

MASON, MICHIGAN. Located approximately twelve miles south of Lansing, Michigan,* the predominantly white community of Mason made a lasting impression on a young Malcolm. At age thirteen, in August 1939, faced with the disintegration of his family and failure in school, a county social worker recommended that Malcolm be placed in a detention home in Mason. The home, run by a white couple, the Swerlins,* was typically regarded as the initial stage of assignment to a reform school. The home's staff liked Malcolm, but the adjustment was difficult for him to make. In the year he spent in Mason, Malcolm made many friends, and he was popular among the town's prominent young white citizens. His white teachers discouraged him, reminding him to stay in his place, and he was frequently called "nigger" by classmates. Despite Mason's acceptance of him, however, Malcolm still faced racial barriers. Outwardly he accepted this, but after a visit with his half sister Ella Collins,* in

Boston, where he observed a thriving and proud black community, he began to feel restless and unsettled around Mason's whites. At the end of his eighth-grade school year, he moved to Boston to live with Ella. In later years Malcolm saw this move as a significant one in his life. Even in Mason, where he had been accepted by his white classmates, Malcolm later realized that despite his intelligence and likeable personality, he was perceived as different because of his skin color. This was dramatically illustrated to him by one of his teachers who told him that "a nigger" could not be a lawyer, a profession that Malcolm aspired to pursue.

SELECTED BIBLIOGRAPHY

Goldman, 1979; Malcolm X with Haley, 1965; B. Perry, 1991; Strickland (Greene, ed.), 1994; Wood, ed., 1992.

Betsy Sakariassen Nash

MASON JUNIOR HIGH SCHOOL. Malcolm (née Malcolm Little) entered Mason Junior High School in Mason, Michigan,* during his eighth-grade year while residing in a detention home operated by a white couple. The only black student, Malcolm was popular with his classmates. He ranked third in his class, played basketball, and was elected class president. While attending Mason Junior High, Malcolm endured racial jokes and slurs, all the while convincing himself that his teachers and classmates meant him no harm. At dances and school affairs, he had to observe white society's taboos regarding his interactions with white female classmates. After visiting his half sister Ella Collins* in Boston during the summer of 1940, where he was exposed to a vibrant, proud, and successful black society, Malcolm returned to Mason Junior High School feeling restless and uneasy. He realized that he had been adopting white attitudes that facilitated his success in school, yet compromised his dignity as a human being. Malcolm, as a result of this revelation, and a negative comment from one of his white teachers, Mr. Ostrowski,* quit school at the end of his eighth-grade year and moved to Boston to live with Ella.

SELECTED BIBLIOGRAPHY

Goldman, 1979; Logan and Winston, eds., 1982; Malcolm X with Haley, 1965; B. Perry, 1991; Strickland (Greene, ed.), 1994; Wood, ed., 1992.

Betsy Sakariassen Nash

MAU MAU. Although there has not been agreement concerning its precise meaning, the term "Mau Mau" has often been used to describe the predominantly Kikuyu-led violent opposition in the early 1950s to Britain's colonial exploitation of the central region of Kenya in East Africa. The origin of the Mau Mau movement could be traced to the 1890s when the British violently incorporated Kikuyuland into their colonial empire. The movement was reinforced among the Kikuyu peasants, largely because their land had not only been taken and apportioned among British settlers but because they were also economically pressured or forced to work on British farms. Against this background, the Kikuyu decided to attack their colonial exploiters in 1953.

While the Kikuyu revolt was brutally crushed and the fact that some 13,000 Kenyan Africans were killed by the British by 1956, one side effect of the revolt was that it eventually forced the British to grant independence to Kenya on December 12, 1963. On occasion, Malcolm would refer to the Mau Mau uprising. Malcolm X would describe the Mau Mau fighters as great liberators, and he would add that such action was needed in America to liberate blacks from what he termed domestic imperialism. Malcolm would frequently cite the Mau Mau revolution in speeches to audiences, as he did once in a Harlem* church when he shared a platform with Fannie Lou Hamer,* as an example of the bloody revolution black Americans would have to launch to resist southern white oppression and violence. Malcolm's glorification of the Mau Mau movement was in line with his view that violence was sometimes necessary to overcome oppression.

SELECTED BIBLIOGRAPHY

Barnett and Njama, 1966; Beyan, 1988; Carson (Gallen, ed.), 1991; Goldman, 1979; Nottington, 1970.

Amos J. Beyan

MAYFIELD, JULIAN. An author, actor, and progressive African American expatriate who lived in the Republic of Ghana,* West Africa, Mayfield, who had met Malcolm in the early 1960s at the home of actor Ossie Davis,* began correspondence with Malcolm during the winter of 1964. In his letters to Malcolm, Mayfield, the leader of the small African American community in Accra, Ghana, spoke of organizing institutional links between native Africans, African Americans, and the Organization of African Unity (OAU).* Mayfield's letters had a profound influence on Malcolm's Pan-Africanist views, and soon this unifying project evolved into the Organization of Afro-American Unity (OAAU),* an African American version of the OAU.

Although Mayfield influenced and stimulated the mind of Malcolm X, he had a negative impact on the Muslim* leader as well. Due to his expatriate status and residence in Ghana, the Federal Bureau of Investigation (FBI)* more closely scrutinized Malcolm's activities. This governmental scrutiny intensified after Malcolm visited Mayfield in Ghana in the fall of 1964 to discuss the formation of the OAAU.

During Malcolm's visit, Mayfield, who worked as a press official in the Kwame Nkrumah* administration, introduced Malcolm to the expatriate colony who feted him enthusiastically. Malcolm also had a chance to meet and talk with the most important international dignitaries in Ghana at the time, including foreign ambassadors and many of the president's cabinet officers. Malcolm despaired about going home, not only because he enjoyed Africa so much but also because he was becoming increasingly aware of the fate awaiting him in New

York. Sadly, he wrote a letter to Mayfield requesting his assistance in getting an African government to take his wife and family in if he were murdered.

After Malcolm's death, Mayfield continued his quest for worldwide African unity. As a member of the Pan-African Solidarity Committee, Mayfield, along with Malcolm's widow Betty Shabazz* and Robert Browne, an economist who espoused a separatist political and economic theory, joined Africans from around the world in fighting against racial oppression.

SELECTED BIBLIOGRAPHY

Forman, 1972; Gallen, ed., 1994; Malcolm X with Haley, 1965; Sales, 1994; Wolfenstein, 1993.

Craig S. Piper

McKISSICK, FLOYD B. An African American attorney, judge, civil rights* advocate, nationalist, Pan-Africanist, and clergyman, McKissick received his education at Atlanta's Morehouse College, North Carolina College, and the University of North Carolina. McKissick's civil rights activism was demonstrated early on by his successful demand for admission to and graduation from the University of North Carolina Law School, which had not accepted blacks before his admission in 1951. McKissick was among the defenders of black students' demands for access to public places in Durham, North Carolina. He was one of the pioneer supporters of the Congress of Racial Equality (CORE)* and, indeed, became its national chairman in 1963 and its national director in 1966.

McKissick and Malcolm had known each other for years, and McKissick considered him to be a friend. But it was a relationship that McKissick knew many mainstream civil rights activists would neither approve of nor understand. In the lobby of the hotel that served as headquarters for the 1963 March on Washington,* the two men encountered each other and warmly embraced during the greeting. One CORE activist who witnessed the friendly meeting quickly pulled McKissick aside to admonish him, informing McKissick that the greeting was an affront to the organization. However, McKissick had little trouble defending his behavior.

It was during McKissick's leadership of CORE that the organization became more militant and moved to the Black Power* position, becoming popular among some other civil rights groups. Like many of the leaders endorsing Black Power, McKissick recognized the importance that Malcolm's philosophy had played in the genesis of the idea. Like Malcolm X, McKissick not only sanctioned the Black Power concept; he also made the conditions of the most socially and economically oppressed black communities part of the civil rights agenda through his economic initiatives. McKissick attempted to put into practice his Pan-Africanism,* as illustrated by his calling upon black Americans to help their brothers and sisters in Africa. Taking the above arguments into consideration, it could be maintained that Malcolm X and McKissick had much in common.

SELECTED BIBLIOGRAPHY

Blackside/PBS, 1987; Bracey, Meier, and Rudwick, eds., 1970; Goldman, 1977; Jenkins (Lowery and Marszalek, eds.), 1992.

Amos J. Beyan

McKNIGHT, SAMMY "THE PIMP." During his years as a New York hustler, there were only two people in Harlem* that Malcolm truly trusted: his brother Reginald Little* and his friend the charismatic Sammy McKnight. Originally from Paducah, Kentucky, Sammy fled to Harlem after impregnating his girlfriend and enraging her parents. Sammy initially worked as a restaurant waiter but supplemented his income by burglarizing the apartments of girlfriends. Sammy then offered to assist them, with loans, which frequently led to a financial and emotional dependence that he readily exploited.

Malcolm and Sammy lived in the same Harlem boarding house. Frequently Malcolm would visit Sammy's apartment, where they ate together and smoked and snorted marijuana and cocaine. Sometimes called Sammy "Pretty Boy," McKnight was also a notable procurer of women for men who frequented New York streets in search of illicit sex. Both black and white women were among those whom he pandered. As Malcolm pondered which hustle he was best suited for, he soon ruled out pimping. He concluded, for the moment at least, that he had no talent similar to Sammy's and thus he would starve. Later, however, Malcolm did get involved in the pimping hustle, guiding white men seeking black women in Harlem for an enterprising madam.

It was Sammy who influenced Malcolm to become a marijuana dealer and loaned him enough money to begin this new business. Malcolm repaid the loan the same night from the almost immediate profits he earned. The two eventually became partners in various criminal ventures, mostly small-scale robberies. One failed burglary left Sammy slightly wounded by gunfire from security guards. Sammy's girlfriend blamed Malcolm, and the two began fighting at Sammy's apartment. Sammy reached for his gun and chased Malcolm into the streets. Although they partially reconciled, Malcolm never again trusted Sammy. But when West Indian Archie,* another of Malcolm's criminal associates, threatened his life, Sammy called Malcolm's friend "Shorty"* in Boston and advised him to take Malcolm out of Harlem. Years later when Malcolm returned to Harlem as minister of Temple Number Seven,* he discovered that Sammy had died.

SELECTED BIBLIOGRAPHY

DeCaro, Jr., 1996; Malcolm X with Haley, 1965; B. Perry, 1991; Rummel, 1989.

Paul J. Wilson

MECCA. Mecca, Saudi Arabia,* is a historical and religious site that played a pivotal role in the life of Malcolm X. When Malcolm made the Hajj* to Mecca in 1964, when he was no longer a member of the Nation of Islam (NOI),* it changed his thinking with regard to whites as well as Islam.* He saw people of all colors and races, including whites, praying together in one of the most magnificent religious events that take place every year in the Islamic world, which draws hundreds of thousands of Muslims* from around the globe. Consequently, after his trip to Mecca he denounced the NOI and publicly converted from a Black Muslim* to an orthodox or Sunni Muslim. Ever since he had been released from prison* in 1952, Malcolm publicly condemned whites for their treatment of blacks, referring to them as evil people. Now he publicly moderated that position and admitted that he had been following a false religion. Mecca was the turning point.

Mecca is considered the holiest site and city in Islam. It is the birthplace of the Prophet Muhammad,* considered the last prophet of Allah* (Arabic for God), to bring the eternal message regarding Islam. It was in Mecca that Malcolm with Muslims from around the world, all dressed in white clothing, circled the Kaaba (place of worship) seven times, went seven times between the hills of Safa and Marwa, stood together at Arafa, and asked Allah for forgiveness (a prelude to Judgment Day), and ended with a festival known as Eid Al-Adha, which was celebrated with prayers. This event, coupled with Eid al-Fitr, which was a feast day, marked the end of Ramadan (period of fasting). Never had Malcolm been so humbled by an event of any nature as this one in Mecca during the Hajj.

SELECTED BIBLIOGRAPHY

Clegg, 1997; DeCaro, 1998; Ibrahim, 1997; Malcolm X with Haley, 1965.

Mfanya Donald Tryman

MEIER, AUGUST. A liberal white historian and civil rights* activist, August Meier has been, for more than fifty years, one of the most reputable scholars of the African American experience. As a young scholar, Meier taught for a number of years at southern black institutions of higher learning, most notably at Mississippi's* Tougaloo College, but has served most of his teaching career on the faculty of Kent State University. He has authored, coauthored, edited, and coedited more than a dozen books and scores of articles and essays. In 1962 while teaching on the faculty of Maryland's Morgan State College, Meier participated in a program sponsored by one of the campus's black fraternities in which he debated Malcolm X on the merits of black nationalism* versus racial integration.* Meier, who had seen a similar debate at nearby Howard University,* where Malcolm had scored the prominent civil rights strategist Bayard Rustin,* was apprehensive about the challenge his formidable opponent would make. Howard University undergraduates Stokeley Carmichael* and Courtland Cox, future Student Non-Violent Coordinating Committee* leaders, helped Meier prepare for the debate. Tense, but composed throughout the affair, Meier's fears about the debate proved unfounded. Tactically reluctant to disagree with Malcolm about the mission of his black nationalists in fighting for human dignity, Meier, nevertheless, skillfully argued the case for racial integration and by his own admission acquitted himself well. The black Baltimore newspaper the *Afro-American* reported on the debate and substantiated Meier's claim that student sentiment was clearly in his corner.

The debate with Malcolm left a lasting impression on Meier. During the course of the debate, in typical Malcolm fashion, the Muslim* leader had denounced whites as "blue-eyed devils," Meier specifically included. In the aftermath of the program, however, Malcolm showed his graciousness and professionalism by extending real courteous comments to Meier. Hence, Meier also left from the encounter favorably convinced of Malcolm's basic humanity and would later regret not having taken the opportunity to get to know him better.

SELECTED BIBLIOGRAPHY

Baltimore Afro-American, March 31, 1962; Meier, 1992.

Robert L. Jenkins

MEREDITH, JAMES HOWARD. James Meredith could have been described as a militant black civil rights* advocate in the 1960s. His successful demand for admission to and graduation from the University of Mississippi despite opposition from white students and state leaders are examples of his strong stands in the 1960s.

Apparently, Malcolm never met Meredith personally, but Malcolm was aware of his accomplishment at the university. Malcolm thought little of Meredith's success and criticized the government for spending millions of dollars to ensure Meredith integrated the university. The money, he said, could have been better used to help poor blacks prosper in Mississippi.*

Meredith's statement that blacks could never win their rightful place in America through nonviolent means corresponded with Malcolm X's legitimate emphasis on self-defense.* Like Malcolm X, Meredith not only held Pan-Africanist ideological views, but he also put them into practice when he went to West Africa, where he studied at the University of Ibadan in Nigeria* from 1964 to 1965. Hence, Meredith and Malcolm X, despite Malcolm's comments to the contrary, had a lot in common, especially on matters relevant to nonviolence in the civil rights movement* and Pan-Africanism.*

SELECTED BIBLIOGRAPHY

Breitman, 1967; Meredith, 1966; J. White, 1985.

Amos J. Beyan

MEREDITH, JAMES—MARCH AGAINST FEAR. James Meredith* was the Mississippi*-born Air Force veteran who integrated the University of Mississippi (Ole Miss) in the fall of 1962. His admission has been called the "Battle of Oxford." On June 5, 1966, Meredith gained additional national notice when he began a lone march from Memphis, Tennessee, to Jackson, Mississippi. The slogan of the march was a call to black Mississippians to register to vote after

Mississippian James Meredith (center) leads his famous "Meredith March against Fear" on a highway near Winona, Mississippi, in March 1967. General Photograph File, Special Collections Department, Mitchell Memorial Library, Mississippi State University.

passage of both the Civil Rights Act of 1964* and the Voting Rights Act of 1965.* During the first day of the march, however, Meredith was shot and wounded by a sniper. The Southern Christian Leadership Conference (SCLC),* the Student Non-Violent Coordinating Committee (SNCC),* and the Congress of Racial Equality (CORE),* led by Martin Luther King, Jr.,* Stokeley Carmichael,* and Floyd McKissick,* respectively, continued the march. After a brief hospitalization, Meredith rejoined the march on June 25. When the march reached Greenwood, Mississippi, Carmichael used the national focus to introduce the slogan "Black Power!"* This call to black empowerment represented an ideological transition in the civil rights movement* from passive nonviolence to self-defense.* The assassination of Malcolm X and the posthumous publication of his autobiography in 1965 legitimated his intellectual militancy.

The growing militancy of the civil rights movement illuminated by the black Power term was alarming to many black and white conservatives who had helped forge the modern black struggle. It also raised fear among Americans in general. These concerns grew out of the ambiguity of the slogan's meaning, but most understood that it was symbolic of the ascendancy of Malcolm who had long disdained the passive nature of the civil rights movement. Meredith's march was the opportunity for one aspect of Malcolm's ideology to become more manifest.

SELECTED BIBLIOGRAPHY

Lawson, 1991; Sitkoff, 1981; Woodward, 1974.

Fon Louise Gordon

"MESSAGE TO THE GRASS ROOTS." *See* Theme Essay "Message to the Grass Roots."

THE MESSENGER **MAGAZINE.** As a high-ranking official in the Nation of Islam (NOI)* frequently in the national limelight, Malcolm X quickly came to realize the power of the press. More important, however, he understood the important role that visible images could play in helping to convey his mentor's messages to a people where reading was not always a high priority. Hence, almost single-handedly, Malcolm established the NOI's permanent presence in the print media with the founding and initial editing of the group's official organ, *Muhammad Speaks.** Similarly, he was also responsible for launching a short-lived pictorial magazine entitled *The Messenger.* The idea behind starting the magazine surely had a practical basis of publicizing the NOI, but it might have also been a natural outgrowth of Malcolm's own interest in photography. Notwithstanding the criticism of his friends and admirers about the poor quality of the pictures he took, Malcolm was himself a devoted amateur photographer and was rarely seen without his camera when visiting aboard. The pictorial magazine was slated to be a permanent publication that would periodically convey significant NOI activities. Its initial but short-lived appearance in 1959 showed great promise with the inclusion of pictures of NOI successes in educating children, depictions of the splendor of Muslim* women in their traditional family and homemaking roles, and illustrations of the organization's numerous business enterprises. *The Messenger* magazine folded, however, almost as soon as it appeared. Malcolm and NOI officials gave no indication of why it ceased publication after only one issue.

SELECTED BIBLIOGRAPHY

Clegg, 1997; Lincoln, 1994.

Robert L. Jenkins

MICHAUX, ELDER LIGHTFOOT SOLOMON. Elder Michaux was a clergyman, social activist, and radio and television personality who came to national prominence in the late 1920s as the founder of the Church of God Movement and its social component, the Gospel Spreading Association. Michaux began his ministry in Newport News, Virginia, but did not become particularly successful until he moved his church to the national capital in 1928. From there he launched what eventually became a weekly radio broadcast that reached thousands of black homes. By 1940, the self-identified "Happy Am I Preacher" had organized a nationally famous choir and as many as seven other churches in various urban centers. His newspaper the monthly *Happy News* would eventually have 8,000 subscribers. A supporter of interracial approaches to solving social and political problems, his congregations were integrated. Yet largely because of the tendency of nonviolent street activism to provoke violence, he was neither a supporter of Martin Luther King, Jr,* nor an enthusiastic advocate of the civil rights movement.*

Michaux was also not impressed with the Nation of Islam's (NOI)* religious doctrine nor their support of black nationalism.* During the early 1960s he and NOI leader Elijah Muhammad* engaged in a spirited dispute over the issue of Christianity* versus Islam.* The clash of views resulted in a September 1961 program, where the two religious leaders debated each other before a large crowd of partisan followers in Washington, D.C.'s Griffith Stadium. Malcolm had led a large contingent of Muslims* from his Harlem* temple to the program, but by then he was already personally familiar with Michaux, having met the religious leader in the famous Harlem bookstore owned by his brother Lewis Michaux.*

It was largely out of the context of this religious dispute between the Messenger and Michaux that Michaux and Malcolm also confronted each other. As a prelude to the Washington debate, Michaux invited Malcolm to speak to his New York City congregation to inform his members about exactly what the Muslims believed in. Whites, Michaux said, were becoming fearful of the Black Muslim* movement. Michaux's brother, Lewis, the black nationalist owner of the National Memorial African Bookstore in Harlem, was a personal friend of Malcolm's and apparently served as the facilitator of Malcolm's appearance. Malcolm, who typically had very little good to say about black preachers, praised Michaux as an intelligent and charming leader. He referred positively to numerous comments that Michaux made in the sermon he gave before Malcolm spoke. As he so frequently did whenever he spoke about religion, Malcolm talked considerably about the Christian Bible* and the relationship of biblical characters to the Arabic language and Islam. He then spoke at length about his own religion and its growth among black Africans and focused his attention on Elijah Muhammad and his effort to lead black Americans to real freedom in their own homeland.

Malcolm was gracious and respectful during his sermon in Elder Michaux's church. In turn, Michaux, who did not share his brother's appreciation of Malcolm, apparently showed little obvious disdain for Malcolm before the mixed Muslim and Christian audience. If Michaux had any expectations that Malcolm would discredit himself and the Black Muslim movement, as his biographer claims, he was sorely disappointed. Malcolm continued to maintain a close friendship with the elder's brother. Apparently, however, after the Washington,

Malcolm in the Harlem bookstore of his close friend, black nationalist Lewis Michaux. © Bettmann/CORBIS.

D.C. encounter between Michaux and Elijah Muhammad, Malcolm and Elder Michaux had no further dealings.

SELECTED BIBLIOGRAPHY

DeCaro, 1998; Marszalek (Garraty and Carnes, eds.), 1988; Mills (Lowery and Marszalek, eds.), 1992.

Robert L. Jenkins

MICHAUX, LEWIS H. Lewis Michaux was a black nationalist who owned the National Memorial African Bookstore (known in Harlem* simply as Michaux's) and headed as president the African Nationalist Council in America. In the 1930s and 1940s he supported Marcus Garvey* and later led an organization called the African Nationalists in America. His bookstore, begun on April 1, 1930, with only 5 books, eventually contained over 200,000 titles by and about black people. Michaux's philosophy was contained in the motto painted on a sign hanging above his store's front: "Knowledge is power; you need it every hour. Read a book." Outside this store at the intersection of 125th St. and 7th Avenue (Adam Clayton Powell, Jr.* Boulevard), the area Michaux called Harlem Square, was the site for most black nationalist public activities.

Malcolm X often spoke here, and he frequented the bookstore. Michaux considered Malcolm a close personal friend and urged Elijah Muhammad* to use moderation in treating Malcolm's suspension from the sect. Though his brother Solomon Lightfoot Michaux* was a noted evangelist and Lewis Michaux had been a deacon in his church, he came to oppose religion and, unlike Malcolm, couched his black nationalism* in secular terms. He narrowly missed witnessing Malcolm's assassination because he arrived late for the meeting to which Malcolm had invited him. Instead of anger, he urged black unity. Michaux stated that Malcolm's death was similar to that of Patrice Lumumba* in the Congo.* He urged blacks not to fight but to come together.

SELECTED BIBLIOGRAPHY

Jet, September 16, 1976; Malcolm X with Haley, 1965; *New York Amsterdam News*,* February 29, 1960; *New York Times*, August 27, 1976; *Publishers Weekly*, September 6, 1976.

John F. Marszalek

MIDDLE-CLASS BLACKS. Malcolm held considerable disdain for the black middle class. He frequently referred to them as "house" and "yard" servants, anxious to do the bidding of the "Good massa." His contempt probably began while growing up in Lansing, Michigan.* He later spoke of "complacent and misguided" middle-class blacks whose idea of status was simply to integrate with whites. This class of blacks in Lansing was actually waiters and bootblacks, who thought of themselves, and were often regarded by many other blacks, as economically "successful."

In Boston, Malcolm once worked as a soda fountain clerk waiting on middle-class blacks. He later called them "Hill clowns," mocking their phony accents and snobbery. They believed themselves more dignified than their ghetto brethren, when they were actually menial workers and servants, claiming status by working for whites. In an interview for the New York journal the *Liberator*,* Malcolm in his role as a militant black leader criticized the black middle class for coveting the crumbs from the white man's table.

He referred to many intellectuals, though he counted numerous ones as his friends, as Uncle Toms* and castigated them for being in a position to lead their people but being too preoccupied with achieving "white" success. The most misguided of the black intellectual middle class were the civil rights* leaders, for whom Malcolm spewed the most public contempt. No other subject so dominated Malcolm X's speeches and autobiography as did his spurn for this group of people, the black middle class, except for his views of racist whites.

SELECTED BIBLIOGRAPHY

Cone, 1992; Malcolm X with Haley, 1965; B. Perry, 1991; Sales, 1994.

Brenda Ayres

MIDDLE EAST. Malcolm X's sojourns in the Middle East exposed him to, and opened his eyes concerning, orthodox Islam* as opposed to the Nation of

Islam (NOI)* in the United States. He first traveled to the Middle East in 1959 as Elijah Muhammad's* ambassador to address and get answers to the NOI's relationship to global Islam and a number of political and religious issues. Malcolm knew that a vicarious relationship existed between the revolutions taking place in Islamic countries in Africa, Asia, and the Middle East and the black political struggle in the United States. He became a good friend of President Gamel Abdel Nasser* of Egypt,* who also served as a religious and political mentor for Malcolm. Because of the friendly relationship Malcolm had built with the Egyptian government, he was able to obtain twenty scholarships for African Americans to study at the University of Al-Azhar in Cairo, Egypt.

His last trip to the Middle East and Africa in 1964 was motivated, in part, by his faith in Islam as well as a fear for his life, as the tension increased between his followers and the NOI. He visited numerous countries in both regions of the world, including Saudi Arabia,* Lebanon, Sudan, Ethiopia, Egypt, Kenya, Tanzania, Nigeria,* Republic of Ghana,* Algeria,* and Liberia. He spoke to various groups, including heads of state, prime ministers, other state officials, and college students on important issues they were concerned with, including nationalism, racism, colonialism, religion, and related topics. After his Hajj* to Mecca,* Malcolm formally changed his name to El-Hajj Malik El-Shabazz,* replacing the X* associated with the NOI with an Arabic name based upon his religious conversion.

SELECTED BIBLIOGRAPHY

Gallen, ed., 1992; M. Lee, 1996; Sales, 1994; R. Turner, 1997.

Mfanya Donald Tryman

MILITANT. The *Militant* was the official newspaper of New York's Socialist Worker's Party.* The paper espoused the philosophy of the party and published news relative to its programs, but it also carried a considerable amount of local, state, national, and even international news. Apparently, its readership was international because Malcolm stated on one of the party's Militant Labor Forums* that he had seen its newspaper being read by Parisians and Africans during his recent visits to France and the African continent.

Almost from the outset of Malcolm X's official duties with the Nation of Islam (NOI)* in Detroit, Michigan,* the paper seemed enamored with him and recognized his work in the black community as an emerging leader. The paper had on staff a number of journalists, including Fred Halstead, Robert Vernon, and George Breitman,* who were close to Malcolm and followed his work and life through the various changes that it took. Seldom was there an issue published that did not contain news about Malcolm, especially after he broke with the NOI in 1964. The paper took a decidedly favorable slant in behalf of Malcolm during his troubles with Elijah Muhammad* and the NOI.

Malcolm, who flirted with the Socialist Party in the waning days of his life, was equally impressed with the *Militant*. He encouraged his followers to subscribe to the weekly paper and allowed it to be sold outside of his Organization of Afro-American Unity* headquarters. He occasionally praised the *Militant* and its writers for their objectivity and commonsense approach to black American problems.

SELECTED BIBLIOGRAPHY

Malcolm X, 1965; *Militant*, December 21, 1964; B. Perry, 1991.

Robert L. Jenkins

MILITANT LABOR FORUM. The Socialist Worker's Party* was one of the more recognizable militant political groups among New York's diverse leftist organizations. At one time the group had been a part of the American Communist Party.* Dedicated to elevating the working class, the largely white Trotskyite organization sponsored numerous programs in pursuit of their goals. Occasionally, it also nominated candidates for local, state, and national political offices, including the presidency.

Among the frequent activities that the party sponsored were the Militant Labor Forums. These events highlighted various kinds of programs of interest, including speeches from party dignitaries, debates, and panel discussions. Malcolm became one of the most popular speakers and panelists on these forums, held largely before white audiences. The forums became the stage from which Malcolm articulated and clarified in the last months of his life his position on numerous issues, including black nationalism,* voting rights, his revised views on Islam,* and the initiative to indict the United States' racial policy before the United Nations.* Exactly how much money Malcolm received in speaker's fees for his participation on the programs is not known; and though he was allowed to keep whatever was voluntarily collected, compensation was likely meager at best.

In his last year, Malcolm spoke on three separate Militant Labor Forums. It was the frequency of his participation on these programs and the strong support that he received from the Socialist Party itself that gave many Malcolm observers and students the incorrect impression that he had abandoned his views about nonalignment with political parties to become a Socialist and official party member.

SELECTED BIBLIOGRAPHY

Malcolm X, 1965; *Militant*, April 27, 1964; B. Perry, 1991.

Robert L. Jenkins

MILITARY. Long before he articulated a position on the military, Malcolm showed a disdain for participating in the service. During World War II* he feigned insanity to evade being drafted into the army. While Malcolm was hardly a coward, neither was he particularly patriotic. Living the life of a hustler at the time, he neither wanted to give up the sporting life nor jeopardize his own for a nation that he was already beginning to see as exploitive of blacks. Throughout his adulthood, Malcolm X became extremely critical of America's military establishment. To Malcolm, the military represented the hypocrisy of the U.S. government. The military's involvement in South Vietnam also symbolized white oppression against African Americans and minorities throughout the world.

This hypocrisy was most evident in how the government treated blacks. On the one hand, the government preached pacifism to African Americans in their quest for civil rights;* on the other hand, the military was told to kill as many of its enemies as possible in the name of safeguarding or expanding the ideology of democracy. While defending democratic ideals overseas, the U.S. government ignored its own domestic civil rights violations such as the denial of voting rights to African American citizens. Hence, Malcolm found it easy to denounce the government's prosecution of Adolf Hitler and the Nazis* and to advise blacks not to fight against the North Koreans during this police action of the early 1950s.

Malcolm also believed that deceit and oppression were intertwined with the federal government's hypocritical military policies. In a January 28, 1964, radio interview with Harry Ring over the New York radio station WBAI-FM, for example, Malcolm stated that the government used the Vietnam conflict* as a convenient alibi not to end oppression of blacks in places like Mississippi.* Malcolm warned, however, that this continuous oppression would lead to black unity and an eventual uprising against whites.

To Malcolm X, the military was a symbol of Uncle Sam's* hypocritical and oppressive racial policies. During the early 1960s he emphasized these themes in his opposition against the nation's war against North Vietnam. By focusing on the Vietnam War, the Muslim* leader had ample fodder for his stinging criticisms of the white establishment and its racially biased policies. His denouncement of the U.S. military also served as a rallying point for Pan-African unity to which Malcolm devoted the remainder of his life.

SELECTED BIBLIOGRAPHY

Breitman, 1967; Gallen, ed., 1994; Malcolm X, 1965; Malcolm X (Breitman, ed.), 1965; Malcolm X with Haley, 1965.

Craig S. Piper

MING, WILLIAM. William Ming was a Chicago* civil rights* lawyer, teacher, and public servant for more than thirty years. He graduated a cum laude student at the University of Chicago, where he also received his law degree. He had a distinguished career as a law professor at the law school of Howard University* and the University of Chicago, where he taught courses in civil rights at both schools. A prominent leader in Chicago's National Association for the Advancement of Colored People (NAACP)* branch office, Ming was one of the leading legal architects of the strategy in the *Brown v. Board of Education, Topeka,*

Kansas case and several other landmark civil rights cases including, *NAACP v. Alabama, Sweatt v. Painter, McLaurin v. Oklahoma, Sievet v. Oklahoma*, and Missouri ex rel *Gaines v. Canada*. In 1947, Ming collaborated with W.E.B. Du Bois* in drafting a petition urging the United Nations* to acknowledge that the claims for human rights* by American blacks were the same as those of colonized people around the world.

Despite his NAACP affiliation and a close association with Martin Luther King, Jr.,* Ming served as the legal counsel to Elijah Muhammad* and the Nation of Islam (NOI).* He worked to acquire a passport for the NOI leader when, in 1958, the Federal Bureau of Investigation (FBI)* and the State Department sought to prevent Muhammad from taking a Middle East* tour. He worked unsuccessfully to prevent Muhammad's son, Wallace,* from being convicted and imprisoned for draft evasion, and he handled Muhammad's personal tax matters in the face of FBI attempts to indict him on tax evasion charges. While there was obviously a relationship between Ming and Malcolm X, it was largely based on that which existed between the lawyer, Elijah Muhammad, and the NOI. During the times when illness prevented Muhammad from meeting with Ming about NOI legal matters, it was Malcolm, as the group's number-two man, who had the responsibility to confer with the attorney. On at least one occasion, however, Malcolm and Ming appeared together on a weekly television show panel hosted by Chicago television personality Irv Kupcinet.* Malcolm articulated his views about taking the case of the black plight to the United Nations and the World Court. Ideologically opposed to what the NOI and Malcolm supported, Ming, nevertheless, had little trouble defending the Islamic group to which Malcolm was so closely tied. In the early 1970s Ming experienced major problems himself with the Internal Revenue Service and was convicted and sentenced to federal prison on income tax evasion charges. He died in 1972 shortly after he was paroled.

SELECTED BIBLIOGRAPHY

Branch, 1988; *Ebony*, October 1947, December 1954, December 1973; Evanzz, 1992; *Jet*, November 12, 1970.

Charles Holmes

MISSISSIPPI. Perhaps the mention of no other state's name did more to raise the northern black consciousness about the lowly place of black people than did Mississippi during the 1950s and 1960s. Located in the heart of the segregated South,* Mississippi, once the nation's quintessential cotton-producing state, had the nation's greatest percentage of blacks in its population during the era. Arguably, however, in no state did blacks fare worse than in the Magnolia State. Economically impoverished, educationally deprived, and politically powerless, they sweltered under an oppressive racial system that frequently employed the most violent means to ensure their subordinate status. Hence, during the civil rights movement,* activists worked diligently throughout the state's local com-

Civil rights marchers demonstrate in Hattiesburg, Mississippi, a state that was a major flashpoint in civil rights violence and a frequent target of Malcolm's criticism. Courtesy of Mississippi Department of Archives and History.

munities, helping to mobilize blacks to overcome their racial barriers. Malcolm X certainly understood the activism, even if he disagreed with the tactics, for in his view Mississippi was clearly symbolic of the triumphant ascendancy of white racism and black victimization in America. In his view, Mississippi-dominated groups like the Ku Klux Klan* and the White Citizen's Council,* the latter originating in Mississippi in the mid-1950s, could only be eliminated by the same kinds of tactics they utilized to oppress blacks.

In his speeches and public comments, Malcolm was quick to point out black suffering in the state and the role of nationally known white segregationist leaders like Senator James Eastland and Governor Ross Barnett in the perpetuation of the black Mississippi plight. In some of his most impassioned remarks, he adroitly recalled the names of Emmett Till,* Mack Charles Parker, and Medgar Evers,* all three of whom were victims of an insidious racism prevalent in Mississippi, and he condemned as well the cold-blooded Klan murder of the three civil rights* workers in Philadelphia, Mississippi,* during the 1964 Mississippi Freedom Summer* campaign. All of these deaths, Malcolm exclaimed, were examples of either the federal government's inability to protect black lives or an unwillingness to do so. It was imperative that blacks in Mississippi with their majority population in dozens of counties take matters into their own hands and wrest political control, by either the ballot or the bullet,* Malcolm said. He promised the aid of his fledgling Organization of Afro-American Unity (OAAU).* Occasionally Malcolm related parallels between the race situation in Mississippi and problems in Africa and hoisted Mississippi as a model among African leaders as a way to mobilize their support for his human rights* violations campaign against the United States. As suggestions frequently emerged about sending black mercenaries to the Congo* to oppose U.S.-backed Moise Tshombe,* Malcolm suggested that Mississippi too be a target for black guerrilla freedom fighters; Harlem,* he said, was filled with blacks ready to descend on the Magnolia State to take on the infamous Ku Klux Klan.

It was not, however, always about the physical harm that black people endured in Mississippi that prompted Malcolm's disdain for the state. It was also through poverty and poor education that white racists managed to keep Magnolia State blacks subjugated. Even with all that James Meredith* went through to desegregate the University of Mississippi, he exclaimed, it was far from adequate compensation for the fact that the state refused to provide even "grade-school level" education for its large black minority. During the last month of his life Malcolm hosted at an OAAU rally the most well-known female Mississippi grassroots leader Fannie Lou Hamer* and served as a sounding board for a contingent of young activists from the state visiting Harlem. He informed the Mississippi delegation of his plans for a summer visit to the state, a part of his scheduled foray into the Deep South, and promised to come fully prepared to help them achieve their human rights goals. Unfortunately, his death a week before the proposed trip prevented the fulfillment of the journey and perhaps the revelation of exactly how he would fit into the evolving radicalization of the black rights struggle.

SELECTED BIBLIOGRAPHY

Davies, 1990; Gallen, ed., 1992; Malcolm X (Breitman, ed.), 1970a; Malcolm X (Clark, ed.), 1992; The *Militant*, January 18, 1965.

Robert L. Jenkins

MISSISSIPPI FREEDOM DEMOCRATIC PARTY (MFDP). The Mississippi Freedom Democratic Party (MFDP) was an offshoot of the Student Non-Violent Coordinating Committee (SNCC),* which, in turn, was the youth arm of the Southern Christian Leadership Conference.* The MFDP was created as an alternative to the racist and segregated Mississippi* Democratic Party, which was all white and a manifestation of the system of racial apartheid known as Jim Crow. A number of black women stood in the forefront of the MFDP, including Fannie Lou Hamer,* Unita Blackwell, Victoria Gray, Ruby Hurley, and Winnie Hudson. In 1963 the MFDP staged alternative elections to the regular state elections in which blacks were still disenfranchised. Eighty thousand black voters turned out for MFDP candidates. The election was organized by the Mississippi Council of Federated Organizations (COFO). In 1964, the MFDP traveled to Atlantic City, New Jersey, where the national Democratic Party* was holding its presidential and nominating convention. The MFDP challenged the credentials of the all-white Mississippi Democratic Party, arguing that the latter party was not truly representative of all Mississippians because of its policy of racial segregation.* The national Democratic Party wanted to make sure that it secured the black vote in the 1964 presidential election, but it also did not want to alienate white southerners. President Lyndon B. Johnson* manipulated officials behind the scenes, which resulted in only a token presence of the MFDP at the convention and the seating of the segregated state entourage.

Malcolm had talked of the need for a black political base similar to the MFDP, for he considered the political parties as merely different wings of the same "bird." Malcolm threw the weight of the Organization of Afro-American Unity,* which he headed, behind the MFDP and efforts in Mississippi of the MFDP to register black Americans to vote. But Malcolm advocated that black Mississippians must use their political participation in a strategic manner. He warned that the slogan "register and vote" could be misleading. First register, but he advised prospective voters to cast their ballot intelligently. Malcolm had been scheduled to speak before the MFDP in Jackson, Mississippi, but had to cancel because of other commitments. When he was assassinated on February 21, 1965, the MFDP was holding its state convention. It called proceedings to a halt and commenced praying in remembrance of him.

SELECTED BIBLIOGRAPHY

Malcolm X (Clark, ed.), 1992; *Militant*, December 28, 1964; Woodard, 1999.

Mfanya Donald Tryman

MITCHELL, SARAH. Sarah Mitchell was a former female follower of Elijah Muhammad's* Nation of Islam (NOI).* After denouncing the NOI in 1964, Sarah joined Malcolm X's Organization of Afro-American Unity (OAAU).* The OAAU, unlike the NOI, encouraged women to play an active role in the organization. Malcolm had moved increasingly away from the belief that women's roles were limited to domesticity after his break with the NOI, and he worked to give women leadership roles in his fledgling organization.

As a member of the OAAU, Mitchell, a schoolteacher by profession, served on Malcolm's public relations team. Malcolm, who rarely stayed at home with his wife, Betty Shabazz,* and their children, occasionally spent the night at Mitchell's house, the sleep overs always dictated by the lateness of the hour and the length of his drive home.

Mitchell was an intelligent single black female with professional aspirations and dreams whom Malcolm trusted implicitly. Likewise, she had the utmost regard for Malcolm, and her loyalty to him was boundless. In fact, she was one of the last persons to talk with him before his assassination. She recalled that Malcolm seemed on edge in the hours before his death. In particular, Malcolm appeared to her to be nervous, short-tempered, and troubled. This clearly seemed the case when she asked him whom he wanted to introduce him that day. Uncharacteristically, his response was for her to leave him alone. Never had she recalled Malcolm losing his temper. Shortly after the conversation, Malcolm was assassinated. Like most of those close to Malcolm, the murder left Mitchell stunned and saddened.

SELECTED BIBLIOGRAPHY

Goldman, 1973; B. Perry, 1991; Sales, 1994; Weiss, 1977.

Bridgette Stasher

MOORE, CARLOS. A Cuban patriot, who left the island-nation in the early 1960s in exile, Moore was one of many black nationalists who acquired a following in Harlem* during the Malcolm X era. Small in stature, he was affectionately called "Little Carlos" by those who knew him well. As it was with many of the militants who functioned in Harlem during the late 1950s and early 1960s, and who shared a similar philosophy about black liberation struggles, Malcolm personally knew Moore. Beyond their work facilitating the 1960 visit to Harlem of Cuban dictator Fidel Castro,* the two men, however, did little initially in concert to act out their shared ideas. This was certainly true when Malcolm was a leader in the Nation of Islam (NOI).* In 1961, for example, Moore led a demonstration at the United Nations* in protest over the murder of Congo* Prime Minister Patrice Lumumba.* Malcolm, who knew Lumumba personally, had constantly denounced the Congo* leader's death and the criminal complicity, he charged, of the United States, Belgium, and American-backed Congolese leader Moise Tshombe* in the murder. Although he sympathized with the effort, he had been unwilling to join with Moore and other militant Lumumba supporters, including poet-activist Maya Angelou,* in the protest, both because it went against NOI policy and because he thought the march unwise. It was a good decision. The planned protest attracted an unexpectedly large crowd and a cadre of city police. The mixture turned ugly, the ensuing "riot" prompting considerably negative national news reports and, of course, unjustified and erroneously ascribed culpability to Malcolm.

Moore and Malcolm did not always agree politically either. For example, Moore, who eventually became rabidly anticommunist, was critical of the Cuban Marxists' failure to do more to recognize the role of blacks in their revolution and to be more inclusive in the affairs of the government; Malcolm welcomed the emergence of Fidel Castro's Cuban dictatorship and was optimistic about the future of black people on the island. That Moore and Malcolm became more than mere acquaintances, however, is evidenced by the time they spent together conferring in Paris in late November 1964 when Malcolm stopped in the French city en route home to deliver a speech before African scholar Alioune Diop's group Presence Africaine. Moore, who was residing in Paris as a student and working in journalism at the time, was involved in the establishment of a small cell of Malcolm's Organization of Afro-American Unity,* which appeared soon after his departure from the historic city. It was Moore who acted as Malcolm's translator and escort in the French city and who introduced him to many of the celebrities in the black expatriate community. The bond is further noted in France's controversial decision to deny Malcolm's return entry into Paris to fulfill a February 1965 speaking engagement. Moore met Malcolm at the airport gate where the two held a brief conversation. Understandably, Moore was outraged over the government's decision. Malcolm returned immediately to London after the failed entrance and gave Moore a telephone interview, which was taped and relayed to the black Parisian group that had organized the visit. During the interview, punctuated with occasional inferences to their respect for each other, Malcolm rapped the French for their action, talked about the theme of black unity, which he had intended to discuss in his Paris lecture, reemphasized his well-known criticism of black American conditions and their struggle against white racism, and related to Moore his recent speaking appearances in Selma, Alabama, and London, England. Malcolm suggested that the planned Parisian rally occur as scheduled; Moore replaced Malcolm as the principal speaker, reading to the crowd the lecture that Malcolm had planned to deliver himself.

SELECTED BIBLIOGRAPHY

Angelou, 1981; Clarke, 1990; Cruse, 1967; Goldman, 1979; Himes, 1976; Malcolm X (Breitman, ed.), 1970a; Mealy, 1993; Moore, 1988; Stovall, 1996.

Robert L. Jenkins

MOSAIC DIETARY LAW. The Nation of Islam's (NOI)* Mosaic Dietary Law establishes guidelines for maintaining a healthy mind, soul, and body. One of the NOI's primary sources of nourishment is provided from beans. Beans are prepared in a variety of ways, from appetizers (soup and salad) to desserts (bean pie). The bean pie* is a delicacy that is very similar in taste to the sweet potato pie and very popular with both NOI members and nonmembers alike. Muslims* exclude alcoholic drinks, pork,* and pork by-products from their diet. Additionally, they avoid soaps and lipsticks that contains pork fat and/or pork by-products. These sources of food are considered slave foods and detrimental to the body. Meats consumed by Muslims include lamb and chicken. Homemade whole wheat bread is prepared, along with many other pastries, with grain and raw sugar. All types of fruits and vegetables are consumed, except collard greens. Rice is also a primary staple for the NOI; however, they only consume brown rice. Muslims eat slowly in order to savor the taste. Elijah Muhammad* provided the recipes for preparing most Muslim dishes. However, all Muslim sisters are respected as culinary specialists and inject their own secrets to enhance the flavor.

The Muslim diet consists of one main meal daily, which is usually eaten at sundown. Malcolm X held fast to the Mosaic Dietary Law. His Sunday evening feast would include soup, hors d'oeuvres, entrees, and a variety of garden vegetables and fruits. His favorite meat was braised lamb. He was also an avid milk drinker and usually consumed a quart of the drink with his evening meal. Desserts consisted of cakes and pies topped with Haagen-Dazs vanilla ice cream, foods he frequently indulged. He also loved to eat banana splits.

Fasting is also incorporated into the Mosaic Dietary Law. Muslims fast for three days during each month, commencing on Friday and concluding on Sunday evening. All Muslims are required to fast, except during pregnancy, illness, and travel-related activities. Muslims regard fasting as a means to enhance their spiritual awareness. Further, fasting is recognized as a means of curtailing obesity.

SELECTED BIBLIOGRAPHY

Karim with Skutches and Gallen, 1992; Muhammad, 1967; B. Shabazz, 1969.

Patricia Jernigan

MOSES. Throughout most of his career as a spokesman for the Nation of Islam (NOI)* Malcolm followed the line of his mentor Elijah Muhammad* in criticizing Christianity.* But in their teachings, Malcolm, before his conversion to orthodox Islam,* and most other Muslim* ministers typically referred to the Holy Bible* more than they did to the Holy Qu'ran.* They found the prophets of the Bible particularly appealing. Indeed, the Qu'ran itself is filled with references to prophets of the Bible, none more prevalent than Jesus Christ, as one of God's greatest prophets. There was no biblical figure whom Malcolm admired more than Moses, however. When Malcolm was a member of the NOI, he often equated Moses with his Muslim leader Elijah Muhammad. Like God had endowed the prophet Moses with knowledge and vision, so had Allah* "raised up" Elijah Muhammad as a similar prophet. Like Moses, Muhammad's job was to lead his people and tell whites, the pharaoh of contemporary America, to free his people from slavery, so that he could lead them to a land of their own. This view coincided with the NOI's demand for a separate black state within the confines of the United States, though Malcolm would not answer questions put to him about exactly where this black state should be located. More often, Malcolm liked to quote Moses as an ardent opponent of racial integration.* Had not Moses, Malcolm would frequently ask assertively, demanded of Pharaoh to let his people go! It was largely because of these words, Malcolm stated, that Moses could never have supported an integrated society. What Moses desired was for Pharaoh to let the Israelites go their separate way. For Malcolm, the Bible passage was a convenient tool to justify the NOI's doctrine of black separatism and their advocacy of a separate territory. More telling was Malcolm's use of Old Testament law to biblically support his view of blacks defending themselves from white violence. There was nothing wrong with blacks believing in a God that could tell Moses, one of his God's favorite people, "an eye for an eye, a tooth for a tooth," Malcolm would occasionally say.

SELECTED BIBLIOGRAPHY

Branch, 1988; DeCaro, 1998; Pickthall, 1953; Samuels (Meier, Rudwick, and Bracey, eds.), 1991.

Robert L. Jenkins

MUHAMMAD, AKBAR. A professor of history at the State University of New York at Binghamton, Akbar Muhammad, the youngest son of Elijah Muhammad,* was heavily involved in the Nation of Islam (NOI)* prior to his father's death. One of his duties included serving as the NOI's Egyptian correspondent for the official newspaper *Muhammad Speaks.**

Akbar, like his oldest brother Wallace,* had considerable contacts in the Arab world, much of which grew out of his college education at Cairo's University of El-Azhar. It was while in Egypt,* the heart of the Islamic world, that Akbar converted to orthodox Islam,* a source of friction between him and his father. What seems to distinguish Akbar Muhammad from some other members of Elijah Muhammad's family was his continued sympathy with, and loyalty to, Malcolm X during Malcolm's strained relations with the established members of the NOI. Malcolm had always been influential in Akbar's life. Akbar respected Malcolm for his intelligence and manly leadership. In turn, Malcolm respected Akbar, especially Akbar's success at transcending the religious chasm that Malcolm publicly crossed toward the end of his life.

After a meeting with Malcolm X in Cairo, Egypt, Akbar Muhammad wrote a letter to his father demanding an explanation for the accusations that had been leveled against Malcolm. When no suitable explanation emerged, Akbar in 1964 left the NOI. Elijah Muhammad's eldest son, Wallace, preceded Akbar Muhammad in leaving the sect. Akbar denounced his father for his sexual transgressions, and he criticized Muhammad's religion as "stifling" and "homemade." Needless to say, the NOI blamed Malcolm X for Akbar's defection, though tensions between Akbar and his father had been apparent for several years. What ensued was a litany of physical attacks against anyone who was viewed as a dissident in the NOI. It was alleged that Malcolm X was directly responsible for all of the disenchantment within the NOI and the defections from it. Thus, it was Malcolm who bore the brunt of the NOI's wrath, not individual defectors like Akbar Muhammad who were related to Elijah Muhammad.

SELECTED BIBLIOGRAPHY

DeCaro, 1996; Goldman, 1979; B. Perry, 1991.

Franklyn Tate and Sharron Y. Herron

MUHAMMAD, CLARA. Clara Muhammad, the former Clara Evans, was the wife of Elijah Muhammad,* whom he married in 1919 in Cordele, Georgia. Her role was that of a mother and a Nation of Islam (NOI)* follower. She had eight children by Elijah Muhammad. In her role as Muhammad's wife, Clara lived according to the ideals and principles of her husband and the NOI. Like most Muslim* women, she was expected to support her husband in whatever endeavor that he undertook and yet remain in the background. She also had to deal with the allegations of adultery and misconduct that swirled around her for many years prior to Muhammad's break with Malcolm X.

It has been argued that Muhammad was a father figure to his followers, even though at times this image appeared to be far from the truth. Muhammad virtually abandoned Clara and their children for approximately seven years during their early marriage. The family survived on handouts received from followers during Muhammad's drift from city to city during this time.

Clara Muhammad supported her husband because of her beliefs in the religion as taught by Muhammad. Occasionally her commitment to Muhammad's wishes might not have been strong, but she seldom dissented. But Clara played more than just the wife's role in the NOI. When Elijah was imprisoned during World War II* for failing to register for the draft, Clara helped to hold the sect together, serving as supreme secretary of the organization. While Elijah was away, she relayed messages to his ministers and captains. She helped to establish the first University of Islam* in Detroit, Michigan,* in 1934 and served as a model for Muslim women.

In relation to Malcolm X, Clara Muhammad often reminded Malcolm of his own mother, who had been unswerving in her support and loyalty to her husband. Malcolm stayed several months in Muhammad's Chicago, Illinois,* home after his release from prison* and during the stay became close to Clara, whom he regarded as a second mother. He visited the Muhammad's Chicago home frequently thereafter, where he engaged in conversation with Clara and her mother-in-law who resided with the messenger. Many of Clara Muhammad's children became closely associated with Malcolm, almost like brothers and sisters. Some of her children, like Malcolm, eventually came to denounce their father and, like Malcolm, separated from the NOI. Clara was understandably angered over her husband's adultery, and on one occasion she supposedly lashed out against him over Muhammad's veiled threats against Wallace, their eldest son, for his involvement with Malcolm in revealing Muhammad's infidelities. Despite rumors to the contrary, she did not divorce Muhammad but temporarily moved to Egypt to live with her son Akbar. She remained a part of the sect until her death in August 1972.

SELECTED BIBLIOGRAPHY

Clegg, 1997; Evanzz, 1992; Malcolm X with Haley, 1965; B. Perry, 1991; R. Turner, 1997.

Franklyn Tate and Sharron Y. Herron

MUHAMMAD, ELIJAH, JR. Elijah Muhammad, Jr., the senior Elijah's* namesake, was the next to the youngest son and born on June 29, 1931, to Clara

Muhammad* during the Great Depression.* Muhammad Jr. was the first in command in orders that came directly from his father regarding the organization, and he controlled the Fruit of Islam (FOI)* at one time. He was sent to the Boston mosque in 1962 after fellow male Black Muslims* there rebelled against the *Muhammad Speaks*￼ newspaper policy, which required them to sell as many as 200 copies a week and to pay for them in advance. He went not to provide direction or guidance on how to sell more newspapers. Rather, he went to Boston and threatened that those who disobeyed the policy would meet with death at the direction of his father Elijah Muhammad. Similarly, at a meeting in which he addressed FOI members in Harlem* in January of 1965, Elijah Jr. noted that the home that Malcolm X occupied in East Elmhurst* belonged to the Nation of Islam (NOI)* and suggested that Malcolm would face greater trouble for not moving out as ordered by the organization. He made it clear that if the NOI decided to kill Malcolm, nothing could be done about it. Indeed, the younger Elijah suggested that Malcolm should have been killed already.

A month later, at the NOI's annual Savior's Day Convention* in Chicago, Illinois,* and only five days after the assassination of Malcolm X,* Elijah Jr. was responsible for saving a black reporter from an attack by Black Muslims as he sat in the audience. The reporter had infiltrated the NOI and published an exposé in the *Chicago Sun Times*. Minister Louis Farrakhan,* when it was his turn to take the podium, identified the reporter as Benjamin Holman* and verbally castrated him as Black Muslims surrounded him. Elijah Jr. yelled for the Muslims to back off and calm down, and they acceded to his command. Elijah Jr. was one member in a committee of five put in place to administer the affairs of the NOI shortly before the death of his father.

SELECTED BIBLIOGRAPHY
Barnette, 1965; Goldman, 1973; B. Perry, 1991.

Mfanya Donald Tryman

MUHAMMAD, ELIJAH, SR. *See* Theme Essay "Elijah Muhammad, Sr."

MUHAMMAD, EMMANUEL. Emmanuel Muhammad was the first child born to Clara and Elijah Poole in Georgia in 1921. Along with his mother, at five years of age, Emmanuel was responsible for rescuing his father, who had passed out on the railroad tracks from drinking too much one night. Like Malcolm, he endured poverty as a child during the Great Depression.* Whereas Malcolm, often starving, often went into town and stole fruits from the market to eat, as a nine-year-old Emmanuel went through numerous alleyways, collecting anything that could be salvaged to help feed himself and his family.

Like Malcolm, Emmanuel spent time in prison* His father would not let him join the military or fulfill his military duty as required by federal law. In 1942 in Chicago, Illinois,* Emmanuel was sentenced along with thirty-eight other Black Muslims,* but, as the son of Elijah Muhammad,* received a five-year sentence rather than the three years that thirty other Muslims received. While Malcolm was referred to as incorrigible and as "Satan" while spending time in prison, Emmanuel showed similar signs of rebellion just before being incarcerated. When sentenced, he stated to the court that he hoped that the "Japs" won the war, because then all Negroes would be free. While in prison, he received inspiration on a fairly regular basis from quotes and citations in the Holy Qur'an,* the most sacred book of the Black Muslims, and from Clara Muhammad,* his mother. Malcolm had a similar experience and was exalted in corresponding with Elijah Muhammad while he was incarcerated.

Shortly before his father's death on February 24, 1975, Emmanuel met with his brothers to chart a path of succession. In 1978 during a probate hearing in Cook County Circuit Court, Emmanuel testified that all thirteen of the children that Malcolm had accused Elijah of fathering out of wedlock had been acknowledged by his late father as his own flesh and blood.

SELECTED BIBLIOGRAPHY

Clegg, 1997; Evanzz, 1992, 1999.

Mfanya Donald Tryman

MUHAMMAD, ETHEL. Ethel Muhammad was born as Frances Lee Poole on October 24, 1922, the second child born to Elijah and Clara Poole. Her name was later changed to Ethel, and she took the last name of Muhammad when the family's name was changed. Ethel married Raymond Sharrief,* the Supreme Captain of the Fruit of Islam (FOI),* and she was designated as the Sister Instructor of the University of Islam.* Virtually all of Elijah Muhammad's* children were given formal positions in the Nation of Islam (NOI)* based upon the advice of Malcolm X. Malcolm had noticed that too many whites were associated with the affairs of the NOI, which stressed independence and self-determination. Upon receiving this advice from Malcolm, Muhammad, the Messenger, began to move his own family members and children, including Ethel, into strategic and instrumental positions dealing with the affairs of the organization. Later, Malcolm may have realized that his advice was a mistake that contributed to his own problems because of the jealousy of family members toward him. Ethel's husband, Raymond, became one of Malcolm's chief rivals and a bitter enemy.

Standards and rules for the rank and file in the NOI often did not apply to the children of Muhammad. Ethel ran a profitable clothing store in the early 1960s in Chicago, Illinois,* with NOI money. It was from her store that every woman in the Chicago mosque had to purchase white apparel for the Savior's Day Convention* in 1961. Profits from the sales did not go into the NOI treasury but to Ethel. Ethel was known, contrary to NOI rules, for extravagant spending on furs and diamonds, although other women in the NOI were expected to live a more stoic and less elegant existence. Malcolm's wife, Betty Shabazz,* was one of the women role models and teachers of these values. Women were expected to remain "streamlined" and petite, while Muhammad's daughters, including Ethel, clearly were on the heavy side.

SELECTED BIBLIOGRAPHY

Clegg, 1997; Essien-Udom, 1962; Evanzz, 1999; B. Shabazz (Clarke, ed.), 1990.

Mfanya Donald Tryman

MUHAMMAD, HERBERT. Herbert Muhammad was one of Elijah Muhammad's* six sons. Like every other recognized member of Muhammad's family, he was heavily involved in the Nation of Islam (NOI).* It had been Malcolm X who suggested to Muhammad that he appoint members of his family to key positions in the NOI. However, Herbert's role, though in many ways more powerful than his other brothers' because of his father's trust, was certainly less public than that of the others in the NOI inner circle. At one time Herbert served the NOI as public relations director. Herbert is often credited as having been the financial brains of the NOI. The NOI had a number of financial ventures, the most prosperous perhaps being the newspaper *Muhammad Speaks*.* With the assistance of professional journalists as well as others, Herbert is credited with efficiently managing the paper once it was removed from Malcolm's control, who founded the paper. In addition to the newspaper, Herbert Muhammad, along with his father Elijah and John Ali,* National Secretary of the NOI, supervised the organization's financial affairs. Herbert also served as manager for former boxing champion Muhammad Ali.* He was allowed to do so by his father as a way to protect the champion from unscrupulous influences, but clearly it was a lucrative arrangement for Herbert, considering the millions of dollars that Ali earned.

Herbert had little direct relationship with Malcolm X. His influence over what was printed in *Muhammad Speaks*, however, had a significant impact on how the rest of the NOI viewed Malcolm. When Malcolm's troubles with the NOI began, however, Herbert, unlike his older and more influential brother Wallace,* sided with his father and the NOI against Malcolm. He printed a number of critical articles on Malcolm and denounced him as a traitor for his attacks against his father and the NOI.

SELECTED BIBLIOGRAPHY

Clegg, 1997; Goldman, 1979; B. Perry, 1991.

Franklyn Tate and Sharron Y. Herron

MUHAMMAD, LOTTIE. Lottie Muhammad was the second daughter born to Elijah* and Clara Muhammad,* on January 2, 1925, the same birth year as Malcolm X. Lottie was often exposed to the harassment that her father was subjected to as the leader of the Nation of Islam (NOI)* as it grew exponentially in membership in the 1940s and 1950s. She observed, on occasion, how police and other legal authorities questioned her father regarding activities of the NOI and questioned her regarding her father's whereabouts at times. Lottie had planned to take a trip to Africa and the Middle East* with her father, brothers, and Malcolm X in 1959, but the federal government and bureaucrats used several ploys to deny her siblings and father the necessary passport. While Lottie and Malcolm were the same age and Malcolm was often in the home of her father, there is little to indicate that they had a close and enduring relationship.

SELECTED BIBLIOGRAPHY

Clegg, 1997; Evanzz, 1999.

Mfanya Donald Tryman

MUHAMMAD, SULTAN. Sultan Muhammad was the minister of Temple Number Seven* in Harlem* in the early 1950s. Arguably the mosque had the largest black constituency, and with three-quarters of a million African Americans alone in Harlem and over a million in five boroughs in a city of close to 7 million, it also had the largest potential membership in the nation. Previously, he had served as the minister of the Milwaukee mosque and, as a cousin, was one of Elijah Muhammad's* strongest supporters. While Elijah was serving a jail sentence in the 1940s Sultan attempted to seek his release, and for doing so he was put in jail himself after an investigation by the Federal Bureau of Investigation (FBI)* for failing to register for the draft.

However, on another level Sultan's wife had compared Elijah Muhammad to a dog. In 1954 he informed Malcolm that Elijah Muhammad wanted him to discipline or divorce his wife, which he was reluctant to do because he loved her. At the same time, Malcolm was proving to be highly successful in building the Boston and Philadelphia temples. Consequently, Malcolm replaced Sultan Muhammad and became the full minister over Temple Number Seven. Malcolm's replacement of Sultan Muhammad would provide him with public acclaim and a strategic position among Harlem's masses that could not be obtained in any other city in the United States. While Malcolm benefited directly by replacing Sultan, controversial statements by the former minister's wife would serve as a harbinger of things to come for Malcolm and help shape his changing perception of Elijah Muhammad during the next ten years. In fact, only one year later, in 1955, Malcolm begin to hear rumors of Elijah Muhammad's involvement in adulterous relationships.

SELECTED BIBLIOGRAPHY

Evanzz, 1999; B. Perry, 1991.

Mfanya Donald Tryman

MUHAMMAD, WALLACE (Warith Deen Muhammad; Warith Deen Mohammed). Malcolm X considered Wallace Muhammad, the second youngest son of the Elijah Muhammad,* as a close and respected friend. The two men always shared an exceptionally close relationship and trust when they were un-

Wallace Deen Muhammad, son of Elijah Muhammad, appears here in the 1970s, in typical attire of the Muslim sect that he led after his father's death. Courtesy of Iman Johnny Hasan.

derstudies of Muhammad and were key leaders in the Nation of Islam (NOI).* To Malcolm, Wallace was viewed as the most objective and spiritually inspired of Elijah's eight children.

Wallace instructed Malcolm in interpreting the Holy Qu'ran* and the Holy Bible* for guidance and documentation when formulating major philosophical decisions. Wallace had become more knowledgeable about orthodox Islam* while serving a three-year federal prison term between 1960 and 1962 for draft evasion. In prison, Wallace had embraced Sunni Islam. Such deliberation and dedication to fundamental scripture would be premier in the evolving character and philosophy of both men and subsequently led to their departure from the NOI and the teachings of Elijah Muhammad.

There were several significant events in the lives of Malcolm and Wallace that resulted in the shifts in their religious and political ideologies. One event involved the discovery by Malcolm that Elijah Muhammad had several illegitimate children and that while the NOI leader praised him publicly, he disliked his growing popularity. Greatly disturbed by this revelation, Malcolm confronted Wallace in 1962. Malcolm felt that the NOI was slowly self-destructing; Elijah needed to be confronted with the truth, and Muslims* in general thought Muhammad would respond positively to such admission of human weakness, particularly in light of their leader's accomplishments. Wallace, though in agreement, felt instead that his father would neither listen nor welcome such an effort by either of them.

Another milestone event late in Malcolm's life was his decision to visit Mecca.* He conferred with Wallace on the matter, and his friend's advice was that a Muslim should learn everything possible about Islam. Malcolm made the pilgrimage to Mecca, and the exposure to the larger Islamic community gave him a greater understanding of Sunni Islam and broadened his philosophy of black nationalism.* In Mecca, he witnessed all races worshiping Allah* as Muslims. An Algerian revolutionary, who considered himself white, challenged Malcolm's definition of black nationalism in that it excluded true white revolutionaries everywhere who fought the exploitation and alienation of oppressed peoples. Clearly, the trip helped to influence and modify Malcolm's racial theology.

Armed with an enlightened concept of Islam and the world, Malcolm returned to America. No longer associated with the NOI, he began expanding and in some cases modifying his political philosophy in 1964. Angered and disillusioned over his father's indiscretions and unable to reconcile his evolving orthodox Islamic knowledge with Muhammad's teachings, Wallace, too, broke completely with his father. Another brother, Akbar Muhammad,* college educated in an Egyptian Islamic University, also left the NOI and was labeled a hypocrite. His defection, like Wallace's before him, was attributed to the influence of Malcolm. To be sure, the Malcolm-Wallace alliance was strengthened by Malcolm's feud with Elijah Muhammad over the Messenger's paternity scandal. After Malcolm's assassination, Wallace would publicly acknowledge the troubles his father had caused for Malcolm and the NOI.

Upon the death of Elijah Muhammad in 1975, Wallace became the leader of the NOI. Inspired with the similar beliefs of his friend Malcolm, Wallace seized the opportunity to initiate a change in the teachings of his father. He renamed New York's Temple Number Seven* in honor of Malcolm, renounced his father's purported divinity, and began to shape the religion in the tradition of orthodox Islam in the East. To distance himself further from Elijah Muhammad and the NOI, he changed his own name to Warith Deen Muhammad and later to Warith Deen Mohammed. The NOI was opened to whites, and Muslims were allowed to enter politics and serve in the U.S. Army.

SELECTED BIBLIOGRAPHY

A&E Entertainment, 1995; Blackside/PBS, 1994; Branch, 1998; Clegg, 1997; Davies, 1990; Goldman, 1979; Malcolm X (Breitman, ed.), 1970a; Malcolm X with Haley, 1965; Parks (Clarke, ed.), 1990; Wolfenstein, 1993.

Otha Burton

MUHAMMAD'S SECRETARIES. As the Nation of Islam (NOI)* grew in size, there was an increase in the demand for staff. No longer could administrative affairs be the domain of one person, such as Clara Muhammad,* the wife of the Messenger, which occurred in the 1940s when he was serving time in prison* for draft evasion. By the early 1950s the NOI had fifteen mosques nationwide. Elijah Muhammad* needed personal secretaries to address the increasing administrative and clerical demands. However, rumors quickly began to circulate that Muhammad was having extramarital affairs with his secretaries that were just teenagers. In more than one instance, impregnated young women were given a "trial" at the mosque where they also worked, found guilty by Muhammad who served as judge, and as punishment banished to another out-of-state mosque or suspended from the NOI. Muhammad ruled in some cases that the young women did not know who the father was, implying that they were promiscuous.

Initially, few if any members of the local mosque realized that the out-of-wedlock partner was Muhammad himself. However, some of the young women who were the victims discussed their predicament with others. In addition, the Federal Bureau of Investigation (FBI)* approached Black Muslims* of the local mosque and bluntly told members that Muhammad was fathering illegitimate children. Wallace Muhammad,* one of Elijah's younger sons, and Malcolm X both began to investigate the rumors, and both came to the same conclusion: that the rumors were true. Wallace had become suspicious of his father hiring teenage secretaries as part of his personal staff, of whom each, after several months of employment, became pregnant and strangely disappeared. Both Wallace and Malcolm confronted Muhammad on different occasions about the rumors. Wallace was the first to engage his father and after meeting with him was convinced of his indifference regarding his philandering ways. When Malcolm confronted him during a visit to the latter's Phoenix home, he was shocked that not only did Muhammad admit to such affairs, but he used biblical justification for his misdeeds. Malcolm left dejected and disappointed that the rumors were true.

Because Muhammad continued to hear stories of his own son spreading word of his transgressions, he was suspended from the NOI as minister of Temple Number Twelve in Philadelphia. Malcolm's questions regarding the secretaries angered Muhammad, and Muhammad subsequently suspended Malcolm permanently, ostensibly for his impolitic remarks regarding the assassination of President John F. Kennedy.*

When Malcolm realized that he would not be reinstated in the NOI, he began to publicly accuse Muhammad of extramarital affairs in various appearances. Malcolm was deeply hurt and felt betrayed, not only because he felt at one time that Muhammad was infallible but because he had recommended two of his former girl friends for personal secretary jobs with the Messenger, and both had become pregnant.

A Nation of Islam member poses beside one
of the sect's newspaper stands on a Detroit,
Michigan street. Courtesy of Iman Johnny
Hasan.

SELECTED BIBLIOGRAPHY

Clegg, 1997; Gardell, 1996; Lincoln, 1994.

Mfanya Donald Tryman

MUHAMMAD SPEAKS. Malcolm was a master in "one-upsmanship."
Throughout his life he was creative enough to ensure that his cause, regardless
of what it was, would get the proper attention. As a child, whenever he did
something that warranted punishment, he realized that by crying loud and creating havoc, his parents would be less inclined to discipline him severely. He
outwitted the draft board by pretending to be psychotic. He played Russian
roulette to prove to his associates in crime, Shorty* and his white female counterparts, that he was not to be betrayed. While in prison* he baited a Harvard
University* Seminary student to admit that Jesus was not a white man. After
joining the Nation of Islam (NOI),* Malcolm consistently debated learned individuals and artfully used words in his responses that were designed to disarm

his opponents or make them defensive. Clearly, Malcolm was a leader and an innovator who consistently looked for ways to be more effective in his causes.

Malcolm's commitment to realizing the growth potential that the NOI possessed was unmatched. He organized or assisted in the organization of temples in cities from Massachusetts to Georgia to California. As an astute organizer, he also realized the importance of the media in successfully carrying out his aim of significantly increasing the NOI's membership. The documentary "The Hate That Hate Produced,"* and C. Eric Lincoln's* *The Black Muslims In America*∗ catapulted the NOI into America's mind-set. Malcolm's articles in the *New York Amsterdam News*∗ and later the *Los Angeles Herald-Dispatch*∗ created a desire to develop an organ to highlight weekly activities in the NOI specifically and, in general, black communities throughout the world. Malcolm achieved this goal by establishing *Muhammad Speaks*. The official newspaper of the NOI was an immediate success and was responsible for generating a considerable amount of the organization's income, once estimated to be more than $100,000 per week. Members of the NOI, aware of the required individual selling quotas, hawked the paper with zeal on city street corners throughout America. Initially published biweekly, Malcolm operated the paper out of the basement of his Queens home until his impending break with Muhammad. The Messenger then vested control over the newspaper from Malcolm and moved the operation to the national headquarters in Chicago, Illinois.* In the tradition of Marcus Garvey's* *The Negro World* of the 1920s, *Muhammad Speaks* challenged the myth of black inferiority and championed self-help and black independence. Its readership was not restricted to members of the NOI. Many non-Muslims eagerly awaited the paper each week. This was especially true of younger readers who had a more radical orientation.

Muhammad Speaks was developed as an alternative newspaper that challenged the validity of mainstream news and perspectives and set an example for others to emulate. Its circulation eventually rose to an estimated 900,000 copies, its popularity necessitating a weekly issue. At its peak, it had the largest circulation of any black newspaper in the nation. Each issue included a section entitled "What the Muslims Believe." In 1967 the Black Panther Party for Self-Defense* established a similar newspaper called *The Black Panther*; it included a section entitled "What We Want/What We Believe," patterned after the section in *Muhammad Speaks*.

Although Malcolm was frequently honored initially in the columns of *Muhammad Speaks*, it is ironic that as the brainchild of the paper and as the national spokesperson for the NOI, in a very crucial period Malcolm's voice was missing from the newspaper. Nevertheless, the paper served a critical need in the development of a crucial period in the history of black nationalism.*

SELECTED BIBLIOGRAPHY

Foner, ed., 1970; M. Lee, 1996; Malcolm X with Haley, 1965; B. Perry, 1991; Pinkney, 1976.

Horace Huntley

MUSLIM. The term *Muslim* is a reference to one who believes in the religion of Islam.* *Islam* means one who has submitted his or her will to Allah* (God), and it is a derivative from a word meaning "peace." A Muslim is often mistaken with "Mohammedanism," or the worship of Allah's final messenger who brought the Holy Qur'an* (Bible)* verbally to the world. Faithful Muslims pray five times daily. One becomes a Muslim by simply stating that "there is no god apart from God, and Muhammad is the messenger of God." By uttering this phrase, one not only becomes a Muslim but expresses his or her faith in all of Allah's prophets and the scriptures that they brought from Allah. There are over 1 billion Muslims in the world, with the largest populations in the Middle East.* However, not all Muslims are Arabs, as many people in the West believe, and not all Arabs are Muslims.

Orthodox Islam is synonymous with Sunni Islam, and followers are referred to as Sunni Muslims. Most Muslims in the world are Sunni Muslims. However, there are other significant segments such as the Shi'ite, a large contingent of which resides in Iran. A more mystical cult is referred to as the Sufi Muslims, who are considered a radical fringe religious group that believes in superstition and other dramatically different beliefs than Sunni Muslims.

Malcolm X was a follower of Elijah Muhammad,* leader of the Nation of Islam (NOI)* in the United States, from his conversion in prison* in the early 1950s until 1964 when he broke from the NOI to form the Muslim Mosque, Inc.* While a member of the NOI, Malcolm was considered a "Black Muslim,"* a term that the media used to described all members of the organization. But Malcolm referred to himself as a Muslim, not a Black Muslim.

In 1964, after Malcolm made the Hajj,* (the Fifth Pillar of Islam—five tenets that every Muslim is obliged to carry out, with the last one, the Hajj, or trip, if one is financially able to) to the Middle East, he formally converted to Sunni Islam. He changed his name from Malcolm X (the X* a derivative of the NOI's policy of changing a black person's last name or "slave name" to this letter) to the Arabic name of El-Hajj Malik El-Shabazz.* During his lifetime, Malcolm had three legal names, two of which were related to his faith as a Muslim. His name was changed from Malcolm Little to Malcolm X when he became a Black Muslim, and, as noted, from Malcolm X to the Arabic name referenced here when he became a Sunni Muslim. When he was assassinated in February 1965, his body was prepared for burial utilizing Muslim religious traditions.

SELECTED BIBLIOGRAPHY

Hitti, 1970; Islamic Affairs Department, 1989; Lincoln, 1994.

Mfanya Donald Tryman

MUSLIM GIRLS' TRAINING CLASSES. The Nation of Islam (NOI)* was more than an organization that sought to teach the tenets of Islam;* it also worked to influence the lives of its membership in a more practical way. To this end, the sect was organized into several branches with activities that targeted both its male and female membership. Women were typically relegated to secondary roles in the NOI, even the practice of having them sit in a different section of the mosque from the men during their Sunday service. Yet despite the traditional place that the NOI reserved for them in temple life and the organization infrastructure, the role of women in the NOI cosmos and the women's sphere was not neglected. Hence, for its female members, the Muslim Girls' Training (MGT) classes, the counterpart to the males-only Fruit of Islam,* strove to teach females a variety of practical things dealing with the home and family and the proper support of Muslim* men. These formalized classes normally met in each temple on Thursday night and came under the immediate supervision of a female Supreme Captain assisted by several lieutenants. Women were inculcated first with the doctrines and history of the NOI and received instruction in domestic arts such as cooking, cleaning, sewing, and child care. They were taught to shun vices like alcohol, tobacco, and dancing and to embrace the general virtues of womanhood—gentleness, submissiveness, and deference to male leadership. Most classes also included self-improvement* components in calisthenics, hygiene, and the English language. Typically, when warranted, a junior class for younger females functioned. Normally instructors were required to make at least one journey to the NOI Chicago* headquarters for training and to meet with the Messenger, Elijah Muhammad.*

As leader of New York's Temple Number Seven* Malcolm, like other temple ministers, had overall responsibility for the affairs and conduct of the MGT classes. He occasionally lectured the women about NOI doctrine, advised them of their proper roles as Muslim women, encouraged them to eschew gossip and issues that fractured normal female relationships, and even admonished them about the dangers of being recruited as spies by potential infiltrators from outside forces like the Federal Bureau of Investigation (FBI).* Before he married her, Malcolm's wife, Betty Sanders Shabazz,* taught hygiene in the MGT classes. Malcolm could be and often was stern and uncompromising with women in these classes, but he was devoted to the NOI and its ideology, and he sought to ensure that what women learned conformed with the best interest of the organization that at one time consumed his life and work.

SELECTED BIBLIOGRAPHY

Carson (Gallen, ed.), 1991; Clegg, 1997; Collins with Bailey, 1998; DeCaro, 1996; M. Lee, 1988; Lomax, 1963; Malcolm X with Haley, 1965; Marsh, 1996; Tate, 1997.

Robert L. Jenkins

MUSLIM MOSQUE, INC. (MMI). This organization was started by Malcolm X on March 12, 1964, after he was suspended from the Nation of Islam (NOI)* for his controversial statement regarding President John F. Kennedy's* death. Believing there was a conspiracy against him by NOI Chicago, Illinois,* officials, Malcolm decided to make the break complete by establishing his own separate organization.

In a press conference at New York's Park Sheraton Hotel, Malcolm stated his new philosophy. He said that the Muslim Mosque, Inc. (MMI)* would provide a religious base for attacking numerous problems, especially in the black community. He indicated that the MMI's new political and economic program would be based on black nationalism* and armed resistance. Although there would be cooperation with established civil rights organizations* and with whites, whites would be unable to join.

Malcolm started the MMI as a religious organization because most of his forty to fifty followers wanted to remain Muslims.* He wanted to be recognized as a minister with political interests. Religion, he claimed, should not be a barrier to a united black effort to fight racism. He was a Muslim, he said, because it was the kind of religion that encouraged fighting against evil. It did not, as Christianity* did, believe in turning the other cheek. Rather, Islam* preached appropriate retribution as a form of justice. Initially, his headquarters was in the Hotel Theresa,* one of Harlem's* major landmarks, where he conducted services in a manner similar to those held in the NOI. The organization progressed slowly, however. Fearing it would drive secular people away, he stopped the formal prayers to Allah* during the services. There were other obvious questions that needed answers: Why did an organization for all people have a religious name? Why start a religious organization if the philosophy was to be black nationalism? Obviously, as Malcolm came to see, the new organization lacked clear goals and strategies.

Realizing the failure of the MMI as a religious organization, in 1965 Malcolm started a secular alternative, the Organization of Afro-American Unity (OAAU).* He brought together a black brain trust to produce a six-page statement of aims and objectives. But the OAAU was a mixture of artists, Maoists, and nonsectarian revolutionaries, including some charged with conspiracy to blow up the Statue of Liberty and to assassinate renowned civil rights* leaders. They frequently argued with members of the MMI, forcing them to leave the Hotel Theresa headquarters.

Writing from Africa and Mecca* in 1964, Malcolm stated that his holy trip, or Hajj,* would officially establish the religious connection of the MMI with the 750 million Muslims of the world. The Muslim world would be forced to address the human rights* plight of African Americans. While in Mecca, Malcolm also stated that he had secured the services of a spiritual adviser for the MMI, Shiek Ahmed Hassoun,* a Sudanese imam. But the chasm grew larger between Malcolm's old and new followers. Many old Muslim hardliners found Malcolm's embrace of orthodox Islam and his public denouncement of Elijah Muhammad quite disturbing. After returning to the United States, Malcolm attempted to smooth over the problems, but he was soon assassinated. Neither organization survived very long after his death.

SELECTED BIBLIOGRAPHY

Cone, 1991; Goldman, 1973; Malcolm X (Breitman, ed.), 1965, 1967; *Militant*, December 7, 1964; Murphy, Melton, and Ward, eds., 1993.

Lawrence H. Williams

MUSLIM WORLD LEAGUE. The Muslim World League, also referred to as the World Muslim League, was started in 1962 in Mecca* based upon the initiative of the Saudi Arabian monarchy. In the United States, the Muslim World League addresses the social and spiritual needs of American Muslims* but particularly foreign Muslims and second- and third-generation immigrant Muslims in American mosques. The League assists these groups in setting an Islamic agenda in various Islamic associations. The League, stationed in Mecca, Saudi Arabia,* along with Malcolm's close friend Dr. Mahmoud Shawarbi,* endorsed and recognized Malcolm's conversion to orthodox Islam,* something Malcolm deeply cherished, given his split with the Nation of Islam (NOI).* As an association, they not only recognized the fact that Malcolm had been converted to Sunni Islam but made him their official representative in the United States in September 1964. This happened after Malcolm had visited the Middle East* in July and August of the same year, a visit that was hosted by the Supreme Council of Islamic Affairs in Cairo, Egypt.*

The League hoped that Malcolm could assist in correcting the distorted image of Islam in the West and particularly in the United States. An endorsement by the League is considered of great honor in the Muslim world. The League's endorsement occurred after the rector of the University of Al-Azhar in Cairo, Egypt, considered the intellectual and scholarly center for the study of Islam, certified Malcolm as an Islamic minister. Later, once Wallace D. Muhammad,* Elijah Muhammad's* son, took over the NOI and changed the name to the World Community of Islam in the West* he was elected to the Supreme Council of Masajid of the Muslim World League. In this capacity he carried on Islamic work similar to that of Malcolm in the United States.

SELECTED BIBLIOGRAPHY

DeCaro, 1996; Gardell, 1996; R. Turner, 1997.

Mfanya Donald Tryman

N

NAEEM, ABDUL BASIT. Abdul Naeem was a Pakistani Muslim* who lived and worked as a journalist, entrepreneur, and missionary in Brooklyn, New York, during the late 1950s and 1960s. Naeem established a relationship with Elijah Muhammad* after having produced a booklet in 1957 entitled *The Moslem World and the U.S.A.* dealing with Muhammad and the Nation of Islam's (NOI)* annual Savior's Day Convention.* Naeem also published a magazine of the same title that highlighted much of the NOI's work and religious ideology, much to the disappointment and criticism of many of his more traditional churchmen. Hoping to move the NOI closer to the orthodox Muslim standard, initially Naeem and Malcolm X maintained something more than a mere casual relationship. Occasionally he featured Malcolm in his magazine. Apparently, it was the Muslim missionary who helped pave the path for Malcolm's initial visit to the Middle East* and Africa in 1959 as Muhammad's advance man. Naeem soon became a close confidant of Muhammad, part of the inner circle among whom Muhammad listened to for advice. According to one biographer, the Federal Bureau of Investigation* recruited Naeem as a reliable informant in the agency's ongoing effort to disrupt the NOI and drive a greater wedge between Muhammad and Malcolm X, his chief lieutenant. An apologist for Muhammad and his brand of Islam,* Naeem understandably sided with the NOI chieftain in the rift that developed with Malcolm X. During a 1964 Savior's Day Convention speech Naeem ripped Malcolm as an unstable instigator of rumor and innuendo and urged the audience to disregard Malcolm's accusations and criticisms of Muhammad. This message, along with similar ones that extolled the virtues of Elijah Muhammad and the NOI, was printed in the official newspaper, *Muhammad Speaks.** They had as their design not only the repudiation of Malcolm but also the elevation and legitimation of the Black Muslim* movement in the eyes of orthodox Muslims. However, Naeem had little success in changing the NOI's image in the larger Muslim world.

SELECTED BIBLIOGRAPHY

DeCaro, 1996; Evanzz, 1999; Friedly, 1992; Lincoln, 1994.

Robert L. Jenkins

NASSER, GAMEL ABDEL. As a young military officer, Gamel Nasser took part in the overthrow of Egyptian King Farouk. Thereafter, his political rise was mercurial. He became premier in 1954 and president in 1956, an office that he held until his death in 1970.

In July 1959 Nasser met Malcolm X when the Black Muslim* leader, on an exploratory trip to the Middle East,* visited Egypt* for the first time. In a subsequent visit to Africa shortly before his death, Malcolm again had an occasion to visit Nasser, and they embraced each other as fellow Muslims.* One of the results of these trips was Nasser's generous grant of twenty scholarships to be distributed to black Americans to study orthodox Islam* at Cairo's University of Al-Azhar. Malcolm had the responsibility of naming the scholarship recipients. He used the opportunity of both visits to study the Holy Qu'ran* in Cairo, which was the only Muslim university in the world. Furthermore, Malcolm used both 1964 visits as the springboard for traveling to other parts of Africa and meeting heads of state and other important African dignitaries. He solicited their support to bring charges of racism against the United States before the United Nations.* After his first 1964 visit, Malcolm announced the formation of the Organization of Afro-American Unity (OAAU)* in New York.

In his July 1959 visit, Malcolm attended the Egyptian independence celebration and was impressed with that country's display of weaponry. However, Malcolm X's proudest moment came when, as chairman of the Organization of African Unity (OAU),* President Nasser allowed him to attend the organization's meeting on July 17, 1964, in Cairo as an official observer. In a memorandum that he submitted to the OAU delegates, Malcolm appealed to the African heads of states in his quest for United Nations redress. Malcolm always admired President Nasser's independent thinking and the Egyptian leader's refusal to accept American aid with strings attached. In addition, Malcolm considered Nasser to be one of his foremost mentors.

SELECTED BIBLIOGRAPHY

Blaxland, 1966; Evanzz, 1992; Gallen, ed., 1992; Metz, ed., 1980; *Militant,* November 2, 1964.

Napoleon Bamfo

NATIONAL ADVISORY COMMISSION ON CIVIL DISORDERS (Kerner Commission). In the last year of his life, Malcolm X often forecast that disenchanted black Americans in the inner cities would rise in mass rebellion against white oppression. Black people, he said, would succeed in their freedom struggle "by any means necessary." While many desired the ballot, when the bullet became a necessity, the masses would not be opposed to its use. In 1964 when Harlem,* New York, became the first large black northern community to erupt from racial rioting, his prediction seemed on target. Thereafter, blacks in many of the nation's larger ghettos resorted to serious rebellion, patterned, it seemed, on the bloody and costly summer outburst in Los Angeles' Watts community less than five months after Malcolm's death. It was a force being unleashed not only consistent with Malcolm's prediction but identified with his ideas as blacks went into the streets shouting, "Long live Malcolm X."

Occurring at the height of the civil rights movement* when black gains in the South* were accumulating, albeit slowly, for many Americans, white and black, these were troubling times. In an effort to understand the basis and nature of this black urban frustration President Lyndon B. Johnson* established the National Advisory Commission on Civil Disorders, popularly referred to as the Kerner Commission for Illinois governor Otto Kerner, who presided over the eleven-member bipartisan body. It took two years before the commission rendered its report, citing many of the realities about the American racial milieu that Malcolm had long noted. Indeed, it was white racism, the report bluntly concluded, that was the underlying cause of the disorders, for the racial abyss separating blacks and whites was historical and deep. Had he been alive, Malcolm would likely have found it difficult not to reiterate and reaffirm some of the commission report's salient, but disheartening, points about the history and current conditions of blacks in America. Conversely, however, it is difficult to believe that he would not have taken issue with one of the report's most quoted passages—that the nation was "moving toward two societies, one black, one white—separate and unequal." Malcolm and many others had long argued that America was already a largely divided society, and it was clearly unequal.

SELECTED BIBLIOGRAPHY

Clarke, ed., 1990; *Kerner Report*, 1988; Malcolm X (Breitman, ed.), 1970a; Sitkoff, 1981; Waskow, 1966.

Robert L. Jenkins

NATIONAL ASSOCIATION FOR THE ADVANCEMENT OF COLORED PEOPLE (NAACP). The National Association for the Advancement of Colored People (NAACP) came into being as a biracial group in 1909. It started as the National Negro Committee, which sought equal justice for blacks. Its original black members came from the militant Niagara Movement, which was organized by W.E.B. Du Bois.* The *Crisis* magazine became the NAACP's chief organ, and it helped to make the association the nation's most influential civil rights organization* in the twentieth century.

The NAACP attempted to gain equality for blacks mainly through legal action. Its Legal Defense Fund won impressive legal victories, including *Smith v. Allright* (1944), which outlawed white Democratic primaries, and *Brown v. Board of Education, Topeka, Kansas** (1954), which declared racial segregation* in public education unconstitutional. Later, the NAACP lobbied for such landmark legislation as the 1964 Civil Rights Act* and the 1965 Voting Rights Act.*

Malcolm X disagreed with much of the NAACP's agenda, because he believed its nonviolent, legalistic approach to achieve racial equality was doomed to failure. He criticized the organization for its strong Jewish influence and generally characterized it as a black body dominated at the top by whites. He had little respect for Roy Wilkins,* who headed the NAACP during the 1960s and who was notably critical of Malcolm and the Nation of Islam (NOI).* In early 1961 students of Howard University's* NAACP created a firestorm when the organization invited the increasingly popular minister to speak on campus. When the program was moved off campus to sidestep university objections about Malcolm's appearance, an NAACP official overruled the students and canceled the invitation.

Malcolm did not support racial integration,* hence, philosophically, he opposed all of the major civil rights* groups during the early years of his prominence. In 1961, black nationalists associated with Malcolm X disrupted an NAACP rally. However, on a radio show, he suggested that his organization could work with civil rights groups, including the NAACP, on the things that they found mutually agreeable. Before his death, Malcolm sought an accommodation with the NAACP and similar groups.

SELECTED BIBLIOGRAPHY

Clegg, 1997; DeCaro, 1996; Kellogg, 1967; *New York Amsterdam News*, June 10, 1961; *New York Times*, February 20, 1995; Ross, 1972.

Napoleon Bamfo

NATIONAL URBAN LEAGUE (NUL). The National Urban League (NUL), which was founded in 1911, became the first national interracial organization dedicated to protecting the political rights of African Americans and advancing their economic and social status. The NUL was designed to accommodate the needs of the large influx of African Americans to northern cities who faced de facto employment and housing discrimination. In southern cities, blacks faced similar conditions of discrimination as well as persecution by their white neighbors. The League opened branches in many large cities and directed migrants to jobs and lodging. During the 1960s civil rights movement,* the Urban League embarked on a program of helping inner-city dwellers to increase their political and economic powers through grassroots involvement. Its historical role in fighting discrimination against urban blacks gave it status as one of the big four civil rights* groups of the midtwentieth century.

Malcolm X was less critical of the Urban League than he was of the National Association for the Advancement of Colored People (NAACP)* and the other civil rights groups because he believed the Urban League was more racially integrated. However, he had little respect for the Urban League because of its middle-class orientation and because he felt it too tolerant of white victimization of African Americans. He frequently referred to Whitney Young,* national leader of the Urban League, as "Whitey" Young, though privately he claimed great respect for him. The League, Malcolm X believed, was willing to swallow its pride to beg at the white person's door for accommodation.

In the months prior to his death, Malcolm sought to work more closely with the National Urban League, and he even supported the League and the other civil rights groups in a boycott against New York's segregated schools. Moreover, he and Young became better acquainted, resulting in a greater degree of mutual respect for each other.

SELECTED BIBLIOGRAPHY

Malcolm X (Perry, ed.), 1989; Moore, 1981; Morris, 1984; N. Weiss, 1989.

Napoleon Bamfo

NATION OF ISLAM. *See* Theme Essay "Nation of Islam."

NATION OF ISLAM (NOI) BUSINESS ENTERPRISES. The Nation of Islam (NOI) has been engaged in a number of business enterprises over the years. Elijah Muhammad,* the architect of Black Muslim* business ventures, started preaching in the 1940s that the economic philosophy of the NOI must be economic independence and doing "for self." Five economic propositions guide their economic philosophy. These are knowing oneself and uniting as a result, pooling physical and financial resources, eliminating criticism of all black-owned and black-operated businesses, removing all jealousy, observing the work habits of whites, and working hard collectively as a group. Black Muslims have been successful in owning and operating department stores, restaurants, groceries, bakeries, and a number of service enterprises. In addition, they have owned a number of farms in northern as well as southern states and a meatpacking plant in Chicago.* A dual approach to attract both the lower-class and the middle-class blacks* had different levels of success. Muhammad often berated the middle class as "Uncle Toms"* in his pitch to attract low-income blacks to the movement, which constituted the majority of the membership. At the same time, he often praised the skills and education of successful and middle-class blacks to lure them into the NOI. This class, of course, had more money and entrepreneurial skills for the types of investments that the NOI would pursue. Finance and religion became intertwined, and Muhammad preached that blacks who donated generously would be divinely paid back in full for their charitable efforts. Economic self-help and "Buy Black" campaigns became fashionable among the Black Muslims in the 1950s, more than a decade before these slogans caught on in the era of Black Power* in the middle 1960s.

During the years that Malcolm was a member of the NOI, their economic enterprises grew significantly. If Muhammad was the business architect, Malcolm was the builder. Malcolm was one of the most skilled members in recruit-

Malcolm helped to develop the idea of business ownership for the Nation of Islam. Here
an NOI member poses in front of a Chicago
bakery, one of many profitable enterprises
the sect owned nationally in the 1970s.
Courtesy of Iman Johnny Hasan.

ing and proselytizing new members, who, in turn, brought different abilities to
the organization. Malcolm was very successful in raising money at various
mosques that he supervised to finance many of the economic ventures that the
Black Muslims would undertake. In addition, Muslim* ministers were required
to raise money for the annual Savior's Day Convention* in Chicago, Illinois,
and Malcolm would raise more money than each minister every year. It was
Malcolm who suggested that Elijah Muhammad move Black Muslims into strategic economic and fiscal positions. Based upon his recommendation, Muhammad gradually moved many of his offspring into important jobs in the Chicago
headquarters.

Malcolm started *Muhammad Speaks*,* the Black Muslim newspaper that had
a national circulation and netted considerable profits for the NOI. The efforts of
Muhammad the architect and Malcolm the builder were designed not only to

serve their own Muslim constituency but also to provide jobs for them. Later, a significant component of Malcolm's ideology of economic black nationalism* was developed as the result of his experiences in the NOI and the economic tenets that were espoused by Muhammad. He also charged that white right-wing extremists like H. L. Hunt of Texas were financing the NOI for their own purposes. By the mid-1960s, it was estimated that the total assets of the NOI ran into the millions of dollars, but Malcolm never was the recipient of any of the business income of the organization.

SELECTED BIBLIOGRAPHY

Clegg, 1997; Lincoln, 1994; Malcolm X (Clark, ed.), 1992.

Mfanya Donald Tryman

NEGRO REVOLUTION. The movement of African Americans in the 1950s and 1960s to obtain civil rights* in the United States was often referred to as "the Negro Revolution." More than anything else, this movement was aimed at racial integration* and the elimination of racially discriminatory laws that prevented blacks from utilizing their basic civil rights that are listed in the U.S. Constitution. The Negro Revolution, as it was coined by the media, civil rights activists, and others, was based upon peaceful change through nonviolence. The mobilization and organization of African Americans, which included whites, for this cause has often been referred to as the civil rights movement.*

Malcolm X expressed disdain for what he termed "the so-called Negro Revolution" as well as those who really thought that a revolution* was taking place. He mocked use of the term *revolution* as it applied to civil rights in the United States, stating that a real revolution means complete change and independence from one type of political system to another type of political system. He stated that revolutions are violent and bloody encounters for the political liberation of a people based upon land, and he pointed out that the American Revolution was a classical example. Malcolm stated that a people cannot obtain their freedom by singing "We Shall Overcome," a major theme song of civil rights marchers, noting that the Negro Revolution was the only nonviolent revolution in the whole world. He said that one could not "sing upon some freedom," but one could "swing upon some freedom." He stated that once blacks really understood what a revolution is all about, they would take the word out of their vocabulary and "get back in the corner," out of the way of more militant youth who would not suffer the indignities of state violence, racial injustice, and beatings and killings by racists. Essentially, Malcolm viewed Martin Luther King, Jr.,* and other civil rights leaders engaged in the Negro Revolution as Uncle Toms* who really did not have a clue about what a political revolution entails. During the last year of his life, Malcolm would change his confrontational style toward King and others, but he never changed his mind about the concept of a political revolution and what it involves.

SELECTED BIBLIOGRAPHY
Malcolm X (Breitman, ed.), 1965, 1992, 1998; T'Shaka, 1983.

Mfanya Donald Tryman

NEWARK MOSQUE. The infamous Newark Mosque Number Twenty-five of the Nation of Islam (NOI),* located in Newark, New Jersey, is perhaps best known for its alleged connection to the assassination of Malcolm X. It has been suggested that the actual assassins were members of the NOI and from the Newark mosque. Minister Louis Farrakhan,* head of the NOI, has admitted that he contributed to the violent climate and rhetoric calling for the assassination of Malcolm X,* but he denies that he had any direct involvement in the actual assassination. On the day of the assassination, Farrakhan was absent from his Boston mosque for Sunday services, which he then headed. Strangely enough, no one there knew of his whereabouts. In fact, Farrakhan was at the Newark mosque, a mere thirty minutes from the site of the assassination of Malcolm in New York, and Talmadge Hayer,* one of the assassins and a member of the Newark mosque, asserted that the four Black Muslims* who conspired with him to assassinate Malcolm were also from the Newark mosque. These five allegedly met with another party that trained them for the assassination of Malcolm and paid them for their time and training. For several months after the assassination of Malcolm, the Federal Bureau of Investigation (FBI)* focused on the Boston, New York, and Newark mosques. Violence and assassinations related to the Newark mosque continued years after Malcolm's death. The Newark mosque was known to be one of the two most corrupt Black Muslim mosques, along with the one in Philadelphia.

SELECTED BIBLIOGRAPHY
Evanzz, 1992, 1999; Friedly, 1992; Lee with Wiley, 1992.

Mfanya Donald Tryman

NEWTON, HUEY P. Huey P. Newton was a black political activist who symbolized opposition to racism and classism by invoking Marxist-Leninist principles, rhetoric, and revolutionary action. In October 1966, Newton and his college friend Bobby Seale* founded the Black Panther Party for Self-Defense.* The Black Panthers advocated a combination of incendiary oratory related to aggressive and armed self-defense* along with self-determination. This was coupled with a left-wing ideology and community-based activism and self-help.

Malcolm's revolutionary ideas, speeches, and writings as they related to black nationalism* were a part of Newton's revolutionary rhetoric and practice. Newton was Minister of Defense for the Black Panther Party. Like Malcolm, Newton believed that blacks had a right to arm and defend themselves against violent attacks by the state as well as racist groups like the Ku Klux Klan.* In Oakland, California, the Panthers developed a practice of following the police around in the black community with loaded weapons to ensure that blacks were not mistreated or brutalized by the police when stopped. This led to a 1967 shootout between white policemen, Newton, and a fellow Panther. Newton was seriously wounded in the affair and charged with the murder of one of the officers. Though he was later freed from prison, his release the result of a cause célèbre in the "Free Huey" campaign, his frequent flirting with dangerous situations eventually resulted in his 1989 death from a shooting in an Oakland, California, drug house.

If Malcolm was distinct and representative of the Nation of Islam* by his dress suit, perennial bow tie, and short haircut, Newton was just as distinct and representative of the Black Panther Party by the black beret, black leather coat, and his openly carrying guns and other weapons around for self-defense. Newton, like Malcolm, did not believe that black Americans could achieve justice in the American economic system of capitalism.* Like Malcolm, Newton came from humble, low-income origins. Perhaps because of both of their lower-class backgrounds, as well as their study of revolution,* both Newton and Malcolm believed that the urban ghetto masses who were most alienated from the American political and economic system would constitute the primary vehicle for revolutionary change. Both leaders considered making alliances with radical white groups who supported their cause.

SELECTED BIBLIOGRAPHY

Foner, ed., 1970; Fredrickson, 1995; Pearson, 1994.

Monte Piliawsky

NEW YORK AMSTERDAM NEWS. The *New York Amsterdam News* was the major African American newspaper in the City of New York covering issues, personalities, and events in Harlem,* the state, and the nation. The paper also carried news of what occurred abroad. The newspaper was and still is black owned and operated, with most of its readership and subscription people of color. From the beginning of Malcolm X's meteoric rise in the Nation of Islam (NOI),* the *New York Amsterdam News* carried stories related to both the organization as well as Malcolm X. This was especially true once Malcolm moved to New York as the minister of Temple Number Seven.* Some of the material that the paper carried on Malcolm was objective in nature and some of it subjective. Generally, the paper covered Malcolm in a favorable light. The editor of the newspaper at the time, James Hicks,* had a friendly relationship with Malcolm X. In fact, Hicks gave Malcolm a weekly column in the *Amsterdam News*, a column Malcolm used expeditiously. However, Elijah Muhammad* began using it for himself and relegated Malcolm's column to the less prestigious black newspaper in California, the *Los Angeles Herald-Dispatch*,* which was far from Malcolm's home base in Harlem.

A number of major events and issues related to Malcolm X were carried in the *New York Amsterdam News*. In a column entitled "Pulse of the Public," the newspaper reprinted a letter sent from Malcolm X while in Africa. The letter stated that Africans should determine the sincerity of the U.S. government's offer of assistance by how well it treated black Americans. This would be an appropriate measuring stick. A story was carried in the March 21, 1964, edition in which Malcolm claimed that the Black Muslims* had sent an assassin to kill him. However, the potential assassin refused to try to kill Malcolm. Instead, he told Malcolm of the plot and informed him that he was wanted dead by the organization. The April 18, 1964, edition carried an article related to the eviction proceedings of Malcolm X from the home that he was living in. The home was in East Elmhurst,* Queens, New York, and was owned by the NOI.

Malcolm was silenced by the NOI for his "chickens coming home to roost"* statement over the assassination of President John F. Kennedy* in November 1963. But he was still able to publicize a number of statements and news items in the *Amsterdam News* through Jimmy Booker, a columnist for the paper.

SELECTED BIBLIOGRAPHY

New York Amsterdam News, March 21, 1964, April 18, 1964; B. Perry, 1991.

Mfanya Donald Tryman

NEW YORK TIMES. Except for *Muhammad Speaks*,* perhaps no newspaper provided greater coverage of the life and times of Malcolm X than the *New York Times*. This does not mean that the coverage was always positive or that it always shed a good light on his statements, views, and activities. Until 1964, Malcolm was often described in the *New York Times* as an extremist, preaching violence, racial supremacy, and racial separation.* The *Times* covered almost everything that Malcolm said or did. This included his views on racial segregation* and legal racial separation,* the eviction from his home in East Elmhurst,* Queens, human rights* and civil rights* of African Americans, a confrontation between police and Black Muslims* in Los Angeles (which the *Times* described as a Black Muslim riot), Malcolm's support for Barry Goldwater* over Lyndon B. Johnson* in the 1964 presidential election, his suspension from the Nation of Islam* after the assassination of President John F. Kennedy,* the firebombing of his home, and his assassination.

But Malcolm also received positive coverage from the *New York Times*. When he denounced Elijah Muhammad* as a religious fake, the paper gave him positive coverage for his change in views as well. When Malcolm threatened to bring the case of human rights to the United Nations,* the *Times* not only covered it but also pointed out Malcolm's contention that it was hypocritical of the United States in attacking apartheid in South Africa* when the United States had the same situation in the American South.* Similarly, when Malcolm argued that black Americans needed to return to Africa culturally, philosophically, and spiritually, the *Times* gave him positive press coverage. He reminded black Americans that Africa was their homeland and that they should have a psychological and cultural identity related to the continent. Malcolm argued in the *Times* article that the United States Information Agency (USIA)* was attempting to give Africans an idyllic picture of African Americans in the United States.

At times, given its circulation, Malcolm sought out the newspaper, and often the newspaper would seek him. Both parties realized that it was advantageous in connecting with the other. Malcolm could make certain of his ideas public to a wide audience, and the *Times* could sell more newspapers given Malcolm's controversial public persona.

SELECTED BIBLIOGRAPHY

New York Times, February 28, April 23, December 5, 1963, August 13, December 13, 1964, February 22, 1965.

Mfanya Donald Tryman

NICKNAMES. Throughout his life Malcolm X, formerly Malcolm Little, was known by his various nicknames, aliases, and titles. Some of these names reflected references to his physical characteristics, whereas others were directly related to the changes that occurred in his life. Malcolm's first nicknames came from other children who ostracized him for the reddish color of his skin and hair. "Chink," "Chinaman," "Snowflake," and "Eskimo" were some of the first names that, according to Malcolm, increased his bitterness about having a white rapist's (his maternal grandfather's) blood in his veins. One of his brothers, a favorite of his mother's apparently because of his darker skin, was called "Blackie" in contrast to Malcolm, who was called "Milky." The friction between Malcolm and his brother Philbert* once led to a fight in which Philbert knocked out the inside corners of Malcolm's two front teeth; thereafter, some called Malcolm "Toothless Blondie."

As was the case with the other few black kids in Lansing, Michigan,* Malcolm was called "Nigger," "Darkie," and "Rastus" so often that he once jested that he thought them to be his natural names. Because he was always such a free spirit, notably happy in his disposition on the streets of New York, friends and acquaintances nicknamed him "Happy." But the nicknames that caused him much anxiety were those that drew attention to his skin color. While working on a train, he came to be known as "Sandwich Red." In his days as a hustler, he was "Harlem Red," "Detroit Red," and "Big Red." When the Federal Bureau of Investigation (FBI)* established its first files on him in 1953, a notation indicates that he was also referred to as "Rhythm Red," likely a reference to his dancing reputation during his "hipster" days in Roxbury* and Harlem.* In prison he was called "Satan" because of his antireligious hostility. He was also called "Mr. Know-How" and the "Green-Eyed Monster."

Once converted to Islam,* Malcolm took the last name of "X" to signify the unknown African name stolen from his ancestors when they came to the New World as slaves. Some Muslims* referred to him as Big M. During his estrangement from the Nation of Islam (NOI),* Elijah Muhammad* would call him the "Child Hypocrite," although it would not detract from the more serious and respectful names of honor bestowed on him such as Omowale and El-Hajj Malik El-Shabazz.* The former name meant "the child has come home" and was bestowed upon him by Nigerian traditionalists and students during his 1964 African tour; the latter name in honor of his pilgrimage to Mecca* and conversion to Sunni Islam. While Malcolm continued to answer to and refer to himself as Malcolm X, his new Islamic name represented a new phase of his life, and the honorable recognition was very important to him. Hence, El-Hajj Malik Shabazz was the name that was engraved on his gravestone at his burial site in New York's Ferncliff Cemetery.

SELECTED BIBLIOGRAPHY

Cone, 1992; DeCaro, 1996; Goldman, 1979; Malcolm X with Haley, 1965; Myers, 1993; O'Reilly (Gallen, ed.), 1994; B. Perry, 1991; Sales, 1994.

Brenda Ayres

NIGERIA. Malcolm X made two 1964 journeys abroad that included stops in thirty African countries. Malcolm's West Africa tours influenced his political and religious identity tremendously. The trips gave him a greater connection to his African origins and to his black Islamic roots. He was the first black leader of the 1960s to speak in Africa directly about the plight of blacks in the United States. Malcolm X visited the West African country of Nigeria in May 1964 and returned in the fall of 1964 on a more extensive African tour. He met with President Neramdi Azikiwe, appeared on Nigerian radio and television programs, and spoke at the University of Ibadan, where students intimidated a West Indian professor who tried to defend the United States against Malcolm's criticisms. According to Nigerian scholar E. U. Essien-Udom,* who knew Malcolm personally from his time in the United States, Malcolm excited the Nigerian crowds whenever he spoke with his rare combination of oratorical brillance and "naked honesty." It was while in Nigeria that Malcolm seemed to abandon any idea of a large-scale African American physical return to Africa; rather, blacks should seek a philosophical, social, and cultural return to their homeland in order to develop a better working framework for Pan-Africanism.* The Muslim Student Society of Nigeria made Malcolm an honorary member, giving him the name "Omowale," Yoruba for "the child has returned." Malcolm regarded the recognition as one of his greatest honors.

During his second 1964 trip to Africa, Malcolm's speeches took on an increasingly anti-imperialist cast. He hoped to internationalize the African American struggle by connecting the problems of blacks in the United States with those of the black community throughout the world. He met with African heads of states, which included Nigerian President Azikiwe, and lobbied to bring the issue of racism and discrimination against African Americans before the United Nations.* The receptions that Malcolm received in West Africa solidified his position as an international figure.

SELECTED BIBLIOGRAPHY

Essien-Udom, 1971; Malcolm X (Breitman, ed.), 1987; *Militant*, June 1, December 7, 1964; Sales, 1994; R. Turner, 1997.

Monte Piliawsky

Richard Nixon during a dinner speech in Mississippi in the early 1960s. Mississippi Republican Party Papers, Special Collections Department, Mitchell Memorial Library, Mississippi State Unitersity.

NIXON, RICHARD MILHOUS. A graduate of Whittier College in 1934, and Duke University Law School in 1937, Richard Nixon narrowly lost the 1960 presidential campaign to President John F. Kennedy.* In 1968, Nixon won the presidency and was reelected in 1972. The Watergate scandal caused him to resign the presidency on August 9, 1974.

Malcolm X taught that only under exceptional conditions could blacks make lasting gains in the electoral arena. He argued for an all-black political party, independent of the two major parties. An example of Malcolm's standard references to Nixon was his January 23, 1963, speech entitled "Twenty Million Black People in a Political, Economic and Mental Prison." Malcolm noted that in the 1960 presidential election, because whites were closely divided between the two candidates, the black vote made Kennedy president.

As it was with all white political figures, Malcolm thought little of Richard Nixon. He once referred to him sarcastically as "Tricky Dick," a term that forecast America's later impressions of Nixon's politics. Malcolm's rhetoric of black nationalism,* by fostering urban rebellions in the United States during the mid-1960s, may have contributed to Nixon's 1968 presidential victory. Certainly, a goal of Nixon's "law and order" political campaign was to exploit the white backlash against the Black Power* movement.

SELECTED BIBLIOGRAPHY

Ambrose, 1987; Malcolm X (Breitman, ed.), 1965, 1970a.

Monte Piliawsky

NKRUMAH, KWAME. Born in 1909 in western Ghana (formerly the Gold Coast) to one of the wives of a goldsmith, Nkrumah early benefited from a relatively affluent background. One of a few Ghanaians to be formally educated abroad prior to the mid-twentieth century, between 1935 and 1947 he attended college in Pennsylvania at Lincoln University and the University of Pennsylvania before relocating to England to attend the London School of Economics. While in the United States he spent time in Harlem,* where he found work selling fish. When he occasionally fell on hard times in New York, he slept in the city's subways, joining others whose economic struggles also left them destitute. After returning to West Africa in the late 1940s, he used his western education well and rose rapidly to political prominence in the emerging Ghanaian movement toward independence. In 1957 Ghana received its independence from Great Britain, and in 1960 Nkrumah became its prime minister and later president. A Pan-Africanist and Marxist Socialist whose preachments about African unity helped to lead to the establishment of the Organization of African Unity,* Nkrumah symbolized the possibilities for black Africa. In the years of his leadership, his name and that of the Republic of Ghana* were synonymous as he worked to make the small nation the continent's showplace.

Few black Americans caught up in the black nationalist movement of the era were not impressed with the charismatic leader. He helped to solidify his position among them when he made a visit to the United States shortly after he became Ghana's leader. It was while Nkrumah was in New York in a fall 1960 visit that he first met Malcolm during a Harlem rally. The keynote speaker at the rally, the Ghanaian president spoke about the inherent possibilities accruing from the linkage of African and African American interests, the idea of which was gaining greater currency in Malcolm's own thinking. Hence, Malcolm, too, was impressed with the African leader, Ghana's Osagyefo (Redeemer), and reveled over being in Ghana in mid-1964 on his return to the United States from Mecca.* Celebrated by Accra's small African American community and given a chance to meet many of the country's most important governmental officials, Malcolm felt particularly privileged to have a private audience with Nkrumah. The meeting was arranged by Shirley Graham Du Bois,* W.E.B. Du Bois's* widow, who was an official in Nkrumah's government and a close friend of the president.

Malcolm, who wrote of Nkrumah's warmth and graciousness in receiving him, was also impressed with the president's knowledge of black American conditions. Their brief conversation included some attention to Pan-Africanism* and the idea of black unity throughout the African diaspora, topics dear to both men, but there is no substantive account of what the two actually discussed. However, Julian Mayfield,* then leader of Accra's small African American colony, seems creditable in his assessment that Malcolm received few positive expectations from Nkrumah that he would support Malcolm's effort to pursue a United Nations'* case against America's treatment of blacks. Ghana was experiencing dire economic problems at the time, and Nkrumah simply did not want to alienate the United States and preclude the possibility of aid. Still, Malcolm regarded the meeting with Nkrumah as the highlight of his African tour, and he mentioned it, along with meetings he had with other African heads of state, in numerous speeches during the remaining months of his life.

Apparently, Malcolm came away from the Nkrumah visit having impressed the African leader. According to one Malcolm biographer, Nkrumah, concerned about the threat to Malcolm's life, offered the black American leader refuge in Ghana and a government job. Unwilling to abandon his causes at home, however, Malcolm refused to entertain the invitation. Nkrumah remembered Malcolm in death, his letter of condolence one of many that came from the international community that Malcolm had come in contact with during the last years of his life. In 1966, the year after Malcolm's death, a military coup ousted Nkrumah, and he lived the remaining six years of his life in exile in Guinea, West Africa.

SELECTED BIBLIOGRAPHY

Angelou, 1986; Apter, 1972; DeCaro, 1996; Evanzz, 1992; Goldman, 1979; Jackson and Rosberg, 1982; Malcolm X with Haley, 1965; Wallerstein, 1967; G. M. Williams, 1969.

Robert L. Jenkins

NONVIOLENCE PHILOSOPHY. The roots of the nonviolence philosophy can be found in the tradition of Christian pacifism and in the teachings of Mahatma Gandhi. In the wake of the Protestant Reformation, some dissenting sects, such as the Quakers, embraced doctrine that proclaimed the inherent God-like nature of all individuals, beliefs that ultimately led them to renounce the use of force and oppose slavery and war. Gandhi claimed in his writings that nonviolence was the only ethical way to achieve any meaningful political goal, and he employed nonviolent protest in the twentieth century to resist British colonialism, to challenge the Indian caste system, and finally, to create an independent Indian state.

By the 1940s, the Congress of Racial Equality,* an American civil rights organization,* had adopted nonviolence as its working philosophy, but Martin

Luther King, Jr.,* following a visit to India in 1959, became the one who popularized the philosophy as the best method to attack the racial caste system in the United States. King believed nonviolent tactics offered the only sensible approach for the civil rights movement,* considering the fact that African Americans constituted only one-tenth of the U.S. population.

Although Malcolm X eventually moved toward supporting some of the aims of the civil rights movement—especially after the break with Elijah Muhammad* freed him from the Nation of Islam's* nonengagement policy—he rejected the idea that nonviolence was the best method to achieve freedom and justice for African Americans. He deplored the violence used by white supremacists against innocent black victims in the South's* civil rights* struggle and said he could not be nonviolent toward his oppressors if they were not nonviolent in their relationship with him. He encouraged blacks not to be nonviolent when violence was necessary to protect themselves, and he scored black leaders in the most strident of voices for their views on nonviolence. Ultimately, Malcolm repudiated the basic tenet of the nonviolence philosophy: that the end can never justify the means used to achieve any specific goal. In contrast, Malcolm felt that African Americans needed as many weapons in their arsenal of tactics as they could amass. They should achieve their freedom and rights without limiting their options, including violence. Malcolm believed that his approach actually provided an opportunity to expand the black struggle for civil rights by offering an alternative to achieving political freedom beyond merely nonviolent direct action.

Malcolm opposed nonviolence for other reasons as well. Noting that nonviolence was a moral tactic, he claimed that such maneuvers could only be used to fight moral people, certainly not the definition of American racists. Malcolm also rejected the idea that because African Americans were in modest numbers in the U.S. population that a nonviolent approach was their only option. Especially after he returned from his trip to the Middle East* and Africa in 1964, Malcolm linked the black struggle in the United States with the fight of people of color around the globe confronting oppression, a perspective that highlighted African Americans' status as part of a world majority and challenged one of King's justifications for a nonviolent approach to achieving civil rights.

SELECTED BIBLIOGRAPHY

I. Bell, 1968; Cone, 1991; Malcolm X (Breitman, ed.), 1970a.

Charles C. Bolton

NORTHERN NEGRO GRASS ROOTS LEADERSHIP CONFERENCE. In November 1963 the popular Detroit* Baptist minister the Reverend C. L. Franklin hosted a two-day gathering of black civil rights* leaders, the objective being to organize a northern version of Martin Luther King, Jr.'s* Southern Christian Leadership Conference.* However, dissension soon enveloped the meeting over issues relative to excluding the participation of black nationalist representatives and adopting King's nonviolent conservative philosophy. The resulting walkout led to the organization of a rump meeting under the militant leader of the Black Church of the Madonna, the Reverend Albert Cleage, Jr.,* an admirer of Malcolm X. Organized under the auspices of the Michigan-based Freedom Now Party* and the Group on Advanced Leadership (GOAL), the conclave, called the Northern Negro Grass Roots Leadership Conference, tabbed Malcolm, who had not been invited to the initial gathering, as the keynote speaker. Two days of workshops and participant interaction interspersed the conference's major speeches. In biting criticism of the traditional civil rights movement* and its leaders, and the damaging effects of white racism on Black America, Malcolm delivered perhaps his most impressive, certainly most enduring address, "Message to the Grass Roots."* Implicit in his comments were numerous references to his support of violent revolution* against continued resistance to black American advancement.

Some Malcolm X scholars mark the leadership conference as a notable turning point in the black leader's activism. On the verge of permanent disassociation with Elijah Muhammad* and the Nation of Islam (NOI),* Malcolm's appearance at the conference and memorable speech strongly supported the idea of militant grassroots political and civil rights activism, a marked departure from his largely muffled voice in the NOI on matters of civil rights advocacy and participation in the political process. Malcolm's role in the conference was well received in the overwhelmingly non-Muslim conclave and gave him increased visibility and respect, if not immediate credibility, even among those listeners who had previously been strong in their anti-Malcolm views.

SELECTED BIBLIOGRAPHY

Branch, 1988; Carson (Gallen, ed.), 1991; Goldman (Franklin and Meier, eds.), 1982; Malcolm X (Breitman, ed.), 1965.

Robert L. Jenkins

NUMBERS RUNNER. During the twentieth century, one of the most popular illegal gambling practices was what is popularly referred to as playing the numbers. Formally called the policy game, it was particularly prominent in American urban centers, often controlled by organized crime. In Harlem* during the 1920s and 1930s, the illegal lottery was one of the most lucrative rackets for local black crime lords, so profitable that major white mobsters like the infamous Dutch Schultz eventually moved to tap the multimillion-dollar market. Poor urban dwellers often played daily small sums of money (sometimes as small as a one-cent wager) from their meager earnings, hoping to "hit" the numbers. Although the game was occasionally associated with numerical combinations related to attendance at horse races, it was more typically based on a bettor duplicating the final three digits in the day's total sale of stock in the United States and foreign exchanges. The odds were staggering against someone actually duplicating the numbers in correct order, but when accomplished, and it happened with considerable frequency, the payoff, depending on the wager, could also be just as staggering. As is usually the case with games of chance, however, the banker was the one who gained the most.

During his hustling* days as "Detroit Red" in Harlem in the 1940s, Malcolm was a numbers runner, responsible for turning into "controllers" the numbers of the wagers from whom he collected. This, too, could be a profitable aspect of the game since he and others in the army of runners normally received as much as 10 percent of the money they shuttled to their bosses. Further, a winner was expected to tip his runner generously when fortune smiled on him or her. Malcolm also played the numbers. During the time, he relished the fact that he was a client of the reputable runner West Indian Archie,* a holdover from the strong-armed days of Dutch Schultz. Archie, according to Malcolm, only handled the numbers of heavy bettors, and Malcolm was certainly a heavy bettor, frequently spending as much as $40 daily on the lottery, especially when some of his other illegal activity brought him a considerable cash flow. Like many of his own clients, Malcolm occasionally hit for small combinations, never the big payoff. Indeed, it was a dispute with his friend Archie over the payoff of a small winning combination that nearly got Malcolm killed and soon prompted a permanent rupture in their personal and business relationship.

As he did when he later reflected on other seamy aspects of his youthful life, Malcolm found little in this activity about which to be proud. Moreover, though he understood the proclivity of impoverished blacks to seek simplistic solutions to their economic conditions, he nevertheless regarded spending hard-earned money on any form of gambling as a foolhardy practice. From both a practical and moral standpoint, Malcolm during his ministry could speak about the evils of gambling. It is doubtful that his view would be different today about the legalized state lotteries that have rendered the old numbers game insignificant.

SELECTED BIBLIOGRAPHY

D. Lewis, 1981; Malcolm with Haley, 1965; Smitherman, 2000.

Robert L. Jenkins

O

OMAHA, NEBRASKA. Malcolm X was born Malcolm Little in Omaha, Nebraska, on May 19, 1925. He was one of eight children. His parents were the Reverend Earl Little, Sr.,* a large, dark-complexioned itinerant Christian preacher from Reynolds, Georgia, and Louise,* a fragile West Indian woman who was so light-skinned that she could "pass" for white. Little, a dedicated organizer for Marcus Aurelius Garvey,* moved from Omaha to Milwaukee after Malcolm was born. During the years when Malcolm lived in Omaha, the city had a thriving black population. But the black population hardly found a paradise in Nebraska's largest city. Indeed, only six years before Malcolm's birth in Omaha, like some twenty-five other cities across the nation, it had been part of the 1919 "Red Summer" of race riots. To be sure, like elsewhere, blacks had not been mere victims; they fought back in the rioting, though they suffered casualties in brutal ways.

Malcolm's family left Omaha after their house was vandalized and terrorized by members of the Ku Klux Klan,* who also physically threatened Mrs. Little. The Littles were asked to leave town because Malcolm's father was accused of spreading trouble among "the good Negroes" of Omaha. The Klan, which enjoyed considerable popularity in many midwestern cities like Omaha during the 1920s, was largely agitated over Earl Little's Garvey activities. Not only was Earl Little grounded in the Garvey tradition, he also held the top leadership position in the Omaha Branch of the Universal Negro Improvement Association* as president. Omaha represented Malcolm's first encounter with racism and bigotry. The incident with the Klan would affect his thinking his entire life.

SELECTED BIBLIOGRAPHY

Clarke, ed., 1969; Franklin and Moss, 1994; Goldman, 1992; Malcolm X with Haley, 1965.

Morgan Ero

ON RELIEF. Malcolm X was opposed to blacks being "on relief" or what is often referred to as welfare. Malcolm believed that depending on free food and subsidies from the government created laziness in the recipients.

Malcolm, as a Muslim,* believed that Negroes should advocate and practice black nationalism* as a solution to their economic deprivation and desist from accepting relief from the government. He urged blacks to control their economic destiny, instead of being permanently dependent on welfare. Malcolm believed that by accepting relief one's confidence, racial dignity, and incentive to excel as a people were destroyed.

He never forgot the humiliating and destructive nature of the welfare system that his mother was exposed to after his father's death in Michigan. He often referred to the dehumanizing and negative effect of welfare on his proud mother, the constant intrusion of workers from the state welfare department in their private lives, and how his mother was eventually devastated physically and psychologically as a result of the persistent invasion of officials in her family's private life. Malcolm's family unit was subsequently destroyed and his mother confined to a mental institution, in part as a result of being on public relief.

SELECTED BIBLIOGRAPHY

Clarke, ed., 1969; Goldman, 1973; Malcolm X with Haley, 1965.

Morgan Ero

ORGANIZATION OF AFRICAN UNITY (OAU). The Organization of African Unity (OAU) is a regional organization founded in 1963 in Cairo, Egypt,* with its headquarters in Addis Ababa, Ethiopia. The organization was established to develop unity, end colonialism, foster economic development, and provide security for African states. Malcolm X was so impressed with the OAU, especially its Pan-African philosophy, that it became the impetus for the establishment of his new organization in June 1964, the Organization of Afro-American Unity (OAAU).*

Malcolm X visited Africa twice in the year prior to his death. During his second visit to African capitals in the summer of 1964, he attended a meeting of the fledgling Organization of African Unity. African leaders, including Dr. Kwame Nkrumah* of Ghana,* Ben Bella* of Algeria,* and Gamel Abdel Nasser* of Egypt, extended an invitation to Malcolm as chairman of the OAAU to attend the conference of heads of states as an observer and a representative at that time of 22 million American blacks. Malcolm was also given the opportunity to submit a memorandum to the group.

In his memorandum, Malcolm urged members of the OAU to lend their support to his effort to indict the U.S. government before the United Nations.* He accused the United States of being morally incapable of protecting the lives and property of black Americans. Malcolm attempted to elevate the demands of American blacks from civil rights* to that of human rights,* contending that the issue was a threat to world peace. On July 17, 1964, thirty-three heads of independent African nations passed a resolution condemning the brutal treatment of black Americans by the U.S. government.

Malcolm was scheduled to attend another meeting of the OAU in Algiers at the invitation of Ben Bella in March of the following year, but fate had a different plan. In February 1965, he was killed.

SELECTED BIBLIOGRAPHY

Clarke, ed., 1969; Goldman, 1979; Malcolm X with Haley, 1965; Sales, 1994.

Morgan Ero

ORGANIZATION OF AFRO-AMERICAN UNITY (OAAU). Shortly after his departure from the Nation of Islam,* Malcolm started his own organization, the Muslim Mosque, Inc. (MMI).* Primarily a spiritual body, the MMI did not serve Malcolm's interest in having a more politically oriented institution that would serve as a platform for his ideas to address the plight of blacks in the United States. He soon found what he believed would be the vehicle. On June 28, 1964, six weeks after returning to New York from his pilgrimage to Mecca,* Malcolm X called a press conference to announce a new organization, the Organization of Afro-American Unity (OAAU). John Henrik Clarke,* a well-known college professor, Malcolm, and several of his followers helped organize the OAAU. Indeed, it was Clarke who suggested the name of the Organization of Afro-American Unity to Malcolm and in whose Harlem* living room, where one of the organizational meetings occurred, that the organizers finalized the Clarke-written draft of the body's Aims and Objectives. The organization was patterned after the Organization of African Unity (OAU)* established at Addis Ababa, Ethiopia, in May 1963. Malcolm had come to understand much about the goals and workings of the OAU while visiting Africa in 1964. The purpose of the OAAU was to provide a medium through which Americans of African descent, regardless of their socioeconomic or religious background, could coalesce to fight against the inhumane indignities allowed by the U.S. government. Additionally, the OAAU endeavored to develop a coalition between the peoples of Africa and those of African descent throughout the diaspora. The coalition was sought in order to present a united front in the fight for human rights* for all races of people. The OAAU constitution declared that African Americans have the right of self-defense,* asserting the right as the first law of nature.

The constitution also called for the "proper education" of African Americans. The educational goals of the organization included developing African studies programs that would tell the truth about the existence of the African in world history. The constitution also envisioned a community-based school board, along with a cooperative parent/teacher association that would contribute to parental involvement in the educational process. Hopefully, the result would be well-rounded and well-grounded students, who ultimately would become productive citizens of the world.

The OAAU's economic and political agenda emphasized a commitment to voter registration. Such an emphasis was designed to combat existing economic exploitation and poverty and to promote the material liberation of the African American community. In a speech delivered at the Audubon Ballroom* in Harlem, Malcolm also indicated several other OAAU domestic programs. The organization wanted to rid the community of crime, violence, and drugs by starting public speaking programs, a newspaper, and outreach political and economic programs. These programs were expected to allow blacks to help themselves and to bring positive values back into their community.

Significantly, the OAAU expected to bring charges of human rights violations against the United States before the United Nations,* with the support of the newly independent nations of Africa. The plan was to internationalize the struggle of African Americans in an effort to enhance human rights. To implement the plan, Malcolm returned to Africa as a delegate to the OAU Summit Conference, held in Cairo, Egypt,* in July 1964. As the OAAU's representative, Malcolm appeared in an unofficial delegate status. At the conference he appealed to the delegates of the thirty-four member nations to bring the cause of 22 million Africans before the United Nations. He got a positive response from some of the delegates that they would support his efforts.

After the conference concluded, Malcolm extended his visit in Africa by traveling to several countries, meeting many political leaders, and discussing the proposed involvement of those countries in the OAAU's expected case against the United States. However, neither at the African Summit Conference nor in later meetings with African political leaders was Malcolm able to gain their full support. Malcolm's return to the United States on November 24, 1964, found the OAAU coming apart. The group lacked financial support, a crucial problem, and its members were quarreling over how to initiate its programs. Malcolm's eighteen-week tour of Africa had left the organization without leadership, which proved costly to its youthful development.

Malcolm, realizing the urgency of the situation, set a new organizational thrust for the OAAU, which emphasized assisting the civil rights organizations* in their push for African American rights. During an interview with reporter Claude Lewis,* Malcolm was asked where he and his group were headed. He answered that he was for the freedom of 22 million African Americans "by any means necessary." He further suggested that the OAAU would formulate coalitions with all of the organizations that promoted African American progress, from the most radical to the more moderate organizations. In February 1965, just days prior to Malcolm's assassination, the OAAU issued a statement regarding its interracial and human rights posture. This statement outlined the African American origins of the OAAU but reemphasized the body's effort to unify with other organizations, regardless of their racial makeup, to ensure African American progress.

However, before the OAAU had an opportunity to have an impact on the fight for human rights, its outspoken and brilliant leader was gunned down by assassins' bullets during a Sunday speech at the Audubon Ballroom in New

York's Harlem community. Consequently, no one will ever know the extent of success that Malcolm and the OAAU could have realized for African Americans. Nevertheless, the spirit of Malcolm endures, and his legacy in the human rights movement remains firm.

SELECTED BIBLIOGRAPHY

Gallen, ed., 1992; Goldman, 1973; Karim with Skutches and Gallen, 1992; Malcolm X with Haley, 1965; Sales, 1994; T'Shaka, 1983.

Saul Dorsey

ORGANIZATION OF AFRO-AMERICAN UNITY ABROAD. On the eve of his death in 1965, Malcolm X had become a true international figure. His travels in the Middle East* and Africa and speaking tours in France and England helped to enhance his reputation as an ardent critic of White America's treatment of its black minority and a legitimate champion of his race's causes. As his stature rose both at home and abroad, so did his following in the Organization of Afro-American Unity (OAAU).* By the time of his death, small cells of the organization could be found in West Africa, France, and Canada. In West Africa, Alice Windom,* whom Malcolm had spent some time with while visiting the Republic of Ghana,* and personal friend, journalist, and writer Julian Mayfield,* nominal leader of Accra's small black American expatriate community, spearheaded the establishment of the OAAU in Africa; in Montreal, international law scholar and university professor Dr. Y. N. Kly held the post of International Chairman of Canada's branch. Little is known about these groups. Exactly who took the initiative in establishing the group in Paris, France, for example, is not clear, although Carlos Moore,* a close friend of Malcolm's, is suggestive. Malcolm X biographer Peter Goldman* noted that the branch, composed of African American and Latin American students, was certainly "active." In his autobiography, Malcolm did not mention these affiliates, perhaps because they had not taken significant shape at the time of his work on the book and because he wanted to maintain secrecy about his organization similar to the confidentiality that he once maintained about aspects of the Nation of Islam (NOI).* Only tacitly did he refer to the organizing work under way in West Africa after his return from the continent in late 1964.

Malcolm realized that his death was imminent long before his murder, and he had hoped that the OAAU would survive him. Essentially, it did not. With no one available to fill the charismatic void that Malcolm left in the organization, it had only a nominal existence following his death in 1965. Apparently, efforts to sustain and further develop the branches outside of the United States suffered a similar fate about the same time.

SELECTED BIBLIOGRAPHY

Angelou, 1986; Goldman, 1979; Kly, 1986; Stovall, 1996.

Robert L. Jenkins

ORGANIZATION OF AFRO-AMERICAN UNITY LIBERATION SCHOOL. Established by one of Malcolm X's chief lieutenants, James Campbell,* the Organization of Afro-American Unity's (OAAU)* Liberation School was the educational component of Malcolm's fledgling organization. Although more comprehensive in design and structure than the elementary nature of the freedom schools of the southern civil rights movement,* the OAAU's version was clearly influenced by them. Indeed, Campbell, a longtime Pan-Africanist, was himself a veteran civil rights* activist, having labored in the early 1960s' Student Non-Violent Coordinating Committee*–led southern summer projects where the idea of freedom schools first took hold. The intent of the OAAU's Liberation School was to merge, through a curriculum framework for adults, both members and nonmembers, and younger children, orientation in practical and citizenship education and Pan-Africanism.* Through weekly Saturday morning classes, young "students" were exposed to heavy doses of African and African American history and politics and training sessions designed to elevate their consumer skills. Wednesday night classes were reserved for adults when they were similarly instructed with an added emphasis for married couples on practical matters relating to family development and household management. A variety of people associated with Malcolm and the OAAU made themselves available to teach in the school, including scholars like the prominent Africanists John Henrik Clarke* and Dr. Keith Beard. One of Malcolm's most trusted associates, James Shabazz,* considered a major intellectual force in both the Muslim Mosque, Inc.* and the OAAU, as well as former Garveyites Eddie "Pork Chop" Davis and Dr. Ben Jochanan, also contributed as participants to the classes. Such personalities were capable and often did present and lead high levels of discussion in these classes. Malcolm X was seldom present when classes were conducted, but on at least one occasion, he led a spirited debate with a graduate student on the question of East African slavery.

Malcolm certainly supported the concept of the Liberation School and willingly signed the graduation certificate recognizing student accomplishments. Unfortunately, the Liberation School, like its parent the OAAU, ended soon after Malcolm's death, the potential for all three entities to do good work in the international black community unrealized.

SELECTED BIBLIOGRAPHY
Militant, October 5, 1964; Sales, 1994.

Robert L. Jenkins

OSTROWSKI (Richard Kaminska). Ostrowski, as Malcolm referred to him in his autobiography, was an English teacher at Mason Junior High School* and had a profound impact on Malcolm X during his eighth-grade year. Mr. Ostrowski, prone to advising students about their future, told Malcolm, who aspired to become a lawyer, that he was not being realistic and that Malcolm should consider an occupation suitable for a black man, such as carpentry. This discussion and a trip to visit his half sister in Boston forced Malcolm to change his views about white society and his present situation. He realized that he had outstanding grades, yet was advised to accept menial occupations because he was black. He began to resent the racial jokes and racial slurs he had light-heartedly endured and became embittered toward his white classmates. Malcolm, disenchanted with this experience, dropped out of school at the end of his eighth-grade year. Later, reflecting on these experiences, he considered Mr. Ostrowski's advice to be a major turning point in his life. Had he become a lawyer or doctor, Malcolm may have been content to live in a society where his self-image and his mind would have always been molded by whites who would have demanded racial integration* based upon their terms and beliefs.

SELECTED BIBLIOGRAPHY

Goldman, 1979; Malcolm X with Haley, 1965; B. Perry, 1991.

Betsy Sakariassen Nash

P

PAN-AFRICANISM. Upon returning in 1964 from the first of two trips to Africa and the Middle East,* Malcolm X became a convert to Pan-Africanism. He had visited the Republic of Ghana,* the fountainhead of Pan-Africanism, where apparently he became convinced that black nationalism,* as he had earlier defined it, was incomplete without an international dimension. His founding in June 1964 of the Organization of Afro-American Unity (OAAU)* reflected his conversion to the belief that the war on racism could only be effectively waged internationally.

Pan-Africanism, a political movement that advocates the unification of all African rule and leadership and the unity and solidarity of black peoples everywhere, had its origins in the nineteenth century. Led initially by blacks from the United States and the West Indies who promoted the worldwide solidarity of all blacks who struggled against white domination and colonialism, the Pan-African movement held its first international congress in London in 1900. Early on, international leaders of the movement disagreed about strategy. W.E.B. Du Bois* and Marcus Garvey* favored black separatism. Blaise Diagne of Senegal and other conservative leaders advocated international cooperation. At the next Pan-African Congress, hosted by the Tuskegee Institute in 1914, Du Bois held to his separatist arguments. In the post–World War I congresses Du Bois continued to be a dominant voice.

Not until after World War II* did the Pan-African movement become truly African. In the 1945 Pan-African Congress held in Manchester, England, Gold Coast political leader Kwame Nkrumah* called for African independence. Twelve years later his homeland, Ghana, gained its independence from Great Britain. Colonial rule soon yielded to independence movements elsewhere in Africa. Nkrumah became the leader of the more extreme or revolutionary Pan-Africanists, who thought that African political unification should move forward without waiting for economic integration to occur. The moderate wing of the movement, led by men from former French colonies, argued that economic unity was the essential precondition of political confederation.

In 1963, the year before Malcolm X visited Nkrumah in Ghana, the two wings of the movement met in Addis Ababa, Ethiopia, to reconcile their differences. Out of this conference, attended by thirty of the thirty-three African heads of state, came the Organization of African Unity (OAU).* This became the primary continent-wide organization and included all of the independent African states except South Africa,* which was still dominated by whites. In a late 1964 visit to Africa, Malcolm attended an OAU meeting in Cairo, Egypt.* Although not allowed to speak, he was officially received by the African heads of state as the special representative of his OAAU organization.

It was this organization that inspired Malcolm X, a year later, to found the OAAU, and he tried to pattern the fledgling organization on the African model. Malcolm's return from Africa not only strengthened his ideas about his organization, but it also informed his views on how the average black American could further Pan-Africanism. Blacks simply had to follow the strategy and model of American Jews.* Jews never returned to Israel physically; rather, they were linked "culturally, philosophically, and psychologically" to Israel, ties that enhanced their political, economic, and social status at home. African Americans could do the same for Africa, allowing Pan-Africanism to accomplish for blacks throughout their diaspora what Zionism accomplished for the Jewish diaspora. After Africans overthrew colonial rule and organized additional independent nations, the Pan-African movement, which requires the surrender of individual state sovereignty, declined. Malcolm X did not live to develop fully his Pan-African ideas or to see the OAAU mature as an organization.

SELECTED BIBLIOGRAPHY

Geiss, 1974; R. Hill, ed., 1987; Martin, 1984; *New York Amsterdam News*, May 23, 1964; B. Perry, 1991; Sales, 1994.

Charles D. Lowery

PARADISE VALLEY. Paradise Valley was a mostly black community in the Hamtramck area of Detroit, Michigan,* an industrial area with a number of primarily white-owned enterprises. Originally the ghetto that blacks inhabited was dominated by Jews.* It was here that Elijah Muhammad* first moved in the early 1940s from Georgia, in search of a better life. It was also here, in Paradise Valley, that W. D. Fard,* the mystical prophet of the Nation of Islam (NOI),* arrived in 1930. Both Fard and Muhammad were successful in proselytizing a number of African Americans, who joined the NOI in Paradise Valley. Fard preached on street corners in Paradise Valley, just as Malcolm preached on street corners in Harlem,* both attempting to recruit new members to the NOI. Malcolm frequently made references to W. D. Fard in Paradise Valley in his talks with new recruits and in his Sunday sermons.

During the summer of 1943 Paradise Valley served as the flashpoint for a riot by African Americans after a rumor circulated that a black woman and her baby had been drowned by a white mob. Tension had been building in Paradise Valley as the result of a number of racial incidents. A riot commission blamed the racial turmoil, in which thirty-four people, mostly blacks, were killed, on the NOI and the Ku Klux Klan.* Muhammad and Fard were constantly harassed by the police while in Paradise Valley, and Muhammad's continuous cautions to Malcolm regarding confrontations with police over incidents involving Black Muslims* were influenced by his former experiences in this Detroit community.

SELECTED BIBLIOGRAPHY

Clegg, 1997; Evanzz, 1999; Malcolm X with Haley, 1965; Platt, 1971.

Mfanya Donald Tryman

PARKS, GORDON. Gordon Parks was a personal friend of Malcolm X and worked for *Life* magazine during the 1960s. At the time, a great deal of his work was related to photography, and he took a number of pictures and photos of Malcolm X that are considered among the best. In fact, Parks did a number of photo essays not only for *Life* but for *Ebony* magazine* and other publishing entities as well. In addition, Gordon Parks has gained notoriety as an author and film producer. Among other works, one of his best known movies is *The Learning Tree*, produced in the early 1970s. The movie is an autobiography of Park's childhood and his experience with racism and oppression. In an interview Malcolm had with Parks a week before he was mowed down by assassins' bullets, Malcolm explained that his conceptualization of brotherhood in America had gotten him caught, to use Malcolm's words, "in a jam," implying that he knew that death was near. And two days before the fatal ending, Malcolm again met with Parks. Malcolm told Parks that the days with the Black Muslims* were mad and sick ones. He stated that he was glad to be free from them and that it was now time for him to be a martyr in the name of brotherhood and reach out to others that were not Muslims.* Parks joined Malcolm's family and a close circle of friends and followers gathered in mourning the evening of Malcolm's assassination.

Less then a week before his assassination, Malcolm had revealed a note to one of his close aides that contained the names of five people. These were the people that he felt would be responsible for carrying out his assassination. When Malcolm was assassinated, his wife, Betty Shabazz,* removed from his jacket pocket the blood-stained note with the names. The evening of his assassination, when Parks joined Malcolm's wife and others, Betty showed him the note that contained the list of conceivable assassins. Parks copied down the names, presumably with the intention of revealing them in a later *Life* magazine story reflecting on his friendship with the slain leader. However, in a story carried by *Life* in the March issue of 1965, the last interview of Malcolm by Gordon Parks, he makes no mention of the assassins list. Neither Betty Shabazz nor Parks subsequently revealed the names that were in the note.

SELECTED BIBLIOGRAPHY

Blackside/PBS, 1994; Evanzz, 1992; Parks, 1965; Parks (Clarke, ed.), 1990.

Mfanya Donald Tryman

PARKS, ROSA. Frequently called the "Mother of the Civil Rights Movement," former seamstress Rosa Parks is best known for her role in inspiring the 1955 Montgomery, Alabama, Bus Boycott. Her steadfast refusal to abandon her seat for a white rider not only initiated the boycott that led directly to the desegregation of bus transportation in Montgomery; but the success was also catalytic in propelling nonviolent civil rights* activism throughout the South.* It also led to the rise of Martin Luther King, Jr.,* as the preeminent symbol of the black rights struggle. Despite her historic act in 1955, Parks left Alabama permanently in 1957 to live in the safety of Detroit, Michigan.* Detroit was the city where Malcolm X began his career as Nation of Islam (NOI)* spokesperson, and he visited the city frequently. Though she had heard him speak before, Parks did not meet Malcolm until February 1965, a week prior to his death. Invited by his close friend, attorney Milton Henry,* a future leader in the Revolutionary Action Movement (RAM),* Malcolm was in the Motor City to make a speech on a program sponsored by the Afro-American Broadcasting Company, which Parks attended.

As a longtime follower of King's nonviolent activism, Parks seemingly had little in common with Malcolm X. Actually, however, there was much about Malcolm and his brave "stand" on behalf of black people that impressed her. Not only was Malcolm "eloquent and forthright" in his speech, but Parks saw much to admire about him for redeeming himself from a "rough background" and devoting himself to his wife and family. She considered him to be a "brilliant" man whom she believed had changed his message from what she remembered when he was in the NOI. Though she regarded King's nonviolent strategy as the best one for defenseless blacks to follow, she claimed that she never completely accepted all the tenets of the philosophy herself. It was difficult in her mind, she once wrote, to accept "brutality with love." Hence, she maintained, there was much about Malcolm's views, especially when he was in the NOI, that she did not disagree with.

How Malcolm responded to the chance meeting is not recorded, but it is difficult to believe that he was not as charmed with Parks as she was impressed by him. The two greeted each other warmly, and Malcolm autographed the civil rights legend's program. Perhaps more significantly, the meeting, occurring during a period of Malcolm's life when he was reaching out to the traditional symbols of the civil rights movement,* might have been an opportunity for developing a stronger relationship with Parks and thus strengthening his effort for greater credibility as a black leader among them.

SELECTED BIBLIOGRAPHY

Branch, 1988; Hines, ed., 1990; Malcolm X (Breitman, ed.), 1965; Malcolm X (Clark, ed.), 1992; Parks with Haskins, 1991; J. Robinson (Garrow, ed.), 1987.

Robert L. Jenkins

PATTERSON, FLOYD. In 1956, at age twenty-one Floyd Patterson defeated the aging Archie Moore to win the vacant World Boxing Association heavyweight championship. His victory at the time made him the youngest person to win the title, which he won on two separate occasions, and also the first heavyweight fighter to accomplish this feat. Humiliating defeats as the champion against Swedish opponent Ingemar Johansson and former convict Sonny Liston, and in a later comeback fight against Muhammad Ali,* however, would cast a pall over Patterson's boxing reputation as a great champion.

For Malcolm X, Floyd Patterson was an easy target of criticism. Patterson, though not a notable social activist, supported Martin Luther King, Jr.,* and his nonviolent civil rights* initiatives. At King's invitation he made an appearance in Birmingham, Alabama,* in the aftermath of King's 1963 confrontational campaign with police commissioner Bull Connor.* Malcolm criticized Patterson's presence as an affirmation of the bankruptcy of King's nonviolent methods with Birmingham's black masses. It was purely an attempt by the white liberals* who controlled the civil rights movement* to bolster King and his tactics by sending to the besieged city a black celebrity,* Malcolm said. It was, however, Patterson's aspersions against Islam* and his apparent black middle-class* status that prompted Malcolm's strongest tirade against the former champion. In his preparation to fight the converted Ali in 1965, Patterson claimed that the Nation of Islam (NOI)* was no different than the Ku Klux Klan,* and he made the fact that Ali was Muslim* an issue with the press. Patterson, who was a Catholic, regarded the bout as a kind of holy crusade, a war that he had to win in order to remove the title from the hands of the Muslim infidel. Patterson seemed so driven by the Christian versus Islam issue that he claimed he would fight Ali without a purse, if necessary, in order to return the title to Christendom. Some of this banter was likely prefight hype, and though Patterson may have had legitimate anti-Islamic views, he clearly allowed himself to be merchandised by whites into condemning Ali and the Muslims as the "anti-Christ."

Malcolm certainly believed that Patterson was being duped by whites, and he took him to task for it. In his autobiography, he attacked the "brainwashed" ex-champion, whose public comments about Ali and the Muslims seemingly spoke for liberals and white Christians. These were people who had already rejected Patterson, evidenced, Malcolm emphasized, from information gleaned from the press. Patterson had integrated an expensive Yonkers, New York, white neighborhood, but he and his family had been so badly treated, Malcolm pointed out, that he was being forced to sell the expensive home at a $20,000 loss.

To be sure, Malcolm himself was no less conscious of the symbolic meaning of the fight in respect to the ideological and doctrinal differences between Islam and Christianity* vis-à-vis Ali and Patterson. He had had little trouble, for example, emphasizing to Ali in his 1964 bout with Sonny Liston when he won the heavyweight crown that this was the first significant prize fight between "the Cross and the Crescent." Unlike his mentor, Elijah Muhammad,* however, he believed in Ali, and such remarks were made to bolster Ali's confidence that "Allah"* would ensure his ring victory. In the case of Patterson, there seemed to be real mutual dislike between the two men for both religious and political reasons, though Patterson would later admit that Malcolm was a very impressive man; in Malcolm's opinion, however, Patterson was the typical "Uncle Tom"* that he so frequently sought to expose to the black masses.

SELECTED BIBLIOGRAPHY

Gardell, 1996; Malcolm X with Haley, 1965; McCallum, 1974; *New York Amsterdam News*, May 25, 1963; Patterson with Goss, 1962; Patterson with Talese (Early, ed.), 1998; Roberts (Gorn, ed.), 1995; Sammon (Gorn, ed.), 1995.

Robert L. Jenkins

PERRY, BRUCE. During the decade of the 1990s there were numerous books and articles written about the life and times of Malcolm Little. However, it is arguable that no book had a more significant impact on the current knowledge about Malcolm Little than Bruce Perry's *Malcolm: The Life of the Man Who Changed Black America*. Perry is also the editor of several other publications on Malcolm X. Perry attended graduate school at Harvard University* and later received his doctorate at the University of Pennsylvania. Perry has lectured in the field of political science in various schools in the University of Texas system, the University of Pennsylvania, and other colleges. The biography interprets and analyzes the thought patterns of Malcolm after he had traveled to Mecca* and changed his ideas about Elijah Muhammad's* version of Islam,* as compared to the international tenets of Islam that are taught in Africa, Asia, and the Middle East.* Perry points out in his work how Malcolm moves from being a supporter of black nationalism* to an advocate of internationalism. Essentially, Perry's biography is an attempt at a psychological study of the life of Malcolm and assesses Malcolm's relationship with Adam Clayton Powell, Jr.,* Elijah Muhammad, and Martin Luther King, Jr.* However, the critical reviews that Perry's book has received note that his sometimes bizarre interpretations of Malcolm combined with a lack of documentation limits the book's value to serious Malcolm X scholarship.

SELECTED BIBLIOGRAPHY

DeCaro, 1996; B. Perry, 1991; Rampersand (Wood, ed.), 1992.

Kenneth H. Williams

PERSONALITY TRAITS. One of the most outstanding contradictions regarding the personality of Malcolm X was the difference between his public persona and his private demeanor. In public, he was often cast by his opposition as a demagogue and hate teacher, spewing forth black racism and racial supremacy and castigating whites as inherently evil, intent on keeping people of color in a subordinate position. In the eyes of the public, Malcolm was contrived as a fanatic black militant who was always angry at white people. A military psychiatrist once described him as one who was asocial with paranoid tendencies. But his public persona was quite different from his private deportment, and anyone who met him in person in a one-on-one conversation or in a private exchange was shocked to know that the public Malcolm was the same man.

His more esoteric attitude and behavior reflected an individual who spoke in soft tones, was deeply respectful of others' views, pleasant, with a good sense of humor, and kind. At times he appeared almost timid and shy with certain individuals. The crown ruler of Saudi Arabia,* for example, noted some of these characteristics about Malcolm. His interpersonal skills showed thoughtfulness, accessibility, receptivity, and courteousness. He was a deeply moral man who did not smoke, drink, use drugs, run after other women, or engage in unethical behavior of any kind after his religious conversion. He was known to have deep religious convictions. He displayed excellent manners, and his puritanical disposition was noticed by virtually everyone who engaged him. He possessed an aura about him, and his presence notably filled rooms to capacity when he was there for any extensive time. In the introduction to his autobiography, the wife of journalist M. S. Handler,* who wrote for the *New York Times,** described her encounter with Malcolm as similar to having tea with a black panther. A panther is the aristocrat of the animal kingdom, beautiful yet dangerous. That was Malcolm. His inner confidence was that of a born aristocrat. He was often described as a tall man, almost six feet four inches in height, handsome, with a reddish bronze skin tone, with hazel or bluish gray eyes, and a lean build that still suggested physical strength.

Malcolm's public oratorical and debate skills were second to none, and as his popularity grew, it became increasingly difficult to find critics that would be foolish enough to engage him in such a forum. A cult of personality began to develop around him, which he strongly discouraged. He displayed an inquisitive and creative mind and almost always had two or three books that he carried with him as he traveled domestically and internationally. Consequently, it was obvious that Malcolm was a first-rate scholar who loved to enunciate as well as to read the written word.

SELECTED BIBLIOGRAPHY

Harper, 1972; Karim with Skutches and Gallen, 1992; Strickland (Greene, ed.), 1994; Wolfenstein, 1993.

Mfanya Donald Tryman

PHILADELPHIA, MISSISSIPPI, MURDERS. In June 1964 three civil rights* workers, Michael Schwerner and Andrew Goodman, both white, and James Earl Chaney, a black, after undergoing training in Oxford, Ohio, became Congress of Racial Equality (CORE)* field workers in Meridian, Mississippi, to help launch the Freedom Summer* of 1964. The Freedom Summer project was composed largely of a massive black voter registration program. On June 21, the three civil rights workers visited a church site in an outlying area that had been recently burned by the Ku Klux Klan.* While returning to Meridian, they were arrested and placed in the Neshoba County jail in Philadelphia, Mississippi. They were later released, but after leaving town, they were stopped again and murdered by local whites. After an exhaustive search, Federal Bureau of Investigation (FBI)* agents located their bodies in an earthen dam on August 4, 1964. In 1967, seven whites were convicted in federal court of conspiring to deprive the three men of their civil rights, including officials from the county sheriff's department. Referring to this incident as well as other violent incidents, Malcolm X criticized the nonviolent approach of the southern civil rights movement.* He regarded the deaths as a travesty and occasionally mentioned the youthful Chaney and his particularly brutal assassination—which included breaking every body bone—as an example of white insanity and the depth of Mississippi's* racism. He asserted that when the federal government was either unable or unwilling to protect the lives of blacks, then black citizens were within their rights to defend themselves by whatever means necessary. This advocacy of self-defense* can be found in the Statement of Basic Aims and Objectives of the Organization of Afro-American Unity,* an organization founded by Malcolm after his split with the Nation of Islam.*

SELECTED BIBLIOGRAPHY

Cagin and Dray, 1988; Carson, 1981; Malcolm X (Breitman, ed.), 1967; Malcolm X with Haley, 1965; McAdam, 1988; J. Williams, 1987.

Horace D. Nash

PIMPS. Malcolm began to get exposure to the life of a pimp in the 1940s while living on St. Nicholas Avenue in Harlem,* an area of Upper Manhattan in New York City. The room that he rented was in a building in the domain of prostitutes and pimps, and many of the prostitutes were actually white women. As a student of the profession, Malcolm learned the intricacies of the trade from prostitutes who would get high on drugs with him during their spare time. He received a hands-on course in race relations and sex from these women, who detailed the sexual idiosyncracies of white and black men and their perverse proclivities for pleasure. He also became familiar with all of the big names and other vices that coexisted with the pimping profession.

Malcolm became a "steerer," particularly for rich white men, who were looking for deviant and unusual sexual gratification. His "classroom" education was hanging out in several well-known black nightclubs that prostitutes, their clients, and others seeking perverse pleasures frequented. Malcolm would lead clients and seekers to their euphoric destinations. As people became more familiar with him, he acquired the name "Detroit Red," reflecting his reddish hair, complexion, and Michigan roots. This name distinguished him from "Chicago Red," a comedian who became the renowned Redd Foxx,* and "St. Louis Red," who came to be one of Malcolm's buddies.

SELECTED BIBLIOGRAPHY

Lomax, 1963; Malcolm X with Haley, 1992; Wood, ed., 1992.

Mfanya Donald Tryman

PITTSBURGH COURIER. Started in 1910, the *Pittsburgh Courier* was one of the most influential black newspapers during the life of Malcolm. In fact, along with the *Baltimore Afro-American* and the *Chicago Defender,** the *Pittsburgh Courier* had a national circulation and could be purchased in virtually every major city in the country. In New York, it was published as the *New York Courier*. For several years, the *Courier* published "Mr. Muhammad Speaks," a column that was first started by Malcolm. In addition, the *Courier* published a column written by Malcolm entitled "God's Angry Men." The newspaper, black-owned and operated, often carried other news related to Elijah Muhammad,* Malcolm X, and/or the Nation of Islam (NOI).* By the late 1950s, influenced by the contributions of Malcolm, Muhammad, and the NOI, the *Courier* had become the largest-selling black newspaper in the country, with a circulation of over 100,000. The *Courier* developed black nationalist undertones in the 1960s and, like Malcolm, questioned the viability of racial integration* and the goals related to it in the civil rights movement.* Malcolm thought so highly of the paper that, according to a nephew, he personally sold the papers on the street corners of Harlem.* J. A. Rogers,* a noted black columnist for the *Courier,* and a historian, like Malcolm, challenged the motives of civil rights* leaders.

Malcolm's experience selling copies of the *Courier* may well have been a factor in influencing him to start *Muhammad Speaks,** the newspaper that would have the largest national circulation of any black newspaper by the mid-1960s. After Malcolm's nephew Rodnell Collins* initially joined the NOI, Malcolm suggested that he sell the *Pittsburgh Courier,* which was publicizing the NOI in its publications. When Wallace Muhammad,* the son of Elijah Muhammad, was indicted for draft evasion in 1958, the *Pittsburgh Courier,* speculating about the poor health of Elijah, editorialized that Malcolm may have to take over the leadership of the NOI. The *Pittsburgh Courier* was also one of the first black newspapers to publish Elijah Muhammad's mythology regarding a black scientist named Yakub* and the creation of an evil people that came to be known as Caucasians.

SELECTED BIBLIOGRAPHY
Collins with Bailey, 1998; Evanzz, 1999; Lomax, 1963; Senna, 1994.

Mfanya Donald Tryman and Keith O. Hilton

POITIER, SIDNEY AND JUANITA. Juanita Poitier was the wife of perhaps the most renowned black actor in American history, Sidney Poitier. Juanita and Sidney, whom Malcolm said he greatly admired because he was one of the few black entertainers who refused to degrade himself by conking his hair, were part of an inner circle of black celebrities* and intellectuals who lived in New York during the 1960s. Like many of these personalities, Sidney and Juanita were involved in a number of local and national social causes and were especially supportive of Martin Luther King, Jr.* and the nonviolent civil rights movement.* They also became friends of Malcolm X, perhaps a logical result of Malcolm's work in Harlem* and their own interests. It was the Poitiers who in 1964 sought to bring Malcolm X into the larger civil rights movement, inviting him, the major leaders of the movement, and a contingent of intellectuals and artists to a strategy meeting in their luxurious home. Whitney Young* of the National Urban League,* whom Malcolm had frequently criticized but personally liked, and several writers and artists, including Ossie Davis* and Ruby Dee,* were among the attendees; the other major civil rights* leaders (including King), however, were unable to come. King, who was in jail at the time, sent instead one of his legal advisers, New York lawyer Clarence Jones,* who had by this time become a close acquaintance of Malcolm. Malcolm used the opportunity to advance his ideas about internationalizing the plight of black Americans and bringing their case to the United Nations.* What role the Poitiers played in the work of the gathering beyond that of facilitators is not clear.

It was also Juanita who came to the aid of Betty Shabazz* and her children after Malcolm's death. Malcolm, who had always seemed to put the financial interest of Elijah Muhammad* and the Nation of Islam* foremost in his life and work, had left his family little money and no insurance. Poitier helped organize a major benefit to assist Malcolm's family, hosting a gathering in her home where more than a thousand guests responded. Juanita and the committee that worked in this effort reportedly raised more than $40,000 to help Malcolm's destitute family. Juanita's work on behalf of Malcolm's family was inspired by more than mere humanitarianism, but also out of respect for Malcolm as a friend and for what he sought to do for black America. Malcolm would certainly have appreciated the effort, for blacks helping other blacks was the kind of philosophy that he often preached.

SELECTED BIBLIOGRAPHY

Branch, 1998; Friedly and Gallen, eds., 1993; Goldman, 1979; Malcolm X with Haley, 1965; B. Perry, 1991.

Robert L. Jenkins

POLICE BRUTALITY. Few issues have done as much to antagonize African American communities as those having to do with questions of police brutality. Historically, a tenuous relationship has almost always existed between these communities and police departments, typically dominated by white officers and black victims. Often driven by their own racism in dispensing enforcement practices, or prone to blatant overreaction to blacks, even for the most trivial or minor infractions, police tactics have resulted in untold deaths and have occasionally been the fuse that sparked bloody and costly racial rioting in America's urban areas during the twentieth century. Many of the most radical black organizations of the 1960s and 1970s, such as the Black Panther Party for Self-Defense* and the Black Liberation Army,* largely nonsouthern urban groups, based much of their opposition to the white power structure on their association of it with police oppression against black people. The brutality tradition, of course, has had no regional boundaries, but most of the violent black reactions to the problems have been in the northern urban ghettos.

Malcolm X, like so many of the nation's black leaders during his life and afterward, was quick to criticize how the police frequently responded to blacks. Many of the problems that gripped the nation domestically, he said, resulted from "the Gestapo tactics" that white policemen employed in the black neighborhoods. Members of the Nation of Islam (NOI),* known for their militant language and prone to challenge aggressive police action, were frequent targets. On numerous occasions Malcolm intervened on behalf of members of his sect who were ruthlessly treated or harassed by the police. In one instance, he traveled south to Flomaton, Alabama, to give assistance, and in another, to Los Angeles in 1962, where reluctantly he helped to stave off a potential mass uprising to the police's fatal shooting of Ronald Stokes* and serious injury to several others.

By this time, of course, Malcolm had long established a reputation among Muslims* and non-Muslims alike for effectively challenging unfair police actions. It was an incident in Harlem* in 1957 and his response to it that did more than anything else he ever did to establish his own credibility and his recognition among New York law enforcement officials as a powerful leader. This resulted from the police's brutal beating and jailing of Muslim Johnson X (Hinton),* an innocent bystander in a street crowd watching a confrontation between officers and a drunk. Malcolm not only helped to secure medical attention for Johnson but aided in averting a major riot outside of the precinct where Hinton was being held. In the weeks that followed, Malcolm understandably found considerable cause to criticize New York's "finest," labeling them as "sadistic" "criminals" and acquiring greater fodder after officials could not substantiate any law that Hinton violated.

In many of his speeches and public comments before his death, Malcolm talked about acts of police brutality. Opposed to the nonviolent civil rights* strategy employed by Martin Luther King, Jr.,* it was easy to criticize both King's Birmingham* campaign and the brutal police tactics that Commissioner

Eugene "Bull" Connor* used against women and children demonstrators. He sought to inform the comfortable middle-class professional black that they were no safer than the poorest dweller in the community from police attacks. As a part of the black community, their very blackness, he said, meant whites labeled them "as a community of criminals." He condemned the white media* for helping to project this image of blacks.

Malcolm made it clear that he did not advocate breaking the law, and he established an admirable record in seeking to lessen provocations between the black community and the police. Perhaps this was one of the reasons that many of New York's policemen who came to know him well liked and respected him. But he was uncompromising in his criticism of policemen who violated black human rights,* and in the charter of his Organization of Afro-American Unity* the passage affirming the right of blacks to arm and defend themselves against racist whites included racist police departments.

SELECTED BIBLIOGRAPHY

DeCaro, 1996; Dyson, 1993; Evanzz, 1999; Kelley, 1996; Library Distributors of America, 1993; Malcolm X (Breitman, ed.), 1965; Malcolm X (Clark, ed.), 1992; Malcolm X with Haley, 1965; B. Perry, 1991; Thernstrom and Thernstrom, 1997.

Robert L. Jenkins

POLITICAL PARTIES. Political parties are groups of individuals or an enduring coalition of a loosely knit philosophical entity who are engaged in various sorts of party activities, donating substantial amounts of money, running party organizations, organizing members to win elections, operating government, and determining public policy. Parties differ from pressure groups in that the former's basic objective is to win control of the machinery of government. In the United States, parties are highly centralized, meaning that most of the power they wield emanates from their national base. Political parties serve numerous functions, including recruitment of candidates, holding and winning elections, educating the public, and serving as a link between government and various constituencies.

Malcolm X and the Black Muslims* did not participate in the political process as a matter of philosophy. The Nation of Islam (NOI)* had consistently labeled electoral politics as rift with selfishness and corruption. Little would come from blacks voting anyway, they argued, since so much in America was stacked against them, and whites, especially white politicians, could not be trusted. Besides, the reasoning went, blacks were not really American citizens anyway.

Malcolm angrily held the Muslim* line about the political process until his eventual break with Elijah Muhammad.* Especially after he started his own separate groups, the Muslim Mosque Inc. (MMI)* and the Organization of Afro-American Unity (OAAU),* he began a movement toward greater involvement and support of black voting rights. Increasingly, he began to engage electoral politics as one of the tools to help eliminate barriers to black elevation in the United States. In 1964 he gave consideration to running as the candidate of the Freedom Now Party* for U.S. senator from Michigan. He told black youth from Mississippi* that he supported the goals of Freedom Summer,* Fannie Lou Hamer* and the Mississippi Freedom Democratic Party,* and the efforts to widen the franchise for black Mississippians, and he went to Selma to support Martin Luther King, Jr.'s* effort in the Selma voting rights campaign.

Yet Malcolm never abandoned his suspicion of both the Democratic* and Republican* Parties. Politicians from these two parties, he often said, were under the influence of white southern racists like the Ku Klux Klan.* It was the liberal white politician whom he viewed with the most disgust. Hence, he often spoke disparagingly about Presidents John F. Kennedy* and Lyndon B. Johnson,* men who represented the Democratic Party and made promises to win the black vote but did little of substance for the race when they were in office. To Malcolm, the Democrats were simply the old "Dixiecrats,"* and they did not have to disguise themselves to maintain subjugation over blacks.

SELECTED BIBLIOGRAPHY

Clegg, 1997; Edwards, 1985; Goldman, 1979; Malcolm X (Breitman, ed.), 1965; Perry, ed., 1989.

Charles Holmes and Robert L. Jenkins

POOLE, MARIE (MUHAMMAD). Marie Poole (née Hall) was the mother of Elijah Muhammad,* who, before he changed his last name to an Arabic one, was known as Elijah Poole (legally) and a number of other aliases. When Elijah changed his last name to Muhammad, he influenced his father (Willie) and mother to do the same, which they did. Born in Georgia in 1871, she was described as a quiet woman with an ebony complexion like that of a Hershey chocolate bar; she married when she was only sixteen. Willie was a minister who moved a number of times in order to improve his occupational mobility and opportunity to provide more income for his growing family. She gave birth to thirteen children, of which Elijah was the seventh child, born in 1897.

In 1958, Muhammad's mother, who was now known as Marie Muhammad and whom Malcolm X was very fond of, died. Malcolm took the death very hard. He always referred to her as Mother Marie, indicative of his affection for her. Mother Marie, in turn, referred to Malcolm as her son, as did Elijah, and Muhammad at this time was seriously considering Malcolm, rather than one of his sons, as the heir apparent to the Nation of Islam.* Mother Marie's funeral was one of the largest that had ever taken place in Chicago, Illinois.*

SELECTED BIBLIOGRAPHY

Clegg, 1997; Evanzz, 1999.

Mfanya Donald Tryman

PORK. In order to truly understand Malcolm X, one must consider the drastic transformation that he underwent from a Christian to a Muslim.* This occurred while he was in prison* when he began to study and follow the teaching of Elijah Muhammad.*

When Malcolm went to prison, he was a street-smart hustler, a drug user, and a robber. What prison taught him was discipline and patience. While in prison he converted to the Muslim faith. To be a Muslim one was required to follow a very strict Muslim code. Some of the major tenets of the Muslim code Malcolm adopted included abstinence from using alcohol or tobacco and eating pork or pork products. Malcolm did not find it difficult to abide by the code. Muhammad taught him and his followers that the pig was a combination of cat, rat, and dog, and hence it was unfit for human consumption. Malcolm and his fellow Muslim inmates simply refused to consume pork and protested vehemently against having pork placed on their plates, even to be given to a non-Muslim. Throughout the remainder of his life Malcolm made many changes and adaptations, but he never wavered from his refusal to consume pork and pork products.

SELECTED BIBLIOGRAPHY

Karim with Skutches and Gallen, 1992; Lomax, 1963; Strickland (Greene, ed.), 1994.

Reginald Colbert

PORTER, HERMAN. Herman Porter was a New York journalist who spent most of his career writing for the New York *Militant*,* the official organ of the Socialist Workers Party.* He was among a number of journalists who found Malcolm good copy and wrote extensively about him, especially after Malcolm broke with the Nation of Islam (NOI)* and founded his own organizations. Porter and Malcolm established a friendly relationship, each highly respecting the other. Malcolm considered Porter to be a good journalist and often praised the *Militant* as one of the most balanced newspapers reporting on issues of importance to blacks. He advised his supporters to purchase it and even sold it outside his Organization of Afro-American Unity (OAAU)* headquarters. Porter claims to have attended every rally that Malcolm held in Harlem* and was in attendance at the Audubon Ballroom* the afternoon of Malcolm's murder. He was struck by the noticeable lack of security that day, an absence, he said, that had never occurred before. Porter wrote a firsthand account of the tragedy and played an important role in recording for his newspaper details of the ensuing trial that resulted in the conviction of three NOI members for Malcolm's murder. He would later team with fellow Socialist and major editor of Malcolm X writings George Breitman* in the publication of a book that contained coverage of most of the trial activity.

SELECTED BIBLIOGRAPHY

Breitman, Porter, and Smith (Miah, ed.), 1976; Kondo, 1993.

Robert L. Jenkins

Adam Clayton Powell and Malcolm respected each other though the two maintained a rather ambivalent relationship.
Library of Congress.

POWELL, ADAM CLAYTON, JR. Adam Clayton Powell, Jr., was a clergyman with political interests and ambitions. Ivy League educated, flamboyant,
and outspoken, he succeeded his father in 1937 as pastor of the Abyssinian
Baptist Church in Harlem,* one of the nation's largest black congregations.
Shortly thereafter, he became a New York City councilman, the city's first black
councilman, and in 1945 won election to the U.S. House of Representatives.

Malcolm's admiration for Powell started while Malcolm was in prison.* After
his release, he occasionally attended Powell's Abyssinian Baptist Church on
Sunday mornings. This was the beginning of their friendship. In June 1956,
Powell introduced Malcolm to various Third World leaders, including Achmad
Sukarno of Indonesia, Dr. Kwame Nkrumah* of the Republic of Ghana,* and
Ben Bella* of Algeria.* Malcolm spoke at Powell's church for the first time in
March 1957. Praising Powell for his church's "open door policy," Malcolm
explained the tenets of the Islamic faith as practiced by the Nation of Islam
(NOI)* and urged "Black unity" and "Black love." Malcolm spoke on subse-

quent occasions at the Abyssinian church, though not without objection on the part of the church's board. His controversial views were becoming more wide-spread and clashed with the Christian doctrines of the church's membership. On one occasion, Powell had to intercede from his congressional duties in Washington to force church officials to allow Malcolm to speak during a series of scheduled lectures entitled "Which Way the Negro."

Malcolm respected Powell, although it did not prevent him from occasionally criticizing the minister. Nevertheless, Malcolm once remarked that he would consider retiring from the black rights struggle if black Americans had ten people like Powell in Washington to represent their interests.

To a very large extent, the affinity between Powell and Malcolm had much to do with Powell's outspokenness, although Powell admitted to sharing few similar views with Malcolm. Like Malcolm, however, he was strident in his criticism of the traditional civil rights organizations* and their leaders. Also, Malcolm was attracted to Powell because of his occasionally strong black nationalist rhetoric. As a member of the Congress, Powell's district included Harlem. He was denied a seat by fellow members of the House in 1967, in part, because of his controversial and flamboyant political style and confrontational approach. On June 16, 1969, the U.S. Supreme Court declared that the House exceeded its constitutional authority in denying Powell his membership to the body. However, he still lost his seniority. Malcolm and Powell were controversial leaders of their times.

SELECTED BIBLIOGRAPHY

Dionisopoulos, 1990; Goldman, 1992; Hamilton, 1991; Malcolm X with Haley, 1965; *New York Amsterdam News*,* June 15, 1957, April 14, 1962, and April 28, 1963.

Morgan Ero

PRISON. Malcolm Little was incarcerated in three different Massachusetts prisons for a total of seventy-seven months. His first year of imprisonment was spent at Charlestown State Prison in Charlestown, Massachusetts, near Boston, beginning on February 27, 1946. He was a very troubled inmate at Charlestown and was given the moniker Satan by his fellow inmates because of his contempt for organized religion. Malcolm's rehabilitation, however, began at Charlestown State Prison with the help of John Elton Bembry,* a fellow inmate convicted of the same offense as Malcolm. Bembry was an intelligent and charismatic prisoner whom all of the inmates respected, including the recalcitrant Malcolm. He convinced Malcolm to educate himself while in prison and to take advantage of the prison library. Malcolm began to spend hours in the library and take correspondence courses in English and Latin, but it was Malcolm's discovery of black history* and the advances made by African civilizations, especially the ancient Egyptian civilization, that created his insatiable appetite for knowledge. His thirst for knowledge was so intense that he would read into the early hours of the morning with the small amount of light that managed to refract into his cell from the guard quarters. He also copied down every word in the dictionary and studied the copied words for hours.

Malcolm was transferred to Concord Reformatory in January 1947. It was there that his spiritual rehabilitation began. It started with a letter from his brother Reginald Little* informing Malcolm about a religious group headquartered in Chicago.* Although Malcolm was informed of this group by his other siblings, he felt close to Reginald and took stock in what he had to say, especially the part in the letter that advised Malcolm to stay off pork* and to give up cigarettes. Malcolm was also told by Reginald that if he did these things, he could get out of prison. He soon converted to Islam,* accepting the doctrine of Elijah Muhammad.*

Malcolm was next transferred to Norfolk Prison Colony in March 1948 in Massachusetts. This occurred at his request and as a result of the efforts of his half sister Ella Collins.* This prison was more modern and had a state-of-the-art library with excellent educational programs that inmates were encouraged to use. At Norfolk, Malcolm developed his oratorical and debating skills. After his parole from Charlestown State Prison in August 1952, Malcolm gave his heart to Allah* (God) and committed himself to Muhammad and the Nation of Islam.* He left prison as Malcolm X, his newly acquired name signifying membership in the organization.

SELECTED BIBLIOGRAPHY

Diamond, 1994; Grimes, 1992; Wolfenstein, 1989; Xenon Studio, 1991.

Byron E. Price

PROPHET MUHAMMAD. In orthodox Islam,* the Prophet Muhammad is considered the last prophet to bring the word of Allah* (Arabic for God) and a reaffirmation of his eternal message to true believers. The Prophet Muhammad was from Mecca,* Saudi Arabia.* When Malcolm X joined the Nation of Islam (NOI),* Elijah Muhammad,* the leader of the sect, taught that he (Elijah) was the last prophet of Allah, not the Prophet Muhammad who was born in 570 in Mecca. Hence, an important distinction must be made between the Prophet Muhammad, considered the Messenger of Allah, and Messenger Elijah Muhammad, whom Malcolm initially believed in as the last Messenger; the former is the last prophet according to orthodox or Sunni Islam and the Holy Qu'ran* (the Bible* for Muslims*), while the latter Muhammad is the last prophet according to the NOI. The Prophet Muhammad was forty years old when he obtained his first revelation from Allah through the Angel Gabriel, and the revelations continued for twenty-three years, culminating in the Qu'ran. While the Prophet Muhammad was illiterate, his recitations of the revelations from Allah over a twenty-three-year period, and his organization of them, is considered a miracle by Muslims. He preached the word of Allah and recited the word of the Qu'ran to nonbelievers, who persecuted him in Mecca. As a result, the Prophet Muhammad and his followers, after receiving orders from Allah in 622, migrated to

Medina, more than 250 miles from Mecca to the north, only to return years later to forgive their persecutors. The Prophet Muhammad died at the age of sixty-three. In Islam, the Prophet Muhammad is considered the last and most important of a long line of visionaries that included Jesus, Noah, Isaac, Jacob, Moses,* and Abraham.

Malcolm often taught classes at Temple Number Seven* and other NOI temples around the country, making numerous references to the Prophet Muhammad, the Messenger of Allah, even while still a member of the NOI. He cited him when he preached as well. After his conversion to Sunni Islam, Malcolm believed only in the Prophet Muhammad, Allah's Messenger from Mecca, who turned his life around, at least from a religious standpoint, with his conversion to Sunni Islam. This conversion and new religious beliefs about Islam, Allah, and the Prophet Muhammad were also reflected in Malcolm's new Arabic name, El-Hajj Malik El-Shabazz.* Malcolm, like the Prophet Muhammad, lived a simple life and, when he died, like Muhammad, had few material or worldly goods.

SELECTED BIBLIOGRAPHY

Abrahim, 1997; Clegg, 1997; DeCaro, 1998; Evanzz, 1999; Hitti, 1970; Malcolm X with Haley, 1965.

Mfanya Donald Tryman

PULLMAN PORTER. During the era of racial segregation* in America, when the doors to numerous employment opportunities were closed to blacks, one of the more prestigious jobs for an African American man was that of a Pullman porter on the railroad. The Pullman workers, although servants, were highly respected among African Americans because it paid reasonably well and accorded them middle-class status, provided them an opportunity to travel, and had a long history of being union organized.

With the assistance of his half sister Ella Collins,* Malcolm was able to enter the Pullman porter's world. The opportunity opened to Malcolm, even though he was only sixteen, because many porters were forced to leave the railroads as draftees during World War II* and because he had no problem passing for age twenty-one. Ella believed the railroad job would launch her brother into the black middle class in Boston's Roxbury* community, but for Malcolm, it was the road to Harlem* and its big bands, ballrooms, and Lindy Hopping. Later, the railroad would cement Malcolm's hustling* career. Technically, Malcolm was not a Pullman porter. Rather, he worked for the New Haven railroad as a dishwasher and later as a sandwich man in the coaches of the "Yankee Clipper," which ran from Boston to New York.* Malcolm enjoyed his frequent visits to New York and used the opportunity to explore Harlem's nightlife and underworld.

It was not long before Malcolm's disruptive behavior caused him to lose his job on the railroad; however, Malcolm's course in hustling in the "Big Apple" had already begun. Eventually, after schooling himself in various hustles, Malcolm used his old railroad identification to travel throughout the East Coast, selling reefer* to his friends who were on tours with their bands. This narcotics hustle allowed Malcolm to travel closely with the musicians he admired.

SELECTED BIBLIOGRAPHY

Malcolm X (Epps, ed.), 1991; Malcolm X with Haley, 1965; Perata, 1996; B. Perry, 1991.

Nancy J. Dawson

PYNE, JOE. Joe Pyne was a local Los Angeles, California television personality. He was little known outside of the Southern California area. During the early and mid-1960s he hosted a popular live television interview show on one of the city's most watched independent stations, KTTV. Audiences were allowed to participate by asking invited guests questions. Pyne was arrogant, his interview style aggressive and often antagonistic, especially if his guests were controversial figures. His blistering questions and personal attacks, typically delivered in a cloud of smoke from the ever-lit cigarettes that he chain smoked, often proved intimidating to his guests.

Malcolm was certainly a controversial personality. When he came to Los Angeles in the early 1960s to quell the crisis over the death of black Muslim* Ronald Stokes,* he occasionally appeared on Pyne's show. Seemingly the Joe Pyne show was the very kind Malcolm found the most appealing. As he had shown on so many other occasions when interviewed in the electronics media,* he excelled; the host typically proved no match for Malcolm's knowledge and logical analysis of American race issues. Malcolm proved to be a popular draw for the show and apparently Pyne was not troubled by his extraordinary displays of intelligence and wit. For many blacks in the Los Angeles areas, Malcolm's appearance on the Joe Pyne show was their first opportunity to see and hear the man whose reputation back East as a bold leader and magnetic speaker had already been long established. Pyne died in the early 1970s from lung cancer.

SELECTED BIBLIOGRAPHY

Les Brown, 1992; Horne, 1995; Jamal, 1973.

Robert L. Jenkins

Q–R

QUAISON-SACKEY, ALEXANDER. Alexander Quaison-Sackey became one of the most prominent African allies of Malcolm X. Born into a family of modest means in the fishing village of Winneba in the former British colony of the Gold Coast, Quaison-Sackey rose to prominence in the 1950s and 1960s as a statesman for the newly independent Republic of Ghana.* After training as a Latin teacher and demonstrating a keen interest in politics, Quaison-Sackey completed his education in the United Kingdom, obtaining an Honors degree from Exeter College, Oxford University (1952), reading law at Lincoln's Inn (1954), and undertaking postgraduate study in international relations at the London School of Economics (1955). As a student, Quaison-Sackey agitated for Ghanaian independence, joining Kwame Nkrumah's* Convention People's Party and participating in the transitional government. After independence, President Nkrumah appointed Quaison-Sackey as Ghana's Permanent Representative to the United Nations* in 1959, a post that he held until 1965.

A fiery opponent of colonialism, racism, and apartheid and a staunch Pan-Africanist, Quaison-Sackey developed a personal friendship with Malcolm X. Like Malcolm, he viewed the African American struggle in the United States as part of a larger African struggle. Both men condemned U.S. intervention in Third World revolutions, particularly in the Congo.* As president of the United Nations General Assembly, the first black African to be elected to that office, Quaison-Sackey assisted Malcolm in mobilizing UN opposition to U.S. violations of African American human rights.*

SELECTED BIBLIOGRAPHY

Evanzz, 1992; Moritz, ed., 1966; Quaison-Sackey, 1963.

Richard V. Damms

RACIAL INTEGRATION. During most of his public career, Malcolm X was adamantly opposed to racial integration. Although at one time he had hailed

A white crowd, including many students, protest public school integration in Alabama. Copyright, Photo by *The Birmingham News*, 2001. All rights reserved. Reprinted with permission.

Jackie Robinson's integration of professional baseball, by the time that he had been released from prison* in 1952 he was advocating the Nation of Islam's* position on racial separation.* By then, the U.S. Supreme Court had handed down its famous school desegregation decision, and blacks were beginning to launch a massive drive to integrate all aspects of American society, especially in the South.* Although Malcolm supported racial separation, not racial segregation* as White America practiced it, he saw integration and its advocates as misguided at best. As the national spokesman for the Black Muslim* sect, he frequently pointed out the folly of blacks pursuing a policy of racial integration when whites made it clear that they could not truly accept them as equals. In the harshest of language, he denounced whites as racists and devils who could never be brotherly toward black people because they did not want to be around them. Was it not true, he asked, that whenever blacks moved into their neighborhoods, whites quickly moved out? Moreover, whites had proved their antipathy to integration through both a historical and contemporary pattern of violence against blacks. Besides, he argued, racial integration not only went against biblical teaching, as he often equated it to Moses's* pleas to Pharaoh to let his people go, it was also demeaning to black people, because it affirmed white supremacists' assumptions that blacks were inferior to them. Why else the drive to become accepted in White society? he questioned.

Near the end of his life, Malcolm abandoned his sweeping indictment against all whites as pariahs incapable of accepting blacks as equals. The moderation came as a direct result of his experiences with white Muslims during his Hajj* to Mecca.* Still, he remained mistrustful of most whites until his death, and he never believed that they could put aside their racial supremacy views sufficiently to live with blacks in a truly integrated society.

SELECTED BIBLIOGRAPHY

Carson (Gallen, ed.), 1991; DeCaro, 1998; Goldman, 1979; Malcolm X (Breitman, ed.), 1970a, 1982; Strickland (Greene, ed.), 1994.

Robert L. Jenkins

RACIAL SEGREGATION. Racial segregation in the United States was relentlessly attacked by Malcolm X as a by-product of black slavery,* which he said created rivalries among blacks as well as antagonistic attitudes between the races. Segregation in the United States divided a society into classes and a caste system on the basis of race, with a primary emphasis on skin color that was legally sanctioned and, in turn, had legal sanctions. Dichotomous relationships were developed between superior (whites) and inferior (blacks) racial groupings, with whites in power at the expense of blacks. Malcolm saw this phenomenon not only as a domestic problem but as a global problem affecting Third World countries where people of color were subordinate to white colonizers from European countries.

Malcolm supported racial separation.* Because of his views, he was attacked as a segregationist. But he made a distinction between racial segregation and racial separation. Malcolm argued that racial segregation, on the one hand, was a malicious system involving force that dehumanized and stigmatized people on the basis of color. Racial separation, on the other hand, involved people voluntarily splitting apart from another racial group with whom they could not coexist in peace.

Malcolm believed that all discriminatory and exploitative practices against a race of people of a systemic nature stemmed from racial segregation and kept a white ruling elite in power. Racial segregation, he felt, had its own internal trappings for a racially subordinate group. He felt that once the subordinate group was made to feel inferior, as in the case of African Americans, racial self-hate would continue to breed internal rivalries and retard any effort toward political freedom and justice for this oppressed group. Social distance between black and white people, who might find common grounds for political unity and action, was maintained in a number of ways in a system of racial segregation. This included the use of mob violence, racial hatred, legal barriers, lynchings,

A segregated bus in Birmingham, Alabama. Malcolm tried to make clear his views about the differences between segregation and separation. Birmingham Public Library, Department of Archives and Manuscripts (Catalog Number 49.59).

stereotypes, and numerous other devices to reinforce superiority-inferiority racial attitudes. Ultimately, Malcolm viewed this system of racial segregation as one that must be destroyed; otherwise, black Americans would have to develop their own sovereign political system based upon their indigenous needs.

SELECTED BIBLIOGRAPHY

Cox, 1970; Maglangbayan, 1972; Malcolm X (Karim, ed.), 1971.

Lee E. Williams II

RACIAL SELF-IDENTIFICATION. Historically, African Americans have often been determined to find acceptable ways to identify themselves. Even during black slavery,* the derisive terms that whites often used to identify their bondsmen were not universally accepted by the slaves themselves. During the late nineteenth century, blacks accommodated themselves to the term *colored* as the popular reference to them, though many—including organizations and institutions—even then preferred such names as African or Afro-American.

During most of Malcolm's lifetime the term *colored* was often used synonymously with the word *Negro*. Malcolm had little use for either and, like his mentor Elijah Muhammad,* usually prefaced his pronouncement with the term *so-called*. Malcolm, who was a student of etymology and frequently taught word meanings in his temple classes, regarded the word *Negro* with disdain. He understood its negative connotations in Western culture, especially how white Americans historically disparaged both the name *Negro* and those whom it identified.

Although he often used the word *Negro* in both his writings and speeches without the prefix—"the so-called"—he preferred to identify black people as African, as Afro-American, or simply the black man. (Indeed, when he unconsciously used the word *Negro* in reference to American blacks in a news conference in West Africa, he was severely criticized and told that the word was considered in poor taste; their preference was *Afro-American*, a correction that Malcolm graciously accepted and understood.) These terms were used with increasing regularity after his break with the Nation of Islam,* and he articulated a growing support for Pan-Africanism.* Thus, just as his views about black nationalism,* self-defense,* and historical awareness preceded the Black Power* movement of the late 1960s, Malcolm's consistent use of such words as *African, Afro-American*, and *black* to identify black Americans popularized their acceptance and usage among race-conscious black youths and greatly influenced the black pride* movement of the 1970s.

SELECTED BIBLIOGRAPHY

Malcolm X (Breitman, ed.), 1965, 1970b; Malcolm X with Haley, 1965; Strickland (Greene, ed.), 1994; Xenon Studio, 1991.

Robert L. Jenkins

RACIAL SEPARATION. Racial separation was a major tenet in the teachings of Elijah Muhammad* and the Nation of Islam (NOI).* The idea is also embodied within one of the few Black Muslim* "hymns," "The White Man's Heaven Is the Black Man's Hell." Black Muslims believe that racial separation must be completed before God's Armageddon* punishes white people for being so evil.

Separation, as an idea, predates the NOI's immediate secular antecedent, Garveyism. By the 1920s, Marcus Garvey's* advocacy of separatism and the "Back to Africa" movement continued a formal tradition that dates to numerous attempts in the nineteenth century to establish a "New Africa" safe haven without slavery and white racist oppression. In 1815 Paul Cuffee, a New Bedford maritime merchant, took thirty-eight free blacks back to Freetown, Sierra Leone. By 1847, other returnees declared the establishment of the new state of Liberia. Soon, many more black advocates of separatism appeared, including Henry H. Garnett, Martin Delany, and Alexander Crummell. By the 1920s, Garvey's Universal Negro Improvement Association (UNIA)* had tens of thousands of members throughout the world. Malcolm X's father was the regional recruiter for Garvey in several midwestern cities. As Garvey's movement declined, many of his followers eventually found a new spiritual home in the NOI.

In his many speeches, Malcolm X explained, following the teaching of Elijah Muhammad, why separation was ordained by God. In a 1962 speech delivered at Yale University, Malcolm X declared that Muhammad's biblical prophecy was the basis for separation of the two races. Malcolm outlined how white supremacy and the system of colonialism had enslaved, persecuted, and exploited the people of color throughout the world and how these same exploited people were rising against their oppressors "to cast aside colonial slavery" and demand liberty. These newly independent nations of Africa and Asia had regained control of their freedom and their land. Malcolm argued further that America faced the same winds of change from her own colonized subjects, the black race in America. He noted that Muhammad described a cancerous lump in America's body politic: the black man. For America to regain its health and to avert its own destruction by the divine will of God, he said, it had to provide for racial separation for blacks.

After criticizing middle-class integrationist blacks, Malcolm told his audience that even Jesus Christ advocated separatism. With this separatism also came compensation, reparations,* and justice for the 20 million "so-called Negroes."* God's justice would demand a high price for the untold years in which the white man robbed the black man of his pride, identity, and culture.

Typically, when Malcolm spoke at length about separation, he made sure to distinguish it from racial segregation.* The latter, he said, was something that a superior group tried to impose on an inferior group. Blacks were historically victims of segregation, where they had no control over their communities. They owned nothing because everything in their community—businesses, politics, civic organizations—was controlled and regulated by outsiders: whites. Communities should choose to be separate, he said, because it would benefit them to own and control their own destinies, as did the Chinese in the nation's Chinatowns, on equal footing with whites. After Malcolm's split with the NOI, his trips to Mecca,* and his discussions with African leaders, he moderated his earlier view of separation.

SELECTED BIBLIOGRAPHY

Bracey, Meier, and Rudwick, eds., 1970; Lomax, 1963; Malcolm X (Breitman, ed.), 1967; Malcolm X (Perry, ed.), 1989; Malcolm X with Haley, 1965.

Malik Simba

RAHMAN, ALMINA (Sharon 10X). Almina Rahman was one of several women who gained prominence in Malcolm X's Organization of Afro-American Unity (OAAU).* Rahman first met Malcolm as a fourteen-year-old teenager in Harlem* when he headed the Nation of Islam (NOI)* Temple Number Seven.* Rahman and some of her classmates were part of a civil rights* demonstration group protesting the exclusion of black construction workers from a hospital building project in Harlem. Malcolm, who as an NOI official could not support direct action movements, was, nevertheless, at the site and engaged Rahman in a spirited forty-five-minute debate, primarily over the merits of the demonstration. Malcolm left an indelible impression on the fourteen-year-old Rahman, as he so frequently did with numerous other encounters with young people. While still in high school she joined the NOI, where she soon became Sharon 10X, and worked alongside Malcolm in the publication office of *Muhammad Speaks.** She also taught in the Muslim Girls' Training Classes.* She was with Malcolm in the NOI restaurant the day that he received the news regarding the murder of President John F. Kennedy* and later validated Malcolm's interpretation of the comments regarding the death that prompted his suspension from the NOI.

No longer wanted in the *Muhammad Speaks* office or as instructor in the girls' training classes because of her close ties to Malcolm when he left the Muslim* group to form his own religious and political organizations, Sharon 10X also left. She subsequently acquired the new Arabic name of Rahman. When the OAAU was in its earliest stages, she performed office work in its Hotel Theresa* headquarters. But her value to Malcolm extended beyond mere secretarial duties. Quick to show that his ideas about the role of women in the OAAU would not follow the secondary role that women traditionally played in the NOI, after reading a version of the speech that Student Non-Violent Coordinating Committee* Chairman John Lewis* did not deliver at the 1963 March on Washington,* Malcolm tabbed Rahman to deliver it before a Harlem street rally.* The speech was considerably more militant in its tone than the one that Lewis actually delivered, which captured Malcolm's interest in it in the first place. The fact that the rally drew an unusually large crowd to hear Malcolm's analysis of the Martin Luther King, Jr.*–led Washington march and that women had not even been allowed on the OAAU's speaking dais before that day made

Rahman apprehensive about the appearance. Malcolm, however, bolstered Rahman's confidence and insisted that his female understudy deliver it before the audience. The speech went over well.

Rahman considered herself an activist and did not always agree with the NOI's nonengagement program. But she became a Malcolm X follower because she appreciated his work in the black community and because, as she wrote, she "admired" and "trusted" him. There is nothing to indicate that he did not return the sentiment.

SELECTED BIBLIOGRAPHY

Blackside/PBS, 1994; B. Perry, 1991; Sales, 1994; Strickland (Greene, ed.), 1994.

Robert L. Jenkins

RAMADAN, SAID. Said Ramadan was an Arab Muslim* who held the post of director-general of the Islamic Centre in Geneva, Switzerland, during the 1960s. Malcolm first met Ramadan when he was abroad in the fall of 1964 on his second African and Middle East* visits. During the tour, he also made two brief side trips to Geneva, one of which, according to biographer Bruce Perry,* Ramadan claimed resulted in "quite a visit." Recently returned from his second visit to Mecca,* the off-season Omra, Malcolm was eager to promote orthodox Islam;* he hoped to spread "true Islam" to a larger number of American blacks and perhaps build a large Islamic center in Harlem.* Ramadan was supportive of his proselytizing intentions, though Malcolm failed to acquire the desired and promised financial assistance for his Muslim Mosque, Inc.* from the Islamic world through Ramadan's contacts. According to one of Malcolm's biographers, Ramadan liked and respected Malcolm, but he clearly found cause to rebuke him for some of Malcolm's previously unorthodox Islamic beliefs and pronounced racial views. In a long letter, Malcolm responded to a series of questions that Ramadan posed to him that sought to explain and justify his political, racial, and religious views. He did so largely in the context of how he and other black Americans felt bound to react to the realities of white racism. Shortly before his death, Malcolm accepted an unfilled invitation to return to the Geneva center in 1965 to speak personally about himself and Islam among black Americans. Although Malcolm never got back to Switzerland, his widow Betty Shabazz* visited extensively with Ramadan in Geneva as his invited guest en route to Mecca on her own pilgrimage, accompanied by Ramadan.

SELECTED BIBLIOGRAPHY

DeCaro, 1996; Gwynne, ed., 1993; B. Perry, 1991.

Robert L. Jenkins

RANDALL, DUDLEY. Born on January 14, 1914, in Washington, D.C., Randall was educated in the public schools of Washington, East St. Louis, Illinois, and Detroit, Michigan.* He earned his undergraduate education at Detroit's

Wayne State University. Poet, editor, writer, and publisher, he achieved prominence in the mid-1960s as the owner/publisher of Broadside Press in Detroit. The press, which he started in 1965, became one of the major black publishing and distribution outlets for little-known but talented artists in the 1960s and 1970s. It was Broadside Press, for example, that highlighted the early work of poets and writers such as Nikki Giovanni,* Gwendolyn Brooks, Sonja Sanchez,* Haki R. Madhubuti (formerly Don Lee), Marvin X (Marvin Ellis Jackmon), and Margaret Alexander, literary figures whose poetry and writings soon garnered them international recognition. These artists, along with Randall and a number of other prominent writers, were a part of the 1960s Black Arts Movement, a broad-based black literary and cultural rebirth in literature and fine arts similar in significance to the 1920s Harlem Renaissance. In many ways, it was Randall and his Broadside Press that stood at the forefront of the movement, helping to propel its national development during the height of the civil rights movement.*

One of the earliest literary pieces to come out of the movement and the second book published by Broadside Press appeared in 1967 under the title *For Malcolm X: Poems on the Life and Death of Malcolm X*. Edited by Dudley and Margaret Burroughs, the anthology of poems contained the work of forty-five poets and celebrated the life of ten top black leaders of the twentieth century, including Malcolm X, who had influenced the thinking of many in the black poet community. Randall and Burroughs wrote the introduction to the anthology, though Randall did not include a poem in the volume; it became an immediate success, selling more than 8,000 copies alone in the year of its appearance.

Randall was a strong supporter of the civil rights movement, especially Detroit's black struggle, and though Malcolm's ideas on Black Power,* black pride,* and the disinherited of the world left an indelible impression on him, if the two had met prior to Malcolm's murder, they were hardly close. It was Randall's enduring fascination and appreciation of the fallen leader's life and work, however, that inspired the publication of *For Malcolm X*. This appreciation still informs Randall's participation on popular programs celebrating Malcolm's legacy and the promotion of themes relative to black identity and equality through literature, themes that Malcolm endorsed during his lifetime.

SELECTED BIBLIOGRAPHY

Baraka, 1984b; Draper, ed., 1992; Randall and Burroughs, eds., 1969; Reilly, ed., 1994; Thompson, 1999; Woodard, 1999.

Robert L. Jenkins

RANDOLPH, ASA PHILIP. A. Philip Randolph received his elementary and secondary education at the Cookman Institute, in Jacksonville, Florida. He went on to receive his postsecondary education at the City College of New York. Randolph was considered a key black leadership figure in the labor movement during the period from the 1940s through the 1970s. Ironically, he was one of the few blacks who advanced through the ranks of leadership in the labor move-

Noted civil rights leader Asa Philip Randolph worked to include Malcolm in the black leadership of New York. Despite the differences in their ideas, the two greatly admired and respected each other. Library of Congress.

ment. Randolph is often acknowledged for his leadership in organizing the 1963 March on Washington.* The political and social climate of the civil rights movement* was the context and relationship of discourse and debate between Malcolm X and Randolph. Relative to the 1963 March on Washington, Malcolm X was critical of the organizers' motives, and he labeled them as the "Big Six." Malcolm identified Randolph as one of the leading Big Six spokesmen.

Paradoxically, Randolph represented the moderate typology of black leadership. Malcolm X represented the radical typology of black leadership. The relationship between these two men was extremely controversial. In fact, Malcolm X was one of Randolph's leading critics concerning his tactics and strategies regarding the enforcement of civil rights* legislation. Malcolm was also extremely critical of Randolph's participation in the 1963 March on Washington. Malcolm believed that Randolph allowed the movement to be coopted into mainstream politics. Malcolm added that white liberals'* participation in the March neutralized and regressed the efforts made by blacks to seek and demand equality. Moreover, Malcolm X queried the moral and ethical conduct of Randolph and other black leaders' public squabbling in their attempt to solicit funds from white liberal organizations. Malcolm X voiced several reservations concerning Randolph's emphasis on indoctrinating African Americans to an assimilationist mode in their attempt to obtain liberation, human rights,* and civil rights.

Yet Malcolm did not believe that Randolph was as badly "confused" in his efforts as other black leaders. Consequently, Malcolm and the Black Muslims* trusted Randolph more than they did others from the civil rights leadership core. Conversely, Randolph was not an outspoken critic of Malcolm. While he dramatically opposed many of the Black Muslim spokesman's views, he held him in high personal regard, "a friend and admirer of Malcolm." Moreover, Randolph made sincere efforts to break the isolation that mainstream black civil rights leaders had ascribed to Malcolm. He invited Malcolm to participate in some of the community meetings that Randolph and his labor union held in their headquarters, some of which Malcolm accepted. Randolph even defended the right of Malcolm as a Nation of Islam* representative to participate in a 1962 community meeting and threatened to withdraw his own involvement after a group of Harlem* members protested against Malcolm's presence.

SELECTED BIBLIOGRAPHY
J. Anderson, 1973; D. Davis, 1972; W. Harris, 1977; Jacobson, ed., 1968; Pfeffer, 1990.
James L. Conyers, Jr.

REEFER. Malcolm X, like many people of his generation, used drugs and alcohol.* For Malcolm and his cohorts, "reefer," or marijuana, was used to help people temporarily escape from the harshness of life. During his life on the streets of Roxbury* and Harlem,* Malcolm was a regular user of narcotics. Although he often smoked opium, marijuana was apparently his drug of preference. Accordingly, he lamented in his autobiography that at one stage of his abuse he smoked as much as an ounce at a time, well above the typical "wooden-match-sized" amount that smokers consumed. Consequently, Malcolm was frequently high from reefer or some other drug and alcohol abuse. As a petty criminal, Malcolm also sold reefer to a steady stream of customers, especially the musicians with whom he maintained close ties. Narcotics policemen eventually forced him from the streets of New York, but he actually increased his business by following the big bands of the day on their road dates, amply resupplying himself with the drug from his friend and major provider Sammy "The Pimp."

Unable to get reefer while imprisoned, Malcolm, like so many other inmates, found a substitute in the smoking of nutmeg; it produced a marijuana-like high. After Malcolm's transition to Islam* and his subsequent rise to fame in America, however, he began to view reefer and other illicit drugs as deliberate ploys by whites to destroy black and other oppressed communities. Malcolm often blamed the government and so-called legitimate businesses for the sanctioning and maintenance of the corruption, vice, and drug addiction in America's inner cities. Malcolm also claimed that reefer was one of the main obstacles for many blacks working to free themselves from the conditions of poverty, unemployment, and illiteracy.

While Malcolm's self-appointed heirs, the Black Panther Party for Self-Defense,* often used reefer as a recreational drug, so much so that they had to develop rules against it, a large number of Panthers saw the presence of the drug in the black community just as Malcolm saw it. Both Malcolm and the Panthers argued that the overwhelming presence of reefer in the black community gave police and other government agencies the excuse to harass and brutalize young blacks and movement activists alike.

SELECTED BIBLIOGRAPHY

Gage, 1971; Malcolm X with Haley, 1965; New York Chapter of the Black Panther Party, 1971.

Curtis Austin

REPARATIONS. A fundamental tenet of the Nation of Islam's (NOI)* message in the early 1960s was that the United States owed its African American denizens land as a reparation, or repayment, for the generations their ancestors spent in slavery. While a member of the NOI, Malcolm preached this doctrine faithfully. It became one of the most controversial and intriguing parts of Malcolm's public addresses and thus one of his biggest drawing cards.

While this doctrine resembled the ideologies of earlier black separatist groups, it is distinguished from them by its religious rationale and its demand for land within the borders of the United States. Whereas most other black nationalists advocated emigration from the United States and often repatriation to Africa, the NOI advocated separatism within the United States. Likewise, while most other black nationalists cited white supremacy and discrimination as reasons for the need to separate, the NOI also cited religious reasons.

The idea, as both Malcolm and Elijah Muhammad* generally expressed it, was that the 22 million blacks in the United States constituted a nation within a nation. Because the people of this black nation had been brought to "the wilderness of North America" as slaves, they had lost their true identity as Allah's* (God's) "chosen people." To restore that identity, it would be necessary for the nation to separate from the evil white society of the United States and create an independent political entity. With this plan accomplished, the NOI would then become more than merely the name of a religious sect; it would constitute a geographic region and a sovereign state.

Since the NOI preached that heaven and hell existed on earth in the present, this new state would represent the promised land, the "Black Kingdom" of Allah on earth. Malcolm repeatedly referred to Moses* and the Hebrews as an example of how Allah intended for the children of slaves to enjoy independence in a land of their own. In the analogy, he threatened that if the United States would not agree to the demand for freedom and separation of its black population, it would incur the same judgment that befell Egypt.*

To justify the demand to white Christian listeners, Malcolm pointed out that Jesus preached the separation of Jews* and Gentiles, calling Samaritan Gentiles "dogs." He also pointed out how, in 1948, the Jews had won an independent homeland and Israel had been recognized as a sovereign nation. African Americans in the 1960s, he said, should be satisfied with no less.

The location of preference for this black nation would be somewhere in the southern part of the United States. The demand, therefore, was that the United States should surrender anywhere from one to eight states of the Union in the South* for the creation of the African American nation. Since black Americans were actually entitled to twenty-five states because of their centuries of unpaid and underpaid labor, according to the NOI, the demand for a fraction of that total was quite reasonable. Furthermore, there was a precedent: The United States had given millions of acres of land to the various Native Americans it had victimized over the years.

The NOI also demanded that the United States support the new nation financially for twenty to twenty-five years until it could become economically stable. This demand, too, was quite reasonable, Malcolm proclaimed, because the United States regularly gave billions in aid to Latin American and East European nations for the purpose of supporting friendly, stable governments in those regions.

Over time, Malcolm began to realize the impracticality of the demand for land within the United States and changed his demand to merely money with which to buy an island in an undisclosed location. This, however, was seldom ever addressed. By late 1963, he was even amenable to the idea of a wholesale repatriation to Africa, though he soon replaced such an idea with support for a black cultural, spiritual, and psychological return to Africa only. After leaving the NOI, his demands lessened even more. By 1965, he no longer held any hope that the United States would meet any demand for land or reparations and, consequently, began espousing equality for African Americans within the Union instead.

SELECTED BIBLIOGRAPHY

Clegg, 1997; Gallen, ed., 1992; Lomax, 1963; Malcolm X with Haley, 1965; Malcolm X (Perry, ed.), 1989; Xenon Studio, 1991.

Thomas Upchurch

REPUBLICAN PARTY. Malcolm X often criticized the Democratic Party* as a racist party that did little to fulfill its promises to blacks or reward them for their loyalty. Blacks, he would say, had only themselves to blame for any abuse because the Democratic Party knew that they could count on their vote and hence took them for granted. But Malcolm's criticism of the Democrats was hardly an endorsement of the Republican Party or the two-party system as it presently functioned. He told blacks that from the outset the Republican Party and Abraham Lincoln, long regarded as "a God" to black people because he signed the Emancipation Proclamation, and the reason for their original fidelity to the Republican Party, actually did little for the race. Lincoln supported black freedom because it was a necessity of war, but the document hardly freed the slaves, else there would be no reason for civil rights* legislation a hundred years later. Lincoln, he said, was no different than any other white liberal* who used black people to their advantage. Malcolm asserted that the Republicans were no less racist than the Democrats, and like the Democrats, Republicans also sold out black people. He would urge blacks to register as neither Democrats nor Republicans but as independents. In the political statement of the Organization of Afro-American Unity's* charter, he promised to support political parties that would run independent candidates who had black American interests at heart.

SELECTED BIBLIOGRAPHY

Carson (Gallen, ed.), 1991; Haley, 1993; Library Distributors of America, 1993; Malcolm X (Breitman, ed.), 1970a; *Militant*, July 13, 1964.

Robert L. Jenkins

REPUBLIC OF GHANA. The West African country of Ghana is the former Gold Coast. The name was changed in 1957 when the colony attained its independence from Great Britain. The late President Kwame Nkrumah* was its first elected indigenous leader.

Malcolm first visited the country in 1959 when Elijah Muhammad* sent him there and to Egypt* and Mecca* as his special ambassador. Little is known about Malcolm's first visit to the African continent. In his autobiography he discusses the trip in only one brief paragraph. He returned to the country in 1964 en route home from his Islamic pilgrimage, the Hajj,* to Mecca. This time, however, Malcolm's visit to the Moslem holy land left an indelible impression on him; his interest in Ghana was certainly heightened by the many Ghanaian orthodox Muslims* that he met there.

Nowhere, he said, was the black continent's wealth and natural beauty more abundant than in Ghana. But it was its people that most impressed him. He described the country as the very fountainhead of Pan-Africanism.* He marveled over how blacks controlled the nation, though he seemed concerned over the large number of whites who lived there. In Malcolm's view, whites were in Africa only to exploit it.

The highlight of Malcolm's visit to Accra was a meeting with a number of black Americans who constituted a colony of expatriates in the capital city. Poet Maya Angelou,* who Malcolm had first met in 1961 in New York, was a part of this group. Angelou had headed the local arrangement committee that set the agenda for Malcolm's stay in Accra. Malcolm was an honored guest, the center of attention as he met large numbers of Ghanaian officials and foreign dignitaries. The Chinese ambassador to Ghana gave a state dinner in his honor, and President Nkrumah, whom Malcolm had previously met on one of his trips to the United States, set aside time for a private conversation with the former Nation of Islam (NOI)* spokesman. During his visit, Malcolm spoke to a large gathering of American and African students at the University of Ghana where he emphasized an African–African American united front against white oppression of blacks.

Malcolm basked in the attention he received in the West African republic, but the visit resulted in a major refocusing of his life and work. When he left Ghana, he left with the form of a new organization in his mind, one that he hoped would help eliminate the lowly place of black people in the United States.

SELECTED BIBLIOGRAPHY

Assensoh, 1986; Gallen, ed., 1992; Goldman, 1979; Lacy (Clarke, ed.), 1990; Malcolm X (Breitman, ed.), 1967, 1982; Malcolm X with Haley, 1965; Myers, 1993.

Akwasi B. Assensoh and Yvette Alex-Assensoh

REPUBLIC OF NEW AFRICA (RNA). Malcolm X is often considered to be the inspiration for the founding of many Black Power* organizations. He best articulated not only the aspirations of Africans throughout the diaspora for recognition as men and women but also the various ways in which blacks could and should successfully pursue those aspirations. One of the more visible groups attempting to implement some part of Malcolm's philosophy was the Republic of New Africa (RNA).

Founded by Yale-educated lawyers Milton Henry* (Brother Gaidi Obadele) and his brother Richard Henry* (Brother Imari Obadele), in Detroit, Michigan,* in 1968, the RNA styled itself a "revolutionary nationalist organization" and regarded Malcolm as one of its "patron saints." At its height in 1970 the group claimed a membership of 2,500 people. The organization's most "revolutionary" philosophy called for the establishment of a separate black nation in the states of Mississippi,* Alabama, Louisiana, Georgia, and South Carolina. As a close friend of Malcolm, who also traveled with him throughout Africa in 1964, Milton Henry became increasingly convinced that separation was the only way blacks would receive justice and equality in North America. After Malcolm's death, the RNA sought to implement its philosophy. In 1971, however, the Federal Bureau of Investigation (FBI),* in conjunction with local and state police, thwarted its plans to obtain and settle on farm land in Hinds County, Mississippi. The state was to be the group's first sovereign territory, and the RNA planned to name it El Malik in honor of Malcolm. Numerous members were imprisoned as a result of the shootout, and though its activities declined, the RNA continued to push toward its goal of a separate nation.

Malcolm's influence on the organization also manifested itself in the group's call for the internationalization of the black struggle. RNA leaders hoped and believed that China, Cuba,* and other nations hostile to the United States would intervene on their sides once the war "for land" was launched. It organized at the grassroots level in the hope of acquiring more political power for blacks.

SELECTED BIBLIOGRAPHY

Hall, 1978; Imari, 1968; Obadele, 1972; Pinkney, 1976; Van Deburg, 1992.

Curtis Austin

REVOLUTION. Malcolm X often called on American blacks to join what he believed was an ongoing revolution of the dark-skinned peoples of the world. In several speeches delivered before his own Organization of Afro-American Unity (OAAU),* he claimed that Africans and Asians were engaged in a struggle to free themselves from the oppression and humiliation of hundreds of years of imperialism and white rule. Like their African brothers, he said, black Americans were also engaged in a fight against white domination. It was a fight, he told his followers, that perhaps could not be won through nonviolent demonstrations but through violent revolution.

According to Malcolm X, successful revolutions were almost always violent. Pointing to America's own revolutionary heritage, he noted that George Washington and Patrick Henry did not embrace nonviolence. On the contrary, they encouraged violence in defense of their rights and liberties. He noted that most revolutionaries also sought to overturn corrupt political systems and to secure for the dispossessed both land and political power. In the West African nations of Ghana, Cameroon, and Kenya, he argued, blacks had taken the first steps toward achieving this goal. Through strikes, boycotts, and guerrilla warfare,* these Africans had overthrown British rule and brought about the creation of independent black African states.

Malcolm X, at times, appeared to advocate a similar revolution for black Americans. In numerous speeches, he argued that the only way that blacks could possibly achieve a real revolution was through black nationalism* and the creation of a separate black state. But his views on revolution and black nationalism changed over time. After his visit to Mecca,* for example, he maintained that whites as well as blacks could be part of a revolution for human rights.*

Yet despite the apparent moderation of Malcolm X's views, he still remained critical of the civil rights movement* and White America. Not long before his death, he complained that blacks were far from achieving anything revolutionary in America. Revolutions, he said, were bloody, and they could not be realized by turning the other cheek or joining hands with the enemy and singing freedom songs. He argued that since the 1954 *Brown v. Board of Education, Topeka, Kansas** decision little, if anything, had been accomplished to benefit African Americans. Racial integration* and civil rights* legislation were of no value to them as long as they still had no economic or political power.

Nevertheless, he did hold out hope that dramatic changes could be achieved if blacks were given the opportunity to vote, and he agreed to help the race, especially southern blacks, acquire the vote. But achieving the right to vote itself might require violence. Whites had proved time and again that they were un-willing to allow African Americans the right to participate in the political system. Bullets, he once announced, might be the only way that blacks would ever get ballots in a racist America.

SELECTED BIBLIOGRAPHY

Malcolm X (Breitman, ed.), 1965, 1967; Malcolm X with Haley, 1965; Sales, 1994.

Phillip A. Gibbs

REVOLUTIONARY ACTION MOVEMENT (RAM). The Revolutionary Action Movement (RAM) was founded in 1963 by Robert F. Williams,* former head of the National Association for the Advancement of Colored People (NAACP)* in Monroe, North Carolina. Believing that revolutionary violence (as opposed to random terrorist acts) was the only way to truly free blacks and other oppressed minorities in America, this Marxist-Leninist group's goal was to assemble a liberation army by educating and mobilizing young blacks. RAM's membership consisted not only of working-class and poor blacks but of businesspeople, lawyers, teachers, and students as well.

Because Malcolm X often publicly suggested armed struggle to overthrow the American government, he became friendly with RAM. Former RAM leader Akbar Muhammad Ahmed (Maxwell Stanford),* in "History of RAM," claimed that before Malcolm's death he had agreed to serve as the international spokesman for RAM, but he did not want to publicize his association with the group until it was ready to confront the white power structure directly. While Malcolm had commented that alleged "Uncle Toms"* like civil rights* leaders Whitney Young* and Roy Wilkins* should be removed from the forefront of the black struggle, some RAM members, according to court testimony, conspired to assassinate these leaders. Like Malcolm's, RAM's militant rhetoric made it a prime target for the now-infamous COINTELPRO (Counter Intelligence Program)* directed toward black activists during the 1960s and 1970s. RAM collapsed in 1968 after years of police raids, Federal Bureau of Investigation (FBI)* violence and the jailing of its members.

SELECTED BIBLIOGRAPHY

Kondo, 1993; *New York Times*, September 28, 1973; Revolutionary Action Movement, 1965; *Time*, June 30, 1967.

Curtis Austin

ROBERTS, GENE X. Gene X Roberts was an undercover New York police officer who infiltrated Malcolm X's inner camp in 1964. Assigned to work within Malcolm's Organization of Afro-American Unity (OAAU)* by the city's special investigative intelligence agency, the Bureau of Special Services (BOSS),* Roberts ingratiated himself sufficiently with Malcolm and his assistants to acquire an appointment as one of Malcolm's bodyguards. As such,

Roberts was frequently in Malcolm's presence and privy to considerable information and conversation regarding Malcolm's activities and rising influence. What information about Malcolm that was not learned by BOSS and the Federal Bureau of Investigation (FBI)* through the wiretap on Malcolm's home and office apparently came from Roberts or from the several other undercover agents working within the OAAU. Roberts, like many of those inside and outside of Malcolm's immediate circle, was keenly aware of the personal danger that surrounded the Muslim* leader. On one occasion during an OAAU meeting, shortly after Malcolm's home was firebombed, Roberts claimed to have witnessed a "dry run" of Malcolm's assassination when several members of the Nation of Islam* appeared in the audience. Although he filed a report to his superiors about the matter, no preventive action occurred.

On the evening of Malcolm's assassination, Roberts was performing his usual guard duty in the Audubon Ballroom.* Apparently he noticed nothing extraordinary about the meeting or the crowd until the diversionary commotion that preceded the shots that felled Malcolm shortly after his welcoming remarks. Roberts's wife was in the audience to hear Malcolm speak, and after seeing her to safety, he rushed to assist Malcolm. He knew immediately, he said, that Malcolm was dead but nevertheless sought to revive him through mouth-to-mouth resuscitation. One of Malcolm's friends and associates, the Harlem* activist Yuri Kochiyama,* was astounded by Roberts's life-saving efforts; apparently, in her opinion, Roberts was not totally trustworthy, and a cloud of suspicion soon swirled around his true feelings about Malcolm, especially after the revelations regarding his police connection.

Although Roberts obviously had firsthand knowledge about the course of events leading up to and after Malcolm's mortal wounds, intriguingly he was not called as an eyewitness by either side in the Malcolm X assassination trial.* Robert's career as an undercover agent would continue in the years that followed Malcolm's death when he worked within the Black Panther Party for Self-Defense,* regarded by the FBI during the late 1960s and 1970s as America's most dangerous subversive group.

SELECTED BIBLIOGRAPHY

Blackside/PBS, 1994; CBS News, 1992; Evanzz, 1992, 1999; Gallen, ed., 1992; Goldman, 1979; Strickland (Greene, ed.), 1994.

Robert L. Jenkins

ROBESON, PAUL. Few people could deny Malcolm X's great awareness of the world around him. An astute student of contemporary issues, especially those that most affected the plight of black people throughout the diaspora, he kept keenly abreast of world affairs. He was also an astute student of history, especially black history.* In both his Temple Number Seven* classes and public lectures, he frequently remembered those whom he regarded as bona fide race heroes. One such person was the internationally renowned performer and political activist Paul Robeson. Educated at Rutgers University, where he excelled in three team sports and achieved Phi Beta Kappa honors, and the Columbia University Law School, where he earned a law degree in 1923, Robeson is best remembered for his remarkable talent as a concert singer and stage and film actor. *Porgy and Bess, Othello, King Solomon's Mine*, and the *Emperor Jones* were among the numerous stage and film credits that won Robeson considerable acclaim. His concert appearances took him across Europe,* including performances in the Soviet Union. At great personal risk physically, Robeson also achieved notable attention for his often controversial activist roles in politics and fights against social injustice. During the 1940s he was a major crusader for anti-lynching legislation, and as an internationally known peace advocate, he advised blacks in the World War II* era and afterward to resist conscription. As a stronger supporter of working men's rights and unionism, much of his unabashed anti-American rhetoric during the 1940s and 1950s was the kind of radicalism that was easily, but erroneously, equated by many, including the Federal Bureau of Investigation (FBI),* as a card-carrying member of the Communist Party.* These were often courageous stands for a black man of his international professional status, and they seriously jeopardized his career.

It was precisely because of his courageous positions, especially about blacks participating in the draft, however, that Malcolm found Robeson appealing. Malcolm regarded Robeson as one of his heroes, and during his imprisonment he kept abreast of Robeson's activities through the newspapers and via prison* radio. One Malcolm biographer suggests that Malcolm thought so highly of Robeson that he even copied the performer-activist's speaking and oratory style. Though influenced more by his pacifist views, Robeson could still express ideas similar to Malcolm against blacks being conscripted to defend a nation that accorded few, if any, citizenship rights to the race. Like Robeson, Malcolm, too, would come under major criticism by many Americans because of his often volatile rhetoric; and the FBI would also erroneously label him a radical with sympathies toward communism.

By the time that Malcolm had achieved his national stature, Robeson, though still championing causes, had toned down much of his activism. However, as Malcolm was aware of Robeson, Robeson was similarly aware of Malcolm. The old activist had little sympathy for the separatist ideological and religious views of the Nation of Islam (NOI),* but supposedly he held Malcolm in high esteem, especially after his break with the NOI and move toward internationalizing the black struggle. Robeson found imperialism particularly loathsome and had argued incessantly against it during his many years of activism. The United States had restricted his travels abroad during the mid-1950s; hence, Robeson had been unable to accept a speaking engagement at the international Bandung Conference* of emerging Third World African and Asian countries meeting in Indonesia. He did, however, send a strong message commending the idea and aims of the Afro-Asian Conference. Like Robeson, Malcolm was a strong supporter of the anticolonial movement and frequently raised the Bandung standard as a

rallying cry for black unity. Robeson was impressed with Malcolm's denouncement of African colonialism.

In late 1963, during a conversation with Robeson's son, Paul Jr., Malcolm
related his affection for his father and the courageous stand he had taken against
the American government. An opportunity to meet Robeson, however, would
not come until much later. At the January 1965 funeral of noted black playwright
Lorraine Hansberry,* which both Malcolm and Robeson attended, Malcolm approached his friend Ossie Davis* to arrange a meeting for him to meet Robeson.
Apparently, Robeson consented, but Malcolm was murdered before the two
could come together. Robeson, however, would live another eleven years. His
death at nearly age seventy-eight ended the life of one of twentieth-century
Black America's most talented intellectuals and performers and an indefatigable
human rights* activist.

SELECTED BIBLIOGRAPHY

Jervis Anderson, 1997; Duberman, 1989; Evanzz, 1992; O'Reilly (Gallen, ed.), 1994;
Plummer, 1996; Robeson, 1971; Von Eschen, 1997; White (Lowery and Marszalek, eds.),
1992; C. Wright, 1984.

Robert L. Jenkins

ROBINSON, JACK ROOSEVELT "JACKIE." Jackie Robinson, the first
black man to break the color barrier in major league baseball, attended Pasadena
Junior College and the University of California at Los Angeles between 1937
and 1941. At both colleges Jackie excelled in football, baseball, basketball, and
track. When World War II* broke out in 1941, he entered the army. After
receiving an honorable discharge in 1945, he played baseball in the Negro American League. Two years later, team owner Branch Rickey asked Jackie to join
his Brooklyn Dodgers. In prison,* Malcolm regarded Jackie as a hero and recalled later in his life how he and the other inmates proudly cheered Jackie's
exploits broadcast over the radio. After a stellar career, in 1956 Jackie retired
from professional baseball to a business career.

In the years that followed, Jackie became active in both politics and the civil
rights movement.* Robinson's strong support of Martin Luther King, Jr.,* and
racial integration,* however, resulted in a number of public disputes with Malcolm X. The two traded barbs against each other, Robinson finding Malcolm so
distasteful that he refused to accept Malcolm's invitation to meet with him and
other notable black leaders of New York to participate in a Harlem* rally in
1960. The dispute between the two men became so bitter, and of interest to
Harlemites, that it was played out in the pages of the *New York Amsterdam
News** through the exchange of a series of letters. Robinson criticized Malcolm
X and the Black Muslims* for promoting race hatred and violence. Too many
black lives had been lost in the quest for equality, Jackie said, for the black
community to abandon the fight in support of the Muslims* and their "vicious
ideas," especially the idea of a separate state. He also argued that, unlike King,

Malcolm X did little but snipe from the sidelines, while others put their lives on the line for freedom. Despite Malcolm's militant rhetoric, Jackie wrote that it was being expressed only in Harlem where it was safe.

Although Robinson was one of Malcolm X's former heroes, he dismissed the veteran baseball star as a pawn of the white man and condemned him for campaigning for Richard Nixon* and Nelson Rockefeller. In Malcolm's opinion, Robinson was one of a number of "phony" black leaders. He knew nothing about the black community, Malcolm said, except what whites told him.

SELECTED BIBLIOGRAPHY

Falkner, 1995; Lincoln, 1973; B. Perry, 1991; Robinson (Tygiel, ed.), 1977; Xenon Studio, 1991.

Phillip A. Gibbs

ROCKWELL, GEORGE LINCOLN. George L. Rockwell was the American Nazi Party* leader who was shot and killed on August 25, 1967, as he sat in his car in an Arlington, Virginia, shopping center parking lot. Like Malcolm X, Rockwell was a key target of the Federal Bureau of Investigation's* COINTELPRO* program and was supposedly killed by an associate. COINTELPRO is an acronym for a series of covert programs that were directed against domestic groups in America by the FBI.

Rockwell shared the same views with Elijah Muhammad* regarding racial separation.* Reportedly, Rockwell even made small monetary contributions to the Muslims* because he agreed with their separatist policy. Muhammad's policy on establishing an alliance and secret meetings with Rockwell was not well received by Malcolm X and some other Black Muslims.* Malcolm X and other Muslim leaders felt that such meetings would create friction within the Nation of Islam (NOI).* Besides, Rockwell represented the very issue—white racism—that Malcolm devoted his energies to eradicate and that he regarded as the stumbling block to black elevation the world over. The invitation to Rockwell to attend the Muslim annual Savior's Day Convention* in 1962 further increased the discord between Malcolm X and Elijah Muhammad. As a result, Malcolm X used the partnership between Muhammad and Rockwell to publicly criticize his former mentor once he left the NOI.

Although Rockwell tried to align his racist ideology and crusade in a coalition with the doctrines of the Black Muslims, he was scorned by Malcolm and the majority of them who followed a religious doctrine of strict racial separation. Rockwell is best remembered as a neo-Nazi race-baiter who supported white injustice against blacks.

SELECTED BIBLIOGRAPHY

Carson (Gallen, ed.), 1992; Goldman, 1979; *New York Amsterdam News*, February 1, 1961; Schmaltz, 1999; Simonelli, 1999.

Felix A. Okojie

ROGERS, JOEL A. Born in Jamaica, British West Indies, in 1883, Joel Augustus Rogers arrived in the United States in 1906 and became an American citizen in 1917. He is noted as an international journalist, writer, novelist, lecturer, and historian. Throughout his many careers one theme emerges: his devotion to black nationalism.* The origins of his ideological position can be traced to his involvement with Marcus Garvey.* Described as one of the "Apostles of race" by author Roi Ottley, Rogers was a member of Garvey's inner crowd. Ottley credited him with making black pride* and nationalism acceptable to America's black population.

Much of Rogers's reputation is based on his various works as a self-taught historian, where he emphasized the contributions of blacks to world civilization. Rogers's historical works have often been criticized for their lack of accuracy in documentation and interpretation, but scholars also recognize his contribution to popularizing the formal study of African Americans. His first major work appeared in 1917 as *From Superman to Man*. He achieved his greatest popularity with an illustrated feature column entitled "Your History" and "Rogers Says" for the *Pittsburgh Courier*.* In both columns, Rogers continued his crusade against the idea of white racial superiority, which also was the basis for his 1934 study *100 Amazing Facts about the Negro* and *The World's Greatest Men of Color* (1935). Rogers also published three novels; he continued to write until his death in 1966 at the age of eighty-five.

Like many Black Muslims,* Malcolm respected Rogers's work and was impressed with his publications on black history,* Malcolm's favorite subject. His first encounter with Rogers's work began while he was in prison* when he read his books on sex and race. During this period Malcolm read deeply the studies of other intellectuals, including H. G. Wells, W.E.B. Du Bois,* Frederick Bodmer, Plato, Kant, and Nietzsche, as he sought to understand the place of black people in the history of man and the relationship of that place to Black Muslim doctrine. Long after his release from prison, Malcolm continued to rely on Rogers's research, occasionally praising what are perhaps Rogers's most enduring historical works on great men of color and Africa's contribution to human history.

SELECTED BIBLIOGRAPHY

Boris, ed., 1927–1940; Gallen, ed., 1992; Ivy, 1966; Malcolm X with Haley, 1965; Ottley, 1968; Thorpe, 1969; Xenon Studio, 1991.

Thaddeus M. Smith

ROLE MODEL. Talk in the African American community about role models never ends. All too often, however, this talk centers on athletes and their performance in their particular domain of excellence. As a result, consequently, their physical excellence is equated with moral character and certain social values related to motivation, success, work ethic, and law-abiding citizenship. Unfortunately, many athletes make poor role models because of their socioeconomic background, and one wonders why they were selected in the first place to fulfill this role.

Malcolm X, not withstanding his background, represented one of the best role models not only for his time but for future generations as well. As much as any other leading black figure, Malcolm showed how a young black raised in a large poverty-stricken family, an eighth-grade dropout, who led a life of criminality, drug abuse, alcohol misuse, and among other activities, hustling women, could, as an ex-convict, reform himself and become one of the most dynamic and charismatic leaders of the twentieth century. His leadership and role model legacy reflect the embodiment of a number of traits, absent athletics and physical prowess, that most African American parents would highly value in their children. Once Malcolm became a Muslim,* he never womanized or cheated on his wife, never drank another drop of alcohol, never again used drugs, never engaged in crime again, and was very religious. In addition, he was a self-taught scholar who debated top professors from top colleges and universities in the United States and Europe.* Because of his busy itinerary and speaking schedule, what is often overlooked is his positive role as a father to his children and as a husband to his wife, Betty Shabazz.*

Like any human being, Malcolm had his faults, particularly the habit of making off-the-cuff remarks that got him in trouble with Elijah Muhammad,* such as "the chickens coming home to roost"* statement after the death of President John F. Kennedy.* While many of his contemporary as well as current critics have attempted to minimize his role in the struggle for black political liberation, no one has been able to successfully launch an attack upon his morals, ethics, lifestyle, religious zealotry, scholarly pursuits, family orientation, and character, values sorely needed among youngsters in the African American community as traits to emulate in a role model.

SELECTED BIBLIOGRAPHY

Collins with Bailey, 1998; DeCaro, 1998; Malcolm X (Epps, ed.), 1991; Malcolm X with Haley, 1965.

Mfanya Donald Tryman

ROOT, GLADYS TOWLES. This flamboyant but shrewd Los Angeles attorney was retained by Malcolm X to represent Lucille Rosary and Evelyn Williams, two former secretaries of Elijah Muhammad* who had filed paternity suits against him in a Los Angeles Superior Court. In the lawsuits, Elijah Muhammad was alleged to have fathered three children by the two women and a possible fourth child about to be born. It was also alleged that he once acknowledged paternity by contributing to the children's economic support but later denied he was the father. Malcolm X agreed to testify about Muhammad's admission of paternity.

Press savvy, Root's skills had been recently honed as counsel for the Frank Sinatra family in their recent ordeal in the kidnapping of Frank, Jr. Root, as

Malcolm hoped, attempted to mobilize the press against Muhammad, occasionally sensationalizing the matter by holding news conferences with the plaintiff mistresses and their illegitimate children alongside her. Many of the black newspapers, however, reported favorably on Muhammad, and the white press paid scant attention to the scandal. Malcolm was noticeably vexed over the white media's* broken promise to provide widespread coverage over the sex tempest.

During this turbulent period, when the relationship between Malcolm X and Elijah Muhammad grew confrontational, Gladys Root became one of Malcolm X's strongest supporters, a friend, legal enforcer, and protector. At the height of the charged atmosphere, when Malcolm's fear over Muslim* death threats was most intense, Root called for police protection for Malcolm X while he was visiting her Los Angeles office to discuss the paternity suits.

Ironically, shortly after Root filed the paternity suit against Muhammad, she was indicted for perjury and obstruction of justice. This new challenge forced her to put the suit aside in order to defend herself. The charges against her were dismissed, but it was after Malcolm X's assassination. The timing and disposition of these charges gave credence to the viewpoint that there was a concerted effort by those forces hostile to Malcolm X and to Root to deprive them of their rightful place in American history.

SELECTED BIBLIOGRAPHY
Branch, 1998; Evanzz, 1992; Goldman, 1979.

Felix A. Okojie

ROSELAND BALLROOM. For those blacks in the 1940s seeking entertainment in the nightlife, the Roseland Ballroom was to Boston's black community what Small's Paradise Club* and the Savoy* were to New York's Harlem* African American community. To be sure, Boston's black population hardly equaled the size of Harlem's, but social life in the after hours there was no less vibrant for fun seekers. For Malcolm X, who had moved to Boston early in the decade to live with his half sister Ella Collins,* the Roseland Ballroom represented his entry into virtually a whole new world. He was young and impressionable, and life in the streets mesmerized him. He quickly became a fixture, a recognizable figure among the regulars at the Roseland, Boston's largest and most prestigious entertainment facility, and other night spots.

The Roseland was particularly special to Malcolm X because he found a job in the club as a shoeshine boy thanks largely to his closest friend, a hustler nicknamed Shorty.* Malcolm's sister Ella, a proud black woman well known in the elite circle of Boston's black Roxbury* section, had real lofty employment and social goals for Malcolm and frowned on the idea of her younger brother working as a "boot black." But Malcolm was immediately captivated by the prospects. With the liberal tips that he received, the job not only gave Malcolm

Patrons of a New York City nightclub dance in a scene similar to one
Malcolm often found himself in during his youth in Roxbury and
Harlem nightlife. © Bettmann/CORBIS.

a good source of self-earned income for the first time, but it also provided him
an opportunity to meet and fraternize with a diverse group of patrons and the
major entertainment acts that worked the Roseland. Malcolm came to know
personally such people as Duke Ellington,* Count Basie,* and Lionel Hampton*
and numerous members of their bands. These were among the many "black
acts" that played at the Roseland on the nights set aside for black patrons.

Making the rounds with Shorty at a number of "pad parties," Malcolm had
learned how to dance the latest dance craze, the Lindy Hop,* and soon showed
how prolific he had become at it. As he shined shoes he often danced to the
"pop" of his shine rag and the beat of the music coming from the large ballroom,
working at his menial task and entertaining his patrons at the same time. After
he quit his job he became an instant celebrity himself, dancing the Lindy in the
club's "showtime" contests where he was spotlighted with the most talented and
acrobatic female partners. His acumen impressed band landers and patrons alike,
especially the ladies, all of whom encouraged and acknowledged his talent and
spirit with phrases like "Go get 'em Red!" and "Go Red, go!" Dressed in his
zoot suit* with its baggy pants, Malcolm, according to Shorty, seemed to be
virtually floating on air when he danced at the Roseland.

In Boston, Malcolm learned the customs and etiquette of the street hipster culture, a phase of life that brought him both pain and joy. Malcolm's Roseland experience was catalytic in influencing his transformation from an innocent youth to a rougher kind of life as "Detroit Red."

SELECTED BIBLIOGRAPHY

Blackside/PBS, 1994; CBS News, 1992; Malcolm X with Haley, 1965; B. Perry, 1991.

Robert L. Jenkins

ROWAN, CARL THOMAS. Born in Ravenscroft, Tennessee, Carl Rowan, a syndicated columnist, was the director of the United States Information Agency (USIA)* during the 1960s and the first African American to serve on the National Security Council.

He was a vocal critic of Malcolm X—Malcolm's philosophy, beliefs, and representations of white Americans' racial oppression and discrimination against African Americans. Rowan often stated in public speeches that Malcolm X's views should not be supported. When Malcolm X criticized the Civil Rights Act of 1964,* Carl Rowan rebutted him, maintaining that the Civil Rights Act was a positive approach in achieving equality between the races in America.

Carl Rowan's criticisms continued even after Malcolm's assassination. Rowan was critical of the worldwide protest and sympathetic outpouring that followed the assassination. In speeches given before groups such as the American Foreign Service Association, the Cleveland Bar Association, and groups on visits to the African continent, he described Malcolm X's assassination as a nonnational, noninternational tragedy. Citizens of most foreign countries, he said, did not know much about the circumstances surrounding Malcolm's death and misunderstood the negative and hateful position that Malcolm X and his followers represented. In spite of Carl Rowan's criticisms, however, Malcolm X continued to be regarded as a martyr, particularly in the Third World.

SELECTED BIBLIOGRAPHY

Carson (Gallen, ed.), 1992; Friedly, 1992; Malcolm X with Haley, 1965.

Felix A. Okojie

ROXBURY SCENE. Malcolm first visited Roxbury, a section in black Boston, Massachusetts, in 1940 when he spent the summer with his half sister Ella Collins.* Roxbury left an indelible impression on Malcolm, especially the section's affluent black middle class. After the summer was over, he returned to Lansing, Michigan,* to resume life with the Swerlin family* in a detention home. The remark of Malcolm's eighth-grade English teacher that Malcolm's dream of someday becoming a lawyer was unrealistic for a "nigger" disillusioned Malcolm and encouraged him to isolate himself from his classmates and the Swerlin family. Somewhat uncomfortable with Malcolm's new disposition, Mrs. Swerlin arranged for Malcolm to be transferred to a different detention home managed by a black couple, Harold and Ivy Lyon. Malcolm's uneasiness was soon communicated to Ella, who arranged to get official custody of Malcolm after he completed the eighth grade. Ella took Malcolm home with her to Roxbury.

Shortly after arriving in Roxbury, Malcolm met Malcolm Jarvis (Shorty*), who took an interest in him. The two shared a common first name, and this, perhaps, is what initially strengthened their attraction to each other. Shorty arranged for Malcolm to get a shoeshine job at the Roseland Ballroom.* While working at the Roseland, Malcolm not only got the opportunity to hear and see the jazz bands of Duke Ellington,* Count Basie,* and Lionel Hampton*; he also got the chance to observe some of the latest and more popular dances of the period, such as the Lindy Hop.* Malcolm eventually became very proficient at dancing the Lindy, an accomplishment that enhanced his popularity in Roxbury nightclubs. His employment at the Roseland soon led him to drinking, gambling, and smoking cigarettes and reefers.* It was in Roxbury that Malcolm also got his first "conk,"* which changed his hair texture, and a bright blue zoot suit.* To be prepared for what often violently erupted in Roxbury's street life, he also began to carry a pistol. Roxbury women "swooned" over the tall, attractive Malcolm X. With his conked hair and flashy clothing, which he normally changed twice daily, Malcolm electrified Roxbury's street life, often stopping the traffic up and down Humboldt Avenue, one of the district's central streets.

Malcolm left Roxbury shortly after the Japanese bombed Pearl Harbor in 1941 and took a new job with the railroad, selling sandwiches and other refreshments to passengers between Boston and New York. For a while he lived in Harlem,* where he got involved in gambling, drugs, and numbers running. When things began to sour in New York, Malcolm hurriedly returned to Roxbury. As a way of obtaining money he organized a burglary ring that targeted homes in affluent neighborhoods. Malcolm and his accomplices were eventually caught when he attempted to have an expensive stolen watch repaired at a jeweler. On February 23, 1946, Malcolm was convicted of burglary and sentenced to serve ten years in Boston's Charlestown State Prison.

SELECTED BIBLIOGRAPHY

Collins with Bailey, 1998; Malcolm X with Haley, 1965; B. Perry, 1991.

Lauren Larsen

RUDY. Rudy was one of Malcolm X's partners in crime during his 1940s period of his lawbreaking in Boston. Little is known about this figure beyond what Malcolm revealed about him in his autobiography. Indeed, given Malcolm's tendency not to reveal the real identity of controversial or shadowy personalities from his past, the name Rudy may have been a fictitious one for this individual. A native Bostonian, Rudy was of mixed African American and Italian ancestry and was already a veteran hustler when Shorty,* Malcolm's closet friend, introduced the two. From the outset they established a good relationship. Rudy was fascinated with Malcolm's burglary ideas and was equally enthusiastic about working with him and the other members of the gang. Rudy's employment as an exclusive itinerant waiter gave him knowledge of potential victims. Hence, his primary job as an accomplice was to designate a burglary site and monitor the targeted building or home before the actual crime occurred; occasionally, he also drove the "getaway" car. Apparently, Rudy was either lucky or much shrewder than Malcolm and the others. When Malcolm and his ring were apprehended for their crimes, Rudy, though implicated, avoided capture and, according to Malcolm, was never arrested for his involvement.

For a period in their lives, Malcolm and Rudy played important roles in shaping each other's behavior. But as it was with many of the other personalities that he associated with during this phase of his life, Malcolm no longer shared much in common with them after his imprisonment and subsequent release, and they remained little more than distant memories for him.

SELECTED BIBLIOGRAPHY

Malcolm X with Haley, 1965; B. Perry, 1991.

Robert L. Jenkins

RUSTIN, BAYARD. As a pacifist and a preeminent civil rights* theorist of nonviolent protest, Bayard Rustin played a significant role in the original March on Washington Movement, the founding of the Congress of Racial Equality,* the Montgomery Bus Boycott, and the actual 1963 March on Washington.* Considered among the more "moderate" of black civil rights leaders—defined by Malcolm as black with white minds—Rustin and Malcolm were ideologically at odds. Both men engaged in several, sometimes heated, debates chiding the other for having policies that were at best misguided. Their most memorable debate confrontation was a 1962 engagement organized by students at Washington, D.C.'s Howard University.* In the debate Malcolm clearly bested Rustin, a real intellectual noted as a gifted logical analyst. Malcolm's criticism of middle-class blacks* and support of black nationalism* rendered in his "biting and uncompromising style" unexpectedly moved the pro-Rustin audience and, at least for the night, won him converts.

Malcolm ridiculed Rustin's commitment to nonviolence and racial integration* and later called the March on Washington, which Rustin played a major role in organizing, the "Farce on Washington." Rustin accused Malcolm of engaging in emotionalism rather than logic and criticized his reluctance to participate in civil rights demonstrations in the South.* Nevertheless, Rustin was one of many former Malcolm adversaries in attendance at the fallen militant's funeral. But Rustin's condemnation of Malcolm continued after his assassination. In 1965 he wrote three essays in which he questioned Malcolm's legacy. He declared that Malcolm was a man of contradictions whose charisma should not be confused with greatness. After all, Rustin argued, Malcolm had no actual program or movement: He was essentially a black conservative whose vitriolic

Bayard Rustin, a prominent civil rights leader, considered himself an adversary of Malcolm X because of their different views on achieving black uplift. Library of Congress.

rhetoric was useless. Nevertheless, Rustin was able to put his views of the living Malcolm aside to pay respect to him in death.

SELECTED BIBLIOGRAPHY

J. Anderson, 1997; Branch, 1988; DeCaro, 1996; Goldman, 1979; Malcolm X (Breitman, ed.), 1967.

Paul J. Wilson

S

SABBATINO, PETER L. F. A veteran New York criminal lawyer, Sabbatino was hired by the family of accused Malcolm X murderer Talmadge Hayer* (also know as Thomas Hagan) to defend him in the assassination trial.* The seventy-four-year-old Sabbatino, who was white and had defended more than 300 persons accused of murder, and his co-counsel Peter Yellin, also white, were the only privately retained attorneys of the six lawyers defending the three men accused in Malcolm's death. The trial began on January 12, 1966, and lasted for two months. Hayer pleaded innocent, but numerous eyewitnesses, including Malcolm's widow Betty Shabazz,* who placed him at the scene where he was captured, and considerable physical evidence virtually locked up the prosecution's case even before the trial began. Early in the trial Sabbatino tried unsuccessfully to distance Hayer from the other two defendants and to deny that his client, although a Muslim,* was neither a member of the Nation of Islam (NOI)* nor had a motive in desiring Malcolm's death. Consequently, Sabbatino planned his defense arguments around procedural questions involving his client's arrest and subsequent preindictment and pretrial incarceration.

Perhaps largely disillusioned by the trial judge who almost instinctively ruled in favor of the prosecution, and who failed to follow standard legal practices about ensuring the defense's access to relevant information about the state's case, Sabbatino's defense was hardly spirited. This proved true even in raising the procedural issues addressed in his introductory statements. And on the stand Hayer helped his own cause very little. In his initial testimony, he denied a multiplicity of prosecution allegations, from motive and association with any of the physical evidence, including the diversionary smoke bomb found near the murder scene containing his thumbprint, to actually firing the initial and additional shots into Malcolm's prone body. In a remarkable turn of events several days later, however, Hayer made a full confession of his guilt, given, he said, to exonerate the other two falsely accused men by simply telling the truth. To

Hayer's anger, Sabbatino tried to downplay the confession, saying it was an act of "Christian" charity for his client to try to help the others, but the jury should ignore the testimony as untruthful.

Despite Hayer's confession to the contrary, the other two defendants were also found guilty, and all three were sentenced to life imprisonment. Sabbatino, however, remained convinced that his client's confession was largely untrue and correctly predicted that the trial would not resolve the controversy over who was actually responsible for commissioning Malcolm's murder. Conspiracy theories, some of which involved federal agencies, continue to surround the mysteries over Malcolm's life and death.

SELECTED BIBLIOGRAPHY

Evanzz, 1992; Friedly, 1992; Goldman, 1979; *Militant*, January 31, 1966, February 14, 1966, March 7, 1966, March 21, 1966.

Robert L. Jenkins

AL-SADAT, MUHAMMAD ANWAR. During the late 1950s, the Nation of Islam (NOI)* began to generate considerable interest from leaders of the Middle East.* The organization and Malcolm X, its national spokesman, had strongly supported the ideals of the developing nations articulated in the Bandung Conference,* many of which were Islamic. Elijah Muhammad's parallel interest in the Arab world resulted in a 1959 invitation from Egypt's* leader Gamal Abdel Nasser* to visit the country as his official guest and then to take the Hajj* to Mecca.* Involved in a major legal tiff with the U.S. government, Muhammad could not accept the invitation but sent his lieutenant, Malcolm X, as his emissary. Malcolm declined the opportunity to meet with President Nasser, believing that this privilege should be reserved for his mentor. Similar reasoning might also have influenced him not to enter Mecca as the first of the NOI's inner circle to make the Hajj. He did, however, spend a considerable amount of time with high-ranking government officials, especially Vice President Anwar Sadat. Like Malcolm, who supported freedom struggles worldwide and philosophically considered himself a revolutionary, Sadat was, in fact, a revolutionary leader who had assisted Nasser in the overthrow of the King Farouk monarchy in 1952. He would himself become president of the nation, serving in the capacity from 1970 to his murder in 1981. Like Malcolm's murderers, Sadat's assassins came from disgruntled members of Islam.*

Although Nasser and Sadat had hoped to use Malcolm and the NOI for political purposes, apparently little came from Malcolm's official visit. Malcolm and Sadat talked about Islam, but little is actually known about the nature of their discussions. Indeed, in his autobiography, Malcolm barely mentions this first trip to Egypt, and no reference is made to Sadat at all. Moreover, if Sadat himself felt particularly impressed from his meetings with Malcolm, he too left no indication of it. Apparently, Malcolm's favorable views of Egypt and its leadership became more definitive after his second trip to the African continent in 1964.

SELECTED BIBLIOGRAPHY

Carson (Gallen, ed.), 1991; Clegg, 1997; Evanzz, 1999; Malcolm X with Haley, 1965.
                                                                        Robert L. Jenkins

SANCHEZ, SONIA. Sonia Sanchez is an award-winning poet, playwright, activist, editor, and educator who was born in Birmingham, Alabama,* on September 9, 1934. After graduating with a Bachelor of Arts degree from Hunter College in 1955, she studied poetry at New York University. She soon became a part of the 1960s Black Arts Movement. The movement was part and parcel of the new "Black Renaissance," which Malcolm X influenced. Malcolm naturally affected the movement, Sanchez says, because it was centered in New York, where Malcolm maintained his headquarters and where Malcolm so greatly influenced black intellectuals. Malcolm had been demonized by the media, and Sanchez, like so many others, had initially accepted the negative portrayal. When Sanchez worked with the Congress of Racial Equality* in Harlem,* she had the opportunity to hear Malcolm speak. Sanchez found him to be electrifying, and she admired his eloquence. She became a follower and helped to spread the news that Malcolm was truly reflecting the views and aspirations of African Americans. There is an unmistakable Malcolm X influence in her early poems, which are characterized by a revolutionary critique of America. Sanchez had intended to be in the Audubon Ballroom* the evening of Malcolm's murder but changed her mind about going at the last moment. She was so stricken with the news of his death that her emotional scream was a "primal" response as much as it was a display of "outrage." Sanchez is credited for having helped immortalize Malcolm X in two of her poems, "Malcolm" and "For Unborn Malcolms."

SELECTED BIBLIOGRAPHY

Blackside/PBS, 1994; Gallen, ed., 1992; Gwynne, ed., 1993; J. Smith, ed., 1991; M. Williams, ed., 1993.
                                                                        Lehlohonolo Tlou

SANDIFER, JAWN. A New York attorney, Jawn Sandifer was also a justice in the New York court system and a state National Association for the Advancement of Colored People* official. Along with his partner, Edward Jacko,* Sandifer did considerable legal work for the Nation of Islam (NOI)* during the 1960s. Sandifer's office was located in Harlem* not far from Malcolm's Temple Number Seven.* The proximity of the attorney's office to the temple, along with his professional work for the NOI, influenced the establishment of an important personal and professional relationship with Malcolm. Sandifer had great respect for Malcolm's work among New York's lowly classes, but it was his ministry in the state's prison* system that he claims was one of Malcolm's greatest contributions to the grassroots. Based on his own influence and legal work within New York's penal system, Sandifer helped to open doors for Malcolm to begin his prison ministry. According to the justice, once Malcolm started his prison outreach he soon worked wonders reaching this criminal element, his pastorate being especially important in establishing or restoring self-esteem among the inmates. But it was not just self-improvement* that Malcolm succeeded in with these convicts. Sandifer extolled the long-term effects of Malcolm's immense proselytizing success converting inmates to Islam.* It was Malcolm, he claims, who actually began the NOI's systematic work among the incarcerated, and his pathbreaking efforts literally set the pattern for later NOI successes in converting larger numbers of convicted felons. The Messenger, Elijah Muhammad,* realized that recruits who came from backgrounds similar to the ones that landed him and Malcolm behind bars often made the most loyal and committed followers. Hence, many of these former inmates helped to increase the membership of the NOI once they won release, some of whom found their place in Malcolm's Harlem temple.

SELECTED BIBLIOGRAPHY

Cassity, 1984; DeCaro, 1998; Evanzz, 1999.

Robert L. Jenkins

SAUDI ARABIA. In April 1964, Malcolm traveled to Saudi Arabia to undertake a pilgrimage to Mecca.* Although Malcolm received the requisite letter of approval from the Islamic scholar Dr. Mahmoud Youssef Shawarbi,* who had tutored him in orthodox Islam,* in Jedda, Malcolm was immediately detained to allow the Muslim* high court to determine his religious authenticity. Malcolm called Omar Azzam,* an engineer in Jedda and the son of Dr. Abd ar-Rahman Azzam, author of *The Eternal Message of Muhammad*, a book given to Malcolm by Dr. Shawarbi. The Azzam family got Malcolm released and gave him a warm reception at their home. This cordial reception by dignitaries occurred throughout his Saudi Arabian tour.

Prince Mohmaed Al-Faysal,* the Saudi ruler, and the royal family welcomed Malcolm as a state guest. The prince's Deputy Chief of Protocol brought Malcolm before the high court, which promptly approved his visit to Mecca. The prince met with Malcolm, his first meeting with a head of state, and criticized the Black Muslim* movement for deviating from orthodoxy. Malcolm's unusual reticence prompted the Saudi leader to later remark that he found the American Muslim shy and timid. The prince, however, provided him with a chauffeured car and a guide for his travels in Arabia, air-conditioned accommodations, and servants wherever he visited. Malcolm's experience in Saudi Arabia and the Hajj* were the real beginnings of major changes in his thinking about Islam and views of whites. His new perspective reflected his conversion to Sunni Islam and his new name El Hajj Malik El-Shabazz.* Malcolm also returned from Saudi

Arabia with a gift from the government of fifteen scholarships for students to study at the University of Medina.

SELECTED BIBLIOGRAPHY

Malcolm X with Haley, 1965; *Militant*, November 2, 1964; B. Perry, 1991; Wolfenstein, 1993.

Paul J. Wilson

SAVIOR'S DAY CONVENTION. The Nation of Islam's (NOI)* national gathering, the annual event is normally held beginning on February 26 to coincide with the birthday of the NOI's founder, the mysterious W. D. Fard.* Fard's successor Elijah Muhammad* declared the first Savior's Day in 1934 and inaugurated the sacred annual celebrations in 1950. The earliest of these events were held in Detroit, Michigan,* site of the first NOI mosque, but then moved to Chicago, Illinois,* where Muhammad established the national headquarters. The several days celebration, which attracted busloads of enthusiastic rank-and-file Muslims* from across the nation during the 1960s, was an impressive demonstration of the increasing power and influence of the group. They had as their mission the teaching of the views of Fard but more often resulted in emphasizing Muhammad's own interpretation of NOI doctrine. Believers and nonbelievers alike got hours-long doses of Muhammad's nonorthodox views of Islam,* NOI history, particularly the role of the central figure Fard, the NOI's positions on black nationalism* and economic development, and the group's position on territorial demands. Participants also heard the NOI's standard fare denouncing Christianity* and condemning the "white devils"* and a rousing criticism of the racial integration* goals of black civil rights* leaders.

Although such subject matter in Muhammad's highly anticipated address, regarded as his most important speech of the year, dominated the event, other speakers also had roles to play. They occasionally included orthodox Muslims, personalities like converted boxer Muhammad Ali,* and non-Muslim militants who sympathized with aspects of the NOI's ideology as well as various influential temple leaders. Other presentations during the convention exposed members to a variety of familiar subjects and training activities relative to NOI dogma, but always the emphasis was on the importance of self-help and blacks having the "freedom" to do for themselves.

Malcolm X, who played an integral role in the evolution of the conventions and who helped to organize many of these annual celebrations, was also a major draw. As Muhammad's chief national representative, he convened the 1963 gathering because Muhammad's bout with asthma confined him to his Phoenix, Arizona, home. Normally, however, Malcolm spoke as a preliminary to the appearance of his mentor. On stage with Muhammad and Malcolm would be a core of regional ministers and other national officers attentively awaiting Malcolm's fiery speech and adulatory introduction. In his presentation of Muhammad to the audience, in their customary separate men and women seating

A national gathering of Nation of Islam members, typical of the annual Savior's Day Convention in its attraction of rank and file members. Library of Congress.

arrangement, the latter clothed in their all-white garb, Malcolm would hail Muhammad as Allah's* prophet and messenger, the "most fearless" black man in the country. These were, of course, times when Malcolm was in the good graces of Muhammad and had much to say that Black Muslims* everywhere revered. By the time that Malcolm had convened the 1963 convention, strains were already appearing in his relationship with the Messenger. In the years that followed his ousting from the NOI, the gatherings were often used as another platform to denounce Malcolm as a traitor to both Muhammad and the movement.

In early 1965, Malcolm had claimed inside information from the NOI that his murder was to occur before the year's Savior's Day Convention began. The information proved highly creditable; he was killed five days before the February opening celebration and buried on the same weekend of the Muslim's Chicago conclave. Ironically, in 1993 NOI leader Minister Louis Farrakhan,* one of Malcolm's protégés and closest friends who later turned on him and to many was implicated in Malcolm's fall and eventual death, used the Savior's Day Convention as a platform to formally address the assassination controversy and to honor the memory of both Muhammad and Malcolm X.

SELECTED BIBLIOGRAPHY
Branch, 1998; Clegg, 1997; DeCaro, 1998; Karim with Skutches and Gallen, 1992; Marsh, 1996; B. Perry, 1991; Rummel, 1989.

Robert L. Jenkins

SAVOY BALLROOM. The Savoy Ballroom was once the largest dance hall in Harlem,* affectionately called the "Home of the Happy Feet." The Savoy opened in 1926, at Lenox Avenue (now Malcolm X Blvd.) and 141st Street, and was credited with being the incubator of the famous dance the Lindy Hop,* created in 1927 and named for aviation pioneer Charles Lindbergh, who made the historic flight to Paris that year. The Savoy was an important social institution in Harlem and was the best place to experience some of the most popular swing bands in the country during the 1930s and 1940s.

Malcolm X frequented the Savoy and was part of its glory status in the 1940s. His first mesmerizing tour of Harlem's nightlife included a visit to the Savoy, which made the Roseland Ballroom* (where Malcolm was first introduced to hustling* in Boston's Roxbury* section) seem shabby in comparison. It was also at the Savoy that Malcolm first saw the famous singer Dinah Washington,* with whom he later became friends. The Savoy, unlike the historic Cotton Club (which only catered to whites), was known for its interracial gatherings. Malcolm was particularly impressed by the various attractions that the club offered, such as "Thursday Kitchen Mechanics Nights," beauty contests, and the new car giveaway every Saturday night. According to Malcolm and many other Harlemites, it was the Savoy's interracial touch that caused the temporary closing of the ballroom during World War II* by New York City Mayor Fiorello LaGuardia.

SELECTED BIBLIOGRAPHY

J. Anderson, 1982; Malcolm X (Epps, ed.), 1991; Malcolm X with Haley, 1965.

Nancy J. Dawson

SCHAPP, DICK. A notable journalist and television commentator, for more than thirty years Schapp has been at the forefront of national sports news. The author of thirty-two books, Schapp has worked as an editor of *Sports Magazine* and in the 1990s became a familiar face as a television sports personality as host of ESPN's *Classics, One on One* and the network's weekly sports "magazine" show *The Sports Reporters*. Although his natural interest has been in sports journalism, where he began his career, Schapp established his early and most impressive journalistic reputation during the mid-1960s with his work as the city editor of the *New York Herald Tribune* and later as senior editor with *Newsweek* magazine. In these capacities, national political and social issues consumed his attention. It was during this period that his interest and fascination with the Nation of Islam (NOI)* developed. At the time, Elijah Muhammad's* organization was at its zenith in national attention. Much of this occurred as a result of the work of Malcolm X, its most articulate spokesman. Schapp knew Malcolm personally and regarded him not only as a compassionate, articulate, and "gifted man" but also as someone almost regal in his bearing and physical qualities. Malcolm, in Schapp's view, was hardly the acerbic white-hating personality that he often depicted himself as; rather, he was a compassionate man who disdained injustice and those who practiced racism. In Schapp's opinion, Malcolm was frequently misunderstood by the public. A prime example of this, he claimed, was in how America angrily reacted to Malcolm's "chickens coming home to roost"* remarks about President John Kennedy's* assassination. It was an impolitic comment, Schapp affirmed, but Malcolm hardly meant it as any more than his public explanation indicated: that the murder resulted from an existing climate of national violence; Kennedy was simply its latest and most prominent victim.

There is much to indicate Schapp's deep admiration for Malcolm. Although close to heavyweight boxer Muhammad Ali* as well, Schapp nevertheless found much to criticize the former champion about in his break with Malcolm and eventual alliance with Elijah Muhammad* when the two Muslim* leaders permanently parted in 1964. Schapp, who considered Malcolm as one of the most important personalities to exist during the 1960s, understandably lamented Malcolm's murder and personally wrote the obituary for his New York journal. Apparently, Malcolm regarded Schapp favorably as well. He thought enough of their relationship to send Schapp a postcard from Mecca* during his Hajj* in the Holy Land and to later seek his personal company in the search for a new headquarters for his Organization of Afro-American Unity.* While the two men

Noted journalist and civil rights activist George Schuyler sits with Malcolm awaiting their interview together at a New York radio station. © Hulton-Deutsch Collection/COR-BIS.

were hardly social companions, apparently their relationship was considerably more than a casual one, an indication of the diverse associations that existed in Malcolm's world.

SELECTED BIBLIOGRAPHY

Gallen, ed., 1992; Halberstam, ed., 1999; *New York Herald Tribune*, March 22, 1965.

Robert L. Jenkins

SCHUYLER, GEORGE. Born in Providence, Rhode Island, on February 25, 1895, George Schuyler acquired a national reputation as a journalist and editor for one of the nation's largest circulating black weekly newspapers during the twentieth century, the *Pittsburgh Courier*.* He began his journalist career in the early 1920s, however, with A. Philip Randolph's militant journal *The Messenger** and during the decade flirted with socialism.* His writing talents later drifted to serious work as a novelist, but he achieved only minimal success. During the 1930s and 1940s, he wrote critically and frequently about America's hypocrisy in denouncing Nazi racism while refusing to address adequately its treatment of blacks. Yet he extolled the virtues of being a black conservative. As such, he opposed Randolph's controversial wartime proposed March on Washington to support black employment in the defense industries and later often criticized Martin Luther King, Jr.'s* nonviolent civil rights* initiatives. Like so many other prominent blacks of the 1960s, Schuyler, who wrote a column for the *Courier* from New York during the decade, became increasingly aware of Malcolm X's urban following. On at least two occasions Schuyler and

Malcolm faced each other on radio and television broadcasts. A member of the black middle class, a natural and popular target of Malcolm's criticism, Schuyler certainly did not escape from such meetings without drawing Malcolm's scorn, but their encounters were hardly confrontational. According to one prominent black leader of the period, only Schuyler among the prominent black leaders, however, fared well in debate with the quick-minded Malcolm.

Clearly the two men had little in common. As an arch political conservative, Schuyler could not endorse Malcolm's militantly articulated black nationalist views or some of his political opinions about marshaling black voters as independents; he frowned on black history* being taught as a separate discipline, a position that Malcolm staunchly supported as a precursor to black self-identity. Still, he expressed respect for Malcolm the man and especially his courage. Perhaps this was conditioned by the *Courier*'s long association with the Black Muslims*; Elijah Muhammad* once wrote a weekly column for the paper, and Schuyler occasionally defended the group for its positive social impact on black communities in his "View and Review" column. In Schuyler's opinion, Malcolm was hardly the "horrendous ogre" that many of both races made him out to be. Acknowledging what most observers of the period well knew, it was Malcolm, "intelligent and gifted," Schuyler once wrote, who was the real brains behind the Black Muslim movement. Nor did Malcolm publically express contempt for the old journalist. Besides their penchant for casting aspersions on several of the period's black leaders, however, they shared little other common ground.

SELECTED BIBLIOGRAPHY

Goldman, 1979; Grill and Jenkins, 1992; Leeming, 1994; Lincoln, 1994; *Pittsburgh Courier*, March 21, 1964; Resh (Lowery and Marszalek, eds.), 1992; Schuyler, 1966.

Robert L. Jenkins

SEALE, ROBERT G. (BOBBY). Born in 1937 in Dallas, Texas, Bobby Seale came to the front of the civil and human rights* movement in the 1960s as a founder of the Black Panther Party for Self-Defense.* The party was nurtured on the outrage expounded by Malcolm X before his death. Indeed, it was Malcolm to whom Seale said the party owed its ideological and philosophical basis. The Panthers considered themselves to be the "heirs of Malcolm."

A militant, Seale and his family moved to Oakland, California, when he was seven years old. He spent three years in the U.S. Air Force and then attended Merritt College in Oakland, California, where he met Huey P. Newton,* another admirer of Malcolm's militancy and urgency of action. The two founded the Black Panther Party in October 1966, some twenty months after Malcolm's assassination. Seale, though he never met Malcolm, had heard him speak. Malcolm's wisdom captivated Seale, and thereafter he had "mesmerized enthusiasm" about Malcolm's leadership. He read *Muhammad Speaks** weekly to find out what Malcolm was saying to his followers. Seale so strongly embraced Malcolm as an icon that news of his murder prompted a major emotional outburst from him. He not only "cried like a baby" but threw bricks at passing cars driven by whites, broke windows in two houses, and cursed incessantly at whites, especially the Federal Bureau of Investigation (FBI)* and the law enforcement establishment, whom he blamed for the assassination. Once the party was established, Newton and Seale assigned Malcolm's autobiography as mandatory reading for new recruits.

The Panthers spearheaded a revolutionary movement that departed from the nonviolent philosophies of other national African American groups. The party emphasized self-defense* and self-determination for the oppressed, as did Malcolm and the Black Muslims* for whom Malcolm spoke. They proposed a ten-point program, largely written by Seale, that included reparations* for past abuses of African Americans, release of all blacks in prisons,* and trials for African Americans by all-black juries. Seale, in classic Malcolm X style, was notable for his angry rhetoric. He maintained that violence took two forms: It was either directed at one to maintain subjugation or it was a defensive tool used against oppression in order to obtain freedom. As a result of Malcolm's philosophy of self-defense, gun battles and other violent confrontations between party members and police were frequent. Thus, within three years of its founding, the Panthers had become the best-known and the most formidable (and vilified) of all African American political/nationalist movements in America. As chairman of the party, Seale was in the center of many of the party's controversies, catapulted into the national limelight by a media that was similar in the way they portrayed Malcolm: The press depicted Seale and the Panthers as evil revolutionaries who hated all whites. The FBI considered Seale and his party followers the nation's greatest national security threat.

Seale, as had Malcolm X, succeeded in luring many youngsters away from the rootlessness and spiritual starvation of ghetto streets. But also like Malcolm X, largely because of his militant ideology, Seale was unable to attract the kind of support to the party from black intellectuals and professionals that would establish a lasting and respectable organization. Much of this failure occurred because Seale and other party leaders were constantly in the justice system and thus in the public eye. In 1969, for example, Seale found himself on probation for a gun law violation and was indicted in Chicago, Illinois,* as a member of the "Chicago Eight" for conspiracy to disrupt the 1968 Democratic National Convention. A sensational trial ensued with Seale's inflammatory behavior causing Judge Julius Hoffman to separate his case, declare an individual mistrial, and sentence him to four years in prison for contempt of court. Earlier in 1969, Seale had been arrested and held on $25,000 bail, charged with the murder of Alex Rackley, an alleged Panther informer in New Haven, Connecticut. On October 19, 1970, the government dismissed conspiracy charges against Seale in connection with the Chicago riot of 1968, but he still had to contend with the murder charge that was finally dismissed on May 3, 1971. In 1974 Seale resigned as chairman of the Black Panther Party. But clearly there was more to Seale than revolutionary ideology, inflammatory behavior, and vitriolic rhetoric. He has authored two books, one of which is his autobiography, run successfully for political office, and lectured widely. By 1980 he was no longer a participant in the Black Power* movement, involving himself in rather orthodox politics and professional and business activities.

SELECTED BIBLIOGRAPHY

Anthony, 1970; Franklin and Moss, 1988; Low and Clift, eds., 1981; Pearson, 1994; Ploski and Williams, 1983; Seale, 1968, 1978; Smythe, 1976.

Lee E. Williams II

SELF-DEFENSE. In the short period that Malcolm X was on the international scene as a leader, a number of phrases and ideas came to be associated with his name and message. "By any means necessary," "the ballot or the bullet," "House Negro,"* and "Field Negro"* are among some of the more easily identifiable and enduring ones. Obvious, too, is the expression or idea "self-defense." Indeed, perhaps no phrase has become more synonymous with Malcolm than the frequently expressed phrase "self-defense." It was largely because of his articulation of it that many during the period of his leadership and thereafter greatly misunderstood Malcolm, falsely labeling him an apostle of violence. But Malcolm, though he often expressed himself in the most threatening language, was hardly an advocate of violence for the sake of violence. To be sure, he talked often and boldly about not being nonviolent with those who were nonviolent with him, but this was expressed largely out of the assertion of his right for self-preservation. It was everyone's right, regardless of color or race, whenever one's personal safety was threatened with violence. Moreover, according to Malcom, his religion of Islam* sanctioned the right for Muslims* to defend themselves.

Along these lines, Malcolm talked considerably about the importance of self-defense. If this required arming oneself to achieve, Malcolm claimed that Americans, including blacks, were well within their constitutional rights to do so. It mattered little if they were innocent demonstrators participating in a peaceful demonstration that turned violent because of brutal police tactics or whether they were simply potential victims of racist whites adhering to the philosophies of organizations like the Ku Klux Klan* or the White Citizen's Council.* Malcolm condemned as hypocritical American whites who glorified white historical figures who resorted to violence to fight for independence or supported wars in far-off places in the name of American honor but who criticized blacks like himself who advocated armed self-defense from white terrorism. No group, he said, had been victimized more by systematic practices of violence than black Americans, and understanding this, it made little sense to encourage black demonstrators "to go to Mississippi* unarmed." Protecting oneself by resorting to violence when necessary, Malcolm would say, had nothing to do with being violent but everything to do with being intelligent.

It was this issue that Malcolm had to address constantly to whites who refused to accept his reasoning. He claimed incredulity about the white public's lack of understanding about his position on the issue but blamed white liberals* for deliberately distorting his ideas as examples of reverse violence and then influencing the press to further exaggeration. But Malcolm never wavered from his uncompromising stand on the importance of blacks individually or as a group banding together, if necessary, to protect themselves from whatever source of violent harm that confronted them. He took this to an alarming and unrealistic extreme, perhaps, with his advocacy of blacks forming rifle clubs as a way to instill this protective solidarity. Certainly more practical was his invitation to those who wished to become proficient at self-defense to join his Organization of Afro-American Unity (OAAU),* which had made self-defense a key component in its programs, to learn the best methods to ensure their physical safety. If few accepted Malcolm's OAAU offer, after his death his view about self-defense found greater currency in the appearance of numerous black militant groups, the very embodiment, for example, in the Black Panther Party for Self-Defense.*

SELECTED BIBLIOGRAPHY

Anthony, 1970; Blackside/PBS, 1987; Hampton and Fayer with Flynn, eds., 1991; James, 1997; Malcolm X (Breitman, ed.), 1965, 1967; Malcolm X (Clark, ed.), 1992; Malcolm X with Haley, 1965; Seale, 1968, 1978.

Robert L. Jenkins

SELF-IMPROVEMENT. During most of its history, few outside of the leadership of the Nation of Islam (NOI)* knew much about the actual size of the organization. Estimates that often ran into the tens of thousands were hardly close to being accurate. Clearly, it was because of some of their views that recruitment into the sect was negatively affected. Its wholesale condemnation of all whites, its pointed political assessment of the United States as a corrupt and evil nation, and its views about black nationalism* and racial separation* gained little currency among many blacks striving to move into the American mainstream as first-class citizens. In addition, the NOI's often harsh restrictions on the membership regarding an assortment of vices and personal habits made it difficult for many urban blacks to formally embrace the sect. That it was able to attract significant numbers in the 1950s and 1960s, the period when Malcolm X's influence was most felt, however, had as much to do with the group's views about black self-esteem and racial solidarity as it did with its antiwhite rhetoric and proposed solution to the dilemma of the black American condition. Moreover, it was precisely the group's teachings about certain issues of personal habit and tendencies that some blacks found especially appealing. The NOI taught blacks to abstain from harmful practices such as smoking and drinking alcohol, and it condemned drug abuse in the most emphatic language. Because of the importance of good health, the NOI reasoned, common sense dictated the avoidance of certain foods, especially pork,* because of its influence on high blood pressure. Muslims* should be conscious of their appearance and do nothing to deprecate themselves. They encouraged black men and women to accept and respect traditional roles in marriage and family life and to avoid adulterous relationships. Men were expected to accept the responsibility of adequately providing for their families and to protect them with their lives if necessary. Though it advised men to be dominant as the family head, it scorned any tendency of husbands and fathers to resort to abuse in maintaining their control.

Before his imprisonment and Islamic conversion, Malcolm had lived a life where many of the vices and personal shortcomings helped to define who he was; consequently, he understood well how ruinous some of them were on health, the home, and the race itself. Hence, like all of the other NOI ministers, in the temple where he ministered, in his prison* outreach, and in his public lectures and comments, Malcolm taught about the detrimental effects of some of these frailties, and he warned his followers to avoid them as obstacles to race advancement and self-improvement.

Malcolm believed that adhering to a value system that championed resisting these vices was morally right and central to individual and race elevation. Such ideas, of course, were not new; black leaders, such as Booker T. Washington, seeking to elevate the race had long advocated the importance of self-improvement as a means to racial progress. But in many ways, Malcolm X and the NOI took the message to a higher level, and it helped many in the urban communities and prisons. Malcolm and the NOI, for example, enjoyed a wide reputation for their reform and rehabilitation work among substance abusers, petty criminals, and prison inmates. Unlike many who preached one thing and practiced another, Malcolm closely followed the line himself, and as a Muslim, a husband, and father, he exemplified the virtuous life that he encouraged other blacks to live.

SELECTED BIBLIOGRAPHY

D. Bailey (Wood, ed.), 1992; Cleaver, 1970; Clegg, 1997; Cone, 1992; Jamal, 1971; Lincoln, 1994; Lomax, 1963; Malcolm X with Haley, 1965; Silberman, 1964; Warren, 1965.

Robert L. Jenkins

SHABAZZ, BETTY SANDERS. On June 23, 1997, the call for an Islamic ritual came once again for the Shabazz family. This time it was for Betty Sanders Shabazz, the widow of Malcolm X. Betty's life was lost due to a serious accident in her home, a fire set by her grandson, whom she was raising, that burned over 80 percent of her body. In the days that followed the accident and her hospitalization, the black community responded with flowers, cards, and prayer, and when the call went out for blood, they also came forward in great numbers out of love for her. During Betty's ordeal in the hospital, her six daughters stayed by her side and prayed endlessly for her life. But they understood the gravity of the situation and knew their responsibilities as the daughters of Malcolm X and Betty Shabazz. Ultimately, Betty's injuries consumed her three weeks after the tragedy. The young daughters—Attallah, Qubilah, Ilyasah, Gamilah Lamumbah, Malikah Saban, and Malaak Saban—demonstrated their love for their mother by giving her the last rites as required by Islamic law. Patiently and lovingly, they cleansed and oiled Betty's body, wrapping the shroud around her while reciting prayers and expressions of their love.

Betty Sanders Shabazz was born in Detroit, Michigan,* on May 28, 1936. She was adopted by the Malloy family (relatives), who raised her with love and care, and they taught her to have wholesome expectations about life. They also gave her a strong foundation in the Methodist religious faith and the best education that they could afford. After she graduated from high school in 1952, she attended Tuskegee Institute, where she majored in nursing. This was a profession that not only prepared Betty for the work that she expected to do in her career but also prepared her for adjusting to the physical and mental challenges that would become a part of her life with Malcolm X. After transferring from Tuskegee, Betty entered New York's Brooklyn State Hospital for additional training.

It was in New York where she attended a Nation of Islam (NOI)* service in 1956 that led to her eventual meeting with Malcolm X. Malcolm, serving at the time as minister of Temple Number Seven,* had shown little interest in establishing a serious romantic relationship with anyone, especially a woman from his temple. He considered most of them to be little more than gossipers and bickerers. Though he was regarded as "a good catch"—regal in his countenance, articulate, and influential—it was his work that consumed him, not the prospect of keeping company with women. Sanders joined the NOI after her arrival in Harlem* and found her place as Betty X, a teacher in the temple's Muslim Girl's Training* program. Despite his professed lack of interest in a serious relationship, Malcolm also began to notice Betty's intelligence and her quiet and unassuming qualities. After what turned out to be a brief courtship, during a telephone conversation Malcolm surprisingly proposed marriage to her, which she promptly accepted. Elijah Muhammad,* leader of the Muslim* sect, gave his blessings to the proposed union, and the two were married on January 15, 1958, in Lansing, Michigan.*

At Malcolm's insistence, Betty did not work in the profession for which she was educated but stayed in the home where she performed the responsibilities of wife and mother. She strongly supported Malcolm's work, sharing his passion for international black liberation causes, and she proved to be understanding of his frequent travels in the United States and abroad. On his private side, Malcolm was often a considerate husband who teased Betty humorously and left affectionate notes around the house for her to find. They acknowledged that the bond between them was sincere and strong.

The marriage, however, did not come without hardships for Betty. This was especially true after Malcolm's break with the NOI. Betty naturally suffered the horror with Malcolm of having their home bombed in the middle of the night, and she worried about his safety in the midst of harassing phone calls and death threats. It was both discomforting and frustrating for her to realize that she could not save Malcolm from the inevitable. Yet he always seemed to return rejuvenated to Betty and his family after a long trip and again went out among the masses of his people, setting the table for his enemies to feed upon. Betty endured each test, however, determined to follow her husband, no matter what the outcome. During their private moments, they certainly talked about their future, but the doubt always remained as to whether there would truly be one for the both of them. Malcolm himself would often say that he would not live to grow old. In the end, of course, only Betty, who sadly witnessed her husband's death, would have a future, however brief that it turned out to be.

After Malcolm's death with no money and the responsibility of raising her family of small children entirely alone, she returned to college, eventually earning master's and doctorate degrees in public health administration and education administration, respectively. At the time of her death, she was a longtime administrator in New York's Medgar Evers* College, named after the Mississippi* civil rights* leader whose assassination Malcolm had often commented on during his speeches and interviews. Betty also remained close to the black community after Malcolm's murder. A contemplative and eloquent speaker, she made frequent guest appearances at various Malcolm X celebrations and spoke at numerous places for a variety of causes, frequently invoking his name and his spirit and analyzing his work. Protective of her family, she defended her daughter Qubilah in an alleged murder plot to kill NOI leader Louis Farrakhan.* She sought to further Malcolm's work in the Organization of Afro-American Unity* while accepting gestures of reconciliation with Farrakhan, whom many believed was intricately involved in Malcolm's murder. She visited many of the same international cities that Malcolm visited and, like her husband, made the important Hajj,* after which she was officially known as El-Hajj Dr. Betty Sanders Shabazz. Until her own death, as Malcolm's widow Betty became the living legacy of his meaning to millions of people who had also loved, respected, and honored Malcolm's life and work.

SELECTED BIBLIOGRAPHY

J. Brown, 1998; Evanzz, 1992; Gallen, ed., 1992; *New York Post*, June 24, 1997; B. Shabazz (Clarke, ed.), 1990; B. Shabazz, 1992.

Zainabu Sipiowe Netosh Jones

EL-SHABAZZ, EL-HAJJ MALIK (Malcolm Little; Malcolm Shabazz). Although he was known publicly most of his adult life as Malcolm X, Malcolm changed his name upon returning from Mecca* to El-Hajj Malik El-Shabazz. The term *El-Hajj* derives its significance from the fact that he had made the pilgrimage to the Holiest City in Islam.* The surname of Shabazz was the family last name that identified his wife as well as his children after the Hajj,* rather than the traditional "X"* that black Muslims* adopted when first joining the Nation of Islam (NOI).* While a number of members of the NOI had publicly adopted Arabic and Muslim* names prior to Malcolm, including his mentor and leader Elijah Muhammad,* Malcolm's new name carried a special meaning. The name suggested not only that he had become a Sunni Muslim but that he had taken on a new religious and cultural identity that was reflected in the name.

Traveling in the United States, he used the name Malik Shabazz when he stayed overnight in hotels. Malcolm maintained that the name change alone provided not only a new identity but also newfound respect from whites and others. Malcolm suggested that there is more in a name than just one's personal identity. Pride, culture, history, and self-respect were integral components of a name, especially with regard to African Americans, who, he argued, were a lost people. Malcolm's emphasis upon the meaning of his name change was consistent with his views on black nationalism* and racial self-identitification.* But even after his name change, most of the public as well as blacks still knew him as Malcolm X. Indeed, Malcolm said that he would not abandon use of the name Malcolm X until conditions in America changed sufficiently enough to warrant it. When Malcolm died, however, his Arabic name of El-Hajj Malik El-Shabazz was printed in a bronze plate above his casket. Yet part of his legacy is reflected in the numerous blacks who adopted African and Arabic names after his death.

SELECTED BIBLIOGRAPHY

Gallen, ed., 1992; Library Distributors of America, 1993; Malcolm X with Haley, 1965; B. Shabazz (Clarke, ed.), 1990.

Mfanya Donald Tryman

SHABAZZ, JAMES (James 67X; Abdullah Abdur-Razzaq). James 67X, as he was previously referred to, would emerge as Malcolm's preeminent aide and confidant. Initially, however, he was a friend and aide of Malcolm's chief rival Captain Joseph Gravitts,* commander of the Fruit of Islam (FOI)* at Temple Number Seven* in Harlem.* As Malcolm's acclaim and notoriety grew, the relationship between the two flowered as well.

One of the attributes that attracted Malcolm to James was his intellect. He was college educated and fluent in Japanese and spoke some French and German. He also counseled Malcolm in many regards, most significantly about refraining from provoking Elijah Muhammad.* He soon became known as Malcolm's chief "man Friday." James's hard work and association probably paid off when he was appointed Executive Secretary of Temple Number Seven. From that position, he managed the day-to-day affairs of the mosque most efficiently. Malcolm's trust in him seemed only to grow and Malcolm confided in him on numerous occasions. Malcolm made James privy to his changing views about race even before his Hajj* to Mecca.*

Likewise, Malcolm shared with James the offer of the Freedom Now Party,*
an all-black political party, for Malcolm to run in the November 1964 general
election as a U.S. senatorial candidate in Michigan. James strongly urged Malcolm to decline the offer, which he eventually did. He confided in James as well
regarding his early plans to prove extramarital allegations against Muhammad.
In fact, he sent James to Phoenix, Arizona, to escort and protect the two women
who accused Muhammad of paternity. He was further instructed by Malcolm to
obtain written statements from the women confirming that Muhammad fathered
their children. James was unable to do so, which left Malcolm fuming. Even
so, their relationship apparently remained a close one. As one of Malcolm's
most trusted associates and his chief secretary, James played a central role in
Malcolm's new organizations, the Muslim Mosque, Inc. (MMI)* and the Organization of Afro-American Unity (OAAU).* In the latter, he assumed an important leadership role, frequently making key decisions in the office during
Malcolm's absence.

SELECTED BIBLIOGRAPHY

Carsino, 1982; Clarke, ed., 1969; Malcolm X with Haley, 1965; B. Perry, 1991; Rummel,
1989; Sales, 1994.

Dernoral Davis

SHABAZZ, (MINISTER) JAMES. Minister James Shabazz (not to be mistaken with James 67X, one of Malcolm's lieutenants, who later changed his
name to James Shabazz*) was a member of the Nation of Islam (NOI)* and
minister of the Newark mosque* in New Jersey until 1973. After Malcolm had
established his own organization, Shabazz was one of a number of NOI members
that contributed to the climate of violence that surrounded Malcolm everywhere
he turned, by publicly calling him a hypocrite who had spread lies and rumors
about Elijah Muhammad.* Later, Shabazz was one of several Black Muslims*
who flanked Muhammad during a press conference in which Muhammad disavowed any knowledge of, or participation in, the death of Malcolm X one day
after his murder.

In 1973 a rival organization to the NOI, the New World of Islam, was en-
tangled in a turf war for control of the Newark mosque. Shabazz was killed in
a hail of bullets in the driveway of his home as he was attempting to get into
his car. Eleven men, all affiliated with the New World of Islam, were arrested
for the fatal shooting.

SELECTED BIBLIOGRAPHY

Friedly, 1992; Karim with Skutches and Gallen, 1992.

Mfanya Donald Tryman

SHABAZZ, JOHN. John Shabazz was the minister of the Los Angeles, California, Nation of Islam (NOI)* temple during the late 1950s and 1960s. As he

did with a number of other NOI temples, Malcolm X had established the Los Angeles temple in 1957, and because of his unique leadership role in the NOI, had considerable influence in Shabazz receiving the ministerial appointment. During the early 1960s, Shabazz's notoriety and influence in black Los Angeles grew largely as a result of the crisis emanating from police confrontation with NOI members that ended with the death of Ronald Stokes,* the severe injury of several others, a controversial investigation of the incident, and the trial and conviction of several Muslims* involved in the affair. A continuation of brutal police incidents against black Los Angelinos, especially black Muslims,* during the remaining years of the decade gave him virtual celebrity status; he was frequently quoted in the local press and interviewed on news programs. This was especially the case during the charged atmosphere in Los Angeles's "Long Hot Summer"* of 1965 and the months following this deadly race riot.

During the crisis over Stokes, Malcolm was often in Los Angeles, sent initially by Elijah Muhammad* to quell the prospects of NOI retaliation against whites and all-out warfare between police and sect members. Malcolm and Shabazz, understandably, worked together closely during the time. Shabazz often praised Malcolm as a gifted speaker and knowledgeable Muslim. Whenever Malcolm came to Los Angeles to handle NOI business and to speak, Shabazz personally chauffeured Malcolm around the city and publicized his temple presentations in the most superlative language. But if Shabazz and Malcolm were ever really close, their relationship ruptured shortly after the Stokes affair. Like so many of the other NOI ministers, Shabazz was devoted to Elijah Muhammad and sided with him in the rift that emerged with Malcolm X. Jealousy of Malcolm no doubt played a significant part. Regardless of his motivation, Shabazz soon exhibited considerable hostility toward Malcolm. He excoriated Malcolm in the columns of *Muhammad Speaks*, describing him in one article as someone beneath even an "Uncle Tom"* and resembling "a dog."According to one of Malcolm's relatives and followers, Hakim Jamal,* on at least one occasion members of Shabazz's temple were implicated in an effort to physically harm Malcolm when Malcolm went to Los Angeles in 1964 to pursue matters regarding Elijah Muhammad's paternity suits.

As Malcolm's stature in the NOI fell, Shabazz's rose; he eventually became Elijah Muhammad's West Coast representative. With all of the hostility he directed toward Malcolm during the last months of his life, he understandably expressed no remorse over Malcolm's death.

SELECTED BIBLIOGRAPHY

Cone, 1991; Evanzz, 1992; Freidly, 1992; Gallen, ed., 1992; Horne, 1995; Jamal, 1973; Lomax, 1968; Malcolm X with Haley, 1965.

Robert L. Jenkins

SHABAZZ TRIBE. The mythology of the Nation of Islam (NOI)* teaches that the original inhabitants of the earth were a black race known as the Shabazz tribe 60 trillion years ago. Malcolm often taught this mythology in the mosques to instill black pride* in members and to provide them with a sense of hope and identity. According to the story, an explosion separated the earth from the moon, which the Shabazz tribe survived. However, 6,600 years ago, a boy named Yacub* was born in Mecca,* and he created an evil people that came to be known as the white race. The Shabazz tribe migrated into Africa and the Nile Valley 50,000 years ago after a scientist by the name of Shabazz wanted to give his people an experience that would toughen them. Living in a different climate in Africa and eating different kinds of food, according to Malcolm, brought about a number of mutations, including "kinky" hair rather than the silky black hair the Shabazz originally had, a broader nose, and a different and darker skin. Malcolm would lecture that the only remaining original trait was the straight black hair that constitutes the eyebrows of blacks. The white race was destined to rule for 6,000 years, which was coming to an end as World War I began. The black race, or Shabazz, had to be aware of their own identity, however, before they could resurrect their rule. This purpose would be carried out by Elijah Muhammad,* the Messenger of Allah,* as communicated to him by W. D. Fard.* Muhammad taught this mythology to Malcolm, who passed it on through his teachings. The Shabazz tribe would again enjoy paradise as they had in Mecca before the rule of the "white devil."* Indeed, after Malcolm's fulfillment of the Fifth Pillar of Islam, the Hajj* or travel to Mecca as the holiest of all Islamic places, he changed his name to El-Hajj Malik El-Shabazz,* but it is safe to say that he no longer believed in a superior black race after becoming an orthodox Muslim.*

SELECTED BIBLIOGRAPHY

M. Lee, 1996; Malcolm X (Karim, ed.), 1971; McCloud, 1995.

Mfanya Donald Tryman

SHARRIEFF, RAYMOND. Raymond Sharrieff was married to Elijah Muhammad's* eldest daughter, Ethel Muhammad.*He was given the title of Supreme Captain and as such commanded the Nation of Islam's (NOI)* Fruit of Islam (FOI).* The FOI was composed of male members of the NOI mosques who received weekly training in the martial arts. Each mosque unit was headed by a captain, who served under Sharrieff's overall leadership. Ethel, the Supreme Instructor over the Muslim* women, was said to be the real power behind Sharrieff.

As part of the Muhammad family, Sharrieff was also responsible for working with the family businesses. Sharrieff served as president of two of the NOI's firms and as president of the NOI's parent corporation. When Sharrieff's stepson Hassan defected from the NOI, he accused his relatives of embezzling money that was supposed to be used for the movement's poor. Hassan cited corruption, embezzlement, and fraud as his reasons for leaving the NOI.

Malcolm X was outwardly impressed with Sharrieff mainly because this man took his orders directly from Muhammad. Malcolm displayed his approval of Sharrieff publicly, showing his allegiance to the NOI and the teachings of Muhammad. It was Sharrieff, however, who became one of Malcolm's archenemies in the NOI and may have been responsible for attempts on Malcolm's life.

During the scandalous period when news of Muhammad's extramarital affairs had spread, two Muslim women left their children outside of the home of Muhammad. They were left in order to force Muhammad to claim that he had fathered the children, but instead, Raymond Sharrieff called the police to settle the matter. The police took the children into custody while they searched for the women.

After returning from a trip to England to speak at Oxford University, Malcolm received a telegram on December 7, 1964, from the NOI. The telegram, signed by Raymond Sharrieff, warned him against scandalizing the name of Elijah Muhammad. Malcolm knew those words did not come from Sharrieff but directly from Muhammad, because Sharrieff had no right to speak independently of Muhammad. Hence, similar to relationships that Malcolm had with several other Muslims close to Muhammad, his friendship with Raymond also unraveled as tension grew between Muhammad and Malcolm.

SELECTED BIBLIOGRAPHY

Friedly, 1992; Goldman, 1979; Malcolm X (Clark, ed.), 1992; Malcolm X (Perry, ed.), 1989; B. Perry, 1991.

Sharron Y. Herron

SHAWARBI, MAHMOUD YOUSSEF. Dr. Mahmoud Youssef Shawarbi, of Arab descent, was the director of the Federation of Islamic Association in the United States and Canada in the 1960s. One of Shawarbi's responsibilities was to recommend Muslims* in North America who wanted to make the pilgrimage to Mecca,* Saudi Arabia.* Shawarbi knew Malcolm from their related religious and political activities of the past. Perhaps the most significant event that tied Malcolm X and Shawarbi together was Malcolm's desire to make the Hajj* or holy trip to Mecca, a requirement of every Muslim who is financially able to do so. Malcolm turned to Shawarbi for the letter of recommendation.

Malcolm posited that when he met Shawarbi at the latter's Riverside Drive office in New York City, Shawarbi gave him the letter of recommendation. However, Shawarbi had a different version of the encounter. Shawarbi stated that Malcolm wanted to learn more about Sunni Islam* rather than the Black Muslim* version that he had been taught by Elijah Muhammad* and the Nation of Islam (NOI).* After several sessions on religion in which Malcolm learned more about Islamic orthodoxy, Shawarbi advised him to take the pilgrimage to Mecca. Shawarbi provided Malcolm with the necessary letter of recommendation and introduction for officials in Saudi Arabia as well as for selected dignitaries in Egypt,* Shawarbi's native country. One of the officials in Saudi Arabia was Dr. Omar Azzam,* the son of Abdel Rahman Azzam. The older Azzam was a noted scholar and important dignitary in Saudi Arabia and Egypt. Shawarbi's introduction of Malcolm and his traveling guest to the Azzam family reduced the obstacles and red tape in Malcolm's quest to go to Mecca. The Hajj, aided by Shawarbi, represented one of the high points as well as one of the most humbling experiences of Malcolm X's life.

SELECTED BIBLIOGRAPHY

Breitman, 1967; Husain, 1995; Malcolm X (Breitman, ed.), 1993; Malcolm X with Haley, 1992.

Zuberi Mwamba

SHERRILL, CAPTAIN EDWARD 2X. Throughout Malcolm's years as a Black Muslim,* Los Angeles was considered one of the toughest cities in America for the Nation of Islam (NOI)* to win converts. Malcolm's occasional trips to the West Coast city convinced him that the claim was accurate. Malcolm attributed this recruiting difficulty to a general reluctance of Californians to readily accept non-Western religious ideas. But he was impressed with the work of Edward 2X Sherrill in Los Angeles.

The Los Angeles NOI temple was fortunate to have a leader of the caliber of Sherrill, captain of the city's mosque. Sherrill was first and foremost a devout Muslim* who accepted the teaching of Elijah Muhammad* without question. Malcolm gained some sense of his religious devotion and ability to energize a crowd on one of his trips to Los Angeles. On the occasion when Captain Sherrill stepped to the podium, according to Malcolm, the crowd seemed unruly and hardly ready for religious edification. Within five minutes, though, the throng had been whipped into a frenzy because Captain Sherrill's religious devotion was infectious. Malcolm was convinced, after observing Edward at work, that he deserved to be a captain in the Los Angeles temple. Sherrill, however, later turned on Malcolm, the two men parting their relationship in the wake of Malcolm's problems with Elijah Muhammad.

Sherrill was also noted for his work on the sale and distribution of the Black Muslim newspaper *Muhammad Speaks** in Los Angeles. In a mosque meeting following the 1962 death of unarmed Muslim Ronald Stokes* by the Los Angeles police, it was Sherrill who spoke before a large gathering of believers to convey Elijah Muhammad's message not to resort to violence in retaliation. Muhammad's message to "Hold fast to Islam" and show the world what the NOI thought of Los Angeles whites by exposing them through the massive sale of newspapers was hardly what Sherrill and other Muslims expected, but they carried out the instructions. With the work of men such as Sherrill, Malcolm predicted that the Los Angeles temple would eventually prove as successful as its East Coast counterparts.

SELECTED BIBLIOGRAPHY
Clarke, ed., 1969; Jamal, 1971; Malcolm X with Haley, 1965; B. Perry, 1991.

                                                           Dernoral Davis

SHIFFLET, LYNN. Lynn Shifflet was a former female follower of Elijah Muhammad's* Nation of Islam (NOI).* As a woman, she was not allowed the
freedom of expression permitted men followers; she and all women sat in a
special section of the temple during weekly services. The repression of women
in the NOI, coupled with allegations that Muhammad fathered several children
out of wedlock, may have prompted Shifflet to renounce her allegiance to Muhammad. She subsequently played a leading role in establishing Malcolm's Organization of Afro-American Unity (OAAU).* It had been Shifflet who helped
gather the small group of intellectuals and activists in the spring of 1964 that
formed the core of the new group. In the four deliberations that preceded the
OAAU's formal founding, Shifflet, an NBC television producer, presided over
the meetings, although Malcolm was clearly recognized as the most important
force in attendance. Malcolm described her as strong and extremely articulate.
As office manager, nominally head of the OAAU, Shifflet went on to become
instrumental, if not essential, in the actual day-to-day operations of Malcolm's
black nationalist organization.

   Malcolm's association and work with Shifflet helped him in his struggle to
trust and to confide in women. Shifflet's leadership, however, was challenged
repeatedly by others, most notably one of Malcolm's male followers and confidants, James Shabazz,* formerly James 67X. Shabazz nominally headed the
Muslim Mosque, Inc.* in New York, the religious component of Malcolm's
movement. Many of the men in Malcolm's OAAU believed Shifflet was simply
not capable of running such an important organization as the OAAU, because
she was a woman and thus a "weak vessel." But Malcolm, who personally
recruited Shifflet, had considerable respect for her ability. It was his growth and
development regarding women following his break with the NOI that gave the
aggressive and able Shifflet the chance to prove herself. Years after leaving the
movement, Shifflet became one of the first black female television newscasters,
a role she served in with honor and distinction, just as she had with the OAAU.

SELECTED BIBLIOGRAPHY
Kly, 1986; B. Perry, 1991; Sales, 1994; Wolfenstein, 1981.

                                                           Bridgette Stasher

"SHORTY" (Malcolm Jarvis). Prior to his conversion to Islam,* Malcolm X's
dearest and most trusted friend, if not confidant, was probably "Shorty,"
whose real name was Malcolm Jarvis. Much of what the world has come to
learn of Malcolm during his days on the street has been a result of Jarvis's
revelations about his friendship with him. The two, according to Malcolm X,
met in the Roxbury* section of Boston, Massachusetts, where he moved

in 1941 from Lansing, Michigan,* after finishing the eighth grade to live with his half sister Ella Collins.* More specifically, they met at a local Roxbury poolroom where Shorty racked balls and catered to the whims of the patrons.

Shorty immediately befriended Malcolm and began schooling him in the ways and etiquette of Roxbury. The lessons included instructions in the proper attire, betting on the numbers, drinking and smoking, womanizing, and how to culti-vate a lifestyle of idle enterprise. Malcolm proved a quick study, learning fast and well. Indeed, Shorty later remarked, he eventually became the student and Malcolm the teacher when it came to Boston's streetlife. For both Shorty and Malcolm, these were exciting times in their lives when this black section of Boston was alive with wine, women, and "always a lot of action." Although the two remained the closest of friends from 1941 to 1946, Malcolm spent part of the World War II* years in New York. Apparently, while his friend Malcolm was in New York, Shorty continued to enjoy the street life of Roxbury, fre-quenting the nightclubs, smoking reefer,* and fraternizing with prostitutes.

Malcolm's move to New York was prompted by a job with the railroad. After approximately a year, however, Malcolm was fired from his railroad job largely because of customer complaints against him. After his stint with the railroad, Malcolm's life took a decided turn toward criminality. He became a drug dealer and involved himself in prostitution and the numbers racket. Occasionally, Shorty would meet Malcolm in Roxbury, where he would return with his over-coat lining filled with marijuana to be sold on the town's streets. Early on, Malcolm seemed to have a flair for such a life but quickly made a sufficient number of enemies to make him a marked man. After hearing of Malcolm's dilemma and possible life-threatening circumstances, Shorty drove to New York to retrieve his old friend and to return him to the safety of Roxbury.

Once back in Roxbury, Malcolm again shared an apartment with Shorty. Malcolm, Shorty quickly realized, was no longer the country bumpkin he had met several years earlier. Instead, he had now graduated to hard drugs and gave every indication of being a seasoned hustler. But with no job and a daily cocaine and marijuana habit, Malcolm needed a hustle. The solution seemed clear: house burglary in the most affluent sections of Boston. Malcolm had no trouble con-vincing Shorty of the ingenuity of his idea. Indeed, Shorty was impressed with Malcolm's ability to think quickly and outwit the police. The burglary ring of Malcolm and Shorty soon expanded to include a male friend of Jarvis and two white females. The two women, Beatrice and Joyce Caragulian, were romanti-cally involved with Malcolm and Shorty. The specific role of the women in the burglary ring was to "case" the homes to be burglarized.

The break-ins and a partnership in crime for Malcolm and Shorty lasted all of six weeks, from the beginning of December 1945 to mid-January 1946. The operation's downfall was triggered by two critical mistakes, both committed by Malcolm. The first was pawning a stolen ring with the owner's initials still evident. The second was attempting to have a diamond-studded watch, also stolen, repaired. In both instances, Malcolm used his real name and the address of Ella, and in the case of the watch, he gave an expected date of pickup. These blunders led to his arrest and the unraveling of the operation.

In the criminal proceedings that followed, Malcolm and Shorty never posted bond, which was set at $10,000 each. Jarvis was represented by counsel, but Malcolm offered no defense and had no attorney. In the end, each was found guilty and sentenced to eight to ten years at hard labor. With their sentencing, the lives of Malcolm and Shorty, which had been so intertwined for the preceding five years, began to move in somewhat different directions. Occasionally, when in the Boston area, Malcolm would look up or run into Shorty after Malcolm converted to and became a member of the Nation of Islam.

SELECTED BIBLIOGRAPHY

Blackside/PBS, 1994; CBS News, 1992; Clasby, 1974; Goodheart, 1990; T. Johnson, 1986; Malcolm X with Haley, 1965; B. Perry, 1991; Strickland (Greene, ed.), 1994.

Dernoral Davis

SILBERMAN, CHARLES E. During the 1960s Charles Silberman attained a notable reputation as a journalist for *Fortune* magazine, one of the nation's foremost monthlies. In 1964 he published one of the civil rights* era's most revealing books, *Crisis in Black and White*, an outgrowth of an assignment to research and write about poverty, migration, and racism in the nation's urban environment. In a number of references in his book, Silberman wrote sympathetically about Malcolm X and the disaffected ghetto residents for whom Malcolm spoke. During the height of Malcolm's popularity in the mid-1960s, he and Silberman, also a New Yorker, became acquainted, perhaps as a result of the research that Silberman conducted in Harlem* for his book. Malcolm was not only a controversial figure; he was easy for many of those who came in contact with him to like. In turn, in Malcolm's world numerous relationships with whites, especially white journalists, flourished, despite the antiwhite rhetoric for which he was most condemned. Apparently, his relationship with Silberman, as it did with so many other journalists, was genuine, and it grew into one of mutual respect. The two certainly came to know each other better after serving on a television panel together. What made Malcolm's affinity for Silberman even more unusual was Silberman's recognition as one of New York's leading white liberals,* a class that Malcolm frequently maligned. Indeed, among the nation's prominent black intellectuals, Silberman was often the target of criticism.

Malcolm especially liked Silberman's book and spoke highly of it. Shortly after its appearance, he criticized a black reviewer whose published analysis of *Crisis in Black and White* in the *New York Times** was uncomplimentary, and he telephoned Silberman to convey his views about it. Occasionally, Malcolm would express similar respect for books by white authors who wrote compassionately about blacks and whose works truthfully depicted the extent of white racism in America.

SELECTED BIBLIOGRAPHY

Cruse, 1967; Goldman, 1977; Silberman, 1964; Vernon, 1968.

Robert L. Jenkins

SMALL'S PARADISE CLUB. In his autobiography, Malcolm X dealt a great deal with his life as a youth enjoying the nightlife in cities like Boston and New York. During this period he frequented most of Black America's most popular nightspots, where he often performed the era's latest dance crazes far into the night and associated with some of the most well-known black celebrities.* One of the "hippest" of the New York places that he frequented was Small's Paradise Club. Located on 135th Street and Seventh Avenue, the club, which originally opened in 1925, was owned by Ed Small. Ed and his brother Charlie, who helped manage the establishment, were two of Harlem's* most respected veteran black businessmen. With its large and beautifully decorated Orchid Room, cozy Clover Leaf Bar, and downstairs cabaret, exclusively for Small's "Seniority Club" members, the club was a strong draw for New York's "sophisticates" and "ultra-smart set." The club attracted the best of the day's stars and often booked major revues that included an array of singers, acrobatic, shake, and comedy dancers that performed several shows nightly. Considered "safe" by New York police standards, the club was often recommended to entertainment-starved whites as one of the best places to go in Harlem for nightlife merriment.

Malcolm's greatest influence from his association with Small's nightspot came as a result of his employment there. Recently fired from his job on the railroad, in 1942 at age seventeen, he used his experience to land a waiter's job in the establishment. Malcolm claimed that the job gave him a real learning experience; he acquired considerable knowledge listening to "old timers" talk about Harlem's history, and he absorbed everything that he could to make himself "indispensable" to both his coworkers and customers. Working there also gave him the chance to meet and establish relationships with a number of unsavory characters, including pimps, prostitutes, and other hustlers. From these elements, Malcolm learned much about the seamy side of life, which he would use to his financial benefit when he devoted himself full-time to street hustling* and petty crime. His activities soon resulted in his dismissal. Nevertheless, working at and patronizing places like Small's Paradise Club were good times for Malcolm in his carefree youth, and while he wrote about this phase of his life with nostalgic passion, after his conversion to Islam* he never gave any indication of a desire to return to that kind of life.

SELECTED BIBLIOGRAPHY

Atlanta Daily World, December 7, 1943; Blackside/PBS, 1994; CBS News, 1992; Malcolm X with Haley, 1965.

Robert L. Jenkins

SMITH, TOMMY. During the 1960s, Tommy Smith was one of the most heralded sprinters in international competition. A student-athlete at California's

San Jose State College, Smith made the U.S. Olympic Team in 1968. The squad, with its numerous black athletes, however, was being assembled in the midst of the emerging Black Power* movement and was influenced by the initiatives of militants such as Stokley Carmichael* calling for blacks to boycott the international event. The Black Power movement, though ambiguously articulated by Carmichael in James Meredith's* 1966 Mississippi March Against Fear,* was a natural result of the growing youthful activists' disillusionment with the nonviolent civil rights movement.* Such activists endorsed the black nationalist and black pride* ideas espoused by the slain Malcolm X.

Rather than boycott the Olympics collectively, leaders and athletes supported participation but advocated the alternative of displaying individual protests during the victory stand celebrations. Smith won the gold medal in the 100 meters event and, along with his San Jose State friend and teammate John Carlos,* who captured the Bronze medal, demonstrated on the victory platform in a fashion that provoked a national outrage, the eventual confiscation of their medals, and their expulsion from the team. Smith and Carlos appeared on the stand shoeless, each wearing black knee-length stockings and a black glove on their right hand. Smith also wore a black scarf around his neck. Rather than look directly at the flag, as is customarily done when the national anthem played, the two lowered their chins and raised their black right-gloved fist above their head, the recognized Black Power salute. Their gesture left a memorable impression on Olympic history. More immediately, however, it symbolized their affirmation of Malcolm's ideas: support of the black liberation struggle that Malcolm had so articulately advanced and identification with the increasingly militant response over the black American condition.

SELECTED BIBLIOGRAPHY

McCartney, 1992; Van Deburg, 1992.

Robert L. Jenkins

SO-CALLED NEGRO. Malcolm strongly suggested that descendants of Africa had been brainwashed and reshaped in the image of their enslaver "the White man." In one generation, according to Malcolm, Africans had been "de-Africanized" and taught to hate everything and everyone black. Because history had been "whitened," and accepted by the "so-called Negro," Malcolm said they simply failed to recognize or know themselves. Not only did "the so-called Negro" not know themselves, but even when they were informed of who they were, they still rejected the message and the messenger. They were taught and internalized lies about Africans and themselves. They believed, for example, that they were descendants of savages and devoid of culture. They worshiped the image of an "alien God" and accepted beauty standards that demeaned the texture of their hair, the thickness of their lips, and their broad noses. These so-called Negroes simply despised their own color and race. In fact, the acceptance of white beauty standards demanded that it was proper to glorify light complexion and European features. Malcolm explicitly declared the insanity of Americans on the issue of race and racist rationales because of the more than 300 years of black slavery,* racial segregation,* and the total indoctrination of and about people of African descent.

Even though this brutal indoctrination was complete and exceptionally successful, segments of the so-called Negro were ripe for the "debrainwashing" that was being administered by Malcolm and the Nation of Islam (NOI).* Rejection of the NOI's "truths" was evident by the more "educated" Negro. The less educated were more receptive to redefining their reality in relationship to that of the white world.

One of the devastating changes that was necessary in the enslavement process was the changing of Africans' names. The older black slaves who had experience on the plantations of the old South* attempted to alert the "raw African" to the necessity of divesting themselves of Africa and all of its cultural traits in order to avoid brutal treatment. There was always resistance by those newly arrived Africans to attempts to acculturate them to the slave system and disengage them from their African roots. In the Alex Haley* *Roots* television series, the fiddler character instructed Kunta that his name was no longer Kunta Kinte; rather, he should answer to Toby. Kunta resisted; however, time was not on his side. Symbolically, as Malcolm would likely have said, this represented the changing of the African to the so-called Negro.

Malcolm, of course, argued that the so-called Negro was an aberration and served the purpose of helping to maintain white dominance. He said that references to all other people in America associated them with a defined land and a nation. Reference was often made, for example, to Italian Americans, German Americans, English Americans, and Japanese Americans. However, descendants of Africa are referred to as Negroes. Malcolm asked, "Where is Negroland?" The term *Negro* is Spanish for "black," and he suggested that if blacks are to speak Spanish, then whites should be referred to as blancos, the Spanish term for white.

These arguments, in regard to the so-called Negro, were not Malcolm originals. They had been developed by Elijah Muhammad,* and Malcolm simply added to and escalated the dialogue.

SELECTED BIBLIOGRAPHY

Haley, 1976; Library Distributors of America, 1993; Malcolm X with Haley, 1965; West, 1993.

Horace Huntley

SOCIALISM. Some white leftists and white liberals* have argued that Malcolm was moving toward a socialistic outlook at the end of his life as a solution to the capitalism* of the United States. One thing was perfectly clear, and that was that Malcolm was definitely against a capitalistic system of government. He felt that based upon the history of Western and European colonialism, capitalism and racism were inseparable and that to be a capitalist, one had to believe in the exploitation of other human beings. Malcolm felt that African countries with socialistic systems could be used as a model of development for African Americans. He castigated blacks who were all too quick to embrace racial integration* and capitalism, given the pitfalls of the American system. Malcolm felt that the social, economic, and political system in America was inherently evil and incapable of reform from within. He did realize, however, that socialism, like Islam,* could be effective in eradicating both the theory and the practice of racism.

Malcolm rarely used the word *socialism*, but he often spoke about the need of blacks in America to pool their resources. This was part of his conceptualization of economic black nationalism,* in which blacks would not only unify economically but independently own and operate their own businesses and economic enterprises. But individual ownership is not the same thing as state ownership, which is consistent with socialism. Malcolm was also aware of the fact that advocating socialism in America was synonymous with supporting communism. Hence, use of the word *socialism* was a red flag. Nevertheless, Malcolm agreed to speak on three occasions in 1964 and 1965 at the Militant Labor Forum* organized by the Socialist Workers Party.* However, he realized that African Americans as a working class in a caste system were all treated alike by working-class whites. Consequently, Malcolm rejected the idea that blacks could coalesce with whites in the struggle to overcome racism and capitalism, because even the working-class white had racist views toward blacks. He felt that if such a coalition ever were to occur, it would have to be after blacks had solved their own internal problems and contradictions.

SELECTED BIBLIOGRAPHY

R. Franklin, 1990; Malcolm X (Breitman, ed.), 1970a; Malcolm X (Oglesby, ed.), 1969; Marsh, 1987.

Mfanya Donald Tryman

SOCIALIST WORKERS PARTY (SWP). Established in New York in 1938, the Socialist Workers Party (SWP) is the oldest and largest Trotskyite communist organization in the United States. The organization was expelled by the Socialist Party because of the SWP's insistence on the use of violence and terrorism as a primary means of achieving their goal of liberation from capitalism.*

In the early and mid-1960s, the SWP, though predominantly white, actively supported Malcolm and his Organization of Afro-American Unity (OAAU).* Malcolm also supported the SWP by agreeing to speak at many of their fundraisers and labor forums, small conferences set up to address the various issues confronting labor in the 1960s. In 1969, in their "Transitional Program for Black Liberation," the SWP adopted and expanded Malcolm's doctrines on the course of black liberation. Clifton DeBerry,* the black former U.S. presidential candidate in 1963 and president of the SWP, openly supported the activities of the OAAU. In many of his campaign speeches, he made it clear that he agreed with Malcolm on the issues of black nationalism,* self-defense,* and the civil rights movement.* According to recently released Federal Bureau of Investigation (FBI)* documents, J. Edgar Hoover* identified the SWP as one of the many "subversive groups" supporting Malcolm. The FBI subsequently used counter-intelligence tactics to prevent a coalition between the SWP and Malcolm's organization.

SELECTED BIBLIOGRAPHY

Clarke, ed., 1969; Goldman, 1979; McDonald, 1977; *New York Amsterdam News*, July 18, 1964.

Curtis Austin

SOLEDAD BROTHERS. Malcolm X's life events were quite similar to those of at least one of the Soledad Brothers. During the early part of the 1970s, a radical group of men, John Cluchette, Fleeta Drumgo, and George Jackson, symbolized the black consciousness and revolutionary cause influenced by Malcolm X at the height of the civil rights movement.* While, like Malcolm in Massachusetts, they served prison* time in California's Soledad correctional facility, Drumgo and Cluchette also were accused of murdering a prison guard. These two men were acquitted by an all-white jury. The third Soledad Brother was George Jackson, a prison leader and Black Panther Party for Self Defense* member. Jackson is best remembered as the author of the book *Soledad Brothers*. During his incarceration, Jackson maintained a collection of personal letters detailing his life in prison and wrote an autobiography, which seems to mirror the events in Malcolm X's life. It was soon after his transfer to San Quentin that he was shot and killed during an alleged escape attempt. After his death, like Malcolm, he became a martyr and a folk hero to many black as well as white radicals.

SELECTED BIBLIOGRAPHY

Estell, ed., 1994; Ploski and Williams, ed., 1989; M. Williams, ed., 1993.

Demond S. Miller and Melvin C. Ray

THE SOUTH. During the years of his political activism, Malcolm spent a considerable amount of time traveling. These travels often involved special work on behalf of the Nation of Islam (NOI)* as he moved through numerous urban centers establishing new Muslim* mosques. Typically, the NOI focused this work in the northern ghettos. Occasionally, however, Malcolm's organizing work found him in the urban South, as was the case with cities like Atlanta, Georgia, where, in 1955, after establishing Temple Number Fifteen, he conducted the NOI's first meeting in the Deep South. Although less decisive, he apparently played an important role in the permanent establishment of temples in Richmond, Virginia, Miami, Florida, and Birmingham, Alabama.*

Unafraid to condemn white racists in the most scathing language, his presence in the South during the height of the civil rights movement* naturally created a potentially dangerous personal situation for him, especially after he attained national prominence. Yet, he did not allow this to deter him from the message he sought to convey to Black Americans and the warnings he had for whites. He often volunteered to go to the South to fight against Ku Klux Klan* violence and seemed determined to assist black activists in the 1963 Birmingham campaign; his mentor Elijah Muhammad,* however, refused Malcolm's request. Andrew Young,* a close aide of Martin Luther King, Jr.,* claims that Malcolm often visited Atlanta and the Southern Christian Leadership Conference (SCLC)* headquarters when he came to the city.

Occasionally, Malcolm did speak before interested southern crowds. Unlike his appearances in the North, however, these were almost always before black audiences. In December 1960 he initiated a brief southern speaking tour that began in Birmingham, Alabama, soon to be the site of one of King's major civil rights* initiatives. He became a favorite among southern black college students, drawing large and enthusiastic crowds at institutions such as Maryland's Morgan State College (now University), Washington, D.C.'s Howard University,* and Georgia's Morehouse College, Clark College, and Atlanta University (now Clark Atlanta University). In the midst of King's 1965 Selma campaign, he spoke to a group of young people in a Selma church, the day after a similar engagement at Tuskegee Institute, founded, ironically, by the black advocate of racial segregation,* accommodationist Booker T. Washington. Prior to his death, Malcolm had committed to the Mississippi Freedom Democratic Party* leader Fannie Lou Hamer* and members of the Student Non-Violent Coordinating Committee (SNCC)* to come to Mississippi* to speak in support of their struggle. Mississippi, a hotbed of racial strife during the turbulent 1960s, was regarded by Malcolm as the nation's most oppressive state for black Americans, and his references to it typically prompted some of his most acerbic commentary.

* Reportedly, Malcolm's Mississippi itinerary included plans to expand recruitment for his black nationalist movement to the region as well. His murder, however, precluded not only a visit to the Magnolia State but also an extensive national tour of college campuses being arranged by his friend, religion scholar C. Eric Lincoln,* that surely would have included a major foray on to numerous black campuses in other Deep South states.

SELECTED BIBLIOGRAPHY

Adams, 1965; DeCaro, 1996; Lincoln, 1994; Malcolm X (Breitman, ed.), 1970a, 1970b; *New York Amsterdam News*, February 11, 1961; B. Perry, 1991; Plummer, 1996; Young, 1996.

Robert L. Jenkins

SOUTH AFRICA. According to Malcolm X, the apartheid system in South Africa stood on the same ideological grounds as racial segregation* in America.

There was, however, a difference. South Africa's government, he told Alex Haley* in the *Playboy* interview, was more honest. South Africa both preached and practiced apartheid. The United States, he said, preached freedom and racial integration* but practiced slavery and segregation. Hendrik Verwoerd, the architect of South African apartheid, was, accordingly, an honest racist, while many American leaders were hypocrites.

Malcolm saw the white government in South Africa as illegitimate and believed that the nation's whites did not belong on the African continent at all. When asked, in 1963, if the type of racial separation* sought by the Nation of Islam (NOI)* was not the same as apartheid, Malcolm responded by noting that apartheid was more than mere separation. South Africa's white government, he pointed out, would not allow black Africans to build a society in which they could be the political or economic equals of the whites. That, he said, was segregation, while the NOI wanted separation. South Africa's segregation belonged to the past; the separation sought by the NOI, Malcolm then argued, was the way of the future.

Malcolm never embraced nonviolence. In his support of self-defense,* he pointed to South Africa, where members of the African National Congress (ANC) rejected nonviolence after the Sharpeville Massacre of 1960. He explained that Nelson Mandela and other leaders of the ANC had come to understand that nonviolence was outdated and that it only helped their oppressors. By 1964, he believed the same was true in the United States, where increasing numbers of blacks were beginning to see nonviolence as a white man's trick that prevented them from defending themselves.

Finally, Malcolm observed United Nations* delegates who attacked South Africa's apartheid but remained silent on the issue of American racism. After inquiring among the delegates, he came to understand that as long as black leaders in America demanded civil rights,* the struggle could never be internationalized. It had to be framed in terms of human rights,* like the situation in South Africa. Then the United Nations might be used to launch an attack against American racism.

SELECTED BIBLIOGRAPHY

Clarke, ed., 1969; Haley (Fisher, ed.), 1993; Malcolm X (Breitman, ed.), 1970a, 1993; Malcolm X (Perry, ed.), 1989; Malcolm X with Haley, 1965.

Alan Scot Willis

SOUTHERN CHRISTIAN LEADERSHIP CONFERENCE (SCLC). In 1957, Martin Luther King, Jr.,* was one of the organizers of the Southern Christian Leadership Conference (SCLC) to coordinate deliberate, nonviolent direct action in the South.* Its antecedent was a network of southern churches that had mobilized in support of the King-led Montgomery Bus Boycott. The SCLC would be organized in a manner similar to the National Association for the Advancement of Colored People (NAACP),* except that it would be a Christian organization with black Baptist preachers as the leaders.

The SCLC conducted numerous marches, demonstrations, boycotts, and related public protests over racial segregation* in southern cities and towns during the 1950s and 1960s. The organization would provoke white segregationists to commit violence as a tool for Congress and civil rights* sympathizers to develop federal legislation in support of black civil rights, which were denied them in the South. Younger members of the SCLC broke away from the central organization and formed the Student Non-Violent Coordinating Committee (SNCC)* in 1960. This organization initially assumed a more militant posture closer to the thinking of Malcolm X.

According to Andrew Young,* a King associate and fellow SCLC leader, Malcolm frequently came to the SCLC headquarters office in Atlanta whenever he visited the city but was unable to meet King there. But Malcolm was especially critical of the SCLC and King for their tactics of nonviolence in the face of racist police brutality,* especially against women and children. Still Malcolm would not be able to deny the SCLC's role in getting the 1964 and 1965 Civil Rights Acts* passed by Congress, however much he disparaged both the work of organizations like SCLC and the legislation they promoted.

SELECTED BIBLIOGRAPHY

Fairclough, 1987; Garrow, 1986; Raines, 1983.

Lee E. Williams II

STATE DEPARTMENT. Malcolm realized that the U.S. Department of State had him under surveillance as early as 1959 when he first traveled abroad to visit a number of countries in the Middle East* and Africa. Because he was also constantly watched in the United States by the Federal Bureau of Investigation (FBI),* he never discussed political and business affairs over the telephone. There was, of course, ample reason for the State Department to monitor his every move and statement. The concern of the State Department may initially have been the racial hatred espoused by the Nation of Islam (NOI)* regarding whites, but it was obviously intensified in 1964 when Malcolm again traveled to Africa and the Middle East, this time to mobilize support for his human rights* campaign against the U.S. government. He argued that the government continued to deny African Americans not just their civil rights* but their human rights as well. Consequently, Malcolm intended to take the case of the African American to the United Nations* and was trying to line up votes in the international arena. He also met with controversial international figures that did not hold the U.S. government in high esteem, including Gamel Abdel Nasser* of Egypt* and Fidel Castro* of Cuba.*

The concern of the State Department for Malcolm's activities was compounded by the message that he brought to Third World countries, that democracy in the United States did not extend to the African American. This message contradicted the United States Information Agency (USIA),* a propaganda arm of the State Department that constantly attempted to indoctrinate Third World countries regarding the political virtues of American democracy. The USIA ran the "Voice of America," an international radio system that propagated American political values.

Perhaps one of the State Department's most successful anti-Malcolm activities occurred in late 1964, shortly before his death, in preventing Malcolm from entering Paris, France. Malcolm had been invited to deliver a speech at one of the city's largest lecture halls. But he could get no farther than the lounge at Paris's Orly Airport and was forced to return immediately to London. French authorities claimed they feared that Malcolm would incite violence in the country, although he had been allowed to visit and speak in the country two months prior to this invitation. Malcolm initially believed that it had been the State Department that was really at the bottom of his denied entrance into Paris, but he eventually claimed that France had been simply duped by Washington, D.C.

In fact, while he traveled in Africa in 1964, Malcolm was constantly "shadowed" by a U.S. government agent. Even when he dined, Malcolm noticed the same man sitting not far away, and he confronted him. Malcolm suspected that the man was from the State Department. Malcolm became violently ill in the middle of the night while in Cairo, Egypt,* and had to be rushed to the hospital and have his stomach pumped. Undoubtedly, he was a victim of food poisoning, but the question remains as to whether someone deliberately tried to poison him or if it was a question of his eating bad or spoiled food. While it has been speculated that the State Department, or even the Central Intelligence Agency (CIA),* may have had something to do with the poisoning, it has never been proven.

SELECTED BIBLIOGRAPHY

Clarke, ed., 1990; Evanzz, 1992; Garrow, 1981; Goldman, 1979; B. Perry, 1991.

Demond S. Miller and Melvin C. Ray

STOKES, RONALD X. Twenty-nine-year-old Ronald Stokes was a veteran of the Korean War and secretary of the Muslim Temple in Los Angeles, California, in April 1962. He was killed during an altercation between police and Black Muslims.* On April 27, 1962, two police officers questioned two Muslims* suspected of selling stolen clothes from the trunk of a car on South Broadway in Los Angeles. Muslim Temple Number Twenty-seven was on South Broadway, and several Muslim brothers witnessed the police's rough treatment of the suspects, who were actually working for a dry cleaners. Seventeen Muslims came to the defense of the suspects. The situation developed into a brawl as more police officers arrived on the scene. One police officer had his revolver taken away and was shot in the elbow; seven other officers were injured during the encounter. As the number of patrolmen increased to seventy-five, Muslims were lined up and kicked as they lay on the ground to be arrested. A total of six Muslims were wounded, and one, Stokes, was killed. Stokes was shot through the heart and left lung by officer Donald Weese, who later testified that Stokes had his hands up like he was going to choke him.

The incident sparked racial unrest in Los Angeles. Muslim brothers from around the country assembled at Temple Twenty-seven to await word from Elijah Muhammad* on how they should respond to the incident. They brought guns and knives in preparation for a race conflict. However, Muhammad discouraged his followers from responding to whites with violence.

Malcolm X was deeply disturbed by the Los Angeles episode, since he had organized the Los Angles temple. He went to Los Angeles and charged the officers with police brutality* in killing Stokes and arresting Muslims. The men were victimized by white policemen, he said, simply because they were black. In his speeches, he criticized the national white media* for their refusal to address issues of police brutality,* a refusal, he said, that amounted to media cover-ups.

Malcolm was very much interested in the Stokes case, and he mourned his death. He gave a tribute at Stokes's funeral, eulogizing the man whom he knew personally. Later he spoke at a rally organized to inquire about the incident. Malcolm's rhetoric was so inflammatory, said one of his former associates, that Los Angeles officials asked Muhammad to tone Malcolm down, a request with which the Muslim leader complied. Malcolm did quiet down, which helped to defuse the black anger in Los Angeles.

The National Association for the Advancement of Colored People* was also critical of the police's handling of the situation and requested state and federal investigations. Yet despite the concerns of blacks, a coroner's jury ruled "justifiable homicide" in the police shooting of Stokes. It took an all-white jury twenty-three minutes to reach this verdict. A grand jury later indicted nine Muslims for assaulting the police in the incident related to Ronald X Stokes. This was especially crucial in halting a number of the more aggressive Muslims' acts of descending on skid row during the night hours to exact vengeance on drunken and unsuspecting white men. Malcolm called this "small-time" gangsterism and "cowardly," certainly no fitting way to avenge a fellow Muslim.

SELECTED BIBLIOGRAPHY

Goldman, 1973; Jamal, 1971; Karim with Sketches and Gallen, 1992; *Los Angeles Times*, April 29, May 5, May 6, May 10, May 14, May 15, May 23, 1962; B. Perry, 1991.

Gerald L. Smith

STONE, CHUCK. Chuck Stone was a former aide to the late Harlem* congressman Adam Clayton Powell.* He also wrote for the *Philadelphia Enquirer*. Perhaps influenced by Powell's rhetoric and exhortations about Black Power* and Malcolm's views regarding black nationalism,* as an author and newspaper columnist, Stone, a journalism faculty member at the University of North Carolina at Chapel Hill, wrote the book entitled *Black Political Power in America*. A number of concepts in the book reflect Malcolm's advocacy of black nationalism. In his work on black political power, Stone argues that black Americans should not have allegiance to either of the major political parties* in America, the Republicans or the Democrats. Rather, Stone called for "political oscillation," in which African Americans would swing their vote to the political party that was the highest bidder and most committed to uplifting the socioeconomic status of blacks in America. Stone frequently has written columns and articles regarding black politics in urban, state, and national arenas. As a reporter and an advocate, Stone attended the Black Power* conferences that were held and that drew nationwide attendance in the late 1960s.

Stone's argument is similar to, but not the same as, Malcolm's analysis of the two major American political parties. He argued that neither party could really be trusted and that both parties were simply different sides of the same coin. Malcolm saw American politics as a game, in which both of the parties were in "cahoots" with one another. Like Stone, he realized that the black vote could be used very effectively if it were cast correctly. Hence, Malcolm attacked the often-used phrase of "register and vote," arguing that one must analyze who and what he or she is voting for, rather than blindly casting a vote based on superficial campaigns or information.

SELECTED BIBLIOGRAPHY

Malcolm X (Breitman, ed.), 1965, 1970a; Pohlmann, 1999; Stone, 1964.

Mfanya Donald Tryman

STRICKLAND, WILLIAM. William Strickland is a longtime professor at the University of Massachusetts, Amherst, Department of Afro-American Studies. In the 1970s he was a central figure in the establishment and work of the Atlanta-based black think tank, the Institute of the Black World. During the 1960s he served as director of the Northern Student Movement (NSM), an urban-based national student organization that worked to mobilize inner-city black neighborhoods to address for themselves the many social and economic ills that hampered their progress. Under Strickland's leadership the organization expanded from its initial involvement in inner-city tutorial work to emphasis on issues addressing welfare rights, police brutality,* inadequate housing, poor education, and unemployment. The work that these college students were involved in was precisely the kind of self-help efforts that Malcolm X sanctioned and preached to the black masses. Like so many other young black activist-intellectuals of the 1960s, Strickland was fascinated with Malcolm the man and his message. But their relationship predated Malcolm's rise to national prominence. Strickland, who was born and reared in Boston's Roxbury* section, knew Malcolm as a youth when Malcolm moved to the community to live with his half sister Ella Collins.* Though Malcolm was older than Strickland, the two became fast friends, largely as a result of Malcolm's close association with one of Strickland's older relatives. They reestablished their contact with each other following one of Malcolm's lectures at Harvard University,* where Strickland matriculated.

Although Malcolm claimed little respect for highly educated blacks like Strickland, he seemed attracted to them and they to him. Before Malcolm's death, the two established a personal working relationship in New York. Strickland was one of several intellectuals and Malcolm associates in Malcolm's core group that helped to organize the Organization of Afro-American Unity.* Moreover, through his activities in the NSM, Strickland coordinated the visit of Fannie Lou Hamer* and a delegation of young civil rights* activists from Mississippi* to Harlem* in 1965 and worked to bring them together with Malcolm. Strickland was expected to play a major role in arranging Malcolm's scheduled visit to the Magnolia State in support of the Mississippi movement, but Malcolm's murder prevented the visit.

Long after Malcolm's death, however, Strickland maintained an avid interest in Malcolm's life and work. This interest manifested itself with his involvement in the Blackside/Public Broadcast System's documentary video production of Malcolm's life entitled *Malcolm X, Make It Plain*. An acclaimed author who had already published about Malcolm's death, Strickland also penned the narrative in a 1994 photographic biography of Malcolm that bore the same title as the documentary. Always impressed by Malcolm's diverse interests and his commitment to effect real change, Strickland's *Malcolm X, Make It Plain* is a convincing and passionate interpretation of a man he obviously greatly admired and the positive legacy Malcolm left to the world.

SELECTED BIBLIOGRAPHY

Blackside/PBS, 1994; Jenkins, interview with Strickland, June 2, 2000; Medina (Lowery and Marszalek, eds.), 1992; B. Perry, 1991; Strickland (Greene, ed.), 1994.

Robert L. Jenkins

STROTHER, GLORIA. Gloria Strother was a young, fair-skinned black Bostonian girl whom Malcolm dated while she was in high school in the early 1940s. Gloria was considered a "Hill" girl, that is, a part of the upper-Roxbury* section of Boston, an elite area of the community where these more privileged blacks looked down on the black lower class. Gloria was tall and shapely and reminded Malcolm of his own mother, but he broke up with her once he began to work on the New Haven Railroad.

Later, while serving time at Norfolk Prison, he began to communicate with Gloria again through a series of letters and told her of his newfound religion and newly acquired extensive reading habits. She, in turn, wrote him back fairly regularly, but she appeared to be more interested in the possibility of recidivism on his part rather than his new interests. Perhaps because of their different concerns, they did not reestablish their old relationship.

Student Non-Violent Coordinating Committee workers in Mississippi. Malcolm admired these young activists for their militancy and bravery. Courtesy of Mississippi Department of Archives and History.

SELECTED BIBLIOGRAPHY

Malcolm X with Haley, 1965; B. Perry, 1991.

Mfanya Donald Tryman

STUDENT NON-VIOLENT COORDINATING COMMITTEE (SNCC). The Student Non-Violent Coordinating Committee (SNCC) was one of the "Big Five" civil rights organizations* of the 1960s. It was organized on the campus of Shaw University in Raleigh, North Carolina, in April 1960 by veteran civil rights* leader Ella Baker and a large representation from college students and other established protest groups. Founded to serve as a vehicle through which the various and numerous young college students involved in the lunch counter sit-in movement could be unified and better mobilized in the broader black rights struggle, the organization functioned autonomously, though initially it worked closely under Southern Christian Leadership Conference (SCLC)* guidance. As such, it endorsed the nonviolence philosophy* of the SCLC's president, Martin Luther King, Jr.*

During the activism of the period, SNCC was involved in some of the South's* most difficult civil rights struggles. Not only were SNCC members victimized by the violence that emanated from the effort to desegregate Deep South interstate bus terminals through the famous "Freedom Rides," but through massive and sustained voting rights campaigns in states like Mississippi,* Alabama, Georgia, and South Carolina, they constantly placed themselves in danger that daily threatened their lives. Almost everywhere that they organized demonstrations and protest drives, SNCC members were intimidated, beaten, and unlawfully jailed. Perhaps no work drove home the inherent dangers in attacking the white southern racial monolith more than its involvement with Mississippi's Congress of Federated Organizations (COFO), a coalition of the major civil rights groups seeking to enfranchise and empower Magnolia State blacks and improve the quality of educating the youth through the establishment of freedom schools. The lead group in COFO's 1964 Freedom Summer,* SNCC was notably shaken when three of the student workers involved in the campaign were found brutally murdered in an earthen dam near Philadelphia, Mississippi,* after a massive hunt. International attention had been turned to the ordeal of the missing students, and though the Federal Bureau of Investigation* had coordinated the task of locating the missing civil rights workers, it adhered to its policy of serving only as an investigative agency, not one committed to protecting the vulnerable activists. The policy both frustrated and angered many in SNCC and helped to push them into a more militant position in their advocacy of black rights.

Although Malcolm X frequently railed against the racial integration and political participatory goals of the civil rights movement,* he had a special affinity for young people. No other group commanded the kind of respect with him that he had for SNCC. He often brought attention to their bravery and lambasted white racists for their crimes against SNCC workers. For its failure to secure the lives of the group's activists, he characteristically expressed his wrath and disdain for the federal government. Malcolm occasionally singled out SNCC leaders John Lewis* and James Forman,* both of whom he had met and dialogued with, as his good friends. Similarly, he held SNCC's Fannie Lou Hamer* in great respect, considering her a real freedom fighter. After meeting with her and a delegation of Mississippi SNCC activists in Harlem* in late 1964, he volunteered to come to Mississippi in support of their work. Before his death, he had made other unaccepted offers of his service to the organization.

Though many SNCC activists were reluctant to accept Malcolm initially because of his often acrid rhetoric, that he eventually had a tremendous influence on the organization is clear. Becoming increasingly disillusioned with King's nonviolent movement, SNCC workers soon gravitated toward militancy, espoused in the ambiguous but threatening term of Black Power.* First uttered by SNCC leader Stokely Carmichael* in 1966, Black Power, as it was espoused and practiced by SNCC, not only advocated black people exerting a greater amount of control over their own communities, but it also meant divorcing themselves from whites, who had always been integral in SNCC, and confining the leadership positions to blacks. Moreover, many abandoned their tolerance for nonviolence in the face of so much violent resistance that they and innocent blacks confronted. Hence, during the late 1960s, few of the more militant SNCC activists such as Forman, Carmichael, and H. Rap Brown* had little trouble in readily invoking Malcolm's memory and supporting his views about black empowerment "by any means necessary" as the keys to black liberation in America. To be sure, Malcolm's death predated by several years the highwater period of the Black Power movement and SNCC's close association with it, but in many ways the spirit of the term paralleled much of what Malcolm believed and advocated.

SELECTED BIBLIOGRAPHY

Carson, 1981; Forman, 1985; J. Grant, 1998; Lewis with D'Orso, 1998; Malcolm X (Breitman, ed.), 1970a, 1992; K. Mills, 1993; Robnett, 1997; Sellers with Terrell, 1973.

Robert L. Jenkins

STUDENT YOUTH MOVEMENT. Malcolm X inspired a generation of young Americans to empower themselves and attempt to transform their communities across the country during the 1960s. More specifically, his emphasis on learning history taught African Americans how they have been affected by social problems. Further, his use of history was a constant theme found in his public dialogue and pedagogical messages to black people. After his departure from the Nation of Islam (NOI)* in 1964, Malcolm focused his discussions on political action as he attempted to show solidarity with the civil rights movement.* In 1965 Malcolm spoke to members of the Student Non-Violent Coordinating Committee (SNCC),* the youth arm of the Southern Christian Leadership Conference (SCLC),* about fighting racism in the South.* At this time Malcolm linked the struggle of African Americans for civil rights* with the struggle of African countries for independence from European colonial rule.

Malcolm X's message of cultural pride, self-study, critical analysis, and social protest would later be expressed in the student movements of the 1960s that would object to race, gender, and class discrimination. The Free Speech movement at the University of California at Berkeley in 1964 and the Black Studies* movement starting at San Francisco State College in 1966 were events led by young people in their communities demanding curriculum reform in higher education to reflect the diversity of American society. This emphasis on community empowerment is a direct result of the public discourse of Malcolm X in the early and mid-1960s. The student movement and black nationalist groups have borrowed heavily from Malcolm X's discussion of black nationalism,* his strong critical rhetoric, and his uncompromising call for social, economic, and political justice.

As a major African American leader and social critic, Malcolm X utilized a pedagogical approach from a multidisciplinary perspective to communicate his overall message. Thus, Malcolm was a forerunner to the Black Studies movement in the context of nonformal community education (community-based learning outside of a traditional school setting). His former associate A. Peter Bailey* referred to him as a "Master Teacher," in which he used an interpretive analysis and insight about black life similar to a college professor's. Malcolm X inspired a generation of young African Americans to reexamine American history and black history* and reaffirm their cultural heritage and traditions through systematic study, both inside and outside of educational institutions. Malcolm X's public exploration of black nationalism served as an ideological model for youth activism that eventually led to the establishment of Black Studies as an academic discipline in higher education. More specifically, Malcolm X's ministry, public lectures, and debates as a lay scholar served to educate black youth in the 1950s and 1960s about the importance of self-study as a means of empowering their communities.

SELECTED BIBLIOGRAPHY

Karenga, 1994; Karim with Skutches and Gallen, 1992; Malcolm X (Clark, ed.), 1992.

Andrew P. Smallwood

SUGAR HILL. Malcolm Little, later to be known as Malcolm X, after finishing the eighth grade asked his Aunt Ella (Ella Collins*), who was actually his half sister from his father's first wife, if he could visit her in Boston during the summer. Before his death, Malcolm's father had bragged about Ella owning property and her status as a socialite. In the summer of 1940, Malcolm boarded a Greyhound bus for Boston. When he arrived there, Ella met him at the bus station and drove him to her home on Waumbeck Street in the "Sugar Hill" section of Roxbury.* This was where all of the so-called black elite or black bourgeoisie lived in Boston. This group was proudest of being homeowners, even though many had to take renters to make the mortgage notes.

Malcolm did not fit in well there. He despised those blacks whom he felt were trying to be white in the way they talked and treated other less privileged blacks. The irony of it all was that these "elites" were housekeepers, floor sweepers, and butlers for whites. In the words of southern aristocrats, former slaves, and later Malcolm himself: These were the "House Negroes."* Malcolm was, however, impressed by the black churches that rivaled any white church that he had seen. At the end of the summer, he returned to Mason, Michigan.* Malcolm was a bright student and received good grades in school before his Sugar Hill visit. But after experiencing the Sugar Hill environment and the other black ghettos of Boston, Malcolm was not content with the life planned for or expected of him in Mason. His favorite teacher discouraged him from becoming a lawyer and suggested that he become a carpenter instead. That was more than he could take, so he returned permanently to his "Aunt Ella's" on Sugar Hill and subsequently began his teenage life as a street hustler in Roxbury and Harlem.*

SELECTED BIBLIOGRAPHY
Collins with Bailey, 1998; Malcolm X with Haley, 1992; Strickland (Greene, ed.), 1994.
                                    Melvin C. Ray and Demond S. Miller

SUSSKIND, DAVID. Former journalist and Malcolm X scholar Peter Gold-man* once said that no American during the height of Malcolm X's prominence understood the power of the media more than Malcolm did. Even the most successful white politician had not, like Malcolm X, mastered the effectiveness of the media "sound bite." Malcolm had numerous opportunities to master these skills because he was such a popular draw for many of the media giants of the period. This was true for both the print press and electronic media.* One of the major television personalities of the era who found Malcolm an attractive guest was David Susskind. Susskind, a New York television personality during the industry's "golden age" in the 1950s and 1960s, is most noted for hosting his "Open End" talk show. As moderator–interviewer of the Sunday night show, the blunt-speaking Susskind often came across as combative. But he was a recognized white liberal* who attracted many of the era's most important and activist black leaders to his show, including Martin Luther King, Jr.* Susskind was the kind of media personality that never seemed to affect Malcolm adversely. Indeed, he appeared to relish sparring with him. A long-time Harlem* leader by the time he appeared on Susskind's show for the first of several interviews, probably in late 1961, Malcolm was certainly a known entity and Susskind was aware of what to expect from his guest. Regardless of the format or the venue, Malcolm never minced his words or significantly moderated his often repeated views on a variety of race-related topics. Apparently Susskind found Malcolm's ideas about the plight and solution to problems affecting black America of such importance that he sought unsuccessfully to bring Malcolm and King together on the show. Philosophically and tactically opposed to Malcolm's ideas, King adamantly refused to sit in dialogue with Malcolm on the show, prompting Malcolm to label King more emphatically "a coward." It was the kind of dispute that both Malcolm and King claimed they wanted to avoid, but it initially added to the harsh views each had for the other and accentuated the philosophical differences that clearly separated them.

Malcolm seldom turned down opportunities to reach larger audiences than his temple lectures and Harlem street rallies* permitted. There was added benefit personally. While Malcolm did not profit financially from these appearances, there is certainly nothing to indicate that he did not bask in the spotlight from this increased visibility. Television shows like Susskind's "Open End" helped to elevate Malcolm's national stature, but the downside was clearly an increase in the internal jealousy that he would have to contend with as a member of the Nation of Islam.*

SELECTED BIBLIOGRAPHY
Les Brown, 1977; CBS News, 1992; DeCaro, 1998; Goldman, 1979; Newcomb, 1997.
                                              Robert L. Jenkins

SUTTON, PERCY. Percy Sutton, a lawyer and politician of great refinement in Harlem,* New York, was Malcolm's close friend and legal adviser. Sutton was borough president of Harlem at the same time that Malcolm X served as minister of Harlem's Temple Number Seven.* The two became acquainted when Sutton began attending the Harlem street rallies* that Malcolm frequently held on 125th Street. Although strongly committed to the conservative National Association for the Advancement of Colored People (NAACP),* Percy frequented Malcolm's street meetings because he believed that someone respectable from the black community should do so. Malcolm soon won him over, though an air of formality always seemed to exist between them: Malcolm referred to Sutton as "Mr. Counselor," Sutton to Malcolm as "Mr. Minister." Sutton's first call to duty on Malcolm's behalf occurred during the break with Elijah Muhammad* and the Nation of Islam (NOI)* over Malcolm's occupation of his Queens, New York, home. Although legally titled to the NOI, Malcolm had lived in the house with his family since 1959 with the understanding that it had been purchased by the Muslims* for him. The Muslims sought to evict him through the courts, a case that Malcolm eventually lost. During this time, Malcolm lacked sufficient funds to pay Percy Sutton for his services. However, with Sutton's recent declaration of candidacy for a seat in the New York State Assembly, Malcolm was able to compensate his lawyer in another way. Sutton sought and received Malcolm's active support for the seat. Malcolm attended Sutton's political rallies and simply made himself visible in support of the borough chief's candidacy, something he had never done for any other political candidate. Malcolm sent dozens of his followers into the streets to campaign for Sutton, knocking on doors to encourage voter registration and making telephone calls in the Democratic candidate's behalf; enough votes were gathered to enable Sutton to win the election.

Sutton's relationship with Malcolm proved especially beneficial. It improved his image among the Harlem militants, who might otherwise have labeled him an Uncle Tom,* and provided an opportunity for Sutton to be identified with a real celebrity. Sutton, however, had a genuine affection for Malcolm and remained loyal to him until the end. Upon Malcolm's death, Sutton worked with several other black celebrities* as a committee to raise enough funds to bury the fallen leader and support Malcolm's family.

SELECTED BIBLIOGRAPHY

A&E Entertainment, 1995; Evanzz, 1992; Goldman, 1979; Strickland (Greene, ed.), 1994.

Terri Earnest and Robert L. Jenkins

SWERLIN FAMILY. After his father's death in 1931 and the subsequent mental breakdown of his mother, Malcolm and his siblings were divided and placed in foster homes. Shortly after this separation, Malcolm began misbehaving in school, with the underlying intention of being expelled so that he might "hang out" or perhaps find a job. Instead, Malcolm was sent to a juvenile home in Mason, Michigan,* operated by a white couple with the last name of Swerlin.

According to Malcolm, he and the Swerlins cared for each other quite a bit. Malcolm fondly describes Mr. Swerlin as a quiet, polite man; he describes Lois "Ma" Swerlin as a jovial, buxom woman who exercised her authority in a wise, compassionate manner, invariably gaining the respect of the youth at the home. The Swerlins' support of Malcolm helped him deal more positively with his defiance against school officials; thus, Malcolm's school performance and behavior improved tremendously during his stay with the Swerlins.

Malcolm did not realize until years later, however, that he had been visible to the Swerlins only through the perspective of contemporary racial perceptions. Malcolm interpreted this as meaning that he was no more than the Swerlins' pet during his two-year stay in their home, based upon their paternalistic and patronizing treatment of him. The Swerlins eventually sent Malcolm to live in a foster home owned by blacks because they believed he would feel more comfortable around other African Americans.

SELECTED BIBLIOGRAPHY

Malcolm X with Haley, 1965; B. Perry, 1991; Wolfenstein, 1981.

Terri Earnest

T

TEMPLE NUMBER SEVEN. For his organizational and proselytizing successes at Temple Eleven in Boston and Temple Twelve in Philadelphia, in June 1954 Malcolm X was appointed minister of Temple Number Seven in Harlem,* New York City, replacing Sultan Muhammad,* who had fallen out of favor with Elijah Muhammad.* When Malcolm took control of Temple Seven, it was little more than a storefront building located at West 116th Street on the corner of Lenox Avenue. New York's five boroughs contained over a million black people in 1954, but Malcolm noted that there were not enough Muslims* in Harlem to fill a city bus. "Fishing"* in Christian storefront churches and at competing black nationalist meetings, Malcolm immediately began to increase the membership of Temple Seven. Branches of Temple Seven were established in Brooklyn and Queens, and he continued to minister the Philadelphia mosque as well. Indeed, from his New York headquarters Malcolm fanned out nationally, establishing new temples and serving Elijah Muhammad as the national spokesperson.

In 1956, Malcolm's future wife, Sister Betty X (eventually Betty Shabazz*), joined Temple Number Seven. She was a nursing student, and Malcolm quickly tapped her expertise for the temple; he assigned her to teach hygiene in the Muslim girls' and women's classes. Muslim temples are organized around daily events, including the training of the Fruit of Islam (FOI),* the group's elite paramilitary force; a Unity night, which promotes socializing among temple members; a day that concentrates on Student Enrollment and Islamic teaching; Muslim Girls' Training* and General Civilization night where females are taught proper domesticity; a Civilization night when classes are devoted to teaching the proper relationship between the sexes; and Sunday temple services. Malcolm reenergized these functions as minister of Temple Seven.

The famous Johnson X (Hinton)* incident benefited Temple Seven and its members tremendously in respect and adulation from their fellow Harlemites. Malcolm quelled the potentially explosive affair resulting from the police beating and jailing of Hinton, which made the news of many of the major African American newspapers, including the *New York Amsterdam News*.* Temple Seven's fame was heightened even further in 1959 when Mike Wallace* and Louis Lomax's* televised piece "The Hate That Hate Produced"* introduced Malcolm X's and the Nation of Islam's (NOI)* views to the general American public. Temple Seven, Malcolm, and Elijah Muhammad became hot copy for weekly white magazines and other publications.

Eventually, Temple Seven became the place where Malcolm would have to wrestle with his congregation vis-à-vis Elijah Muhammad's moral digressions, where he became aware of traitors in his midst, and where he was "silenced" by Elijah Muhammad for impolitic remarks about President John Kennedy's* death. He was even forbidden to teach at Temple Seven, the mosque that he had done so much to build and develop though his eloquence, magnetism, and organizational ability.

SELECTED BIBLIOGRAPHY

Evanzz, 1992; Lincoln, 1994; Lomax, 1963; Malcolm X with Haley, 1965.

Malik Simba

TEMPLE NUMBER SEVEN RESTAURANT. Originally a storefront, Harlem's* Temple Number Seven* was a four-story building located on 116th Street and Lenox Avenue. Putting Malcolm X in charge of it in 1954 demonstrated Elijah Muhammad's* early confidence in him. Its restaurant was just around the corner.

Malcolm's ministry at Temple Seven grew tremendously, a result of his immense energy and dedication to Muhammad and the Nation of Islam (NOI).* As his national reputation and popularity rose, Muslim* and non-Muslim alike (especially the media) sought him out for counsel and interviews. Many of these meetings took place in the confines of the restaurant. It was in the restaurant where Malcolm met and scared a white Harvard University* co-ed who had heard him speak at the university. The young student who wanted to know if Malcolm really believed that all whites were bad left the restaurant in tears, emotionally torn over Malcolm's answer that she could not do anything for black equality.

The restaurant's proximity to the temple made it a natural and popular hangout where Malcolm regularly visited and ate the standard Muslim fare of fish and bean dishes. Occasionally, Malcolm held audiences with important dignitaries at the restaurant as he did with emerging poet Maya Angelou.* More than a simple eating place, the restaurant, a part of the NOI vast economic and business empire, was a mecca for social gatherings, and Malcolm's presence enhanced its popularity.

SELECTED BIBLIOGRAPHY

Cone, 1993; Gallen, ed., 1992; Malcolm X with Haley, 1965; B. Perry, 1991.

Brenda Ayres and Robert L. Jenkins

TEMPLE RELATIONSHIPS. Elijah Muhammed* taught that the Nation of Islam (NOI)* was not an organization but a world. The accepted social norms and religious practices within the confines of the temple or mosque where services were held were numerous. The religion of the NOI, as taught by Muhammad, was based, in part, on issues of race and the relationships of power among different racial groups.

Appearance and mannerisms within the temples were very stern. Men dressed tastefully in dark suits, pressed white shirts, and ties. The women, or sisters as they were referred to in the temple, wore ankle-length gowns and no makeup and covered their heads with scarves as a sign of modesty. The children in the temples were not exempted from temple etiquette. Muslim* men and children treated Muslim sisters with honor and respect. When inside the temples, men sat on one side of the room and women on the other.

In addition to the strict codes of manners and dress, NOI members were also punished for violating rules, such as eating more than one meal a day, drinking alcohol, and taking drugs. These rules were internally enforced by the Fruit of Islam (FOI),* the paramilitary wing of the NOI.

In his early days as a member of the NOI, Malcolm spent many hours in the temples listening to ministers and leaders speak to the followers. Understandably, he came to respect the mosques with great reverence. The temples were not only places to pronounce Muslim doctrine and worldviews; they were first and foremost religious structures. Malcolm himself became a minister and leader who attracted many followers to temples across the nation. As such he held to the NOI standards. Meetings began promptly. Messages and lessons had specific goals and objectives, as Malcolm always sought to teach his followers "the duty of a civilized man." Inside the temple he emphasized modes of conduct, adherence to morality and decency, and commitment to the Muslim laws and principles.

SELECTED BIBLIOGRAPHY

Friedly, 1992; Goldman, 1979; Karim with Skutches and Gallen, 1992; Lincoln, 1961; Malcolm X with Haley, 1965.

Terri Earnest

THIEL, BETTY JEAN. As a Muslim* minister Malcolm X blamed women for the woes of men and often preached against the seductive ways of women. It is ironic that he would have held such attitudes. He had numerous positive relationships with women, including several females with the given name Betty (Thiel, Girven, Kennedy, and Sanders, the latter who became his wife). One of the first of these relationships occurred during his childhood with Betty Jean Thiel. Thiel was a white girl who lived across the street from the Littles in Lansing, Michigan.* Like Malcolm, she had a wide gap between her two front teeth. Apparently she and Malcolm were constant playmates in their youth.

Despite happy childhood playtimes with Thiel, Malcolm developed a negative white race consciousness. His very dark father seemed to favor Malcolm over the other children because Malcolm was light in complexion; conversely, his very light-skinned mother apparently beat Malcolm more because he was lighter than his siblings. In addition, he had negative experiences at school with white students and teachers. Strangely, Malcolm X did not mention Thiel or any other childhood white friends to Alex Haley.* Perhaps this was because when he began writing his autobiography, his antiwhite feelings were still strongly negative, though his dislike of whites simply because of their color was beginning to change.

SELECTED BIBLIOGRAPHY

Malcolm X with Haley, 1965; B. Perry, 1991.

Brenda Ayres

THOMAS, CARY (Cary 2X; Abdul Malik). In the months following his break with the Nation of Islam (NOI),* Malcolm X seemed keenly aware of the likelihood of his murder. Predictions about his death notwithstanding, Malcolm and those close to him understandably took precautionary measures to safeguard his life by establishing a security force. Composed of several bodyguards, the security around Malcolm was most prominent during his weekly Organization of Afro-American Unity (OAAU)* speaking engagements at the Audubon* auditorium. Cary Thomas, also known as Cary 2X and Abdul Malik, was one of the men who served as Malcolm's bodyguard. Thomas, who was on duty the evening of Malcolm's assassination, played a central role in identifying the three men arrested in Malcolm's murder as the perpetrators and provided the prosecution with the most damaging testimony of the trial against them.

Thomas was regarded as a rather mysterious character. A native New Yorker, he was a former heroin addict, drug dealer, and convicted felon. Except for marital problems that had caused a four-year separation from his family of five, his rehabilitation seems to have paralleled the story of many converts to the NOI. He officially joined the Black Muslim* sect in 1963, acquiring his "X"* as a member of New York's Temple Number Seven.* In 1963, however, he suffered from a mental breakdown and was briefly held at New York's Bellevue Hospital for psychiatric evaluation. Although Thomas's background is vague about the extent of his association with Malcolm and the New York temple, apparently he left the next year after the Elijah Muhammad*–Malcolm X rift to support Malcolm. Reportedly, however, Thomas knew little about either the NOI and their practices or what Malcolm had come to represent in the months after his break with the NOI. Hence, if there was much of a relationship between him and Malcolm, it was apparently not a close one.

Despite his background, however, Thomas was, nevertheless, considered so important to the success of the murder case that he was arrested as a material witness and, for security reasons, detained for nearly a year until the trial began. In the interim as a detainee, he continued his bizarre behavior, on one occasion setting fire to the mattress in his jail cell. His testimony in the 1966 assassination trial* was filled with flaws, as he frequently failed to answer crucial questions about his own relationship with the NOI and Malcolm and contradicted previous statements given to the grand jury that he had actually seen the accused, Talmadge Hayer* and Norman 3X Butler,* pump bullets into Malcolm's felled body. Nevertheless, in the three days of testimony, he provided convincing testimony about what occurred in the Audubon auditorium. His testimony challenged that of Hayer's, the only one of the three accused captured at the scene, that Hayer was a member of the Black Muslim sect, and it was certainly one of the most important, though disputed, factors tying Hayer to the other Muslim* defendants and to the murder.

Thomas claimed to have fallen on the floor during the melee that ended Malcolm's life. Hence, as one of Malcolm's bodyguards, Thomas sadly did little to perform the security tasks for which he was responsible.

SELECTED BIBLIOGRAPHY

Breitman, Porter, and Smith (Miah, ed.), 1976; Friedly, 1992; Goldman, 1979; *Militant*, March 14, 1966.

Robert L. Jenkins

TILL, EMMETT. For Black Americans living in the twentieth-century Deep South, life was often filled with sheer terror. The record of this terror is replete with examples of lynchings as white mobs, determined to keep the African American population subordinate, committed some of the most gruesome acts of murder in the nation's history. In 1955, Emmett Till, a fourteen-year-old Chicago* youth visiting his grandfather in the Mississippi* delta, was brutally murdered and his corpse thrown into the Tallahatchie River for allegedly whistling at a white woman. Although several persons were tried for the atrocity, no one was ever punished. Till's death not only horrified the nation but became the catalyst in inspiring civil rights* activism among many people in the South.* The lynching also angered many black Americans. Malcolm X exhibited a kind of controlled anger over the murder. Long after the national revulsion over the lynching subsided, he continued to raise Till's name as an example of the oppression that southern blacks in general and Mississippi blacks in particular faced daily from white racists. He criticized the innocent verdict of the white men charged in the crime as predictable and reminded blacks that this kind of justice did not, in turn, warrant their patriotic support of the nation. Malcolm recalled Till's murder, along with the death of his father, Earl Little, Sr.,* and Medgar Evers* and the lynchings of Mack Charles Parker, Michael Schwerner, Andrew Goodwin, and James Chaney, as representative of the evil and pervasiveness of southern white racism. He also talked about them as a way to raise the consciousness of black Americans about the importance of defending themselves, violently if necessary, from the possibilities of these kinds of acts.

Mississippi courtroom scene of the woman whom Emmett Till whistled at and her husband during his trial for Till's murder. Courtesy of Mississippi Department of Archives and History.

SELECTED BIBLIOGRAPHY

Carson (Gallen, ed.), 1991; Evanzz, 1992; Malcolm X (Breitman, ed.), 1970a; Whitfield, 1988.

Robert L. Jenkins

TOURÉ, SÉKOU. Twice in 1964 Malcolm X traveled to Africa. On his second journey, Malcolm visited Guinea and President Sékou Touré. Despite efforts by the U.S. State Department* to convince Touré not to give Malcolm a cordial welcome, he was Touré's house guest for three days. After returning to the United States, Malcolm told an audience at the Audubon* Auditorium that Touré was deeply concerned about the plight of African Americans.

Ideologically, Touré and Malcolm saw the problems of Africa and African Americans in similar ways. Both understood neocolonialism. Touré, alone of French West Africa's leaders, rejected the French community, while Malcolm insisted on economic nationalism for African Americans. Touré and Malcolm agreed on the need for Africans and African Americans to control their own economic and political destiny. Both Touré and Malcolm understood, too, the common cause of Africans and African Americans; Malcolm credited Touré with a "sincere desire" to help African Americans.

Touré and Malcolm had considerable common ground. Yet Malcolm said little specifically about Touré after returning from Africa. He noted that Touré had offered excellent advice on solving the race problem in America but did not elaborate on what that advice entailed. He frequently included Touré among the leaders who had helped broaden his understanding of the race struggle but did not single him out for discussion in the way he did Gamel Abdel Nasser* and Kwame Nkrumah.*

SELECTED BIBLIOGRAPHY

Adamolekun, 1976; Collins with Bailey, 1998; Gallen, ed., 1992; Malcolm X (Perry, ed.), 1989.

Alan Scot Willis

TSHOMBÉ, MOISE. Moise Tshombé was a wealthy businessman and political leader in the Congo,* later renamed Zaire, who in 1960 declared the secession of the Katangan province. Katanga was a rich copper-mining region in the southern part of the Congo, which was experiencing a serious political crisis under the leadership of Patrice Lumumba,* the elected nationalist leader of the country who Malcolm X idolized. Lumumba was an outspoken critic of Belgium, the Congo's former colonial ruler, and still intricately involved in Congolese affairs. While the United Nations* responded to Lumumba's request to help him bring stability to his country, the body, under the pressure of the United States and other Western powers, decided not to use its forces in the Congo against Tshombé. Hence, Tshombé's military forces were led by mercenaries from Belgium, South Africa,* Rhodesia, England, France, and the United States. In fact, the secession had been encouraged and financed by the Belgian mining company of Union Muniere and other western companies in Katanga. Against this background, especially following the well-plotted conspiracy that murdered Lumumba in January 1961 in Katanga by forces loyal to Tshombé, Malcolm X would portray Lumumba as a great nationalist and Pan-Africanist who died for the cause of his people. In speech after speech, especially following his return to the United States from his second African trip, in the fall of 1964, he condemned Tshombé as a cold-blooded murderer, an international thug who should never be permitted to visit the United States. In no uncertain terms, he criticized Tshombé as an "Uncle Tom"* and a puppet of the United States. Malcolm's frequent criticism of Tshombé gave him the occasion to dig at President Lyndon B. Johnson,* to whom he claimed Tshombé answered.

SELECTED BIBLIOGRAPHY

Breitman, 1968; Carson (Gallen, ed.), 1991; Gerard-Libois, 1967; Heing and Doonay, 1966; *Militant*, December 21, 1964.

Amos J. Beyan

TURNER, HENRY McNEAL. A chaplain of the Freedman's Bureau, Bishop College president, and newspaper editor, Turner became one of America's most radical and articulate black nationalists and Pan-Africanists during the nineteenth century. As a former Union soldier during the Civil War and as a Georgia Reconstruction legislator, Turner strongly protested the continued subjugation of blacks and is on record as declaring that blacks had no reason to love America or to be patriotic. He later described the Constitution of the United States as a cheap document and stated that he wished every black person would spit on it. Turner believed that whites would never stop persecuting blacks until blacks had absolute control of their own destiny. Like Malcolm X after him, Turner believed that by identifying with Africa, blacks could win self-respect, which would, in turn, serve as a powerful force against their oppression in America. Turner argued that White America should pay $40 billion to African Americans for having exploited blacks; he suggested that $100 million of the total amount be used to send 5,000 to 10,000 blacks to Africa annually. Malcolm also advocated pronounced reparation* ideas. Turner and his International Migration Society sent two large groups of blacks to Liberia in 1896. Indeed, Turner himself took four trips to Africa between 1891 and 1898. How much Malcolm knew about Turner is not clear.

According to his nephew Rodnell Collins,* Malcolm acknowledged Turner's contribution to Black America. Considering the parallels between the Pan-African views of Malcolm and Turner and the fact that Malcolm was well read on a variety of subjects, including black history,* it is suggestive that Malcolm was aware of Turner's ideas and perhaps coopted some of his thoughts. It could be said that Malcolm X and Turner not only advanced Pan-Africanism* and black nationalism* as ideologies but also gave them a practical application.

SELECTED BIBLIOGRAPHY

Berry and Blassingame, 1982; Collins with Bailey, 1998; F. Miller, 1975; Moses, 1978; Stuckey, 1987.

Amos J. Beyan

22 WEST COFFEE SHOP. Located on 135th Street, "22 West," as it was popularly called, was a favorite meeting place for Malcolm X. As minister of Harlem's* Muslim* Temple Number Seven* when he was not out of town or teaching in the temple, Malcolm X could usually be found in the Temple Restaurant on 116th Street and Lenox Avenue. The Muslim restaurant not only served as a favorite eatery for Malcolm but also doubled as his office and where he typically met people who sought him out for various reasons. After he left the Nation of Islam (NOI)* and established the official headquarters of his Organization of Afro-American Unity (OAAU)* in the Hotel Theresa,* many of the meetings and other activities that he once frequently reserved for the Temple Number Seven Restaurant* moved to the 22 West Coffee Shop. The coffee shop was a convenient place for him to hold court. There, over the simplicity of coffee and perhaps ice cream, his favorite dish, he met and gave interviews to journalists, entertained dignitaries and black celebrities,* or merely fraternized with the large crowds that gathered in the shop. Though not a particularly heavy coffee drinker, Malcolm, who was so disciplined about virtually everything that might negatively impact on his health, could nevertheless consume considerably more than usual when his encounters with friends and acquaintances were long, as they often were. Malcolm always sat at the same table, conveniently located at the back of the luncheonette where it was easy to watch for his enemies. Especially in the last months of his life, a time filled with apprehension and trepidation, Malcolm liked to frequent the coffee shop because it was always filled with his friends and admirers.

SELECTED BIBLIOGRAPHY

Angelou, 1993; DeCaro, 1996; Gallen, ed., 1992; Goldman, 1977.

Robert L. Jenkins

U

UNCLE SAM. The term *Uncle Sam* was one of Malcolm's favorites when making reference to the U.S. government. While the title and name is a pejorative one that was used widely by African Americans after World War II,* it was initially used with a degree of reverence, if not awe, for the power of the government. Uncle Sam (which abbreviated stands for U.S.) has been personified and caricatured as a tall and somewhat gangly white man with a thin face and chin whiskers or small white goatee. Uncle Sam is pictured as dressed in a red, white, and blue outfit with a long coat with a tail on it and striped pants. A tall hat decorated with a band of stars completes the outfit. During wartime as well as peacetime, it has not been uncommon to see Uncle Sam with a scowl on his face and pointing his finger straight ahead, giving the appearance that anyone who stood directly in front of a picture or poster of him was the one that he was targeting. A common caption at the bottom of the poster is the phrase "Uncle Sam Wants You!" This is usually a reference to volunteering to fight during wartime or, alternatively, making sure that males register with the Selective Service System when they are eighteen years of age. An uncle in one's family usually denotes warm feelings and affection associated with familial bloodlines. So while Uncle Sam has a serious look on his face, it is also clear that he is subliminally considered to be an authority figure in the "family."

Malcolm constantly "roasted" Uncle Sam, but there was no humor intended by him. This roast was intended to ridicule and point out the contradictions, hypocrisy, and racism of Uncle Sam with regard to how the government treated, and allowed inhumane treatment of, African Americans in the United States. Uncle Sam was responsible for violations of human rights,* failure to uphold civil rights,* and relegating black Americans to second-class citizenship, a citizenship that Malcolm stated no other people in the world had.

Malcolm lambasted Uncle Sam in the international arena as well. He made it clear that black men have been willing to die for Uncle Sam, fighting abroad against people of color they do not know, despite the fact that Uncle Sam has committed, or allowed, atrocities against blacks at home throughout their presence in America. *Uncle Sam* is a common term used in many of Malcolm's speeches, but it is almost always used in a sardonic, sarcastic, hypocritical, and acrimonious manner. He also used the slang phrase *Uncle Tom** in a similarly derogatory manner, referring to blacks who thought that whites were superior to them and always thought, acted, and talked in a manner that showed their own inferiority. These "uncles" of Malcolm's constituted two of his favorite metaphors in describing what he often referred to as the American Nightmare for blacks.

SELECTED BIBLIOGRAPHY

Lomax, 1963; Malcolm X (Breitman, ed.), 1970a; Malcolm X (Clarke, ed.), 1990; T'Shaka, 1983.

Mfanya Donald Tryman

UNCLE TOM. This is a literary and stereotypical term used by antebellum southern white writers to describe slaves who identified more closely with their masters than other slaves. Portrayed as docile, faithful, musical, dishonest, and irrational house slaves, the Uncle Tom slave would often fight and even die in defense of his master.

While the image associated with Uncle Tom was emphasized in the antebellum South* by white novelists, dramatists, journalists, and historians to justify the perpetual subjugation of blacks, Malcolm X used the term in the 1960s to condemn those blacks he considered as serious obstacles in accomplishing black nationalist, Pan-Africanist, and human rights* objectives. Against this background, Malcolm X would argue that the Uncle Toms of the early 1960s were the black leaders who continued to emphasize nonviolent and integration-oriented approaches to the civil rights movement.* Clearly, the opposite of the Uncle Tom in the 1960s were the militant black nationalists and Pan-Africanists like himself, Floyd McKissick,* Stokely Carmichael,* Imamu Amiri Baraka,* Frantz Fanon,* Patrice Lumumba,* Kwame Nkrumah,* and Sékou Touré.*

SELECTED BIBLIOGRAPHY

Allen, 1969; Berry and Blassingame, 1982; Breitman, 1967; J. White, 1985.

Amos J. Beyan

UNITED NATIONS. As an official observer Malcolm X presented a memorandum to the Organization of African Unity* conference in Cairo, Egypt,* that detailed the long history of racial injustice in America. In the memorandum he asked the African nations to condemn the United States for its ruthless disregard for its African American citizens. According to Malcolm, the U.S. government's failure to prevent the brutal treatment of civil rights* activists in Alabama, Mississippi,* and other parts of the nation demonstrated that it was not able or did not care to protect black citizens. Malcolm's plea to these African leaders was for support in taking the African American cause to the UN. Malcolm's decision to ask for UN support grew out of his conviction that African Americans would never receive justice at the hands of whites in America. African Americans, said Malcolm during one television interview, had asked the United States for justice, believing that "the criminal would solve the crime." If African Americans wanted justice, they would have to take their case to the United Nations. There, they would appeal to member nations (particularly those that had suffered under Western colonialism) to pass a resolution charging the United States with violating the UN Charter on Human Rights. A UN resolution condemning the United States for human rights* violations, Malcolm believed, would embarrass the United States and compromise its struggle with the Soviet Union to win the hearts and minds of postcolonial peoples. Malcolm was convinced that such a resolution would receive UN support. After years of colonialism, the peoples of Africa, Asia, and Latin America were now forming their own independent governments. And by the early 1960s, the darker peoples were fast becoming a majority in the United Nations. But Malcolm failed to realize the extent to which the newly created African states, as well as other nations, were dependent upon American foreign aid. Despite their warm embrace of Malcolm's call for African unity, few, if any, African leaders were willing to jeopardize U.S. dollars to support their African American brethren. Thus Malcolm's hope that the United Nations would become an effective voice for African American grievances was never realized. And because of his premature death, his petition for a UN resolution denouncing the United States for its violation of human rights was never completed.

SELECTED BIBLIOGRAPHY

Goldman, 1973; Malcolm X (Breitman, ed.), 1965; Sales, 1994.

Phillip A. Gibbs

UNITED STATES INFORMATION AGENCY (USIA). The United States Information Agency (USIA) was a federal propaganda agency with outlets around the world. Under the guidance and direction of the State Department,* the USIA had the responsibility of presenting the United States in the most favorable light in an effort to thwart the spread of communism. During the 1960s, it was headed by former journalist Carl Rowan,* who became a bitter critic of Malcolm X. Rowan regarded Malcolm as little more than a black version of the small but vocal minority of white bigots that did nothing to advance the real interest of the nation. Under Rowan, the USIA greatly expanded its radio broadcast operations, targeting key emerging Third World countries in Africa and Asia. Occasionally, it worked in conjunction with the Central Intelligence Agency* to influence the internal politics of some African countries least favorable to the United States.

Concerned over his growing influence among some of the continent's more radical leadership, the agency took special note of Malcolm, beginning with his tours of Africa in 1964. Indeed, after Malcolm spoke before a university audience in Lagos, Nigeria,* during his first African tour, disgruntled students precipitated a near riot in front of the USIA headquarters in a protest of the organization's portrayal of him as a hate monger.

Malcolm had little respect for the USIA, contending that it was more vicious than the propaganda machine operated by the Nazis during World War II.* He accused it of spreading false information in Africa about the plight of race relations in the United States. The agency, Malcolm said, sought to convey that black Americans enjoyed an enviable status, one no longer repressed by lynching and police brutality* and where their social and political rights were being greatly enhanced by passage of measures such as the 1964 Civil Rights Act.* Malcolm's claim that the agency went through great pain to discredit him personally on the African continent was an accusation that gained considerable stock after his death. Almost immediately after Malcolm's murder, the USIA, under the directive of its leader, inundated Africa with reports of the murder. However, it was largely unsuccessful in its effort to minimize the importance of Malcolm as a world leader and his work as a just cause.

SELECTED BIBLIOGRAPHY

Evanzz, 1992; Goldman, 1979; Krenn, 1999; Malcolm X (Breitman, ed.), 1970a; *Militant*, March 15, 1965; Sales, 1994.

Robert L. Jenkins

UNIVERSAL NEGRO IMPROVEMENT ASSOCIATION (UNIA). The Universal Negro Improvement Association (UNIA) was the organization started by Marcus Garvey,* a black nationalist who exhorted African Americans in the 1920s to be proud of their race, their culture, and their history and African roots. The UNIA originated in Garvey's native Jamaica in 1914, but it quickly spread to the United States. By the end of World War I in mid-1919, Garvey claimed, perhaps somewhat exaggeratedly, more than thirty branches in the United States and a membership of 6 million followers by 1923. Similarly, the Nation of Islam (NOI)* grew exponentially under the influence of Malcolm's organizing and leadership skills, and numerous mosques were established by the late 1950s. Malcolm's father had been a strong and open supporter of the UNIA in the 1920s, and Malcolm felt that his death at the hands of white supremacists was related to his black nationalist activities as a "Garveyite." Malcolm's mother was also an avid Garveyite, doing secretarial work for the UNIA and writing for the organization's newspaper. One of the goals of the UNIA was to assist African Americans in returning to Africa as the motherland on a permanent basis. Malcolm had once argued, similar to his mentor Elijah Muhammad,* that blacks should be given fertile land in the United States to start their own nation, since they could not coexist with whites.

Before its decline in 1923, the UNIA was primarily directed at the poor and lower-class black American who felt excluded by the black middle class–oriented National Association for the Advancement of Colored People (NAACP),* which was associated with liberal whites and affluent blacks. Similarly, the recruitment and appeal of the NOI and recruitment activities of Malcolm X focused on black Americans who felt like Garvey and the UNIA that the "American Dream" was an ideal that they could never obtain. Consequently, the NOI, like the UNIA, advocated that blacks return to their African homelands. Before Malcolm changed his views to support only a cultural, philosophical, and psychological return to Africa, he was, like Garvey and the UNIA, a strong proponent of African repatriation. Garvey asserted that the NAACP and W.E.B. Du Bois,* a middle-class black leader, were white oriented and wanted African Americans to become white through racial integration.

Garvey felt that it would be impossible for blacks to integrate with whites, who he felt were much too ethnocentric, if not racist, to accept blacks on an equal level in a democratic system. When Malcolm joined the NOI, he expressed feelings similar to those of Garvey, though he would outgrow them as he matured politically. He had argued that it was foolish for blacks to try to integrate themselves into a "burning house." Like Garvey, he felt that the solution was racial separation,* not racial integration.* Like Garvey, Malcolm excoriated the middle-class black leadership as "Uncle Toms"* and "House Negroes."* Malcolm, too, argued that whites would not accept blacks on an equal level.

In 1923, Garvey was imprisoned for mail fraud. President Calvin Coolidge pardoned him in 1927, but for all practical purposes, the UNIA was an organization in decline after Garvey's conviction and deportment, just as the NOI became fractured with the departure of Malcolm X.

SELECTED BIBLIOGRAPHY
Bracey, Meier, and Rudwick, eds., 1970; Cruse, 1987; Franklin, and Moss, 2000; Gallen, ed., 1992; Segal, 1995; United American Video, 1998.

Mfanya Donald Tryman

UNIVERSITY OF ISLAM. Throughout its history the Nation of Islam (NOI)* strove to inculcate its followers with a philosophy that would enhance their understanding of the religion and strengthen their ties to the organization and its leaders. A number of institutions such as the University of Islam emerged to play critical roles in this endeavor. First established in Detroit, Michigan,* in 1933, the original headquarters of the NOI, the sect would also establish a "university" in Chicago,* after Elijah Muhammad* assumed leadership and relocated the official headquarters to the "Windy City." As the national membership of the NOI grew, "campuses" of the university became associated with temples in other cities. Members were normally required to remove their children from the public schools and to enroll them in the university. Elijah Muhammad's daughter Lottie Muhammad* supervised these "universities," a job that she assumed largely because Malcolm had insisted that Muhammad's family be employed in the NOI's business enterprises.*

The term *university* in the schools' name, however, is actually a misnomer, for from the beginning the institutions were actually the equivalent of grammar and high schools. The schools' curricula consisted of typical grade school subjects, including English and the nontraditional Arabic. There also existed a considerable focus on personal improvement where students were encouraged to shun some of the denigrating vices like gambling, drinking, drugs, and smoking. Rules were strict when it came to behavior, and dress codes and respect for school mates and elders was demanded. The schools also emphasized uplifting the black self-image through the teaching of black history* and the history of the NOI and its basic doctrines on racial separation,* white demonology, and the coming Armageddon* as expounded originally by Master Wallace D. Fard* and Muhammad. As an NOI leader, occasionally Malcolm had to defend the schools' detractors, who accused them of teaching hate and spreading false and damaging doctrine among the young. The schools' offerings were legitimate, he said, even doctrines about black divinity and white devilry. And there was certainly nothing wrong in not fostering a black inferiority complex by refusing to teach Muslim* children the "Black Sambo" story typically offered children of his public school days. As a Muslim minister and a leader truly interested in the education of black children, Malcolm frequently played a highly visible role as a "teacher" of youth from the schools. Occasionally, for example, he took them on field tours around New York to places like the Museum of Natural History, where the youngsters listened attentively to him expound authoritatively on a variety of subjects dealing with the exhibits on display.

Almost from the outset of their establishment, the Universities of Islam have had to confront local controversy. On at least one occasion controversy forced the temporary closure of a school. Yet they still thrive in those cities where the NOI temples exist, the membership continuing to show pride about the schools' low dropout rate, number of college admissions, and other student accomplishments.

SELECTED BIBLIOGRAPHY

Carson (Gallen, ed.), 1991; Clegg, 1997; Evanzz, 1999; Lomax, 1963; Strickland (Greene, ed.), 1994; Tate, 1997.

Robert L. Jenkins

US. US is an organization started by Maulana Ron Karenga* in the aftermath of the Watts uprising during the summer of 1965 in south-central Los Angeles. As a black nationalist organization located primarily on the West Coast, US stresses cultural nationalism as a necessary phase before revolutionary black nationalism.* African dress is emphasized among US advocates, and Kwi-Swahili is offered as an alternative to English. US stresses that the mental battle for the minds of blacks must be won before serious talk of a physical revolutionary war begins. US has been influenced both by the Nation of Islam (NOI)* and Malcolm X.

During Malcolm's last year, he began to emphasize a return culturally, socially, and psychologically to Africa rather than a physical return to the land. US stresses African culture as necessary to develop the appropriate value system and ethos to determine African American "identity, purpose, and direction," or, as Karenga would put it, to determine who one is, what one must do, and how one must do it. Karenga argues that it is useless to speak of or pray to God, for people of African descent are gods themselves. Elijah Muhammad* made similar statements, which suggested that Black Islam as it is known in the West was moving toward Sufism, a mystical form of Islam,* near the end of his life in 1975. US emphasizes African traditions, rituals, and race pride. Similarly, Malcolm used to teach about the great kingdoms of Africa and the influence of Islam in Africa among his constituency and at various mosques before he broke with the NOI.

SELECTED BIBLIOGRAPHY

Halisi, 1965; Malcolm X (Karim, ed.), 1971; C. Williams, 1976.

Mfanya Donald Tryman

V

VAN PEEBLES, MELVIN. During the 1970s America witnessed a virtual rebirth of Hollywood black filmmaking. In many ways, the 1970s resurgence was a recapturing of the 1930s and 1940s explosion of films produced, directed, and starred in by black entrepreneurs and artists, and it brought large black audiences to the theaters to view a variety of film genres, including the so-called Blaxploitation movies. One of the most notable cinema makers of this era was Melvin Van Peebles. A quasi-independent filmmaker, Van Peebles's most successful, though controversial, work was the 1971 film *Sweet Sweetback's Baadasssss Song*. Filled with a zigzag of sexual, violent, and flight scenes, the outlaw-hero character, Sweet Sweetback, played by Van Peebles, fights successfully against an oppressive police system victimizing an inner-city black community. The movie, written, directed, and produced by Van Peebles, attracted a large crossover and youthful audience from many of the nation's urban centers.

Van Peebles's interest in filmmaking was long-standing, and though his major impact on American filmmaking did not occur until the *Sweetback* movie, he had already made a name for himself in films while in Paris, France, where he had lived among a sizable population of black American expatriates since the early 1960s. There he associated with such black notables as Richard Wright* and Chester Himes.* In the French capital he had originally devoted himself to writing before turning to his first love. It was while he resided in Paris that he first came into contact with Malcolm X. In 1964 on the return from his second African tour, Malcolm had stopped in Paris, where he spoke to his followers in the black community and initiated the Paris branch of his Organization of Afro-American Unity.* Hired as a freelance writer by a Parisian newspaper, Van Peebles spent considerable time shadowing Malcolm in Paris to ascertain his views about a variety of issues for the paper, including Malcolm's impressions about China's recent detonation of its first atomic bomb. Van Peebles learned much about Malcolm during their encounters. Like a host of other black intellectuals and professionals who came to know Malcolm beyond the media's hostile portrayal of him, Van Peebles was immediately struck with Malcolm's intelligence and knowledge of world affairs. He was, however, most impressed with the black leader's "decolonized mind." It was a quality that he obviously respected and that was clearly celebrated in Sweet Sweetback, his most notable film character.

SELECTED BIBLIOGRAPHY

Cripps, 1993; Goldman, 1979; Guerrero, 1993; Himes, 1976; Stovall, 1996.

Robert L. Jenkins

VIETNAM CONFLICT. A former French colony in Southeast Asia, Vietnam during the Cold War became an Asian battlefield. Alarmed over nationalist Ho Chi Minh's effort to unify a country ideologically divided into northern and southern halves since the mid-1950s, the United States during the 1960s found itself embroiled in arguably the nation's most controversial military conflict. Minh was an avowed Marxist-Leninist, but he was hardly solidly in the Soviet Union's sphere. Still, the American government was determined to ensure that South Vietnam not be overrun by Minh's nationalist army, and theoretically beginning a domino effect propelling other Asian nations toward communism. Despite an increasing American military presence in South Vietnam against the communist insurgency, Minh and his guerrilla force proved to be formidable adversaries for the United States and the South Vietnam military.

From the outset Malcolm found much in the Vietnamese situation to criticize. In the speech that initially got him into trouble with Elijah Muhammad* over President John Kennedy's* murder, he accused the late president of negligence in Asia that led to a climate responsible for the slaying of South Vietnam's president Ngo Dinh Diem and his brother Ngo Dinh Nhu. Military escalation began in earnest in February 1965, the month of Malcolm X's assassination, but he had already seen enough of the communist guerrillas' tenacity and determination to be impressed. The United States, like France before it, was clearly a superior military force, but like France, it too was being handled effectively by the North Vietnamese communists. The United States, he said, was "trapped" in a losing cause in a determined effort from a people whose only resources were sneakers, a gun, and "a bowl of rice." Long before American antiwar opposition became a veritable crusade, Malcolm railed against American involvement in the Vietnam conflict. As the war escalated, he praised the North Vietnamese effort, regarding it as a struggle of dark-skinned people to resist white racial oppression. In Malcolm's opinion, what the United States was doing in Vietnam was simply another example of the nation's long history of resorting to violence to achieve selfish ends. Malcolm declared that the country's violent effort to sustain its interest in Asia paralleled the nation's historical pattern of violence that oppressed black Americans. He suggested that young blacks should learn from the motivations and guerrilla warfare* tactics of the North Vietnamese and become freedom fighters in their own right at home. Black Americans, he said, should be fighting in places like Alabama, not Vietnam.

In many ways, the Vietnam conflict proved to be one of twentieth-century America's defining events, shaping politics and social issues for more than two decades. Prior to his death, Malcolm correctly predicted that the American people would not long support the nation's involvement in the war. It is likely that had he lived, he would have had much more to say against the nation's continuous expansion of the war and the concomitant emotionalism that grew out of the antiwar movement.

SELECTED BIBLIOGRAPHY

Carson (Gallen, ed.), 1991; Herring, 1979; Malcolm X (Breitman, ed.), 1970a; Malcolm X (Clark, ed.), 1992; Malcolm X (Perry, ed.), 1989.

Robert L. Jenkins

VIOLENCE VERSUS NONVIOLENCE. Malcolm X, the man behind the statement "by any means necessary," was viewed as an advocate of violence in American society. His teachings were considered radical. Despite the fact that Malcolm never committed a violent act himself as a public figure, he was readily accused of being a "black supremacist" who urged his followers to resort to violence. Malcolm never professed having all of the answers to the political, economic, and social problems faced by African Americans, but he was one of those willing to try to bring an end to the injustices African Americans suffered.

Malcolm's philosophy on violence versus nonviolence focused on his belief that African Americans should fight against those who fight against them and that this was the best course of action in any situation. More specifically, he believed that one should protect oneself against violent acts by others. He did not advocate violence merely for the sake of violence but only as a mechanism of self-defense.* Malcolm spoke often about white racists in powerful positions who worried about the changing mood and behavior of African Americans, especially if that mood and that behavior became what whites called violent. According to Malcolm, white racists even called it violence if and when a black man protected himself against the attacks of a white man. White racists, he argued, did not even use the word *violence* until someone gave the impression that a black person was enraged. Hence, when the time came for blacks to physically explode, whites called it violence, but when whites acted similarly against blacks at any time, it was not called violence. Malcolm noted that all African Americans were victims of violence, but they were so victimized that they could not always recognize it for what it was.

Malcolm generally expressed his thoughts on nonviolence in racial terms. He stated that most whites who professed support for the black struggle for equality were usually allies as long as blacks were nonviolent. These whites were the ones who encouraged blacks to be nonviolent, to love their enemies, and to turn the other cheek. Seemingly, blacks in the United States began to see that they were tricked by nonviolence in order to keep them from even being able to defend themselves. Malcolm explained that whites resorted to giving out peace prizes to try to strengthen the image of nonviolence, but everyone did not accept this image; he certainly was not fooled by it, and he warned other blacks not to be fooled either. He noted that in America whites had been violent toward blacks for over 300 years, and this practice was not likely to change. Few, however, looked beyond Malcolm's fiery words to seek a rationale for and understanding of his views.

SELECTED BIBLIOGRAPHY

Dinwiddie-Boyd, 1996; Malcolm X (Brietman, ed.), 1965, 1970a, 1992.

Phyllis Gray-Ray

VOTING RIGHTS ACT OF 1965. Although President Lyndon B. Johnson* did not sign the 1965 Voting Rights Act* until five months after Malcolm X's assassination, the former Nation of Islam (NOI)* spokesman took a keen interest in increasing the African American vote. Even while he was still in the NOI, Malcolm had joined the 28th Precinct Community Council in Harlem* and assisted in voter registration. Elijah Muhammad* disliked any of his supporters allying with civil rights* groups and ordered Malcolm to criticize the 1963 March on Washington.* The NOI believed that Allah* (God), and not man, would solve the problems of the black race. Malcolm became frustrated with this nonactivist stance of the NOI, and this frustration played a part in his breakup with the organization.

When Malcolm finally broke with the NOI, he began to develop his more flexible political strategy and his ideas for the Organization of Afro-American Unity (OAAU).* Voting rights were a central part of this new direction. Malcolm went to Washington, D.C. to observe the progress of the 1964 civil rights bill and later attacked it for not going far enough to protect black citizens. He pointed out that the views of segregationist white politicians would change if black southerners could vote. He defended the voter registration drives of Freedom Summer* in Mississippi* in 1964 and condemned the murders of the three civil rights workers in Philadelphia, Mississippi.* But it was not just in the South* that he saw the potential of the ballot. In New York, too, he realized that black voters could wield considerable influence in their communities if they voted proportionately with their numbers. During the height of discussion over the 1964 civil rights bill, he pledged to lead "a massive voter registration drive in Harlem" to ensure that every black was registered. Increasingly, Malcolm took a more active role in the broader civil rights movement's* attempts to expand the franchise.

Malcolm invited students from McComb, Mississippi, to New York City to encourage them in their struggle for civil rights. When the police in Selma, Alabama, arrested Dr. Martin Luther King, Jr.,* during the voting rights cam-

Civil rights demonstrators supporting voter registration efforts in Mississippi. Wilson F. "Bill" Minor Papers, Special Collections Department, Mitchell Memorial Library, Mississippi State University.

paign in early 1965, Malcolm went to speak at nearby Tuskegee Institute to express solidarity with the efforts of Dr. King and other activists.

Just before his death, Malcolm went to Europe* and articulated his new belief in the power of the ballot. Voting became an integral part of Malcolm's new philosophy shortly before his death. He saw the change it could possibly bring to his people. His untimely death cut short his evolution toward voting and Black Power.* Had he lived longer, he may have taken a more active role in conventional black politics and the fruits of the 1965 Voting Right Act, even to the extent of seeking public office.

SELECTED BIBLIOGRAPHY

Malcolm X (Breitman, ed.), 1970a; Malcolm X with Haley, 1965; *New York Amsterdam News*, April 4, 1964; Strickland (Greene, ed.), 1994.

David T. Gleeson

W

WALLACE, GEORGE C. George Wallace represented the antithesis of Malcolm X and the Nation of Islam (NOI)* and assisted the NOI in its evolution. His demonstrated belief in racial segregation* and the subjugation of people of African descent was, in many ways, the raison d'être for Malcolm and the NOI.

Wallace, whose political career had been rather uneventful until his election as Alabama governor in 1962, soon came to symbolize southern segregationists' resistance to black social elevation. He gained notoriety in June 1963 when he personally blocked desegregation of the University of Alabama, defying a federal court order and provoking a tense confrontation with President John F. Kennedy.* The forces of Alabama white supremacy, whose views Wallace gave greater currency and courage, would precipitate major outbreaks of violence against black civil rights* activism.

Malcolm often condemned Wallace's Alabama for the violence perpetrated against blacks during the civil rights movement.* In a comparison with President John F. Kennedy, he once called Wallace a "wolf" because of his intemperate personality. Many equated Wallace with Malcolm on the issue of segregation. Malcolm, though, was not a segregationist; he was a separatist. *Segregation* connotes debilitation and subjugation of one people by the other. Racial separation,* as defined by Malcolm, is the act of parting from an undesirable existence because of the inability for races to coexist. The *Plessey v. Ferguson* U.S. Supreme Court decision of 1896 dictated to black people that African Americans would be "separate but equal" from whites, although the "equal" concept of the doctrine was a fallacy. For more than one-half century black people would be humiliated by segregation and segregationists. During the civil rights movement of the 1950s and 1960s, George Wallace became a symbol of this humiliation.

The reaction to racial segregation was a call for separation rather than integration by the Black Muslims.* Separation, said Malcolm, entailed making a conscious choice between the rejection and dejection of a segregated and sub-

Popular segregationist governor of Alabama George Wallace waves at an adoring white crowd during a parade in downtown Jackson, Mississippi, during the early 1960s. Courtesy of Mississippi Department of Archives and History.

ordinate existence, mandated by the white-controlled state, and gaining self-respect and control of one's own destiny by leaving the debilitating circumstances that characterized race relations in this country. Therefore, to many, Wallace symbolized black subordination and rejection, whereas Malcolm represented independence and self-determination.

SELECTED BIBLIOGRAPHY

C. Clark, 1993; Kennedy, 1978; Lesher, 1994; Malcolm X with Haley, 1965.

Horace Huntley

WALLACE, MIKE. The senior correspondent for the longtime popular CBS News feature program *60 Minutes*, Mike Wallace is one of America's most recognizable and trusted television commentators. Wallace's relationship with Malcolm X dates back to the late 1950s when his interest in Elijah Muhammad* and the Nation of Islam (NOI)* led to the exposé airing of the organization on a special five-part documentary entitled "The Hate That Hate Produced."* It was

Wallace's documentary that was largely responsible for introducing the little-known Muslim* sect to White America. For some blacks, the exposure was clearly overdone, its negative tone unwarranted. This was a view suggested by several prominent leaders, including baseball great Jackie Robinson* and Roy Wilkins* of the National Association for the Advancement of Colored People,* who participated in a local television panel discussion that Wallace hosted following the airing.

Although the documentary featured Malcolm along with other Muslim leaders, Wallace did not personally meet Malcolm until after the broadcast. Louis E. Lomax,* the prominent black journalist–author who worked with Wallace on the documentary and who had already established a friendship with Malcolm, invited Wallace to meet with Malcolm one morning over breakfast. Admittedly, the meeting left a notable impression on Wallace and would be the beginning of a lasting and what Wallace would identify as "a curious friendship" between the two. At once, Wallace would later say about this first encounter, Malcom showed that he was someone both "strange and special." As they learned more about each other, a strong bond of trust also developed, though, according to Wallace, Malcolm was slow to acknowledge this. Eventually, however, Malcolm came to trust Wallace, even to the extent of confiding in him before it became public about the flawed moral character of Elijah Muhammad. In June 1964 shortly after his formal break with the NOI, Malcolm made an appearance on Wallace's New York radio news show. Wallace asked the most searching questions, some of which had little to do with questions of race, and Malcolm respected Wallace for recognizing his interests in a diversity of contemporary issues.

Wallace, who spoke glowingly of Malcolm during the 1999 dedication services for the Malcolm X commemorative postage stamp,* regarded Malcolm as an intelligent, compassionate, honest, and sincere leader whose devotion to Black America was unswerving. Despite how some people unfairly depicted him, Wallace maintains that Malcolm actually strove to effect a meaningful "reconciliation" between blacks and whites. Understanding that Malcolm had considerably more to offer his people than Muhammad and the NOI, the journalist lamented the failure of Malcolm to find immediately a wider constituency following his break with the Black Muslims* and later adequate funding to support his fledgling Organization of Afro-American Unity (OAAU).* Wallace truly liked Malcolm and, as articulated in one of his books dealing with the history of his media career, expressed pride about the fact that they considered each other to be friends. Clearly, Wallace had moved far away from his first impressions of Malcolm as a dangerous extremist—one of the "merchants of hate" described in the 1959 documentary.

Malcolm's murder, though not totally unexpected because Malcolm had himself widely predicted it, nevertheless shocked Wallace. If he was once convinced of the guilt of Norman 3X Butler* and Thomas 15X Johnson* in Malcolm's murder, however, he would eventually abandon the premise. By the 1980s Wallace would, through his *60 Minutes* television show, work to help exonerate the two men and win their release from prison.

SELECTED BIBLIOGRAPHY

CBS News, 1992; Gallen, ed., 1992; Hampton and Fayer with Flynn, eds., 1991; Malcolm X with Haley, 2000; Wallace and Gates, 1984.

Robert L. Jenkins

WALLACE, THOMAS 13X. Thomas 13X Wallace was the brother of actress Ruby Dee,* a close friend of Malcolm's. He became a member of the Nation of Islam (NOI)* in the early 1960s. It was Wallace who introduced Malcolm to his sister and her husband, Ossie Davis.* Wallace was one of a number of high-level officials in the NOI who defected from the NOI when Malcolm X publicly announced his break from the organization led by Elijah Muhammad.* Wallace was a member of Harlem Temple Number Seven* over which Malcolm had presided as the chief minister. After his defection from the NOI, Wallace was brutally attacked and beaten by members still loyal to the NOI.

When Malcolm's house was set on fire in East Elmhurst,* Wallace, a close friend who did not live far from Malcolm, offered to let Malcolm and his family reside at his home until they could get back on their feet. But Malcolm moved by himself into a motel, presumably to protect his family from retaliation from the NOI for his own defection. When Talmadge Hayer,* who would later be convicted as one of the assassins of Malcolm X, was found residing at a Hilton Hotel not far from Wallace's residence shortly before Malcolm was murdered on February 21, 1965, police patrols were witnessed on the street of the home. A voice sounding like that of Wallace Muhammad,* the son of Elijah Muhammad and a close friend of Malcolm's, may have been the one calling the Wallace residence, asking for Malcolm, on the day of Malcolm's assassination, perhaps to warn him of the fate that awaited him.

SELECTED BIBLIOGRAPHY

Collins with Bailey, 1998; Evanzz, 1992; B. Perry, 1991.

Mfanya Donald Tryman

WASHINGTON, DINAH (Ruth Lee Jones). Born Ruth Lee Jones, this undisputed "Queen of the Blues" first crossed paths with Malcolm in the early 1940s at the Braddock Hotel in Harlem* during Malcolm's introduction to black Manhattan's nightlife. Malcolm, who was a teenager at the time, was mesmerized by the young songstress, who was described by her biographer as having a high clear voice resembling the tenor sax and the clarinet. Washington was also known for her forthright blues style with jazz qualities.

In his autobiography, Malcolm describes his first encounter with the singer during her appearance at the Savoy Ballroom* as the vocalist for jazz musician

Lionel Hampton.* At the time, Malcolm was working on the New Haven railroad, the Yankee Clipper, which ran from Boston to New York.* Young and immature, Malcolm was captured by the Harlem nightlife. He had never experienced such intensity on the dance floor, but his fascination with Harlem was heightened when Washington sang her famous recording "Salty Papa Blues." In his autobiography, Malcolm notes that he and Washington became great friends, although he did not explain the nature of their relationship.

SELECTED BIBLIOGRAPHY

Haskins, 1987; Hine, Brown, and Terborg-Penn, eds., 1993; Malcolm X with Haley, 1965; *New York Times*, December 15, 1963.

Nancy J. Dawson

WATTS, DANIEL. Daniel Watts was one of the many black intellectuals and contemporaries of Malcolm X in New York who supported black liberation movements. The two men knew each other well, bonded by mutual interests. An architect by education and training, Watts turned to African liberation causes in the late 1950s. In 1960, he founded an organization called On Guard to further liberation goals on the African continent; he claimed that the organization was active in several large American cities. Watts was especially agitated over the murder of Congolese leader Patrice Lumumba* and played a role in some of the demonstrations that protesters held at the United Nations* over the African leader's death. Activist leaders had been unable to enlist Malcolm's support for the demonstrations, though Malcolm was outraged over Lumumba's death.

Watts's greatest association with the militancy of the 1960s, however, resulted from his editorship of the journal the *Liberator*,* a popular black nationalist journal that published the articles of many of the era's most recognizable intellectuals and ardent supporters of black liberation, including James Baldwin,* Amiri Baraka (LeRoi Jones),* Harold Cruse, Robert Williams,* and, of course, Malcolm X. As editor in chief of the journal and part of the Harlem Writer's Guild, Watts also worked to further the New York aims of the Freedom Now Party (FNP),* though his own involvement in the party's internal dissension led to a failed and misguided effort to start a rival political organization and eventually the FNP's demise. As it was with many of his associates, his political activity made him a target of Federal Bureau of Investigation* surveillance.

It was to Watts that Malcolm broached the subject of pursuing in behalf of blacks a genocide charge against the United States at the United Nations. Watts, whom one biographer claims was familiar with the workings of the United Nations, reportedly advised Malcolm of the futility of such an effort, given the American government's influence with many of the member nations. During the last year of his life, Malcolm and Watts were apparently in each other's company occasionally. Like many of Malcolm's other associates, Watts was concerned about Malcolm's prediction of his imminent death, but he too was helpless to do anything to prevent it. He was part of the large crowd that attended Malcolm's funeral* and left behind a record of the outpouring of affection that mostly blacks displayed for their fallen leader.

SELECTED BIBLIOGRAPHY

Cruse, 1967; Daniels, ed., 1982; Goldman, 1979; O'Reilly (Gallen, ed.), 1994; Woodard, 1999.

Robert L. Jenkins

WECHSLER, JAMES. James Wechsler was a *New York Post* editor who had a controversial encounter with Malcolm shortly before the latter's death. The conflict grew out of the death of a prominent white minister from Cleveland, Ohio, the Reverend Bruce Klunder,* who as a participant in a Congress of Racial Equality* protest demonstration against the city's segregated schools was accidentally run over and killed by a bulldozer. Following a speech that Malcolm made in April 1964 at the Militant Labor Forum,* a white member of the audience rose and suggested to Malcolm that he lead the audience in a moment of silence in special recognition of Klunder. Malcolm, who had been in Cleveland the day of Klunder's death, responded to the suggestion acridly, showing a side of him that appeared callous to the memory and effort of a white liberal* working for black uplift. In a brief exchange that soon included Wechsler, Malcolm indicated that he could show no special deference to any white person for such a sacrifice when 22 million blacks daily were suffering similar tortures. In Mississippi,* African Americans Medgar Evers,* Emmett Till,* and Mack Charles Parker were lynched; even his father had been murdered, and no one gave them special honors. It was past the time, Malcolm said, that whites should die in the cause of black liberation.

Malcolm's irritated logic did not augur well with Wechsler. A notable northern white liberal, someone precisely among the class whom Malcolm frequently scorned publicly for what he generally described as insincerity, Wechsler struck at Malcolm through the press. The journalist attacked Malcolm first through the columns of his own press and later wrote a scathing criticism of Malcolm in *The Progressive*, a liberal monthly journal, where he denounced him as selfseeking and arrogant. Wechsler, who had first met Malcolm in 1963 during Malcolm's association with the Nation of Islam (NOI),* neither liked nor respected the Muslim* firebrand, and this was clearly manifest in his journal pieces. In his opinion, under Malcolm's leadership, blacks could hardly expect anything except to be led "down a dead-end road."

Strangely, however, Malcolm's death revealed another side of the newspaperman. Seemingly foregoing the wrath and disdain that anti-Malcolm forces often expressed about Malcolm at the news of his murder, Wechsler was relatively compassionate, writing a tempered account of their previous confrontation and articulating a rather veiled admiration for Malcolm's genius and leadership qualities. More revealing, Wechsler expressed disappointment about what others, including himself, might have learned from Malcolm, had they been more open-minded.

SELECTED BIBLIOGRAPHY

DeCaro, 1996; Malcolm X (Breitman, ed.), 1970a; *New York Post*, April 13, 1964; Vernon, 1968.

Robert L. Jenkins

"WEST INDIAN" ARCHIE. As a young, brash, hip, and enthusiastic "student," Malcolm X was to be "educated" in the ways of the "Big Apple" slicksters by older and more experienced hustlers on the streets and in the enclaves of Harlem.* The streets were filled with many young "hotheads" who blew off steam "at the drop of a hat." However, the real hustlers were calm and universally feared and respected. This group included such notables as "Black Sammy," "Bub" Hewlett, "King" Padmore, and "West Indian Archie." West Indian Archie was a member of the noted "Forty Thieves," who specialized in supplying their clientele with the finest of clothes for very reasonable prices.

Archie, according to Malcolm, was impressed with "Detroit Red," one of Malcolm's street nicknames before converting to Islam,* and took him on as a prodigy. West Indian Archie was also a genius with numbers. A numbers runner,* Archie was unique because he mastered the technique of remembering all of his daily "plays" and never wrote numbers down. Therefore, he was never susceptible to arrest for having number slips on his person. It is ironic that West Indian Archie and Malcolm, given this close association, would nearly kill each other because of a misunderstanding over a numbers bet. Years later, after Malcolm's conversion to the Nation of Islam (NOI)* and Archie's retirement from the streets, the two reminisced about the "old days." Malcolm often used Archie in educational settings to illustrate how the two had been "victims of the white man's society" and how under different circumstances many black minds, similar to their own, could have benefited the world with contributions in mathematics and science.

SELECTED BIBLIOGRAPHY

Malcolm X (Epps, ed.), 1968; Malcolm X with Haley, 1965.

Horace Huntley

WHEN THE WORD IS GIVEN. *When the Word Is Given* is the title of a book written by black journalist-activist Louis E. Lomax,* published in 1963. This book is the story of the origin and rise of the Black Muslims* in America and the leaders, Elijah Muhammad* and Malcolm X, who stood in the forefront of this insurgency organization.

Biographical sketches are provided of W. D. Fard,* Elijah Muhammad, and Malcolm X in the first part of the book. The work then traces the Nation of Islam* back to W. D. Fard, the mystical peddler of silks and satins in the

Depression-era black neighborhoods of Detroit, Michigan.* Fard, who appeared to be of Middle Eastern or Arab origin, greatly influenced the thinking and beliefs of Muhammad and brought the message of Islam* to Muhammad. Lomax, also the author of *The Negro Revolt*, provides a good early account of the organizational practices, religious rituals, dogma, and beliefs of Black Muslims.

The second major part of the book focuses primarily on the speeches of Malcolm X but includes one by Elijah Muhammad in Atlanta. The other speeches by Malcolm cover ones given at Harvard,* Atlanta University, Queen's College, and Yale and at a Harlem street rally* in New York City. The book concludes with an interview of Malcolm X by the author, who knew Malcolm on a personal as well as professional level.

SELECTED BIBLIOGRAPHY
Lomax, 1963, 1968, 1971.

Wanda T. Williams and Mfanya Donald Tryman

WHITE CITIZEN'S COUNCIL. The White Citizen's Council was initially organized in Indianola, Mississippi, in response to the 1954 *Brown v. Board of Education, Topeka, Kansas** decision. In attendance at the first meeting were respected white businessmen as well as the rabble-rouser element associated with the physical terrorism that characterized the image of a racist, white Mississippi.* The conservative element carried the day and mouthed disavowal of physical violence. However, just as plain as that disavowal was the threat and eventual practice of using "economic terrorism" against African Americans who insisted upon utilizing the *Brown* decision to ensure the adequate education of their children. Landlords evicted, employers fired, and wholesalers refused to sell or provide credit to those black people that insisted upon becoming a functional part of a predominantly white society.

Malcolm frequently criticized the White Citizen's Council, regarding them as no better than the Ku Klux Klan.* The fact that some might have respected the white middle- and upper-class contingent of professionals that largely comprised the body, the so-called Uptown Klan, mattered little to him because these people also sought to deny black social, political, and economic elevation in the South.* And some sought to do so violently. Malcolm declared before a group of black Mississippi youth visiting Harlem* in December 1964 that as long as groups like the White Citizen's Council committed violence against blacks, it was unfair to urge nonviolence for blacks. In 1965 in Alabama the second trial of those accused of killing the white Michigan housewife, mother, and civil rights* volunteer in the Selma campaign, Viola Liuzzo, contained eleven jurors who were or had been members of the White Citizen's Council. Despite the overwhelming evidence against the defendants, after two hours of deliberation, the White Citizen's Council–dominated jury found them not guilty. Malcolm would suggest that these examples, at the least, represented the social disdain for blacks by whites. In a broader sense, it was evidence of the deterioration of American society.

SELECTED BIBLIOGRAPHY

Ashmore, 1982; Kennedy, 1978; Malcolm X (Breitman, ed.), 1965; Malcolm X (Epps, ed.), 1968; Malcolm X with Haley, 1965.

Horace Huntley

WHITE CONSCIOUS. Malcolm often used the conscious of his white listeners to attack the racist social policies that existed in the United States. Previously, few African American leaders had effectively forced white Americans to examine their own individual racial attitudes. Malcolm explained that many whites considered themselves to be fair-minded and racially tolerant, but they failed to look upon their economic and social positions as a product of racial privilege. He claimed that white Americans would not change their social attitudes until they felt individually responsible for the actions of the entire white race. White guilt became one of Malcolm's most powerful tools in his attempt to expose whites to their own immoral conduct toward blacks. Liberal white Americans began to examine their own racial attitudes and preconceptions. Malcolm successfully made race and racism a daily issue and reality in the lives of many American whites. The attack on the white conscious also made whites aware of the vast cultural and economic differences that separated the races. Among a growing number of white Americans, the United States ceased being a homogenous white culture and became a country of varied cultures and ethnic groups.

SELECTED BIBLIOGRAPHY

Blauner, 1989; Caditz, 1976; Campbell, 1971; Fager, 1967.

James W. Stennett

WHITE DEVILS. One of the favorite idioms of members of the Nation of Islam (NOI)* was a reference to Caucasians as "white devils." This was a reference to the demonology and mythology taught by the NOI in which a mad scientist created an evil people 6,600 years ago, supposedly the white race. Presumably, the white race, evil by nature, would rule the world for 6,000 years, which was to end in the early twentieth century.

Malcolm and the NOI used the phrase "white devil" as a part of their lexicon and mechanism of recruitment to proselytize new members. All of the evils of modern society that blacks encountered, whether it was drugs, alcoholism, prostitution, poverty, poor housing, unemployment, racism, and other social ills, were blamed on the white devil. Malcolm was exposed to this devil premise while still in prison,* and it seemed to make sense to him. He and other ministers constantly emphasized to potential recruits that the white devil was responsible for all of the problems that blacks encountered. Not only was this phrase a major tool in recruitment, but it proved critical in keeping Black Muslims*

Malcolm speaking before a largely white audience of college students. ©
Bettmann/CORBIS.

unified against a common enemy. Since most of their clientele were low-income
and poor blacks, as a group typically scorned in American society, this reasoning
seemed to make complete sense to new recruits as well as established members.
When Malcolm went "fishing"* for new recruits, or was lecturing behind the
podium, he would often accentuate the fact that all of the social, political, and
economic power in the United States and the Western world was controlled by
white devils. Since it was clear that most of the positions of economic and
political power were controlled by whites, it was hard to refute his reasoning.

   Even publicly, Malcolm X, Elijah Muhammad,* and later Louis Farrakhan,*
Muhammad's successor, referred to Caucasians as white devils in their pronun-
ciations, news releases, radio talk shows, press conferences, debates, and other
arenas. *Muhammad Speaks*,* the official newspaper organ of the NOI in the
1960s, often ran cartoons and caricatures showing whites with pointed noses,
horns, and an arrow or point on the end of tails. Such boldness became one of
the factors involved in the labeling of members of the NOI as a "hate group."
Once Malcolm converted to Sunni Islam* and became an orthodox Muslim,*
he dropped the white devil rhetoric from his lexicon.

SELECTED BIBLIOGRAPHY

Gallen, ed., 1992; Hitti, 1970; Levinsohn, 1997; Muhammad, 1965.

Mfanya Donald Tryman

WHITE LIBERALS. In both his public and private utterances, Malcolm X frequently singled out for criticism specific classes of blacks whom he considered hostile to the race's interests. Middle-class blacks,* so-called Uncle Toms* (modern version of slave-era blacks whose identity with and deference to whites subordinated their interest as well as the race's interest), black intellectuals, and the nationally recognized civil rights* leaders were among those whom Malcolm typically targeted. Understandably, he bitterly denounced white racists who openly strove to prevent the elevation of the black masses, but to the chagrin of many whites and blacks, Malcolm did not leave unscathed white liberals. In many ways, Malcolm equated whites who were regarded as liberal on the race issue as insincere at best and no different than the avowed racists at worst. It was this group, Malcolm would often declare, that told blacks that they supported their advancement but who actually sought to keep the "knee-grow" (Negro) subjugated and dependent. They made promises to the race, and though they might have treated them slightly better, most of their promises went unfilled. These were the whites, Malcolm said, who were the first to run out of the better neighborhoods when blacks integrated them; they simply did not wish to be around them, and subsequently, as history showed, the community became a ghetto.

It was the liberal white political leaders for whom Malcolm expressed the greatest contempt. Presidents Abraham Lincoln, John F. Kennedy,* and Lyndon B. Johnson* led the group as the most obvious of those who duped blacks about being their friends. President Lincoln pronounced the Emancipation Proclamation, yet blacks a hundred years later were still not free; white liberals in Congress prompted the Reconstruction amendments, he said, yet blacks were still striving for acceptance as American citizens. Had each of them accomplished what they said, or what many thought they accomplished, there would clearly have been no need for additional laws to give black people the equal rights that supposedly they had already acquired. Even the U.S. Supreme Court displayed similar characteristics; it clearly had the power to enforce the U.S. Constitution when it came to black civil rights, but it blatantly refused to order the South's* public schools immediate desegregation because the justices own racial proclivities did not differ materially from professed southern segregationists. It was ridiculous, Malcolm said in 1963, for the schools to still be segregated nearly ten years after the *Brown** decision.

Fundamentally, Malcolm believed that the liberals were in a terrible predicament because of their need to please both the racists and the integrationists: It was a case, he said, of "smiling at one" while "whispering to the other." Because some of these whites believed they were nobly making sacrifices for blacks with their superficial support, they also thought they had the right to dictate both the aims and the tactics of the black struggle; in most cases neither coincided with legitimate black goals or effective strategies. Only when African Americans learned of the importance of internationalizing their struggle by elevating it to one of human rights* rather than civil rights, Malcolm would suggest, would it be easy to abandon the effort to ally with duplicitous or misguided white liberals who controlled the civil rights movement.*

SELECTED BIBLIOGRAPHY

Carson (Gallen, ed.), 1991; Malcolm X (Clark, ed.), 1992; Malcolm X (Perry, ed.), 1989; *Militant*, June 22, 1964, September 14, 1964; *New York Amsterdam News*, November 17, 1962.

Robert L. Jenkins

WHITE MEDIA. From his earliest days in public life, Malcolm X was intensely cognizant of the power of the media. He was fully aware that the white media would avail itself of every opportunity to make all that he uttered and did privy to the world. Malcolm's ascent into the national limelight began in July 1959, following the airing of a documentary entitled "The Hate That Hate Produced,"* which suggested that black prejudice was prompted by white racism. Whites in New York City, where the documentary was aired, were particularly distressed, if not horrified, for two reasons. The first was Malcolm's admission that Elijah Muhammad,* the Nation of Islam (NOI)* leader, taught that the serpent in the Garden of Eden was actually in the image of a white man and not a snake. More disturbing still, and the second reason for white horror, was the revelation from the documentary that students of the University of Islam* in Chicago, Illinois,* at all grade levels were taught whites were devils.

Following the controversial documentary, the NOI became instantly newsworthy. Several national weekly publications began immediate and extensive coverage of the Black Muslims.* For his part, Malcolm was not only asked to host a weekly talk show at a Harlem* radio station, but he was increasingly besieged by the media. This media attention and coverage quickly catapulted Malcolm into national prominence, thereby enabling him to speak often and directly to White America. The mass media assumed, of course, that such coverage would allow it to expose the NOI and Malcolm as frauds, racists, demagogues, and subversives. Malcolm, however, cultivated the press much like a seasoned and experienced politician. He skillfully manipulated his journalistic pursuers by providing them with snippets of sensationalism, which only intensified the pursuit. Malcolm's success at this media gamesmanship allowed him to keep the NOI riveted in the national consciousness and at the same time plead the case of the black man's plight in America in a historical as well as contemporary context.

Malcolm's willingness to engage the media on occasion led to reprimands and censure, as in the case of comments made after President John Kennedy's* assassination. In response to a reporter's question about the assassination, Malcolm suggested it was a case of "the chickens coming home to roost."* The public reaction among blacks and whites was one of outrage, prompting Muhammad to ban Malcolm from any public speaking, including his weekly sermon at the Harlem* temple, which began what was to become a permanent rift between the two.

Between 1959 and 1964, Malcolm had succeeded in generating precisely the kind of public persona he sought via the media. But his increasingly strained relationship and ultimate break with the NOI no doubt gave him pause for thought as to the public persona he had purposely projected over the years. Indeed, some of Malcolm's public statements prior to his death suggest that he was reevaluating his image and hoping it could be recast in certain respects. Apparently, too, Malcolm thought he, as much as the media, was to blame for his image, both having endeavored to manipulate the other for their own vested interest. Ironically enough, it is that very image/persona with which Malcolm was seemingly concerned that has endeared, if not immortalized, him in the eyes of many African Americans.

SELECTED BIBLIOGRAPHY

Barnette, 1965; Cone, 1991; *New York Village Voice*, February 25, 1965; B. Perry, 1991; Shabazz, 1969; T'Shaka, 1983; S. Weiss, 1977.

Dernoral Davis

WHITNEY, GEORGE 28X. George 28X Whitney was a former Black Muslim* who was a personal bodyguard of Malcolm X. He was on the scene the day of Malcolm's assassination and scrutinized and questioned a number of people who entered the Audubon Ballroom* on that fateful Sunday afternoon. Because Malcolm had instructed his security detail not to search audience members for weapons, Whitney was confined to asking questions. He did identify one Fruit of Islam* member who had forgotten to remove his identifying pin, and Whitney requested that he take off the pin if he wanted to stay to hear Malcolm speak.

As the assassination plot unfolded against Malcolm, Whitney was one of two bodyguards that moved from the back of the ballroom to quell a disturbance in the audience as other bodyguards converged upon the two men involved in what appeared to be an altercation. Whitney, like the other bodyguards, did not realize that the event was staged and that the assassins were left with an unfettered aim of Malcolm for their deadly assault. Once the shooting took place, and Malcolm lay dying on the stage, Whitney was able to slow down one of the fleeing assassins as he left the Audubon Ballroom by grabbing him by the collar. As the angry crowd continued to assault the man, several policemen came to his rescue, with one of them firing a shot into the air. This froze the crowd and allowed the police to get the man into a squad car. Whitney testified that he saw Talmadge Hayer,* one of three convicted assassins, in the ballroom that fateful day.

SELECTED BIBLIOGRAPHY

Friedly, 1992; Goldman, 1979.

Mfanya Donald Tryman

Longtime head of the NAACP, Roy Wilkins
and the conservative civil rights leadership
were often Malcolm's target of biting criticism. Library of Congress.

WILKINS, ROY. With the death of Walter White in 1955, Roy Wilkins became
executive secretary of the National Association for the Advancement of Colored
People (NAACP),* serving in this capacity until 1977. He was proud of the
NAACP's team leadership approach, in which he led the administrative operation and Thurgood Marshall* the legal one. His racial philosophy was integration, and his primary civil rights* approach was litigation. Unlike Martin Luther
King, Jr.,* he believed the Ghandian approach would only work in places like
Montgomery, Alabama, where blacks were in the majority. Unlike Malcolm X,
he saw black nationalism* as suicidal. Yet Wilkins respected Malcolm X as a
leader, believing he was a masterful debater. He contended that none of the
black leaders of the period could come near Malcolm X in debate, including
King. The closest black leader to Malcolm, according to Wilkins, was George
Schuyler.* Schuyler, like Malcolm, who had a quick wit and sharp tongue, was
a well-known journalist and activist who in the 1960s represented the extreme

Right. Wilkins received numerous invitations to speak at Malcolm's meetings, just as other leaders did. While he never accepted the invitations, he did take them seriously enough to include a response.

Wilkins had tremendous respect for Malcolm as a man, especially his puritanical preaching and advocacy of developing black businesses. However, he did not agree with Malcolm's hard line answers to racial problems, such as the belief that all whites were devils, his generalization that the black church was "devil-in-chief," his anti-Semitism, or his views about black separatism. A major player in the historic 1963 March on Washington,* Wilkins criticized Malcolm for being in the city but said that he was not surprised to find him there, insinuating that Malcolm had a penchant for publicity. News of Malcolm's death surprised Wilkins, and during an impromptu news conference following the news, Wilkins became one of the first leaders to tie Malcolm's death to "international implications." Though Wilkins seldom had positive things to say about him, he did not engage in a war of words against Malcolm. For Wilkins, Malcolm made an outstanding contribution to the civil rights movement* by forcing whites to deal with moderate black leaders, realizing that Malcolm X was the alternative. He was not opposed to saying so.

SELECTED BIBLIOGRAPHY

J. Anderson, 1997; Branch, 1988; Fairclough, 1987; Lowery and Marszalek, eds., 1992; Matney, ed., 1978; Wilkins with Mathews, 1982.

Lawrence H. Williams

WILLIAMS, JOSEPH. Joseph Williams was a lawyer, along with co-counsel William Chance, for Norman 3X Butler,* one of three defendants tried for the murder of Malcolm X. Williams and Chance were both court-appointed lawyers for Butler and as such were on a statutory fee of only $2,000 each for the trial. Williams had no witness list, and tried unsuccessfully to advance the theory that a discontented faction of Malcolm X supporters was really responsible for the assassination. Williams was also a lawyer for the Nation of Islam (NOI)* in trying to get Malcolm evicted from his home in East Elmhurst,* New York.

Williams wanted an investigation by the district attorney and the grand jury to locate the source of a mysterious check sent to his client for "a job well done" after Malcolm's murder. The check was made out to Butler for $10,000, and a note was sent with it. After it was traced, the check turned out to be counterfeit and was written on the Harlem* Progressive Labor Party account, though the account had been closed for several years. Williams asserted that the check was an attempt at character assassination of Butler and/or the Progressive Labor Party. No action was taken as the result of Williams's request.

SELECTED BIBLIOGRAPHY

Friedly, 1992; Goldman, 1979; *New York Times*, April 15, 1966.

Mfanya Donald Tryman

WILLIAMS, MR. Malcolm X had a number of experiences as a teenager that had a great influence on his life. After relocating to Mason, Michigan,* from Lansing, Michigan,* and staying with Mr. and Mrs. Swerlin, his foster parents, Malcolm was enrolled in Mason Junior High School,* a school that was almost all white in a town that was almost all white except for one black family who had children in lower grades than Malcolm. Mr. Ostrowski,* his English teacher, and Mr. Williams, his history teacher, would both have a profound impact on Malcolm's thinking and attitude toward whites. Malcolm was one of the top students in the eighth grade. He had a good relationship with his white classmates, who routinely called him "nigger," not meaning it as a racial slur but uttered as a commonplace expression among whites when making reference to blacks in Mason at the time. Malcolm often bought candy for his classmates from a part-time job that he had. But Mr. Williams, Malcolm recalls, was fond of telling "nigger jokes," which always degraded African Americans and humiliated Malcolm.

In fact, the first week of school, Malcolm recalls, when he walked into the classroom, Mr. Williams starting singing a song about "niggers" in the cotton field who did not steal. Malcolm did not like Mr. Williams's characterization of African Americans in the jokes that he often told the class, which always portrayed blacks as indolent, stupid, and shiftless. When Mr. Williams talked about black history,* he did it in a comical way to indicate that their contributions were worthless. Malcolm specifically remembered Mr. Williams telling the white students in his history class that black people had feet so big that when they walked, they did not leave footprints but holes in the ground. Mr. Williams, Malcolm contended, could not control himself for his laughter. While Malcolm continued to like history, it became clear that he was not fond of Mr. Williams. The experience in this class, as well as others in junior high school, made Malcolm withdraw from most whites, including the teachers and the classmates with whom he had established a friendship in Mason, Michigan.

SELECTED BIBLIOGRAPHY
Malcolm X with Haley, 1965; B. Perry, 1991.

Mfanya Donald Tryman

WILLIAMS, ROBERT FRANKLIN. Drafted to the chairmanship of the Union County, North Carolina, chapter of the National Association for the Advancement of Colored People (NAACP)* in 1956, Robert Williams vocally advocated the use of black violence and armed self-defense* to combat attacks by white "racist terrorists" such as the Ku Klux Klan.* His language eventually led to his dismissal from the NAACP. In 1961 a state grand jury indicted him for allegedly kidnaping Mr. and Mrs. G. Bruce Stegall during an antisegregation riot in his hometown. He fled the country and found political asylum in Cuba.* A Marxist, Williams spent the next eight years of his life traveling to various communist nations, speaking against foreign and domestic policies of the United States.

It is not clear if Malcolm ever personally met Williams, although he claimed in a 1964 radio interview show that Williams was a "very good friend of mine." But he was certainly aware of the controversy surrounding Williams in North Carolina. While in Ghana on his 1964 African tour, the Chinese ambassador honored Malcolm with an official state dinner. Afterward films celebrating the Chinese Revolution* and China's support of the black American struggle were shown; one of them included clips and comments by Williams, whose views on blacks arming themselves Malcolm later acknowledged. He approved of Williams's strong stand on the right to armed self-defense. In 1964 on a Philadelphia talk show, he defended Williams against such critics as Martin Luther King, Jr.,* praising Williams for making a historic though premature stand in following his own armed self-defense philosophy. Because a large segment of the black masses seemed to be rejecting the methods of the nonviolent civil rights movement,* Williams, like Malcolm, had simply been "ahead of his times."

SELECTED BIBLIOGRAPHY

Barksdale, 1984; Brisbane, 1974; Forman, 1985; Malcolm X with Haley, 1965; Meier, Rudwick, and Bracey, eds., 1971; R. Williams, 1962; Wolfenstein, 1993.

James W. Stennett

WILSON, GERTRUDE. Wilson was a liberal white newspaper journalist whose popular column "White on White" appeared regularly during the 1960s in the *New York Amsterdam News*.* Wilson was among a corp of white media* figures with whom Malcolm X apparently enjoyed a relatively close relationship during the latter years of his life, though he left no personal account of the basis or extent of their association. Wilson also greatly admired Malcolm's wife Betty Shabazz,* establishing a personal relationship with her that was rather unusual given Betty's tendency not to maintain strong ties with personage linked to Malcolm professionally. Despite the misinformed views about Malcolm that whites often entertained, Wilson hardly fit into that mold. She wrote passionately about Malcolm and honorably defended him in death from the harsh criticism of fiercely anti-Malcolm voices like that of Carl T. Rowan,* director of the United States Information Agency.* Malcolm's life and work, and especially his manliness, she wrote, had significant meaning for black people in Africa and throughout the diaspora. He was not only highly regarded by his friends but even among many who were reluctant to openly acknowledge their admiration for him. Perhaps Wilson had a special sensitivity to Malcolm, his work, and his ideas because of her association with the African American community through her featured column in the black press. Clearly, however, she understood the extent of Malcolm's influence among his people long before some scholars and other students of the black icon would detail it in the decades following his assassination.

SELECTED BIBLIOGRAPHY

DeCaro, 1996; *New York Amsterdam News*, February 27, March 6, 1965.

Robert L. Jenkins

WINCHELL, WALTER. Walter Winchell was one of the most recognizable personalities in the print media and on radio between the 1930s and the 1960s. During the period, his gossip columns and commentaries went literally into millions of American homes via syndicated newspapers, over the air waves, and eventually via national television broadcasts. Based in New York City, Winchell could often take the most caustic course in his analysis of a variety of topics and assessment of personalities. This was certainly true about Malcolm X. Like so many in the press, Winchell was aware of Malcolm's work and ideas but apparently paid little attention to him on a regular basis. He was, however, agitated over a callous statement that Malcolm made regarding the death of a white minister, the Reverend Bruce Klunder,* a civil rights* activist who was tragically killed in Cleveland, Ohio, in 1964 when a bulldozer ran over him. Already a controversial media issue because the incident angered noted liberal white journalist James Wechsler,* Winchell joined in the condemnation, similarly criticizing Malcolm in his news column. Black supporters quickly responded to the Winchell bashing, noting his lack of understanding of Malcolm and the fervor that he often expressed in support of his work for his people.

But it was Winchell's response to Malcolm's murder that clearly tabbed him as vehemently anti-Malcolm and unappreciative of his influence. Winchell recounted Malcolm's earlier criminal life for his readers and excoriated the fallen leader as "a petty punk" who became little more than a hate monger. Winchell found nothing to be remorseful about in Malcolm's death, and he erroneously told his readers that Malcolm's murder had nothing to do with ideological differences with fellow Black Muslims* but resulted instead from a rift over the sect's property holdings. Winchell failed to understand the influence that Malcolm had among his people and the commitment and passion that defined his efforts; he was also hardly atypical among whites who refused to acknowledge the changes that had occasionally marked Malcolm's adult life.

SELECTED BIBLIOGRAPHY

Les Brown, 1977; DeCaro, 1996; Settel, 1967.

Robert L. Jenkins

WINDOM, ALICE. A sociologist educated at Ohio University and the University of Chicago, Windom came from a family of university professors in St. Louis, Missouri. In 1962, shortly after the independence of Ghana, she moved to this West African republic bent on establishing a community of African social workers. Other less professional and demanding work, however, would command her time. For several years she lived in the capital city of Accra, one of approximately 200 black American expatriates who had accepted the invitation of Ghanaian president Kwame Nkrumah* to reconnect to their ancestral African homeland.

Windom first met Malcolm in the early 1960s after attending a meeting where he had lectured in the Nation of Islam's* Chicago* temple. Like so many other young activists excited about the vibrancy of the black rights struggle, Windom left the meeting impressed with Malcolm's oratorical skills and his militant views. Even in Africa she kept abreast of Malcolm's work and was enthusiastic about the prospects of seeing him again in Africa during his 1964 visit to Ghana. On his trip, Malcolm visited the home of the black novelist, playwright, and journalist Julian Mayfield,* the nominal leader of Accra's black American community, who was hosting a reception for him. Windom was a key member of the "Malcolm X Committee," established to plan and coordinate Malcolm's visit in Ghana. Like many of the others present, she was mesmerized by the black celebrity as he told of his Hajj* to Mecca* and how it transformed his thinking about aspects of the white race and black nationalism,* his travels through Black Africa, and his plans to argue the plight of African Americans before the United Nations.* He was so impressed with Windom and several of the others that he met that he suggested that they return to the United States and teach other blacks what Africa had taught them.

Windom recorded many of the events of Malcolm's trip, including his speech at the University of Ghana and his meetings with top governmental officials. She spent much of her time taking official photographs of Malcolm during his visit, but the moments that they shared talking about the future of black people and Malcolm's continued activism in the United States bolstered their budding friendship. It also inspired her association with his Organization of Afro-American Unity (OAAU),* formed in Accra as the first African chapter during his visit in the country. By mid-1964 Windom had relocated to Ethiopia, where she saw Malcolm for the last time during his second visit of the year to Africa. By then Windom was working for the United Nations in the East African country and helping to build OAAU branches on the African continent, only to see them largely stillborn because of Malcolm's murder.

SELECTED BIBLIOGRAPHY

Angelou, 1986; Gallen, ed., 1992; Malcolm X (Breitman, ed.), 1970a; Malcolm X with Haley, 1965; Strickland (Greene, ed.), 1994.

Robert L. Jenkins

WOMEN, ROLE OF. *See* Theme Essay "Malcolm X and the Role of Women."

WOMEN IN AFRICA. The imposition of colonial rule and the fight for independence caused the male leaders of many African countries to involve women in every phase of the liberation movement. Many African leaders believed that the only way to become self-sufficient was to utilize all available manpower—men, women, and children—in the development of political, economic, and educational institutions. For African women, survival and the struggle for liberation were synonymous. Thus, it was, and continues to be, important that women be involved in the revolution* and nation-building process.

This is why Malcolm X's trips to Africa had a profound effect on his perspective on women. In countries like the Republic of Ghana,* Kenya,* Egypt,* and Tanzania, he noticed how progressive women were; and where the country was underdeveloped and backward, the women were underdeveloped and backward. Malcolm maintained that in African countries that opted for mass education and participation, there existed a more legitimate and progressive society. He was particularly complimentary of W.E.B. Du Bois's* widow, Shirley Graham Du Bois,* for the work she was doing as head of Ghanaian National Television.

Within traditional African and contemporary society, women are of an intrinsic value and form the link for continuity. African women's involvement in the revolutions affecting their countries made it possible for them to obtain positions of authority within various social, economic, political, and educational spheres.

SELECTED BIBLIOGRAPHY

Malcolm X (Perry, ed.), 1989; Malcolm X with Haley, 1965; Ogundipe-Leslie, 1994; B. Perry, 1991; Steady, 1981; Terborg-Penn, 1987.

LaVerne Gyant

WOMEN IN THE MUSLIM MOSQUE, INC. When Malcolm X founded the Muslim Mosque, Inc. (MMI)* following his break with Elijah Muhammad* in 1964, his goal was to establish a religious, moral, and cultural base for African Americans. Through the MMI, Malcolm X hoped to combine Muslim* practices with political action.

Women in the MMI came out of the Black Muslim* community. Black Muslims stressed that men and women were different and had separate social roles. Black Muslim men were obligated to respect women, who in return should be modest, particularly in their dress. Muslim women were instructed in "female-only" skills, like homemaking arts. In the temple women dressed in white and were seated separately from men.

The traditional Muslim structure was transferred to the mosque. The Muslim-oriented MMI failed to attract a large following. The membership never reached 100, and only about a dozen members were really active. Active women members served in the traditional positions like clerical work and light administration. They did not make the decisions but carried them out efficiently. This pattern was reinforced when the short-lived MMI became affiliated with orthodox Islam.* When Malcolm founded the Organization of Afro-American Unity (OAAU),* the role of women expanded and they occupied high-level administrative and organizational positions.

SELECTED BIBLIOGRAPHY

Breitman, 1967; Carson (Gallen, ed.), 1991; Clasby, 1974; Myers, 1993; B. Perry, 1991.

Carolyn Williams

WOMEN IN THE NATION OF ISLAM. With his conversion to Islam,*
Malcolm X reassessed and radically altered many of his traditional behavior
patterns and moral assumptions. His perception of women, especially African
American women, also underwent a fundamental transformation. While Malcolm initially continued to regard women as inferior to men, a view basic to
orthodox Islamic beliefs, he increasingly respected black women and viewed
their protection from abusive white males as a primary precept of the Nation of
Islam (NOI).*

The Islamic tradition in North America originated among some of the earliest
African slaves forcibly exported to the colonies. Although enslaved, African
Muslims* tenaciously clung to their theological ideals, even while losing their
personal freedoms and identities. With emancipation, African Americans sought
to recreate their own sense of community and religious beliefs separate from
their former slave owners. Organized religion offered blacks an opportunity to
develop their own values and beliefs independent from the dominant white society.

After hundreds of years of close interaction, however, African Americans
adopted certain cultural aspects of white society, especially ideas concerning the
role and status of women. In redefining their own identity, freedmen and freed-
women desired to replicate the separation of gender roles as defined by white
society. Ideally, men would resume the role as breadwinners, and women would
remain in the home and care for their husbands and children. This arrangement
offered many potential benefits for African American women, most importantly
protection and isolation from white males. Unfortunately, the institutionalization
of Jim Crow barred African American men from professional and well-paying
occupations, requiring that black women join the labor pool to support their
families. Many African American men resented their economic dependence on
black women, and negative stereotypical images of women emerged within the
black community.

These characterizations often depicted black women as bossy, critical, and
domineering. Before his Islamic conversion, Malcolm also held these negative
female stereotypes and considered women really weak and manipulative. During
Malcolm's childhood and adolescence two individuals prominently shaped his
views toward women—his mother and his half sister Ella Collins.*

In his autobiography, Malcolm X portrays the relationship between his mother
and father, Louise* and Earl Little,* as riddled with tension and physical abuse.
Earl often beat his wife when she questioned his decisions or flaunted her educational background. After the violent murder of Malcolm's father in 1931,

Malcolm sits in a courtroom with Nation of Islam women during the trial of several black Muslims in Los Angeles. © Bettmann/CORBIS.

Louise faced the formidable task of raising her children alone with little money and prospects for the dim future. For six years, she fought to keep her family together, but constant economic and emotional stress resulted in her complete mental breakdown. With her commitment to a state hospital, Malcolm and his siblings became "state children."

While Malcolm deeply loved his mother, her inability to support the family helped to formulate his views of women as weak and incompetent. Malcolm's half sister, however, challenged this assumption. Ella, a strong and independent woman, helped Malcolm and many other relatives relocate in the North. Malcolm respected Ella's character and cultural values. Malcolm, though, criticized Ella's outspoken nature and blamed her domineering personality for her previous failed marriages.

Even before his religious conversion, many of Malcolm's views toward women paralleled their role and definition within the NOI. Islam defines men as inherently strong and protective and women as innately weak and dependent. Based on this interpretation, Elijah Muhammad,* the founder of the NOI, barred women from political participation and all leadership roles. The NOI viewed women solely as wives and mothers and considered marriage and childbearing as religious duties. Within the family, wives obeyed and followed their husbands' decisions, and husbands respected and provided financial support for their wives.

Both male and female Muslims followed a strict, almost "puritanical," moral code. Islamic tenets forbade physical contact between nonrelated men and women, discouraged dating, and severely punished adultery and interracial liaisons. Muslim women bore a large responsibility for maintaining the morality of their fellow Islamic brothers. To discourage sexual fantasies, women wore floor-length dresses, head scarves, and no makeup. This attire not only served to mute sensual desires among Muslim males but also protected African American women from the advances of white men.

The NOI helped to fulfill the earlier desires of freedmen and women to implement separate ideological orientations within their communities. The NOI's economic cooperative programs and its members' patronage of Muslim businesses were designed to provide Muslim men with well-paying jobs, enabling husbands to solely support their wives and children. This freed Muslim women from working for often hostile and abusive white employers. Although women's social roles were restricted to the private sphere and discouraged their public contributions, Islamic tenants mandated that Muslim men respect and protect their fellow sisters within the home and the broader community. One historian of the movement, E. U. Essien-Udom,* claims that many black women found the NOI appealing because of the promise of this respect in the organization.

As a new NOI member, Malcolm X marveled over the respect and admiration accorded to black women. His previous experiences with women, however, still governed his general perception of them; he continued to view women as untrustworthy and weak and as barriers to black men's advancement. Muslim women often complained to Elijah Muhammad concerning Malcolm's sermons, criticizing women's inherent diabolical nature and urging black men to control "their" women to gain social respect.

With his marriage to Betty Shabazz* and later separation from Elijah Muhammad, Malcolm X reevaluated his views. In an interview with Alex Haley,* Malcolm expressed his love and trust in Betty. Malcolm claimed that only Islam provided its adherents with a true understanding of love based on the compatibility of attitudes, dispositions, behaviors, and thoughts. Islamic teachings stressed a person's inner nature rather than outside appearance.

After he broke with the NOI, Malcolm increased his contact and interaction with Muslims throughout the world. From observing Third World countries, Malcolm concluded that a country's progress was directly related to the social status accorded its women. If women lacked incentive and education, they inhibited the development of their children and therefore the nation. To incorporate this idea within his own community, Malcolm took the initiative and put women in leadership roles in the Organization of Afro-American Unity (OAAU).* Indeed, his sister Ella replaced Malcolm as head of the fledgling organization after Malcolm's assassination in 1965.

SELECTED BIBLIOGRAPHY
Burrow, 1992; Essien-Udom, 1962; Goldman, 1973; Haddad and Lummis, 1987; Lincoln, 1994; Malcolm X (Perry, ed.), 1989; McCloud, 1995.

Pattie Dillon

WOMEN IN THE OAAU. When the Muslim Mosque, Inc. (MMI)* failed to attract followers, Malcolm X founded the Organization of Afro-American Unity (OAAU),* loosely based on the Organization of African Unity (OAU)* and Marcus Garvey's* Universal Negro Improvement Association (UNIA).* Unlike the Islamic-based MMI, the OAAU was entirely secular. Its aim was to unite a variety of people, in part to promote human rights.* The immediate goal was to "internationalize" the American civil rights* struggle by taking it to the United Nations* and elevating it to the level of human rights concerns.

The inclusive nature of the OAAU allowed for a different level of participation for women and a greater focus on women's issues. The earlier black nationalist organization that served as a model for the OAAU, the UNIA, provided an important precedent for women activists. While lending sympathy and support to the early twentieth-century feminist movement (constructed primarily by privileged white women), Amy Jacques Garvey and women members of the UNIA concentrated more on the particular plight of women of the African diaspora. UNIA women leaders had influence in the decision-making process of the organization.

The women who responded to Malcolm X's call to create a nonreligious and nonsectarian human rights organization followed in the footsteps of their foremothers. Gloria Richardson Dandridge,* the Student Non-Violent Coordinating Committee (SNCC)* chapter director in Baltimore, helped write the OAAU charter. Although Malcolm X was the undisputed leader, Lynn Shifflet* (later one of the first African American television newscasters) was the nominal head of the organization. Maya Angelou,* who renewed her contact with Malcolm X during his travels on the African continent, wanted to help him develop the organization he envisioned, but Malcolm's premature death precluded her involvement.

Although many attended the rallies held by the OAAU, the organization had a small membership. The only component of the organization that actually functioned was the education committee. This committee reflected the OAAU focus on issues of particular concern to women and children. The charter statement composed by Dandridge and others listed the chief priorities as helping unwed mothers and improving the quality of the education of black children and adults.

Concerns with women's issues and their participation in the OAAU can be attributed to the fact that Malcolm X (by then known as El Hajj Malik El-Shabazz*) began to trust and rely on women in his family and beyond in the political arena. Association with individuals like Gloria Richardson Dandridge and Maya Angelou increased his respect for the intellectual competency and political activism of women. His awareness of the exploitation and oppression women were subjected to was heightened by his attempt to help two of the young women, Robin X and Heather X, who accused Elijah Muhammad* of seducing them and fathering children by them. It was especially his travels in Africa that opened his eyes to the possibilities that women offered in the black struggle. In Africa, women were playing leading roles in virtually all aspects of life, and this impressed Malcolm. He would claim that women were the most crucial element in determining whether a country would remain "backwards" or move progressively ahead.

Malcolm was killed in February 1965, less than a year after the MMI and OAAU were formed. His half sister Ella Collins* then proclaimed herself the "Caretaker Head" of the OAAU until a successor could be chosen. Her leadership provided a faint glimpse of the possibility of female activism in concert with one of the most vital and electric leaders America has produced.

SELECTED BIBLIOGRAPHY

Carson (Gallen, ed.), 1991; Malcolm X (Breitman, ed.), 1970a; Matthews, 1979; Myers, 1993; B. Perry, 1991; Strickland (Greene, ed.), 1994.

Carolyn Williams

WOODWARD, YVONNE LITTLE. Yvonne Little Woodward is the youngest sister of Malcolm X, born five years after Malcolm's birth when the Little family had moved to Lansing, Michigan.* In the aftermath of their father's death, as the family strove to work through the crisis of a fatherless household, Yvonne and Malcolm maintained a close sibling relationship. Understandably, at age nine, she found it traumatic when the family was broken up after their mother's commitment to a mental institution. But her ties to the family remained strong; and she later encouraged Malcolm and his other siblings to work toward achieving their mother's release from the mental facility. Early on, young Yvonne had acquired a fascination and healthy respect for Malcolm's natural leadership ability that would endure until his death. From Michigan, where she continued to live with her husband and family, she followed Malcolm's mercurial rise in the Nation of Islam (NOI)* and took pride in his accomplishments as one of America's most brilliant and recognizable leaders. She acknowledged that Malcolm had always been influential in her life but that influence increased once he became a Muslim* leader. She marveled over his ability to accurately analyze the plight and solutions to black urban problems. Yvonne had not been a member in the NOI. So, unlike the case with a couple of her siblings, apparently no estrangement developed between the two during the rift that Malcolm eventually had with the NOI. Like much of Black America, Woodward was saddened over her brother's murder. Although she and several others of her family members went to New York shortly after the slaying, alleged threats against their personal safety prevented them from attending the funeral.

SELECTED BIBLIOGRAPHY

Blackside/PBS, 1994; Collins with Bailey, 1998; Lee with Wiley, 1992; Strickland (Greene, ed.), 1994.

Robert L. Jenkins

WORLD COMMUNITY OF ISLAM IN THE WEST (WCIW). The World Community of Islam in the West (WCIW) was the name of the organization started by Wallace Muhammad.* Wallace would later change his name to Warith Deen Muhammad. He was one of the younger sons of Elijah Muhammad* and had been the heir apparent to the Nation of Islam (NOI)* after the death of his father in 1975. Warith took over the leadership of the NOI, after meeting with three of his brothers, with whom he had discussed the direction that the NOI would take in the post–Elijah Muhammad period. As an orthodox Muslim,* Warith began to reorient the former NOI toward a more traditional Islam,* which differed greatly in beliefs and practices from Elijah Muhammad's organization. One of the most significant changes was allowing whites to become members of the WCIW. This was a major change from the beliefs of the NOI that not only had refused to allow whites to join but had referred to them as "white devils."* Warith's efforts at reorienting the NOI may have been influenced by Malcolm, who was a close friend and orthodox Muslim as well. After his ouster from the NOI, Malcolm started the Muslim Mosque, Inc.* As with Malcolm, Warith's reorientation with the WCIW brought the wrath of some and the warmth of others.

In 1980 the World Community of Islam in the West was renamed the American Muslim Mission. The newspaper, which had originally been called *Muhammad Speaks** under the old NOI, was initially changed to *The Bilalian News* under the WCIW and after several other name changes became known as the *Muslim Journal* when the WCIW became the American Muslim Mission. The American Muslim Mission continued outreach programs, and unlike the old NOI that forbade its members from any type of political participation, it encouraged its members to become involved in politics. Malcolm had made numerous efforts to involve the NOI in politics before he was ousted, but his attempts were vetoed on every occasion by Elijah Muhammad. The Mission also continued economic development enterprises and engagement in economic investments. Their efforts were similar to Malcolm's emphasis on economic black nationalism,* which involved investment and ownership of economic enterprises in the black community. While Warith's efforts to deracialize Islam as practiced by American blacks has been successful in the context of the American Muslim Mission, the membership remains overwhelmingly black. The Mission is aware of this, and its ongoing ties to the black community are reflected in such things as clean-up campaigns in black ghettos and a black perspective in its newspaper. It advocates the same type of self-help that Malcolm supported. Like Malcolm, Warith was able to bring about a number of changes. Unlike Malcolm, he had no one over him to veto his policy initiatives as Malcolm had under Elijah Muhammad.

SELECTED BIBLIOGRAPHY

Estell, 1994; Gellner, 1983; M. Lee, 1996.

Mfanya Donald Tryman

WORLD WAR II. When America entered World War II in December 1941, black as well as white men were conscripted for service in the armed forces.

But for Malcolm X, who at this time was a pimp* and a hustler in Harlem,* New York, military service held little appeal. Blacks served in segregated units and were treated as inferior soldiers. Malcolm X had no desire to fight and perhaps die in what he saw as a white man's war.

When Malcolm X received his induction notice in 1943, he concocted a clever ruse in order to avoid military service. On the day in which he was to report to the induction center, he donned a zoot suit* and the demeanor of a psychopath. During his session with the army psychiatrist, Malcolm asserted that he was eager to join the army. His secret wish, he told the psychiatrist, was to be stationed in the American South* where he could organize his black comrades and kill some "crackers." The psychiatrist concluded that he was mentally unfit for military service. Soon after, Malcolm X received his 4-F card in the mail. Philosophically, Malcolm remained opposed to the draft. In prison* he had once debated against compulsory military training, and as a spokesman of the Nation of Islam (NOI)* he criticized blacks serving in the military for a country that accorded them few citizenship rights.

SELECTED BIBLIOGRAPHY

Malcolm X with Haley, 1965; B. Perry, 1991; Wynn, 1976.

Phillip A. Gibbs

WORTHY, WILLIAM. Trained as a journalist, William Worthy lived in New York City and had a public following in Harlem.* He was known in part for his radical writings. Worthy was the New York leader of the Freedom Now Party,* committed to running blacks for national as well as state and local offices. He was one of a number of speakers, along with Malcolm X, on the Northern Negro Grass Roots Leadership Conference* program on November 9–10, 1963. The conference was held in Detroit, Michigan,* as an alternative to the Northern Leadership Conference, which had rebuffed black nationalists like Malcolm X. When this occurred, the Reverend Albert B. Cleage, Jr.,* pastor of the Shrine of the Black Madonna, in conjunction with the Freedom Now Party and the Group on Advanced Leadership, decided to hold their own meeting. Worthy knew Malcolm X and was one of a number of leaders to whom Malcolm wrote in 1964, inviting him to attend the founding rally of the Organization of Afro-American Unity (OAAU)* on June 28, 1964.

While Worthy took his work seriously, he often displayed a lighter side. On one occasion in the early 1960s, Worthy had visited Boston, Massachusetts, and met with a number of black businessmen who had converted to Islam* and became members of the Nation of Islam (NOI).* Worthy had known these Muslims* before their conversion. Now they seemed so antiwhite. In a playful manner, Worthy reminded them that in 1955 they had given him a pin-up calendar of a nude Marilyn Monroe, a white movie star, and that he still had the poster. One of Worthy's featured articles on the NOI and Malcolm X appeared in *Esquire* magazine in February 1961 entitled "The Angriest Negroes."

SELECTED BIBLIOGRAPHY

Cone, 1991; DeCaro, 1998; Sales, 1994.

Mfanya Donald Tryman

WRIGHT, RICHARD. Richard Wright was one of the most accomplished and well-known black writers of the twentieth century. Although the novel was his genre, as a keen observer of the American and international scene, he also wrote occasional serious journal pieces and essays that dealt with social issues. The author of nearly a dozen books, he is best known for his prizewinning 1940 novel *Native Son* and autobiography *Black Boy*. Born in Natchez, Mississippi, and raised in Arkansas and Tennessee during the height of the segregated era, Wright understood from the perspective of both a victim and intellectual observer the pain of white racism, a theme central in his literature and key to understanding both his most accomplished books. During the 1930s, as a resident of Chicago* and later New York City, he became a communist, though his affiliation with the party was short-lived. His worldview about human rights* issues gave him wide recognition, both in the United States and abroad. By the time that Malcolm X had reached national prominence in the late 1950s, Wright had already left the United States to live in the more racially hospitable environment of Paris, France. By the end of 1960, the dawn of Malcolm's celebrated international status, Wright had already died.

If the literary sage was a personal hero of Malcolm's, Malcolm certainly left no knowledge about it. But Malcolm was likely aware of Wright; few black intellectuals could have escaped him. Besides, Richard and Malcolm had much in common. The two men, for example, were clearly concerned about the state of American race relations. Moreover, they mutually shared a great appreciation for what the African and Asian worlds tried to accomplish in 1955 when their leaders convened to denounce imperialism and advance the various independence movements at the Bundung Conference* in Indonesia. Wright wrote a book about the conference, published in 1956 as *The Color Curtain*, which, perhaps, Malcolm read. Malcolm often extolled the virtues of the conference and held it up as an example of what black Americans could accomplish if their leaders worked harmoniously to advance the race's peculiar plight.

In the summer of 1964, Malcolm visited Paris, where he spoke before a group of black expatriates, primarily artist and intellectuals, long disillusioned with America's racial order. While there he had the occasion to visit with Wright's daughter Julia, who entertained Malcolm in her home. Before he left the city he would also have the opportunity to meet with Wright's widow. Shortly thereafter, Paris's Noir cell, sympathetic to the plight of blacks in America and becoming increasingly conscious of international liberation movements, established a small branch of Malcolm's Organization of Afro-American Unity (OAAU)* in the city. French authorities denied Malcolm a second visit to Paris in early 1965. Presumably he would have had the occasion to visit again with Wright's family and other blacks in the Parisian community.

SELECTED BIBLIOGRAPHY

M. Alexander, 1988; Malcolm X with Haley, 1965; Stovall, 1996; R. Wright, 1956.

Robert L. Jenkins

X–Z

X SYMBOL. The Nation of Islam (NOI)* adopted the *X* as a symbol to replace the "slave" name of blacks who joined the religion. Malcolm Little's name became Malcolm X to signify his conversion to Islam* as a member of the Black Muslims.* For members who possessed the same first name, a number preceded the *X*, signifying the order of conversion. Hence, Malcolm 2X, 3X, 4X revealed the sequence in which men with the name Malcolm became members of the NOI.

The Black Muslim *X* was regarded as a "badge" representing the rejection of the slave name and the beginning of a symbolic search for one's ancestral identity. The letter *X* represents the unknown name because white slave masters stripped the ancestors of blacks of their original African names, customs, religions, and knowledge of self. Indeed, Malcolm even had trouble with the name "Negro" to identify blacks. Malcolm cited nationalities such as German and French, pointing out how they connected persons with a nation, a language, and a culture. There was no place on the globe called "Negro Land." Such examples were used to support the NOI position for blacks to reclaim their African names. Prior to officially assuming his *X*, a new convert was required to write a letter indicating that he had attended all of the scheduled and required temple meetings and that he "believed in the truth" as told in the services. Under NOI practices, after a period of time, the *X* is often replaced with an Arabic name, signifying a closer relationship with Islam. Hence, though Malcolm was almost always referred to as Malcolm X, when asked about his "last name," he would typically give it as Shabazz, especially after he made the Hajj.*

SELECTED BIBLIOGRAPHY

Lincoln, 1961; Malcolm X (Karim, ed.), 1971; Malcolm X with Haley, 1965.

Wanda T. Williams

YACUB, DR. According to the cosmological and theological beliefs of the Nation of Islam (NOI),* Dr. Yacub (sometimes spelled Yakub) was a brilliant but evil scientist who rebelled against Allah.* Born near Mecca* in 8400 B.C., Dr. Yacub resided in the Holy City, which, according to NOI lore, was founded by black people. Hard times had come to Mecca due to the machinations of Dr. Yacub. The authorities forced Dr. Yacub and his 59,999 followers into exile onto the remote island of Pelan in the Aegean Sea, west of Turkey. There, Dr. Yacub resolved to seek revenge for his outcast.

Over 6,600 years ago, according to the NOI belief, Dr. Yacub, the "big-head scientist," had conducted genetic experiments that eventually resulted in the creation of an inferior "bleached-out" white race who were really devils in disguise. This was accomplished through "grafting" the weak brown gene apart from the black gene in the Original Black Man. The creation of the white race was one that Dr. Yacub did not live to see, although he supposedly lived to be 152 years of age. Nonetheless, his devoted followers carried out his experiments to the letter. Black children were not allowed to live; only brown or light-skinned babies were not killed. Constant mixing of light and brown couples was conducted. If a dark-skinned baby was born, the child was immediately killed. The result over many generations was the creation of a white-skinned, blue-eyed inferior race, which eventually migrated back across the Arabian Peninsula, where they caused a great deal of disruption among the Meccans. The Meccans drove these so-called white devils* into Europe,* where they lived in caves and began to resemble apes.

The first to leave the caves and become civilized, Black Muslim* lore contends, were the Jews.* Later, others followed and Allah allowed this civilized white race to rule the world for 6,000 years, after which the original black race would be resurrected and returned to its rightful place of superiority. The end of the 6,000-year reign of the white race, according to the Black Muslims, occurred in 1914.

Since that time Allah had sent a Messenger in the form of Elijah Muhammad* to teach the "so-called Negro"* that he is the Original Man, a Muslim,* and that he must separate himself from the white devil, who has brainwashed him and held him in slavery.

The story of Dr. Yacub, whose name is very similar to the Hebrew patriarch Jacob, has long been a central tenet in the belief system of the Black Muslims. The sect's founder W. D. Fard* originated the mythology. According to the book that sets down the main beliefs and myths of the sect, *The Supreme Wisdom*, Dr. Yacub had founded the science of genetics 6,600 years before Gregor Mendel. He was also responsible for experiments that caused the creation of the moon.

Malcolm X initially learned about these beliefs from his sister Hilda (Little).* He followed those beliefs at first. His rhetoric before black and white audiences and in the press was filled with references to the white devils of Yacub history.

Almost all of his remarks publicly were prefaced with the term "the honorable Elijah Muhammad," whom he believed was the true prophet of Allah who had come to teach the so-called Negro the truth. However, Malcolm began to have doubts about Yacub when he broke with the NOI and visited other Muslim nations. None of these Muslim nations held similar views about a Dr. Yacub and the evolution of black and white races. Eventually, Malcolm outgrew those beliefs and rejected most of them in their entirety.

SELECTED BIBLIOGRAPHY

M. Lee, 1996; Lincoln, 1994; Magida, 1996; B. Perry, 1991.

Charles Pete Banner-Haley

YORTY, SAMUEL WILLIAM. Born in Lincoln, Nebraska, in 1909, Sam Yorty migrated to southern California in the late 1920s, where he graduated from Southwestern University Law School and quickly became a political force. During the era of the Great Depression* he won a seat to the state legislature and, following a World War II* stint in the air force, was elected to the U.S. House of Representatives. In 1961 Yorty won election as mayor of Los Angeles, then the nation's third largest city. A Democrat by party affiliation, Yorty, like many other political leaders outside of the South,* spoke favorably to the interests of black Americans, and they rewarded him with their support. This support, however, waned precipitously during the latter part of his term and subsequent administration. Much of the decline occurred because of numerous controversies that involved his solid support of the city's police chief, William Parker, hardly a favorite among black Los Angeles because of the department's consistent use of force and harassment practices in their communities. Yorty, known for his strong anticommunist politics, found an equally strong opponent of subversive groups in Parker. The police chief had a tendency of labeling virtually any militant group un-American and undertook deliberate steps to destroy them. It took him little time to so designate the Los Angeles Nation of Islam (NOI)* members as communists. Tensions between the NOI and Yorty's administration came to a head following the April 1962 death of unarmed Black Muslim* Ronald Stokes* by the police in a confrontation with NOI members outside the temple headquarters. During the shootout a police officer and a number of Muslims* were wounded.

Malcolm's association with Los Angeles began during the late 1950s after he established and helped develop the NOI in the central city, Temple Number Twenty-seven. For a while he wrote a regular column in the city's militant black newspaper, the *Los Angeles Herald-Dispatch.** Following Stokes's death, he returned to the city at Elijah Muhammad's* request to deliver the eulogy and to prevent the police-NOI affair from becoming more confrontational. Malcolm spoke all over the city during his visit and appeared on local television programs denouncing the atmosphere that led to Stokes's death and Los Angeles officials' handling of the whole affair. Understandably, Malcolm and Yorty had little appreciation for each other. While he was personally opposed to Muhammad's decision for the NOI to harness any vengeance, exchanges between Malcolm and Yorty became heated. Malcolm labeled the mayor as "a professional liar" and criticized his investigation of the conflict that exonerated Parker and the police of any wrongdoing. Clearly he said, Yorty and Parker were in "cahoots" with each other in brutalizing the black community. Yorty retaliated with invectives of his own. He regarded the NOI as a Nazi-type group and condemned them for teaching race hatred. He attempted to discredit Malcolm as the chief hate monger after acquiring a tape of a speech that Malcolm made before Los Angeles followers praising Allah* (God) for an airline crash that killed more than 120 whites. Long after the Stokes affair, Malcolm and Yorty continued to show disdain for each other. Though no other violent outbreaks necessitated Malcolm's appearance in the city, Yorty sought to recruit conservative black church leaders in his campaign to destroy the NOI chapter in Los Angeles. He failed in the effort.

SELECTED BIBLIOGRAPHY

Ainsworth, 1966; Clegg, 1997; Evanzz, 1992; Horne, 1995; Jamal, 1971; *New York Times*, July 27, 1962; Simitar Videos, 1994.

Robert L. Jenkins

YOUNG, ANDREW. A clergyman and civil rights* activist, Andrew Young is a native of New Orleans, Louisiana. At Howard University* and the Hartford Theological Seminary, he earned his Bachelor of Science and Bachelor of Divinity degrees, respectively. It was as a lieutenant of Martin Luther King, Jr.,* and a major official in the Southern Christian Leadership Conference (SCLC)* that Young first acquired a name for himself. In virtually every campaign that King launched after the Montgomery Bus Boycott, Young played a visible role. After the civil rights movement* ended, Young became a notable Georgia political figure and statesman. In 1972, he won a seat to Congress, the first African American to represent a Georgia district since the Reconstruction era. President Jimmy Carter in 1976 named him the first black to serve as ambassador to the United Nations;* from 1982 to 1990 he became the second African American elected to the office of mayor in Atlanta.

Young's acquaintance with Malcolm began before Malcolm became a nationally prominent figure. During the late 1950s as an employee of the National Council of Churches, Young met Malcolm in the Queens, New York, home of his journalist friend Louis Lomax.* Young was immediately struck by Malcolm's "intelligence" and "gentleness." The meeting had occurred just prior to television personality Mike Wallace's* 1959 documentary exposé on the Black Muslims,* "The Hate That Hate Produced."* The program helped to make Malcolm famous, but Young lamented the harsh and misleading portrayal of Malcolm, which he dubbed "a terrible distortion" of a "just man" trying to do good for his people. In Young's opinion, Malcolm was a genuine freedom fighter

Andrew Young was one of Martin Luther
King, Jr.'s chief aides. Library of Congress.

and he respected him for his commitment. Malcolm offered, Young would
later admit, potentially the best insight into problems confronting black urban
America.

Apparently the paths of Young and Malcolm crossed periodically. Young
claims, for example, that Malcolm visited the SCLC office in Atlanta whenever
he came to the city, though Malcolm made no more than casual references to
Young in his speeches and autobiography. Nevertheless, Young maintains that
he appreciated Malcolm's seriousness and always enjoyed the opportunity to
talk to him.

Positive impressions notwithstanding, Malcolm offered solutions to the Af-
rican American dilemma philosophically and tactically different from Young's.
These differences were potentially explosive during the 1965 Selma Voting
Rights campaign when Malcolm spoke before a large church rally at the invi-
tation of young Student Non-Violent Coordinating Committee* activists.
Alarmed over the prospect of Malcolm inciting violence in King's absence,
Young quickly diffused the possibility by recruiting two of King's closest as-
sociates, Baptist ministers James Bevel and Fred Shuttlesworth, to address the

gathering and by persuading the reluctant Coretta Scott King,* Martin King's wife, to also speak. Accounts vary about the effectiveness of Malcolm's presentation, but he really had no intention of aggravating an already tense situation in Selma. Clearly, however, he understood at the time, though expressed more disdainfully later, what had been Young's concern and especially the reason behind Coretta's presence in the church. Apparently, in Selma, Malcolm was continuing to moderate his views toward the civil rights* leadership in order to gain wider acceptance among them, a transition that was not lost on Andrew Young.

SELECTED BIBLIOGRAPHY

Branch, 1998; CBS News, 1992; Hampton and Fayer with Flynn, eds., 1991; Malcolm X (Clark, ed.), 1992; Sellers with Terrell, 1973; Young, 1996.

Robert L. Jenkins

YOUNG, WHITNEY M., JR. In 1961, Whitney Young became the executive director of the National Urban League.* Under his leadership, the league broke with its tradition by identifying more significantly with the activism of the civil rights movement.* To be sure, the League did not actively participate in demonstrations; rather, it negotiated between the demonstrators and the white power structure. Young spoke at the March on Washington* in August 1963 and, along with the other national civil rights* leaders sponsoring the march, was severely criticized by Malcolm X for participating in a white farce, "with white clowns, and black clowns." Malcolm's comments were typical of his views about the nonviolent civil rights movement and its leaders. But he seemed to have held more contempt for Young than he did for others, and his name-calling of Young was especially telling. In what Malcolm often tried to portray as a slip of the tongue, he sometimes referred to Young as "Whitey Young" or "Uncle Whitney." But Malcolm accused almost all of the leaders of being Uncle Toms* and sellouts, and Young seems not to have been overly offended by the connotations. Still, he struck back, on one occasion simply dismissing Malcolm and his views on racial separation* as belonging "to the past." An America with "two nations" in one was an idea a century old, he said.

After leaving the Nation of Islam (NOI),* Malcolm extended the olive branch to the national leaders. According to biographer Peter Goldman,* Malcolm "hungered" for acceptance "as a national leader," but he was ignored. In early 1965, Malcolm X met with a group of national civil rights leaders, including Young, and a friendship developed between the two men that led to several other meetings. Goldman stated that Malcolm actually liked Young as a person, believing he was "more down to earth" than the other leaders. Although he had once suggested in a late 1964 interview that Young lacked understanding of the black problem because he had not spent much time around the people he sought to lead, he eventually exclaimed that the Urban League leader was "blacker . . .

than his board room manners suggested." Malcolm's opinion of Young had apparently undergone a metamorphosis.

Young believed that Malcolm X played a valuable part in the 1960s civil rights movement, asserting, as other leaders often did, that Malcolm's "hell-raising" scared the more timid blacks into the National Urban League and the National Association for the Advancement of Colored People.* Young's effective use of the threat of "the iron fist of the militant" got results from white corporate executives, who feared being contacted by more militant blacks, such as Malcolm X.

SELECTED BIBLIOGRAPHY

DeCaro, 1996; Gallen, ed., 1992; Goldman, 1973; Malcolm X (Breitman, ed.), 1993; B. Perry, 1991; N. Weiss, 1989.

Lawrence H. Williams

YOUNG SOCIALIST ALLIANCE (YSA). Malcolm felt that youthful white groups such as the Young Socialist Alliance (YSA) could be instrumental in breaking down and eliminating racism. In an interview granted to Jack Barnes and Barry Sheppard, representatives of the YSA, on January 18, 1965, he cautioned, however, that this had to be done by having such groups go into white communities where there was a great deal of opposition to African American freedom, justice, and equality. The work of young white groups would be in these areas, Malcolm reasoned, not in black communities sympathizing with the plight of oppressed African Americans or by having young whites join black organizations. The problem, he said, was not with blacks but with whites. Malcolm felt that young people in general had a role to play in eliminating racism and oppression and often cited youthful revolutionary groups in other countries as examples.

The YSA, a mostly white organization, wanted Malcolm to consider a national speaking tour on college campuses during the year of 1965. Malcolm realized that students in general and many white students in particular on college campuses were more open-minded than the rank and file that he experienced in everyday life. Malcolm argued that if white radicals on college campuses were going to make a difference, however, they could not afford to be bought off by the government with jobs and other enticements. Hence, they would have to organize independently and keep their distance from professors and other agents who would do the government's bidding. Malcolm felt that white radicals committed to black liberation could serve as missionaries or revolutionaries. This was the message Malcolm conveyed to members of the YSA, an organization that he came into contact with the last year of his life.

SELECTED BIBLIOGRAPHY

Malcolm X (Breitman, ed.), 1992; Malcolm X (Clark, ed.), 1991.

Mfanya Donald Tryman

ZOOT SUIT. The zoot suit was a fashion fad made popular by African American youth in the early 1940s. The dress included baggy pants worn waist high, a long jacket with broad shoulders, wide-brimmed hat, and a long chain. "Zooters" used an exaggerated "jive speech" pattern and danced the boogie woogie, jitterbug, and Lindy Hop.* The black press and civil rights* leaders were extremely concerned about the negative effects of the zoot suit upon American society, obviously seeing the zoot suit culture as a reaction against white authority. They believed the zooters confirmed white negative stereotypes of blacks.

Like hundreds of thousands of African Americans before him, young Malcolm Little, when he arrived in the northern urban centers in 1940, acquired the typical ghetto attire, habits, and image, consisting of a zoot suit, conked hair, liquor, and smoking reefers.* He bought his first colorful zoot suit on credit, flashy attire that made him stand out. Apparently, he acquired several of the colorful outfits. The outfits gave Malcolm not only a new kind of identity but a real sense of pride. At age sixteen when he made his initial purchase, Malcolm's world, both his social and political world, expanded. Dressed in his hipster attire, he was well known in the Boston and New York nightclub scene. However, after becoming a Black Muslim,* Malcolm X criticized this phase of his life, claiming that in his zoot suit days he had simply been a clown, only he did not know it at the time.

SELECTED BIBLIOGRAPHY

Auerbach, ed., 1994; Kelley, 1994; Malcolm X with Haley, 1965; Tyler, 1994.

Lawrence H. Williams

BIBLIOGRAPHY

A&E Entertainment. *Biography: Malcolm X: A Search for Identity*. Video. (1995).

Abernathy, Ralph David, Sr. *And the Walls Came Tumbling Down: An Autobiography*. (1989).

Adamolekun, Lapido. *Sékoure Touré's Guinea: An Experiment in Nation Building*. (1976).

Adams, Alvin. "Malcolm Seemed Sincere About Helping Cause: Mrs. King." *Jet* (March 11, 1965): 28–30.

Ainsworth, Ed. *Maverick Mayor: A Biography of Sam Yorty, Mayor of Los Angeles*. (1966).

Aldon, Jesse Thomas Moore, Jr. *A Search for Equality: The National Urban League, 1910–1961*. (1981).

Alexander, Amy. *Fifty Black Women Who Changed America*. (1999).

"Alex (Palmer) Haley." In *Current Biography Yearbook*. Edited by Charles Moritz. (1977).

Alexander, Margaret Walker. *Richard Wright, Daemonic Genius: A Portrait of the Man, a Critical Look at His Works*. (1988).

"Alexander Palmer Haley.'" In *Who's Who among Black Americans*. Edited by Iris Cloyd. (1990).

Alkalimat, Abdul. *Malcolm X for Beginners*. (1990).

———. "Studies on Malcolm X." *Sage Race Relations Abstracts* 17 (November 1992): 4–22.

———, ed. *Perspectives on Black Liberation and Social Revolution: Proceedings of Malcolm X: Radical Traditions and a Legacy of Struggle Conference*. (1990).

Allen, Robert L. *Black Awakening in Capitalist America: An Analytical History*. (1969).

Ambrose, Stephen E. *Nixon: The Education of a Politician*. (1987).

Anderson, Jervis. *A. Philip Randolph: A Biographical Portrait*. (1973).

———. *Bayard Rustin: Trouble I've Seen: A Biography*. (1997).

———. *This Was Harlem: A Cultural Portrait, 1900–1950*. (1982).

Anderson, Jon Lee. *Che Guevara: A Revolutionary Life*. (1997).

588   BIBLIOGRAPHY

Anderson, Terry H. *The Movement and the Sixties: Protest in America from Greensboro to Wounded Knee*. (1995).

Angelou, Maya. *All God's Children Need Traveling Shoes*. (1986).

————. *The Heart of a Woman*. (1981, 1993).

Anthony, Earl. *Picking Up the Gun: The Story of the Black Panthers*. (1970).

Apter, David E. *Ghana in Transition*. 2nd rev. ed. (1972).

Ashmore, Harry S. *Hearts and Minds—The Anatomy of Racism from Roosevelt to Reagan*. (1982).

Assensoh, A. B. *Dr. Martin Luther King, Jr., and America's Search for Racial Integration*. (1986).

Auerbach, Susan, ed. *Encyclopedia of Multiculturalism*. (1994).

Bacon, Donald C., Roger H. Davidson, and Morton Keller, eds. *The Encyclopedia of the United States Congress*. (1995).

Baer, Hans A., and Merrill Singer. *African-American Religion in the Twentieth Century*. (1992).

Bailey, A. Peter. "He Was a Master Teacher: Time Spent with Malcolm Was a Lesson in Liberation." *Emerge* (February 1990): 27–28.

Bailey, Deidre. "The Autobiography of Deidre Bailey: Thoughts on Malcolm X and Black Youth." In *Malcolm X: In Our Own Image*. Edited by Joe Wood. (1992).

Bak, Richard. *Joe Louis: The Great Black Hope*. (1996).

Baker, Houston A. *Afro-American Poetics*. (1988).

Baldwin, James. *The Fire Next Time*. (1962).

————. "Negroes Are Anti-Semitic Because They're Anti-White." In *Black Anti-Semitism and Jewish Racism*. Edited by Nat Hentoff. (1969).

————. *One Day When I Was Lost: A Scenario Based on Alex Haley's The Autobiography of Malcolm X*. (1973).

Ballard, Allen B. *The Education of Black Folks: The Afro-American Struggle for Knowledge in White America*. (1973).

Banks, William M. *Black Intellectuals: Race and Responsibility in American Life*. (1996).

Banner-Haley, Charles. *The Fruits of Integration: Black Middle-Class Ideology and Culture, 1960–1990*. (1994).

Baraka, Amiri. *The Autobiography of LeRoi Jones*. (1984b).

————. *Daggers and Javelins: Essays, 1974–1979*. (1984a).

————. *Eulogies*. (1996).

————. *Funk Lore*. (1996).

————. *Home: Social Essays*. (1966).

————. *The LeRoi Jones/Amiri Baraka Reader*. Edited by William J. Harris. (1991).

————. "Malcolm as Ideology." In *Malcolm X: In Our Own Image*. Edited by Joe Wood. (1992).

————. "Toward the Creation of Political Institutions for All African Peoples." *Black World* (October 1972): 54–78.

————. *Wise Why's Y's*. (1995).

Barboza, Steven. *American Jihad: Islam after Malcolm*. (1994).

Bardolph, Richard, ed. *The Civil Right's Record: Black Americans and the Law: 1849–1970*. (1970).

Barksdale, Marcellus C. "Robert F. Williams and the Indigenous Civil Rights Movement in Monroe, North Carolina, 1961." *Journal of Negro History* 69 (Spring 1984): 73–89.

Barnes, Jack, and Barry Sheppard. "Interview with Malcolm X." *Young Socialist* (March–April 1965): 2–5.

Barnett, Donald L., and Karari Njama. *Mau Mau from Within: An Analysis of Kenya's Peasant Revolt.* (1966).

Barnette, Aubrey. "The Black Muslims Are a Fraud." *Saturday Evening Post* (February 27, 1965): 23–29.

Bell, Derrick. *And We Are Not Saved: The Elusive Quest for Racial Justice.* (1987).

Bell, Inge Powell. *CORE and the Strategy of Non-Violence.* (1968).

Benson, Thomas. "Rhetoric and Autobiography: The Case of Malcolm X." *Quarterly Journal of Speech* 60 (1974): 1–13.

Berger, Morroe. "Die Schwarzen Muslims." *Der Monat* (March 1965): 13–25; (April 1965): 58–67.

Berry, Mary Francis. "Slavery, the Constitution, and the Founding Fathers: The African American Vision." *In African Americans and the Living Constitution.* Edited by John Hope Franklin and Geena Rae McNeil. (1995).

Berry, Mary Francis, and John W. Blassingame. *Long Memory: The Black Experience in America.* (1982).

Bethune, Lebert. "Malcolm X: in Europe." In *Malcolm X: The Man and His Times.* Edited by John H. Clarke. (1990).

Beyan, Amos J. "The Development of Kikuyu Politics during the Depression, 1930–1939." *Journal of Third World Studies* 6 (1988): 29–47.

Beyon, E. D., and Prince A. Cuba. *Master Fard Muhammad: Detroit History.* (1990).

Biographical Directory of the United States Congress, 1774–1989. (1989).

Black Media News. "The Malcolm X Commemorative Stamp." (Summer 1999): 5–7.

Blackside/PBS. *Malcolm X: Make It Plain.* Video. (1994).

———. *Eyes on the Prize: America's Civil Rights Years. The Time Has Come, 1964–1966.* Video. 6 vols. (1987).

Blair, Thomas. *Retreat to the Ghetto: The End of a Dream.* (1977).

Blauner, Bob. *Black Lives, White Lives: Three Decades of Race Relations in America.* (1989).

Blaxland, Gregory. *Egypt and Sinai.* (1966).

Blount, Mildred. "The Waldorf of Harlem: Million Dollar Theresa Is Most Famous Negro Hotel in Nation." *Ebony* (April 1946): 8–12.

Boggs, James. *Racism and the Class Struggle: Further Pages from a Black Worker's Notebook.* (1970).

Bontemps, Arna, and Jack Conroy. *Any Place But Here.* (1966).

———. *They Seek a City.* (1945).

Boris, Joseph J., ed. *Who's Who in Colored America.* Vols. 1–3. (1927–40).

Borowitz, Eugene B. *Liberal Judaism.* (1984).

Boulware, Marcus. "Minister Malcolm Orator Profundo." *Negro History Bulletin* 30 (November 1967): 12–14.

Boyd, Todd. *Am I Black Enough for You? Popular Culture from the Hood and Beyond.* (1997).

Bracey, John H., Jr., August Meier, and Elliot Rudwick, eds. *Black Nationalism in America.* (1970).

Branch, Taylor. *Parting the Waters: America in the King Years, 1954–63.* (1988).

———. *Pillar of Fire: America in the King Years, 1963–65.* (1998).

Branham, Robert J. " 'I Was Gone on Debating': Malcolm X's Prison Debates and Public Confrontations." *Argumentation and Advocacy* 31 (Winter 1995): 117–138.

Breitman, George. *Malcolm X: The Evolution of a Revolutionary.* (1967, 1968, 1973, 1982).

Breitman, George, Herman Porter, and Baxter Smith. *The Assassination of Malcolm X.* Edited by Malik Miah. (1976).

Bridges, Tyler. *The Rise of David Duke.* (1994).

Brigsby, C.W.E. *The Second Black Renaissance: Essays in Black Literature.* (1980).

Brink, William, and Louis Harris. *The Negro Revolution in America.* (1964).

Brisbane, Robert H. *Black Activism: Racial Revolution in the United States, 1954–1970.* (1970, 1974).

———. *The Black Vanguard: Origins of the Negro Social Revolution.* (1969).

Brock, Ann K. "Gloria Richardson and the Cambridge Movement." In *Women in the Civil Rights Movement: Trailblazers and Torchbearers, 1941–1965.* Edited by Vicki Crawford, Jacqueline Rouse, and Barbara Woods. (1990).

Broderick, Francis L. *W.E.B. Du Bois: Negro Leader in Time of Crisis.* (1959).

Brotz, Howard. *The Black Jews of Harlem.* (1970).

Brown, H. Rap. *Die Nigger Die.* (1969).

Brown, Jamie Foster, ed. *Betty Shabazz: A Sisterfriend's Tribute in Words and Pictures.* (1998).

Brown, Leonard Lewis. "Malcolm and the Music." In *Teaching Malcolm X.* Edited by Theresa Perry. (1996).

Brown, Les. *Les Brown's Encyclopedia of Television.* (1992).

———. *The New York Times Encyclopedia of Television.* (1977).

Bullard, Sara. *Free at Last: A History of the Civil Rights Movement and Those Who Died in the Struggle.* (1989).

———. *The Ku Klux Klan: A History of Racism and Violence.* (1988).

Burk, Robert Frederick. *The Eisenhower Administration and Black Civil Rights.* (1984).

Burrow, Rufus, Jr. "Some African American Males' Perspectives on the Black Woman." *Western Journal of Black Studies* 16 (1992): 64–73.

Bush, Roderick D. *We Are Not What We Seem: Black Nationalism and Class Struggle in the American Century.* (1999).

Caditz, Judith. *White Liberals in Transition: The Current Dilemmas of Ethnic Integration.* (1976).

Cagin, Seth, and Philip Dray. *We Are Not Afraid: The Story of Goodman, Schwerner, and Chaney and the Civil Rights Campaign for Mississippi.* (1988).

Campbell, Angus. *White Attitudes toward Black People.* (1971).

Carew, Jan. *Ghosts in Our Blood: With Malcolm X in Africa, England, and the Caribbean.* (1994).

Carmichael, Stokley. *Stokley Speaks: Black Power to Pan Africanism.* Edited by Ethel N. Minor. (1971).

Carmichael, Stokely, and Charles Hamilton. *Black Power: The Politics of Liberation in America.* (1967).

Carsino, Louis. "Malcolm X and the Black Muslim Movement." *Psychohistory Review* 10 (1982): 165–84.

Carson, Clayborne. *In Struggle: SNCC and the Black Awakening of the 1960s.* (1981).

———. *Malcolm X: The FBI File.* Edited by David Gallen. (1991, 1993).

Carson, Clayborne, et al., eds. *The Eyes on the Prize Civil Rights Reader: Documents, Speeches, and Firsthand Accounts from the Black Freedom Struggle, 1954–1990.* (1991).

Carter, Dan T. *From George Wallace to Newt Gingrich: Race in the Conservative Counterrevolution 1963–1994.* (1996).

Carter, Rubin. *The Sixteenth Round.* (1976).

Cashman, Sean Dennis. *African Americans and the Quest for Civil Rights, 1900–1990.* (1991).

Cassity, Michael J. *Chains of Fear: American Race Relations since Reconstruction.* (1984).

CBS News. *The Real Malcolm X: An Intimate Portrait of the Man.* Video. (1992).

Chaiton, Sam, and Terry Swinton. *Lazarus and the Hurricane: The Freeing of Rubin "Hurricane" Carter.* (2000).

Chalmers, David. *Hooded Americanism: The First Century of the Ku Klux Klan: 1865 to the Present.* (1965).

Christian, Charles M. *Black Saga: The African American Experience.* (1995).

Clark, Culpepper. *The Schoolhouse Door: Segregation's Last Stand at the University of Alabama.* (1993).

Clark, Kenneth B., ed. *King, Malcolm, Baldwin: Three Interviews.* (1985).

——. *The Negro Protest.* (1963).

Clarke, John H., ed. *Malcolm X: The Man and His Times.* (1969, 1990, 1993).

Clasby, Nancy. "The Autobiography of Malcolm X: A Mythic Paradigm." *Journal of Black Studies* 5 (September 1974): 18–34.

Clay, William. *Just Permanent Interest: Black Americans in Congress.* (1992).

Cleage, Albert D., Jr. *Black Christian Nationalism: New Directions for the Black Church.* (1972).

Cleage, Albert D., Jr., and George Breitman. *Myths about Malcolm X: Two Views.* (1968).

Cleaver, Eldridge. "Initial Reactions on the Assassination of Malcolm X." In *Malcolm X: As They Knew Him.* Edited by David Gallen. (1992).

——. *Post-Prison Writings and Speeches.* Edited by Robert Scheer. (1969).

——. *Soul on Ice.* (1970, 1978).

Clegg, Claude Andrew, III. *An Original Man: The Life and Times of Elijah Muhammad.* (1997).

Cloyd, Iris, ed. *Who's Who Among Black Americans.* (1990, 1994–1995).

Cohen, Robert Carl. *Black Crusader: A Biography of Robert Franklin Williams.* (1972).

Collins, Patricia Hill. "Learning to Think for Ourselves: Malcolm X's Black Nationalism Reconsidered." In *Malcolm X: In Our Own Image.* Edited by Joe Wood. (1992).

Collins, Rodnell P., with A. Peter Bailey. *Seventh Child: A Family Memoir of Malcolm X.* (1998).

Condit, Celeste Michelle, and John Louis Lucaites. "Malcolm X and the Limits of the Rhetoric of Revolutionary Dissent." *Journal of Black Studies* 24 (March 1993): 291–313.

Cone, James H. *A Black Theology of Liberation.* (1970).

——. *Martin & Malcolm & America: A Dream or a Nightmare.* (1991, 1992).

Conot, Robert. *Rivers of Blood, Years of Darkness.* (1967).

Conyers, James, Jr., ed. *Black Lives: Essays in African American Biography.* (1999).

Cook, James Graham. *The Segregationists.* (1962).

Corliss, Richard. "The Elevation of Malcolm X." *Time* (November 23, 1992): 64.

Cox, Oliver C. *Caste, Class and Race: A Study in Social Dynamics.* (1970).

Crawford, Vicki L., et al. *Women in the Civil Rights Movement.* (1990).

Cripps, Thomas. *Making Movies Black: The Hollywood Message Movie from World War II to the Civil Rights Era.* (1993).

Cronon, David E. *Black Moses: The Story of Marcus Garvey and the Universal Negro Improvement Association.* (1969, 1995).

Cross, Theodore. *The Black Power Imperative: Racial Inequality and the Politics of Nonviolence.* (1984).

Croussy, Guy. "Il y a les blancs et les noirs. Promenades a New York." *Esprit* 33 (March 1965): 502–13.

Cruse, Harold. *The Crisis of the Negro Intellectual from Its Roots to the Present.* (1967).
———. *Plural But Equal.* (1987).

Current Biography Yearbook, 1966. (1991).

Cushmeer, Bernard. *This Is the One: Messenger Elijah Muhammad, We Need Not Look for Another.* (1971).

Cwiklik, Robert. *Malcolm X and Black Pride.* (1991).

Daniels, Walter C., ed. *Black Journals of the United States.* (1982).

Davenport, Christian A. "Reading the 'Voice of the Vanguard': A Content Analysis of the Black Panther Intercommunal News Service, 1969–1973." In *The Black Panther Party [Reconsidered].* Edited by Charles Jones. (1998).

Davies, Mark. *Malcolm X: Another Side of the Movement.* (1990).

Davis, Angela. "Meditations on the Legacy of Malcolm X." In *Malcolm X: In Our Own Image.* Edited by Joe Wood. (1992).
———. *Women, Race and Class.* (1983).

Davis, Daniel S. *The Story of A. Philip Randolph, Father of the Civil Rights Movement.* (1972).

Davis, Ossie. "Why I Eulogized Malcolm X." In *Malcolm X: The Man and His Times.* Edited by John H. Clarke. (1990).
———. "Why I Eulogized Malcolm X." *Negro Digest* (February 1966): 64–66.

Davis, Ossie, and Ruby Dee. *With Ossie Davis and Ruby Dee: In This Life Together.* (1998).

Davis, Thulani. *Malcolm X, the Great Photographs.* Edited by Howard Chapnick. (1993).

DeCaro, Louis A., Jr. *Malcolm X and the Cross: The Nation of Islam, Malcolm X, and Christianity.* (1998).
———. *On the Side of My People: A Religious Life of Malcolm X.* (1996).

Deffaa, Chip. *Swing Legacy.* (1989).

Dent, Gina, ed. *Black Popular Culture.* (1983).

Diamond, Arthur. *Malcolm X: A Voice for Black America.* (1994).

Dickerson, Dennis C. *Militant Mediator: Whitney M. Young.* (1998).

Dinwiddie-Boyd, Elza. *In Our Own Words.* (1996).

Dionisopoulos, P. A. *Rebellion, Racism and Representation: The Adam Clayton Powell Case and Its Antecedents.* (1990).

Dittmer, John. *Local People: The Struggle for Civil Rights in Mississippi.* (1994).

Draper, James, ed. *Black Literature Criticism: Excerpts from Criticisms of the Most Significant Works of Black Authors Over the Past 200 Years.* (1992).

Draper, Theodore. *The Rediscovery of Black Nationalism.* (1971).

Duberman, Martin Bauml. *Paul Robeson.* (1989).

Du Bois, David. *And Bid Him Sing.* (1975).

Du Bois, Shirley Graham. *His Day Is Marching On: A Memoir of W. E. B. Du Bois.* (1971).

Du Bois, W.E.B. *The Souls of Black Folk.* (1903).

Dyson, Michael Eric. *Between God and Gansta Rap: Bearing Witness to Black Culture.* (1996).

———. *Making Malcolm: The Myth and the Meaning of Malcolm X.* (1995).

———. *Race Rules: Navigating the Color Line.* (1997).

———. *Reflecting Black: African-American Cultured Criticism.* (1993).

Dyson, Walter. *Howard University, The Capstone of Negro Education: A History: 1867–1940.* (1941).

Early, Gerald, ed. *The Muhammad Ali Reader.* (1998).

Ebony. "A Case of Black and White." (December 1973): 126.

———. "Gloria Richardson: Lady General of Civil Rights." (July 1964): 23–26.

———. "In Chicago's Legal Circle, He Is a One Man Brain Trust." (December 1973): 23.

———. "Negro Profs at White Colleges." (October 1947): 14–18.

———. "Whatever Happened to Eldridge Cleaver." (March 1988): 66–68.

Edwards, Audrey. "The Fire This Time." *Essence* (October 1997): 74–76, 155–156.

Edwards, David V. *The American Political Experience.* (1985).

Emery, Lynne Fauley. *Black Dance from 1619 to Today.* 2nd ed. (1988).

Epps, Archie. "The Theme of Exile in Malcolm X's Harvard Speeches." *Harvard Journal of Negro Affairs* 2 (1968): 40–54.

Epstein, Howard M., ed. *Revolt in the Congo.* (1965).

Eskew, Glenn T. *But for Birmingham: The Local and National Movements in the Civil Rights Struggle.* (1997).

Essien-Udom, E. U. *Black Nationalism: A Search for an Identity in America.* (1962, 1971).

Essien-Udom, E. U., and Ruby M. Essien-Udom. "Malcolm X: An International Man." In *Malcolm X: The Man and His Times.* Edited by John H. Clarke. (1969, 1990, 1993).

Estell, Kenneth. *African America: Portrait of a People.* (1994a).

———, ed. *The African American Almanac.* 6th ed. (1994b).

Evanzz, Karl. *The Judas Factor: The Plot to Kill Malcolm X.* (1992).

———. *The Messenger: The Rise and Fall of Elijah Muhammad.* (1999).

Evers, Mrs. Medgar, with William Peters. *For Us, the Living.* (1967).

Evers-Williams, Myrlie with Belinda Blau. *Watch Me Fly: What I Learned on the Way to Becoming a Woman.* (1999).

Fabre, Michel, and Robert E. Skinner, eds. *Conversations with Chester Himes.* (1995).

Fager, Charles E. *White Reflections on Black Power.* (1967).

Fairclough, Adam. *To Redeem the Soul of America: The Southern Christian Leadership Conference and Martin Luther King, Jr.* (1987).

Falkner, David. *Great Time Coming: The Life of Jackie Robinson, from Baseball to Birmingham.* (1995).

Fanon, Frantz. *The Wretched of the Earth.* (1963, 1968).

Farmer, James. *Lay Bare the Heart: An Autobiography of the Civil Rights Movement.* (1985).

Fauset, Arthur H. *Black Gods of the Metropolis: Negro Religious Cults of the Urban North.* (1971).

Fax, Elton C. *Garvey: The Story of a Pioneer Black Nationalist.* (1972).

Ferruccio, Gambino. "Transgression of a Laborer: Malcolm X in the Wilderness of America." *Radical History Review* 55 (Winter 1993): 7–31.

Films for the Humanities. *Malcolm X: Black American Leader.* Video. (1998).

Flick, Hank, and Larry Powell. "Animal Imagery in the Rhetoric of Malcolm X." *Journal of Black Studies* 18 (1988): 435–51.

Foner, Phillip S. *American Socialism and Black Americans: From the Age of Jackson to World War II.* (1977).

———, ed. *The Black Panthers Speak.* (1970).

Ford, Nick Aaron. *Black Studies: Threat or Challenge.* (1973).

Forman, James. *The Making of Black Revolutionaries: A Personal Account.* (1972, 1985).

Franklin, John Hope. "Race and the Constitution in the Nineteenth Century." In *African Americans and the Living Constitution.* Edited by John Hope Franklin and Geena Rae McNeil. (1995).

Franklin, John Hope, and August Meier, eds. *Black Leaders of the Twentieth Century.* (1982).

Franklin, John H., and Alfred A. Moss, Jr. *From Slavery to Freedom: A History of Negro Americans.* (1967, 1988, 1994, 1999, 2000).

Franklin, Robert. *Liberating Visions: Human Fulfillment and Social Justice in African-American Thought.* (1990).

Franklin, Vincent P. *Living Our Stories, Telling Our Truths; Autobiography and the Making of the African American Intellectual Tradition.* (1996).

Fredrickson, George M. *Black Liberation: A Comparative History of Black Ideologies in the United States and South Africa.* (1995).

Friedly, Michael. *Malcolm X: The Assassination.* (1992).

Friedly, Michael, with David Gallen. *Martin Luther King, Jr.: The FBI File.* (1993).

Gage, Nicholas. *The Mafia Is Not an Equal Opportunity Employer.* (1971).

Gallen, David, comp. *Malcolm A to X: The Man and His Ideas.* (1992).

———, ed. *Malcolm X: As They Knew Him.* (1992).

———, ed. *A Malcolm X Reader: Perspectives on the Man and the Myth.* (1994).

Gardell, Mattias. *In the Name of Elijah Muhammad: Louis Farrakhan and the Nation of Islam.* (1996).

Gardner, Jigs. "The Murder of Malcolm X." *Monthly Review* 16 (April 1965): 802–5.

Garrow, David J. *Bearing the Cross: Martin Luther King, Jr., and the Southern Christian Leadership Conference.* (1986).

———. *The FBI and Martin Luther King Jr: From Solo to Memphis.* (1981).

Gates, Henry Louis, Jr. "The Charmer." *The New Yorker* (April 29 and May 6, 1996): 116–131.

Geiss, Immanuel. *The Pan-African Movement: A History of Pan-Africanism in America.* (1974).

Gellner, Ernest. *Nations and Nationalism.* (1983).

Gerard-Libois, Jules. *Katanga Secession.* (1967).

Geyelin, Philip. *Lyndon B. Johnson and the World.* (1966).

Giddings, Paula. *When and Where I Enter: The Impact of Black Women on Race and Sex in America.* (1984).

Gilliam, Reginald Earl, Jr. *Black Political Development: An Advocacy Analysis.* (1975).

Giovanni, Nikki. *Black Feeling, Black Talk, Black Judgment*. (1970).

―――. *Racism 101*. (1994).

Glanville, Brian. "Malcolm X." *New Statesman* (June 12, 1964): 901–2.

Glick, Brian. *The War at Home: Covert Action against U.S. Activists and What We Can Do About It*. (1989).

Goldfield, Michael. *The Color of Politics: Race and the Mainsprings of American Politics*. (1997).

Goldman, Peter. *The Death and Life of Malcolm X*. (1973, 1977, 1979, 1992).

―――. "Malcolm." In *A Malcolm X Reader: Perspectives on the Man and the Myth*. Edited by David Gallen. (1994).

―――. "Malcolm X: Witness for the Prosecution." In *Black Leaders of the Twentieth Century*. Edited by John Hope Franklin and August Meier. (1982).

―――. *Report from Black America*. (1969).

Goodheart, Lawrence. "The Odyssey of Malcolm X: An Eriksonian Interpretation." *The Historian* 53 (Autumn 1990): 47–62.

Gorn, Elliott J., ed. *Muhammad Ali, the People's Champ*. (1995).

Grant, Earl. "The Last Days of Malcolm X." In *Malcolm X: The Man and His Times*. Edited by John H. Clarke. (1990).

Grant, Joanne. *Ella Baker: Freedom Bound*. (1998).

Greaves, William. *Malcolm X: Nationalist or Humanist?* Video. (1990).

Gregory, Dick, with Robert Lipsyte. *Nigger: An Autobiography*. (1972).

Gregory, Dick, with James McGraw. *Up from Nigger*. (1976).

Griffin, John Howard. *Black Like Me*. (1960).

Grill, Johnpeter, and Robert L. Jenkins. "The Nazis and the American South in the 1930s: A Mirror Image." *Journal of Southern History* 58 (December 1992): 667–94.

Grimes, Nikki. *Great Lives, Malcolm X: A Force for Change*. (1992).

Guerrero, Ed. *Framing Blackness: The African American Image in Film*. (1993).

Guevara, Ernesto. *Venceremos! The Speeches and Writings of Ernesto Che Guevara*. (1968).

Gwynne, James B., ed. *Malcolm X: Justice Seeker*. (1993).

Hacker, Andrew. *Two Nations*. (1992).

Haddad, Yvonne, and Adair T. Lummis. *Islamic Values in the United States: A Comparative Study*. (1987).

Haines, Herbert H. *Black Radicals and the Civil Rights Mainstream, 1954–1970*. (1988, 1989).

Halberstam, David, ed. *The Best American Sports Writing of the Century*. (1999).

Haley, Alex. *Alex Haley: The "Playboy" Interviews*. Edited By Murray Fisher. (1993).

―――. *Roots*. (1976).

Halisi, Clyde. *The Quotable Karenga*. (1965).

Hall, Raymond. *Black Separatism in the United States*. (1978).

Hamilton, Charles V. *Adam Clayton Powell, Jr.: The Political Biography of an American Dilemma*. (1991).

Hampton, Henry, and Steve Fayer, with Sarah Flynn, eds. *Voices of Freedom: An Oral History of the Civil Rights Movement from the 1950s through the 1980s*. (1991).

Hampton, Lionel, with James Haskin. *Hamp: An Autobiography*. (1989).

Hansberry, Lorraine. *The Movement: Documentary of a Struggle for Equality*. (1964).

Hare, Nathan. "The Contribution of Black Sociologists to Black Studies." In *Black So-*

ciologists: Historical and Contemporary Perspectives. Edited by James E. Black-well and Morris Janowitz. (1974).

Harlan, Louis R. *Booker T. Washington: The Making of a Black Leader, 1865–1901.* (1972).

———. *Booker T. Washington: The Wizard of Tuskegee, 1901–1915.* (1983).

Harper, Frederick D. "A Reconstruction of Malcolm X's Personality." *Afro-American Studies* 3 (June 1972): 1–6.

Harris, Robert, Nyota Harris, and Grandassa Harris, eds. *Carlos Cooks and Black Nationalism from Garvey to Malcolm.* (1992).

Harris, Trudier, ed. *Dictionary of Literary Biography: Afro-American Writers, 1940–1955.* (1988).

Harris, William. *Keeping the Faith: A. Philip Randolph, Milton Webster, and the Brotherhood of Sleeping Car Porters, 1925–1937.* (1977).

———, ed. *The LeRoi Jones Amiri Baraka Reader.* (1991).

Haskins, Jim. *The Queen of the Blues: Biography of Dinah Washington.* (1987).

Hauser, Thomas. *Muhammad Ali: His Life and Times.* (1991).

Hawkins, Walter L. "Spike Lee." In *African American Biographies.* (1992).

Hazzard-Gordon, Katrina. *Jookin': The Rise of Social Dance Formations in African-American Culture.* (1990).

HBO and *Sports Illustrated. Boxing's Best: Muhammad Ali.* Video. (1989).

Heath, Louis G. *Off the Pigs: The History and Literature of the Black Panther Party.* (1976).

Heing, G., and H. Doonay. *The Last Fifty Days.* (1966).

Herring, George C. *America's Longest War: The United States and Vietnam, 1950–1975.* (1979).

Hill, Herbert, and James E. Jones, eds. *Race in America: The Struggle for Equality.* (1993).

Hill, Robert A., ed. *Pan African Biography.* (1987).

Hilliard, David, and Lewis Cole. *This Side of Glory: The Autobiography of David Hilliard and the Story of the Black Panther Party.* (1993).

Himes, Chester B. *My Life of Absurdity: The Later Years: The Autobiography of Chester Himes.* (1976).

———. *The Quality of Hurt: The Early Years: The Autobiography of Chester Himes.* (1972).

Hine, Darlene Clark, ed. *Black Women in United States History: The Twentieth Century.* (1990).

Hine, Darlene Clark, Elsa B. Brown, and Rosalyn Terborg-Penn, eds. *Black Women in America: An Historical Encyclopedia.* (1993).

Hirsch, James S. *Hurricane: The Miraculous Journey of Rubin Carter.* (2000).

Hitti, Phillip K. *Islam: A Way of Life.* (1970).

Hopkins, Ellen. "Their Fathers' Daughters." *Rolling Stone* (November 30, 1989): 76–77.

Hopson, Chuck. "Malcolm X Liberation University." *Negro Digest* (March 1970): 41–42.

Horne, Gerald. *Black Liberation/Red Scare: Ben Davis and the Communist Party.* (1994).

———. *Fire This Time: The Watts Uprising and the 1960s.* (1995).

Hornsby, Alton, Jr. *Milestones in 20th-Century African-American History.* (1993).

House Committee on Internal Security, 93rd Congress, Second Session. *Terrorism* 1 (August 1974).

Hughes, Langston. *The Best Short Stories by Negro Writers: An Anthology from 1899 to the Present.* (1967).

Husain, Mir Zohair. *Global Islamic Politics.* (1995).

Ibrahim, I. A. *A Brief Illustrated Guide to Understanding Islam.* 2nd ed. (1997).

Illo, John. "The Rhetoric of Malcolm X." *Columbia University Forum* (Spring 1966): 5–12.

Imari, Brother (Obadele, Abubakari). *War in America: The Malcolm X Doctrine.* (1966, 1968).

Islamic Affairs Department. *Understanding Islam and the Muslims.* (1989).

Ivy, James W. "Joel Augustus Rogers (1883–1966)." *Crisis* (April 1966): 201.

Jaaber, Heshaam. *The Final Chapter: I Buried Malcolm (El Haj Malik El-Shabazz).* (1992).

Jack, Hulan E. *Fifty Years a Democrat: The Autobiography of Hulan E. Jack.* (1982).

Jackson, Robert H., and Carl G. Rosberg. *Personal Rule in Black Africa: Prince, Autocrat, Prophet, Tyrant.* (1982).

Jacobson, Julius, ed. *The Negro and the American Labor Movement.* (1968).

Jamal, Hakim A. *From the Dead Level: Malcolm X and Me.* (1971).

James, Joy. *Transcending the Talented Tenth Black Leaders and American Intellectuals.* (1997).

Jeffreys-Jones, Rhodri. *The CIA and American Democracy.* (1989).

Jenkins, Robert L. "Floyd McKissick." In *Encyclopedia of African-American Civil Rights: From Emancipation to the Present.* Edited by Charles D. Lowery and John F. Marszalek. (1992).

Jet. " 'Anti-Material Neurosis' Cited in Tax Case." (November 12, 1970): 19.

———. "Drop Conspiracy Charges against Bobby Seale." (November 5, 1970): 10–11.

———. "How Blacks Remember Malcolm X." (May 2, 1976): 4, 22–27.

———. "Lewis Michaux, 92, Dies." (September 1976): 5–6.

Johnson, Jacqueline, and Richard Gallin, eds. *Stokely Carmichael: The Story of Black Power.* (1990).

Johnson, John. *Succeeding against the Odds.* (1993).

Johnson, Timothy. *Malcolm X: A Comprehensive Annotated Bibliography.* (1986).

Jones, Charles E., ed. *The Black Panther Party [Reconsidered].* (1998).

Kahn, Tom, and Bayard Rustin. "The Ambiguous Legacy of Malcolm X." *Dissent* (Spring 1965): 188–92.

Karenga, Maulana Ron. *Introduction to Black Studies.* (1982).

———. *Kawaida Theory: An Introductory Outline.* (1980).

———. "The Oppositional Logic of Malcolm X: Differentiation, Engagement, and Resistance." *Western Journal of Black Studies* 17 (Spring 1993): 6–16.

———. "Socio-Political Philosophy of Malcolm X." *Western Journal of Black Studies* 3 (Winter 1979): 251–62.

Karim, Benjamin, with Peter Skutches and David Gallen. *Remembering Malcolm: The Story from Inside the Muslim Mosques by His Assistant Minister, Benjamin Karim.* (1992).

Karriem, Kamal. *Black Women Back Door to Racism.* (n.d.).

Kelley, Robin D. "Black Like Mao: Red China and Black Revolution." *Soul* 1 (Fall 1999): 6–41.

———. *Race Rebels: Culture, Politics, and the Black Working Class.* (1994, 1996).

————. "The Riddle of the Zoot: Malcolm Little and Black Cultural Politics during World War II." In *Malcolm X: In Our Own Image*. Edited by Joe Wood. (1992).

————. *Yo' Mamma's Disfunktional! Fighting the Culture Wars in Urban America*. (1997).

Kellogg, Charles Flint. *The National Association for the Advancement of Colored People, 1909–1920*. (1967).

Kempton, Murray. "Malcolm X." *Spectator* (February 26, 1965): 252.

Kennedy, Robert F., Jr. *Judge Frank M. Johnson, Jr.: A Biography*. (1978).

Kerner Report: The 1968 Report of the National Advisory Commission on Civil Disorders. (1968, 1988).

Kharif, Wali Rash. "Ralph David Abernathy, Sr." In *Encyclopedia of African-American Civil Rights: From Emancipation to the Present*. Edited by Charles D. Lowery and John F. Marszalek. (1992).

King, Coretta Scott. *My Life with Martin Luther King, Jr*. (1969).

King, Martin L., Jr. *The Autobiography of Martin Luther King, Jr*. Edited by Clayborne Carson. (1998).

Klein, Jeffery L. "Hulan Edwin Jack." In *Encyclopedia of African-American Culture and History*. Vol. 3. Edited by Jack Saltzman, Daniel Lionel Smith, and Cornel West. (1996).

Kluger, Richard. *Simple Justice: The History of Brown v. Board of Education and Black America's Struggle for Equality*. (1975).

Kly, Yussuf N. *The Black Book: The True Political Philosophy of Malcolm X*. (1986).

Knebel, Fletcher. "A Visit with the Widow of Malcolm X." *Look* (March 4, 1969): 74–80.

Kochman, Thomas, ed. *Rappin' and Stylin' Out*. (1972).

Kondo, Baba Zak A. *CONSPIRACYS: Unraveling the Assassination of Malcolm X*. (1993).

Kopel, D. B. "Canadian Gun Laws and Crimes." *Journal of the American Rifleman* (September 1988): 56–58.

Krenn, Michael L. *Black Diplomacy: African Americans and the State Department*. (1999).

Krieg, Robert. "Malcolm X: Myth and Truthfulness." *Journal of Religious Thought* 36 (Fall–Winter 1979–80): 37–44.

Lacy, Leslie Alexander. "Malcolm X in Ghana." In *Malcolm X: The Man and His Times*. Edited by John H. Clarke. (1990).

Laurino, Maria. "Who Were the Killers." In *Malcolm X: As They Knew Him*. Edited by David Gallen. (1992).

Lawson, Steven. *Running for Freedom: Civil Rights and Black Politics in America since 1941*. (1991, 1997).

Lear, Leonard. "An Ancient African Religion Makes a Comeback." *Sepia* (November 1976): 16–24.

Lee, Martha F. *The Nation of Islam: An American Millenarian Movement*. (1988, 1996).

Lee, Spike with Ralph Wiley. *By Any Means Necessary: The Trials and Tribulations of the Making of Malcolm X*. (1992).

Leeman, Richard W. *African-American Orators: A Bio-Critical Sourcebook*. (1996).

Leeming, David. *James Baldwin: A Biography*. (1994).

Lesher, Stephen. *George Wallace: American Populist*. (1994).

Levine, Daniel. *Bayard Rustin and the Civil Rights Movement*. (2000).

Levine, Lawrence W. *Black Culture and Black Consciousness: Afro-American Folk Thought from Slavery to Freedom*. (1978).

Levinsohn, Florence Hamlish. *Looking for Farrakhan*. (1997).

Lewis, David Levering. *W.E.B. Du Bois: Biography of a Race 1868–1919*. (1993).

———. *W.E.B. Du Bois: The Fight for Equality and the American Century, 1919–1963*. (2000).

———. *When Harlem Was in Vogue*. (1981).

Lewis, John, with Michael D'Orso. *Walking with the Wind: A Memoir of the Movement*. (1998).

Library Distributors of America. *The True Malcolm X Speaks*. 2 Vols. Video. (1993).

Lincoln, C. Eric. *The Black Muslims in America*. (1961, 1973, 1994).

———. "The Meaning of Malcolm X." In *Malcolm X: The Man and His Times*. Edited by John H. Clarke. (1990).

———. *Race, Religion and the Continuing American Dilemma*. (1984).

———. *Sounds of the Struggle: Persons and Perspectives in Civil Rights*. (1968).

Lincoln, C. Eric, and Lawrence H. Mamiya. *The Black Church in the African American Experience*. (1990).

Lippy, Charles H., and Peter W. Williams, eds. *Encyclopedia of the American Religious Experience: Studies of Traditions and Movements*. Vol. 2. (1988).

Logan, Rayford W. *Howard University: The First One Hundred Years, 1867–1967*. (1969).

Logan, Rayford W., and Michael R. Winston, eds. *Dictionary of American Negro Biography*. (1982).

Lomax, Louis E. *The Negro Revolt*. (1971).

———. *To Kill a Black Man*. (1968).

———. *When the Word Is Given: A Report on Elijah Muhammad, Malcolm X and the Black Muslim World*. (1963).

Low, Augustus, and Virgil Clift, eds. *Encyclopedia of Black America*. (1981).

Lowery, Charles D., and John F. Marszalek, eds. *Encyclopedia of African-American Civil Rights: From Emancipation to the Present*. (1992).

Lynn, Conrad. *There Is a Fountain: The Autobiography of a Civil Rights Lawyer*. (1979).

Magida, Arthur J. *Prophet of Rage: A Life of Louis Farrakhan and His Nation*. (1996).

Maglangbayan, Shawna. *Garvey, Lumumba and Malcolm: Black Nationalist Separatists*. (1972).

Malcolm X. "Black Muslims and Civil Rights." In *Freedom Now! The Civil Rights Struggle in America*. Edited by Alan F. Westin. (1964).

———. *By Any Means Necessary: Speeches, Interviews, and a Letter by Malcolm X*. Edited by George Breitman. (1970a, 1987, 1992).

———. "Definition of a Revolution." In *Malcolm X: The Man and His Times*. Edited by John H. Clarke. (1969, 1990, 1993).

———. *The End of White World Supremacy*. Edited by Benjamin Goodman Karim. (1971).

———. *February 1965: The Final Speeches of Malcolm X*. Edited by Steve Clark. (1992).

———. "I Don't Mean Bananas." In *The New Left Reader*. Edited by Carl Oglesby. (1969).

———. *The Last Year of Malcolm X*. Edited by George Breitman. (1967).

———. *Malcolm X on Afro-American History*. Edited by George Breitman. (1970b).

————. *Malcolm X: Speeches at Harvard.* Edited by Archie Epps. (1968, 1991).

————. *Malcolm X Speaks: Selected Speeches and Statements.* Edited by George Breitman. (1965, 1982, 1993).

————. *Malcolm X Talks to Young People.* (1965, 1969).

————. *Malcolm X Talks to Young People: Speeches in the U.S., Britain, and Africa.* Edited by Steve Clark. (1991).

————. *Malcolm X: The Last Speeches.* Edited by Bruce Perry. (1989).

————. *Two Speeches by Malcolm X.* (1965, 1987, 1990).

Malcolm X, with Alex Haley. *The Autobiography of Malcolm X.* (1965, 1992, 2000).

Malcolm X College. *Catalogue, 1998–2000.* (1997).

Mamiya, Lawrence H. and C. Eric Lincoln. "Black Militant and Separatist Movements." In *Encyclopedia of the American Religious Experience: Studies of Traditions and Movements.* Vol. 2. Edited by Charles H. Lippy and Peter W. Williams. (1988).

Manis, Andrew M. *A Fire You Can't Put Out: The Civil Rights Life of Birmingham's Reverend Fred Shuttlesworth.* (1999).

Marable, Manning. *Black American Politics.* (1985).

————. *Black Leadership.* (1998).

————. *Black Liberation in Conservative America.* (1997).

————. *Race, Reform, and Rebellion.* (1991).

————. *Race Reform and Rebellion: The Second Reconstruction in Black America, 1945–1982.* (1984).

————. *W.E.B. Du Bois: Black Radical Democrat.* (1986).

"March on Washington." In *Encyclopedia of African-American Civil Rights.* Edited by Charles D. Lowery and John F. Marszalek. (1992).

Marsh, Clifton E. *From Black Muslims to Muslims: The Resurrection, Transformation and Change of the Lost-Found Nation of Islam in America, 1930–1995.* 2nd ed. (1996).

————. *From Black Muslims to Muslims: The Transition from Separatism to Islam, 1930–1989.* (1984).

————. "Malcolm X—From Detroit Red to Mecca: The Evolution of a Black Leader's Vision from Separation to Third World Liberation." *Journal of African Civilizations* 9 (December 1987): 74–92.

Marszalek, John. "Michaux, Lightfoot Solomon." In *Dictionary of American Biography, Supplement Eight, 1966–1970.* Edited by John A. Garraty and Mark C. Carnes. (1988).

Martin, Tony. *The Pan African Connection: From Slavery to Garvey and Beyond.* (1984).

Massaquoi, Hans J. "Mystery of Malcolm X." *Ebony* (September 1964): 38–46.

Matney, William C., ed. *Who's Who among Black Americans.* (1978).

Matthews, Mark D. " 'Our Women and What They Think,' Amy Jacques Garvey and the Negro World." *Black Scholar* 9 (May–June, 1979): 2–13.

McAdam, Doug. *Freedom Summer.* (1988).

————. *Political Process and the Development of Black Insurgency: 1930 to 1970.* (1985).

McCallum, John D. *The World Heavyweight Boxing Championship: A History.* (1974).

McCartney, John T. *Black Power Ideologies: An Essay in African-American Political Thought.* (1992).

McCloud, Aminah Beverly. *African American Islam.* (1995).

McDonald, Lawrence P. *Trotskyism and Terror: Their Strategy of Revolution.* (1977).

McEvoy, James, and Abraham Miller. *Black Power and Student Rebellion*. (1969).

McFeely, William. *Frederick Douglass*. (1991).

Mead, Margaret, and James Baldwin. *A Rap on Race*. (1971).

Mealy, Rosmari. *Fidel and Malcolm X: Memories of a Meeting*. (1993).

Medina, Mark E. "Northern Student Movement." In *Encyclopedia of Civil Rights: From Emancipation to the Present*. Edited by Charles D. Lowery and John F. Marszalek. (1992).

Meditz, Sandra W., and Tim Merrill, eds. *Zaire: A Country Study*. (1994).

Meier, August. *The Transformation of Activism*. (1970).

———. *A White Scholar and the Black Community, 1945–1965: Essays and Reflections*. (1992).

Meier, August, and Elliott Rudwick. *CORE: A Study in the Civil Rights Movement, 1942–1968*. (1973).

Meier, August, Elliot Rudwick, and John Bracey, Jr., eds. *Black Protest in the Sixties*. (1990, 1991).

———. *Black Protest Thought in the Twentieth Century*. (1971).

Meredith, James. *Three Years in Mississippi*. (1966).

Merriam, Sharan B., and Rosemary S. Caffarella. *Learning in Adulthood*. (1991).

Metz, Helen Chapin, ed. *Egypt: A Country Study*. (1980).

Miller, Floyd. *The Search for Black Nationalism: Black Colonization and Emigration 1787–1863*. (1975).

Miller, Ross. "Autobiography as Fact and Fiction: Franklin, Adams, Malcolm X." *Centennial Review* 16 (1972): 221–32.

Mills, Gary B. "Michaux, Solomon Lightfoot." In *Encyclopedia of African-American Civil Rights: From Emancipation to the Present*. Edited by Charles D. Lowery and John F. Marszalek. (1992).

Mills, Kay. *This Little Light of Mine: The Life of Fannie Lou Hamer*. (1993).

MNTEX. *Malcolm X, A Video*. (1991).

Moore, Carlos. *Castro: The Blacks and Africa*. (1988).

Moore, Jesse Thomas, Jr. *A Search for Equality: The National Urban League, 1910–1961*. (1981).

Moritz, Charles, ed. *Current Biography Yearbook*. (1966, 1977).

Morris, Aldon. *The Origins of the Civil Rights Movement*. (1984, 1989).

Morrison, Allan. "Who Killed Malcolm X." *Ebony* (October 1965): 135–42.

Morrow, Willie. *Four Hundred Years without a Comb*. (1973).

Moses, Wilson J. *Black Messiahs and Uncle Toms: Social and Literary Manipulations of a Religious Myth*. (1993).

———. *The Golden Age of Black Nationalism 1850–1925*. (1978).

Muhammad, Elijah. *History of the Nation of Islam*. (1994).

———. *How to Eat to Live*. (1967).

———. *Message to the Blackman in America*. (1963, 1965).

Murphy, Larry G., J. Gordon Melton, and Gary L. Ward, eds. *Encyclopedia of African-American Religions*. (1993).

Murray, Albert. *The Omni Americans: Some Alternatives to the Folklore of White Supremacy*. (1970).

Myers, Walter Dean. *Malcolm X: By Any Means Necessary: A Biography*. (1993).

Nagel, Carol DeKane, ed. *African American Biography*. (1994).

Nagel, Rob. "King and Shabazz." In *Epic Lives: One Hundred Women Who Made a Difference*. Edited by Jessie Carney Smith. (1993).

National Advisory Commission on Civil Disorders. *Report*. (1968).

Neal, Larry. *Visions of a Liberated Future: Black Arts Movement Writings*. (1989).

Neusner, Jacob. *Christian Faith and the Bible of Judaism: The Judaic Encounter with Scripture*. (1987).

Newcomb, Horace, ed. *Museum of Broadcast Communications Encyclopedia of Television*. 3 Vols. (1997).

Newsweek. "Malcolm's Brand X." (March 23, 1964): 32.

Newton, Huey P. *Revolutionary Suicide*. (1995).

New York Chapter of the Black Panther Party. *Guns Plus Dope Equals Genocide*. (1971).

Norden, Eric. "The Murder of Malcolm X." *The Realist* (February 1967): 22–26.

Nottington, John. *The Myth of Mau Mau: Nationalism in Kenya*. (1970).

Nunnelley, William A. *Bull Connor*. (1991).

Oates, Stephen. *Let the Trumpet Sound: The Life of Martin Luther King, Jr.* (1982).

Obadele, Imari. *America the Nation–State*. (1993).

———. "The Struggle Is for Land." *Black Scholar* 3 (February 1972): 24–36.

Ofari, Earl. *The Myth of Black Capitalism*. (1970).

Ogundipe-Leslie, Molara. *Re-creating Ourselves: African Women & Critical Transformation*. (1994).

Ohmann, Carol. "The Autobiography of Malcolm X: A Revolutionary Use of the Franklin Tradition." *American Quarterly* 22 (1970): 131–49.

O'Meally, Robert. *Lady Day: The Many Faces of Billie Holiday*. (1991).

O'Reilly, Kenneth. *Black Americans: The FBI Files*. Edited by David Gallen. (1994).

———. "Racial Matters." *The FBI's Secret File on Black America, 1960–1972*. (1989).

Osofsky, Gilbert. *Harlem: The Making of a Negro Ghetto, 1890–1920*. 2nd ed. (1971).

Ottley, Roi. *New World A-Coming*. (1968).

Page, James A. *Black Olympian Medalists*. (1991).

———, comp. *Selected Black American Authors: An Illustrated Bio-Bibliography*. (1977).

Parks, Gordon. "I Was a Zombie Then—Like All Muslims I Was Hypnotized." *Life* (March 5, 1965): 29–31.

———. "Malcolm X: The Minutes of Our Last Meeting." *Malcolm X: The Man and His Times*. Edited by John H. Clarke. (1990).

Parks, Rosa, with Jim Haskins. *Rosa Parks: My Story*. (1991).

Patterson, Floyd, with Milton Goss. *Victory over Myself*. (1962).

Patterson, Floyd, with Gay Talese. "In Defense of Cassius Clay." In *The Muhammad Ali Reader*. Edited by Gerald Early. (1998).

Pearson, Hugh. *The Shadow of the Panther: Huey Newton and the Rise of Black Power in America*. (1994).

Perata, David D. *Those Pullman Blues: An Oral History of the African American Railroad Attendant*. (1996).

Perkins, Kathy A. "The Unknown Career of Shirley Graham." *Freedomways* 25 (1985): 6–17.

Perry, Bruce. *Malcolm: The Life of a Man Who Changed Black America*. (1991).

Perry, Theresa, ed. *Teaching Malcolm X*. (1996).

Pfeffer, Paula F. *A. Philip Randolph, Pioneer of the Civil Rights Movement*. (1990).

Pickthall, Mohammed Marmaduke. *The Meaning of the Glorious Koran: An Explanatory Translation.* (1953).

Pinkney, Alphonso. *Red, Black, and Green: Black Nationalism in the United States.* (1976).

Pitney, David Howard. *The Afro-American Jeremiad: Appeals for Justice in America.* (1990).

Plano, Jackson C., and Milton Greenbert. *The American Political Dictionary.* (1985).

Platt, Anthony M. *The Politics of Riot Commissions 1917–1970: A Collection of Official Reports and Critical Essays.* (1971).

Plimpton, George. "Miami Notebook: Cassius Clay and Malcolm X." *Harpers* (June 1964): 54–61.

———. "Miami Notebook! Cassius Clay and Malcolm X." In *The Muhammad Ali Reader.* Edited by Gerald Early. (1998).

Ploski, Harry A., and Ernest Kaiser, eds. *The Negro Almanac: A Reference Work on the Afro-American.* (1971).

Ploski, Harry A., and James Williams. *The Negro Almanac: A Reference Work on the Afro-American.* (1983, 1989).

Plummer, Brenda Gayle. *Rising Wind: Black Americans and U.S. Foreign Affairs, 1935–1960.* (1996).

Pohlmann, Marcus D. *Black Politics in Conservative America.* 2nd ed. (1999).

Porterfield, Ernest. "Birmingham: A Magic City." In *Search of the New South: The Black Urban Experience in the 1970s and 1980s.* Edited by Robert D. Bullard. (1989).

Powledge, Fred. *Free at Last? The Civil Rights Movement and the People Who Made It.* (1991).

Price, Joe X. *Redd Foxx, B. S. (Before Sanford).* (1979).

Protz, Roger. "The Real Reason Why Malcolm Went to Africa." *Sepia* (October 1964): 42–46.

Publishers Weekly. "Obituary. Lewis Michaux." (September 6, 1976): 18.

Quaison-Sackey, Alexander. *Africa Unbound: Reflections of an African Statesman.* (1963).

Quarles, Benjamin. *Black Mosaic: Essays in Afro-American History and Historiography.* (1988).

Raboteau, Albert J. *A Fire in the Bones: Reflections on African-American Religious History.* (1995).

Raines, Howell. *My Soul Is Rested: The Story of the Civil Rights Movement in the Deep South.* (1983).

Rampersand, Arnold. "The Color of His Eyes: Bruce Perry's *Malcolm* and Malcolm's Malcolm." In *Malcolm X: In Our Own Image.* Edited by Joe Wood. (1992).

Randall, Dudley, and Margaret G. Burroughs, eds. *For Malcolm: Poems on the Life and the Death of Malcolm X.* (1969).

Rashad, Abid. *The History of Islam and Black Nationalism in the Americas.* (1991).

Reed, Adolph Jr., ed. *Race, Politics, and Culture: Critical Essays on the Radicalism of the 1960s.* (1986).

Reedy, George B. *Lyndon B. Johnson, a Memoir.* (1982).

Reilly, Charlie, ed. *Conversations with Amiri Baraka.* (1994).

Reitan, Ruth. *The Rise and Decline of an Alliance: Cuba and African American Leaders in the 1960s.* (1999).

Resh, Richard W. "George S. Schuyler." In *Encyclopedia of African-American Civil*

Rights: From Emancipation to the Present. Edited by Charles Lowery and John Marszalek. (1992).

Revolutionary Action Movement. *"Why Malcolm X Died: An Analysis."* (1965).

Richardson, Judy, and James Turner. "Malcolm X: Make It Plain: The Documentary and Book as Education Materials." In *Teaching Malcolm X.* Edited by Theresa Perry. (1996).

Roberts, Randy. "The Wide World of Muhammad Ali: The Politics and Economics of Televised Boxing." In *Muhammad Ali: The People's Champ.* Edited by Elliott J. Gorn. (1995).

Robeson, Paul. *Here I Stand.* (1971).

Robinson, Jackie. As told to Alfred Duckett. "An Exchange of Letters." In *The Jackie Robinson Reader: Perspectives on an American Hero, with Contributions by Roger Kahn, Red Barber, Wendell Smith, Malcolm X, Arthur Mann and More.* Edited by Jules Tygiel. (1977).

Robinson, Jo Ann Gibson. *The Montgomery Bus Boycott and the Women Who Started It: The Memoir of Jo Ann Gibson Robinson.* Edited by David Garrow. (1987).

Robnett, Belinda. *How Long? How Long? African American Women in the Struggle for Civil Rights.* (1997).

Roche, John P. "The Founding Fathers: A Reform Caucus in Action." *American Political Science Review* 60 (December 1965): 719–816.

Rodgers, Raymond and Jimmie M. Rogers. "The Evolution of the Attitude of Malcolm X toward Whites." *Phylon* 44 (June 1983): 108–119.

Rosberg, Carl G., Jr., and Peter Goldman. *The Life and Death of Malcolm X.* (1979).

Ross, B. Joyce. *J. E. Spingarn and the Rise of the NAACP, 1911–1939.* (1972).

Rossiter, Adam. *Of Long Memory: Mississippi and the Murder of Medgar Evers.* (1994).

Rothschild, Mary Aiken. *A Case of Black and White: Northern Volunteers and the Southern Freedom Summers, 1964–1965.* (1982).

Rummel, Jack. *Malcolm X: Militant Black Leader.* (1989).

Rummel, Jack, Ben Richardson, and William A. Fahey. *Great Black Americans.* (1976).

Rustin, Bayard. *Down the Line: The Collected Writings of Bayard Rustin.* (1971).

Sagay, J. O. and D. A. Dawson. *Africa: A Modern History, 1800–1975.* (1978).

Sales, William H., Jr. *From Civil Rights to Black Liberation: Malcolm X and the Organization of Afro-American Unity.* (1994).

Salter, John. *Jackson, Mississippi: An American Chronicle of Struggle and Schism.* (1987).

Salzman, Jack, et al. *Bridges and Boundaries: African Americans and American Jews.* (1992).

Sammon, Jeffrey T. "Rebel with a Cause: Muhammad Ali as Sixties Protest Symbol." In *Muhammad Ali: The People's Champ.* Edited by Elliott Gorn. (1995).

Samuels, Gertrude. "Two Ways: Black Muslim and NAACP." In *Black Protest in the Sixties.* Edited by August Meier, Elliot Rudwick, and John Bracey. (1991).

———. "Two Ways: Black Muslim and N.A.A.C.P." *New York Times Magazine* (May 12, 1963): 26–27.

Schlesinger, Arthur M., Jr. *Robert Kennedy and His Times.* (1978).

Schlessinger Video Productions. *Malcolm X, 1925–1965, Militant Black Leader.* Video. (1992).

Schmaltz, William H. *Hate: George Lincoln Rockwell and the American Nazi Party.* (1999).

Schuyler, George. *Black and Conservative: The Autobiography of George S. Schuyler.* (1966).

Seale, Bobby. *A Lonely Rage: The Autobiography of Bobby Seale.* (1978).

———. *Seize the Time: The Story of the Black Panther Party and Huey P. Newton.* (1968).

Segal, Ronald. *The Black Diaspora.* (1995).

Sellers, Cleveland with Robert Terrell. *The River of No Return: The Autobiography of a Black Militant and the Life and Death of SNCC.* (1973).

Semmes, Clovis. *Cultural Hegemony and African American Development.* (1992).

Senna, Carl. *The Black Press and the Struggle for Civil Rights.* (1994).

Settel, Irving. *A Pictorial History of Radio.* (1967).

Shabazz, Attallah. "Introduction." In *The Autobiography of Malcolm X.* Malcolm X with Alex Haley. (2000).

———. "The Longest Prayer." *Essence* (October 1997): 72–74, 154–55.

Shabazz, Betty. "From the Detroit Riot to the Malcolm X Summit." *Ebony* (November 1995): 62, 64.

———. "The Legacy of My Husband, Malcolm X." *Ebony* (June 1969): 172–82.

———. "Loving and Losing Malcolm." As told to Susan L. Taylor and Audrey Edwards. *Essence* (February 1992): 51, 104, 107–10, 112–13.

———. "Malcolm X as Husband and Father." In *Malcolm X: The Man and His Times.* Edited by John H. Clarke. (1990).

Shafritz, Jay M., E. F. Gibbons, Jr., and Gregory E. J. Scott. *Almanac of Modern Terrorism.* (1991).

Siegel, Beatrice. *Marian Wright Edelman: The Making of a Crusader.* (1995).

Sikora, Frank. *Until Justice Rolls Down: The Birmingham Church Bombing Case.* (1991).

Silberman, Charles E. *Crisis in Black and White.* (1964).

Simitar Videos. *The Life and Death of Malcolm X.* Video. (1994).

Simonelli, Frederick J. *American Fuehrer: George Lincoln Rockwell and the American Nazi Party.* (1999).

Sinclair, Andrew. *Che Guevara.* (1970).

Sitkoff, Harvard. *The Struggle for Black Equality, 1954–1980.* (1981, 1992).

Smallwood, Andrew P. "An Intellectual Aesthetic for Black Education." In *Black Lives: Essays in African American Biography.* Edited by James L. Conyers, Jr. (1999).

Smith, A. N. *Afro-American History since 1954.* (1982).

Smith, Edward, and Arnold Zurcher. *Dictionary of American Politics.* (1955).

Smith, Jessie Carney, ed. *Notable Black American Women.* (1991, 1992).

Smith, Suzzane E. *Dancing in the Street: Motown and Cultural Politics of Detroit.* (1999).

Smitherman, Geneva. *Black Talk: Words and Phrases from the Hood to the Amen Corner.* (1994, 2000).

Smythe, Mabel. *The Black American Reference Book.* (1976).

Sollors, Werner. *Amiri Baraka/LeRoi Jones: The Quest for a "Populist Modernism."* (1978).

Sollors, Werner, Caldwell Titcomb, and Thomas A. Underwood, eds. *Blacks at Harvard: A Documentary History of the African-American Experience at Harvard and Radcliffe.* (1993).

Solomon, Irvin D. "Albany, Georgia, Sit-in." In *Encyclopedia of African-American Civil*

Rights: From Emancipation to the Present. Edited by Charles D. Lowery and
John F. Marszalek. (1992).

Southern, David W. *Gunnar Myrdal and Black–White Relations: The Use and Abuse of
"An American Dilemma," 1944–1969.* (1987).

Spitz, Barry N. "The End of Malcolm X." *Sepia* (May 1965): 14–17.

Standley, Fred L., and Louis H. Pratt, eds. *Conversations with James Baldwin.* (1989).

Steady, Filomina C. *The Black Woman Cross-Culturally.* (1981).

Steigerwald, Donald. *The Sixties and the End of Modern America.* (1977).

Stein, Judith. *The World of Marcus Garvey: Race and Class in Modern Society.* (1986).

Stone, Chuck. *Black Political Power in America.* (1964).

Stovall, Tyler. *Paris Noir: African Americans in the City of Light.* (1996).

Strickland, Arvarh. "March on Washington." In *Encyclopedia of African-American Civil
Rights: From Emancipation to the Present.* Edited by Charles D. Lowery and
John F. Marszalek. (1992).

Strickland, William, with the Malcolm X Documentary Production Team and edited by
Cheryll Greene. *Malcolm X, Make It Plain.* (1994).

Stuckey, Sterling. *Going Through the Storm: The Influence of African American Art in
History.* (1994).

———. *Slave Nationalist Theory and Foundations of Black America.* (1987).

Stull, Bradford. *Amid the Fall: Du Bois, King, Malcolm X, and Emancipatory Compo-
sition.* (1999).

Tate, Sonsyrea. *Little X: Growing Up in the Nation of Islam.* (1997).

Taylor, Clarence. *Knocking at Our Own Door: Milton A. Galamison and the Struggle
to Integrate New York City Schools.* (1997).

Telephone conversation [between Malcolm X and Carlos Moore]. In *Malcolm X: The
Man and His Times.* Edited by John H. Clarke. (1990).

Terborg-Penn, Roslyn, et al. *Women in Africa and the African Diaspora.* (1987).

Thernstrom, Stephen, and Abigail Thernstrom. *America in Black and White: One Nation
Indivisible.* (1997).

Thompson, Julius E. *Dudley Randall, Broadside Press, and the Black Arts Movement in
Detroit, 1960–1995.* (1999).

Thorpe, Earl. *Black Historians: A Critique.* (1969, 1971).

Time. "Busting RAM." (June 30, 1967): 20.

Tirro, Frank. *Jazz: A History.* (1977, 1993).

T'Shaka, Oba. *The Political Legacy of Malcolm X.* (1983).

Turner, Patricia. *I Heard It Through the Grapevine: Rumor in African American Culture.*
(1999).

Turner, Richard Brent. *Islam in the African American Experience.* (1997).

Tygiel, Jules, ed. *The Jackie Robinson Reader: Perspectives on an American Hero.*
(1997).

Tyler, Bruce. "Zoot Suit Culture and the Black Press." *Journal of American Culture* 17
(Summer 1994): 21–33.

Tyson, Timothy B. *Radio Free Dixie: Robert F. Williams and the Roots of Black Power.*
(1999).

United American Video. *Death of a Prophet: The Last Days of Malcolm X.* Video.
(1998).

Urquhart, Brian. *A Life in Peace and War: Memoirs.* (1991).

———. *Ralph Bunche—An American Life.* (1993).

U.S. Riot Commission. *Report of The National Advisory Commission on Civil Disorders.* (1968, 1988).

Van Deburg, William L. *Modern Black Nationalism from Marcus Garvey to Louis Farrakhan.* (1997).

———. *New Day in Babylon: Black Power Movement and American Culture, 1965–1975.* (1992).

Van Peebles, Mario, Ula Y. Taylor, and J. Tarika Lewis. *Panther: A Pictorial History of the Black Panthers and the Story behind the Film.* (1995).

Vernon, Robert. *The Black Ghetto.* (1968).

Vincent, Ted. "The Garveyite Parents of Malcolm X." *Black Scholar* 20 (March 1989): 10–13.

Vincent, Theodore G. *Black Power and the Garvey Movement.* (1971).

Von Eschen, Penny M. *Race against Empire: Black Americans and Anticolonialism, 1937–1957.* (1997).

Wagoner, Fred E. *Dragon Rouge.* (1980).

Wagstaff, Thomas, ed. *Black Power: The Radical Response to White America.* (1969).

Waldron, Clarence. "Minister Louis Farrakhan Sets the Record Straight About His Relationship with Malcolm X." *Jet* (June 5, 2000): 4–7, 10–11.

Walker, Wyatt T. "Nothing But a Man." *Negro Digest* (1965): 29–32.

Wallace, Mike, and Gary Paul Gates. *Close Encounters: Mike Wallace's Own Story.* (1984).

Wallerstein, Immanuel. *Africa, the Politics of Unity: An Analysis of Contemporary Social Movement.* (1967).

Walters, Ronald, and Robert C. Smith. *African American Leadership.* (1999).

Walton, Hanes, Jr. *African American Power and Politics: The Political Context Variable.* (1997).

———. *Black Political Parties: An Historical and Political Analysis.* (1972).

———. *Invisible Politics: Black Political Behavior.* (1985).

———. "Moral Man and a Moral Journey." In *Morality, and Higher Education: Essays in Honor of Samuel Du Bois Cook.* Edited by F. Thomas Trotter. (1997).

———. *The Political Philosophy of Martin Luther King, Jr.* (1971).

———. *Reelection: William Jefferson Clinton as a Native-Son Presidential Candidate.* (2000).

Ward, Hiley. *Prophet of the Black Nation.* (1969).

Warner Studio. *Malcolm X: His Own Story.* Video. (1972).

Warren, Robert P. *Who Speaks for the Negro?* (1965).

Waskow, Arthur I. *From Race Riot to Sit-in: 1919 and the 1960s: A Study in the Connection between Conflict and Violence.* (1966).

Weinstein, James. *Ambiguous Legacy: The Left in American Politics.* (1975).

Weiss, Nancy J. *Farewell to the Party of Lincoln: Black Politics in the Age of FDR.* (1983).

———. *Whitney M. Young, Jr.: And the Struggle for Civil Rights.* (1989).

Weiss, Samuel. "The Ordeal of Malcolm X." *South Atlantic Urban Quarterly* 76 (1977): 53–63.

Weissman, Stephen R. *American Foreign Policy in the Congo, 1960–1964.* (1974).

Wesley, Charles S. "Black Studies and History Week." *Negro History Bulletin* (February 1972): 28–29.

West, Cornel. *Race Matters.* (1993).

White, John. *Black Leadership in America:From Booker T. Washington to Jesse Jackson.* (1985).
White, Mark B. "Malcolm X." In *African American Orators: A Bio-Critical Sourcebook.* Edited by Richard W. Leeman. (1996).
White, Shane, and Graham White. *Stylin': African American Expressive Culture from Its Beginnings to the Zoot Suit.* (1998).
White, Vibert. "Paul Robeson." In *Encyclopedia of African-American Civil Rights: From Emancipation to the Present.* Edited by Charles D. Lowery and John F. Marszalek. (1992).
Whitfield, Stephen J. *A Death in the Delta: The Story of Emmett Till.* (1988).
Wicker, Tom. *A Time to Die.* (1975).
Wiggins, David K. "Victory for Allah: Muhammad Ali, the Nation of Islam, and American Society." In *Muhammad Ali: The People's Champ.* Edited by Elliott J. Gorn. (1995).
Wiley, Ralph. "Great Xpectations." *Premier* (November 1992): 88–93.
Wilkins, Roy with Tom Matthews. *Standing Fast: The Autobiography of Roy Wilkins.* (1982).
Williams, Chancellor. *The Destruction of Black Civilization.* (1976).
Williams, G. Mennen. *Africa for the Africans.* (1969).
Williams, Juan. *Eyes on the Prize: America's Civil Rights Years, 1954–1965.* (1987).
———. *Thurgood Marshall: American Revolutionary.* (1998).
Williams, Michael W., ed. *The African-American Encyclopedia.* 8 vols. (1993).
Williams, Robert F. *Negroes with Guns.* (1962).
Wilson, Amos. *Black on Black Violence.* (1990).
Wilson, Moses. *Classical Black Nationalism: From the American Revolution to Marcus Garvey.* (1991).
Wolfenstein, Eugene V. *The Victims of Democracy: Malcolm X and the Black Revolution.* (1981, 1989, 1993).
Wolseley, Ronald. *The Black Press, U.S.A.* 2nd ed. (1990).
Wood, Joe, ed. *Malcolm X: In Our Own Image.* (1992).
Woodard, Komozi. *A Nation within a Nation: Amiri Baraka (LeRoi Jones) and Black Power Politics.* (1999).
Woodward, C. Vann. *The Strange Career of Jim Crow.* 3rd ed. (1974).
Wright, Charles H. *The Peace Advocacy of Paul Robeson.* (1984).
Wright, M. Frank. "Franz Fanon in Historical Perspective." *Black Scholar* 6 (July–August 1975): 19–29.
Wright, Richard. *The Color Curtain: A Report on the Bandung Conference.* (1956, 1994).
Wynn, Neil A. *The Afro-American and the Second World War.* (1976).
Xenon Studios. *Malcolm X: El Hajj Malik Shabazz.* Video. (1991).
Yakubu, Owusu Yaki. "The Meaning of Malcolm for Imprisoned Afrikans in the United States." In *Teaching Malcolm X.* Edited by Theresa Perry. (1996).
Yinger, Milton J. *Religion, Society, and the Individual.* (1968).
Young, Andrew. *An Easy Burden: The Civil Rights Movement and the Transformation of America.* (1996).

NEWSPAPERS

Atlanta Daily World.
Baltimore Afro-American.
Clarion-Ledger (Jackson, MS).
Dallas Express.
Detroit News.
Economist (London).
Los Angeles Herald-Dispatch.
Los Angeles "Not Born Yesterday" Citizen.
Los Angeles Sentinel.
Los Angeles Times.
Militant (New York).
Montgomery Advertiser.
Muhammad Speaks.
New Crusader (Chicago).
New Statesman (London).
New Jersey Paterson Morning Call.
New York Amsterdam News.
New York Herald Tribune.
New York Post.
New York Times.
New York Village Voice.
Now (Detroit).
Pittsburgh Courier.
Times (London).
Washington Daily News.
Washington Evening Post.
Washington Post.

ELECTRONIC SOURCES

Archives of Malcolm-X. Listservdiscussion available at: http://maelstrom.stjohns.edu/archives/malcolm-x.html
Malcolm X: A Research Site. Available at: http://www.brothermalcolm.net
Malcolm X College. Available at: http://www.ccc.edu

ORAL INTERVIEWS

Jenkins, Robert. With Iman Johnny Byrd. October 15, 1999.
————. With William Strickland. (Telephone) May 7, 2000.
Tryman, Mfanya. With Brenda Council. (Telephone) July 25, 2000.

INDEX

Page numbers in **bold** indicate main entries.

612

INDEX

for Defense and Justice and, 183;
Founding Fathers and, 225; Freedom
Summer and, 230; Harlem rent strike
and, 261; King and, 314; Malcolm X
Society and, 369; March Against Fear
and, 380; Newton and, 418–19;
Organization of Afro-American Unity
and, 431; Philadelphia murders and,
443; Seale and, 494; South Africa and,
515; Williams and, 565
Self-hatred, black, **123–24**
Self-improvement, **496–97**
Selma, Alabama, 32, 34, 199–200, 547,
582–83
Senegal, 59
Sengstacke, John A., 147
"Separation or Death," 73
Sepia, 107, 110
*Seventh Child: A Family Memoir of
Malcolm X,* 47, 168
Sex and Malcolm X, **365–66**
Sexism, 23–24
Shabazz, Attallah, 149–50, 170, 498
Shabazz, Betty Sanders, **497–99;**
assassination and, 438–39;
assassination trial and, 79, 138, 372;
black manhood and, 108; child rearing
by, 150; children of, 148–49; Cooks
and, 176; *Ebony* and, 198; Evers-
Williams and, 210; Farrakhan and, 150;
Internet sites on, 47; Jacko and, 291;
King (Coretta Scott) and, 311;
Malcolm's assassination and, 22;
Malcolm's family life and, 52–53, 347–
48; Malcolm's funeral and, 357;
Mayfield and, 377; Muslim Girls'
Training Classes and, 408; Poitier and,
445; as role model, 399; Sabbatino
and, 484; Wilson and, 565; women's
roles and, 571
El-Shabazz, El-Hajj Malik, 19, 253, 407,
421–22, 487, **499–500**
Shabazz, Gamilah Lamumbah, 149, 498
Shabazz, Ilyasah, 149, 498
Shabazz, James, 434, **500–501**, 506
Shabazz, (Minister) James, **501**
Shabazz, John, **501–2**
Shabazz, Malaak Saban, 149, 498

Shabazz, Malikah Saban, 149, 498
Shabazz, Qubilah Bahiyah, 149, 150,
498, 499
Shabazz Tribe, 19, **502–3**
Sharpeville Massacre, 515
Sharrieff, Raymond, 129, 233, 245, 399,
503–4
Shawarbi, Mahmoud Youseff, 64, 86,
410, 487, **504–5**
Sheppard, Barry, 584
Sherrill, Captain Edward 2X, **505–6**
Sherrod, Charles, 64
Shi'ites, 407
Shifflet, Lynn, 161, **506**, 572
"Shorty" (Malcolm Jarvis), 94–95, 239,
481, **506–8**
Shrine of the Black Madonna, 162
Shuttlesworth, Fred, 582–83
Sierra Leone, 116
Sievet v. Oklahoma, 389
Silberman, Charles E., **508–9**
Sinatra, Frank, 477
60 Minutes, 43, 320, 550, 552
Slavery. *See* Black slavery
Slave uprisings, 116
Small, Charlie, 509
Small, Ed, 509
Small's Paradise Club, 98, 102, 204, 260,
284, **509**
Smethwick, England, 207, 208, 273
Smith, Tommy, 142, **509–10**
Smith Act, 278
Smith v. Alright, 413–14
So-called Negro, **510–11**
Socialism, 140, 141, 184, 492, **511–12**
Socialist Workers Party (SWP), 131, 183–
84, 386, 387, **512–13**
Soledad Brothers, **513**
Soledad Brothers, 513
SOUL ON ICE, 164
Soul Sister, 5
The Souls of Black Folks, 5
The South, **513–14**
South Africa, 60, 437, **514–15**
South Carolina, 469
Southern Christian Leadership Conference
(SCLC), 28, 158, **515–16**; Abernathy

ABOUT THE CONTRIBUTORS

YVETTE ALEX-ASSENSOH is Assistant Professor of Political Science at Indiana University.

ABDUL ALKALIMAT is Professor of Black Studies and Director of the Department of Africana Studies at the University of Toledo.

AKWASI B. ASSENSOH is Associate Professor of History at Indiana University.

CURTIS AUSTIN is Assistant Professor of History and Assistant Director of the Oral History Program at the University of Southern Mississippi.

BRENDA AYRES is Professor of English at Middle Georgia College.

NAPOLEON BAMFO is Associate Professor of Public Administration at Valdosta State University.

CHARLES PETE BANNER-HALEY is Associate Professor of History and Coordinator of the African American Studies Program at Colgate University.

ABDUL AL-BARRAK is Assistant Professor of Public Administration in Saudi Arabia.

AMOS J. BEYAN is Associate Professor of History at West Virginia University.

CHARLES C. BOLTON is Associate Professor of History and Director of the Oral History Program at the University of Southern Mississippi.

OTHA BURTON is city administrator for Jackson, Mississippi, and Assistant Professor of Public Administration at Jackson State University.

REGINALD COLBERT is a high school history teacher in Aliceville, Alabama.

JAMES L. CONYERS, JR., is Chair of the Department of Black Studies and Associate Professor of Black Studies, Sociology, and History at the University of Nebraska at Omaha.

RICHARD V. DAMMS is Assistant Professor of History at Mississippi State University.

DERNORAL DAVIS is Associate Professor of History and Acting Department Head at Jackson State University.

NANCY J. DAWSON is Assistant Professor of Black American Studies at Southern Illinois University.

PATTIE DILLON is Instructor of History at Central Florida University.

SAUL DORSEY is a graduate student at Jackson State University.

TERRI EARNEST is an administrative assistant at the Mississippi State University Social Science Research Center.

MORGAN ERO is an Associate Professor of Political Science at Mississippi Valley State University.

NANCY-ELIZABETH FITCH is Associate Professor of English at the College of New Rochelle.

DAMON FORDHAM is a graduate student at the University of Charleston.

PHILLIP A. GIBBS is Associate Professor of History at Middle Georgia College.

DAVID T. GLEESON is Assistant Professor of History at Armstrong Atlantic State University.

FON LOUISE GORDON is Associate Professor of History at the University of Kentucky.

PHYLLIS GRAY-RAY is Associate Professor of Sociology and Research Co-ordinator, Institute for Disability Studies at the University of Southern Mississippi.

JOHNPETER HORST GRILL is Professor of History at Mississippi State University.

LaVERNE GYANT is Associate Professor of Adult Education and Director of the Center of Black Studies at Northern Illinois University.

SHARRON Y. HERRON is Associate Professor and Director of the Public Administration Program at California State University at Fresno.

KEITH O. HILTON is an Assistant Professor in the Department of Communication at the University of the Pacific.

CHARLES HOLMES is Professor of Political Science at Tougaloo College.

HORACE HUNTLEY is part-time Assistant Professor of History at the University of Alabama at Birmingham.

LaVONNE JACKSON is a Lecturer in History at Bowie State University.

PETER JACKSON is Associate Professor of Economics at Benedict College.

ROBERT L. JENKINS is Associate Professor of History at Mississippi State University.

PATRICIA JERNIGAN is a recent graduate of the doctoral program in Public Administration at Mississippi State University.

FRANKLIN JONES is Professor of Political Science at Texas Southern Univeristy.

ZAINABAU SIPIOWE NETOSH JONES is a doctoral student in Education at Temple University.

KENNETH A. JORDAN is Professor of Public Administration at Savannah State University.

LAUREN LARSEN was formerly an Instructor of History at Morgan State University and currently resides in the West Indies.

MAMIE LOCKE is mayor of Hampton, Virginia, and a former Dean at Hampton Institute.

CHARLES D. LOWERY is Professor Emeritus of History at Mississippi State University.

JOHN F. MARSZALEK is Giles Distinguished Professor of History at Mississippi State University.

DEMOND S. MILLER is Assistant Professor of Sociology at Rowan University.

NAJEE E. MUHAMMAD is Assistant Professor of Education and Coordinator of the Cultural Studies Program at Ohio University.

ZUBERI MWAMBA is Professor of Political Science at Texas Southern University.

BETSY SAKARIASSEN NASH is a middle school administrator in San Antonio, Texas.

HORACE D. NASH is adjunct Instructor of History at San Antonio College.

FELIX A. OKOJIE is Associate Vice President for Academic Affairs at Jackson State University.

WILLIAM A. PERSON is Professor of Curriculum and Instruction and Director of the Graduate Program at Mississippi State University.

MONTE PILIAWSKY is Associate Professor of Education at Wayne State University.

CRAIG S. PIPER is Librarian/Archivist at Mississippi State University.

BYRON E. PRICE is a doctoral student in the Public Administration Program at Mississippi State University.

MELVIN C. RAY is Assistant to the President and Associate Professor of Sociology at Mississippi State University.

WILFRED D. SAMUELS is Associate Professor of English and Ethnic Studies at the University of Utah.

AMILCAR SHABAZZ is Assistant Professor of American Studies at the University of Alabama and Coordinator of the American Studies Program.

MALIK SIMBA is Professor of History at Georgia State University.

ANDREW P. SMALLWOOD is Assistant Professor of Black Studies at the University of Nebraska at Omaha.

GERALD L. SMITH is Associate Professor of History and Director of the African American Studies Research Program at the University of Kentucky.

THADDEUS M. SMITH is Associate Professor of History and Chair at Middle Tennessee State University.

IRVIN D. SOLOMON is Associate Professor of History at the Gulf Coast University.

BRIDGETTE STASHER is a graduate student in History at Jackson State University.

JAMES W. STENNETT is a media consultant for a professional baseball team.

FRANKLYN TATE is a doctoral student in the Public Administration Program at Mississippi State University.

LEHLOHONOLO TLOU is Associate Professor of History and Political Science at Longwood College.

YOSHAWNDA TROTTER is a doctoral student in History at Mississippi State University.

MFANYA DONALD TRYMAN is Professor of Political Science at Mississippi State University.

RONNIE TUCKER is Adjunct Professor of Political Science at Mississippi State University.

THOMAS UPCHURCH is a doctoral candidate in History at Mississippi State University.

G. N. UZOIGWE is Department Head and Professor of History at Mississippi State University.

HANES WALTON is Professor of Political Science and Faculty Associate in the Center of Political Studies in the Institute of Social Research at the University of Michigan.

L. HENRY WHELCHEL is Associate Professor of Religion and Department Chair at Clark-Atlanta University.

CAROLYN WILLIAMS is Associate Professor of History at the University of North Florida.

KENNETH H. WILLIAMS is Associate Professor of History at Alcorn State University.

LAWRENCE H. WILLIAMS is Professor of History at Luther College.

LEE E. WILLIAMS II is Professor of History and Director of the Multicultural Center at the University of Alabama in Huntsville.

WANDA T. WILLIAMS is a television reporter for WATE-TV in Knoxville, Tennessee.

ALAN SCOT WILLIS is Visiting Assistant Professor of History at Texas A&M University at Corpus Christi.

PAUL J. WILSON is Assistant Professor of History at Nicholls State University.

KOMOZI WOODARD is Associate Professor of History at Sarah Lawrence College.